*ADJUSTMENT TO EMPIRE*

Richard R. Johnson

# Adjustment to Empire

## The New England Colonies
### 1675–1715

RUTGERS UNIVERSITY PRESS

*1981*

*Library of Congress Cataloging in Publication Data*

Johnson, Richard R      1942–
  Adjustment to empire.
  Bibliography: p.
  Includes index.
  1. New England—Politics and government—Colo-
nial period, ca. 1600–1775.  I. Title.
F7.J64      974'.02      80-39978
ISBN 0-8135-0907-6

*To my parents*

# Contents

# Preface

This book is a study of the New England colonies—Massachusetts, Plymouth, Connecticut, Rhode Island, and New Hampshire—in the late seventeenth and early eighteenth centuries. It centers upon the events and aftermath of their participation in the Glorious Revolution of 1688–1689, and it takes as the dominant theme of New England's history during this period the colonies' relationship with England and their accommodation to a greater measure of royal supervision. Hence, it pays particular attention to the forces and circumstances that shaped this relationship—the ties of trade and of a common social and intellectual heritage, the pressures of war with the French and Indians, England's attempts to bring the American colonies into a greater dependence upon the crown, and what I judge to be the most significant of all these influences, the tensions, needs, and ambitions of the colonists themselves.

Such an emphasis, while it draws much from the insights and researches of earlier scholars, diverges from the interpretative paths taken by most other recent studies of New England's colonial past. It lies open, in particular, to criticism of the kind first levelled as far back as 1720, by Isaac Watts at the account of New England by Daniel Neal. "I had Hoped," Watts wrote to Cotton Mather of Neal's work, "that I should have found there an abstract of the lives and Spiritual experiences of those great and good Souls that planted and promoted the Gospel amongst you and those remarkable Providences, Deliverances and Answers to Prayers . . . which are recorded in your *Magnalia Christi;* but I am disappointed in my expectation; for he has written with a different view and has taken meerly the task of an Historian upon him."[1] Muted to match the taste of a more secular

---

[1] Watts to Mather, Feb. 11, 1720, Colman Papers, Mass. Hist. Soc. For a modern version of this complaint, see Perry Miller, *The New England Mind: From Colony to Province, passim.*

[ix]

age, Watts's complaint would still win a sympathetic hearing today; for if modern scholars are now less openly concerned with portraying the history of New England as the unfolding of divine providence, they have nonetheless continued to focus with remarkable persistence upon the region's religious and social development and its evolution as an essentially self-contained and self-motivated society. To the numerous studies of Puritan thought and doctrine have been added others tracing the lives of individual families and communities. Historiographically at least, New Englanders remain a chosen people.

As a consequence of these studies, we now comprehend the religious and social history of New England far better than before, to the extent, indeed, that I have deliberately abbreviated my treatment of such matters (and made due reference to this scholarship) in the belief that they have already been expertly explored. This book, therefore, touches only lightly upon the colonists' church and town life during the years under discussion. I have also followed this course in the less complimentary belief that the study of religious and social development, for all its undoubted contribution to an appreciation of the intricacies of the New England way, does not provide the necessary key for understanding the most significant changes through which New England passed during the era of the Glorious Revolution. Rather, such an understanding can best be obtained through analysis of the region's relatively neglected political and institutional history, especially as it focuses upon the colonies' dealings with one another and with the outside world. This perspective no doubt derives in part from my somewhat circuitous approach to New England studies by way of a training in medieval European history and a subsequent interest in the nature of English colonial government. At a deeper level, I believe, it stems from a conviction fostered by my researches, that those who shaped events and attitudes within New England during these years were as much seasoned and often far-sighted politicians and participants in an Atlantic community as they were men with their eyes fixed upon village life or the hereafter—or the one in preparation for the other. A truism as stated, perhaps, but one too often slighted amid the tendency to study New England man as *homo Puritanissimus,* more angel than Englishman.

This reassessment of the colonists' attitudes and actions, moreover, has led me to the conclusion that their part in the shaping of relations between old and New England has been unduly neglected. Here again (though with certain notable exceptions such as David Love-joy's fine account of *The Glorious Revolution in America*), recent studies have encouraged a different perspective by their account of these relations in terms of the institutions and policies of English colonial government as seen from the viewpoint of London. Coupled with the oft-expressed belief of scholars of New England life that the region's development can be portrayed as all but isolated from external influences, this has resulted in a scenario in which the colonists appear as little more than victims trapped in a web of Stuart imperialism or English mercantilist greed. English policy, in fact, was by no means as coherent or purposeful as this scenario would suggest; and I have tried to show in this book that New Englanders, though often ignorant and always suspicious of London's ways, nonetheless learned how to work within the structure and mechanisms of royal government and even to turn them to their advantage. The result, by 1715, was a settlement that amid—and, in part, because of—a greater acceptance of English institutions and procedures preserved much of the colonists' traditional autonomy from external control.

In pursuing these themes, I have held to an essentially chronological organization while moving back and forth across the Atlantic to compare and interweave changing perspectives and events. The opening chapter sets the scene within New England and traces the contours of the interplay between crown and colonists which led up to the creation of the Dominion of New England in 1686. Chapter 2 moves to the heart of the work in analyzing the overthrow of the Dominion and the domestic and international circumstances that prompted New England's leaders to look to London for assistance. Chapters 3 and 4 present a case study of transatlantic interaction by narrating the intricate negotiations in London that culminated in the return of royal government to Massachusetts and New Hampshire, set against the background of the political rivalries of the new reign and the troubles besetting New England at this time.

Three final chapters describe the unfolding of the post-Revolutionary settlement in New England. Chapter 5 examines the forces—the vagaries of royal policy, the pressures of war, and the colonists' own rivalries and anxieties—that made the 1690s a period of exceptional instability and uncertainty. Chapter 6 turns to the ways in which the colonists were beginning to adjust to their closer ties to the crown, especially as seen in their employment of agents to advance their interests in London, their participation in appointments to office, and the emergence of a new pattern of political factionalism in royally governed Massachusetts and New Hampshire. Chapter 7 presents the period between 1698 and 1715 as one in which the post-Revolutionary settlement was reworked and consolidated, in part by the resurgence of strong leadership within the individual colonies and in part by the growth and more careful definition of government and its functions.

I have sought throughout to demonstrate the value of a regional approach for understanding this period in New England's past. This is not, I hope, to homogenize the region's history or to fall into the trap of identifying it with that of its longtime leader, Massachusetts. Rather, my basic approach is comparative, both within the colonies in assessing their common and contrasting problems and solutions and within a transatlantic context in setting these problems and solutions in turn against the aims and policies of royal officials in London. Throughout, also, I have deliberately focused upon the aftermath of the upheavals of 1688–1689, believing as I do that their consequences were of greater long-term significance than their causes and that what subsequently emerged in New England by the early eighteenth century—the foundation of a renewed and lasting political and social stability—is a commodity more precious and hence more worthy of study than the froth of revolution.

A few words must be added concerning the style and content of the work's documentation. It is based upon the great range of manuscripts currently held by archives on both sides of the Atlantic. Fortunately for the scholar and teacher of early American history, a great proportion of this material is available in print, in published state and national records or in the pages of historical journals. Indeed, no historian of New England should deprive him- or herself of the pleasures of browsing through the *Proceedings* of the Massachusetts Historical Society or the *New England Historical and Genealogical Register.* Because such material is far more readily available to the general public in its printed than its manuscript form, I have chosen wherever possible—and where transcriptions appear accurate—to cite from the printed version; to do otherwise would be to defeat the purpose of such documentation, which I take to be that of allowing readers to check the accuracy of the writer's use of such materials and encouraging them to pursue further investigations without excessive inconvenience. Thus, I have persistently cited material from the Massachusetts Archives as it is printed in the volumes of the *Acts and Resolves, Public and Private, of the Province of the Massachusetts Bay,* and from the Winthrop Papers as they appear in the *Collections* of the Massachusetts Historical Society. I have deviated from this rule, however, in citing from the papers in London's Public Record Office printed in the *Calendar of State Papers, Colonial Series,* for up until the volume covering the year 1699, the degree of compression required of the *Calendar*'s editors was simply too great to do justice to the material: an extreme example is the summarizing in two printed pages of over two hundred manuscript pages of material bearing upon the preparation of the Massachusetts charter of 1691. In a number of early volumes, moreover, comparison with the originals reveals serious errors of transcription. The volumes covering the eighteenth century, by contrast, are much fuller in coverage, and wonderfully accurate. In documenting my analysis of the period prior to 1700, therefore, I have generally cited from the manuscripts; the dates given in these citations permit comparison with the chronologically ordered *Calendar.* Citations from the originals for the years after 1700 generally reflect the fact that petitions are not as fully summarized in the *Calendar* as letters.

In keeping with the usual scholarly practice for this period, all dates are given in "Old Style," according to the Julian calendar then in use in England and its American colonies, but with the year considered as beginning on January 1 instead of, as in the "Old Style" calendar, on March 25. Hence a date cited by contemporaries as February 18, 1690, or February 18, 1690/1 (or 18 day 11 month 1690 as it might be written by New Englanders hostile to pagan terminology) is given as February 18, 1691. I have reproduced spelling and punctuation as I have found them in the sources, save for modernizing the old usages of *i* for *j*, *u* for *v*, and *th* for *y*, and expanding abbreviations where necessary for clarity.

This book is the product of the skills and assistance of many people. Long before I ever ventured into the new world of early America, Michael Cherniavsky first convinced me of what I now seek to persuade others, that the study of history can be an absorbing and wide-ranging humane discipline. I am deeply grateful to Rotary International and to the University of California for the opportunity to take up graduate study in the United States; indeed, the latter provided not only sustained financial assistance and many valued friendships but an environment—Berkeley in the 1960s—that gave me a more immediate opportunity than I could have anticipated to study a society in upheaval. Inside the classroom I learned much, in different ways, from Robert Middlekauff, Charles Sellers, and Thomas Barnes. Subsequently, while visiting archives in both old and New England, I received much patient and courteous assistance; in particular, because of the length of time I imposed myself upon them, I give special thanks to Miss Winifred Collins and her fellow saints at the Massachusetts Historical Society, to Mr. and Mrs. Leo Flaherty of the Massachusetts Archives, and to the staff of the Public Record Office in London. A generous fellowship from the William Andrews Clark Memorial Library in Los Angeles allowed me to mine its collections and those of the Henry E. Huntington Library and to enjoy the libraries' splendid hospitality to scholars. The Colonial Williamsburg Library lent me microfilm of their collection of Blathwayt Papers. I have greatly benefited from access to two fine research libraries, those of the University of California at Berkeley and the University of Washington in Seattle.

I am well aware that even though I have tried to blaze new trails I have worked in a field abundantly mapped by other modern writers, and I hope that they will accept my references to their work as testimony of my indebtedness to their scholarship. Less apparent, and hence worthy of special mention, is my debt to those whose devoted labors elucidated and placed in print so many of the materials of New England history, notably James Savage, James Phinney Baxter, Albert Stillman Batchelor, Nathaniel Shurtleff, William H. Whitmore, Robert N. Toppan, Abner C. Goodell, John Russell Bartlett, Charles J. Hoadly, and J. Hammond Trumbull. Further back in the past stand such figures as Thomas Prince, Jeremy Belknap, and Thomas Hutchinson. In drawing upon their work, the student becomes increasingly conscious that, in the medieval metaphor, his vision derives from standing upon the shoulders of giants; it is a privilege to contribute to such a tradition.

Over a number of years, this book has profited greatly from the advice and criticism of my friends. At an early stage, J. William T. Youngs, Jr., and Dauril Alden took the trouble to read the manuscript and give me their advice; my colleagues in the History Research Group at the University of Washington, especially William J. Rorabaugh, have helped to sharpen the style and argument of particular portions. Indeed, I am glad to have this occasion to thank all my colleagues here in Seattle for much encouragement and good fellowship. Timothy H. Breen of Northwestern University kindly provided me with a copy of an unpublished paper. Herbert Mann of Rutgers University Press has counselled and encouraged me over a longer period of years than either of us wish to remember; Leslie Mitchner and Willa Speiser have been exemplary editors. I am especially grateful to two eminent scholars of early America, Wesley Frank Craven and

Robert E. Moody, for their unselfish generosity in reading and criticizing the manuscript in its penultimate form. Above all, I am profoundly indebted to Robert Middlekauff for his constant support and interest, his tolerance of diverse approaches to New England's history, and his superb example as scholar and teacher. None of these friends should thereby incur blame for the errors and infelicities that remain in this book; on the contrary, they deserve the reader's gratitude along with mine for reducing them in number.

Lastly I acknowledge two profound debts of a more personal kind. The first, of longest standing, is declared in the dedication. The second is to a colleague in every sense of the word, my wife and fellow historian, Carol, for her loving friendship.

# *Abbreviations*

Addit. MSS.  Additional Manuscripts, British Library, London.

Adm.  Admiralty Papers, Public Record Office, London.

Amer. Antiq. Soc.  American Antiquarian Society, Worcester, Massachusetts.

*Andros Tracts*  William H. Whitmore, ed. *The Andros Tracts. Being a Collection of Pamphlets and Official Papers issued during the Period Between the Overthrow of the Andros Government and the Establishment of the Second Charter of Massachusetts.* Prince Society Publications, vols. V–VII. Boston, 1868–1874.

*APC Col.*  *Acts of the Privy Council in England, Colonial Series.* Edited by W. L. Grant and James Munro. 6 vols. London, 1908–1912.

*Boston Records*  *Reports of the Records Commissioners of the City of Boston.* 39 vols. Boston, 1876–1909.

C.O.  Colonial Office Papers, Public Record Office, London.

Col. Wmsbg.  Colonial Williamsburg Research Library, Williamsburg, Virginia.

*Commons Journals*  Great Britain. House of Commons. *Journals.* London, 1742–.

Conn. Archives  Connecticut Archives, Connecticut State Library, Hartford.

| | |
|---|---|
| Conn. Hist. Soc. | Connecticut Historical Society, Hartford. |
| *Conn. Records* | *The Public Records of the Colony of Connecticut.* Edited by J. Hammond Trumbull and C. J. Hoadly. 15 vols. Hartford, 1850–1890. |
| *CSP Col.* | *Calendar of State Papers, Colonial Series, America and West Indies.* Edited by W. Noel Sainsbury *et al.* 44 vols. London, 1860–1969. |
| *Doc. Hist. Maine* | *Documentary History of Maine.* Maine Historical Society, *Collections,* 2nd ser., I–XXIV. Portland, 1869–1916. |
| *Doc. Hist. N. Y.* | *The Documentary History of the State of New York.* Edited by Edmund B. O'Callaghan. 4 vols. Albany, 1887. |
| Essex Instit. | Essex Institute, Salem, Massachusetts. |
| HMC, *Finch* | Historical Manuscripts Commission. *Report on the Manuscripts of the Late Allen George Finch of Burley-on-the-Hill, Rutland.* 4 vols. London, 1913–1965. |
| HMC, *Ormonde* | Historical Manuscripts Commission. *Calendar of the Manuscripts of the Marquess of Ormonde Preserved at Kilkenny Castle.* New ser. 8 vols. London, 1902–1920. |
| HMC, *Portland* | Historical Manuscripts Commission. *The Manuscripts of His Grace the Duke of Portland Preserved at Welbeck Abbey.* 10 vols. London, 1891–1931. |
| *House of Lords MSS.* | Historical Manuscripts Commission. *The Manuscripts of the House of Lords.* 3 vols. London, 1889–1895. New ser. 11 vols. London, 1906–1962. |
| Hunt. Lib. | Henry E. Huntington Library, San Marino, California. |

# Abbreviations

| | |
|---|---|
| *Lords Journals* | Great Britain. House of Lords. *Journals.* London, 1767-. |
| *Mass. Acts and Resolves* | *Acts and Resolves, Public and Private, of the Province of the Massachusetts Bay.* Edited by Abner C. Goodell and Melville M. Bigelow. 21 vols. Boston, 1869-1922. |
| Mass. Archives | Massachusetts Archives, State House, Boston. |
| Mass. Hist. Soc. | Massachusetts Historical Society, Boston. |
| *Mass. Records* | *Records of the Governor and Company of the Massachusetts Bay in New England.* Edited by Nathaniel B. Shurtleff. 5 vols. Boston, 1853-1854. |
| N. H. Hist. Soc. | New Hampshire Historical Society, Concord. |
| *N. H. Laws* | *Laws of New Hampshire.* Edited by Albert S. Batchellor. 10 vols. Manchester, 1904-1922. |
| *N. H. Provincial Papers* | *Provincial, State, and Town Papers of New Hampshire.* Edited by Nathaniel Bouton *et al.* 40 vols. Concord, 1867-1943. |
| *N. Y. Col. Docs.* | *Documents Relative to the Colonial History of the State of New York.* Edited by Edmund B. O'Callaghan and Berthold Fernow. 15 vols. Albany, 1853-1887. |
| *Plymouth Records* | *Records of the Colony of New Plymouth in New England.* Edited by Nathaniel B. Shurtleff and David Pulsifer. 12 vols. Boston, 1855-1861. |
| Pubs. Col. Soc. Mass. | Publications of the Colonial Society of Massachusetts, Boston. |
| *Randolph Letters* | *Edward Randolph: Including his Letters and Official Papers from the New England, Middle, and Southern Colonies in America,* |

*Adjustment to Empire*

| | |
|---|---|
| | *with Other Documents Relating Chiefly to the Vacating of the Royal Charter of Massachusetts, 1676–1703.* Edited by Robert N. Toppan and Alfred T. S. Goodrick. Prince Society Publications, vols. XXIV–XXVIII, XXX–XXXI. Boston, 1898–1909. |
| R. I. Archives | Rhode Island Archives, Rhode Island State House, Providence. |
| R. I. Hist. Soc. | Rhode Island Historical Society, Providence. |
| *R. I. Records* | *Records of the Colony of Rhode Island, and Providence Plantations, in New England.* Edited by John R. Bartlett. 10 vols. Providence, 1856–1865. |
| *Sibley's Harvard Graduates* | John L. Sibley and Clifford K. Shipton. *Biographical Sketches of Those Who Attended Harvard College.* 17 vols. Cambridge, Mass., 1873–1975. |
| T. | Treasury Papers, Public Record Office, London. |

Full references to the sources cited in the footnotes, including, in some cases, identification of the particular volume cited from a series, can be found in the bibliography.

[xx]

# *ADJUSTMENT TO EMPIRE*

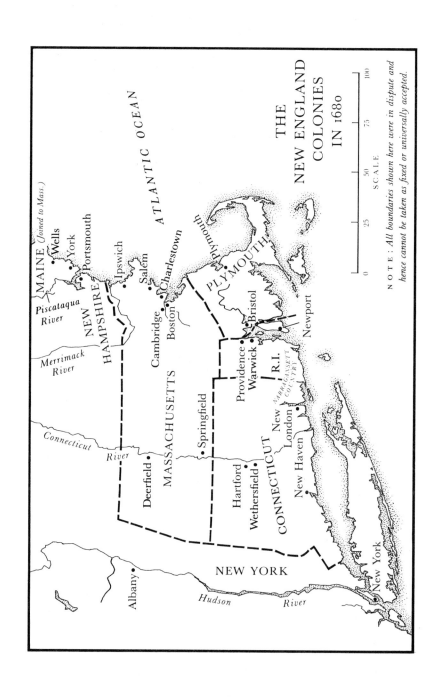

THE
NEW ENGLAND
COLONIES
IN 1680

SCALE

0    25    50    75    100

NOTE: All boundaries shown here were in dispute and
hence cannot be taken as fixed or universally accepted.

ATLANTIC OCEAN

MAINE (Joined to Mass.)

Wells
York
Portsmouth
Piscataqua
River

NEW
HAMPSHIRE

Merrimack
River

Ipswich
Salem
Charlestown
Cambridge
Boston

Plymouth

PLYMOUTH

Bristol

Providence
Warwick    R.I.
New
London    Newport
NARRAGANSETT
COUNTRY

Deerfield
MASSACHUSETTS

Springfield

Connecticut
River

Hartford
Wethersfield    CONNECTICUT
New Haven

Albany

NEW YORK

Hudson    River

New York

# I

## Prologue: Expansion and Confrontation, 1675-1685

"I WRITE the *Wonders* of the CHRISTIAN RELIGION, flying from the Depravations of *Europe,* to the *American Strand.*" Thus Cotton Mather, minister of Boston's Old North Church, began his *Magnalia Christi Americana,* a huge compendium and celebration of the lives and works of those New Englanders who had built a new Jerusalem in America, far from England's shores.[1] In the mid-1690s, as Mather penned these words, he could take pride in the fact that the colonists' Christian institutions still stood firm. Politically, however, as Mather well knew from his own active part in events, the history of New England had taken a different turn, away from virtual independence of the mother country and back toward subordination to the English crown. One attempt by the London government to consolidate the New England colonies into a single royal province had collapsed in the wake of the Glorious Revolution of 1688 in England. But a lasting settlement was emerging even as Mather wrote, setting Massachusetts and New Hampshire under royal government and restoring Rhode Island and Connecticut to rule according to their ancient charters. These events, their impact upon New England's heritage, and the colonists' slow accommodation to closer political ties with England, are the subjects of this study. They were in essence compromises, the consequences of a clash of beliefs and interests that was already well advanced by the early 1680s. Hence the story must begin in earlier years, with the elements from which these compromises were forged—the character of New England's societies, the

---

[1] Cotton Mather, *Magnalia Christi Americana,* "A General Introduction."

[*3*]

forces leading them into contact with the crown, and the aims of royal policy.

As New England entered the last quarter of the seventeenth century, its colonists could look back upon a time of remarkable peace and stability. From the small and scattered settlements of the 1620s their number had grown to some fifty thousand souls. Nearly two-thirds lived within the jurisdiction of the Massachusetts Bay Colony, which by the 1670s had spread north from the half-circle of towns girdling Massachusetts Bay to include what had begun as the independent settlements of Maine and New Hampshire. To the south and west lay the separate governments of Plymouth, Rhode Island, and Connecticut. The tranquility was due in part to a happy isolation, from each other and from the outside world. England and continental Europe were preoccupied with civil wars and national rivalries, and within New England there had been room enough for disagreement to be resolved by schisms and internal migration rather than by open strife. This same circumstance, coupled with a stern policy of repression and reprisal, had also enabled the settlers to avoid all but relatively localized conflicts with the country's first inhabitants, the Indians, although there were signs, as 1675 approached, that a more general confrontation lay at hand.

More fundamentally, however, this tranquility was the fruit of a broad consensus among New England's settlers concerning the forms and functions of human society, a consensus rooted in the soil of homogeneous origins and beliefs. Though they ranged in status from the small farmers and laborers of Plymouth to the affluent merchants of Boston and New Haven, the great majority of the first settlers had been "middling people" from the towns and villages of central and southern England. Some followed their minister or lord of the manor across the Atlantic; others came in response to the reports of life in the new world sent back by friends or relatives. All crossed in a stream of interrelated families that from the very beginning gave New England's societies a much greater internal strength and stability than

[4]

that of early Virginia, for example, where a high proportion of the immigrants were restless young bachelors. With them, these families brought the traditions and customs of English provincial life.[2]

The immigrants were like-minded also in the support they gave to the plans of their leaders to settle where it would be possible to live a godly and orderly life. England, it seemed in the 1630s, was falling into religious reaction and political autocracy: now was the time, in Governor John Winthrop's words, "to seeke out a place of Cohabitation and Consorteshipp under a due forme of Goverment both civill and ecclesiasticall."[3] Winthrop and a majority of his fellow leaders were Puritans, part of a group within the established Protestant Church of England dedicated to purifying the church of what they saw as remnants of papist and unscriptural ceremonies and procedures. They believed that such "a due forme of Goverment" could be established by following the dictates of God revealed in the Bible. Most who went with them shared their religious fervor. The subsequent history of New England, with its frequent schisms and doctrinal disputes, plainly demonstrated that not all were of one mind as to how God's word should be translated into a way of life. The Rhode Islanders, for example, pursued more radical and less disciplined forms of Puritanism, while the first settlers of Maine and New Hampshire generally regarded themselves as orthodox members of the Church of England. Yet, paradoxically, the very frequency of their doctrinal differences testified to a common devotion to a religious purpose. Some did come to New England for more mundane reasons, to catch fish or to find the land so scarce at home. But the soil and climate were rugged, the immediate returns few, and fortune hunters headed farther south, to the fertile plantations of Virginia and the Caribbean. There was justice in the repeated claims of the colonists

---

[2] Charles E. Banks, *Topographical Dictionary of 2,885 English Emigrants to New England, 1620–1650, passim;* Carl Bridenbaugh, *Vexed and Troubled Englishmen, 1590–1642,* 463–465; Edmund S. Morgan, *American Slavery, American Freedom,* 162–163, 235–236, 407–410; Russell R. Menard, "Immigrants and Their Increase," 102–103.

[3] Allyn B. Forbes, ed., *Winthrop Papers, 1498–1649,* II, 293.

and their descendants that New England, in the beginning, was a plantation of religion rather than of trade.[4]

The course of settlement strengthened this common purpose. By force of leadership and armed with the charter granted to the Massachusetts Bay Company by King Charles I, the seven hundred colonists who arrived with Winthrop in 1630 had exercised a predominant influence. From the Bay, emigrants moved north to the Merrimack and west to the Connecticut River. Even Rhode Island, always the maverick in matters of government and religion, received its scattering of early settlers from the Bay, if less by design than by the flight there of such as Roger Williams, Anne Hutchinson, and Samuel Gorton following religious disagreements. Harvard College, "that Artillery Garden from whence we receive our most expert souldiers of Christ," founded in 1636, sent forth a stream of ministers to the pulpits of New England; Boston made all the northern colonies its hinterland. Massachusetts assumed a moral and political leadership in New England that lasted throughout and beyond the colonial period. Neighboring colonies drew liberally and often literally upon its example for their laws and practices of government. The Cape mare—Plymouth Colony—was not alone in trotting after the Bay horse.[5]

By 1675, therefore, the colonists' civil and religious institutions were well established. In structure, the Puritan churches were congregational, each deriving its authority and autonomy from its

---

[4] Thus, among many examples, the General Court of Massachusetts to Oliver Cromwell, 1651, in Thomas Hutchinson, *The History of the Colony and Province of Massachusetts-Bay*, I, 431; and John Higginson, *The Cause of God and His People in New-England*, 11.

[5] John Wise, *The Churches Quarrel Espoused*, 131. For the influence of Massachusetts, see: Nelson P. Mead, *Connecticut as a Corporate Colony*, 30, 35; Frederick R. Jones, *History of Taxation in Connecticut*, 10 and n.; David E. Van Deventer, *The Emergence of Provincial New Hampshire, 1623–1741*, 17; and George L. Haskins and Samuel E. Ewing, "The Spread of Massachusetts Law in the Seventeenth Century," 413–418. For contemporary references to the leading role of "the Bay horse," see: George Bishop, *New England Judged not by Man's But by the Spirit of the Lord*, 130; Ichabod Wiswall to Thomas Hinckley, Nov. 5, 1691, Mass. Hist. Soc., *Collections*, 4th ser., V (1861), 301; and James Noyes to Fitz-John Winthrop, Aug. 29, 1706, *ibid.*, 6th ser., III (1889), 346.

founding by a congregation joined together in covenant. As in England, all persons were gathered into one congregation or another. In contrast to the practice of the parent Anglican church, however, full membership in these churches and admission to the sacraments were generally restricted to those who could demonstrate to the satisfaction of the congregation that they were among the elect singled out by God for salvation. Most churches adopted procedures whereby the saving faith of such "visible saints" could be recognized, as far as was possible in this world, through tests that included personal narratives of religious experience.

These restrictions had important political consequences, most notably in Massachusetts, where in 1631 the colony's legislative body, the General Court, had decreed that henceforth only those men who were full church members could become freemen and so be eligible to vote in electing the magistrates and (after their first summoning in 1634) the deputies who sat in the General Court.[6] By seventeenth-century standards, an unusually large percentage of adult males were thus enabled to vote, since most settlers were then church members. Later, Massachusetts allowed a few men to qualify for freemanship on the grounds of wealth alone, and none of the other colonies, save New Haven Colony, annexed to Connecticut in 1664, were quite as strict in limiting the franchise to church members. Nevertheless, political power in Puritan New England was always closely attuned to godliness, in practice and in the minds of rulers and ruled alike. Such godliness, it was true, tended to be most apparent in those who, like Winthrop, were already persons of substance and standing in society. But power was never automatically accorded, as in England, to those of birth, wealth, or property, or, as nowadays, to all over a certain age. Instead it was a privilege extended by the central governments to those who would, it was believed, share in upholding a godly way of life and in perpetuating religious and social orthodoxy. "The way of God hath alwayes beene to gather his churches out of the world," remarked Winthrop. "Now the world, or civill state, must be raised out

---

[6] *Mass. Records,* I, 87.

[7]

of the churches."[7] Only Rhode Island succumbed to the argument of
Roger Williams that soul liberty and purity of the church required
religious beliefs to be divorced from the business of government.

The bonds of these tightly knit religious and political structures
were further cemented by careful control of the land which formed
New England's most valuable commodity and by a constant process
of selection and exclusion at all levels of society. Claiming the right to
grant all lands within their jurisdictions by virtue of their charters
and compacts of government, the colonial governments supervised
the planting of new communities to ensure that only loyal and godly
families were permitted to establish new towns and churches.[8] Thus
the closed circle of authority was made complete: only the General
Court could create the institutions from which could come the freemen who elected the members of the General Court. The towns in
their turn, since each held its reserves of undivided land in common
ownership, likewise possessed a powerful weapon to ensure conformity among their inhabitants and to regulate the admission of further settlers. Many colonists, like the men of Dedham, had resolved
from the first that "we shall by all means labor to keepe of[f] from us
such, as ar contrary minded. And receave onely such unto us . . . as
may be probably of one harte with us." Rural communities in England had long exercised their own internal discipline, "warning out"
those likely to prove a burden on local morals or resources.[9] Transmitted across the Atlantic, this screening process gained an added authority and intensity from the towns' broad powers of self-government and from the selection and exclusion inherent in the practices of
New England Puritanism. Though God may indeed, as William

---

[7] Forbes, *Winthrop Papers,* III, 467. Timothy H. Breen, *The Character of the Good
Ruler,* provides an excellent analysis of Puritan concepts of leadership during
these years.

[8] In some parts of New England, as in Rhode Island and north of the Merrimack,
lands were divided and towns established before the creation of an effective central government. By mid-century, however, only Rhode Island lacked this centralized control of land.

[9] Don G. Hill, ed., *Early Records of the Town of Dedham,* III, 2; Frederick G. Emmison, ed., *Early Essex Town Meetings, passim.*

Stoughton suggested in his election day sermon of 1668, have "sifted forth a whole Nation that he might send choice Grain over into this Wilderness," it was still necessary to winnow the harvest so as to blow forth the chaff to Rhode Island.[10]

Within New England, therefore, powerful pressures could be brought to bear upon the individual to conform to the will of society. Yet these pressures were no greater, if somewhat different in character, than those exerted by other contemporary societies, and they were tempered and rationalized by the procedures, such as trial by jury and taxation by representative consent, that Englishmen on both sides of the Atlantic regarded as the touchstones of good government. The hand of authority stretched out to regulate every aspect of personal behavior, but it was not extended, as in Europe, to receive bribes or to extort forced loans. Though economic circumstances permitted but a modest prosperity, high wage rates and the widespread ownership of land enabled New Englanders to avoid the extremes of contemporary poverty.[11] Above all, the New England way gave to those who followed it the opportunity to seek the "true liberty" that Winthrop had once defined as "a liberty to that only which is good, just, and honest." Most echoed the quiet contentment expressed by

---

[10] William Stoughton, *New-England's True Interest,* 18. For an example of this winnowing, see the verdict of the Roxbury Church against Robert Potter in *Boston Records,* VI, 187.

[11] A comparison of the scattered figures available for wages and prices in New England compared to those of England in the seventeenth century suggests that, after initial short-term fluctuations, wages settled at a level almost twice that of England while food prices did not vary significantly from those of England. Thus the figures in William B. Weeden, *Economic and Social History of New England, 1620–1789,* II, 877–903; U.S. Department of Labor, Bureau of Labor Statistics, *History of Wages in the United States from Colonial Times to 1928,* 46–142; Brian R. Mitchell and Phyllis Deane, *Abstract of British Historical Statistics,* 484–487; Christopher Hill, *The Century of Revolution, 1603–1714,* 317–319; and the analysis in Herbert R. Cederberg, Jr., "Wages and Prices in Eighteenth-Century England and the Thirteen Colonies"; Roslyn R. Cooperman, "The Free Worker in Colonial Massachusetts"; Terry Lee Anderson, *The Economic Growth of Seventeenth-Century New England,* 146–151; and William I. Davisson, "Essex County Price Trends: Money and Markets in Seventeenth-Century Massachusetts," 144–185. For economic conditions as seen in the demographic history of one town, see Kenneth A. Lockridge, "The Population of Dedham, Massachusetts, 1636–1736," esp. 334–338. Due partly to the availability of land, wage labor was notoriously scarce and costly in early New England.

one humble immigrant, John Wiswall of Dorchester, some years after his arrival. "For the land it is a fyne land," he wrote to a friend back in England, "good for corne, especially Indian, which is a very precious graine for divers uses besides bread, good for pasture, and good haye land, plenty of wood. Truely Sir, I like it very well, and so I thinke any godly man God calls over will when he sees Moyses and Aaron, I mean magistrate and minister, in church and commonwalke to walke hand in hand, discountenancing and punishing sinne in whomsoever, and standinge for the praise of them that doe well." A quarter of a century later, the men of Dedham still testified to their satisfaction with "a Godly righteous and peacable goverment. . . . We may and (we hope) shall say our portions are falne amongst the godly."[12]

Such tributes were common, and they suggest the source of New England's innate conservatism, a conservatism that lingered and continued to shape colonial politics and relations with the outside world long after changing circumstances had rendered the realization of its goals impossible. The colonists believed they had found the Gospel way—and the truth and the life. It could only be defended; it could hardly be improved. Nor was this a spirit shared merely by those who enjoyed the full political privileges of freemanship. Recent studies have shown that, in Massachusetts at least, a decreasing proportion of the adult male population voted in colony-wide elections.[13] Yet there is no evidence that any considerable number of men were being excluded from the political process or were discontented as a result. Some, it seems, were conscientiously unable to narrate the religious experience that remained the main path to freemanship by way of church membership. Others, whether church members or not, apparently felt no compelling desire to assume the privileges (and burdens) of participation in a government with whose course they found

---

[12] John Winthrop, *Winthrop's Journal,* II, 239; Wiswall to George Rigby, Sept. 27, 1638, Historical Manuscripts Commission, *The Manuscripts of Lord Kenyon,* IV, 56; Hill, *Early Records of Dedham,* IV, 276, 278.

[13] See the works cited in B. Katherine Brown, "The Controversy over the Franchise in Puritan Massachusetts, 1954 to 1974," 212–241.

trying to protect native agriculture against foreign competition, and a
1668 petition from Salem spoke of the annual importation of thirty or
forty thousand bushels of grain into the colony "and yett wee have
generaly butt hand to mouth."[19] Some of the grain was reexported by
traders willing to brave popular resentment for the harder currency
and tropical commodities obtainable in the southern plantations.[20]
But contemporaries agreed that by the 1680s the colony had become
dependent upon the rest of New England for such exports and even
for supplies for its own consumption. Massachusetts, reported one
royal official, "though most considerable for Number of Townes and
Inhabitants and well situated for Trade is one of the smallest and
Poorest Tracts of Land and Produces least of any of the other Col-
lonys for Exportation."[21] Well into the next century the colony was
beset by wheat shortages which could only be relieved by relief shipments from Connecticut and elsewhere.[22]

At first, these difficulties were concealed by the capital and credits
brought from England. But the slackening of immigration in the
1640s plunged Massachusetts into an abrupt economic depression,

---

Andros to his Instructions, [Apr.? 1690], C.O., Class 5, volume 855, no. 90 (fol.
240).

[19] Thomas Hutchinson, *Hutchinson Papers*, I, 241; *Mass. Records*, IV, pt. i, 246; *New
England Historical and Genealogical Register*, IX (1855), 84.

[20] Thus the efforts to restrict the export of corn, *Mass. Records*, III, 123, 153, IV, pt.
ii, 43; *Mass. Acts and Resolves*, I, 226, 236, 249, 277, 724. Upon occasion, similar
embargoes were laid in every New England colony. The export of corn led to
bread riots in Boston in 1710 and 1713.

[21] Answer of Sir Edmund Andros to his Instructions, [Apr.? 1690], C.O. 5/855,
no. 90 (fol. 240); Andros to the Lords of Trade, Mar. 30, 1687, C.O. 5/940, 346;
President and Council of New England to the Lords of Trade, read Oct. 21, 1686,
C.O. 1/60, no. 80 (fol. 235v.); Edward Randolph to the Earl of Sunderland, Mar.
25, 1687, Joseph Dudley to William Blathwayt, July 31, 1686, *Randolph Letters*,
IV, 154, VI, 196.

[22] Thus Cotton Mather, *The Diary of Cotton Mather*, ed. Worthington C. Ford, I,
191–193, 196, 223, 241; Samuel Sewall, *The Diary of Samuel Sewall, 1674–1729*, II,
715, 734; and Benjamin Colman to Robert Wodrow, Jan. 23, 1719, Mass. Hist.
Soc., *Proceedings*, LXXVII (1965), 113. The nature of the trade between Connecticut and the Bay is shown well in the letters between Josiah and Henry Wolcott,
Roger Wolcott Papers, I, 16–41, Conn. Hist. Soc.

forcing a search for new sources of income.[23] Schemes to develop domestic iron and cloth industries failed; a promising trade in skins and furs from the back country withered in the 1660s. Only lumber, fish, and New England's agricultural surpluses remained reliable staples for export. None had the scarcity value of tobacco or sugar, and to seek the best returns and markets, the traders of Massachusetts took to the seas to peddle their cargoes in ports as far afield as southern Europe and the Caribbean. Already middlemen linking the lumbermen of New Hampshire and the farmers of Rhode Island and Connecticut to outside markets, the Massachusetts traders increasingly assumed this role within the Atlantic community, profiting from the commissions and freight charges to be earned from the complex interchange of New England products with tropical commodities and European manufactured goods. By the second half of the seventeenth century, the ports of the Massachusetts Bay—Boston, Charlestown, and Salem—were the channels through which flowed the great proportion of New England's trade.[24] Smaller ports fed into the Bay through a network of coasting vessels. Even the important trade in masts and other naval stores from the Piscataqua directly to England was guided by Boston merchants and their agents until the end of the century.[25] Outside these commercial centers, Massachusetts was no

---

[23] Marion H. Gottfried, "The First Depression in Massachusetts," 655–678. For a contemporary comment on the erosion in New England of capital brought from England, see Lord Say and Sele to John Winthrop, July 9, 1640, Forbes, *Winthrop Papers,* IV, 265.

[24] Bailyn, *New England Merchants,* 45–91; Carl Bridenbaugh, *Cities in the Wilderness,* 23–24, 30–34, 38–39. Together, the three Bay towns contained at least a tenth of New England's population in 1675; in the same year they paid 37 percent of a tax levied throughout Massachusetts: *Mass. Records,* V, 55–56. Other coast towns such as Newport were beginning to emerge as ports with a significant overseas trade, but they lagged well behind those of the Massachusetts Bay. For Rhode Island's commerce, see Carl Bridenbaugh, *Fat Mutton and Liberty of Conscience,* chapter V.

[25] Van Deventer, *Emergence of Provincial New Hampshire,* 87–97, 130–131. Additional evidence of the extensive trading ties between the Bay merchants and their New Hampshire hinterland in the late seventeenth century can be found in the papers of Robert Gibbs, Massachusetts Manuscripts, Colonial, 1659–1787, Amer. Antiq. Soc.; of John Usher and David Jeffries, Jeffries Papers, III, Mass. Hist. Soc.; and of Jonathan Corwin and Eleazer Hathorne, Curwen Papers, II, III, Essex Instit.

less agricultural than its neighbors. The representatives of the inland towns continued to have a preponderant voice in government. Yet the importance of commerce was clearly greater than could be gauged from the men or capital which it employed. Its earnings were essential for the redress of the colony's balance of trade. It was the dynamic element in the New England economy, and the evidence suggests that, for Massachusetts at least, it was already indispensable.[26]

With commercial contacts, however, came an inevitable involvement with the affairs of the outside world. As early as the days of Governor John Winthrop, Massachusetts and its merchants had been drawn into an ill-fated intervention in the struggle of two rival French claimants for control of Acadia (the modern Nova Scotia). The subsequent expansion of New England trade, matching that of European settlement along the Atlantic seaboard, brought commercial and diplomatic ties with the French in Canada and the Dutch in neighboring New Netherland.[27] Trade fostered migration: from Barbados, for example, where many New Englanders had relatives and trading correspondents (the first often doubling as the second), a number of prosperous merchants removed to Boston after mid-century.[28] Most important of all, the New England colonies, and Massachusetts in particular, were brought face to face with the ambitions of

---

[26] The importance of external trade even in a predominantly agricultural economy is suggested, for a later period, by Gordon C. Bjork, "The Weaning of the American Economy," 541–560.

[27] John B. Brebner, *New England's Outpost,* chapter I; and, generally, Arthur H. Buffinton, "The Policy of the Northern English Colonies towards the French to the Treaty of Utrecht."

[28] Vincent Harlow, *A History of Barbados, 1625–1685,* chapter VI; G. Andrews Moriarty, "Barbadian Notes," LXVII, 360–371, LXVIII, 177–181, and "New England and Barbadian Notes," XIV, 164–167, XV, 132–136; James D. Phillips, *Salem in the Seventeenth Century,* 284; Richard S. Dunn, *Sugar and Slaves,* 111. Such prominent merchants as Robert Gibbs, Peter Lidgett, and Tobias Payne came to Boston via Barbados: details of Gibbs's extensive trade with the island can be found in Massachusetts Manuscripts, Colonial, and in the early pages of what is somewhat misleadingly termed the Ledger Book of Jonathan Corwin, 1658–1718, Essex Instit. (Corwin married Gibbs's widow). Examples of New England trade to other parts of the West Indies can be found in Howard W. Preston, ed., *The Letter Book of Peleg Sanford of Newport,* and Letterbook of John Hull, 1670–1685 (typescript of manuscript), Amer. Antiq. Soc.

England's mercantile community four thousand miles away. Emerging from the dislocations of civil war between king and Parliament, English traders were likewise seeking to profit from the Atlantic carrying trade and the exchange of colonial raw materials for European manufactured goods. To this end they had secured the passage of an act of Parliament in 1651 aimed at excluding Dutch competition; among other provisions designed to strengthen English commerce and shipping, all vessels not built and owned in either England or its colonies were barred from trading with or between the colonies. This regulation was reenacted in 1660 after the restoration of the Stuart monarchy, with the added stipulation that certain "enumerated" goods produced by the colonies, including tobacco, sugar, and cotton, were to be shipped only to England or to another English colony. Three years later, Parliament completed the circle of regulation by requiring that, with minor exceptions, all goods imported into the colonies from Europe must pass through England and hence through the hands of its merchants.

These Acts of Trade, or Navigation Acts as they were also called, were designed to protect and foster all facets of England's overseas trade, not merely the small portion of it that then lay with the infant plantations in America.[29] Nor did they immediately damage New England's commerce. The acts had been passed without much thought for their execution; those parts most readily enforceable, notably the provisions excluding foreign vessels from colonial ports, favored New England's carrying trade and its growing shipbuilding industry. For their part, the colonists would have found nothing strange in England's attempts to regulate trade with the colonies; other European countries did likewise and the New England governments themselves had long endeavored to subordinate economic activity to the interests of the common welfare, even down to the setting of wages and prices.

---

[29] In the 1660s, trade with all the American colonies was less than one-eighth of the value of London's imports and less than one-twelfth of its exports: Ralph Davis, "English Foreign Trade, 1660–1700," 164–165.

## Expansion and Confrontation

Nonetheless, the passage of the Acts of Trade prepared the way for an open clash of interests between old and New England. Colonies, in the minds of English merchants and royal officials, existed to serve the mother country by furnishing it with commodities and with secure markets for the trade which built up national wealth and a powerful merchant marine. They were alarmed and, ultimately, indignant to find that some colonists, lacking any considerable share of useful commodities, were setting up on their own account as traders and carriers under the aegis of plantation governments seemingly heedless of regulations made in England. Massachusetts was clearly challenging rather than properly complementing England's economic prerogatives. By the 1670s, English merchants were complaining loudly at Whitehall that their New England counterparts were depriving the English treasury of large sums in customs revenue by their extensive and, it was alleged, predominantly illegal trade.[30]

Thus by 1675, the economic enterprise needed to sustain New England's fragile prosperity had already set the colonists upon a collision course with the London government. Simultaneously, developments within New England equally rooted in the circumstances of its founding were also thrusting its affairs upon the attention of royal officials. No single theme was more pervasive in the settlement of colonial America than land and the problems of its distribution. "The Lord give you and me," wrote the devout Boston diarist, Samuel Sewall, to his brother, "skill and oportunity to take up a Lot in Heaven where every Habitant will rejoice in the Strength of our Title and our great Landlord will demand but thanks for our Quit Rent."[31] In clothing religious hopes in the images of his conception of man's earthly rewards, Sewall touched upon aspirations dear to the heart of

---

[30] George L. Beer, *The Old Colonial System, 1660–1754*, I, 45–52; *CSP Col., 1675–1676*, nos. 673, 721, 787, 881.

[31] Samuel Sewall to [Stephen Sewall], Feb. 1, 1687, Curwin Papers, I, 1, Amer. Antiq. Soc.

every colonist: whatever the rewards of commerce, land was still the badge of status and security. In comparison to the wholesale dispersion of unsettled lands in other colonies, the New England governments, both central and local, kept firm hold upon their landed capital. Yet as the population of New England all but quadrupled in the thirty years after 1640, the pressures upon the available reserves of fertile land became severe. Young men seeking larger allotments than their parents could or would provide and immigrants excluded from existing towns by inhabitants fearful of overcrowding petitioned in growing numbers for space to establish new plantations. "God Land," wrote Roger Williams, "will be (as it now is) as great a God with us English as God Gold was with the Spaniards." Men were rushing into the wilderness so fast, cried Edward Johnson, that they could no longer hear "the sweet sound of the silver Trumpets blown by the laborious ministers of Christ."[32] By the 1660s, Massachusetts, "being now increased and wanting convenient places to settle our people," was sending men as far west as Albany in search of land "cleer for the Plough," and many New Englanders were leaving to settle in New York, the Jerseys, and the Carolinas.[33]

Massachusetts stood in the forefront of this expansion, both by reason of its growing population and comparatively limited agricultural resources and because of its keen sense of spiritual and political leadership. Until the 1660s, when both Connecticut and Rhode Island received charters from King Charles II, it alone could claim title to its lands by direct royal grant. Confident of its legal authority and strong in the faith that the blessings of godly rule should be spread among

---

[32] Roger Williams to John Winthrop, Jr., May 28, 1664, *Publications of the Narragansetts Club*, 1st ser., VI (Providence, 1874), 319 (see also Williams to Major Mason, June 22, 1670, *ibid.*, 342); Edward Johnson, *Johnson's Wonder-working Providence, 1628–1651*, 253. Similar laments can be found in [Increase Mather], *The Necessity of Reformation*, 8; Increase Mather, *An Earnest Exhortation to the Inhabitants of New-England*, 9; and William Hubbard, *The Happiness of a People*, 58.

[33] *Plymouth Records*, X, 445, IX, 211; Arthur Buffinton, "New England and the Western Fur Trade, 1629–1675," 188–189; Lois K. Mathews, *The Expansion of New England*, 53–56, 66–67. Numerous plans were floated in these years on both sides of the Atlantic to encourage New Englanders to move to more "useful" parts of America, such as the West Indies.

the heathen, be they Indian or English, Massachusetts took every opportunity to extend its borders. Indeed, in terms of the imposition of government and ideology upon other European colonists, the Bay Colony was the most aggressive and successful expansionist power on the American continent in the seventeenth century. To the north, by a dubious construction of its charter, it asserted its claim to the lands granted by the Council of New England to John Mason and Sir Ferdinando Gorges. By 1643 the last of the New Hampshire towns had submitted, and by 1658 the scattered settlements along the coast of Maine also acknowledged Boston's authority. Westward, the colony secured the upper reaches of the Connecticut River from Hartford's control, and to the south, after restricting Plymouth Colony to a corner which it was ultimately to absorb, Massachusetts harassed and sought to annex the defiantly heterodox settlements in Rhode Island and around Narragansett Bay. Connecticut likewise, once it had received its royal charter, absorbed neighboring New Haven and strove to wrest from Rhode Island the rich lands to the west of Narragansett Bay. Each colony pressed hard upon its remaining Indian inhabitants to give up further portions of their lands.

This internal expansion proceeded, in the main, by way of negotiation rather than conquest. The conflicting titles issuing from the crown gave color to a multitude of claims, and both north of the Merrimack and around Narragansett Bay there were those who welcomed the order and security offered by Boston's or Hartford's rule. Others did not, especially those who had settled there precisely in order to be beyond the reach of Puritan orthodoxy. Indeed, the very policies of selection and exclusion which had preserved consensus and conformity within such colonies as Massachusetts and Connecticut now bred conflict within New England as a whole because of the number of dissidents from each colony who had settled in the path of its subsequent expansion.[34] Many of these settlers feared renewed

---

[34] This point suggests the danger of relying too closely for a picture of New England society upon studies of individual communities alone—though in themselves they might be "peaceable kingdoms," they often clashed fiercely with one another, the more fiercely indeed because of their internal unity and strength.

persecution and dispossession, and they were quick to observe that behind the expansionists' claims lay schemes for personal profit. In the contest for control of the rich Narragansett lands, for example, a group of speculators headed by Humphrey Atherton of Boston claimed ownership by virtue of a series of unusually disreputable purchases from the local Indians. The stakes were large: some of the hundreds of thousands of acres bought for a few hundred pounds were soon being sold for as much as five and ten shillings apiece.[35] All would be lost if the Rhode Island government were permitted to gain control of the region and rescind the purchase. Hence the Atherton proprietors bent all their considerable political influence in Massachusetts and Connecticut toward ensuring that their lands would be taken under the latter's jurisdiction. Was not Rhode Island, as they piously informed Connecticut's governor, "a *rodde* to those that love to live in order,—a road, refuge, asylum to evil livers?" A struggle began which lasted well into the following century.[36] Similarly, the annexation of Maine by Massachusetts set in motion a wave of land acquisitions by prominent inhabitants of the Bay, foremost among them being the magistrates appointed to administer the province. The holdings accumulated by such influential families as the Tyngs, Hut-

---

[35] The price paid can be estimated from Amos Richardson to John Winthrop, Jr., July 9, 1659, Mass. Hist. Soc., *Collections*, 5th ser., IX (1855), 7, and James N. Arnold, ed., *The Records of the Proprietors of the Narragansett, otherwise called the Fones Record*, 1–4, 9, 10, taking the value of wampum to be five shillings a fathom. For the price of land sold, *ibid.*, 26, 83–85, 122–123. All figures are in New England money, then worth 75 percent of English sterling money. A report drafted for the guidance of prospective Huguenot settlers in 1687 spoke of one hundred acres of land in the Narragansett country as costing twenty pounds cash sterling: Société de l'Histoire de Protestantisme Français, *Bulletin Histoire et Littéraire*, XVI (1867), 73.

[36] The Atherton Proprietors to Governor John Winthrop, Jr., c. 1661, Mass. Hist. Soc., *Collections*, 5th ser., IX (1885), 27. General accounts of this complicated struggle can be found in Elisha Potter, "The Early History of Narragansett," *passim;* Clarence W. Bowen, *The Boundary Disputes of Connecticut*, 31–42; and Richard S. Dunn, *Puritans and Yankees*, 109 *et seq.* Among the proprietors between 1660 and 1689 were Atherton, Thomas Deane, John Saffin, John Winthrop, Jr., and his sons, Fitz-John and Wait, Simon Bradstreet, Daniel Dennison, Edward and Elisha Hutchinson, Richard Wharton, William Tailer, Richard Lord, Simon Lynd, and Richard and James Russell, all notable political and mercantile figures in Massachusetts and Connecticut. Sydney V. James, *Colonial Rhode Island*, 75–93, 101–106, elucidates the tangled land disputes within and around that colony.

chinsons, Gedneys, and Leveretts may fairly be seen as an important motive underlying the prolonged and costly commitment of Massachusetts to the defense of Maine in later years.[37]

No single government within New England possessed the power or undisputed legal authority to resolve this tangle of overlapping claims. The three most orthodox Puritan colonies, Massachusetts, Connecticut, and Plymouth, were united in a loose alliance, the Confederation of New England, but this body, composed of commissioners from each colony meeting annually, was too dominated by Massachusetts and too palpably hostile to outsiders such as Rhode Island for its decisions to command any general acceptance. Increasingly, therefore, those who found no satisfactory remedy within New England turned to their nominal sovereign, England, for redress. With the restoration of a monarchy decidedly unsympathetic to Puritanism, the opponents of Massachusetts seized their chance. In London, the heirs of Gorges and Mason sought for the return of their proprietary authority over Maine and New Hampshire, and from settlers within each province came petitions complaining of Boston's domination and requesting their own separate government. Agents from the Rhode Island town of Warwick appealed for protection from the claims of settlers backed by Massachusetts and Connecticut. Even the Atherton proprietors, despairing of a permanent settlement, ultimately enlisted the aid of royal officials at Whitehall.[38] Endless

---

[37] William Willis, *History of Portland from 1632 to 1864*, 224–234, 886; William D. Williamson, *History of the State of Maine*, I, 563, 566. An account of early land speculation in New England is much needed: see, for the eighteenth century, the summary of Roy H. Akagi, *The Town Proprietors of the New England Colonies*, chapter VIII, and, for Maine in particular, the detailed study of Robert E. Moody, "The Maine Frontier, 1607 to 1763." Some impression of the Massachusetts involvement in Maine land can be gathered from the petitions for confirmation of grants printed in *Doc. Hist. Maine*, VI, 222–412, 449–467. For contemporary comments on the link between political decisions in Massachusetts and the land dealings of "particular interests," see Governor John Easton of Rhode Island to Governor Simon Bradstreet of Massachusetts, Nov. 17, 1691, Mass. Archives, XXXVII, 212, and Edward Randolph to the Earl of Sunderland, Mar. 25, 1687, *Randolph Letters*, IV, 153.

[38] *APC Col.*, I, nos. 888, 1014, 1025, 1050, 1222–1224, 1233, 1244, 1291; *CSP Col.*, *1661–1668;* nos. 49–51, 64, 230, 1024i–iii, *1669–1674*, nos. 150, 439, 512, 593,

charges, countercharges, and commissions of enquiry followed. Though other issues contributed to bringing New England affairs to London's attention, none were as fundamental and persistent as those concerning the title and possession of land.

Yet London's attention brought no assurance of effective action, and it seemed at first as though the crown's response to the complaints of merchants and colonists alike would be as ineffectual as its earlier attempts to curb New England's autonomy. In the 1630s, for example, royal officials had tried to annul the Massachusetts charter by legal action and to impose a governor general upon New England. Thirty years later, in the wake of the complaints levelled against Massachusetts and a stinging official report detailing its "many enormities," royal commissioners had been sent with the expedition launched against the neighboring Dutch colony of New Netherland to investigate New England affairs.[39] Several schemes for the reduction of the American colonies to "a more certaine civill and uniforme way of government" had been advanced during the period of parliamentary rule in England, and some officials clearly hoped for New England's inclusion within a coherent scheme of colonial reorganization.[40] All those plans, however, foundered upon the shoals of royal disinterest and colonial opposition. On neither occasion was the crown prepared to push matters to a decisive conclusion; in the 1660s,

---

1247, 1420, *1675–1676*, nos. 412, 413, 753, 754, 1187, *1677–1680*, nos. 1080, 1527, 1532; *N. H. Provincial Papers*, XVII, 510–513; Maine Hist. Soc., *Collections*, I (1831 [reprinted 1865]), 400–402; Joseph H. Smith, *Appeals to the Privy Council from the American Plantations*, 122–126; Dunn, *Puritans and Yankees*, 220–224.

[39] Charles M. Andrews, *The Colonial Period of American History*, I, chapter XIX; Report of the Council for Foreign Plantations, [April 30, 1661], *CSP Col.*, *1661–1668*, no. 75.

[40] This phrase, first appearing in proposals drawn up by the influential merchant Thomas Povey, was incorporated in the instructions drawn up in 1660 for the newly created Council for Foreign Plantations: Charles M. Andrews, *British Committees, Commissions, and Councils of Trade and Plantations, 1622–1675*, 56–60; Beer, *Old Colonial System*, I, 233–234; *N. Y. Col. Docs.*, III, 35. The Council's intent is expressed in minutes of Jan. 7, 1661, *CSP Col.*, *1661–1668*, no. 3.

far from bringing privately governed colonies under closer royal control, Charles II added to their number and autonomy by granting requests for new proprietary governments in the Carolinas and New York (conquered New Netherland) and by giving generous charters of incorporation to Connecticut and Rhode Island. Within New England, the Massachusetts government bluntly rebuffed the commissioners' attempts to sit as a court of appeal within the colony and to restore independent governments to Maine and New Hampshire.

In part, this failure stemmed from what was to prove a perennial problem of England's relations with its American colonies, a lack of accurate information concerning conditions across the Atlantic. Prior to the commissioners' visit, for instance, disaffected settlers had assured royal officials that the great majority of New England's inhabitants were loyal to the crown. A mere show of royal authority would bring down the oligarchic rule of the Boston magistrates just as, in 1660, the facade of Cromwellian government in England had crumbled before the return of Charles II.[41] Hence the crown's expectations, in its instructions to the commissioners, that Massachusetts could be induced to accept a "renewal" of its charter and royal participation in the selection of its leading officials. In any event, the walls of Zion did not fall before the intruders: the only trumpets heard were those blown early in the morning outside the commissioners' Boston lodgings, heralding the General Court's proclamation that it refused to recognize their proceedings. Far from shaking the Puritan hold upon government, the commissioners' visit only proved its strength.

---

[41] Samuel Maverick to the Earl of Clarendon, [c. 1661], *Collections of the New-York Historical Society for 1869* (New York, 1870), 22, 26–27. A measure of London's mixture of ignorance and misinformation concerning New England can be seen in the notebooks of Joseph Williamson, then under-secretary of state: Mass. Hist. Soc., *Proceedings*, X (1867–1869), 377–382, XIII (1873–1875), 132–135. Williamson's version of Massachusetts's theological dispute with Anne Hutchinson was that Governor Vane had seduced Mrs. Hutchinson and one of her followers and that both had subsequently borne monsters. As the Committee of Trade remarked in May 1675 concerning New England, "Things . . . at this distance and where no person appears on the other side seeme very darke:" C.O. 5/903, 23.

Even had Massachusetts meekly submitted, however, it is improbable that the crown would yet have begun a general regulation and reorganization of New England. Engrossed in the pleasurable task of reestablishing the monarchy's position in English affairs, and relishing its fruits, Charles and his ministers had little time or interest to spare for the proceedings of a fanatical remnant several thousand miles away. Their mood was conciliatory, not revengeful.[42] Moreover, despite the greater momentum and consistency imparted by an emerging bureaucracy, the course of official action was still (as it long continued to be) primarily defined and directed by the interplay of private ends and ambitions. Government remained the king's business, not the nation's, and few measures were undertaken without considering their immediate benefits for the royal purse. Down the administrative ladder, public power and private interest were no less closely intertwined: officials held their positions as valuable pieces of property, to be bought, sold and even inherited, and drew their returns from the fees and gratuities exacted from every piece of business transacted.

Until such time as New England and its affairs were better understood in Whitehall, therefore, the character of Stuart government weighed against sustained royal intervention. The commissioners might fulminate against Boston's "Common-wealth-like" ways but their hostility could not be translated into action without more substantial incentives, for the crown or for those willing and able to grease the official wheels. Such incentives were already apparent in colonies to the south, with their rich crops of sugar and tobacco, and the Caribbean colonies of Jamaica, Barbados, and the Leeward Islands were all brought to join Virginia under direct royal government

---

[42] Wesley Frank Craven, *The Colonies in Transition, 1660–1713*, 44–49. For a different interpretation see Michael G. Hall, *Edward Randolph*, 13–15. Hall, however, overstates the implications of the powers accorded the commissioners, and his assessment of the crown's intentions relies on a memorandum not in fact written until the following decade and then most probably by Robert Tufton Mason, a claimant to New Hampshire, rather than by a royal official: Percy L. Kaye, *English Colonial Administration under Lord Clarendon, 1660–1667*, 76–81; and compare the text of the memorandum (C.O. 1/18, no. 46) with that of Mason's proposal in 1675 (C.O. 1/34, no. 68).

within a dozen years of the Restoration. London was also willing to protect these regions and the revenues they generated: English military and naval forces were stationed in the Caribbean and in 1675, upon news of an uprising in Virginia, an expedition of eleven hundred men headed by three royal commissioners was dispatched to the colony to restore order and investigate complaints.[43] No comparable returns were apparent elsewhere; hence other colonies were allowed to rest in the hands of those interested and influential enough to negotiate new proprietary grants or, like Massachusetts, were left to their own devices save for those occasions when the petitions of the king's subjects in those parts prompted investigation. In sum, policy in the sense of systematic procedures carried through into practice was as yet piecemeal and pragmatic; English royal government, in colonial as in domestic matters, remained a fundamentally passive instrument, opportunist upon occasion but shortsighted in its objectives and active primarily when impelled by the numerous interest groups within and around it.

Gradually, however, the London government's tolerance of New England's independent course gave way to an increasing concern over its strength and direction. By the early 1670s, optimism as to Massachusetts's fundamental loyalty had been replaced by an equally exaggerated apprehension. "We understood," recorded the diarist John Evelyn, a member of the royal Council for Foreign Plantations, "they were a people al most upon the very brink of renouncing any dependance of the Crowne." The council's president, the Earl of Sandwich, wrote of his concern that Massachusetts had become

---

[43] The crown drew direct revenues of some £4,500 a year during the 1670s from the West Indies, besides larger sums from customs duties, and it was estimated in 1676 that the rebellion in Virginia was endangering £100,000 in annual revenues: Archibald P. Thornton, *West-India Policy under the Restoration*, 258 (and *ibid.*, 214–252, for the crown's defense commitments to the Caribbean); C. Douglas Chandaman, *The English Public Revenue, 1660–1688*, 352–360; Wilcomb E. Washburn, *The Governor and the Rebel*, 93. Such revenues provided the additional inducement of lucrative fees for officials: thus C. S. S. Higham, "The Accounts of a Colonial Governor's Agent in the Seventeenth Century," 263–285. Significantly, the crown did not hesitate to abandon colonies such as Tangier and Bombay that proved to be financial liabilities.

England's rival in supplying provisions and manufactures to the southern colonies and that its dominance in New England gave it a potential monopoly of the vital trade in masts and naval stores.[44] Reports that the colony could put thirty thousand men under arms seem to rule out any possibility of reducing it by conquest, and the council was inclined to favor suggestions that a naval force should be sent to exert pressure on the colony by imposing an embargo on its trade.[45]

The choice of strategy, in conjunction with Sandwich's observations, made plain the economic logic that was for the first time drawing New England to the forefront of the crown's colonial concerns. The expansion of its commerce under the aegis of the Acts of Trade was depriving English merchants (and the royal revenues) of the benefits which the acts had been designed to garner. Even more alarming were the many reports that the New Englanders were skirting the acts to reap additional profits, exporting colonial commodities directly to continental Europe and returning with foreign manufactures. Clearly, England's commercial system could not be secure until the acts were both tightened and uniformly enforced, in New England no less than in other colonies more directly valuable to the crown. The regulation of trade, therefore, ultimately dictated a greater uniformity of royal control: in contrast to the maxim of a later and more consciously imperial age, the flag followed trade and not trade the flag. Yet it was not a uniformity deriving from any belief that the colonies were all alike. Whereas England had brought its southern plantations under its immediate government in expectation of a more profitable trade in goods and commodities, the inclusion of New England began as an attempt to suppress a dangerous competitor in the work of exploiting American colonial resources. This distinction, and the circumstances which prompted it, remained

---

[44] John Evelyn, *The Diary of John Evelyn*, III, 581 (June 4, 1671); F. R. Harris, *The Life of Edward Mountagu, K. G., First Earl of Sandwich (1625–1672)*, II, 337–341.

[45] Harris, *Life of Sandwich*, 338; Evelyn, *Diary*, III, 582, 584. A naval embargo had also been suggested by two of the royal commissioners to New England some years earlier.

crucial factors in the shaping of royal policy toward New England.

War with the Dutch employed the British navy in more important tasks than blockading Boston harbor, but Parliament took action in 1673 with a new Act of Trade which seemed to one observer to be "wholly made in reference to New England."[46] It imposed new restrictions and duties upon intercolonial (and hence New England's) trade and provided for the appointment by the crown of customs officers in colonial ports. As before, enforcement was first attempted in the southern colonies, but with the return of peace, and following a further flurry of complaints against the New Englanders, royal officials began to press for a broader compliance. Domestic bureaucratic development likewise favored a more general approach: in 1671 responsibility for the collection of trade duties, hitherto farmed out to private financiers, was assumed by an energetic Board of Customs Commissioners appointed by the crown and responsible to the Treasury; in 1675 the various committees and councils which had attended to commercial and colonial matters were united into a single more powerful body, a standing committee of the king's Privy Council known as the Lords of Trade and Plantations. Like its predecessors, this committee continued to forward recommendations and reports for action by the king or his secretaries of state. But with its leading members equally prominent in the Privy Council, advisory and executive functions were effectively telescoped together. Meeting on a regular basis, generally once a week, its sessions were customarily attended by the principal officers of state and even, upon occasion, by King Charles or by his brother James, an active entrepreneur in overseas expansion and proprietor of the colony of New York bordering upon New England.[47] Sustained by this interest and support and guided by an experienced secretariat, the Lords of Trade began

---

[46] "Memoriall concerning the Plantation trade from Ld. Culpeper," n.d., Addit. MSS., 28079, fol. 85.

[47] Thomas C. Barrow, *Trade and Empire*, 4–19; Ralph Paul Bieber, *The Lords of Trade and Plantations, 1675–1696*, 89. Attendance at the committee's meetings can be followed from its journals: C.O. 391/1–6. Both of the secretaries of state during these years, Sir Henry Coventry and Sir Joseph Williamson, were keenly interested in colonial affairs.

to establish the administrative continuity and coordinated supervision of colonial affairs necessary for an active royal policy.

New England was among the first items upon the new committee's agenda, largely owing to the tireless efforts of Ferdinando Gorges and Robert Tufton Mason, grandsons of the original proprietors, in pressing their claims to Maine and New Hampshire and in concerting the chorus of complaints levelled against Massachusetts. In December 1675, the committee recommended that the Boston government be commanded to send agents to London to answer their claims. Three months later, Mason's cousin, Edward Randolph, was dispatched across the Atlantic with a letter to this effect. Randolph was also instructed to return with information on the state of New England and its people's attitude to the crown.[48] There was as yet no threat of any direct action against the Massachusetts government or its charter, although Mason had questioned the charter's validity. A meeting of the Lords of Trade shortly before Randolph's departure had discussed the matters—the irregularity of New England's trade and its reluctance to acknowledge royal authority—"wherin it were necessary to have New England more in Dependence upon his Majesty." But, they concluded, "their Lordships do not suppose that to Consider New England so as to bring Them under Taxes and Impositions or to send thither a Governor to raise a fortune from Them can be of any use or Service to his Majesty."[49] Yet Randolph's mission set in motion events that soon altered this opinion. Less than two years after his arrival in New England, the Lords of Trade recommended that legal proceedings by writ of *quo warranto* be commenced against the Massachusetts charter, a step that led to its annulment in 1684 and the

---

[48] Preamble and Minutes of the Committee for Trade and Plantations, Apr. 22, Dec. 1, 2, 1675, Petitions of Robert Mason and Ferdinando Gorges, Jan. 13, [Dec. 22], 1675, Order of the King in Council, Dec. 22, 1675, *CSP Col., 1675–1676*, nos. 528, 529, 721–723, 412, 413, 753–755. The king's letter to Massachusetts, Mar. 10, 1676, and Randolph's instructions are in *Randolph Letters*, II, 192–194, 196–201. For Mason's hand in the dispatch of Randolph, long suspected but never established, see his letter to Lord Treasurer Danby, Mar. 5, 1676, Egerton Manuscripts, 3340, fol. 155, British Library.

[49] Journal of the Lords of Trade, Feb. 4, 1676, C.O. 391/1, 70.

creation of a royal government in Boston empowered to rule Maine, New Hampshire, and the disputed Narragansett country as well as Massachusetts. By 1688, the boundaries of this "Dominion of New England" had been extended to gather in the remaining New England colonies of Plymouth, Connecticut, and Rhode Island and the neighboring provinces of New Jersey and New York. The Dominion's form of government was as novel as its extent—in place of New England's representative assemblies sat only a single governor and council appointed by the crown.

In retrospect, this shift of policy was clearly part of the larger movement occurring over the course of the late seventeenth century whereby the crown brought the American colonies under its closer supervision. Commercial and strategic considerations led to political intervention and the extension of royal control in the Caribbean colonies and then on the American mainland. This movement assumed new form and intensity amidst the dramatic political changes attempted on both sides of the Atlantic during the last years of Charles II's rule and the brief reign, brought to an end by revolution in 1688, of his brother James. Within England, the two Stuarts strove to remodel and thereby bring to heel the chartered municipal corporations as part of a larger plan to subject church and state to the will of the royal prerogative. In America, likewise, the crown sought to reduce and consolidate all bastions of local particularism: by 1686, as the Dominion of New England took shape, legal action had been ordered against every extant colonial charter.

The strength and scope of this assertion of royal authority has prompted speculation that from as early as 1675 the crown's attempts to regulate Massachusetts were aimed at overthrowing the colony's charter and imposing a common pattern of royal government throughout New England. This "experiment in consolidation" would then have served as model for the reorganization of the remaining American colonies had not the Glorious Revolution supervened.[50]

---

[50] Thus, for example, Philip S. Haffenden, "The Crown and the Colonial Charters, 1675–1688," 298, 300, 308, 461; and Viola Barnes, *The Dominion of New Eng-*

Undeniably, regulation precipitated consolidation, as royal officials capitalized upon the opportunity presented by the successful prosecution of the Massachusetts charter to initiate both the unification of New England and the proceedings aimed at revoking the colonial charters. These proceedings in turn, had they not been overtaken by events in England, would doubtless have extended some form of royal government to every American colony.

Yet the outcome of policy is no certain guide to its original intent, and we must beware of reading back the ultimate breadth and coherence of this extension of royal control into the earlier stages of its development. A closer attention to the sequence of events shows that it was by no means certain, almost until the day when judgment was finally given against Massachusetts, that London's desire to curb the colony would necessarily lead, or even was intended to lead, to the annulment of its charter and the dispatch of a royal governor, let alone the consolidation of the Dominion. At first, despite the damaging information against the colony brought back by Randolph, the Lords of Trade declared their willingness, in July 1677, to preserve the charter providing that reforms were made "to set all things right that are now amiss." It was only upon learning in the following year of Boston's evasion of such reforms that an angry committee declared that "the whole matter ought seriously to bee considered from the Very Root" and recommended the issuance of a *quo warranto*.[51] Moreover, when the recommendation was finally brought before the King in Council, more than three years later, the decision was diluted to a vague threat of "further resolutions" should Massachusetts not comply with the Acts of Trade and dispatch agents to negotiate a settlement in London.[52] And when, after two more years had passed, the

---

*land,* 27–46. A much more balanced and wide-ranging study, but one that, in my opinion, still overstresses the crown's determination and consistency, is David S. Lovejoy, *The Glorious Revolution in America,* esp. 1–31, 122–159.

[51] Journal of the Lords of Trade, July 27, 1677, Apr. 8, May 16, 1678, *Randolph Letters,* II, 280, 297, III, 3–4.

[52] Charles II to Massachusetts, Oct. 22, 1681, *ibid.,* III, 110–113. There has been some confusion concerning the crown's actions at this time. A more severe letter openly threatening legal action and seemingly based upon a report prepared by

crown agreed to order a *quo warranto,* it was still presented to Massachusetts more as bargaining counter than as statement of intent—if the colony would make a free submission to the king, then its charter, in an amended form, might yet be saved.[53]

A similar caution marked the evolution of plans for an eventual settlement of New England. As early as 1677, in debate within the committee, some members had suggested that the governor of Massachusetts should serve under commission from the crown, and others had later urged the creation of "some General Governor, or some Supreme Authority" over New England as a whole. Not until 1681, however, did the committee agree to endorse the appointment of such a governor.[54] In the meantime, following legal advice that the government of New Hampshire assumed by Massachusetts was by law still vested in the crown, it had taken the first step toward royal rule in New England by establishing a royal government in New Hampshire in 1679. But its plans again outran its capacity to implement them: the King in Council took no action on its recommendation concerning a general governor, and both in New Hampshire and in Massachusetts, following the annulment of the charter, the committee had to settle for the expedient of a temporary government of a president and council appointed from among the colonists so as to gain time to prepare a permanent settlement. It was six months after the annulment of the Massachusetts charter before consideration was given to revoking those of Rhode Island and Connecticut, and nearly two years before a royal governor was commissioned to rule the Domin-

---

Sir Robert Southwell some years before was drafted: thus C.O. 1/47, no. 79, and George Chalmers, *Political Annals of the Present United Colonies from the Settlement to the Peace of 1763,* Book I, 443–449. Much to the frustration of the committee's staff, however, a much milder version was dispatched: *Randolph Letters,* I, 150. Some scholars, however, have continued to assume that the more severe version was sent: Viola Barnes, *Dominion of New England,* 20; John Gorham Palfrey, *History of New England,* III, 350; Herbert L. Osgood, *The American Colonies in the Seventeenth Century,* III, 328.

[53] Order of the King in Council, June 13, July 20, 1683, *Randolph Letters,* III, 235, 245-247.

[54] Journal of the Lords of Trade, Aug. 2, 1677, Apr. 8, July 30, 1678, Apr. 16, 1681, *ibid.,* II, 282, 297, III, 32, 92–93.

ion. Not until after the judgment against Massachusetts can the
crown's ultimate intentions be deduced from any wider campaign
against colonial charters: only one other, that of the Bermuda Company, was challenged prior to 1685, and its prosecution was carried
through at the invitation of the islands' inhabitants and dissatisfied
merchants, primarily as a private speculation.[55] Moreover, although
the committee now regarded all private charters with suspicion and
strove to prevent their proliferation, it was unable to stop Charles II
from granting another such charter to William Penn in 1681.[56]

Some of these delays and indecisions were inherent in the workings
of Stuart bureaucracy. Others can be blamed upon the course of
events in England. Just at the moment when the committee was seeking approval for legal action against Massachusetts in 1678, English
politics were convulsed by the hysteria of the Popish Plot, a supposed
Catholic conspiracy to assassinate the king. In addition, the plot and
its reverberations briefly brought to power, and to attendance at the
Privy Council and its committee of trade, members of the opposition
group of Whigs led by the Earl of Shaftesbury. Shaftesbury and his
friends were suspicious of any measure, such as the prosecution of the
charter, which seemed to strengthen royal power at the expense of the
liberties of English subjects; their brief tenure of power during the
summer of 1679 was marked by a significant turn of policy in favor of
the colonists, as in the decision to allow the Massachusetts agents to
share in nominating the leaders of the temporary New Hampshire
government and the drafting of a remarkably liberal constitution for
that government.[57] Later, the death of Charles II delayed the dis-

---

[55] Richard S. Dunn, "The Downfall of the Bermuda Company," 487–512.

[56] The Lords of Trade to the king, [Sept. 1682], *CSP Col., 1681–1685*, no. 696. As
late as 1679, the Lords had been willing to recommend the issuance of a charter
to Plymouth Colony: Report of the Lords of Trade, Dec. 4, 1679, *ibid.,
1677–1680*, no. 1206; Charles II to Gov. Josiah Winslow, Jan. 12, 1680, Mass.
Hist. Soc., *Collections*, 4th ser., V (1861), 31–33.

[57] Secretary of State Coventry to Col. Herbert Jeffreys, Dec. 5, 1678, Addit.
MSS., 25120, fol. 136; Memorandum of the Lords of Trade, Feb. 1679, Names of
Councillors for New Hampshire submitted by the agents of New England, July 7,
1679, *CSP Col., 1677–1680*, nos. 912, 1054; and compare the committee of trade's
report drafted by Shaftesbury and his fellow Whigs, July 10, 1679, *APC Col.*, I,

patch of a royal governor to Boston. Yet throughout these years other government business continued apace, and the distraction caused by these diversions, when set in the context of the evident disagreements within the committee and with its parent Privy Council as to the measures to be adopted, serves as further evidence of the low priority accorded New England affairs and the absence of any truly coherent and self-sustaining policy regarding its ultimate disposition.

There is no convincing evidence, therefore, that the Dominion was the product of a long-planned policy aimed at reducing the charters and consolidating the governments of New England. The protracted negotiations and frequent attempts at compromise in the decade following 1675 were not the unfolding of a grand imperial design of centralization but steps in a gradual acceptance of measures more extreme than those originally thought necessary. Nor should this seem surprising in light of London's earlier relations with New England. Royal officials now perceived ever more clearly the necessity of compelling the New Englanders to obey the Acts of Trade—"without a fair compliance in that matter," reported back one of the agents sent from Massachusetts, "there can be nothing expected but a total breach, and the storms of displeasure that may be."[58] More generally, they were resolved, as one official observed in the midst of compiling a list of the colony's misdeeds designed to spur the Privy Council into action, "to bring that unruly place into some better tune and more apparent dependance upon the Crown."[59] Yet they were far from certain what might be necessary to achieve these ends and how far such measures could or should be prosecuted. The forces of inertia and tradition still hung heavily. "You may now be sensible," wrote a Whitehall acquaintance to Randolph in the summer of 1680, "of the

---

no. 1293 (and *CSP Col., 1677–1680,* no. 1058) with the final form of government prepared for New Hampshire during Shaftesbury's fall from power in *N. H. Laws,* I, 1–8.

[58] William Stoughton to Massachusetts, Dec. 1, 1677, Hutchinson, *History of Massachusetts-Bay,* I, 270.

[59] Sir Robert Southwell to the Duke of Ormonde, Aug. 27, 1678, HMC, *Ormonde,* IV, 447.

great difficulties that have arisen from grasping at too great a power without due advice; matters of Power and Government by new ways and forms being not readily to be proposed nor easily brought to pass, Excentricall motions often meeting with an Icarian fate."[60] Repeatedly, the committee paused to refer such disputed questions as the status of colonial lands and boundaries to the crown's law officers or the judges of the common law and then shaped its proceedings in deference to their opinions—opinions, it may be noted, which were frequently as solicitous of the colonists' rights as of the crown's prerogative.[61] A colonial charter was itself the private property of English subjects and not to be seized without solid evidence of its abuse presented in a court of law. Nor was this concern for legality purely formal. Not only would the confiscation of property without due process set a fateful precedent for all Englishmen, but three of the committee's nine appointed members were themselves colonial proprietors who would not lightly call into question the sanctity of such charters. Other important officials, Lord Privy Seal the Earl of Anglesey and (or so Robert Mason charged) Secretary of State Sir Joseph Williamson, actively sympathized with the cause of Massachusetts.[62]

Practical considerations also governed the crown's deliberations.

---

[60] [William Blathwayt?] to Randolph, Aug. 20, 1680, Blathwayt Papers, I, Col. Wmsbg.

[61] Thus, for example, in regard to New England affairs, Report of Lords Chief Justices Sir Richard Raynsford and Sir Francis North, [July 17, 1677] (accepting the validity of the Massachusetts charter and thus blunting the thrust of Mason's and Randolph's attack), Reports of Attorney General Sir William Jones and Solicitor General Sir Francis Winnington, Apr. 27, Apr., 1678 (ruling that the legal action of the 1630s had not invalidated the charter), Report of Attorney General Sir Robert Sawyer, [Apr. 30, 1681] (accepting the validity of the charter's transfer to New England and limiting appeals from thence to the king), May 30, 1681, *CSP Col., 1677–1680*, nos. 342, 694, 695, *1681–1685*, nos. 92, 122. See also Sawyer's opinion defending the colonists' right to representative government, note 117, following. A striking example of the checks upon policy exerted by such reports can be seen in the crown's abandonment of its struggle with Jamaica in 1680: Thornton, *West-India Policy*, 198–199.

[62] For Anglesey's support, see John Collins to Gov. John Leverett, Mar. 19, 1675, Hutchinson, *Papers*, II, 206; Anglesey to Leverett, May 16, 1676, *idem, History of Massachusetts-Bay*, I, 262n.; and for Mason's charge against Williamson, Robert Mason to the Earl of Danby, Mar. 5, 1676, Egerton MSS. 3340, fol. 155v.

The most important was neatly summarized in the debate among the Lords of Trade in April 1678 which followed Randolph's testimony that the Boston government had effectively spurned the compromise offered the previous year. If "fair persuasions" were ineffective, the committee concluded, then neither would the colonists obey commands "if nobody bee there on the Place to give countenance to His Majesties Orders, and truly to represent from thence, what obedience is given unto them." To some, the solution lay in a royal governor: "yet all agreeing, that it must bee a Governor wholy to bee supported and maintained by his Majestie."[63] Therein lay the rub. Even in the unlikely event that the colony's unpredictable fanatics submitted without a struggle, its government would remain a charge upon a chronically insolvent crown at a time when royal officials were striving to reduce the cost of administering and defending more valuable colonies to the south.[64] Indeed, with this goal in mind, the committee had already embarked upon an ambitious campaign to force the legislative assembly of Jamaica, and later that of Virginia, to furnish permanent revenues to the crown.[65] It was highly unlikely that the Bostoners would consent to provide such aid short of a complete remodelling of their government. Neither did their resources seem to warrant the attempt: as William Blathwayt, secretary to the Com-

---

[63] Journal of the Lords of Trade, Apr. 6, 1678, *Randolph Letters,* II, 297.

[64] Orders of the King in Council, June 6, 27, 1679, *CSP Col., 1677–1680,* nos. 1016, 1038; even after this economy drive, the charges directly paid by the crown still amounted to some £17,500 a year.

[65] This campaign between 1677 and 1680 has more usually been seen as part of a plan to emasculate all colonial legislatures by denying them the power to initiate legislation: Leonard Woods Labaree, *Royal Government in America,* 220–222. It may be conceded that many at Whitehall wished to curb the powers of the assemblies, but two facts suggest that the crown's overriding purpose was to secure a permanent revenue: first, the attempt to limit the two assemblies' power, though remarkably successful in Virginia, was allowed to lapse once some form of permanent revenue was assured to the crown and, secondly, no similar attempt was made in those colonies, Barbados and the Leeward Islands, where such a revenue had already been granted—indeed, William Blathwayt specifically denied in a letter to Gov. Sir Jonathan Atkins, Jan. 17, 1680, that the same tactics were to be pursued against Barbados: Blathwayt Papers, XXIX, Col. Wmsbg. The best account of the crown's colonial finances is still that of Beer, *Old Colonial System,* I, chapter III.

mittee and a strong advocate of greater royal control, acknowledged, "his Majestie can expect no profitable returns from New England besides the use of their men and Shipps."[66] A consolidation of the northern colonies would create a unit economically stronger and politically more loyal. Yet, as one official drily remarked, "the New England disease is very catching," and it might be safer to keep Massachusetts in quarantine.[67]

What considerations, therefore, led the crown to move beyond attempts at regulation and the redress of grievances to royal government and the creation of the Dominion of New England? The most fundamental, if also the one most easily overlooked by too close a focus on the formulation of policy in London, leads us back across the Atlantic to the stubborn refusal of Massachusetts to submit to any form of compromise. Throughout the years prior to the annulment of the charter, a solid majority of the colony's General Court held out against any substantial concessions, contesting the claims of royal officials to exercise their authority within Massachusetts and refusing to delegate powers to negotiate a settlement to the agents it reluctantly dispatched to answer the complaints presented at Whitehall. Typical of this intransigence was the General Court's response to the crown's 1677 offer of a confirmation of the charter providing that certain laws deemed contrary to those of England were repealed and the Acts of Trade henceforth "religiously observed": no laws were repealed and the Acts were declared in force within the colony solely "by Authority

---

[66] [Blathwayt], "Reflections upon a Paper concerning America," n.d., Blathwayt Papers, BL 416, Hunt. Lib. The employment of Randolph in 1676 also indicated the crown's reluctance to spend money on reducing New England, a plan to send commissioners being rejected for reasons of cost: Egerton MSS. 3340, fol. 150. "I can never say too often," wrote Randolph to Blathwayt, June 19, 1686, "that this is a very poore place." *Randolph Letters*, VI, 177.

[67] Observations on the proposals of Mr. Secretary Ludwell of Virginia, [1674?], *CSP Col., 1675–1676*, no. 403; English officials customarily referred to Massachusetts as New England. Quarantine was the policy suggested by the Earl of Sandwich—Massachusetts should be "streightened and environed on all sides with a loyall people:" Harris, *Life of Sandwich*, II, 220.

of this Court" and with no reference to that of king or Parliament. In addition, far from instituting the oath of allegiance required by the crown, the court strengthened the oath of fidelity which placed loyalty to charter government above loyalty to the king. Even as the *quo warranto* proceedings reached their conclusion, Massachusetts still sought, in its instructions to the colony's attorney in London, "to spinn out the case to the uttermost."[68]

The sources of this intransigence are worth examining in some detail, for they throw vivid light upon the colonists' relationship with England and their perceptions of English policy. It was due in part to misapprehensions akin to those that had led the crown to expect swift submission in 1660. Isolated from the flow of events at Whitehall by the fall of English Puritanism from power, the colonists failed to perceive the significance now attached to conformity with England's commercial system. Nor did they realize the scope and gravity of the grievances levelled against them; not until agents Peter Bulkeley and William Stoughton arrived in London early in 1677, for example, did they learn of the grants substantiating Mason's and Gorges's claims or of the judgment given against the Massachusetts charter in the 1630s. "We are greatly surprized at what we finde," wrote Bulkeley back to Massachusetts, "and wonder the Ancient magistrats are, or make themselves, so ignorant of what ha[th] passed in former times, relating to the disposall of the Countrey."[69]

As Bulkeley's words suggest, however, ignorance was also the consequence of aversion and a desire not to know. The restoration of the Stuarts had broadened the differences between New England and the London government into a gulf of suspicion and mistrust. A fresh influx of immigrants brought tales of the reestablishment of the Anglican church and its persecution of dissenters, strengthening fears that the conditions imposed in England would soon be attempted across the Atlantic. The royal design, reported Humphrey Davie upon his

---

[68] *The Colonial Laws of Massachusetts*, 257–258; *Mass. Records*, V, 154–155, 157–161, 439.

[69] Peter Bulkeley to Edward Bulkeley, Jan. 17, 1677, Mass. Hist. Soc., *Proceedings*, 2nd ser., XIV (1900–1901), 213.

arrival in 1662, was "to exterpate the profession and professors of the pure and right waies of the Lord, out of this Collony, if not out of the Country, and to make all to receive the marke of the Beast and his Immage."[70] Davie and others among the newcomers promptly took the lead in opposing concessions to the crown.[71]

Such news as the colonists received from England, therefore, served only to confirm their suspicions that every letter from Whitehall and every intervention on behalf of local malcontents were pieces in a larger plan to bring in "popery" and impose a royal "Generall Governour" upon New England.[72] Negotiations in such circumstances seemed tantamount to complicity, and the Boston government swiftly let lapse the standing agency it had maintained in London before 1660. Only with reluctance did it thereafter send over agents in response to royal commands, and these "messengers," as they were carefully called to avoid any suggestion that they were armed with plenipotentiary authority, were hedged about with peremptory instructions to limit their freedom of action.[73] In place of an agency, Massachusetts occasionally used English sympathizers to present its

---

[70] Davie to John Davenport, c. Oct. 1662, Mass. Hist. Soc., *Collections*, 4th ser., VIII (1868), 204: see, for similar accounts of the Restoration settlement, *ibid.*, 166–216; John Davenport, *The Letters of John Davenport*, Isabel M. Calder, ed., 138–141, 176–179, 195–204, 207–209; Hutchinson, *Papers*, II, 42; Hull, "Diaries," 194, 196.

[71] These immigrants, including such later political leaders as Peter Sergeant, John Foster, and John Walley, and others such as Francis Willoughby, John Leverett, and Increase Mather who now migrated back to New England after long absences, proved themselves ardent defenders of the New England way. They far outmatched in numbers and influence the scattered few, notably Thomas Breedon and Richard Wharton, who also came in this period and sought greater royal control. For a different emphasis, however, see Bailyn, *New England Merchants*, 110–111, 122, 124, 135.

[72] Thus *Mass. Records*, IV pt. ii, 72–73; Richard Frothingham, *History of Charlestown, Massachusetts*, 155; Hutchinson, *Papers*, II, 41; John Davenport to William Goffe, received July 3, 1662, Samuel Nowell to Jonathan Bull, Sept. 25, 1676, Mass. Hist. Soc., *Collections*, 4th ser., VIII (1868), 198, 573.

[73] For the use of the term *messenger* for the three agencies of 1661, 1676, and 1682, see *Mass. Records*, IV, pt. ii, 39, 50, V, 113, 115, 157, 346, and Hutchinson, *Papers*, II, 65–93. In a draft of instructions dated Mar. 1681 the word *agents* is carefully replaced by *messengers:* Mass. Archives, CCXLI, 303.

letters and petitions, including such men as Henry Ashurst, Robert Thompson, and Robert Boyle, the famous scientist; all three were active in the Company (originally founded as the Society) for the Propagation of the Gospel in New England, more commonly known as the New England Company, a charitable organization founded in 1649 to promote missionary work among the American Indians and still largely run by English Puritans.[74] But they and others similarly employed by the colony had little familiarity with Whitehall's new ways—some, as dissenters, feared arrest should they even venture to court—and Boston paid no heed to their repeated advice that permanent agents should be empowered to serve the colony in England and money laid out to "entangle" the crown's proceedings against the charter.[75]

Boston's refusal was not just the consequence of miscalculation or niggardliness. Rather, it reflected the widely held belief that to stoop to such tactics would begin a descent into compromise and self-betrayal. Even at the last there was a striking consensus within Massachusetts that to make voluntary surrender in hope of better terms was to "pull downe the house ourselves which is worse than to be passive." Submission was suicide and self-preservation was a moral duty. God would sanctify the sufferings of his people to them if they were blameless of such apostasy. "It is our undoubted duty," counselled the colony's ministers in 1681, "to abide by what rights and Priviledges the Lord our God in his mercifull providence hath bestowed upon us and

---

[74] George P. Winship, *The New England Company of 1649 and John Eliot, passim,* and William Kellaway, *The New England Company, 1649-1776,* 1-121, give an account of the company's early years and the activities of these men. The company controlled a large endowment, and its yearly remittances to such favored Boston merchants as Peter Sergeant (Ashurst's nephew), Hezekiah Usher, and John Richards were an important source of capital for the currency-starved colonies.

[75] John Knowles to John Leverett, Apr. 16, 1674, letter of Robert Boyle, July 1674, John Collins to Leverett, July 28, 1674, Mar. 19, 1675, Hutchinson, *Papers,* II, 179, 182, 183, 206-207. The one belated attempt by Massachusetts, in 1682, to bribe the crown into dropping its proceedings ended in disclosure and ridicule: Hutchinson, *History of Massachusetts-Bay,* I, 285; Edward Rawson to Joseph Dudley and John Richards, Dec. 10, 1682, Prince Papers, Mass. Hist. Soc.; Peter Bulkeley to Dudley, Aug. 8, 1683, Chamberlain Collection A.2.45., Boston Public Library.

whatever the events may be the Lord forbid wee should be in any way active in parting with them."[76]

Massachusetts's resistance to the crown's demands, therefore, was rooted in its people's profound conviction of the rightness and godliness of the New England way of life. They saw their mission and their sacred trust to be the preservation of a church and society established according to the dictates of the Gospel. If events seemed set against them, it was their duty to hold fast until the tide of history turned back to them again. Yet this faith alone does not entirely explain the absolutism of their stand. Others in New England no less Puritan than they proffered at least token loyalty and accommodation to the crown. Connecticut and Rhode Island successfully solicited in London for their charters, and Plymouth strove to follow their example. All three received the royal commissioners of the 1660s with deference and posed no objection in principle to allowing legal appeals from their courts to England.[77] Only Massachusetts stood out in open defiance, and the fact that in falling it brought down the pillars of the temple upon all New England should not conceal its singular obstinacy.

The roots of this intransigence, it would seem, lay in Massachusetts's differences from its neighbors—the colony's keen sense of its role and duty as leader of New England Puritanism, its confidence in its greater military strength, and its larger stake in protecting commercial and territorial expansion. In particular, the colonists of the Bay consolidated these interests, and took their stand, behind the one central bulwark their neighbors did not possess: a founding charter long interpreted as bestowing both secure title and virtual immunity from external interference. From the first, the charter of 1629 had

---

[76] Samuel Nowell to John Richards, Mar. 28, 1683, Mass. Hist. Soc., *Collections*, 5th ser., I (1871), 435; Gookin, *Daniel Gookin*, 172–176; Answer of the elders, Jan. 4, 1681, Blathwayt Papers, BL 226, Hunt. Lib., and Mass. Archives, CCXLI, 298. For similar sentiments in Connecticut, Thomas Dongan to the Earl of Sunderland, May 27, 1687, C.O. 1/62, fol. 206.

[77] George Carr [George Cartwright?] to [Secretary Lord Arlington], Dec. 14, 1665, *CSP Col., 1661–1668*, no. 1103; George D. Langdon, Jr., *Pilgrim Colony*, 190–200.

furnished a right to land and government superior to the confused blend of proprietorial grant, squatter sovereignty, and Indian purchase upon which surrounding, charterless settlements depended. Its uncomfortable implication that the king, as grantor, held ultimate sovereignty was swiftly overlaid by the contention that it had conveyed an irrevocable grant of authority, giving Massachusetts "a perfection of parts . . . a self-sufficiency." "We claim not as by commission, but by a free donation of absolute government," ran the colony's instructions to agent Edward Winslow in 1646. "Our charter gives us absolute power of government."[78]

This strategy soon became an article of faith: by the 1660s a majority of the General Court had concluded that Massachusetts need have no truck with the London government save for informing it, as often as royal opacity required, of the colony's status as a self-governing "body politique" and of the extent to which even its allegiance to the crown was defined and limited by the charter. Diplomacy assumed the form of incantation. Others, anxious to preserve ties of sentiment or commerce with the mother country, pressed for a less openly provocative stance, yet even these "moderates" differed more as to the tactics to be employed in maintaining the colony's autonomy than as to any question of its existence and necessity.[79] Throughout the contest with England that followed, Massachusetts neither retreated nor

---

[78] Winthrop, *Journal*, II, 290, 314–315. Massachusetts also argued that their grant was, in effect, a purchase paid for by the toil and expenditures of settlement: Hutchinson, *History of Massachusetts-Bay*, I, 445–446, and Gov. Richard Bellingham to Robert Boyle, May 31, 1665, *Collections of the New-York Historical Society for 1869*, 66.

[79] Paul R. Lucas, "Colony or Commonwealth," 88–107, has shown that even during the 1660s, when public debate over the attitude to be adopted toward the crown was loudest, those who wished for royal government in Massachusetts were but a tiny and politically insignificant faction (*ibid.*, 90 n. 6). And even Lucas, I believe, by his "colony or commonwealth" dichotomy (one not made at the time), has overstated the substance and sharpness of factional divisions within the colony at this time, at least as far as they concerned relations with England. For the fundamental documents of this debate, see Mass. Hist. Soc., *Collections*, 2nd ser., VIII (1826), 99–111, and the petitions of the towns in Mass. Archives, CVI, 97–111. Theodore B. Lewis, "Massachusetts and the Glorious Revolution, 1660–1692," 2–30, sets this debate in the larger context of the colony's political history.

advanced beyond reliance upon the charter as a sufficient defense.
Those sent as "messengers" were instructed to do no more than "to
give his majestie sattisfaction touching the rights and extent of our
patent" in such matters as Gorges's and Mason's claims. Regulation
could only be considered insofar as it might adàpt the colony's government more fully "unto the rules of our charter."[80] The instrument
was sacrosanct by reason of both its nature and the purpose it served.
It was, wrote the General Court to Bulkeley and Stoughton in 1678,
"under God, our only security" in preserving "the interest of the Lord
Jesus, and of his churches scittuated in this wilderness." Hence "any
litle breach in the wall would endainger the whole, and therefore . . .
wee would not that, by any concessions of ours, or of yours on our be-
halfe, that any the least stone should be put out of the wall." The colony's choice of weapons, therefore, all but ruled out compromise. "I
know your people cannot think of Submission," wrote Edward Randolph to a friend in Boston, "and therefor they are broken because
they will not bend."[81]

Faced with this unyielding stance, painfully reminiscent of the
smug certainties of Cromwell and his "saints," the Lords of Trade
passed from impatience to exasperation and finally to weary determination. At the last, royal prestige was at stake. Massachusetts, declared the judge presiding at the hearing which confirmed the charter's annulment, was "a Company of Rebells the King should send a
fleet to subdue." It was the colony, wrote Randolph, "by whose example the other plantations mutinie and are uneasy."[82] It could not
be permitted to triumph.

---

[80] *Mass. Records,* V, 115, 386.

[81] *Ibid.,* 202; Randolph to John Usher, Feb. 2, 1685, *New England Historical and Genealogical Register,* XXX (1876), 21.

[82] Roger Morrice, "Entr'ing Book," I, 443, Dr. Williams's Library; Randolph to Sir Leoline Jenkins, Apr. 16, 1681, *Randolph Letters,* III, 93. There were reports in England that such a fleet was being readied: Israel Feilding to the Earl of Arran, Nov. 26, Dec. 2, 1684, HMC, *Ormonde,* VIII, 289, 291.

The peculiar character of Massachusetts's resistance, therefore, compelled the crown to abandon piecemeal regulation and make good its threats against the charter. Yet this does not account for the shape and timing of Whitehall's actions, nor for its pursuit of the issue to a particular conclusion. Here, as in earlier years, private interests on both sides of the Atlantic played an important part. In particular, Robert Mason and Ferdinando Gorges, while far from being cast in the heroic mold of their pioneering grandfathers, proved tenacious and imaginative in their quest to establish their inherited claims to New Hampshire and Maine. In their petitions, which totalled at least sixteen during the decade of the 1670s alone, they were the first to question the validity of the Massachusetts charter and to resurrect the old plea of the colony's opponents that a royal general governor be sent to rule New England.[83] Their intent was plain: for their purposes, regulation alone would not suffice to loosen Boston's grip upon the lands they claimed. Mason also worked behind the scenes to advance his suit—a letter to Lord Treasurer Danby, the king's first minister, pressing for Randolph's dispatch to Boston, reveals that he had promised a share in the proceeds once his claims were vindicated to both Danby's son and James, Duke of Monmouth, Charles II's favorite bastard and a rising figure at court.[84] The extent of these grandees' assistance is unknown, but it may well have been their retirement from court in 1679—Danby to the Tower of London following his impeachment by Parliament, and Monmouth into exile—that, no less than the Popish Plot, checked the prosecution of Massachusetts and brought Mason to accept in New Hampshire a temporary government dominated by colonists hostile to his claims in place of one headed by a royal governor. In the same year, a discouraged Gorges sold out his claim to Maine to the Massachusetts government. Mason,

---

[83] Petitions of Mason, Gorges, and William, Earl of Stirling, [Mar. 20, 1674], of Mason, [Dec. 22, 1675], of Gorges and Mason, [Jan. 12, 1677], [Jan. 9, 1678], *CSP Col., 1669–1674*, no. 1247, *1675–1676*, no. 753, *1677–1680*, nos. 8, 587vii; and, generally, *N. H. Provincial Papers,* XVII, 514–541. For further petitions, see notes 38 and 48, preceding. I have treated Mason's role in more detail in "Robert Mason and the Coming of Royal Government to New England," *Historical New Hampshire* (forthcoming).

[84] Robert Mason to Danby, Mar. 5, 1676, Egerton MSS. 3340, fol. 155.

however, pressed on undaunted, and it was primarily his continued complaints and petitions that prompted a resumption of action against the charter and the subsequent dispatch to New Hampshire in 1682 of a royal lieutenant governor, Edward Cranfield, to whom Mason likewise promised a share in his future profits.[85]

Appeals to the crown from within New England also shaped the course of London's actions. In 1675 the tensions between colonists and Indians stirred up by the steady advance of English settlement at last erupted into open conflict. The struggle, called King Philip's War by the colonists, was severe and losses heavy on both sides, but by the fall of 1676 most of the Indian peoples within the colonized limits of New England had been defeated and dispersed. Broad areas were opened up for settlement and speculation, giving new life to old disputes over boundaries and jurisdictions just at the moment when royal authority was assuming a renewed importance in the minds of many colonists. Hence Plymouth Colony turned to the crown for title to the land taken from the Wampanoag Indians, and a stream of agents and petitions, from Connecticut, Rhode Island, and the proprietors of the Atherton Company descended upon Whitehall to seek confirmation of their claims to the Narragansett territories.[86] These solicitations began enquiries that broadened the focus of London's attention from the Bay Colony's misdeeds to the condition of New England as a whole: it was after listening to accounts of the violence and bitterness aroused by the Narragansett issue that the Lords of Trade concluded that only a general governor could heal New England's dissensions. Six years later, the same concern, together with further solicitations, prompted the committee to expand the royal

---

[85] Petitions of Robert Mason, [Aug. 6, 1680], [Nov. 10, 1681], [Feb. 18, 1682], Address of Mason to the king, [Jan. 23, 1682], *CSP Col., 1677–1680*, no. 1480, *1681–1685*, nos. 288, 421, 375. Mason's arrangement with Cranfield can be seen in *N. H. Provincial Papers*, I, 453, 465.

[86] Governor Josiah Winslow to the king, June 26, 1677, July 1, 1679, *CSP Col., 1677–1680*, nos. 314, 1042; and, for the struggle over the Narragansett lands, *ibid.*, nos. 748, 766–768, 777, 837–838, 844, 853, 872, 890, 1044, 1132, 1309, 1448, 1487, 1530, 1532, and *APC Col.*, I, nos. 1222–1224, 1233, 1234, 1236, 1244. For the career of William Harris, the most persistent and colorful of the Narragansett litigants until his capture by Algerian pirates, see R. I. Hist. Soc., *Collections*, X (1902), *passim*.

government then in preparation beyond Massachusetts and its environs to include the disputed area within the Dominion.[87]

By the 1680s, moreover, the personal ambitions and involvements of royal officials themselves had added a further impetus to the evolution of policy. No individual did more to bring about direct royal intervention than Edward Randolph, the crown's courier to Boston and, after 1678, royal collector of customs in New England. Initially, it would seem, Randolph was merely echoing the strategy of his cousin and patron, Robert Mason, in questioning the validity of the Massachusetts charter and in proposing that the crown should impose a settlement upon New England by force.[88] Yet Randolph soon displayed a keen appreciation of the broader opportunities inherent in a remodelling of New England and the strategy likely to effect it. Over the next decade, in innumerable letters, petitions, and memorials, he furnished his new masters in Whitehall with what they had hitherto lacked in their attempts to fashion a coherent policy toward New England—organized and generally accurate information on such matters as the nature of its trade, the structure of its governments, and the loyalties of its people.[89] Randolph also used his skills as a lawyer to weave this information into a web of specific charges against the Boston government, thereby setting in motion the judicial procedures which led to a prosecution of the charter.[90] Finally, from as early as 1679, he submitted increasingly detailed proposals as to

---

[87] Journal of the Lords of Trade, July 30, 1678, Nov. 17, 1684, *Randolph Letters*, III, 32, C.O. 391/5, 32.

[88] Randolph to the Lords of Trade, May 6, 1677, *Randolph Letters*, II, 265–268.

[89] Thus, for example, Randolph to Secretary of State Coventry, June 17, 1676, to the king, Sept. 20, 1676, to the Lords of Trade, Oct. 12, 1676, *ibid.*, 203–209, 216–259. Other reports fill this and subsequent volumes of the *Randolph Letters*. Still further material has been lost: a correspondent in the Plantation Office, perhaps Blathwayt, thanks him, Aug. 20, 1680, for twenty-six letters over the preceding ten months, none of which have survived: Blathwayt Papers, I, Col. Wmsbg. On this phase of Randolph's career, see the excellent account by Michael G. Hall, *Edward Randolph,* 21–52. Alison Gilbert Olson, *Anglo-American Politics, 1660–1775,* 65–68, stresses the importance of Randolph's role in showing to London officials the possibilities of capitalizing upon internal colonial political divisions.

[90] Randolph to the Lords of Trade, May 6, 1677, Apr. 18, 1678, to the king, [1680], Apr. 6, 1681, *Randolph Letters,* II, 265–267, 318–319, III, 78–79, 89–91.

the shape of a final settlement, for Massachusetts and then for New England as a whole, complete with the names of colonists willing to participate in a royal government and the measures, such as freedom of conscience and security of title, which might best encourage a peaceful transition. Throughout, he stressed the economic and political benefits to the crown of unifying New England.[91] Much of the form and scope of the royal government established in Boston in 1686 derived from these proposals.

Randolph's great strength lay in his readiness to align his own advancement with that of the interests of the crown. Had he been born in Massachusetts, indeed, his pride in his official duties and self-conscious rectitude might well have carried him to high place among the very Puritan leaders against whom he struggled. Other royal officials urging vigorous action were plainly spurred by hopes of personal profit. "As for Boston," wrote Edward Cranfield, the newly arrived lieutenant governor of New Hampshire, to his patron Blathwayt in 1683, "there are some person's to bee Exempt out of the pardon who will buy their pardon att 8 or 10,000 li [pounds] besides there are severall graunts of Towne land's, which will in a yeare or two come to bee renewed to pay above 2,000 li upon their new leases."[92] William Dyre, a much-travelled Rhode Islander appointed surveyor general of customs in America, sent Blathwayt an account of pickings totalling over forty-five hundred pounds which could be garnered from a change of government.[93] To Blathwayt himself, besides a promised share in this bounty, the establishment of royal government in New England would bring a further addition to his already formidable power and patronage as head of the Plantation Office staff and to the handsome income he derived from checking the accounts of royal col-

---

[91] Randolph to the Lords of Trade, Feb. 22, 1679, to Secretary of State Jenkins, Apr. 16, 30, 1681, to the Lords of Trade, Sept. 2, 1685, *ibid.,* III, 38–40, 93–95, VI, 89–94, IV, 43–47; Michael G. Hall, "Randolph, Dudley, and the Massachusetts Moderates, in 1683," 513–516.

[92] Cranfield to Blathwayt, Feb. 20, 1683, *Randolph Letters,* VI, 139.

[93] Dyre to Blathwayt, n.d., Blathwayt Papers, IV, Col. Wmsbg. For Dyre's hostility to Massachusetts, see his letter to Gov. Simon Bradstreet, Mar. 5, 1685, *ibid.,* and Lovejoy, *Glorious Revolution in America,* 153.

onies in his capacity as surveyor and auditor general of crown revenues in America.[94]

Inevitably, officials and opportunists among the colonists soon learned to capitalize upon each other's desires. The most striking example of this cooperation, and one which graphically demonstrated the crown's continued susceptibility to the leverage exerted by well-placed individuals, stemmed from the increasingly desperate attempts of the Atherton proprietors to loosen Rhode Island's grip upon the Narragansett lands. Like Mason before them, they at length concluded that only the carrot of self-interest would quicken the pace of Whitehall's bureaucracy and turn its course to their advantage. Under the aggressive leadership of Richard Wharton, a rising Boston merchant, they solicited support from royal officials on both sides of the Atlantic; in 1680 they offered the governor of Virginia, Thomas, Lord Culpeper, then passing through Boston on his way back to England, a share in their company in return for his promotion of their cause at court. Culpeper promptly persuaded the Lords of Trade to appoint a commission to investigate the rival claims and proposed a list of "substantial, able and (as I was informed in the place) uninterested persons, fit to be Commissioners."[95] All on the list, as Culpeper must have known, were either shareholders of the Atherton Company or their close associates. The committee meekly accepted these names, adding only that of Cranfield to head the commission. Blathwayt was promised "due acknowledgments" and later "a parcel of land" for his aid in speeding proceedings at Whitehall. The venal Cranfield also held out the prospect of more succulent rewards. Both sides had money, he informed Blathwayt, and "3 or 4,000 li: will not be felt in the disposeing [of] those lands."[96] In October 1683, after enough of an

---

[94] Gertrude Jacobsen, *William Blathwayt*, 180; Stephen Saunders Webb, "William Blathwayt, Imperial Fixer: From Popish Plot to Glorious Revolution," 7–8.

[95] Culpeper's proposals, Apr. 20, 1681, Journal of the Lords of Trade, Oct. 18, 1681, Report of the Lords of Trade, [July? 1682], *CSP Col., 1681–1685*, nos. 88, 259, 636. Prior to their alliance with Culpeper, the proprietors had been using the services of John Lewen, an agent and associate of the Duke of York.

[96] Richard Wharton to Blathwayt, Apr. 2, 1683, Cranfield to Blathwayt, Feb. 20, Oct. 5, 1683, *Randolph Letters*, VI, 142, 139, 148. Blathwayt was also solicited by

enquiry to lend a veneer of official impartiality to their intentions, the commissioners duly reported in favor of the Atherton Company's claims and declared the Narragansett territory to be under the jurisdiction of Connecticut. Heartened by this success, other groups of colonial speculators, with the indefatigable Wharton in the forefront, likewise solicited London's support.[97]

These transatlantic contacts further broadened the scope of Whitehall's involvement in New England. Moreover, they gave substance to Randolph's claims that there were now colonists ready to accept and support the establishment of royal government. Randolph undoubtedly exaggerated both the numbers of such men and their devotion to the crown: most, as subsequent events proved, were simply hedging their bets in response to the evident growth of royal power in America. Boston merchants, for example, though anxious to escape an open breach with London and the colonial markets it controlled, were equally concerned with avoiding changes which might precipitate a full enforcement of the Acts of Trade. Few wavered in their fundamental preference for the comfortable ambiguities of New England's existing relationship with the outside world.[98]

As the prosecution of the Massachusetts charter assumed definite shape, however, a handful among the "moderate" faction which had

---

Connecticut and Rhode Island in the matter: John Allyn to Blathwayt, Sept. 21, 1681, Conn. Archives, Foreign Correspondence, I, 23a; Blathwayt to Rhode Island, Apr. 8, 1680, Boundary Documents, Rhode Island and Massachusetts, vol. I, R. I. Archives; and the copies of letters, mostly to and from Rhode Island, 1679–1684, in Blathwayt Papers, XI, Col. Wmsbg.

[97] Report of the Narragansett commissioners, [Oct. 20, 1683], *R. I. Records,* III, 140–145, and, generally, Dunn, *Puritans and Yankees,* 220–224. For subsequent solicitations, see Viola Barnes, "Richard Wharton, a Seventeenth Century New England Colonial," 248–249, and Bailyn, *New England Merchants,* 173.

[98] It is difficult to be precise concerning the merchants' attitudes at a time when almost every well-to-do New Englander still dabbled in trade. To state, however, as does Michael G. Hall in *Edward Randolph,* 58, that the New England merchants were "by and large" Randolph supporters runs quite counter to the available evidence. Many more backed charter government than opposed it, and most stood apart from politics or held a neutral position. For some cogent criticism of the recent scholarship which has stressed the coherence and political role of the merchants (particularly Bailyn's *New England Merchants*), see Stephen Foster, *Their Solitary Way,* Appendix C. See also Chapter 7, note 109, following, and, for more extended analysis, Richard R. Johnson, "Adjustment to Empire," 201–210.

long argued against an open defiance of the crown did embark upon
an active collaboration in the planning of royal government. All were
participants in the Atherton Company or other similar ventures.[99]
This is not to say that land speculation was the original or even the
primary motive for their decision. Those who can be identified as the
leaders in working with Randolph to plan the new regime had all had
firsthand opportunities to appreciate the strength of London's resolve
to regulate New England: Wharton had long cultivated his ties with
English officialdom, and Joseph Dudley, Peter Bulkeley, and William
Stoughton had each passed many months in England in the thankless
mission of defending Massachusetts's cause at court.[100] These experiences and, it would seem, the growth of a common conviction that
their own and New England's future could be served best by negotiation and compromise antedated their involvement in the speculative
ventures of the 1680s. Such involvement, nevertheless, aptly reflected
what manner of men they were—enterprising, outward looking, impatient of the restraints and traditions of charter rule, and, as Wharton's letters to England reveal, keenly aware of the political and
economic opportunities to be derived from royal intervention, partic-

---

[99] Theodore B. Lewis, "Land Speculation and the Dudley Council of 1686,"
255–272.

[100] Stoughton and Bulkeley were in England on behalf of the colony from January 1677 to August 1679, Dudley from August 1682 to August 1683. For Wharton's contacts with London, Viola Barnes, "Richard Wharton," 251, and his letters to Blathwayt in Blathwayt Papers, VI, Col. Wmsbg. Dudley's agency is
described in Everett Kimball, *The Public Life of Joseph Dudley*, 13–20, and William
Andrew Polf, "Puritan Gentlemen," 219–222, 233–240. For evidence of the leadership of these four, see, in addition, Dudley to [Blathwayt], Aug. 13, Dec. 9,
1683, May 4, Sept. 12, Nov. 4, 1684, Bulkeley to [Blathwayt], Dec. 7, 1683,
Blathwayt Papers, IV, Col. Wmsbg.; Dudley to Sir Leoline Jenkins, May 7, 1684,
C.O. 1/54, no. 92; Abstract of letter from Dudley, Stoughton, and Wharton to
Randolph, [Dec. 8, 1684], C.O. 1/56, no. 111; Stoughton, Dudley, Bulkeley, and
Samuel Shrimpton to William Blathwayt, Apr. 21, 1685, C.O. 1/57, no. 94; Edward Randolph to [Sir Robert Southwell], Mar. 12, 1681, Blathwayt Papers, BL
227, Hunt. Lib.; Randolph to Shrimpton, July 26, 1684, to Dudley, Jan. 9, 1685,
*Randolph Letters*, III, 317–318, IV, 12–14; Dudley to Randolph, June 7, Dec. 1,
1684, Mass. Hist. Soc., *Collections*, 4th ser., VIII (1868), 484, 483 (Dudley's reference in the second letter is clearly to Bu[lkeley] and not, as suggested by the editor, to Benjamin Bullivant). This group of four seem to have met regularly at the
house of Stoughton's sister, Mrs. Rebecca Tailer, at the corner of Elm and Hanover streets in Boston.

ularly by those whose ventures, like Wharton's schemes to settle immigrants on his land claims and exploit New England's native commodities, could be promoted in London as furthering and not, like so
much of New England's trade, contravening the purpose of English
commercial regulation.[101] To officials back in London, meanwhile,
the declared readiness of these colonists, in Dudley's phrase, "to sustain some place in the Regulation" gave hope that Massachusetts
would accept a royal government without the trouble and expense of
military intervention.[102]

In the absence of any clear guidelines from the crown, therefore,
private interests and ambitions initiated and shaped a broader royal
intervention. As late as the summer of 1684, its precise form remained
uncertain; Randolph, fresh from consultation with the Lords of
Trade, told a friend in Boston that no decision had yet been reached
as to whether a governor should be set over the whole of New England or over a union of just Massachusetts and Plymouth.[103] Yet the
stage seemed set for a settlement along the lines he had planned with
his colonial allies, for some kind of loose confederation of the New
England colonies under a crown-appointed general governor, retaining at least the principle of elected representation.[104] Neither he nor

---

[101] Thus Wharton to Blathwayt, Dec. 30, 1680, June 5, 1686, Blathwayt Papers,
VI, Col. Wmsbg.

[102] Dudley to Randolph, Dec. 1, 1684, Mass. Hist. Soc., *Collections,* 4th ser., VIII
(1868), 483. As Wharton wrote to Blathwayt, Dec. 6, 1684, the prospect of the
charter's fall "makes all good subjects thoughtful as to how they may best express
their obedience:" Blathwayt Papers, VI, Col. Wmsbg.

[103] Randolph to Samuel Shrimpton, July 26, 1684, *Randolph Letters,* III, 317.

[104] For Randolph's proposals and his role in the making of the Dominion, see
note 91, preceding, and Michael G. Hall, *Edward Randolph,* 83–109. Although
Randolph clearly wished to dispense with assemblies as they had existed under
the charter government, all his proposals include or take account of some form of
elected body or bodies, even the proposal presented after the crown's express pro-
hibition of elected assemblies in the constitution being drawn up for the Dominion. Subsequently, he continued to urge the creation of an assembly for the Dominion: *Randolph Letters,* IV, 45–47, VI, 193. Randolph was no democrat, but he
had a realistic perception of what was necessary for peaceful rule in New England.

they had reason to wish for any more thorough reorganization, which might well stir up armed resistance, cast all land titles into doubt, and dim their hopes of office; as Wharton pointedly reminded Blathwayt, not only would a drastic remodelling impose heavy charges upon the crown, but its accompanying curbs and dislocations would blight the prospects of "those that should be the most active Instruments therein."[105] Even the predatory Cranfield had by now concluded that New England's poverty and its people's uncouth reluctance to grease official palms made it a place unworthy of his and the crown's attentions. Disillusioned of Mason's "fantasticall fiction" that his province was a land flowing with fines and quitrents, the New Hampshire governor secured leave to move to the richer hunting grounds of the Caribbean. "I had rather be in a Warmer Country," he told Blathwayt, "where I can account for more than the Game of the whole Government of New-England is able to produce."[106]

Within a few weeks of the charter's annulment, however, the crown abruptly embarked upon a new and radical course. On November 8, the Lords of Trade were informed that the king had appointed Col. Piercy Kirke, an English army officer and a stranger to the American colonies, to be governor of Massachusetts. Within the month a commission was in preparation, adding New Hampshire, Maine, Plymouth, and the Narragansett lands to Kirke's government and giving him broad and arbitrary powers, including that of ruling without an elected assembly.[107] Charles's death and the brief flurry of rebellion that greeted James's accession kept Kirke in England, however. Wharton and his friends enjoyed a brief taste of power in the temporary government headed by Joseph Dudley. Yet the crown's plans were only delayed and not diverted. In May 1686, Sir Edmund Andros, formerly governor of James's proprietary colony of New York, was appointed governor of "our Territory and Dominion of

---

[105] Wharton to Blathwayt, Dec. 30, 1680, Blathwayt Papers, VI, Col. Wmsbg.

[106] Cranfield to Blathwayt, Dec. 1, 1682, *Randolph Letters*, VI, 121, 123.

[107] Journal of the Lords of Trade, Nov. 8, 17, 22, 1684, *ibid.*, III, 324–326, 332–335, C.O. 391/5, 32–33.

New England" with the princely salary of twelve hundred pounds a year.[108] Writs of *quo warranto* had already been brought against the charters of Rhode Island and Connecticut, and Andros was authorized to bring them under his control. Two years later, in March 1688, New York and New Jersey were added to the Dominion.

Why, in view of Whitehall's long-standing reluctance to assume the burden of government in New England and the existing pressures for a more limited settlement, did the crown create the elaborate and costly structure of the Dominion? The fundamental cause lay in England rather than the colonies, in the marked revival of royal fortunes which followed the collapse of the Whig campaign to exclude the Catholic James from the succession to the throne and the well-publicized exposure, in mid-1683, of a plot against the king's life by Whig extremists. Determined to purge opponents of the prerogative from office and secure a complaisant Parliament, Charles and his Tory advisers began a wholesale remodelling of English local government by means of *quo warranto* proceedings against the borough charters. Simultaneously, the old persecution of Dissenters and other Nonconformists was revived. Massachusetts, both a chartered corporation and a renowned stronghold of dissent, and already under siege, was swept up in this rising tide—as Blathwayt had predicted back in 1682, the "thriving condition" of affairs in England served to accelerate the pace of action against the colony.[109] Moreover, news from New England during the spring and summer of 1684 made it plain that, despite the hopes of Randolph and his allies, the prospects for a negotiated settlement were diminishing rather than growing. Reports of the quickening of Stuart authoritarianism, given added force by

---

[108] Commission of Sir Edmund Andros, June 3, 1686, *N. H. Laws*, I, 146; Journal of the Lords of Trade, May 10, 1686, C.O. 391/5, 263; Memorandum of the Lords of Trade, June 2, 1686, C.O. 5/904, 281–282; Warrant for the establishment of two foot-companies in New England, Aug. 30, 1686, *Randolph Letters*, IV, 122–123; Entry Book of William Blathwayt, T., Class 64, volume 88, 199, 200, 294, 296.

[109] Blathwayt to Gov. Thomas Lynch of Jamaica, Oct. 2, 1682, Blathwayt Papers, XXIII, Col. Wmsbg.; Lovejoy, *Glorious Revolution in America*, 160–169.

the example of Cranfield's corrupt and arbitrary rule in neighboring New Hampshire, had stiffened Massachusetts's will to resist.[110] Increase Mather, the influential minister of Boston's Second Church and hitherto an advocate of negotiation and the sending of agents, now turned to exhort a tearful meeting of the town's freemen into a unanimous opposition to submission.[111] In the colony elections of April 1684, those magistrates who had favored submission were clustered near the bottom of the poll, and Dudley and two others were dropped from office altogether.[112] Clearly, stern measures were needed to bring Massachusetts to heel, measures that now came easily to officials freshly experienced in the handling of recalcitrant corporations.

A further impetus came from plans for a larger reorganization of English America. By December 1684, Blathwayt was informing the governor of Virginia that the crown was preparing to move against the governments of all the proprietary colonies. Three months later, following James's accession, Blathwayt made the royal purpose explicit: the king was resolved "to reduce all Proprieties and Independent Government to an Imediate Dependence upon the Crown."[113] By June 1686, *quo warrantos* had been ordered out against every remaining colonial charter. This was a large step beyond the earlier attempts of the Lords of Trade to prevent the creation of new proprie-

---

[110] Theodore B. Lewis, "Royal Government in New Hampshire and the Revocation of the Charter of Massachusetts, 1679-1683," 28-38.

[111] Diaries of Increase Mather, Oct. 17, 1680, Jan. 6, 1681, Amer. Antiq. Soc.; *idem., The Autobiography of Increase Mather,* 308; *Boston Records,* VII, 164; Extract of a letter from New England, Mar. 14, 1684, *Randolph Letters,* III, 283-285.

[112] The votes cast for the nomination of magistrates are recorded in Prince Papers, no. 43, and Miscellaneous Bound Manuscripts, 1679, Mass. Hist. Soc. Stoughton and Bulkeley, though narrowly elected, refused to serve: Peter Bulkeley *et al.* to Sir Leoline Jenkins, Dec. 7, 1683, Representation of Edward Randolph, read July 16, 1684, *Randolph Letters,* III, 271-273, 309-310.

[113] Blathwayt to Governor Lord Howard of Effingham, Dec. 8, 1684, Mar. 6, 1685, Blathwayt Papers, XIV, Col. Wmsbg. In this context, the oft-quoted recommendation of the Lords of Trade, July 17, 1685, that action be taken against the proprietary governments, is evidently a response to and not an initiation of policy: *N. Y. Col. Docs.,* III, 362.

taries: the crown was seeking, as at home, to restructure all existing charter governments regardless of whether they had abused their privileges.

An appreciation of the scope of these plans for colonial reorganization and their link to Stuart policies within England must be tempered, however, by the fact that none except that involving the Dominion was ever executed. The prosecutions of the remaining colonial charters lagged, and only those directed against governments subsequently incorporated into the Dominion—Rhode Island, Connecticut, and East and West Jersey—were resolved before the Revolution of 1688 put an end to further action. Had James remained king, other consolidations might ultimately have followed among the colonies to the south.[114] But none was officially discussed or attempted prior to the onset of revolution, a fact which suggests that other considerations besides a desire for greater colonial dependence and uniformity prompted the attention given to the settlement of the northern colonies.

The nature of these considerations emerges from a closer examination of the Dominion's evolution. Clearly, the course of events was shaped by decisions made over the heads of the Lords of Trade, hitherto the prime advocates of sterner measures. Curtly informed of Kirke's appointment to Massachusetts, they scrambled to piece together an appropriate province. Similarly, their recommendation that Kirke's commission be patterned after that of the governor of Virginia, with a crown-appointed council and an assembly to "bee called when the Governor shall see occasion," was promptly overruled by a royal command that all mention of an assembly be expunged.[115] None of the Stuarts or their confidants had any love for representative government, but some evidence suggests that both Kirke's appointment and the shape of his commission were due to the influence of James, who was just then restored to predominance in royal counsels after a period of exile in Scotland and who had earlier

---

[114] Haffenden, "Crown and Colonial Charters," 456–465.

[115] Journal of the Lords of Trade, Nov. 8, 22, 1684, *Randolph Letters*, III, 325, 332.

balked at permitting an assembly in his proprietary province of New York. When the denial of an assembly was opposed in council by the Marquis of Halifax as a threat to the liberties of all Englishmen, it was James who then charged Halifax with being an enemy to the interest of monarchy.[116] Some months later, when the Lords of Trade were inclined to follow the opinion of Attorney General Sir Robert Sawyer that the people of Massachusetts retained the right to participate in matters of legislation and taxation despite the loss of their charter, James, now king, again intervened and forbade the inclusion of an assembly.[117]

The overruling of Halifax and Sawyer and their subsequent dismissal from office revealed the extent to which the cautious pragmatism and concern for constitutional propriety that had hitherto governed colonial policy was giving way to an authoritarianism that was contemptuous of half-measures and convinced of the boundless powers of the prerogative. It also demonstrated James's personal interest in the reorganization of New England, an interest evident in other aspects of the Dominion's structure and one which does much to explain both its purpose and uniqueness. The Dominion had from its inception a martial flavor characteristic of James's approach to government. Though a number of earlier reports sent in by Randolph and others in the colonies had commented on the strategic value of a unified New England in the face of French and Indian attack, royal officials had been more concerned with New England's threat to trade and revenue than with the security of settlements remote from the centers of royal government in Virginia and the Caribbean.[118]

---

[116] Helen C. Foxcroft, *Life and Letters of Sir George Savile, Bart., First Marquis of Halifax*, I, 427–429; Viola Barnes, *Dominion of New England*, 40n.; Andrews, *Colonial Period*, III, 113–119.

[117] Minutes of Attorney General Sawyer, Mar. 10, 1685, C.O. 1/57, no. 50; Lords of Trade to Lord President Halifax, Aug. 26, 1685, C.O. 5/904, 251; Journal of the Lords of Trade, Sept. 9, 1685, C.O. 391/5, 193.

[118] [Edward Randolph], "A Narrative of the State of New England," c. 1677, C.O. 1/61, no. 34; Randolph to the Lords of Trade, Feb. 22, 1679, to Sir Leoline Jenkins, Apr. 30, 1681, *Randolph Letters*, III, 40, VI, 90; Randolph to Lord Keeper Sir Francis North, Dec. 3, 1684, Blathwayt Papers, BL 232, Hunt. Lib. Also Gov.

James, by contrast, was an experienced soldier keenly interested in matters of strategy and military organization.[119] His proprietorship of New York had made him thoroughly familiar with the difficulties of defending the northern colonies' borders and the disadvantages of their disunion; King Philip's War, for example, had touched off an acrimonious dispute between the New York and New England governments as to which was responsible for failing to help the other. The appointment of Kirke, a professional soldier whose career had begun under James's patronage and who had just returned from governing England's African outpost of Tangier, evidenced a determination both to set a tight rein upon notoriously recalcitrant colonists and to consolidate the defenses of a region conspicuously vulnerable to attack.[120] Royal officials (or James himself, fresh from Scotland) may have had in mind as a model the marcher lordships long established on England's own borders; these administrative units, vested with broad and arbitrary executive powers, had served to protect the more loosely (and constitutionally) governed heartlands of the kingdom from unruly frontier subjects and foreign incursions. If so, the Dominion was never intended to be the prototype for subsequent colonial consolidations, a conclusion further substantiated by the fact that only those colonies grouped within the Dominion were denied representative assemblies.[121]

---

Sir Edmund Andros of New York to the Lords of Trade, Apr. 16, 1678, *N. Y. Col. Docs.,* III, 263.

[119] Jock Haswell, *James II, Soldier and Sailor,* and John R. Western, *Monarchy and Revolution,* 82–85, pay particular attention to this side of James's character. Stephen Saunders Webb, " 'Brave Men and Servants to His Royal Highness,' " 55–80, reveals how many of the men in James's entourage subsequently held office in the colonies. For reasons evident in my analysis of royal policy toward the American colonies (in this and subsequent chapters), however, I remain in blunt disagreement with Webb in his conclusion (*ibid.,* 80, and embellished at great length in his *The Governors-General,* esp. 445–464) that he has shown such policy to have been dominated until well into the eighteenth century by a "military system," a deliberate design of "militant imperialism" and "imperial militarization."

[120] *Calendar of State Papers, Domestic Series, of the Reign of Charles II, 1665–1666,* 522; Richard L. Ollard, *Pepys,* 272–273.

[121] As Andrews (*Colonial Period,* I, 243–244, III, 118n.) has pointed out, the commission subsequently issued for the government of Bermuda (which had likewise

## Expansion and Confrontation

James's personal interest remained the dominant force in guiding the Dominion's development in the months following his accession, despite the rebellions and purges in England which noticeably distracted Whitehall's attention from colonial affairs. Several of the more experienced members of the committee of trade died or were dismissed, and their replacements were men subservient to James with little knowledge of the plantations. The committee's meetings, once averaging some sixty a year, decreased to barely more than one a month. Yet two of the rare occasions when James presided over its meetings were devoted to the northern colonies' settlement, and his choice of Andros as governor of the Dominion in place of Kirke, at a time when Randolph and others were pressing for the appointment of Joseph Dudley or the rich London merchant Sir Matthias Vincent, ensured that the post would remain in the hands of a professional soldier and close personal associate.[122]

Andros, moreover, had served for many years as James's governor of New York, and that province's problems now required attention no less than the matter of New England's future. Col. Thomas Dongan, New York's governor since 1683, had arrived to find the province facing serious difficulties. James's cession of the Delaware counties and East and West New Jersey to independent proprietors had cut deeply into his province's resources, and the heavy taxes levied upon commerce to pay for the remaining portion's government and defense

---

lost its charter) authorized an assembly. Subsequently, assemblies continued to be authorized in the instructions issued to the governors of the Leeward Islands (1686), Jamaica (1687), and the Bahamas (1688) at a time when the Dominion was again refused an assembly: *CSP Col., 1685–1688*, nos. 1020, 1187, 1832; Petition of Increase Mather, Samuel Nowell, and Elisha Hutchinson, Aug. 10, 1688, C.O. 1/65, no. 39; *Andros Tracts*, II, 10.

[122] Though Vincent's name never appears in the official records, he was confidently spoken of in late 1685 as the new governor: Morrice, "Entr'ing Book," I, 489, 490; Edward Randolph to Sir Robert Southwell, Nov. 27, 1685, *Randolph Letters*, IV, 72. Morrice saw Vincent as a friend to New England and he was described by Samuel Sewall (*Diary*, I, 95) as "Brother to the Minister," doubtless the well-known Puritan cleric, Nathaniel Vincent. Sir Matthias, a London alderman and a landholder in Pennsylvania, had made his fortune in the service of the East Indian Company; he was M. P. for Lostwithiel, 1685–1687. King James presided over the committee's meetings on March 3, 1685, and May 10, 1686.

were diverting trade from New York ports to the point that quantities of goods were being smuggled duty-free across the Hudson from New Jersey. Worst of all, the traffic in furs from Albany, New York's principal export and "the best branch of your Majestyes Revenue," was threatened by both competition from Pennsylvania traders and French encroachment from Canada upon the lands and trade routes from which the furs were gathered.[123] In particular, the French were making new efforts to conquer or win over the confederated Five Nations of the Iroquois, long the most formidable obstacle to their expansion, and New York's essential shield against attack. The Iroquois, though seldom able to muster more than two thousand warriors from their "castles" along the Mohawk River, dominated the lands around the Great Lakes and as far south as Virginia by their swift raids and tactics of calculated terror. Fiercely hostile to the tribes allied with the French, they had developed a bond of mutual profit and dependence with the merchants of Albany, obtaining guns and manufactured goods for furs traded or pillaged from the interior.

Dongan, a soldier trained in French service like his royal master, was keenly aware of the economic and strategic dangers posed by French designs. Once the protection afforded by the Iroquois was removed, he told London, the fur trade and Albany itself would be lost and all the northern colonies open to invasion. He began an aggressive "forward" policy of his own, countering French incursions and Jesuit proselytizing with trading expeditions and conferences at Albany aimed at strengthening ties with the confederacy. To support this policy and restore New York's prosperity, Dongan pleaded for authority to requisition aid from neighboring colonies and for a strengthening of his province's economic base by the annexation of

---

[123] Address of the Mayor and Common Council of New York, read in Council, May 17, 1687, C.O. 1/62, no. 45; Bernard Mason, "Aspects of the New York Revolt of 1689," 169–174; Beer, *Old Colonial System*, II, 346–354. French aims and actions during these years are well summarized by William J. Eccles, *Canada under Louis XIV, 1663–1701*, 99–154.

the Jerseys and the western half of Connecticut, both originally included in James's patent.[124]

Others before Dongan had urged similar measures—Andros had even attempted to annex western Connecticut by force in 1675—but not until now, with the general remodelling of charters and James's supremacy at home, had so favorable an opportunity arisen. James began a reorganization less than a month after his accession, when he directed that New York, now a royal colony, should have a government similar in form to that being prepared for the Dominion of New England. He also announced his intention not to confirm the "Charter of Libertyes" drawn up by the New Yorkers two years before.[125] Four months later, a letter from the city authorities of New York, complaining of the losses suffered because of their separation from the territories east and west of the Hudson, was used in conjunction with charges drawn up by Edward Randolph to justify the issuance of the *quo warranto*s against Delaware, the Jerseys, Rhode Island, and Connecticut. By April 1686, as Randolph learned from a correspondent in the Plantations Office, "a larg settlement" of New York's government was in preparation, one likely to encompass at least part of Connecticut.[126] This settlement, it appeared, would take its place alongside that of the Dominion of New England, now also moving toward

---

[124] Dongan to the Lords of Trade, Feb. 22, 1687, to Lord President Sunderland, Sept. 8, 1687, Feb. 19, 1688, *N. Y. Col. Docs.*, III, 391–393, 428–430, 510–512. The content of earlier reports can be gauged from the replies of James's secretary, Sir John Werden: *ibid.*, 340–341, 349–353. On Dongan's policy and New York's situation, see Arthur H. Buffinton, "The Policy of Albany and English Westward Expansion," 327–366, and Allen W. Trelease, *Indian Affairs in Colonial New York,* chapter X.

[125] Journal of the Lords of Trade, Mar. 3, 1685, *N. Y. Col. Docs.,* III, 357. James ordered the government of New York to "be assimilated to the Constitution that shall be agreed on for New England." Both the immediate context and later policy suggest that *assimilated* is here used in its sense of *make similar to* and not, as some scholars have assumed, *joined to.* For the New York charter, see David S. Lovejoy, "Equality and Empire: The New York Charter of Libertyes, 1683," 493–515.

[126] Mayor of New York to Sir John Werden, [May 13, 1685], Order of the King in Council, July 17, 1685, *N. Y. Col. Docs.,* III, 361–363; Randolph to John Povey, June 27, 1686, *Randolph Letters,* VI, 180.

a final definition. Closely matched commissions were issued to Andros and Dongan; the latter's salary was raised to six hundred pounds a year, part way toward the twelve hundred allotted to Andros; the territory in Maine north of the Kennebec River granted to New York by James's proprietary patent was transferred to the jurisdiction of New England; and the two companies of English red-coats ordered to accompany Andros to Boston matched those already stationed in New York.[127] The lavish scale of these establishments, in sharp contrast to the pennypinching of earlier years, reflected James's grandiose conceptions of kingly government. It was also a consequence of his greater resources, for a dutiful Parliament and economic prosperity at home had given James a net income half again as large as his brother had received five years before.[128]

A complete settlement, however, waited upon the submission of the governments facing *quo warranto*s, and it was at this point that events in New England, together with the colonists themselves, began to regain some of the influence upon Whitehall's decisions that they had exerted prior to James's domination of policy making. Randolph, now returned to Boston as councillor, secretary, and registrar in the temporary Dominion government headed by Joseph Dudley, found the report of New York's impending "larg settlement" alarming, for he and his Boston colleagues had expected that the submission of Rhode Island and Connecticut would be followed by their annexation to the Dominion. Randolph had brought over the *quo warranto*s along with the commission for the Dudley government in May 1686, but delays in England had rendered them legally void. Dudley and his council, therefore, hastily dispatched letters and emissaries to the Connecticut magistrates, "with whom wee have so long had a happy understanding and good agreement in the common interest of Reli-

---

[127] Journal of the Lords of Trade, May 10, 1686, C.O. 391/5, 263–264; Commission of Andros, June 3, 1686, *N. H. Laws,* I, 146–155, of Dongan, June 10, 1686, *N. Y. Col. Docs.,* III, 377–382; Memorandum as to Dongan's salary, May 20, 1686, *ibid.,* 367; Order of the King in Council, June 20, 1686, C.O. 5/904, 282.

[128] Chandaman, *English Public Revenue,* 256–261, 333. The two companies were paid out of English revenues, as was Andros until such time as the Dominion's revenues were settled: T. 64/88, 199–200.

gion and Liberty," in an effort to persuade them to make a swift voluntary submission to the crown and petition for union with Boston.[129] Dongan likewise scented opportunity in this fluid situation and began a similar courtship of both Connecticut and Rhode Island.[130] Connecticut's government flirted with these suitors; that of Rhode Island declared its readiness to submit to the crown, and its Quakers looked to Dongan for protection from its old enemies in Massachusetts. Both colonies, however, hoped to retain their independence if not their charter privileges and so refused a definite commitment.

All parties in this maneuvering evidently believed that, Stuart authoritarianism or no, Whitehall would still pay heed to the two colonies' wishes regarding their ultimate disposition. Further, all sought to influence a decision by lobbying at court. Dongan insisted that New York could hardly subsist without Connecticut and the Jerseys; Randolph and Dudley described the corn and cattle of western New England as essential to Boston's prosperity.[131] Rhode Island dispatched magistrate John Greene as agent to plead its case in London, and Connecticut empowered London merchant William Whiting, brother of the colony's treasurer, to act in a similar cause.[132] Randolph's letters were the first to arrive, and it seems to have been his

---

[129] Randolph to Gov. Robert Treat of Connecticut, May 27, 1686, Joseph Dudley to Treat, July 21, 27, 1686, *Conn. Records*, III, 352–354, 358–359, 363–364; Instructions for Maj. John Pynchon, Maj. John Winthrop, and Capt. Wait Winthrop, July 27, 1686, Winthrop Papers, Mass. Hist. Soc.

[130] Governor Treat to Dongan, June 14, July 3, Aug. 5, 1686, Dongan to Treat, Aug. 13, 1686, *N. Y. Col. Docs.*, III, 385–387, *Conn. Records*, III, 366–367. Dongan's letters to Rhode Island have not survived but are mentioned in John Greene to Dongan, Aug. 8, 1686, C.O. 1/60, no. 24 (information omitted from the printed calendar), and Randolph to John Povey, June 27, 1686, to Sir Edmund Andros, July 28, 1686, *Randolph Letters*, VI, 179, 190.

[131] Tho. D[ongan] to the Earl of Sunderland, Nov. 25, 1686, C.O. 1/61, no. 11 (this letter is not from J[ohn] S[pragge] as in the printed calendar); Dongan to the Lords of Trade, [1686], *N. Y. Col. Docs.*, III, 391–392, to Sunderland, May 20, 1687, C.O. 1/62, no. 50; Randolph to Povey, June 27, 1686, Dudley to Blathwayt, July 31, 1686, *Randolph Letters*, VI, 179, 196; President Dudley and the Council of New England to the Lords of Trade, read Oct. 21, 1686, C.O. 1/60, no. 80 (fol. 235v.).

[132] John Greene to Dongan, Aug. 8, 1686, Commission of Greene, Aug. 6, 1686, Petition of Greene, [Jan. 19, 1687], C.O. 1/60, nos. 24, 25, 53; *Conn. Records*, III, 211–212, 368–375.

arguments, coupled with the news of Rhode Island's submission and the peaceful establishment of the Dominion in Boston, that tipped the scales back in favor of a consolidated New England. Early in September 1686, the Lords of Trade recommended that both Rhode Island and Connecticut should be included in the Dominion.[133] Duly empowered, Andros took charge of Rhode Island soon after his arrival in Boston in December. Hartford continued to hold out against a voluntary submission for ten more months, feeding Dongan's flickering hopes that it might yet choose to fall westward. In pleading to retain its independence, however, it expressed a preference for union with the Dominion rather than New York, a compliance promptly interpreted as capitulation in Whitehall. Andros was ordered to annex Connecticut, and in October 1687 he travelled in state to Hartford to complete the unification of New England.[134]

Whitehall's decision did nothing to relieve the pressures on New York, and that province's difficulties were heightened during the summer of 1687 by an open French assault upon the Iroquois. James, in response, ordered Dongan to claim the Five Nations as English subjects and protect them by all means necessary, but the logic behind the New York governor's long-standing plea for additional resources was now only too painfully apparent.[135] New York was indeed serving as, in Dongan's words, "the Bullwark to Boston," and though its settlers equalled those of French Canada in numbers, the great majority were of Dutch descent with little reason to be loyal to their English conquerors. Few could match Canada's skilled woodsmen or its French regular troops. The New England colonies, by contrast, had more than six times New York's population and a numerous and battle-tested militia.[136] Yet political divisions continued to impede the deployment of these resources—even royal governor Andros

[133] Journal and memorandum of the Lords of Trade, Sept. 7, 12, 1686, *CSP Col., 1685–1688*, nos. 844, 857.

[134] Connecticut to the Earl of Sunderland, Jan. 26, 1687, Journal of the Lords of Trade, May 18, 1687, Order of the King in Council, June 18, 1687, the king to Sir Edmund Andros, June 27, 1687, *ibid.*, nos. 1197vi, 1259, 1308, 1321.

[135] Dongan to the Earl of Sunderland, Sept. 8, 12, 1687, the king to Dongan, Nov. 10, 1687, *N. Y. Col. Docs.*, III, 428, 477, 503–504.

[136] Dongan to Sunderland, Feb. 18, 1688, Oct. 25, 1687, *ibid.*, 511, C.O. 1/63, no.

proved no more helpful than his Puritan predecessors in aiding New York, despite specific orders from the crown. The answer lay in the replacement of voluntary cooperation with institutional responsibility, and in March 1688 James ordered that New York and the Jerseys be added to the Dominion. Dongan had himself advised this step should Connecticut not be given to New York. Undoubtedly, this last consolidation was for reasons of defense. It provided, in the words of Andros' new commission, for "the better protection and security of our subjects in these parts." Such a union, wrote Blathwayt to Randolph, "will be terrible to the French and make them proceed with greater caution than they have lately done."[137] These hopes were never fully tested; barely nine months after Andros had completed this painfully contrived amalgamation, it crumpled into ruin upon the news of its maker's overthrow in England.

Although scholars have differed as to whether the Dominion should be judged a product of Stuart despotism or a monument to constructive statesmanship, they have generally agreed that it was the logical culmination of earlier measures.[138] Undeniably, the Dominion

---

50 (foll. 227v.–228). New York's and French Canada's populations both stood at around 10,000 to 12,000 in 1685, New England's at some 75,000; U.S. Bureau of the Census, *Historical Statistics of the United States, Colonial Times to 1957*, 756; Jacques Henripin, *La Population Canadienne au Début de XVIIIe siècle*, 119–120. English officials had a detailed picture of New England's resources from Randolph's reports and the colonists' answers to questions posed by the Lords of Trade in 1679: *CSP Col., 1677–1680*, nos. 1349, 1352, 1360, 1447. Andros, in urging a unification of the military forces of the northern colonies in 1679, had reported that New England had between 13,000 and 15,700 freemen able to bear arms: *N. Y. Col. Docs.*, III, 262.

[137] Blathwayt to Randolph, Mar. 10, 1688, *Randolph Letters*, IV, 216; Commission of Sir Edmund Andros, Apr. 7, 1688, *N. H. Laws*, I, 226. There is no record of any discussion of the consolidation by the Lords of Trade prior to James's decision.

[138] Viola Barnes, *Dominion of New England*, vii. See also Haffenden, "Crown and Colonial Charters," 297–299, 461–466; and Lovejoy, *Glorious Revolution in America*, 179. For older views of the Dominion as the fulfilment of Stuart despotism, see George Bancroft, *History of the United States of America from the Discovery of the Continent*, chapter XVII; Edward Channing, *A History of the United States*, chapter VI; and Evarts B. Greene, *The Foundations of American Nationality*, 187. Craven, *Colonies in Transition*, 212–217, provides a valuable critique of these interpretations.

was a direct consequence of the commercial and colonial regulation outlined after the Restoration and begun in earnest in the 1670s. Nor were the measures it embodied so eccentric as to be discredited by its downfall in 1689; royal officials continued to advocate the remodelling of proprietary and charter government well into the following century. In attempting to shore up the defenses of a vulnerable northern frontier, the Dominion likewise raised an issue and advanced a solution that remained a staple of royal policy for many years to come. In these respects, the Dominion was indeed a milestone in the relations of England and its colonies.

Seen against the entire span of events prior to the Glorious Revolution, however, the Dominion must be judged as much an anomaly as a consummation. It sprang in large part from the peculiar obduracy of Massachusetts; it was shaped by James's personal interpretation of the character of kingly government; and its lavish scale, autocratic structure, and brusque shuffling together of diverse and discordant colonies were an abrupt departure from a pattern of administration hitherto characterized by a hardheaded caution in financial and political matters and a marked respect for process and procedure. Nor did its novelty escape contemporary notice, both by those who like Halifax and the colonists themselves deplored its incipient tyranny and by those who like Randolph viewed its form as a blunder rather than a crime. Randolph's openly expressed dismay to his London correspondents at the appointment of a "hott, heady passionate Souldier" such as Kirke and the denial of a representative assembly was more than resentment at the ignoring of his own proposals: it revealed his realistic understanding of the difficulties likely to attend the maintenance and funding of a government lacking the hallowed and convenient procedures for popular participation and consent.[139] His forebodings soon proved as prophetic as the words of his Whitehall correspondent at the beginning of the decade: the Dominion,

---

[139] Randolph to Dr. William Lloyd, Bishop of St. Asaph, Mar. 1685, to Sir Robert Southwell, Aug. 1, 1685, *Randolph Letters*, IV, 18, 29–30; E[dward] R[andolph] to Sir Francis North, Dec. 3, 1688, Blathwayt Papers, BL 232, Hunt. Lib. For Randolph and the lack of an assembly, see note 104, preceding.

born of "Eccentricall motions," indeed met with "an Icarian fate."[140]

The drama of the Dominion's rise and fall, therefore, should not obscure the less striking but ultimately more enduring ties spun between England and New England in these early years. They derived, in the beginning, from rival rather than complementary interests as mutual commercial growth and territorial expansion sparked friction and political conflict. On the one hand stood royal officials convinced that England's self-interest and security required a closer supervision of New England; on the other were colonists equally determined to resist the least infringement upon their cherished religious and political heritage. Yet the very consequences of pursuing these conflicting goals to a conclusion led each closer to acceptance of an accommodation. Although English policy makers seeking the regulation of colonial trade had found no solution short of wholesale political intervention, their aim prior to James's supremacy had clearly been to find a middle course that would skirt the difficulties of imposing an expensive and unpopular form of government upon relatively unimportant and unprofitable settlements while still managing to curb an independence that threatened the stability of England's commercial system. The Dominion's fate would soon prove these instincts sound. The colonists, for their part, had found their defenses undermined by their own divisions and then brought down in ruins by the crown's ability to challenge the charters upon which they had centered their claims to political autonomy and legitimacy. "Whatsoever the vicissitudes of affayres be that may happen in England," noted a Boston writer in 1687, "matters will never be againe *in statu quo* here in each respective Colony."[141] The crown's power and presence could no longer be ignored, however distasteful and dangerous it might seem.

Moreover, the means and circumstances necessary to such an accommodation were becoming apparent. Within each colony men had shown their willingness to serve a royal government. Dudley, Whar-

---

[140] See note 60, preceding.

[141] John Saffin to John Allyn, June 14, 1687, *Conn. Records,* III, 382.

ton, and their allies had actively promoted the changes that would advance their own political and entrepreneurial ambitions; others now declared at least a formal loyalty to the new order by accepting office in the Dominion. The great majority had already held similar positions under the old charter governments. Thus twenty-two of the thirty New Englanders who sat on the Dominion council had formerly served as magistrates or colony officials, and of the remaining eight, all from Massachusetts and New Hampshire, most had long been politically and socially associated with the circle of those in power: four were the sons of former magistrates. Of those nominated to the council, only three, from Massachusetts, refused to serve, certainly a tribute to Randolph's skill in suggesting likely candidates to Whitehall yet also a sign of pliancy among New England's leadership scarcely evident ten years before.[142]

Few of these men had sought the imposition of royal government. Rather, they were from among the moderate factions which had emerged within each colony in turn as the crown's pressures intensified, men who urged not so much a political program as a posture, one of respect and conciliation toward the crown. Their principal common bond was mistrust of those diehard opponents of submission who, as Peter Bulkeley complained, "are hugging our priviledges and franchises to death and preferre the dissolution of our Body Politique rather than to suffer amputation of part of its limbs." "If N. Englands Interest come once to be managed by such men, I would not give 2 pence for it," wrote another. "Time will make it appeare who have been the faithfull and wise conservators of N[ew] E[ngland] liberties."[143] To the moderates, less apocalyptic in their vision of events and more confident either of the crown's intentions or its inefficiency,

---

[142] Simon and Dudley Bradstreet and Nathaniel Saltonstall refused to serve. Randolph's nominations for Dudley's council are in *Randolph Letters*, IV, 44–45. The fullest recent analysis of "moderates" and "royalists" in Massachusetts is given by Lewis, "Massachusetts and the Glorious Revolution," 25–29, 90–105, 157–172, 410–440.

[143] Bulkeley to [William Blathwayt], Dec. 7, 1683, Blathwayt Papers, IV, Col. Wmsbg.; letters of Simon Bradstreet, Jr., May 27, 1680, Apr. 11, 1681, Prince Papers.

the truer path was to be as the willow rather than the oak, to bend with the wind and stay in place rather than be uprooted and give way to outsiders or upstarts who knew not New England and its heritage.

Fundamentally, therefore, these men differed with their fellow colonists as to the nature and significance of the changes that had overtaken their relationship with the mother country. Familiarity bred caution, and it was among those most aware, through circumstances and self-interest, of the crown's mounting determination to discipline New England—agents and petitioners at Whitehall, speculative promoters, merchants and gentry in the coastal towns—that the desire for accommodation was greatest. In Massachusetts, where the political fermentation heightened by royal pressures had worked the longest, the division was in part one between generations: where the board of assistants under the old charter had been dominated even into the 1680s by leaders of the first settlements of the colony, those who served on the Dominion council from Massachusetts, with the single exception of Wharton, were the sons of this founding generation, their median age in 1688 a mere forty-six, twenty years less than that of the assistants a decade earlier.[144] The division was far from complete. Other younger leaders, such as Thomas Danforth, Elisha Hutchinson, Samuel Sewall, and Elisha Cooke, clung fast to the cause of the charter. But it nonetheless marks a watershed that grew ever more apparent in the years ahead. These Massachusetts moderates had not passed through the fire of persecution and parliamentary reformation. They were not of the generation of the old-charter magistrates who had fought for the "good old cause" alongside Cromwell's Ironsides and lived in hope of its resurrection.[145] Instead, they had

---

[144] In two cases I have assumed that the age of first marriage was twenty-five. The difference between average ages is less striking—forty-eight to sixty-one instead of forty-six to sixty-six—but this is because of the election to the Massachusetts council by 1678 of a number of young moderates, notably Dudley and Bulkeley, then aged thirty-one and thirty-five.

[145] John Leverett (assistant 1665–70, deputy governor 1671–73, governor 1673–79), Francis Willoughby (assistant 1664, deputy governor 1665–71), and Daniel Gookin (assistant 1652–75, 1677–86) had all served as officers in the parliamentary armies.

[67]

reached maturity in a world where the king had come into his own again and where civil strife had given way to international rivalries and transoceanic trade. Forty years earlier, John Winthrop had spoken with scorn of those states and persons "who walk by politic principles only."[146] Henceforth, the most successful leaders in New England were to be precisely those who could mediate between the conflicting desires and interests of English officials seeking a greater colonial dependence and colonists accustomed to a decisive role in government.

These days, however, still lay ahead. For the present, a common acceptance of office masked a wide diversity of purpose. In drawing together men from every New England colony, Dudley and Andros inherited all the internal divisions which had done so much to open New England to royal intervention. Within the Dominion council sat both active supporters and opponents of the Atherton company's claims, both leaders of Massachusetts's expansion and those from Rhode Island and New Hampshire who had long looked to the crown to redress Boston's overweening influence. Others, such as Edward Palmes and Samuel Willis of Connecticut, seem to have embraced royal government as an opportunity to pursue their personal grievances against the old order. Wait and Fitz-John Winthrop, grandsons of Massachusetts's first governor but hitherto aloof from politics, succumbed to a double temptation: shareholders in the Atherton Company, they also saw their appointment to the council as a proper if belated tribute due their wealth and lineage.[147] It remained to be seen how these diverse ambitions and interests could be harnessed to the work of government.

Further, these men were still a small minority among their fellow colonists. In Massachusetts those who had openly committed themselves to royal government met fierce public resentment despite their social standing: Dudley and Stoughton were labelled enemies to their country by the Boston town meeting and openly abused when they

---

[146] Winthrop, *Journal*, II, 218.

[147] Dunn, *Puritan and Yankees*, 235, 219.

ventured forth.[148] A strong majority of the clergy remained ada-
mantly opposed to submission and to those among them inclined to
moderation: when the Reverend John Danforth suggested that those
who opposed a royal governor's commission would be "Rebels and
Traitors," Increase Mather retorted that had Danforth's grandfather,
a founder and minister of the church in Boston, been alive he would
have boxed his grandson's ears.[149] The deputies of the now dissolved
Massachusetts General Court challenged the new councillors of the
Dominion to consider whether the latter's form of government "be
safe, either for you or us."[150] There could be little hope of an effective
accommodation while these and other colonists were excluded from
their customary part in government.

Yet there were at least a few signs, though more in consequence of
necessity than of sentiment, that New Englanders were learning to
view London as an integral part of their political horizon. Whitehall
could give charters and Whitehall could take them away; it was also
apparent to some that its officials could be influenced and its measures shaped by inducements and pressures ranging from petitions
and the dispatch of agents to outright bribery. Colonists from Connecticut and Rhode Island, doubtless remembering the success of
their missions to solicit charters in the 1660s, had always been more
willing to solicit in this fashion; by 1686, those in Massachusetts had
at least become familiar with the practice even if they could see little
virtue in its results. With the crown now irrevocably entangled in
New England affairs, it was better to attempt to share in decision
making than, as in earlier years, remain aloof in the hope that events
would pass them by. Finally, many colonists were themselves realiz-
ing their dependence upon a wider world. Commercial necessity dic-

---

[148] Sewall, *Diary,* I, 80, 81, 102; Abstract of a letter from New England, Mar. 14,
1684, *Randolph Letters,* III, 284.

[149] Nathaniel Mather, Jr., to his uncle, c. August 1685, Prince Papers; Sewall,
*Diary,* I, 71–72; Mass. Hist. Soc., *Proceedings,* XII (1871–1873), 105–107. For a sim-
ilar stand by the ministers in Connecticut, see Governor Dongan to the Earl of
Sunderland, May 27, 1687, C.O. 1/62, no. 55 (fol. 206).

[150] *Mass. Records,* V, 516; "Dudley Records," 238.

tated conformity (though not conjunction) with English interests; the crown's overriding sovereignty held the key to legitimizing territorial expansion; and New England's deepening involvement in the conflict of nations cast new doubts upon the value and adequacy of its vaunted self-sufficiency. As yet, New Englanders were uncertain how they could come to terms with changes that seemed to sever them from a cherished and inspirational past. "The foundations being destroyed," wrote Samuel Sewall in his diary, "what can the Righteous do?"[151] But a new synthesis to this transatlantic dialectic could yet emerge from the crucible of the Glorious Revolution.

---

[151] Sewall, *Diary*, I, 113.

# II

## *"A Wolfe by the Ears"*:
## *Dominion, Revolution, and Settlement,*
## *1686–1689*

The establishment of royal government in Boston in 1686 marked a turning point in New England's political history and in its colonists' relationship with the English crown. Administratively, the Dominion accomplished little beyond demonstrating that English officials and their colonial allies still had much to learn about the ways royal authority could be rendered palatable to colonists accustomed to conducting their own affairs. Yet by the time of its overthrow by armed rebellion in April 1689 upon the news of William of Orange's successful invasion of England, the Dominion's very existence had completed the challenge to the continuity and legitimacy of charter rule begun by Randolph in the 1670s. Those who now sought to restore the old order found themselves facing a new and baffling world: matters could indeed "never be againe *in statu quo* here in each respective Colony." Tormented by internal division and external attack, New England's leaders were drawn to look back to the crown for guidance and authority. By 1690, moreover, royal officials in turn were ready to moderate their demands. From these new circumstances would come an enduring political settlement.

At first, the transition from charter to royal rule was surprisingly uneventful. Though the great majority of Massachusetts colonists had continued to honor the General Court's authority despite the charter's annulment, the long period of waiting amid reports from England of the defeat of all challenges to James's authority had eroded defiance into resignation. "The symptoms of Death are on us," recorded Samuel Sewall in January 1686. Four months later,

[*71*]

when the commission for Dudley's temporary royal government finally reached Boston, the magistrates debated for three gloomy days in George Monck's Blue Anchor Tavern, then submitted peacefully. Dudley and his new council helped to disarm opposition by retaining many of the procedures and personnel of the old regime.[1]

Once in power, moreover, Dudley and his colleagues further eased the pangs of transition by electing to delay a full enforcement of royal authority in favor of the easier and altogether more congenial work of tending to their own personal interests and ambitions. In particular, aware that a royal governor would soon arrive, they hastened to gratify the territorial ambitions which had been so prominent in their pursuit of office. Cranfield's report in favor of the Atherton Company's claims was adopted, and shareholders and supporters of the company were appointed to oversee government in the Narragansett country. Land along the Merrimack River, where Dudley and six other councillors had invested in a further speculative project, was given separate status as a county. The registering of land titles was placed in friendly hands.[2] Some attempt was made to form a working alliance with the merchants of the coastal towns: a committee was appointed to investigate the decay of trade, and proposals were advanced for a bank to be funded upon the security of mortgages and personal property. But the proposals proved better designed to benefit landowners and farmers than merchants; and the need to raise revenue for government, a particularly delicate problem because of the council's fear of the consequences of levying the traditional direct taxes upon polls and estates without the consent of a representative assembly, soon cut directly across such an alliance. As Randolph noted, the merchants favored taxes upon land, "but Mr. Dudley Stoughton and others who have gott very larg tracts of Land are for Laying all upon the trading party." The results clearly showed the

---

[1] Sewall, *Diary,* I, 93; Mass. Archives, XLVIII, 276 (the tavern bill of £6/1/6d. was not paid until eleven years later); "Dudley Records," 230–237.

[2] *R. I. Records,* III, 197–202, 208–209; James N. Arnold, *Fones Record,* 57–179; Randal Holden to the king, Aug. 21, 1686, C.O. 1/60, no. 30; Jeffries Papers, IV, 111; *N. H. Laws,* I, 119; "Dudley Records," 235, 251, 255, 256.

speculators' political muscle: the only taxes levied were duties upon imported goods and incoming shipping.[3] Little else was accomplished, and Randolph, who had expected both a more thorough royalization of Massachusetts and a larger share in the new government, was bitterly disillusioned. The "Grandees" of the council, he told Blathwayt, "agree in nothing but Sharing the Country amongst themselves." The old ways remained: "the persons onely and not the government is changed."[4]

Randolph was not the last English official to be rudely awakened by the sudden frigidity of despised colonial allies once they had climbed upon his shoulders into office. Yet he was peculiarly a victim of his own strategies. Seeking to be the eminence behind a regulated New England, he had repeatedly proclaimed that the colonies teemed with loyal supporters of the crown, and Whitehall had duly accepted his nominations. Now it became plain that even a Dudley or a Stoughton looked more to his own advancement and political survival than to the interests of the crown as Randolph perceived them. The usable men had used him. The brief span of Dudley's presidency of the Dominion proved how superficial and pragmatic was the royalism of even Randolph's closest colonial allies and how deeply engrained remained the habits and beliefs of the New England way.

Governor Andros's response to this situation upon his arrival in Boston late in December 1686 swiftly revealed the full dimensions of this gulf between colonial and English official conceptions of royal rule. A soldier and a royalist by training and family tradition, Edmund Andros shared with his Stuart master a personal integrity that viewed obstacles with impatient inflexibility—both men, perhaps, were circumscribed as politicians as much by their virtues as by their failings. Andros followed his instructions as James did his conscience. These instructions directed him to assess quitrents upon lands not yet

---

[3] "Dudley Records," 248–249, 272, 241, 242; Andrew M. Davis, ed., *Colonial Currency Reprints, 1682–1751*, I, 153–187; Randolph to Blathwayt, Feb. 3, 1687, *Randolph Letters*, VI, 211; *N. H. Laws*, I, 109–111.

[4] Randolph to William Blathwayt, July 12, 1686, to the Archbishop of Canterbury, 1686, *Randolph Letters*, VI, 187–188, IV, 91.

granted or "confirmed" by the crown, to govern without an elected assembly, and to grant liberty of conscience in matters of religion with "particular encouragement" afforded to the Church of England—requirements striking in turn at the land titles, representative government, and religious orthodoxy that were the cornerstones of New England's way of life.[5] The lapse of charter government gave theoretical sanction for the laying of new foundations, and Andros was conscientious and shortsighted enough to make the attempt. "Sir Edmonds coming over will make a more throw reformation," wrote Randolph.[6] His echo of the notorious policy of "thorough" attempted in England by Charles I in the 1630s, however unwitting, was nonetheless appropriate. Within a few months of his arrival Andros had begun a reconstitution of New England society as radical as any attempted by the Stuarts across the Atlantic.

Crisply self-confident and backed by his small force of sixty English soldiers, Andros immediately tackled the vital issue from which the Dudley government had shrunk, the raising of an adequate revenue. Early in March 1687, over considerable opposition from within his council, he imposed both indirect taxes—customs, excise, and tonnage duties—and a direct tax of the kind formerly levied in Massachusetts and Connecticut. Prompt and widespread resistance to this taxation without representative consent culminated in the arrest and trial of a group of Ipswich men led by their minister, John Wise. The dissidents were imprisoned and heavily fined, and New England submitted to this show of strength.[7] Apologists for the Dominion both then and since have maintained that the direct tax, being only a

---

[5] Andros's Instructions, Sept. 12, 1686, *N. H. Laws*, I, 155–167.

[6] Randolph to William Blathwayt, June 19, 1686, *Randolph Letters*, VI, 177. On Andros and his various governorships, see Jeanne Gould Bloom, "Sir Edmund Andros: A Study in Seventeenth Century Colonial Administration," esp. 71–158.

[7] "Andros Records," 244, 245, 246, 256, 258; *N. H. Laws*, I, 184–190; George A. Cook, *John Wise, Early American Democrat*, 45–57; Viola Barnes, *Dominion of New England*, 80–90. Despite its evident distaste for Puritan "fanaticism," Barnes's study remains much the best account of the events of the Andros administration.

single "country rate" of twenty pence per poll and one penny in the pound upon estates, was small in comparison to those levied in Massachusetts both before and after the Dominion. To the colonists, it was fundamentally a matter of principle—Wise and his fellow resisters appealed to Magna Carta and their rights as "free borne English subjects"—but the tax was also drafted in such a way as to be more than usually onerous.[8] It assessed the value of livestock at an outdated and disproportionately high level, placing a particular burden upon poor farmers such as those of Plymouth Colony; and in setting the terms of payment it abolished the customary discount of one-third for payment in cash and pegged the price at which corn and other produce would be accepted for payment in kind at such an artificially low level that it made the real cost of the tax far higher than that of previous single country rates. Nor was the revenue from these taxes sufficient to meet even the day-to-day administrative costs of a government now burdened with an annual charge of thirty-five hundred pounds for the pay of the governor and his English soldiers, a sum alone exceeding the entire yearly budget of government in Massachusetts during all save a few of the years of charter government.[9] Hence, despite a doubling of the customs and excise duties early in 1688, Andros still sought to levy a second country rate and made preparations to impose a direct tax, measures that would yield two and a half times as much as the rate of 1687.[10]

---

[8] Andros's report of his administration, [May 27, 1690], *N. Y. Col. Docs.*, III, 725; Proceedings of the Ipswich town meeting, Aug. 23, 1687, C.O. 1/63, no. 75iv (fol. 300); Joseph B. Felt, *An Historical Account of Massachusetts Currency*, 242–243; "Andros Records," 479–480; Thomas Hinckley to William Blathwayt, June 28, 1687, Plymouth Colony to the king, Oct. 1687, Mass. Hist. Soc., *Collections*, 4th ser., V (1861), 155, 175; Joseph Dudley to Cotton Mather, June 5, 1689, *ibid.*, 6th ser., III (1889), 504.

[9] The king to Andros, Nov. 7, 1687, *N. H. Laws*, I, 176–177; Sylvester Judd, *History of Hadley*, 198–199; Petition of James Russell, Feb. 12, 1701, Mass. Archives, CI, 177.

[10] *N. H. Laws*, I, 215–218. Viola Barnes, *Dominion of New England*, 93, states that "after the passage of the revenue act in the spring of 1687, there were no other country rates than the one levied under the provisions of the act," seemingly a contention that only one rate was levied, in 1687. But there is evidence that a second was levied (and paid by some towns) in July of the following year: Edward Field, comp., *Tax Lists of the Town of Providence during the Administration of Sir Edmund Andros*, 29–37; *Town Records of Manchester*, 30–31, 34; John G. Metcalfe, comp.,

Taxation without representative consent was but the beginning of the Dominion's autocracy. Government in New England had long been intensely local and particular, run by town meetings, selectmen, and magistrates at little cost to the community at large. A few received small salaries or gratuities; most, as an early writer noted, were "Volunteers, governing without pay from the people." Rulers such as John Winthrop had grown poor in their country's service.[11] Abruptly, with the administration of the new government tightly centralized in Boston, the colonists found themselves confronted by numerous appointed officials, many of them newcomers to New England, who were dependent on their fees and perquisites and eager to turn the reorganization of government to their personal advantage. Large payments were required for all legal transactions. A new judicial system was established. For many the consequences were inconvenient and expensive. Thomas Hinckley, the former governor of Plymouth Colony, cited to William Blathwayt the example of a widow compelled to travel to Boston and pay thirty-five shillings to secure probate of her husband's estate, which was valued at little more than fifty pounds. Others later spoke of arbitrary and corrupt practices, greedy officials, and "Packt and pickt juries."[12] In the eyes of New Englanders, the Dominion steadily assumed all the trappings of a despotism. Besides a "standing army" of English soldiers, censorship was imposed on the press, men committed to prison without benefit of

---

*Annals of Mendon*, 106. Andros had already been authorized to impose a direct tax in the form of quotas levied from each county, and the Jeffries Papers, in which are many of the records of Dominion treasurer John Usher, contains a list (IV, 6) of the revenue raised by rates in the Dominion for 1688 amounting to £3168/12/-, a sum suggesting the levying of a direct tax since it is considerably more than could be raised from a single rate even with the inclusion of Connecticut in the Dominion after October 1687.

[11] Edward Johnson, *Wonder-working Providence*, 141. See, generally, Osgood, *American Colonies in the Seventeenth Century*, I, 483–488.

[12] Hinckley to Blathwayt, June 28, 1687, Mass. Hist. Soc., *Collections*, 4th ser., V (1861), 156; *The Revolution in New England Justified* (Boston, 1691), reprinted in *Andros Tracts*, I, 115–117; [William Stoughton *et al.*], *A Narrative of the Proceedings of Sir Edmund Androsse and his Complices* (Boston, 1691), reprinted in *ibid.*, 144–145; *An Appeal to the Men of New England* (Boston? 1689?), reprinted in *ibid.*, III, 195–198. For the Dominion's fees, see *N. H. Laws*, I, 107, 250.

bail or jury trial, and freedom of travel outside the Dominion curtailed. Town meetings had long been the forums for local political
debate and decision; following the protests against the Dominion's
taxation, Andros pushed through an act restricting such meetings to
one each year and placing the work of the selectmen chosen at these
yearly meetings under the supervision of justices of the peace appointed by the governor.[13]

Still more distressing to Hinckley and his fellow Puritans was the
direction of the Dominion's course in religious matters. Dudley had
not pressed the liberty of conscience he was instructed to permit to
the point of encouraging public heterodoxy. Andros, however, swiftly
moved to displace Puritan Congregationalism from its privileged
legal position. With the support of the Rhode Islanders on his council, he refused to enact laws which would have continued the payment of Puritan teachers and ministers by rates levied upon all inhabitants.[14] Following both his instructions and his own beliefs,
moreover, he actively promoted the cause of Anglicanism and its
small band of local adherents. Having forced the members of Boston's
South Church to open their meetinghouse for weekly Church of England services, provoking embarrassing incidents as the displaced congregation awaited its turn in the street outside, the governor then
seized a plot of common land to begin construction of a separate Anglican chapel. Anglicans received a large share of civil and military
appointments in the new government, and contemporaries noted that
"Common prayer-men," predisposed by their beliefs to support the
cause of royal authority, now figured prominently upon the juries
empanelled to try the Dominion's critics.[15] Their suspicions would

---

[13] "Andros Records," 249, 486; *The Revolution in New England Justified, Andros Tracts,* I, 80; [Stoughton *et al.*], *A Narrative, ibid.,* 141–142; [Increase Mather], *A Narrative of the Miseries of New-England* (London, 1688), reprinted in *Andros Tracts,* II, 5; *ibid.,* III, 92–93; *N. H. Laws,* I, 218–221.

[14] Hinckley to Andros, Feb. 28, to Blathwayt, June 28, 1687, Mass. Hist. Soc., *Collections,* 4th ser., V (1861), 149, 161; Andros to Hinckley, Mar. 5, 1687, Prince Papers; "Andros Records," 257, 469.

[15] Increase Mather, *Autobiography,* 321. Among the known Anglicans preferred were Samuel Ravenscroft, Anthony Haywood, William White, Charles Lidgett,

have hardened could they have read Secretary Randolph's letters to England. To the Archbishop of Canterbury, Randolph proposed that henceforth New England's ministers should be licensed and its schools regulated, and that the funds of the New England Company and even the proceeds of collections in Boston's churches should be diverted for the support of an Anglican ministry. Later, in a blatant attempt to keep up with the changing political scene at home, Randolph repeated these proposals to one of the newly prominent Catholics surrounding King James, with the startling additional suggestion that a Catholic mission and convent (to be staffed by Randolph's brother-in-law) be established in New England.[16]

Even before these schemes could be unveiled, the defenders of a shattered orthodoxy were sadly noting the evidence of their loss of power. Within a few months of the installation of royal government, Samuel Sewall was recording in his diary the drunken rout led by two of the crown's most prominent supporters through the streets of Boston in a coach coming from Roxbury, doubtless from Joseph Dudley's suburban home. "Such high-handed wickedness," concluded Sewall, "has hardly been heard of before in Boston." It was only a beginning. Licentious English games and fashions won sudden popularity. Street brawls and exhibitions of swordplay disturbed the peace. In an episode that must have stirred memories of the exploits of Thomas Morton and his bacchanalian crew at Merrymount half a century before, a garlanded Maypole was set up across the river in Charlestown.[17]

These were visible signs of the decay of the alliance between minister and magistrate which had sustained the settlers of New England

---

Humphrey Luscomb, Francis Foxcroft, Giles Dyer, Benjamin Bullivant, and James Sherlock. The first five were among the eight officers appointed by Andros to command the Boston militia in 1687: Sewall, *Diary*, I, 133; Abstract of the militia of New England, May 13, 1690, C.O. 5/855, fol. 246. The first three served on the jury at the trial of Wise and his fellow protesters, and no less than eight of the twelve jurors contributed toward the building of the Anglican chapel: *Randolph Letters*, IV, 178–179; Henry W. Foote, *Annals of King's Chapel*, I, 89.

[16] Randolph to Archbishop Sancroft, [July 7], Aug. 2, Oct. 27, 1686, to Sir Nicholas Butler, Mar. 29, 1688, *Randolph Letters*, IV, 88–91, 103–110, 131–133, VI, 240–247.

[17] Sewall, *Diary*, I, 121, 133, 135–136, 138–140, 144, 180.

in their search for a godly society. Moses and Aaron no longer walked hand in hand together in government. Yet even these dramatic changes could hardly have sufficed by themselves to arouse the degree and breadth of resentment against the Dominion that were evident by the time of its overthrow in 1689. New Englanders in general, particularly those who had been excluded from full political participation under charter rule, were well accustomed to an authoritarian style of government. Some clearly relished the opportunities opened up by the Dominion and its turn toward the raffish ways of Restoration England. Discontent might have remained factional and unfocused had not Andros ignited an issue even more fundamental than the maintenance of a Bible Commonwealth—the validity of the colonists' title to their lands.

Once again, the government's fiscal needs shaped policy. The crown's instructions permitted Andros some discretion as to the levying of annual quitrents upon landholders. But Randolph had often stressed the potential value of such payments, and Whitehall clearly expected that they would become a key source of permanent revenue for the Dominion, as in all other English colonies in America.[18] At first, Andros required quitrents only from those who sought grants of vacant land or confirmation of disputed titles; in mid-1687, Richard Wharton was assessed ten shillings a year for an estate of seventeen hundred acres in the Narragansett country. But few were willing to take even this first step, and the matter was soon caught up in the larger political issue of Andros's hostility to the independent authority and democratic tendencies of the towns.[19] Throughout his brief tenure of office, the governor consistently strove to subordinate

---

[18] Randolph to Lord Treasurer Rochester, Aug. 23, to the Lords of Trade, Aug. 23, to William Blathwayt, June 19, to John Povey, June 27, 1686, *Randolph Letters*, IV, 115, 118, VI, 177, 179, 181; Joseph Dudley to [Blathwayt], Mar. 30, 1687, Blathwayt Papers, IV, Col. Wmsbg.; Osgood, *American Colonies in the Seventeenth Century*, II, 35–42.

[19] *R. I. Records*, III, 225–226; "Andros Records," 470, 474; Randolph to John Povey, May 21, 1687, to William Blathwayt, Apr. 2, 1688, *Randolph Letters*, IV, 162, VI, 250–251. The Lords of Trade had proposed a quitrent of 2/6d. per hundred acres: *ibid.*, III, 334.

local autonomy to the procedures of centralized rule: he denied, it was later charged, that "wee had any such thing as a Town or Township amongst us."[20] Such a program could never succeed while the towns retained the power to grant the free ownership of land to their inhabitants and held control of lands as yet undivided or held in common. Indeed, royal government could hardly be a reality until colonial landowners were brought to a sense of their direct tenurial dependence upon the crown.

There is no evidence that Andros planned to carry through a wholesale redistribution of lands. His purpose was to change the form of ownership, not its composition. So radical were the means employed, however, that the colonists' worst fears seemed justified. Confronted with resistance to suggestions that all titles should be brought forward for confirmation by the new regime, Andros and his subordinates began to deny that any existing titles remained valid. In particular, since the townships were improperly incorporated according to English law, their proprietors could not hold title to any lands that remained undivided. Randolph and other royal officials promptly filed claims to portions of the common lands of Lynn, Cambridge, and other towns, and several such claims were granted despite local protests.[21]

The colonists had attempted to prepare for such a challenge. In the last months of charter rule, Connecticut had distributed the bulk of its reserves of undivided land among individual proprietors in various towns; Massachusetts and Rhode Island had resurrected, or manufactured, Indian deeds to establish titles based upon purchase from the first inhabitants.[22] Yet neither strategy was proof against the present situation. The surrender of the charters, royal officials maintained, had returned all the lands of New England to the crown, their

---

[20] "A memoriall to explaine ... the Declaration," Miscellaneous Bound Manuscripts, 1679–1693, Mass. Hist. Soc.

[21] *The Revolution in New England Justified, Andros Tracts*, I, 94–99; *ibid.*, 155–156, 161; Viola Barnes, *Dominion of New England*, 195–199.

[22] *Conn. Records*, III, 176–178, 225, 228; *Mass. Records*, V, 470–471, 516; Justin Winsor, ed., *The Memorial History of Boston*, I, 249–250, II, 375; *R. I. Records*, III, 227.

original grantor. As for Indian deeds, the colonies, as part of the crown's dominions, could be apportioned only by the king's grant or under authority of his charter—for half a century, indeed, Massachusetts had itself rested its title to the soil on precisely such a claim. Indian signatures, declared Andros, were of no more value than "a scratch with a Bears paw." John Higginson, the aged minister of Salem, fell back upon the book of Genesis. "We received only the right and power of Government from the Kings Charter," he informed Andros, ". . . but the right of the Land and Soil we had received from God according to his Grand Charter to the Sons of *Adam* and *Noah*, and with the consent of the Native Inhabitants." The governor's reply put the issue with ominous clarity. Since Englishmen had settled the country, its land belonged to the king. "Either you are Subjects," he concluded, "or you are Rebels."[23]

The retort epitomized the domineering style that made the governor's innovations all the more offensive to his subjects. Caution and political skill might have achieved much in the atmosphere of confusion and resignation that had accompanied the establishment of the Dominion. But Andros scorned the judicious distribution of patronage and the profits of office that could have consolidated a court party from the group of moderates who had helped Dudley take office in 1686. Pressing forward with military dispatch, and contemptuous of opposition, he soon outran his local supporters. The Dominion's geographical extent prevented all save a handful of its colonial councillors from attending the meetings in Boston, and several of those who came later complained that Andros pushed through bills with scant regard for discussion and agreement.[24] Even more wounding was his evenhanded indifference to their particular interests and ambitions. In a scathing report to London, Andros advised that the claims of both Wharton and the Narragansett proprietors to unimproved land be rejected. The merchants who might have been drawn to the Dominion government by the prospect of better relations with

---

[23] *The Revolution in New England Justified, Andros Tracts,* I, 92, 88–90.

[24] [Stoughton *et al.*], *A Narrative, ibid.,* 138–141.

England were repelled by strict enforcement of the Acts of Trade and the accompanying decay of commerce. Finally, as property titles were called into question, Dominion councillors like Samuel Shrimpton found that they were the first to be called upon to prove their loyalty by an expensive repatenting of their estates.[25]

In place of the councillors, Andros turned for advice and support to an intimate clique of lawyers and military subordinates. Almost without exception they were recent arrivals in New England. Several had come directly from England with the redcoats; Ens. Joshua Pipon was, like the governor himself, from England's Channel Islands; Lt. Thomas Treffry was a Cornish relative of William Blathwayt. But most, notably John Palmer, James Graham, and John West, now appointed to the posts of attorney general, deputy secretary, and registrar respectively, had served with Andros during his prior governorship of New York.[26] In favoring such men, Andros clearly aimed to supplant those colonists on his council whom he now found, despite their acceptance of office, to be "so wedded to their old wayes and Customes as can hardly admitt asserting the Kings rights to anything they can avoyed."[27] All he accomplished, however, was to replace subordinates who were at least known to their fellow colonists and experienced in New England's ways with others no less greedy but far more threatening and insensitive. Even if the colonists' subsequent desire to blame outsiders is taken into account, there is abundant contemporary evidence to substantiate the charges levelled after the Revolution that it was this "Crew of abject Persons fetched from *New York*" who endowed the Dominion with an indelible record of

---

[25] Andros to the Lords of Trade, Aug. 31, 1687, C.O. 1/63, nos. 21iv, v; Viola Barnes, *Dominion of New England*, 156–160, 169–171, 199; Jeffries Papers, II, 19–73; Samuel Prince to John Chapman, Mar. 18, 1686, Prince Papers.

[26] James Bertrand Payne, *An Armorial of Jersey*, I, 319; *Randolph Letters*, VI, 208; Petition of John Treffrey, [July 22, 1689], C.O. 5/855, no. 19; *N. Y. Col. Docs.*, II, 740n., III, 657; New-York Historical Society, *Collections*, LXXX (1947), 91–98; Paul M. Hamlin and Charles E. Baker, *Supreme Court of Judicature of the Province of New York, 1691–1704*, I, 425.

[27] Andros to William Blathwayt, June 4, 1688, Blathwayt Papers, III, Col. Wmsbg.

misgovernment.[28] Hungry Restoration bureaucrats, they were accustomed by service in a conquered province to view the plantations as a mine of plunder and fast profit. Some settlement of the tangled claims and boundaries, particularly north of the Merrimack, was long overdue. But the colonists found that precedent and equity counted for little against the thirst for exorbitant fees. Both the claims of Robert Mason and of the settlers of New Hampshire were set aside so that all had to be proved anew, to the profit of the bureaucracy. Farther north, around Pemaquid, Palmer and West amassed estates and harassed the existing landowners.[29]

By the summer of 1688 the Dominion had become an alien regime estranged from its subjects. Bloated beyond manageable limits by successive annexations, it remained committed to a policy of centralization which brought even the records of New York and the probate of New Jersey estates to Boston. Andros's personal integrity was not in doubt, but he was unable to control his subordinates. "The Governor," wrote Randolph to London, "is safe in his New Yorke confidents, all others being strangers to his councill."[30] In desperation, especially as it became clear that all land titles were to be called into question, leading colonists resorted to a maneuver fast becoming a staple tactic of those dissatisfied with royal officials stationed in the plantations—they sought to outflank Andros by appealing directly to Caesar in Whitehall. The time seemed ripe, for King James was now attempting to forge a political alliance with English Puritans through his Declarations of Religious Indulgence. Wharton and his fellow Boston merchant, Elisha Hutchinson, were already in London, seek-

[28] *The Declaration of the Gentlemen, Merchants, and Inhabitants of Boston and the Country Adjacent. April 18, 1689* (Boston, 1689), reprinted in *Andros Tracts,* I, 13.

[29] Maine Hist. Soc., *Collections,* V (1857), 107–111, 125; Jeremy Belknap, *The History of New Hampshire,* I, 190–191; *Doc. Hist. Maine,* VI, 219–412, 449–467; Edward Randolph to John Povey, Jan. 24, June 21, 1688, *Randolph Letters,* IV, 198, 226–227.

[30] Randolph to John Povey, June 21, Oct. 7, 1688, *Randolph Letters,* IV, 227, VI, 271; *N. Y. Col. Docs.,* III, 656.

ing direct royal permission to develop mines and other industries in New England and striving to protect their claims to land in Maine and the Narragansett country.[31] In March, Increase Mather made a dramatic overnight escape from Randolph's pursuing officers and sailed for London to lay the colonists' grievances before the king. There they were joined by others, including Samuel Sewall.[32] By now only a handful of native New Englanders, most of them Anglicans, held office in the Dominion. As in England in 1640 and 1688, when the wind of an external crisis struck, those clustered around the edge of the balloon of government proved to be too few and insignificant to prevent it from being blown away.

Developments outside the Dominion in both England and America touched off its fall. All through the early months of 1689, New Englanders received fragmentary reports of the invasion of England by the Prince of Orange and the subsequent overthrow of James II. There were rumors that all charters had been restored. At the beginning of April, a traveller from the West Indies brought into Boston a copy of the Prince's Declaration of October 1688, which instructed unjustly deposed magistrates to resume their posts; the news became common knowledge despite Andros's attempt to suppress it. Two weeks later, when the uprising in Boston began, its partisans knew they could ally themselves with a cause that had already been proclaimed in England.[33]

---

[31] Sewall, *Diary*, I, 172–174; Elisha Hutchinson and Mehitable Warren to Thomas Lake, June 29, 1687, Maine Hist. Soc., *Collections,* 2nd ser., I (1890), 285; Richard Wharton to Wait Winthrop, Nov. 17, 1687, Mar. 14, Apr. 26, Oct. 18, 1688, to Bartholemew Gedney, Mar. 10, 1688, Mass. Hist. Soc., *Collections,* 6th ser., V (1892), 9–18; Petition of Thomas, Lord Culpeper, Richard Wharton, and Thomas Brinley, [Jan. 13, 1688], C.O. 1/64, no. 3i; Viola Barnes, "Richard Wharton," 243–248.

[32] Increase Mather, *Autobiography,* 320–323; Kenneth B. Murdock, *Increase Mather,* 183–189; Sewall, *Diary,* I, 164, 184–242. Other New Englanders then in England included Thomas Brattle, Samuel Nowell, and John and Samuel Appleton.

[33] Channing, *History of the United States,* 198–199; *N. Y. Col. Docs.,* III, 591, 660; John Allyn to Wait Winthrop, Apr. 15, 1689, Mass. Hist. Soc., *Collections,* 6th ser., V (1892), 19, Wait to Fitz-John Winthrop, Dec. 13, 25, 1688, Jan. 5, 1689, *ibid.,* 5th ser., VIII (1882), 486–489; *The Revolution in New England Justified, Andros Tracts,* I, 77–79; C. D., *New-England's Faction Discovered* (London, 1690), reprinted in *ibid.,* II, 209.

Yet not until over a month after their rebellion did the colonists receive definite word of William's success, and it was the difficulties of defending the northern colonies that provided the immediate occasion for the Dominion's toppling, just as they had earlier presided over its birth. Dongan's aggressive policies and the French attempts to cow the Iroquois had heightened tensions all along the frontier, and in the fall of 1688, soon after Andros had taken over the government of New York and New Jersey, fresh trouble broke out on the Dominion's eastern flank. The boundary between Maine and French Acadia was confused, and the attempts of Dongan's officials to establish New York's eastern border at the River St. Croix, the modern line of the state of Maine, had infringed upon French settlement, which extended as far west as the Penobscot, eighty miles closer to Boston. Dongan's men also disrupted a flourishing trade between Acadia and New England, notably by their seizure of the ship *Jeanne* and its cargo of wine, an action which touched off prolonged diplomatic wranglings back in Europe.[34] Boston merchants, led by the influential John Nelson, protested in vain at the disruption of peace and prosperity. Others, such as Jean-Vincent D'Abbadie de Saint-Castin, a nomadic gentleman-trader living on the eastern shore of Penobscot Bay, objected more forcefully. Castine, as he was called by the English, was married to the daughter of a local Abnaki chieftain, and when Andros attempted to expel all French settlers from the area and rifled Castine's trading house during the spring of 1688, the Frenchman roused his Indian allies to retaliate against the outlying English settlements.[35] At sea, a perennial disagreement over the exclusive fishing

[34] Governor Andros to the king, July 9, 1688, C.O. 1/65, no. 20; President Dudley and the Council of New England to the Lords of Trade, [Oct. 21, 1686], C.O. 1/60, no. 80 (fol. 60); Maine Hist. Soc., *Collections*, V (1857), 75–81, 89–91, VIII (1881), 188–189. For the intricate case of the *Jeanne*, part-owned by Nelson, see *CSP Col., 1685–1688*, nos. 807, 925, 960, 1079, 1492, 1509, 1545, 1560, 1608, 1615, and *Randolph Letters*, IV, 96–97, 98–99, 126.

[35] Edward Randolph to John Povey, June 21, 1688, *Randolph Letters*, IV, 224–225; Mass. Hist. Soc., *Collections*, 3rd ser., I (1825), 82–83; *Doc. Hist. Maine*, VI, 446–447; English MSS., II, 6, Essex Instit., Salem; Pierre Daviault, *Le Baron de St. Castin, Chef Abenaquis*. Nelson, nephew to Sir William Temple, onetime proprietor of Acadia, had long traded with Castine; *Collection de manuscrits contenant lettres, mémoires, et autres documents historiques relatifs à la Nouvelle France*, I, 367.

rights claimed by the French in Acadian waters was a further cause of dispute.[36]

Andros was convinced that the Indian wars of the past had been caused by the colonists' undue severity. He endeavored to negotiate with the tribes and reprimanded the local commanders who had surreptitiously seized a number of Indians suspected of participating in earlier attacks. Spurred on by Castine, however, and furnished with powder and shot by the French government in Quebec, the Abnaki were not to be deterred. Unable to find a New Englander willing to accept command of a punitive expedition, the governor was himself forced to spend the winter of 1688 scouring the wastes of Maine in search of an elusive foe. By April of the following year, according to his subsequent report to the committee of trade, no less than seven hundred men were garrisoning a chain of fortified posts beyond the Merrimack.[37]

Andros's strategy proved more deadly to his own power than to the enemy's, for the Indians easily evaded these scattered outposts. Given the nature of New England settlement, the network of fortified towns created during King Philip's War, which allowed the colonists to defend themselves while continuing a semblance of normal life, was probably the best solution to an intractable problem. But Andros was eager to place his first line of defense in the enemy's country, and his suspicion of the townships prejudiced him against any policy that would have strengthened their power. The governor later claimed that he had brought the tribes to the point of surrender; his critics replied that his forts were "but a project to Hedge in the Cuckow" and that his costly and exhausting campaign had not killed a single In-

---

[36] Bruce T. McCully, "The New England–Acadia Fishery Dispute and the Nicholson Mission of August, 1687," 277–290.

[37] Andros to Major Gold, Aug. 25, 1688, to Colonel Tyng, Sept. 20, 1688, Andros's charges against the Massachusetts government, [May 20, 1690], *Andros Tracts*, III, 86–88, 31–33; Edward Randolph to William Blathwayt, Nov. 8, 1688, to the Lords of Trade, May 29, 1689, *Randolph Letters*, VI, 278–281, IV, 276–277; Francis Parkman, *Count Frontenac and New France under Louis XIV*, 220–223.

dian.[38] The question was overshadowed by more sinister speculations. Even before the outbreak of war there were rumors of a "horrid design" to deliver New England into the hands of France. Had not Andros, an alien "Guernsy-man" from the Channel Islands, subverted true religion and the rights of Englishmen to erect "a *French Government?*" Were not several of his subordinates known Catholics? Had not Secretary John West been heard to say that the king's interest would best be served by replacing New England's people by another?[39] "A dreadfull, lengthy, wasting Indian war" now seemed to be the capstone of New England's own Popish Plot, with the children of Israel led into the wilderness "to be a sacrifice to our Heathen Adversaries." Leniency toward the enemy was in reality collusion and betrayal. It was rumored that Andros supplied ammunition to the enemy and encouraged attacks upon the English. His overthrow had forestalled the arrival of a French fleet to receive the surrender of a New England stripped of its defenders.[40]

There was no substance to these suspicions—the French governor of Montreal thought that Andros would certainly side with the rebel

---

[38] Cotton Mather, *Decennium Luctuosum* (Boston, 1699), reprinted in Charles H. Lincoln, ed., *Narratives of the Indian Wars, 1675–1699*, 193; Answer of Sir Edmund Andros to his Instructions, [April 1690], C.O. 5/855, foll. 243–244; A. B., *An Account of the Late Revolutions in New-England* (London, 1689), reprinted in *Andros Tracts*, II, 193; Answer of the Massachusetts Agents to Andros's Account, Mar. 30, 1690, *ibid.*, III, 34.; *The Declaration of the Gentlemen, ibid.*, I, 17. The forts constructed by Governor Berkeley of Virginia twenty years before had aroused similar criticism: see "The History of Bacon's and Ingram's Rebellion, 1676," in Charles M. Andrews, ed., *Narratives of the Insurrections, 1675–1690*, 50.

[39] [Increase Mather], *Miseries of New-England, Andros Tracts*, II, 5, 11; *The Revolution in New England Justified, ibid.*, I, 79–80; Charges against John West, *ibid.*, 163; Abstract of a letter from Boston, Aug. 20, 1688, C.O. 1/65, no. 43. Catholics surrounding the governor included Lt. Anthony Brockholls, Capt. Gervais Baxter, Capt. George Lockhart, and Lt. David Condon of the frigate *Rose* stationed at Boston.

[40] Joshua Moody to Increase Mather, Jan. 8, 1689, Mass. Hist. Soc., *Collections*, 4th ser., VIII (1868), 370; *The Revolution in New England Justified, Andros Tracts*, I, 101–112, 118–122; [Stoughton *et al.*], *A Narrative, ibid.*, 145–147; *A Vindication of New-England* (Boston? 1690?), reprinted in *ibid.*, II, 50–52; *Doc. Hist. Maine*, V, 142–153. For the widespread belief in a Catholic conspiracy throughout English America at this time, see Lovejoy, *Glorious Revolution in America*, 281–288.

Prince of Orange against his lawful king.[41] But they were widely believed, and their effect upon the garrisons in Maine was to snap bonds of discipline already weakened by the rigors of long and seemingly fruitless service. The troops on the frontier were not the rootless and malleable raw material of English regular forces, but husbandmen taken from their farms and families. They were not to be cowed by the jovial brutality of such English officers as Lt. James Weems, who informed new conscripts arriving at the fort at Pemaquid that "Hell is like to be youre winter quarters and the divel your Landlord ... Damn'd Sons of Whores."[42] When, late in March 1689, Andros received word of William's landing and hastened back to Boston from the frontier, it seemed as if the cup might yet be dashed from New England's lips at the very moment of deliverance. Early in April the soldiers at Saco River deserted their post and began to march on Boston. It was the news of this mutiny, according to Cotton Mather, that forced the hands of those who had hoped for a peaceful solution and precipitated an armed uprising.[43]

Much remains obscure about the events of April 18, 1689. One contemporary account tells of simultaneous reports broadcast at each end of Boston that the men of the other end of town were up in arms. The leaders who gathered at the Town House before noon to demand Andros's surrender professed themselves surprised by events, then produced a lengthy and well-prepared indictment of his administration.[44] Their modest reluctance to claim responsibility for rebelling

---

[41] M. de Callières to M. de Seignelay, Jan. 1688, *N. Y. Col. Docs.*, IX, 404.

[42] *Doc. Hist. Maine*, V, 20–21; see *ibid.*, 33–44 and *Andros Tracts*, I, 171–173 for the soldiers' complaints of mistreatment by their English officers.

[43] Orders of Andros, Apr. 12, 1689, Mass. Archives, CXXIX, 368–370; *A Vindication of New-England, Andros Tracts*, II, 52; Samuel Mather, *The Life of the Very Reverend and Learned Cotton Mather*, 42; Cotton Mather, *The Life of Sir William Phips*, 51–52.

[44] Nathaniel Byfield, *An Account of the Late Revolution in New-England* (London, 1689), reprinted in *Andros Tracts*, I, 3–4; *The Declaration of the Gentlemen, ibid.*, 11–20.

against a royal governor at a time when the fate of William's invasion was still in doubt is thoroughly understandable. But if, as some opponents of the revolution later claimed, the popular movement was concerted beforehand, it is curious that none stepped forward to claim credit when treason had prospered and the events of 1689 had become a sanctified chapter in New England's historical folklore.

The most likely explanation is that the plans of an influential minority were overtaken and redirected by spontaneous mass action. Andros's opponents were in touch with Increase Mather and the other colonists in London. Though still in doubt as to the outcome of events there, they realized that developments on both sides of the Atlantic would soon bring matters in New England to a crisis. A meeting of "some of the Principal Gentlemen in *Boston*" was held in mid-April. According to the account given by Cotton Mather eight years later, they agreed to try to "extinguish all Essays in the People towards an *Insurrection,* in daily Hopes of Orders from *England* for their Safety: But that if the Country People by any violent Motions push'd the Matter on so far, as to make a *Revolution* unavoidable, then to prevent the shedding of *Blood* by an ungoverned *Mobile,* some of the Gentlemen present should appear at the Head of the *Action* with a *Declaration* accordingly prepared."[45] These precautions do not seem to have been taken to the point of active conspiracy. Randolph, ever eager to sniff out plots and cabals, could only level the vague accusation after the event that there had been a meeting of armed men at Mather's house on the night of April 17. Judging by those who assumed leadership of the militia the following day and who shaped policy immediately after the coup, it was *not* the old-guard supporters of the charter but a group of Boston merchants, particularly three—John Nelson, John Foster, and David Waterhouse—with most reason

---

[45] Cotton Mather, *Life of Phips,* 52; also the similar account in A. B., *Account of the Late Revolutions, Andros Tracts,* II, 195, a work that textual and other evidence suggests was also written by Mather. Chalmers, *Political Annals,* Book II, 20, suggests that Increase Mather transmitted news of events in England by early January 1689, an account embroidered upon by later scholars, but no evidence survives as to the existence of such a letter or its precise contents.

to resent the governor's actions in Maine, who were readiest to embark upon forcible action.[46]

Within Boston, meanwhile, besides the imminent arrival of the mutinous militia, a further element of instability was provided by the crew of H.M.S. *Rose,* a frigate of the Royal Navy moored in Boston Harbor. Confined to a worm-eaten "leakey ship" commanded by an autocratic captain and an aging and reputedly Roman Catholic lieutenant, several of the sailors, led by the ship's carpenter, Robert Small, had deserted; their stories of plans for an attack upon the town by the frigate as part of the plot to deliver the colonists to the French heightened the general anxiety.[47] On April 16, Andros noted "a general buzzing among the people great with expectation of their old charter or they know not what." A little after dawn on April 18 came reports of disturbances in Charlestown. Soon afterward Captain George of the *Rose* was arrested as he stepped ashore. Again, there was an air of improvisation: it was sound strategy to take a measure which might prevent both the bombardment of Boston and the escape of frigate and governor with news of a treasonable uprising, yet George was seized by Small and his sailors, not by any organized group of conspirators. By nine in the morning, the beat of drums was calling the people of Boston to arms, and flags on Beacon Hill summoned the militia companies from nearby towns.[48]

---

[46] Randolph to William Blathwayt, July 20, 1689, *Randolph Letters*, VI, 291. Nelson, Foster, and Waterhouse are frequently mentioned as commanders of the Boston militia on April 18, yet none had previously served in such a position. For their links to Acadia, see Randolph to the Lords of Trade, May 29, 1689, *ibid.*, IV, 277; *Andros Tracts*, II, 216; and note 35, preceding.

[47] Log of H.M.S. *Rose,* Feb. 11, 1686, Adm., Class 51, volume 3955; Deposition of sailors of the *Rose,* Mass. Archives, CVII, 9–11; Petition of Jervas Coppindale, [Feb. 25, 1690], C.O. 5/855, no. 66; Cotton Mather, *Life of Phips,* 52. For the activities of Capt. John George of the *Rose,* see John H. Edmonds, "Captain Thomas Pound, Pilot, Pirate, Cartographer, and Captain in the Royal Navy," 24–29.

[48] Hutchinson, *History of Massachusetts-Bay,* I, 316; Narrative of John Riggs, July 16, 1689, C.O. 5/855, fol. 35; "A Particular Account of the late Revolution at Boston," and Captain George to Secretary Samuel Pepys, June 12, 1689, Andrews, *Narratives of the Insurrections,* 199–200, 216; Byfield, *An Account, Andros Tracts,* I, 4; Samuel Prince to Thomas Hinckley, Apr. 22, 1689, Mass. Hist. Soc., *Collections,* 4th ser., V (1861), 193. Other detailed modern interpretations, by Dunn,

## Dominion, Revolution, and Settlement

Many of those perceived as loyal supporters of the Dominion were arrested in the streets. Andros, Randolph, and a few others found refuge in the fort completed some months before on the hill overlooking Boston harbor from the south. With most of the English regular forces still on active service in Maine, the governor had little more than a dozen soldiers to defend his position. Out in the harbor, Lt. David Condon of the *Rose* penned what must stand as one of the most unusual log entries in the annals of the Royal Navy: "Thursday, 18 April, 1689: Revolution. This morning Capt George the Doctor and Master was committed by a Mobile to Prison and the Major part of the Church of England People. The Governor forct to his Forte, who was promis under hand writing by those that took the Government [neither] to secure nor to Dammify him nor his Government belonging to him if he would surrender it same. The wind from South-west by West to East-north-east Faire."[49] Late in the afternoon, Condon sent a boat to the fort to rescue Andros and his garrison, but "just at that nick" the besieging militia under Capt. John Nelson came up and chased the governor and his redcoats back inside the fort. The situation was hopeless; toward evening Andros and his remaining supporters walked to the Town House, where they were arrested and placed under guard. On the following day, Ensign Pipon and his garrison on Castle Island commanding the entrance to Boston harbor also surrendered, and, after a mutiny among the crew, the *Rose* was disabled by the confiscation of her sails.[50]

---

*Puritans and Yankees,* 253–255, Lovejoy, *Glorious Revolution in America,* 239–242, and Lewis, "Massachusetts and the Glorious Revolution," 305–307, place greater emphasis on the Revolution as a result of well-conceived plans. The lengthy description by Gerald B. Warden, *Boston, 1689–1776,* 3–11, is novel only by reason of its persistent factual inaccuracy—beginning with its description of the *Rose,* a fifth-rate frigate of twenty-eight guns and two hundred twenty-nine tons, as a "seventy-four-gun ship of the line" (*ibid.,* 4). Cf. Joseph R. Tanner, *Pepys' Memoires of the Royal Navy, 1679–1688,* 94.

[49] Sir Edmund Andros to the Secretary of the Admiralty, Sept. 5, to Lord Dartmouth, Nov. 28, 1687, *Andros Tracts,* III, 75, C.O. 1/63, no. 77; Narrative of John Riggs, July 16, 1689, C.O. 5/855, no. 17 (fol. 35v.); Log of the *Rose,* Adm. 51/3955.

[50] Byfield, *An Account, Andros Tracts,* I, 5–7; Samuel Prince to Thomas Hinckley, Apr. 22, 1689, Mass. Hist. Soc. *Collections,* 4th ser., V (1861), 194–196. Though

The coup was as swift and complete as its English counterpart, and for much the same reasons. The threat of radical change imposed from above drew all ranks of society into a common coalition for the preservation of established rights and privileges. It was a revolution as contemporaries defined the term—a turning of the wheel of change to restore what were conceived to be the ways of the past.[51] The importance of preserving a common front and avoiding bloodshed at such a time was graphically demonstrated by events in neighboring New York. There the situation was complicated by strong internal political rivalries, by ethnic divisions between Dutch and English settlers, and by the degree to which many of the leading landowners and merchants had committed themselves to the administration of the Dominion. Further, when news of the Boston revolt reached New York, Andros's lieutenant governor, Francis Nicholson, deserted his post and fled to England. The vacuum left by his departure set off a bitter contest between the remaining Dominion councillors and opponents led by a militia captain of German origin named Jacob Leisler. Leisler emerged supreme, but shortly before the long-delayed arrival of a new royal governor commissioned by William of Orange, now king, he was goaded into firing upon supporters of the new regime. Convicted of treason, Leisler and his son-in-law, Jacob Milbourne, were hanged in May 1691. The result was a blood feud that poisoned and polarized the politics of New York throughout the remaining years of the century.[52]

In New England, by contrast, the Andros regime's estrangement from its subjects and a stronger tradition of consensus and modera-

---

most accounts place the surrender of the *Rose* on April 19, Condon's log dates it on April 20, when, upon receiving a command "to surrender the Shipp to King William . . . the men gave 3 Chears and Shuck yards and Topmast." The sails were brought ashore on April 22. Adm. 51/3955; Mass. Archives, CVII, 2.

[51] Vernon F. Snow, "The Concept of Revolution in Seventeenth-Century England," 167–174.

[52] Jerome R. Reich, *Leisler's Rebellion;* Lawrence H. Leder, "The Politics of Upheaval in New York, 1689–1709," 203–212, and *idem, Robert Livingston, 1654–1728, and the Politics of Colonial New York;* Thomas J. Archdeacon, *New York City, 1664–1710,* 105–146; and Robert C. Ritchie, *The Duke's Province,* 198–231.

tion in government preserved the colonists from their neighbors' fate. The inhabitants of Boston, wrote Cotton Mather with pardonable hyperbole, rose in arms "with the most *Unanimous Resolution* perhaps that ever was known to have inspir'd any People." In addition, "the Principal Gentlemen" of Boston and their clerical advisers were ready with leadership and direction. Their Declaration, read from the balcony of the Town House at midday on April 18, put forth a mature political program. It was probably drawn up by Cotton Mather from material already gathered for use against Andros at Whitehall and hastily adapted for the occasion. In a few succinct paragraphs, it interpreted past events and charted a course for future action. New England had fallen prey to the far-flung tentacles of the Popish Plot. With its walls breached by a malicious and unreasonable assault upon the charters, the country had fallen under an arbitrary government founded upon an illegal commission. There followed a litany of the sins of the Dominion, its persecutions and corruptions, its threat to life, liberty, and property. New England had borne all this with exemplary patience until the noble undertaking of the Prince of Orange and fears of treachery and French attack had inspired the country to rise up against its oppressors.[53]

With justification came a less explicit plea for domestic reconciliation. It was a foreign tyranny that had laid New England low. Office and preferment were given to "such Men as were strangers to and haters of the People: . . . of all our Oppressors we were chiefly *squeez'd* by a Crew of abject Persons fetched from *New York*." In short, outsiders were to blame. There were New England men on Andros's council, but those who were true lovers of their country had been deliberately excluded from decision and debate: "the Governor, with five or six more, did what they would." The removal of the alien incubus of Dominion rule, it could be concluded, cleared the way for a return to the old tranquility.[54]

[53] Cotton Mather, *Life of Phips*, 53; *The Declaration of the Gentlemen*, Andros Tracts, I, 11-19.

[54] *The Declaration of the Gentlemen*, Andros Tracts, I, 13, 17.

The broad coalition that stood behind the Declaration was made plain a few hours later. In a display of unity doubtless designed to impress upon Andros the indefensible isolation of his position, fifteen leading citizens subscribed to a letter urging the governor to surrender the fort before the fury of the mob became uncontrollable. Five—former governor Simon Bradstreet, Thomas Danforth, John Richards, Elisha Cooke, and Isaac Addington—had been chosen assistants in the last election under charter rule. Three—Wait Winthrop, William Browne, and Samuel Shrimpton—were members of the Dominion council, while two more—William Stoughton and Bartholemew Gedney—were both councillors and former charter magistrates. The remainder—John Nelson, John Foster, David Waterhouse, Peter Sergeant, and Adam Winthrop—were prominent Boston merchants; all save Winthrop had settled in Massachusetts since the Restoration and had hitherto taken little part in the colony's political life.[55] Only one of the colony's leaders from the time of charter rule had become so identified with the Dominion as to be irretrievably involved in its fall: Joseph Dudley was seized in Rhode Island upon his return from judicial duties in New York, brought back to Boston, and imprisoned with Randolph in the common jail. Not the least of Andros's legacies to New England was the reunification of a political establishment divided since the time of the crown's campaign against the charters.

Revolution was one thing, settlement another. "I fear," wrote Samuel Prince to his father-in-law four days after the revolt, "whether or no the matter of settling things under a new Government may not prove far more difficult than the getting from under the power of the former." Added former Deputy Governor Danforth, "I am deeply sensible that we have a wolfe by the ears."[56] The early paragraphs of

---

[55] *Ibid.*, 20. Adam Winthrop was a native New Englander but passed ten years in England before his return in 1680. Little is known of Waterhouse, but his letters in the Jeffries Papers, XI, 31–41, suggest that he spent more time in London than Boston.

[56] Prince to Thomas Hinckley, Apr. 22, 1689, Mass. Hist. Soc., *Collections*, 4th ser., V (1861), 196; Danforth to Increase Mather, July 30, 1689, Hutchinson, *Papers*, II, 312.

the Declaration seemed to argue for a speedy return to charter government. It did not openly declare that the Massachusetts charter
had been illegally vacated, but there was a general understanding
that Increase Mather in London had secured an opinion to that effect
from Attorney General Sir Thomas Powys in the last months of
James's reign.[57] Yet the Declaration ended upon a note of uncertainty
that revealed the differences among its supporters and hinted at the
discord to come. "We do therefore seize upon the Persons of those few
*Ill Men* which have been (next to our Sins) the grand Authors of our
Miseries; resolving to secure them, for what Justice, Orders from his
Highness, with the *English Parliament* shall direct . . . for which Orders
we now humbly wait." In similar fashion, the letter to Andros required him to surrender the government "to be preserved according
to Order and Direction from the Crown of *England.*"[58]

This undertaking became the guiding precept of a new government. On April 20 the fifteen signatories of the letter to Andros constituted themselves a Council for the Safety of the People and Con-
servation of the Peace "until there be a farther and more Orderly
Settlement." Fifteen additional members were admitted to the
council upon their pledge of support for the policy laid down in the
letter to Andros. Twelve of the fifteen were leading merchants of
Boston, Charlestown, and Salem. Bradstreet was chosen president
of the council, Isaac Addington clerk, and Wait Winthrop commander of the militia. Over the next few days the councillors reorganized the frontier garrisons, appointed port collectors and other local

---

[57] Edward Randolph to the Lords of Trade, May 29, 1689, *N. Y. Col. Docs.,* III,
578. There is no record of such an opinion by Powys in the state papers in London, although it may have resulted from the opinions sought from him by the
Lords of Trade, Aug. 10 and Oct. 17, 1688, *CSP Col.,* 1685–1688, nos. 1859, 1913.
Nor does Mather mention such an opinion in any account of his agency, although he might have suppressed it as casting doubt upon the need for a new
charter. It was also rumored in England that James had restored all confiscated
charters, presumably a reference to the royal proclamation of Oct. 17, 1688, restoring corporation franchises: John Allyn to Wait Winthrop, Apr. 15, 1689,
Mass. Hist. Soc., *Collections,* 6th ser., V (1892), 19.

[58] *The Declaration of the Gentlemen, Andros Tracts,* I, 18–19, 20.

officials, and assigned to themselves the powers of justices of the peace.[59]


For half a century Massachusetts had fought against acknowledging more than a nominal dependence upon England. Now its leaders waited passively for an imposed settlement. To many colonists the failure of the council to resume charter government seemed inexplicable. Increase Mather subsequently argued that had Massachusetts promptly exercised its "undoubted Right" to resurrect the charter, the *fait accompli* would have been accepted by the crown. Instead, the colony's decision to inform royal officials that it was awaiting a settlement had undercut his efforts to secure a restoration of the old charter.[60] Diehard supporters of the old government never ceased to believe that a great opportunity had been missed, a revolution betrayed.

By a fine irony, it seems to have been Mather's son who played the most active part in the decision against immediate resumption of the charter. Both the account written by Cotton Mather's bitter critic, Robert Calef, and the posthumous biography by Samuel Mather agree that Cotton strongly urged that affairs be left to the judgment of the English Parliament. According to Calef, Mather argued that to

---

[59] Mass. Archives, Court Records, VI, Apr. 20, 22–25, 1689. These records containing the council minutes show that only fifteen more members were admitted to the council on April 20, not twenty-two as generally supposed. Seven more were admitted on May 1 (as note 71, following); the two groups are set under these different dates in the Court Records. I have chosen to cite these records (and their continuation under the new charter as the council's journal during assembly session and, under the title of Executive Records of the Council, between assembly sessions) by date and not by manuscript page number, in order to facilitate correlation with the widely available microfilm versions of these records, film made of copies of the records having different pagination from the originals. For a listing of this film, see William Sumner Jenkins, *A Guide to the Microfilm Collection of Early State Records*. Extensive extracts from these records are printed, for 1689, in Pubs. Col. Soc. Mass., *Transactions*, XVII (1913–1914), 14–27, and, for 1689–1692, in *N. H. Laws*, I, 271–498.

[60] Increase Mather, *A Brief Account Concerning Several of the Agents of New-England* (London, 1691), reprinted in *Andros Tracts*, II, 291–292. The address is that of June 6, 1689, printed in Mass. Hist. Soc., *Collections*, 6th ser., I (1886), 147n. At the time, however, Mather supported this position and rushed this address into print.

[96]

do otherwise would be to slight his father's work in England.[61] Nevertheless he could not have swayed his compatriots without support from those leading the colony. Many evidently agreed with Mather that, whatever the equity of the proceedings, the Massachusetts charter had been legally annulled by the crown. In the forceful words of one writer, "if a man be killed though never so unjustly it will not bring him to life again though he be taken up and set upon his legs with great complaints how basely and unmanly he was killed."[62] His words, together with the nervous waverings of the revolutionary government, testify to the extent to which the procedures and decisions of English common law remained a fundamental part of the colonists' frame of political reference. That law might be variously interpreted, but its verdicts, once rendered, could not be disregarded. From this perspective, only a legal process in England could resuscitate charter government.

Others who challenged this argument still acknowledged that the old charter was deficient as a basis for government. "It were to be wished," remarked one colonist during the commissioners' visit in the 1660s, "that some things which seem necisarie for good government were more expressly and in termes set down in the Pattent than can be found there."[63] Randolph had quickly perceived this flaw in the colony's position, and there was no defense against his charge that Massachusetts had greatly exceeded the limited powers granted to it as a trading company back in 1629. Hence the revolutionary government came to speak in terms of a restored charter with the addition of new and comprehensive powers. Even Thomas Danforth, leader of the most conservative faction in the General Court five years before

---

[61] Robert Calef, *More Wonders of the Invisible World* (Boston, 1700), reprinted in Samuel E. Drake, ed., *The Witchcraft Delusion in New England*, III, 145–147; Samuel Mather, *Life of Cotton Mather*, 43; Cotton omitted both his father's remark and any description of his own role in 1689 from his biography of his father. Nor did he deny that role in a counterblast to Calef, saying that he had wanted resumption insofar as it was legally possible: Obadiah Gill *et al.*, *Some Few Remarks upon a Scandalous Book*, 45–46.

[62] "Reflections upon the Affairs of New England," 326.

[63] Mass. Hist. Soc., *Proceedings*, XLVI (1912–1913), 297.

and a man accused by Randolph of denying almost every form of English authority, expressed his hope that the charter would be confirmed "with such addition of privileges as may advance the revenue of the crown and be an encouragement of their Majesties subjects here."[64]

More pragmatic considerations also stood in the way of immediate resumption. A policy of procrastination preserved the precious unity of the ruling coalition in a time of chaos. Several members of the Council of Safety were moderates who had always opposed confrontation with England, and present circumstances served only to strengthen their preference for caution and negotiation. William Stoughton, it was reported, had refused to sign the letter to Andros without some mention in the Declaration of the colonists' dependence on the English crown. A large majority of the Council were coastal merchants with overseas investments; this, as Randolph noted in a letter from his prison cell in Boston, made them wary of any course which might incline other colonies and England to view them as rebels.[65] All were keenly aware that Massachusetts was "Briar'd in the Perplexities of another Indian War" and in imminent danger of French attack. The triumph of Europe's Protestant champion gave hope for a new beginning in English colonial policy. It seemed wisest, therefore, to play a waiting game. Only Simon Bradstreet and Elisha Cooke, an unlikely alliance of octogenarian moderate and second-generation conservative, are known to have urged immediate resumption. As a body, the Council of Safety was reluctant to take responsibility for so irrevocable an action; delay was the easiest course.[66]

---

[64] Instructions for the Agents of Massachusetts, Jan. 24, 1690, *Andros Tracts*, III, 59–60; Danforth to Increase Mather, July 30, 1689, Hutchinson, *Papers*, II, 314. Boston merchant William Broughton expressed hope for a parliamentary confirmation of the old charter in a letter to Mather, Apr. 2, 1690, Mass. Archives, XXXV, 378a.

[65] William S. Perry, ed., *Historical Collections Relating to the American Colonial Church*, III, 49; Randolph to the Governor of Barbados, May 16, 1689, Hutchinson, *Papers*, II, 315–316.

[66] *The Declaration of the Gentlemen*, *Andros Tracts*, I, 17. Calef's testimony that Brad-

These scruples, however, were overborne by the strength and rancor of a tide of public opinion that knew no such qualms and anxieties. Its first impulse was vengeance upon Andros and his subordinates. On the day after the uprising, wrote Samuel Prince, "the country people came armed into the town in the afternoon in such rage and heat, that it made all tremble to think what would follow: for nothing would pacify them but he [Andros] must be bound in chains or cords, and put in a more secure place; and that they would see it done ere they went away, or else they would tear down the house where he was to the ground." Nor were fellow citizens exempt from the fury of the "wild bears" of the mob. For all Mather's calculated insistence on the unanimity and moderation of the people, the revolt had begun, as Lieutenant Condon and others noted, with the imprisonment of "the Major part of the Church of England People," the group from which had come the bulk of Andros's most loyal and favored local supporters.[67] If Condon was indeed a Catholic as the colonists believed, it must have seemed a strange irony to one familiar with religious discrimination to observe a revolution carried through in the name of English liberties beginning with a roundup of Anglicans. The majority were released within a week, and only twenty-six men—minor Dominion officials, together with Andros and his New Yorkers—remained in confinement.[68] Yet public feeling continued to run high against those whose ways seemed part and parcel of the Dominion's tyranny, and Anglicans in their turn drew together to pro-

---

street favored resumption would be difficult to accept were it not supported by the testimony of Elisha Cooke: Calef, *More Wonders,* in Samuel E. Drake, *The Witchcraft Delusion,* III, 145–146; Cooke to Simon Bradstreet, Oct. 16, 1690, Mass. Hist. Soc., *Proceedings,* XLV (1911–1912), 652; Hutchinson, *History of Massachusetts-Bay,* I, 333.

[67] Prince to Thomas Hinckley, Apr. 22, 1689, Mass. Hist. Soc., *Collections,* 4th ser., V (1861), 196; "A Particular Account of the Late Revolution, 1689," in Andrews, *Narratives of the Insurrections,* 200, 204, 206; Log of the *Rose,* Adm. 51/3955.

[68] Names of the Persons imprisoned with Sir Edmund Andros, [July 29, 1689], C.O. 5/855, no. 24 (the version in *CSP Col., 1689–1692,* no. 305, omits the name of Lieutenant Jordan); Account of gaoler John Arnold, Mass. Archives, XL, 613. Hutchinson's estimate (*History of Massachusetts-Bay,* I, 317) that fifty were originally imprisoned seems plausible; the records printed in *N. H. Laws,* I, 282, 285, 290, 304, 307, 335, 343, detail their gradual release.

test what they denounced as malicious Puritan persecution of England's established church. The split revealed the religious passions underlying Andros's overthrow and gave the lie to protestations of the colonists' consensus and conformity to English methods. As such, it was to prove a powerful weapon in the hands of those on both sides of the Atlantic who sought to prevent the crown's confirmation of a return to charter government.[69]

Disappointed of vengeance, the colonists turned their frustrations against their new leadership. Popular sentiment had from the first backed a prompt resumption of the charter. Even as they besieged Andros in his fort, the citizens of Boston had ceremoniously escorted the old magistrates to the Town House and cheered the arrival of former Governor Bradstreet.[70] Now they saw government appropriated by a self-appointed group dominated by the very merchants they had consistently excluded from power in earlier years. Some, such as Nelson, Foster, and Waterhouse, who sat on the Council of Safety by virtue of their prominence "at the Head of the Late Action," were not even freemen; several, notably Stoughton and Samuel Shrimpton, were known to have had a hand in undermining charter rule. With the approach of the charter-prescribed election day, the council found itself under strong pressure to take more positive action. Five petitions from Essex County called for the holding of colony-wide elections. On May 1, the council admitted seven more members, three of them former magistrates and all from the smaller rural towns. If this was an attempt to stave off criticism by seeking broader popular support, it came too late. In the judicious words of the court record: "There being some agitation in the Council of the Necessity of settling some forms of Government, and Several Gentlemen appear-

---

[69] For Anglican complaints, see *Andros Tracts,* I, 25, 53, II, 28–32, 210–212; "A Particular Account," in Andrews, *Narratives of the Insurrections,* 207–208; letters of the Rev. Samuel Myles, Nov. 29, Dec. 12, 1690, C.O. 5/855, nos. 124, 127. For a different analysis, concluding from an examination of the rhetoric of apologists for the revolution that "the revolt had little or nothing to do with religion," see Breen, *Character of the Good Ruler,* 152n.

[70] Byfield, *An Account, Andros Tracts,* I, 4; Samuel Prince to Thomas Hinckley, Apr. 22, 1689, Mass. Hist. Soc., *Collections,* 4th ser., V (1861), 194.

ing, out of the Countrey moveing the Same thing, the farther debate there abouts is deferred until the Morrow; and Signification was dispatched to some other Gentlemen of the Council at Salem &c: to desire their Company."[71] There was open disagreement, which found expression in rival broadsheets appropriately entitled "From a Gentleman of Boston To a Friend in the Countrey" and "The Countrey-Man's Answer to a Gentleman in Boston." Both declared themselves in favor of a resumption of charter government. But where the Bostonian urged reconciliation and a simple reinstatement of the General Court of 1686, his opponent (satirically apologizing for the "homespun Attire" of his lines) demanded an election so that the people could judge who had best served their country. Was it likely, he asked, that the magistrates of 1686 would resume the charter when they had already failed to do so after the revolution? Rather than accept those who had collaborated with the Dominion, it would be better to choose from among those active in its overthrow. "The *Sword* now rules," he concluded, a circumstance opening the way for an election to be held without strict attention to the usual procedures.[72] A well-informed contemporary evidently writing with these two sheets before him described the two positions and added a third, that the Council of Safety should be continued as it was. Each had its supporters, and the whole matter was "the occasion of much needless Discourse and of many Heart burnings that might as well have been spared."[73]

On May 2, the enlarged council accepted a proposal calling for consultation with the people. Representatives of the towns were to

---

[71] Mass. Archives, CVII, 8–8a, Court Records, VI, May 1, 1689. The seven were Nathaniel Saltonstall (Haverhill), Richard Dummer (Newbury), Robert Pike (Salisbury), Daniel Pierce (Newbury), John Smith (Hingham), Edmund Quincy (Braintree), and William Bond (Watertown). All were freemen; Saltonstall, Pike, and Smith were former assistants.

[72] The two broadsheets are conveniently reprinted (from C.O. 5/855, nos. 5, 6) in Richard C. Simmons, "The Massachusetts Revolution of 1689," 7–8, 10–12. Dr. Simmons is mistaken, I believe, in asserting that these two were first circulated between the conventions of May 9 and 22, since they speak of the approach of the traditional day of election (May 8 in 1689).

[73] A. B., *Account of the Late Revolutions, Andros Tracts*, II, 200.

convene in Boston a week later. The chosen date, one day after election day, ensured there would be no regular elections in the colony that year. Yet the balance within the council remained so delicate that the next day's meeting first revoked and then reaffirmed the decision to summon representatives.[74] In all likelihood, the issue was decided by a compromise on the wording of the letters dispatched to the towns. Both of the circulated broadsheets had agreed on the wisdom of enlarging the franchise by including freeholders or other men of property, and the council now recommended consideration of this matter to the towns. In consequence, most towns permitted inhabitants who were qualified to vote in town meetings to join with the freemen in choosing and instructing the delegates sent to Boston—an intriguing anticipation of the subsequent belief that a matter as fundamental as the settlement of government requires the participation of a broader segment of the political nation than its customary electorate.[75] The result, as a recent scholar has noted, was a striking departure from the traditional pattern of Massachusetts politics. Of the sixty-six representatives from forty-four towns who met on May 9,

---

[74] Mass. Archives, Court Records, VI, May 2, 3, 1689.

[75] *Ibid.*, CVII, 21. For accounts of the participation by all town inhabitants (and sometimes by all freeholders) see, for example, "Boxford Town Records, 1685–1706," 46–47; "Salem Town Records," 213–214; Myron O. Allen, *The History of Wenham*, 45; John J. Currier, *History of Newbury, Massachusetts, 1635–1902*, 208. No evidence survives to show that this was done in the conscious belief that a broader electorate was needed to legitimize a settlement of government. Nor, on the other hand, have I found an earlier use of the practice in the American colonies or indeed in England. For the debates in England during December 1688 on how a parliament could be called following King James's flight and those within the convention which met the following month to determine the correct procedures for dealing with a "vacant" throne, see Howard Nenner, *By Colour of Law*, 173–196, and Henry Horwitz, *Parliament, Policy and Politics in the Reign of William III*, 6–14. The closest any English leader came to anticipating the radical rhetoric in Massachusetts was Lord Delamere's remark (cited by Horwitz, *ibid.*, 8) that "nothing can be done but by the body of the people in their representatives." Possibly there were memories on both sides of the Atlantic of the advocacy in 1656 by parliamentarian (and onetime resident and governor of Massachusetts) Sir Henry Vane of a form of constitutional convention separate from a legislative assembly for the purpose of establishing a government: Margaret A. Judson, *The Political Thought of Sir Henry Vane*, 44–45. But I have found no evidence to suggest that the colonists were consciously echoing these English debates.

only sixteen had previously served as deputies to the General Court and only half can be identified as freemen of the colony. In part this was due to the sheer size of the gathering—fifty-one deputies from forty-four towns had been the largest previous attendance (in 1672), and eight deputies had then come from towns in Maine and New Hampshire that were not represented in 1689. Thirty-two had been the largest number attending during the last decade of charter rule.[76]

Nonetheless, the delegates were thoroughly traditional in their opinions. Pointedly addressing themselves to those sworn as magistrates in 1686 rather than to the Council of Safety, they informed them that they, with the deputies chosen in 1686, were the colony's lawful present government. If additional magistrates were needed they could be chosen according to charter methods once the number of freemen had been increased. Assuredly, the crown would at length confirm such a settlement.[77] In reply, the magistrates again evaded a decision. They pointed out that several towns had not submitted their views and that others had sent delegates without specific instructions. A further meeting was necessary. The delegates then asserted their right to continue the Council of Safety in power and agreed to meet again on May 22.[78]

Throughout Massachusetts, constitutional issues were now the subject of vigorous public debate. Not since the first years of settlement had American colonists engaged in such a widespread assess-

---

[76] Simmons, "Studies in the Massachusetts Franchise," 132 (with corrections); Mass. Hist. Soc., *Collections,* 3rd ser., IV (1834), 289–292. The contrast should not be overstated: of the thirty-five deputies in the 1686 General Court, sixteen were returned to sit in the first "regular" court which met in 1689 on June 5.

[77] Mass. Archives, Court Records, VI, May 10, 1689; the delegates were thus excluding William Stoughton and John Pynchon who, though elected in 1686, had declined to be sworn.

[78] *Ibid.;* Mass. Archives, CVII, 26; Mass. Hist. Soc., *Collections,* 4th ser., VIII (1868), 708–709. Towns such as Mendon, Newbury, Hatfield, and Westfield had indeed merely ordered their representatives to consult at Boston.

ment of the fundamentals of their government; it would not occur again until the 1770s. They made no attempt to construct a new constitution in the manner that was to become so characteristic of American political life in later years. The only substantial reform sought was the broadening of the franchise, a measure which would merely bring Massachusetts into line with neighboring Puritan colonies. A few hoped for an executive appointed by the crown, but the overwhelming majority wanted a continuance of the form of government preordained by divine and human law and hallowed by half a century's rule. Yet disagreement over how to achieve this common goal revealed significant differences of opinion about the sources of political legitimacy. Those who urged delay in expectation of a royal settlement stressed the colony's dependence upon England and the legal obstacles created by the annulment of the charter. In essence they waited for authority to descend from a higher power. From the wording of the letter sent out to the towns on May 10, a majority of the Council of Safety still favored this position: the letter sought advice as to the settlement of government only until such time as orders (and not merely a confirmation) should be received from England.[79] In reply, the author of a third broadsheet, dated May 18, 1689, boldly asserted the right of the people to erect their own government and laws in times of violent change. He repeated the old arguments that the laws of England did not extend beyond that country's shores and that Massachusetts's allegiance was defined and limited by its charter: far from defying the crown, a reinstatement of charter rule would restore "our legal Acknowledgements of Dependence, which we are in no Capacity of prosecuting any other way but by Charter." In conclusion the writer urged upon his readers the duty of self-preservation often cited by earlier defenders of the charter. Then, however, the object had been the protection of the Bible Commonwealth and its transcendent mission. Now, *"Salus Populi Suprema Lex,"* a portent of the way in which subsequent champions of New England autonomy

---

[79] Samuel A. Bates, ed., *Records of the Town of Braintree*, 26; *Watertown Records*, II, 37.

would seek to legitimize their claims by reference to the welfare of the people rather than obedience to the laws of God.[80]

The safety of the people did indeed seem in jeopardy. War menaced the eastern frontier, and settlers who called for aid upon what they uncertainly addressed as "the superior Power now in being at Boston" found small response. In the seat of government itself, tensions were such that stories spread by deserters from the *Rose* (half of whose crew had by now jumped ship) that a fire in Boston's North End had been deliberately set were enough to incite a crowd to storm aboard the frigate and seize its officers. With them to jail once more went the customary scapegoats from Boston's Anglican community. The Council of Safety was unable to stem the ferment. "It is not in our power," responded Bradstreet and Winthrop to a request for Andros's release, "to set any persons at liberty who are confined and kept by the soldiers."[81]

By May 22, therefore, as the delegates reassembled in Boston, the pressures upon the leadership to settle a stable and respected government were becoming irresistible. More than fifty towns had now responded to the council's request for advice. Fifty-one sent representatives, and sixty-two of the seventy-five delegates had attended the earlier meeting.[82] Known freemen and those with political experience in the General Court were again in the minority. A concise tabulation of their views and the wishes of the towns is rendered difficult by the fact that few of the returns can be placed in clearly defined categories. Some simply requested the restoration of charter government; others,

---

[80] Philo. Angl., *The Case of Massachusetts Colony Considered, in a Letter to a Friend at Boston,* reprinted from C.O. 5/855, no. 4, in Simmons, "The Massachusetts Revolution of 1689," 8–9.

[81] Letter of Samuel Wheelwright and others, Apr. 25, 1689, Pubs. Col. Soc. Mass., *Transactions,* VIII (1902–1904), 127–128; Log of the *Rose,* May 1, 16, 18, Adm. 51/3955; Capt. John George to Secretary Pepys, June 12, 1689, Andrews, *Narratives of the Insurrections,* 218; John Sherrett and others to Governor Bradstreet, June 7, 1689, Prince Papers; Hutchinson, *History of Massachusetts-Bay,* I, 327.

[82] Mass. Archives, Court Records, VI, May 22, 23, 1689; though described as the representatives of fifty-four towns, only those of fifty-one are listed.

following the wording of the council's letter, wished for charter rule until orders came from "the Authority of England." A number asked for the election of additional magistrates to join with either the magistrates of 1686 or the existing Council of Safety.[83] Yet as a contemporary abstract of the returns noted, one basic division was plain: a large majority of the towns, at least forty-two, supported immediate resumption. Only eight favored continuation of the Council of Safety.[84] On May 24, the delegates, now describing themselves as a convention in emulation of the English assembly that had offered the throne to William and Mary, issued a second declaration proclaiming a restoration of charter rule. Seeking to placate all factions, it acknowledged the dependence of Massachusetts upon the realm of England and spoke of the time when "Order shall come from the higher Powers" there. Simultaneously, however, it bluntly declared that the "Method of Settlement of the . . . Government in this present Juncture lieth wholly in the Voice of the People" and demanded that the towns be consulted for "their approbation and compliance" prior to any further constitutional change.[85]

In response, the magistrates elected in 1686 finally agreed to administer the colony "according to the Rules of the Charter." Their reluctance was plain: they consented to govern, they declared, "from the present Necessity, and for Satisfaction of the people . . . until by Direction from England there be an Orderly Settlement of Government." They asked for assurances of popular obedience, for the selection of "Fit Persons" to fill vacancies among the magistrates, and for

---

[83] The town returns are in Mass. Archives, CVII, 14–23a, 24a–25, 36–41b, 43–47, 48a–51. Many can be found printed in individual town histories.

[84] A Breviate or Abstract of the Returns from the Severall Towns," MSS. L. 1689, Mass. Hist. Soc. (a mutilated version is in Mass. Archives, CVII, 52–54). Those supporting the continuation of the council or opposed to a return of the 1686 government were Charlestown, Wrentham, Hingham, Dunstable, Medfield, Bradford, Haverhill, and Sudbury, although the last two seem eventually to have sided with the majority. Eight towns favored an enlargement of the franchise.

[85] A printed copy of the convention's declaration, dated May 24, 1689, "Collected by Some of the Representatives . . . for the Satisfaction of the Several Towns," is in C.O. 5/855, no. 17iv.

acceptance of the actions of the Council of Safety. No mention was made of the convention's expressed desire for an increase in the number of freemen. One final face-saving (and perhaps, for magistrates concerned for England's response, neck-saving) proviso was added upon publication of their acceptance: the magistrates declared that they did "not intend an Assumption of Charter Government; nor Would be so Understood." It was two weeks before the representatives had an opportunity to chastise this apostasy. By threatening to obstruct all public business, they forced the magistrates to retract their words. Five more magistrates, three of them displaced members of the Council of Safety, were elected and sworn to office. On June 22, all laws in force before the coming of the Dominion were revived. Government by charter had returned to Massachusetts.[86]

Step by step, pressure from below had brought the Bay magistrates to accept a policy of resumption despite their misgivings about its wisdom and legality. Like Macaulay's Etruscans at the bridge, those behind cried "Forward!" and those before cried "Back!" Elsewhere in New England, where the hand of the crown and Governor Andros had lain less heavily, matters were more easily resolved. Faint echoes of the issues being debated in Massachusetts were audible in Plymouth Colony. When former governor Thomas Hinckley summoned a meeting of delegates from the towns soon after the revolution in Boston, Marshfield and Duxbury called for a broader franchise and Scituate revived an old complaint against past changes in the system of county government. Hinckley himself was scarcely more anxious than Bradstreet to resume the post of leadership. On the positive side, however, since Plymouth had never managed to obtain a royal charter, no debate comparable to that raging in Massachusetts was necessary. Nor was the colony embarrassed or its resentment aroused by relics of the Dominion—only a few local quislings remained to be disciplined

---

[86] Mass. Archives, CVII, 27, 138, Court Records, VI, May 24, June 7, 22, 1689; C.O. 5/855, no. 17v; *Boston Records*, VII, 195.

by their respective towns.[87] The crucial question was not resumption but whether Plymouth could now use this opportunity to obtain formal recognition of its separate existence from the crown. In June, an assembly of representatives restored the old government of 1686 and directed Hinckley to petition the king "for the reestablishment of their former enjoyed liberties and priviledges both sacred and civil." An elaborate but carefully worded address was dispatched to Sir Henry Ashurst, the son of the colony's old ally in negotiations with the crown and likewise active in the New England Company, for presentation in London. With a fervor more consistent than their metaphors, the colonists reminded King William that their forefathers had been the first "to break the Ice into this vast American desart." They asked for confirmation of their traditional political and religious institutions.[88]

To the north, New Hampshire confronted different problems. There was no thought of returning to the corrupt and unpopular royal administration that had ruled the province before its incorporation with the Dominion, yet those who had welcomed their separation from Massachusetts ten years before still hoped to preserve an independence from Boston's control. Through the remaining months of 1689 the four towns of the colony struggled to piece together a temporary government. But internal dissensions—Hampton refused to cooperate with the others in the election of a president and other officials—and the solvent of war rendered their efforts futile. Indian attacks on the outlying garrisons of Dover in the early summer and the subsequent expeditions against the enemy convinced the settlers

---

[87] Langdon, *Pilgrim Colony*, 224–225; John Walley and Nathaniel Byfield to Wait Winthrop, Apr. 22, 1689, Winthrop Papers.

[88] *Plymouth Records*, VI, 208–209; Thomas Hinckley to Ashurst, June 6, 1689, Mass. Hist. Soc., *Collections*, 4th ser., V (1861), 201–202; Address of the General Court of Plymouth to the king and queen, June 6, 1689, C.O. 5/855, no. 13 (fol. 27). This address, later printed as a broadside in Boston in 1690, differs markedly from the draft in Mass. Hist. Soc., *Collections*, 4th ser., V (1861), 199–200; nor, despite the wording of the precis given in *CSP Col., 1689–1692*, no. 183, does it assert that the colony had ever possessed a charter.

that there was no hope of survival without aid and protection from their more powerful neighbor. After a convention of town delegates in February 1690 and before the protective snows of winter could melt away, a petition was circulated among the towns seeking annexation to the Boston government pending directions from the crown. The petition received nearly four hundred signatures, including those of all the province's leading settlers save for Nathaniel Weare and Henry Green of Hampton and John Hinckes of Portsmouth. A few weeks later Massachusetts accepted the petition and appointed three prominent supporters of the union, William Vaughan, Richard Martyn, and Nathaniel Fryer, as magistrates within the province.[89]

For all their cordial dislike for each other, Rhode Island and Connecticut followed similar paths in the months after the revolution. Unlike Massachusetts, both possessed charters specifically tailored to the requirements of colonial self-government, and both had surrendered them to Andros before legal proceedings had been carried to the point of judgment and confiscation. Hence they could argue that no legal impediment prevented a simple return to charter rule. More by circumstance than design, their claim was allowed to stand. As elsewhere in New England, however, events demonstrated that there could be no easy way back to the days of old.

In Rhode Island, plans for the restoration of government took shape within a week of the Boston uprising. A letter to the towns sent out over the initials of Walter Clarke and John Coggeshall, governor and deputy governor prior to the Dominion, proposed a meeting to discuss a return to "our ancient privileges and former methods." Accordingly, a small group of leaders gathered at Newport on May 1, the usual day of election. By the votes of forty men, and without popular consent, according to one hostile critic, they reinstated charter

---

[89] Mass. Archives, XXXV, 229; *N. H. Provincial Papers*, II, 30–55; Charles W. Tuttle, "New Hampshire in 1689–1690," 218–228.

rule together with the officers elected before the arrival of Andros.[90]
Despite their professed expectations that the crown would confirm
this settlement, it was not until the following January that the colony
dispatched an account of its actions to England. The wheels of Rhode
Island government moved slowly at the best of times, but the delay
may also have been due to disagreement. Although Clarke and his
fellow magistrate and Quaker, Walter Newbury, had signed the declaration of resumption, they subsequently chose to "disclaim the government" and refuse office. Clarke likewise refused to make a voluntary surrender of the colony's charter, which was in his possession. In
the first six months of 1690, no less than six men were successively
chosen to the posts of governor or deputy governor; some declined to
serve and others accepted only brief periods of office.[91]

Within Connecticut, by contrast, disagreement produced a lively
contest for political power centering upon issues similar to those being
discussed in Massachusetts. The survival of Fitz-John Winthrop's
papers allow a rare glimpse of domestic politicking. On the one side
stood those who, like the "Countrey-man" writing in Massachusetts,
demanded both an immediate resumption of the charter and new
elections. At their head stood James Fitch of Norwich, Nathaniel
Stanley and James Steele of Hartford, and the Reverend James
Noyes of Stonington, men hitherto more prominent in local affairs
than in the central government who (or so their opponents charged)
now sought to ride into power upon the wave of popular rejoicing
mixed with resentment against those magistrates who had submitted
to Andros which had followed the Dominion's fall. To the west, the

---

[90] *R. I. Records*, III, 257, 266, 268–269; Francis Brinley to Wait Winthrop, May 6,
1689, Mass. Hist. Soc., *Collections*, 6th ser., V (1892), 20; [Brinley?] to John
Usher, July 7, 1689, C.O. 5/855, no. 16.

[91] *R. I. Records*, III, 258–261, 271. A copy of the May 1 declaration reached England, but there is no indication of when it was received: C.O. 5/905, 109–110.
Clarke and Newbury seem to have been more active than most in the Dominion:
they were accused (though by a prejudiced Bostonian) of using their position as
Dominion councillors to engross land: "A Memorial to explaine the Declaration," Miscellaneous Bound MSS., 1679–93, Mass. Hist. Soc.

towns of the old New Haven Colony, led by magistrates who had resisted incorporation in the Dominion, also favored an immediate election.[92]

In opposition to Fitch and his followers were those who regarded themselves as the natural leaders of Connecticut by birth and breeding. Foremost among them were Samuel Willis, the Reverend Timothy Woodbridge, and the principal "civil servants" of the Hartford government, Secretary John Allyn and the colony's attorney and former treasurer, William Pitkin. They generally favored a return to charter rule but, like the Boston magistrates, feared the consequences to themselves and the colony of a sudden election, suspecting that Fitch intended to use the popular mood to purge the government and give free rein to his extensive speculations in Indian lands. The threat brought together a varied coalition. Willis remained bitter over his imagined legal wrongs, but still stronger was his fear of any threat to rule by a genteel elite. Pitkin, a Hartford lawyer and religious liberal, nursed a similar mistrust of schemes "originated in the Common people." "Popular motions," he wrote to Fitz-John Winthrop, "are seldom wel directed," and he cautioned lest a sudden election spawn a crushing congregational orthodoxy of "narrow spirritted men" and a disloyal neglect of English authority. Finally, the eccentric and learned Gershom Bulkeley, minister of Wethersfield and a justice of the peace under Andros, took the more extreme position of denying the legality of any election or resumption on the ground that the charter had been irrevocably surrendered to the crown.[93]

Both sides strove to enlist the prestige of Fitz-John Winthrop, then recuperating from an illness at New London; though never a charter

---

[92] Gershom Bulkeley, "Will and Doom, or the Miseries of Connecticut by and under an Usurped and Arbitary Power, 1692," 154; Roger Wolcott, "A Memoir for the History of Connecticut, 1759," 331; Franklin B. Dexter, ed., *Extracts from the Itineraries and Other Miscellanies of Ezra Stiles*, 199; Zara Jones Powers, ed., *New Haven Town Records, 1684–1769*, 63, 65.

[93] Pitkin to Fitz-John Winthrop, May 6, 1689, Winthrop Papers; Petition of Pitkin and others, 1664, Conn. Archives, Ecclesiastical Affairs, I, 10b; Gershom Bulkeley, *The People's Right to Election* (Philadelphia, 1689), reprinted in *Andros Tracts*, II, 88, 101.

magistrate, he remained the colony's representative of the first family
of American Puritanism. "As the Winthropps have been a Blessing to
al New-England so we hope God wil continue you to bee stil," wrote
Pitkin, urging him to come to Hartford for the election on May 9.
Fitch and Stanley made a pilgrimage to New London, and Allyn ner-
vously informed Winthrop that, with the "Seaside Townes" divided
in their choice of governor, the proponents of an election planned to
run Winthrop as their candidate. Flattered but wary, Winthrop was
inclined to agree with Bulkeley that the colony should await a royal
settlement under its present leadership. Yet if the people decided otherwise, he added coyly, "there is no striveinge against the streame of
popular resolution." Despite Allyn's pleas that he be on hand to ensure "the preventing of inconveniences" and the thwarting of Fitch's
designs, Winthrop stayed away from the Hartford election.[94]

After a day of excitement on the green at Hartford, Allyn and his
associates escaped the inconveniences they feared through a compromise similar to that about to be adopted in Boston. By the account of
an indignant Gershom Bulkeley, "the Gentlemen" had come to an
agreement with their opponents on the day prior to the election
whereby three propositions were submitted to the representatives sent
by the towns and other assembled freemen. The choice was between
restoring the magistrates elected in 1687, retaining the present government, or choosing a council of safety. With the approval of the
first option, the others were never brought to a vote. Both Fitch and
Allyn were among the restored magistrates; vacancies occasioned by
death permitted some political fence mending as Samuel Willis and
Winthrop, the man for all factions, were named to the council.
Winthrop, however, declined to serve. A second sour note was the assembled representatives' insistence, anticipating the similar demand
by their Boston counterparts, that they and not merely the magis-

---

[94] Pitkin to Winthrop, May 6, Allyn to Winthrop, May 2, 1689, Winthrop
Papers; Timothy Woodbridge to Winthrop, [May 1689], Winthrop to [Wood-
bridge], May 6, to [Allyn], May 6, Allyn to Winthrop, May 6, 1689, Mass. Hist.
Soc., *Collections*, 6th ser., III (1889), 33, 498–501. I have followed the valuable
analysis of Dunn, *Puritans and Yankees*, 286–289, save in the point of who proposed
Winthrop as governor: it was Fitch's Hartford allies, not Allyn and Woodbridge.

trates should be consulted prior to any future alteration of government.[95]

Charter rule had been restored to Connecticut, the General Court declared, "untill there shall be a legall establishment setled amongst us," and the colony's explanation of events to the crown reflected this lingering uncertainty. In a long and apologetic address prepared after much debate, Governor Robert Treat and Secretary Allyn told how the colony's desire to unite with Boston rather than New York had been mistakenly taken as a resignation of its charter; they skirted the dangerous topic of the Dominion and its overthrow and emphasized that only urgent necessity and external dangers had compelled a resumption of charter government.[96] This timidity drew a sharp reproof from Connecticut's representative in London, William Whiting, who refused to deliver the address and told Treat, no doubt at Increase Mather's insistence, that Connecticut would only bring attention upon itself and its neighbors by raising the issue of the charter's validity. There was, he declared, no record of its surrender and no reason why the colony should not continue to enjoy its privileges. The Hartford government later sent a second and more noncommittal address but, as Whiting had suspected, Whitehall's preoccupations made its reception a mere formality. It was late in 1693, four years after the Boston revolt, before either Connecticut or Rhode Island received any official response from the crown.[97]

Traditional ways of government had been reestablished throughout New England, yet they were everywhere beset by new and unexpected difficulties. These did not derive from any concerted desire for political or social change. Andros had been the true revolutionary in

---

[95] Bulkeley, "Will and Doom," 156–160; *Conn. Records*, III, 250–253.

[96] *Conn. Records*, III, 250, 254, 463–466.

[97] Whiting to Governor Treat, Aug. 12, 1689, *ibid.*, 469–470; Connecticut to the king, Jan. 3, 1690, C.O. 5/855, no. 52, Conn. Hist. Soc., *Collections*, XXIV (1932), 24–25.

this respect, and his attempt to remodel New England had only served to strengthen popular attachment to the tried and trusted ways of local community life. In one town, Dedham, the rebellion was followed by the wholesale replacement of the veteran selectmen who had served during the Dominion. But such a convulsion was exceptional. No other towns are known to have followed Dedham's example, and elsewhere the traditional local leadership remained in place.[98] More accurate indicators of the character of New England's political disarray were the towns' aggressive role in the restoration of government and the numbers of individual colonists who stepped forward to take an active part in politics. Far from seeking change, they strove to prevent their leaders from allowing change to continue. As they accurately perceived, the danger lay at the heart and not at the extremities of the body politic—the thread of continuity cherished in the towns lay broken at the center. The ardor and assurance that had carried New England's rulers across the shoals of heresy and through storms of royal displeasure had given way to refusals to serve, to contorted evasions of responsibility such as the request of former Governor Clarke of Rhode Island that the new government seize the colony records from him by a show of force so as to relieve him of any liability for surrendering them, and to the timorous acceptance of office "Until there be a Setlement of Government here by Direction from the Crown of England" (the proviso added to the oaths of office in Massachusetts).[99] Nothing, indeed, better substantiates the hypothesis that the old guard leadership in Boston played little part in initiating the uprising of April 18 than their subsequent actions: they showed themselves singularly reluctant rebels.

Undoubtedly, as with the victors of the Glorious Revolution in England, the act of overthrowing established authority was in itself an intensely unsettling experience for those who had for so long

---

[98] Kenneth A. Lockridge, *A New England Town*, 88. Much has been made of this incident but examination of other town records shows that it was not repeated elsewhere.

[99] *R. I. Records*, III, 261; Mass. Archives, Court Records, VI, June 7, 13, 1689.

preached and expected the virtues of civic obedience.[100] Still more disturbing, as evident in their anxious attempts to justify their actions, was the uncertain status of the charters. This would have mattered little had either the magistrates or the colonists at large been convinced that the people had the right to create and sustain their own governments. True, some part of their careful deference to England and their insistence that they were reassuming only government "according to the Rule of the Charter" and not the charters themselves can be attributed to their desire to protect themselves should the crown decide to restore the Dominion.[101] Yet their consistent use of such language, and the extent to which it shaped their actions, also demonstrated that the great majority still held to those convictions which had rendered a prosecution of the charters so potent a weapon in disarming colonial resistance—a deep-rooted deference to the rule of law and a belief that within New England such law and civil authority itself was grounded upon the charters. "The Voice of the People" might rule in times of violent change, but no colonist, and certainly no magistrate, as yet proclaimed it to be sufficient basis for lasting and legitimate government. Fifty years before, John Winthrop had confidently woven together popular consent, charter right, and divine law in justifying the rule of a godly aristocracy. By 1689, changing circumstances had thrown this harmony out of joint, leaving the traditional underpinnings of leadership badly weakened. Shaken by the crown's determination and ability to transform the authority derived from the charters into a means of direct royal control, and unwilling to submit to being the mere representatives of a giddy and possibly godless multitude, New England's magistrates lost much of their former confidence in their capacity and right to rule.

Their constituents, for their part, saw only dismaying and even sinister vacillation. Emboldened and resentful, some took matters

---

[100] An excellent treatment of this theme's importance in England is John P. Kenyon, *Revolution Principles.*

[101] Governor Bradstreet to the king and queen, June 6, 1689, Mass. Hist. Soc., *Collections,* 6th ser., I (1886), 148n.; *Conn. Records,* III, 465.

into their own hands. In at least seven towns in Massachusetts and Plymouth, bitter disputes erupted following the General Courts' reinstatement of the militia officers who had held commissions in 1686. Typical was the situation in Swansea, where "a young crew that were very heady" insisted upon electing new officers.[102] In Connecticut there was talk of the dangers of "Anarchical Government" and in Rhode Island complaints of the unprecedented turbulence of the people and the invasion of private lands by squatters.[103] The most striking illustration of the erosion of authority occurred in Boston. There, while Joseph Dudley languished in prison alongside other Dominion officials, his well-placed friends and relatives sought pardon for this black but native sheep. His misdeeds were carefully omitted from printed accounts of the Dominion, and after a petition to the council and an exculpatory letter to Cotton Mather he was permitted to return to his Roxbury house under heavy bond.[104] The public reaction was immediate. Gathering on an evening of intense summer heat, a crowd confronted the aged Governor Bradstreet and denounced him as an "old Rogue" for his leniency. Then, several hundred strong, the crowd sallied forth from the town, attacked Dudley's house at midnight, and dragged him back to Boston. There he was chased from one house to another by "women boyes and negros" until Bradstreet was compelled to implore his brother-in-law to return to the security of the common jail.[105] As for the other prisoners, the

[102] *N. H. Laws,* I, 287; *Plymouth Records,* VI, 210; John Walley to Thomas Hinckley, [Aug. 1689], Apr. 16, 1690, Mass. Hist. Soc., *Collections,* 4th ser., V (1861), 208–209, 239–242. For a detailed account of the militia troubles in Charlestown, Northampton, and Woburn, see Timothy H. Breen, "War, Taxes, and Changing Political Brokers."

[103] William Pitkin to Fitz-John Winthrop, May 6, 1689, Gershom Bulkeley to Fitz-John Winthrop, Oct. 28, 1689, Winthrop Papers; Francis Brinley to Wait Winthrop, May 6, 1689, Mass. Hist. Soc., *Collections,* 6th ser., V (1892), 20–21.

[104] Dudley to Mather, June 5, 21, 1689, Mass. Hist. Soc., *Collections,* 6th ser., III (1889), 501–507, 4th ser., VIII (1868), 485; Mass. Archives, CVII, 119, 204.

[105] Edward Randolph to William Blathwayt, July 20, 1689, *Randolph Letters,* VI, 289–290. The transcribed documents which he enclosed concerning Dudley's experiences and an anonymous letter describing the incident are in C.O. 5/855, foll. 57–63, 73.

council's suggestion that they be charged or set at liberty was blocked by a lower house vote that their crimes did not allow their release on bail. In September, "a great Company of Armed Men" assembled to ensure that former secretary John West was not discharged from prison.[106]

Several attempts were made to conciliate this undercurrent of unrest. Following the receipt of a royal letter in November 1689 ordering that Andros and his fellow prisoners should be sent back to England, all joined in the congenial task of collecting evidence to press charges against them before the king. With them, to accomplish this task and to work with Increase Mather and Sir Henry Ashurst to secure "a Confirmation" of the old charter, were sent magistrate Elisha Cooke and, at the insistence of the deputies, "being made more sensible of the Countries desire of the same," their speaker, Thomas Oakes.[107]

The Boston and Hartford governments also took steps to satisfy the widespread desire for greater political participation. In October, the Connecticut General Court offered freemanship to all adult men of "peaceable, orderly and good conversation" holding freehold estate with a yearly value of forty shillings in country pay. Procedural changes eased the admission of men in outlying settlements and gave the towns a larger role in the nomination and election of magistrates.[108] Four months later, Massachusetts took similar action after a

---

[106] Mass. Archives, CVII, 151, 309; *Andros Tracts*, III, 103, 104. In August, public anxiety had been heightened when Andros briefly escaped from prison: *ibid.*, 95–102.

[107] The king to the government of Massachusetts, July 30, 1689, Governor Bradstreet to Capt. Gilbert Bant, Feb. 5, 1690, *Andros Tracts*, III, 111–113; Charges against Andros and others, *ibid.*, I, 149–173; Credential and instructions for the Agents, Jan. 24, 1690, *ibid.*, III, 58–60; Mass. Archives, XXXV, 104b, 142, 171, Court Records, VI, Dec. 7, 1689, Jan. 18, 1690. The pressing of charges was apparently the principal reason for the sending of agents: Lawrence Hammond, "The Diary of Lawrence Hammond," 152, and Edward Rawson to Elisha Cooke, Nov. 14, 1689, Mass. Archives, CCXLII, 391.

[108] *Conn. Records*, IV, 11. There was an evident parallel with the famous forty-shilling franchise in England, although forty shillings in Connecticut country pay was then equivalent to only about sixteen shillings sterling: Conn. Hist. Soc., *Collections*, XXIV (1932), 48–49.

petition reminded the General Court of the loyalty shown by non-freemen during recent events and the many requests by the towns for an enlargement of the franchise. Henceforward, those certified by local selectmen as "not vicious in life" and who paid four shillings in a single country rate (not including the poll tax and meaning possession of a total estate valued at forty-eight pounds) or owned freehold property with a yearly value of six pounds could apply for admission to freemanship. Church members could still become freemen whatever their financial status and, as in Connecticut, the requirement of moral certification preserved an opportunity for the exclusion of the ungodly, however wealthy they might be. Further, both enactments discriminated in favor of those, such as the farmers of the country towns, with a landed stake in society. Deliberately so, perhaps, for the manner in which the Massachusetts measure was put into practice suggests that it was designed to permit a stronger voice in government to those in the rural areas who had been most critical of the magistracy, thus redressing what was seen as the undue preponderance of the seaport merchants and gentry. Over the next year, up until April 1691, over seven hundred men were admitted to freemanship by the Massachusetts General Court, two-thirds of them by reason of property rather than church membership, and together potentially swelling the ranks of the freemen by more than a third.[109] The town of Lynn, for example, which had been especially active in the revolution, presented no less than ninety-one names, almost as many as did Boston, ten times its size. Yet the method employed—not all towns submitted names and those that did generally seem to have listed all those they deemed to qualify—does not suggest a rush by the underprivileged to claim their due. Nor do all those named seem to have taken up or exercised their freemanship, for the

---

[109] Mass. Archives, XXXV, 154, Court Records, VI, Feb. 12, 1690; C.O. 5/855, no. 64. The names and manner of qualification are printed in *N. H. Laws*, I, 355, 363–471; a consolidated list is in *New England Historical and Genealogical Register*, III (1849), 347–352. There was considerable duplication; I follow the figures provided by Simmons, "Studies in the Massachusetts Franchise," 135, partially corrected from Theodore B. Lewis and Linda M. Webb, "Voting for the Massachusetts Council of Assistants, 1674–1686," 632–633.

number of votes cast in the election of magistrates between 1690 and 1692 was actually smaller than in the years prior to the Dominion.[110] Rather, the two governments' measures demonstrate the continuing factional divisions within the two governments and their interest in bolstering their authority and legitimacy, particularly among men of property hitherto either unwilling or unable to participate in political affairs.

Criticism of the magistrates' halfhearted commitment to charter rule was necessarily confined within the boundaries of New England—to appeal to an external power would be to question the very autonomy such critics sought to restore. A less immediate but ultimately more dangerous challenge came from the opposite end of the political spectrum, from those who continued to oppose the restoration of charter rule and looked to England as the only source of a lasting solution to New England's problems. Among them, inevitably, were those who had backed the Dominion and suffered at the revolution. More surprising, and certainly more alarming to the magistrates, were the numbers of those who had supported or even actively led the overthrow of Andros and had since become alienated by the course of events. This disaffection was centered in the port towns of Boston, Salem, and Charlestown and was undoubtedly accentuated if not caused by the steady ebbing of the influence of these communities' leaders within the revolutionary government. The resumption of charter rule under pressure from the rural towns had displaced all save a handful of the merchants who had led the revolution and dominated the Council of Safety. It also compelled them to face the delicate issue of whether a new authority had legitimately succeeded that of Andros. The dimensions of this dilemma were evident in the effort made to bridge it: thirteen of those excluded from the council signed

---

[110] Thus compare, for example, the figures given by Webb and Lewis with those for 1690-1692 in Mass. Archives, XXXVI, 54, C.O. 5/855, no. 99, C.O. 5/856, no. 146, and Mass. Hist. Soc., *Collections,* 3rd ser., X (1849), 120-121. Scholars have always assumed that these men became freemen, but the number of total votes cast steadily declines during this three-year period, from some 22,700 to just over 16,000 by 1692.

a declaration pledging their support to its "future Endeavours for the preservation of the peace." Three, Samuel Shrimpton and Wait Winthrop of Boston and John Phillips of Charlestown, were then among those chosen to fill the vacancies in the board of charter magistrates.[111] Yet the declaration nowhere acknowledged the legitimacy of the new administration, and it pointedly reminded the magistrates of their verbal and written promises to preserve Massachusetts "in Obedience, unto the direction we expect from the Crown of England." Some evidently came to believe that these promises had been broken; three signers of the declaration, John Nelson, David Waterhouse, and Richard Sprague, later joined those who appealed directly to England for aid.

An open confrontation was delayed by the new administration's careful avoidance of such provocations as the levying of taxes. It could hardly be avoided, however; several who had held minor office under the Dominion continued to insist, as did Gershom Bulkeley in Connecticut, that in default of orders from the crown the commissions granted by Andros remained in force. Finally, in September 1689, three of Charlestown's militia officers, Sprague, Lawrence Hammond, and John Cutler, together with former Dominion judge Thomas Graves, openly defied the magistrates' authority. Graves, with Bulkeley and another disgruntled merchant, Charles Lidget of Boston, pressed their opposition in pamphlets surreptitiously printed in Philadelphia. They were aided by a powerful if excessively legalistic defense of Andros and the Dominion circulated in manuscript form by former chief justice John Palmer.[112] The challenge was serious, and the Charlestown leaders, all former deputies to the General

[111] Mass. Archives, Court Records, VI, May 26, 1689; the version from the Winthrop Papers printed in Mass. Hist. Soc., *Collections*, 5th ser., VIII (1882), 491–492, has only eleven signatures.

[112] Bulkeley, *The People's Right to Election, Andros Tracts*, II, 102–108. Lidgett was probably the author of A. B., *Seasonable Motives to Our Duty and Allegiance*—thus Samuel Worden to Thomas Hinckley, Nov. 14, 1689, Mass. Hist. Soc., *Collections*, 4th ser., V (1861), 224. Palmer's tract was printed as *The Present State of New-England, impartially considered in a Letter to the Clergy* (Boston, 1689) and later in its better-known shortened form under his own name, *An Impartial Account of the State of New England* (London, 1690), reprinted *Andros Tracts*, I, 21–62.

Court, received considerable support from within their own community. Committed to prison, they were brought before the council and stripped of their offices; Sprague was expelled from the House of Representatives, and orders were given for the suppression under severe penalties of all papers tending to the subversion of the government. Most of the rebels made formal submission early in the new year, after the publication, amid much fanfare, of a royal letter authorizing a temporary administration in Massachusetts.[113] Even so, a significant undercurrent of disaffection remained. A number of the dissident Charlestowners later petitioned the crown for aid; in April of 1690, Salem's two deputies, backed by the town, protested against the holding of new elections until the crown's wishes were made known.[114] Both towns held back from supporting the government's enlargement of the franchise, only three names coming from Charlestown and none at all from Salem.[115]

Factional division, the questioning of the magistrates' authority, and challenges to the legitimacy of charter rule—New England had met such problems before without endangering its political stability or looking to England for aid. Now, however, they pressed in upon

[113] Frothingham, *History of Charlestown*, 224–234; *N. H. Laws*, I, 329–331; Mass. Archives, XXXV, 35b, 287–288; Elizabeth to John Usher, Oct. 16, Protest of Thomas Graves, Sept. 21, Minutes of a Council at Boston, Sept. 24, Order of the Convention of Massachusetts, Dec. 3, Printed copy of the king's letter to Massachusetts, Aug. 12, 1689, C.O. 5/855, foll. 99, 102–103, 137, 147; Edward Randolph to William Blathwayt, Oct. 8, to John Usher, Oct. 16, 1689, to the Lords of Trade, Jan. 10, 1690, *Randolph Letters*, VI, 297–298, 306–307, V, 28–29. Randolph had numbered both Hammond and Sprague among his opponents in 1682, and both had been actively hostile to the Dominion.

[114] Benjamin Bullivant, "Journal of Dr. Benjamin Bullivant," 107. Subsequent unrest and the appeals to London are discussed in Chapter 4, following. *Andros Tracts*, I, 195–208, reprints a tract, *Further Quaeries Upon the Present State of the New-English Affairs*, written in early 1690 and evidently aimed at the dissidents in Salem.

[115] *N. H. Laws*, I, 381. Eighteen were nominated for freemanship from Salem Village. The three from Charlestown were the only names sent from any of the eight towns (note 84, preceding) which had opposed resuming charter government in May 1689.

the central governments, suddenly the weakest link in the political chain, at the precise moment when the latter's authority and resources began to be tested to the utmost by New England's expanding involvement in a long and wasting war. Whatever Andros's part in precipitating hostilities, his fall and the Dominion's dissolution into its component parts removed the only authority capable of maintaining a coordinated defense of the two hundred miles of frontier between Albany and Maine. The loss of a controlling hand was quickly felt. Within a few weeks of the Boston revolt, most of the garrisons in Maine had deserted or been withdrawn and their English officers dismissed, leaving only a few weakly held outposts north of Falmouth. Bringing the troops home was a popular move and, besides, some thought it possible to convince the Indians that a war supposedly begun by Andros could be ended by his overthrow. But Castine and his Abnaki allies were only emboldened by peace overtures accompanied by such a precipitous withdrawal. Joined by the Pennacook Indians of New Hampshire, they began a series of destructive raids on outlying towns, culminating in the killing or capturing of fifty settlers at Cocheco, the site of modern Dover, late in June. Six weeks later, the depleted garrison of Fort Charles at Pemaquid, the last outpost beyond the Kennebec, surrendered after a two-day siege.[116]

The Boston government's response heralded the trail of difficulties and frustrations that lay ahead. To hundreds of impressed militiamen were added two troops of friendly Indians from Plymouth and Connecticut and colonial volunteers responding to a promise of eight pounds for every enemy killed or captured, a revival of the scalp bounties first offered in King Philip's War. Commissioners summoned according to the rules of the old New England Confederation, the organization which had overseen the winning of that war, blessed

---

[116] Mass. Archives, Court Records, VI, Apr. 20, 1689; *N. H. Laws*, I, 277–278, 288; Cotton Mather, *Decennium Luctuosum*, in Lincoln, *Narratives of the Indian Wars*, 189, 195–197. The collapse of the defenses in Maine can be followed in the plaintive petitions printed in *Doc. Hist. Maine*, IX, 10–21. The attack upon Cocheco and the killing of Maj. Richard Waldron was a long-delayed revenge for Waldron's treacherous capture of a body of friendly Indians thirteen years before.

the expedition as a defensive and hence just enterprise.[117] But it proved no more successsful than Andros's very similar campaign the winter before. Moving as far north as the Kennebec in two unwieldy columns, the expedition was unable to pin down and bring to battle any substantial numbers of the enemy, although several men were killed in a skirmish at Casco where the militia companies charged amid "thundring pealls of shoot."[118] Simultaneously, the colonists' time-honored ways of waging war displayed ominous signs of strain. Intercolonial cooperation had been the key to success in King Philip's War, but the Hartford government, citing suspicions that undue provocation had been given to the Indians (or, more probably, because it saw no reason to participate in a war beyond the traditional boundaries of New England), refused to send more than token aid to its sister colony. Later, it withheld its commissioners from further meetings of the Confederation, bringing to an end the attempt to revive that Puritan alliance just when its services were most needed.[119] Massachusetts was thrown back upon the resources of its militia system, but numbers of men, some questioning the government's authority to act, refused the call to service, and others hampered operations by disobedience and desertion.[120] The onset of winter drove the

---

[117] The preparation and progress of this expedition can be followed in *N. H. Laws,* I, 296–328, and Thomas Church, *The History of Philip's War . . . also, of the French and Indian Wars at the Eastward, in 1689, 1690, 1692, 1696, and 1704,* 152–160. For the efforts of Massachusetts to enlist aid from other colonies, see Mass. Hist. Soc., *Collections,* 4th ser., V (1861), 203–205; Mass. Archives, II, 210a, CVII, 247; Conn. Archives, War, II, 10–16, 20; Conn. Hist. Soc., *Collections,* XXI (1924), 311–312.

[118] Maj. Benjamin Church to Massachusetts, [Sept. 24, 1689], *Doc. Hist. Maine,* IV, 460.

[119] *Conn. Records,* IV, 3–4; Gov. Robert Treat to Massachusetts, July 31, 1689, Mass. Archives, II, 210a; Treat to the Commissioners of Massachusetts and Plymouth, Oct. 1689, Conn. Archives, War, II, 24b; Harry M. Ward, *The United Colonies of New England, 1643–90,* 352–353, 358. In 1677, when Massachusetts had previously clashed with the eastern Indians in Maine after the conclusion of King Philip's War within southern New England, Connecticut had refused to aid or, later, help pay for military expeditions by Massachusetts troops "without [i.e., outside] their patent liberties": *Conn. Records,* II, 497–498, 502–504, III, 496; *Plymouth Records,* X, 463.

[120] Letter from Boston, [July 30, 1689], John Legg to John Browne, Aug. 14, 1689, C.O. 5/855, nos. 25, 29 (fol. 80); *Doc. Hist. Maine,* V, 10, 73, 95, IX, 29, 37, 66; Church, *History,* 160–176.

expedition back across the Merrimack, leaving the remaining frontier communities no better defended than before. By May 1690, New Hampshire's commanders reported that "nothing now remaines Eastward of Welles," seventy miles back from what had been the line of settlement twelve months previously.[121]

At the root of these difficulties, as the colonists themselves were beginning to perceive, lay the fact that New England was now entangled in a different kind of conflict from those of earlier years. For all its skirmishes and ambushes, King Philip's War had been decided by the formal tactics of wasting enemy territory and assaulting fortified bases—it was the last war fought within New England for possession of its soil. The eastern Indians were a less orthodox foe, more elusive because less tied to an agricultural way of life, more inaccessible because they could fade back into the trackless forests of Maine. They were not to be drawn into pitched battles such as those which had broken the strength of the Pequots and the Narragansetts. Nor, as Connecticut's response made plain, were other colonies as willing to share in the defense of a distant frontier as they had been to participate in a war within their own borders.

Still more alarming was the mounting evidence that the war in Maine was but the beginning of New England's involvement in a larger, international struggle. Given the steady inflation of the spheres of influence claimed by both France and England in America, some such collision was doubtless inevitable even had James Stuart retained his throne. Blinkered by racial attitudes, neither side was prepared to credit the Indians with pursuing their own interests and ambitions by their resistance: New Englanders blamed French machinations, "a premeditated Jesuiticall contrivance complotted long before," just as Canadians believed the Iroquois, "vos sauvages loups habituez à Albany," to be the pliant tools of English aggression.[122]

---

[121] Charles Frost, Nathaniel Fryer, and Richard Martyn to Massachusetts, [May] 22, 1690, Mass. Archives, XXXVI, 77. A graphic picture of the hazards of frontier life in these years is given in the journal of John Pike, minister of Dover: Mass. Hist. Soc., *Proceedings*, XIV (1875–1876), 117–152.

[122] Massachusetts to the Secretary of State (draft), Apr. 5, 1676, *Doc. Hist. Maine*,

James's fall and William's triumph, however, swept aside the last shreds of official neutrality. England joined the Dutch and the powers confederated in the League of Augsburg in a grand alliance against the ambitions of Louis XIV; war was declared; and the northern colonies were thrust into place besides Flanders, Ireland, Spain, and the Caribbean as a battleground in a struggle for Atlantic supremacy. It was not a contest New Englanders had sought or, save by their expansion in Maine, precipitated. Yet they were caught up within the polarities it imposed. In French eyes they were as much the "Rebells . . . Hereticks and Traytors" who had deserted their lawful sovereign for a usurper as any other Englishmen.[123] Moreover, with their neighbors in New York and their allies, the Iroquois, they threatened Canada's very survival by their constriction of its lifeline of fish and furs. Hence, even before the formal declaration of war, French leaders had drawn up plans for a direct attack upon New York, by sea and down the Hudson valley. Frontenac, enterprising and autocratic, was sent back to Canada as governor to direct the assault. Fresh supplies of material aid and spiritual comfort were sent to fuel the war in Maine—reports to Boston noted that the conquerors of Pemaquid were Abnaki converts accompanied by their priest and outfitted with French equipment. By the time of Frontenac's arrival early in the fall of 1689, moreover, Canadians of all ranks were thirsting to strike a decisive blow, for in August, avenging the French attack of two years before, the Iroquois had struck across the St. Lawrence near Montreal in the bloodiest massacres in Canadian history.[124]

The impact of this situation upon New England's leaders was pro-

VI, 111; Governor Denonville to Governor Dongan, Aug. 10/20, 1688, C.O. 1/65, fol. 222.

[123] Samuel A. Green, ed., "Two Narratives of Sir William Phips's Expedition to Quebec," 286, 313; Declaration of Sylvanus Davis, [1690], *Doc. Hist. Maine,* V, 146, 147.

[124] M. de Callières to M. de Seignelay, Jan., Feb., May, 1689, Instructions for the Invasion of New York, June 7, 1689, Observations on the State of Canada, Nov. 18, 1689, *N. Y. Col. Docs.,* IX, 404–408, 411–412, 420–426, 433; Parkman, *Count Frontenac,* 224–226, 177–181; Eccles, *Canada under Louis XIV,* 161–165; Account of the loss of Pemaquid Fort, Aug. 3, 1689, C.O. 5/855, no. 27.

found; it can be gauged by the remarkable enlargement of their strategic perspectives during the months following the Dominion's overthrow. For the first time, they openly acknowledged their dependence
upon the security of Albany and the Hudson valley. The town, wrote
Governor Bradstreet of Massachusetts (thereby unconsciously echoing the arguments of a generation of New York governors), was "a
frontier to all the English Colonies against the incursions of the
French."[125] Its loss would open all western New England to attack.
More particularly, Albany was the vital link in the "Covenant-
Chain" sustaining friendly relations with the Iroquois, and it was
from these fearsome warriors that the New England governments
hoped to obtain assistance against the eastern Indians. In June and
again in July 1689, the representatives in Boston voted to open negotiations with the Iroquois nation and to offer the usual bounty of
eight pounds per enemy scalp to those Iroquois who would come to
fight in Maine. Early in September, Colonel John Pynchon, Major
Thomas Savage, and Captain Andrew Belcher, joined on the way by
Captain Jonathan Bull of Connecticut, reached Albany on this mission. There they met with the Iroquois and their dependent tribe, the
River Indians, presenting gifts of wampum, clothes, and powder and
shot.[126]

The plan was not new: Pynchon had been among the commissioners sent to Albany in 1677 in an unsuccessful attempt to persuade the
Iroquois to intervene in the conflict with the eastern Indians which
had flared up at the end of King Philip's War.[127] New, however, were
the lengths to which the New England governments were prepared to
carry their efforts to make it work. Despite many promises from the

---

[125] Bradstreet to Plymouth Colony, to Connecticut, Oct. 5, 1689, Mass. Hist.
Soc., *Collections*, 4th ser., V (1861), 218, Conn. Archives, War, II, 22.

[126] *N. H. Laws*, I, 301, 313, 316; Mass. Archives, CVII, 284, XXXV, 45; *Doc. Hist.
Maine*, IX, 4–5, 38–39, 50–53; Negotiations with the Iroquois, Sept. 24, 1689, Miscellaneous Bound MSS., 1679–93, Mass. Hist. Soc.; Cadwallader Colden, *The
History of the Five Indian Nations Depending on the Province of New-York in America*,
88–93. Captain Bull had previously journeyed to Albany in May to report on the
disposition of the Iroquois: *Conn. Records*, III, 460–463.

[127] Richard R. Johnson, "The Search for a Usable Indian," 634.

Iroquois, no war parties left for Maine. Instead, in a remarkable reversal of roles, the New Englanders aided Albany at the request of the
Iroquois. The commissioners found that the town's refusal to accept
the authority of Leisler's revolutionary government in New York had
left it defenseless against French attack. They recommended, and
Boston and Hartford agreed, that troops should be sent to its aid. The
Iroquois had asked for a hundred men for this purpose, and in November Bull returned to Albany at the head of eighty-seven of the
Connecticut militia, remaining there until the following spring.[128] At
that time, writing to Connecticut, Bradstreet's plea for their retention
demonstrated how far New England's leaders had come in perceiving
the broader strategies required by their predicament. Bull and his
men must stay in Albany, he urged, "that so Reputation may be
gained with the five Nations, when they shall take notice that we
mind the same thing and venture on the same Bottom. Albany is a
strong and well fashioned Curb for our Enemies, which if it should be
broken they would run at a prodigious Rate, Albany is the Dam,
which should it through neglect be broken down by the weight of the
Enemy, we dread to think of the Inundation of Calamities that would
quickly follow thereupon. Certainly in reinforcing of it we do most
industriously consult our own Safety and Interest."[129]

The strategy was still essentially defensive: as commissioner Pynchon pointed out, Albany was the key to the defense of western Massachusetts. Yet it reached beyond the boundaries of New England
and led directly to the attempts, in 1690 and subsequent years, to relieve the pressures on the frontier and gain further "reputation" with
the Iroquois by direct assaults upon the French in Canada.[130] In retrospect, therefore, the commitment to Albany marked a decisive step
in New England's emergence from its self-imposed isolation and the
recasting of its leaders' policies and perspectives. Not since John

---

[128] *Doc. Hist. N. Y.,* II, 96–97, 132.

[129] Bradstreet to Connecticut, Mar. 24, 1690, *Doc. Hist. Maine,* V, 64.

[130] Pynchon to Bradstreet, Sept. 30, 1689, Mass. Archives, XXXV, 32; Bradstreet
to Gov. Thomas Hinckley, Mar. 11, 1690, Mass. Hist. Soc., *Collections,* 4th ser., V
(1861), 230.

Winthrop burned his fingers intervening in the 1640s had the New England governments taken an active part in external affairs. Never before had they committed troops to the defense of a colony outside their borders. Now they were taking up cudgels that were not to be laid to rest for almost a century. Having destroyed the Dominion, they were nonetheless being drawn to assume its role. In seeking to involve others in the defense of New England, they were themselves drawn onto a wider stage.

Simultaneously, war and its demands heightened the pressures impelling the colonists toward a greater dependence upon the crown. Transatlantic differences seemed of less account in the face of the larger conflict, and it was all too evident that the French drew no distinctions as to which particular Englishmen they attacked. If New England had to stand up and be counted, better any Stuart across the ocean than Bourbon rule in Albany. More prosaically, the colonists stood in desperate need of arms and ammunition, and further supplies could come only by royal sanction because of the strict English embargo upon shipping.[131] At sea, the absence of the British frigates which had guarded commerce was keenly felt as French privateers and pirate ships manned by English renegades decimated the fishing fleets of Salem and Marblehead.[132] Both ships and supplies would be needed if the proposals advanced during the winter of 1689 for a naval attack upon Canada were to be pursued. Increase Mather later asserted that the repeated requests of Massachusetts leaders for such assistance had fatally compromised his negotiations in England. To call for aid, he wrote, "was, in effect, to pray for a [royal] Governour.

---

[131] Among many contemporary references to such shortages, see Edward Randolph to the Lords of Trade, Oct. 15, 1689, *Randolph Letters*, IV, 299–300; Gov. Simon Bradstreet to the Earl of Shrewsbury, Oct. 26, 30, 1689, Mar. 29, 1690, C.O. 5/855, nos. 45, 47, 70; Thomas Danforth to Sir Henry Ashurst, Apr. 1, 1690, Hutchinson, *History of Massachusetts-Bay*, I, 337n.; Sgt. Maj. Edmund Quincy to Maj. Gen. Wait Winthrop, Mar. 28, 1690, John Pynchon to Winthrop, July 17, 1690, Winthrop Papers.

[132] Edward Randolph to the Lords of Trade, Oct. 15, 1689, *Randolph Letters*, IV, 300; George F. Dow and John H. Edmonds, *The Pirates of the New England Coast, 1630–1730*, chapter IV; James D. Phillips, *Salem in the Seventeenth Century*, 10–11. The *Rose* was finally allowed to leave Boston in December.

They could not be so weak as to think the King would send the one without the other."[133]

Within New England, also, the financial burden of waging war compounded the political difficulties of governments already uncertain of their authority. At first, Massachusetts sought to rely on loans solicited from leading citizens and on subscriptions from the towns. But with defense costs amounting to as much as £110 a day—a sum sufficient to have exhausted the entire annual budget of the colony ten years before within a month—there was no alternative but to levy taxes, six rates in November 1689 and one and a half the following month. Even the unpaid portions of the supposedly illegal taxes assessed by Andros were ordered to be collected. Connecticut, supporting Bull and his men at Albany, a charge totalling nearly £700 over four months, imposed a rate of one and a half pence on the pound in October and another of four pence the following April.[134] Yet just as some refused service in the army, so others defied these assessments. Five towns on the borders of Essex County were cited in the General Court for their delinquency. In Plymouth Colony, which had sought a public loan and then levied a tax of £750, four towns refused to pay.[135]

These difficulties were but the beginning of a time of trial as faltering governments continued to be plagued by internal dissension and external attack. Ultimately, and in conjunction with the colonists' changing conception of their political purposes and the evolution of English colonial policy, they drew New Englanders toward

---

[133] Increase Mather, *A Brief Account, Andros Tracts,* II, 292.

[134] Mass. Archives, C, 416, 452; *N. H. Laws,* I, 311, 319, 321, 330, 335, 337, 358; Order of the General Court, Feb. 12, 1690, C.O. 5/855, no. 64; Abstract of a letter from Edward Randolph to Francis Nicholson, Oct. 25, 1689, *Randolph Letters,* IV, 304; *Conn. Records,* IV, 13, 16; Conn. Archives, War, III, 10.

[135] Randolph to Lord Privy Seal Halifax, July 23, to the Lords of Trade, Oct. 15, to John Usher, Oct. 16, 1689, *Randolph Letters,* IV, 285–286, 298, VI, 306–307; Bullivant, "Journal," 104, 106; *N. H. Laws,* I, 352; *Plymouth Records,* VI, 215–216, 220, 226.

closer, more regular ties with the London government. Already, by the first months of 1690, within a year of the Boston revolt, signs of change in what had hitherto been predominantly an adversary relationship were apparent. As it had during the time of the prosecution of the charters, Massachusetts unwillingly showed the way. Greater numbers of its citizens than ever before—if still a small proportion of the whole—now looked to London for aid and authority, some petitioning for the restoration of a royal government. Disillusioned by the problems attendant upon the return of charter rule and newly aware, since the Dominion, of the length of the royal arm, they exercised considerable influence upon the negotiations under way in London.[136] Still more significant, in terms of the sentiments of the colony at large, was the shift of opinion within the Massachusetts General Court toward formal participation in those negotiations and acceptance of a political settlement reached in England. In part, perhaps, the selection of Cooke and Oakes as agents in December 1689 was prompted by fears of what Increase Mather might concede were he left unchaperoned amid the corruptions of the English court. Further, Mather's letters predicted the imminent restoration of colonial charters by act of Parliament, and agents could both take advantage of this situation and ensure the punishment of Andros and his accomplices.[137] Nevertheless, not since the Restoration had the colony voluntarily sent agents to London, and never had they been accorded such broad discretionary powers. Their departure in February 1690 was in itself evidence of a quiet revolution in Massachusetts's attitude toward the mother country, as momentous a step in its way as the troops dispatched to Albany.

Straightforward self-interest paved the way for this decision: not only could the crown furnish military assistance but, as Boston merchant Thomas Broughton noted in a letter to Mather in London, "it would greatly silence contemners of our authority to have our Char-

---

[136] For these petitions and their effects, see the following chapter.

[137] Mather's letters were printed in Boston as a broadside late in 1689, probably in early December before the appointment of the agents: *The Present State of the New-English Affairs,* reprinted *Andros Tracts,* II, 15–18.

ter confirmed by our king and parlament."[138] Yet self-interest was also buttressed by the first stirrings of a new confidence that king and Parliament were once more worthy of New England's allegiance. For thirty years, Puritan leaders had watched the course of history with deepening gloom. "These are dying times," wrote the fugitive regicide William Goffe from his refuge in western Massachusetts, "wherein the Lord hath been and is breaking down what he hath built and plucking up what he hath planted."[139] England seemed to be fast slipping into the pit of popery and slavery. Hence it was necessary to stand against change, repel intruders, and preserve a saving remnant as the last best hope of a holy commonwealth on earth. In this hour of need, William's descent upon England and the equally bloodless collapse of the Dominion shone forth as crowning providences worthy of comparison with Cromwell's defeat of the Scots at Worcester or the scattering of the Armada—"a Second EIGHTY-EIGHT out-shining that in the former Century."[140] Together they gave hope that mankind had reached a turning point in history. "God seems to have begun the Reformation of the whole World, and eminently to appear for the True Reformed Religion," cried Increase Mather in London. Back in Boston, his son harnessed the course of events, commencing with the renewed persecution of Protestants in France in 1685, to the chariot of imminent apocalypse foretold in Revelation. "I dare publish it as my Humble Conjecture and Perswasion," wrote Cotton in his election day sermon of 1690, *"That the last Slaughter of the Lord's Witnesses is over;* and that we are got more than two years Depth, into those *Earth Quakes* which will shake yet until they have *shaken* the *Papal Empire* to pieces, and *shaken* out the very Hearts of them, that shall not *come out of her.* "[141] History had come its full cycle:

---

[138] Broughton to Increase Mather, Apr. 2, 1690, Mass. Archives, XXXV, 378a.

[139] Letter of c. 1674, Hutchinson, *Papers,* II, 186.

[140] Cotton Mather, *The Wonderful Works of God,* 33 (preached Dec. 1689).

[141] [Increase Mather], *A Brief Relation of the State of New England* (London, 1689), reprinted *Andros Tracts,* II, 169; Cotton Mather, *The Serviceable Man,* 50 (preached May 1690). See also Cotton's *Wonderful Works of God,* 38, 41, *Souldiers Counselled and Comforted,* 37 (preached Sept. 1689), and *Things to be Look'd For,* 55, 63 (preached

"the Wheel of Divine Vengence," declared another Massachusetts writer, "is now turning apace, upon the French Papists for their late Bloody and Matchless Persecutions."[142]

All tended toward a renewed sense of kinship with a mother country seemingly restored to the path of virtue and good government. "I cannot but think," wrote Increase Mather from London to John Richards in Boston, "that there is a great earthquake happening in this sinfull kingdome."[143] The flight of Protestants from France, many of whom took refuge in New England, drove home the realization that differences within the reformed churches were as nothing compared to the gulf which separated them from Catholicism. Some of the colonial pamphleteers now writing to convince English readers of the propriety of the Boston uprising deliberately exaggerated this community of religious interest. As Boston's Anglicans could and did testify, Puritan antipathy to the Church of England, though decorously concealed in print under the guise of criticism of its vestiges of "Romish worship," continued to run high.[144] Nevertheless, others who wrote only for a domestic audience, including authors as discordant in their opinions as Gershom Bulkeley and the anonymous author of *An Appeal to the Men of New England,* agreed on both the existence and the necessity of Protestant unity against a common foe. New England's afflictions, whether defined as the loss of the charters or, in Bulkeley's very different formulation, the attempt to restore them, were the work of Jesuits hatching their world-wide popish plot. Protestants, concluded Cotton Mather, must stand together: *"War with none but Hell and Rome."*[145] The beguiling vision of Protestant

---

June 1691). Cotton Mather's eschatology is most comprehensively explored in Robert Middlekauff, *The Mathers,* 320–349. The dates of delivery indicate which sermons were preached before the appointment and departure of the agents.

[142] S. E., *Further Quaeries, Andros Tracts,* I, 201.

[143] Mather to Richards, June 9, 1690, Winthrop Papers.

[144] Cotton Mather, *Serviceable Man,* 32, 53; Samuel Willard, *The Sinfulness of Worshipping God with Men's Institutions, passim;* and note 69, preceding.

[145] *Andros Tracts,* II, 98–99, III, 192; Cotton Mather, *Wonderful Works of God,* 40. Also *Andros Tracts,* I, 11–12, II, 21–22.

Christian union was beginning to exert a fascination upon clerical minds that was to ripen into obsession the following century.[146]

Rhetoric is not always a reliable guide to private thought and public action. The Mathers, for example, despite the remarkable predominance of their writings in the printed literature of the time, were clearly more deeply committed to closer ties to England, by reason of Increase's agency and their more sweeping vision of events, than were the bulk of their fellow colonists.[147] New Englanders in general did not lightly suspend a lifetime's suspicions of Stuart rule. Yet their leaders were at least willing to make the attempt to enlist in the larger cause. Addresses to England pledged loyalty to a king whose "Glorious Enterprise" had rescued "the Protestant Interest" from "Popery and Arbitrary Government." Proclamations in Massachusetts called for prayers for "the whole English Israel." Such language breathed optimism that England had resumed its rightful leadership of the cause preserved in New England. In a famous metaphor, Perry Miller has likened the relationship of old and New England in the seventeenth century to the circus act of a clown who enters the arena trailed by another disguised as the first clown's bustle. In mid-century, Miller noted, England had turned aside from traditional ways, leaving the bustle of colonial Puritanism to continue blindly straight ahead. Now England seemed to have turned back, returning to the forefront of the Protestant crusade.[148]

---

[146] Middlekauff, *The Mathers,* 209–230; Carl Bridenbaugh, *Mitre and Sceptre,* 3–22; Alan Heimert, *Religion and the American Mind from the Great Awakening to the Revolution,* 95–158.

[147] Any account of the period that relies upon the contemporary printed literature necessarily cites the Mathers extensively. Cotton, for example, though only twenty-six at the time of the Boston revolt, wrote no less than twenty-three of the forty sermons published within Massachusetts by its ministers up until the end of 1692, and his dominance in the field of "political" sermons was virtually complete. Perry Miller's brilliant analysis of these years, work which has charted the way for all subsequent interpretations, is essentially a digest of the Mathers' writings: *Colony to Province,* 157–172. Set against the context of the debates within the towns and conventions, together with the other letters and papers of the time, however, the Mathers' views are clearly not representative of the sentiments of, for example, a majority of the Massachusetts deputies.

[148] Addresses from Massachusetts, Plymouth, and Connecticut, May 20–June 13,

If so, the colonists could safely follow the advice of those who believed that negotiation with London would bring both a confirmation of charter rule and an end to conflict with the crown. They might even be able to turn the toppling of Andros to their advantage for, as colonial writers hastened to point out, it showed that New England had spontaneously shared in the work of revolution. "Such conformity to the Methods which the English Nations have been driven to take for their Deliverance," declared the leaders of Massachusetts to the new king and queen, persuades us "that we shall not be forgotten nor left without our share in the Universal Restoration of Charters and English liberties." To Cotton Mather, "Nothing in the World could more exactly imitate and resemble the late circumstances of our Mother *England* than the *Revolutions* here, in all the steps thereof; and this though we understood not one another." Here was further reason to believe that New England's purposes could now best be furthered by negotiation and conformity with the crown rather than isolation and defiance. Mather, palpitating with pride in his father's mission and with anxiety lest it be jeopardized by blind prejudice at home, even went so far as to command the General Court in his election sermon of May 1690 "to do *Nothing* for us, but what has a Tendency to maintain our due Dependence on the Authority of *England,* and to preserve and Enlarge the *English* Empire."[149]

Out of the colonists' hopes and needs had arisen an image of England very different from that which had inspired the Mathers to lead the resistance to any compromise with the crown only five years before. Yet it remained to be seen how far this new image corresponded

---

1689, Mass. Hist. Soc., *Collections,* 6th ser., I (1886), 146n.–147n., C.O. 5/855, nos. 7, 12, 13; *Conn. Records,* III, 463; Broadside, "At the Convention," (Boston, [Sept. 7], 1689); Proclamation for a Fast Day, June 28, 1690, Mass. Archives, XI, 53; Perry Miller, *Errand into the Wilderness,* 13.

[149] Address of Massachusetts, May 20, 1689, C.O. 5/855, no. 7—a slightly different printed version is reproduced in Mass. Hist. Soc., *Collections,* 6th ser., I (1886), 147n.; Cotton Mather, *Wonderful Works of God,* 42, and *Serviceable Man,* 61. See also *Andros Tracts,* I, 71, II, 76, 198, III, 202, for similar themes.

to the reality. Englishmen had indeed rejected royal autocracy but not, as in mid-century, for a government of the saints. The Protestant succession, episcopacy tempered by religious toleration, the sanctity of property, and an emerging partnership of crown and parliament fostered by party organization and political management—these were the themes of a revolutionary settlement that was in essence restoring and refurbishing the moderate royalism England had known before the convulsions of the 1680s. The "good old cause" of godly parliamentary rule lay enshrouded in the ideology of a Whiggism even now being drawn by the prospect of political office toward an increasingly tame collaboration in the work of royal government. True, the reaction against James's methods, coupled with the removal of his personal interest in colonial affairs, weighed against any revival of plans for a general remodelling of the chartered colonies. Equally, however, there could be no turning back the clock still further to the days before the crown's intervention in New England. The Blathwayts and the Southwells of Whitehall remained in office, the momentum and the institutions of royal regulation were established. A retreat from James's costly and cumbersome experiments did not mean any lessening of England's resolve to profit from its colonial dependencies. If the clown had returned, he remained in a significantly different costume from that worn in mid-century. Perhaps New Englanders could adapt or camouflage the bustle to match. It was not yet apparent how far they themselves had travelled in their political philosophy since the imposition of the Dominion. For the moment, it was enough that they were committed to negotiations with the English government.

# III

## London Interlude:
## The Quest for the Massachusetts Charter

W hen the two ships carrying the agents of the Massachusetts revolutionary government and the former rulers of the Dominion
reached England in the last days of March 1690 after a tempestuous
passage from the Bay, Increase Mather had already been working on
New England's behalf in London for nearly two years.[1] It would be
another two years before he or his fellow agents could return to Boston. During this brief but critical period, they strove to come to terms
with a royal government uncertain of its colonial policy and distracted by European commitments; they reached a settlement that
determined England's relations with the northern colonies for almost
a century until it was in turn consumed in the fire of a second revolution. Moreover, their diplomacy set an end to the intermittent em-
bassies of earlier years. It inaugurated the semipermanent institutionalized representation of the New England colonies in London
that was both a consequence of the new constitutional framework and
a significant influence on its subsequent development. Finally,
Mather's own lengthy mission in London merits detailed examination as much for its substance as for its result. Beyond its intrinsic importance and despite certain unique characteristics, its exceptionally
abundant documentation affords a rewarding case study of two crucial facets of Anglo-American political adjustment—the strategies
and resources essential for satisfactory accommodation with Whitehall and the perennial problems of transatlantic communication.

Mather's work in the years after his arrival in England in the spring
of 1688 falls into three phases—his lobbying at the court of James II;
his attempts to take advantage of the broader opportunities of a new

---

[1] Elisha Cooke to Simon Bradstreet, Oct. 16, 1690, Mass. Hist. Soc., *Proceedings*,
XLV (1911–1912), 644–645; Hammond, "Diary," 152.

reign by successive applications to King William, the Privy Council and its committee of trade, and the English Parliament; and his final acceptance of the necessity of a new settlement through negotiations with the committee of trade. These phases roughly coincide with stages in the development of his strategy—reform (of Andros and the Dominion); restoration (of the New England charters); and, when all else failed, replacement (of the lost Massachusetts patent by a more comprehensive instrument of government).

In later years Mather and his loyal son Cotton did their utmost to vindicate his service to New England, and this categorization may seem to mirror their insistence on his prescience and dexterity. But other evidence, notably Mather's own manuscript diaries, refutes the possibility that their accounts are merely a belated ordering of chaos. Together, they show Mather's acute perception of the realities of his situation, his incessant search for alternative solutions, and the bold vigor with which he attempted to implement his conclusions. Perhaps a grounding in Biblical exegesis and theological controversy was a natural education for penetrating the mysteries of English colonial administration. He clearly took a scholar's delight in planning—and recounting—the details of his campaign. Mather was convinced of the justice and importance of his chosen cause. But he also relished the opportunity which justified his appearance on a greater stage than the narrow confines of a colonial wilderness and allowed him to sit, like Puritan ministers of his father's generation, amid the councils of the mighty. Mather had always been deeply interested in the slow unfolding of New England's purpose. He rejoiced, and strove with passionate intensity, at the prospect of playing a part in its fulfillment.

Mather began, as he was to continue, by turning apparent handicaps to his advantage. He arrived in London in May 1688 as a fugitive from the Dominion; not until March 1690, with the arrival of the commission authorizing him to act with Cooke, Oakes, and Ashurst on behalf of the revolutionary government in Massachusetts, did he possess either the credentials or financial resources of earlier New England agents. Yet his status as Puritan minister and self-appointed spokesman for colonial grievances gave him a position in English society and a freedom of action that other envoys had lacked. Free from the blinkered vision imposed by instructions drawn up an ocean's breadth from London, Mather was able to shape his solicitations to the circumstances of the moment; his renown in English Nonconformist circles as the leader of colonial Puritanism ensured his prompt admission to a closely knit group well versed in the byzantine complexities of English politics. A voluminous correspondence had ripened and enlarged the friendships formed during a four-year stay in England some thirty years before, and he drew heavily upon this precious capital. Within a few days of reaching London, he met and consulted with leading clergy and laymen of the city's dissenting community. One arranged a meeting with the king. Less than a week after his arrival, on May 30, 1688, Mather presented addresses from the New England churches to James in person at Whitehall.[2] The dissenting connection so often used by New England in the past became the vital thread binding together the several chapters of Mather's work. It contributed much to his success, and it remained a dominant theme of New England's transatlantic relations for many years to come.

Mather's arrival, moreover, was fortunately timed. James's attempts to secure tolerance and office for his fellow Catholics had led him to seek the support of Protestant Dissenters in hopes of forging an alliance strong enough to overcome Anglican resistance to his policies. A new purge of the local corporations, in some instances bringing back into office the very Whigs and Dissenters expelled a few years before, was accompanied by a second Declaration of Indulgence extending the promise of religious toleration. A number of Mather's friends in London held out against this sudden and suspicious court-

---

[2] Increase Mather, *Autobiography*, 324–325; *idem*, Diary, May 26–30, 1688; Mass. Hist. Soc., *Collections*, 6th ser., I (1886), 59n. Murdock, *Increase Mather*, gives a full account of Mather's early life and English contacts.

ship, fearing the truth of Halifax's famous warning in his *Letter to a Dissenter*—"You are therefore to be hugged now, only that you may be the better squeezed at another time." But others succumbed, and New England's cause gained from their new-found influence at court. They assured the king that favor shown to the cause of their colonial brethren would gratify all Dissenters. For the first time since the Restoration, New England's religious idiosyncrasies eased rather than encumbered its dealings with the crown.[3]

Mather matched his strategy to the situation. He made no direct challenge to the Dominion, a government fashioned in part by James himself and ruled by Andros very much in the Stuart manner. Instead, at two further meetings with the king, he poured out the colony's gratitude for the royal gift of toleration and depicted Andros as a governor who sought to suppress congregational religion in favor of the Anglican church.[4] Early in July, he supplemented this plea for liberty of conscience with an appeal for specific political reforms that would have reinstated charter rule in all but name, save for the retention of a governor and council appointed by the crown.[5] His petition was referred to the committee of trade and then in August to Attorney General Sir Thomas Powys with a memorandum that the king would grant New England religious liberty, security of property titles, and protection for the traditional constitution of Harvard College.

---

[3] Foxcroft, *Life and Letters of Halifax*, II, 367; John P. Kenyon, *Robert Spencer, Earl of Sunderland, 1641–1702*, 171–174, 186–194; Western, *Monarchy and Revolution*, 194–238; Increase Mather, *Autobiography*, 325, 326, 330.

[4] Increase Mather, *Autobiography*, 329–330; Cotton Mather follows this account, adding further details in his *Parentator. Memoirs of Remarkables in the Life and the Death of the Ever-Memorable Dr. Increase Mather. Who Expired August 23, 1723* (Boston, 1724), relevant extracts of which are printed in *Andros Tracts*, III, 123–187.

[5] Petition and proposals of Increase Mather, Samuel Nowell, and Elisha Hutchinson, [July 1688], Mass. Hist. Soc., *Collections*, 4th ser., VIII (1868), 701–702, and C.O. 1/65, no. 39 (fol. 95); Murdock, *Increase Mather*, 194–197, 204–208. Murdock, *ibid.*, 204, assumes that the memorial which Mather presented to James on July 2 was that contained in *CSP Col., 1685–1688*, no. 1878i and printed, with glosses, in Mass. Hist. Soc., *Collections*, 4th ser., VIII (1868), 699–700. Probably, however, it was more restrained in its complaints, for this first version seems to have been withdrawn prior to its discussion by the committee of trade: Joshua Moody to Increase Mather, Oct. 4, 1688, *ibid.*, 366; Chalmers, *Political Annals*, Book I, 466.

Conspicuously omitted was any promise to restore representative government to New England, and although Mather had offered, in effect, to purchase the right to an assembly by conceding that it should be chosen by freeholders rather than freemen and that a permanent annual revenue of five thousand pounds be provided for the maintenance of government, these parts of his proposal were struck out of his petition. Mather later discovered that Secretary of State Sunderland had personally blotted out all mention of an assembly. James and his ministers still refused to permit in New England what they tolerated elsewhere in the plantations.[6]

In the meantime, Mather's incessant lobbying at Whitehall led him into paths amid the political labyrinth of the last months of James's reign that would have horrified his faithful congregation in Boston. Though wary of an offer of assistance from Father Petre, the Jesuit priest regarded by many Englishmen as James's evil genius, he gratefully accepted the help of the Quaker William Penn and sought the favor of such other intimates of the king as the notorious Lord Chancellor Jeffreys and the latter's Catholic associates on the Privy Council, Lord Belasyse and Sir Nicholas Butler. Under the mellowing influence of a Saturday-night dinner which cost Mather the sum of thirty shillings and sixpence, Butler agreed that Andros should be curbed and offered to bring the matter to the attention of Sunderland and the king.[7] On the following Thursday, June 21, Mather walked to Whitehall to attend upon the powerful secretary and he spent eleven of the next forty days in "waiting at Whitehall on New England affairs." Small wonder he included a charge of ten shillings for boots among his expenses.[8]

Late in August, Mather twice called upon Sir Thomas Powys to

---

[6] Journal of the Lords of Trade, Aug. 10, 1688, C.O. 391/6, 181; Petition and proposals of Mather, Nowell, and Hutchinson, [Aug. 10, 1688], Memorandum, [Aug., 1688], C.O. 1/65, nos. 39, 53; [Increase Mather], *Miseries of New-England, Andros Tracts*, II, 9-10. Sunderland attended the meeting of Aug. 10.

[7] Increase Mather, *Autobiography*, 325; *idem*, Diary, May 31, June 16, July 11, 14, 30, 1688, and the account of his expenses *sub* March, 1688/9.

[8] Increase Mather, Diary, June 21, 25, 26, 28, 29, July 5-7, 9, 21, 27, 28, 1688, and *sub* March 1688/9.

guide and hasten the attorney general's report on his petition. On September 26 and again on October 16 he was admitted to audience with the king. The following day he wrote to John Richards in Boston of his hope that New England would benefit from the royal proclamation promising a restoration of all the confiscated corporate charters. His diary records ten more visits to Whitehall in the space of the next four weeks.[9] But these months of toil brought no substantial results. From his powerful position as head of the Plantation Office and clerk of the Privy Council, William Blathwayt threw his support behind Andros even though, by a remarkable turn of events, Mather enlisted Blathwayt's wife as a lobbyist in New England's cause.[10] Of the colonists in London who had assisted Mather in his task, Samuel Nowell, another eloquent preacher turned patriot politician, died of apoplexy early in the fall, while Elisha Hutchinson and Richard Wharton were absorbed in a prolonged and not entirely amicable quest to secure their land titles and establish a corporation for mining minerals in New England.[11] James himself would not go beyond his repeated promise to confirm "property, liberty, and our Colledge" to the colonists. Mather drew up a petition asking for a council of landowners drawn from each county in the Dominion as a check upon Andros's legislation if an assembly could not be granted. But the committee of trade met only once more in 1688 after the middle of August, and the petition, if submitted, was among those again referred to Powys. By then, too, a panic-stricken government was bringing the Tories and Anglicans back into office. Nevertheless, Mather played the game to the last. Even after it was known that William of Orange had landed at Torbay, Mather continued to so-

---

[9] *Ibid.,* Aug. 23, 31, Sept. 26, Oct. 16, 22–25, 29, 30, Nov. 7, 8, 10, 13, 1688; Increase Mather, *Autobiography,* 331; Mather to Richards, Oct. 17, 1688, Winthrop Papers. Murdock, *Increase Mather,* 202, errs in saying that Lord Wharton introduced Mather to the king at this time; Wharton was not then at court and Mather's diary speaks of Mr. Wharton, almost certainly the colonist Richard Wharton: Richard Wharton to Wait Winthrop, Oct. 18, 1688, Mass. Hist. Soc., *Collections,* 6th ser., V (1892), 17.

[10] Jacobsen, *William Blathwayt,* 131–133; Murdock, *Increase Mather,* 200–201.

[11] Viola Barnes, "Richard Wharton," 243–245, 267–268.

licit at Whitehall right up until the end of November, meeting ministers such as the Earls of Middleton and Melfort who were soon to join their sovereign in exile in France.[12]

As James's reign flickered to a close, it seemed as if Mather's work had come to nothing. Yet he could justly reflect that time and events rather than any faults of personality or method had frustrated New England's suit. By circumventing the dilapidated machinery of English colonial administration to appeal directly to the king, he had come close to securing many of the constitutional guarantees which Thomas Danforth, in a letter from the Bay, had judged to be the most that New England could hope to obtain from the crown.[13]

Moreover, the means for another venture lay ready to hand. The tide that swept away the short-lived bubble of Mather's influence at a Catholic court left unscathed his standing among the leaders of English Nonconformity. Throughout the year he had cultivated his ties with the dissenting congregations, preaching for their ministers if they would agree to lobby on his behalf and visiting influential laymen in their homes. In particular, he spent many days during the summer of 1688 in Newington Green, a small community clustered around the dissenting meetinghouse a few miles north of the walls of the City of London. This pleasant suburb was as much a focus of transatlantic Puritan culture as was "New England Walk" within the City's Royal Exchange for Boston's trade. Two of New England's most learned ministers, Charles Morton of Charlestown and Samuel Lee of Bristol in Plymouth Colony, had taught there before coming to Boston in 1686.[14] Morton's renowned academy in Newington was now headed by Stephen Lobb, who had first introduced Mather to King James. Here also Mather may have met with one of Morton's former pupils, Daniel Foe (or, as he preferred to call himself, Defoe);

---

[12] Increase Mather, *Autobiography,* 331; Hutchinson, *History of Massachusetts-Bay,* I, 313; Minute of the Lords of Trade, Oct. 17, 1688, C.O. 5/905, 76–77; Increase Mather, Diary, Nov. 13, 27, 1688.

[13] Danforth to [Samuel] Nowell, Oct. 22, 1688, Hutchinson, *Papers,* II, 308–309.

[14] Increase Mather, *Autobiography,* 326; Wilfred H. Munro, *The History of Bristol, R. I.,* 131; Samuel E. Morison, "Charles Morton's *Compendium Physicae,*" vii–xxix.

the struggling young merchant and future author of *Robinson Crusoe* had business interests nearby and later signed a petition in support of New England.[15] Certainly Mather often dined at the Newington homes of two particular friends, Robert Thompson, long active in the New England Company and a warm supporter of the colonists' cause, and Hercules Horsey, son-in-law of Richard Saltonstall, a former Massachusetts magistrate now back in England, and brother-in-law of Nathaniel Saltonstall of Haverhill, Massachusetts.[16]

Through these contacts Mather found fresh allies among the victors of the Glorious Revolution. Three days before James left London for the last time, Thompson took Mather to meet Gilbert Burnet, an Anglican minister who had come to England with William and stood high in the Prince's favor. No doubt it was also he who introduced Mather to his nephew Sir John Thompson, a member of the convention which gathered in London after Christmas and the son-in-law of New England's old ally at court, the Earl of Anglesey.[17] And before the end of the year, Mather met with two more sympathizers whose assistance was to prove invaluable in the months to come. Philip, Lord Wharton had been a patron of English Puritanism since his years as a leader of the Long Parliament. Though aged and soon to retire from active politics, Wharton could draw upon the experience and friendships of a lifetime of opposition to Stuart misrule.[18] The

---

[15] Herbert McLachlan, *English Education under the Test Acts*, 76–80; James Sutherland, *Defoe*, 18–23, 40–42; Petition of merchants trading to New England, [1691], Mass. Archives, XXXVII, 7.

[16] Increase Mather, Diary, *passim;* [Hercules Horsey?] to [Nathaniel Saltonstall?], Apr. 12, 1686, Prince Papers; Robert E. Moody, *The Saltonstall Papers, 1607–1815,* 38–41. For Thompson's contacts with New England, see also Richard R. Johnson, "The Humble Address of the Publicans of New-England," 245n. James Porter, chosen as agent by Connecticut in 1690, was another Newington resident, as were others who, by Mather's influence, were subsequently benefactors of Harvard College: Samuel Eliot Morison, *Harvard College in the Seventeenth Century,* II, 485.

[17] Increase Mather, Diary, Dec. 20, 22, 1688, Jan. 24, 28, 30, Feb. 1, Mar. 9, 1689; *idem, Autobiography,* 327.

[18] Increase Mather, Diary, Dec. 27, 1688. For Wharton, see G. F. Trevallyn Jones, *Saw-Pit Wharton,* and, principally covering the notable career of his son Thomas, John Carswell, *The Old Cause.*

second, Sir Henry Ashurst, a city merchant, was an associate of Robert Thompson in the New England Company and his relative by marriage. Less influential at court than Wharton, he now began a career of service to New England that was to last until his death in 1711.[19]

These new acquaintances signalled Mather's swift reworking of his strategies. James had created the Dominion, and as long as he continued to dominate affairs Mather could do little more than hope to curb Andros's worst excesses by playing upon the king's distaste for Anglican intolerance and his desire to placate Dissenters. James's fall opened the way for a frontal assault upon the Dominion as a remnant of an autocracy now rejected back in England. Politically, Mather could abandon his attempts to capitalize upon the uneasy alliance of the two wings of English Nonconformity, Protestant and Catholic, against the Anglican center and turn back to the more congenial task of building upon the ties which had traditionally aligned Protestant Dissenters with liberal Anglicans and Whigs of all religious persuasions in opposition to popery and prerogative rule.

Mather firmly believed, as his son later wrote, "that in all Affairs, *a Few did all,*" and his first impulse during the two-month interregnum between James's flight and William and Mary's acceptance of the crown in February 1689 was to try the same direct approach which had brought him close to success a few months before. He secured an

---

[19] Increase Mather, Diary, Dec. 31, 1688 *et seq.* Ashurst was the brother of Thompson's son-in-law, Sir William Ashurst, whom Mather had met earlier in the year. Sir Henry, like his father, Henry Ashurst (d. 1680), was also a devoted friend of the great Richard Baxter, whom Mather had met soon after his arrival: Frederick J. Powicke, *The Reverend Richard Baxter under the Cross (1662–1691)*, 144; *idem*, "The Reverend Richard Baxter and his Lancashire Friend Mr. Henry Ashurst," 309–325; F. C. Cass, *History of East Barnet*, 68; and Philip A. Muth, "The Ashursts, Friends of New England." For Sir Henry Ashurst's commercial connections with such New Englanders as William Stoughton and Joseph Dudley during the 1680s, see Letterbook of Sir Henry Ashurst, Ashurst Manuscripts, Bodleian Library, Oxford.

interview with the prince's chaplain, William Carstares, who drafted a memorial on New England to be delivered to Hans Willem Bentinck, the prince's most intimate friend and counsellor.[20] On January 9, he travelled to St. James's Palace in Wharton's coach to an audience with William himself. Wharton, by Mather's account, pressed New England's case, "with great zele and affection." The colonists, he told the prince with a shrewd eye to the priorities of the moment, were a conscientious godly people who did not seek money or soldiers, only "their aunclent priviledges." William promised a reply by way of his private secretary, William Jephson, and Wharton then took Mather to meet the secretary, his distant cousin and political ally.[21] This service quickly proved its worth. Later in the week a routine circular was prepared, authorizing colonial governors to continue at their posts.[22] Andros would be confirmed in power and the Dominion confirmed in its present form until specific orders to the contrary. But Jephson gave Mather advance notice of the letter's dispatch, and the agent's vigorous protests, relayed to William, ensured that the copy destined for New England was delayed to await an investigation of the circumstances of the loss of the charters.[23]

Backstairs diplomacy had saved New England from being grouped with the other plantations in a general sanctification of the status quo. It failed to secure a positive settlement. In three petitions drawn up at this time, two of them in conjunction with a fellow colonist newly arrived in London, Sir William Phips, Mather planned to ask William for a letter "under your hand and signe manual" declaring that New England's charters and privileges were restored. None of

---

[20] Cotton Mather, *Parentator, Andros Tracts*, III, 157; Increase Mather, Diary, Dec. 28, 31, 1688, Jan. 8, 1689.

[21] Increase Mather, *Autobiography*, 331; *idem*, Diary, Jan. 9, 1689.

[22] Order of the King in Council, Feb. 19, 1689, *CSP Col., 1689–1692*, no. 21.

[23] Increase Mather, *Autobiography*, 331–332. The entry book containing the copy of the circular letter to be sent to New England has a memorandum that Mather's application has prevented its dispatch: C.O. 5/905, 42; Andrews, *Narratives of the Insurrections*, 277n.

[ *145* ]

these petitions appear among the official papers.[24] Perhaps William was reluctant; more probably, Mather's Whig allies balked at such a blatant exercise of the prerogative even in a righteous cause. Unable to cut through New England's problems with a single stroke, Mather had to fall back upon the more tortuous and hazardous course of challenging the legality of Whitehall's past actions. Where he had previously written with calculated vagueness that the charters had been vacated "by extraordinary wayes," he now presented a petition claiming that they had been "invaded and taken away by illegal and arbitrary proceedings."[25] Such a charge required proof, and it would inevitably arouse the resentment of royal officials anxious to keep buried the details of their service to a fallen monarch.

Much, therefore, depended upon the attitude of the "jury" which would try his cause, the newly reappointed committee of the Privy Council for trade and plantations to which his petition was referred. Its membership reflected the political reorderings set in motion by William's accession. During the fierce partisan warfare of the 1680s, the factional alignments that in their simplest form derived from the struggle for position and power—the immemorial enmity of court and country—had roughly corresponded with those inspired by principle and belief—the division ultimately enshrined as the rivalry of Tory and Whig. By its very nature, this correspondence could not long survive the abrupt accession to power of a prince who proclaimed his attachment to the cherished liberties of Whiggism. Over the next several decades, Whigs and Tories intermingled and re-

---

[24] *Andros Tracts,* III, 146n., 149n.; Mass. Hist. Soc., *Collections,* 4th ser., VIII (1868), 705. A memorandum of Jan. 22, 1689, linking this request to the policy pursued in regard to Jamaica is in Carte Manuscripts, 81, fol. 756, Bodleian Library: cf. *CSP Col., 1689-1692,* no. 6.

For Phips, a New Englander of humble origins and remarkable enterprise, who had reaped fame, fortune, and a knighthood from the recovery of sunken treasure from a Caribbean wreck, see Viola Barnes, "The Rise of Sir William Phips," 271–294, and Cotton Mather, *Life of Phips.* Phips had returned to Boston in 1688 with aspirations to office in the Dominion but a rebuff at the hands of Andros had sent him back to London to join forces with Mather.

[25] Petition of Sir William Phips and Increase Mather, [Feb. 18, 1689], C.O. 5/751, no. 2; *Calendar of State Papers, Domestic Series, of the Reign of William and Mary, 1689-1690,* 3; *APC Col.,* II, 124.

grouped, some from each faction joining to form a "Country" and ultimately Tory opposition, others rallying to the court and the fruits of office to form a conservative Whiggism very different from its radicalism in the 1680s.[26] In the meantime, a host of anxious politicians jockeyed for place and advantage, each convinced that their past service or suffering gave them title to a claim on the royal gratitude. William himself exacerbated the situation by his efforts to preserve a balance among the factions and so create a government of national unity to prosecute the coming struggle with France. Several of the great offices of state went to men who had faithfully served the Stuarts almost to the end; the Whigs received most of the posts within the royal household and on the commissions set up to administer the Treasury, Admiralty, and Great Seal. Lacking skilful management, however, the result was not fruitful equilibrium but sterile friction. William's new ministers agreed on almost nothing save their resentment of the preferment accorded to the king's Dutch favorites.

The committee of trade shared in this dissension, and Mather's petition came before a body divided against itself. Some of its members—Thomas, Viscount Fauconberg, Halifax, again Lord Privy Seal, and his bitter rival Danby, Lord President of the Council and soon to be Marquis of Carmarthen—were experienced in colonial matters and well remembered the events leading up to the creation of the Dominion. Henry Compton, Bishop of London, John Grenville, Earl of Bath, and Daniel Finch, Earl of Nottingham, soon to take office as second secretary of state, were Tory churchmen unlikely to favor a Nonconformist's plea. The Earl of Shrewsbury, the first secretary, a popular but indolent court Whig, had as yet little knowledge of affairs.

Mather's hopes for a sympathetic hearing lay rather with the other members of the committee. Edward Russell, Henry Powle, Charles, Viscount Mordaunt, Sir Henry Capel, and William Cavendish, Earl of Devonshire were all veterans of the parliamentary opposition to

---

[26] For recent studies interpreting the course of English politics in the 1690s, see Richard R. Johnson, "Politics Redefined," 700–703, 707–708, 729.

Charles II.[27] Their Whiggish views and past ties to dissenting interests predisposed them to sympathize with Mather's argument that New England was entitled to a share in the general restoration of English liberties. Yet there was also the danger that their new enthusiasm for the work of government and their equally close ties to the English mercantile community might now incline them to the official belief that the law and England's economic advantage required a strict colonial dependence upon the crown. At the least, they could be trusted to support a plea for the return of representative government to New England—the principle which Halifax had defended in the face of James's opposition five years before. The whole committee would heed the royal wish expressed in the order referring the petition: William was "graciously disposed to gratifie the Petitioners."[28]

Judging by Mather's entries in his diary, he made no attempt to lobby directly among the Lords of Trade with the exception of a single expedition with Lord Wharton to call upon Secretary Shrewsbury. Others such as Ashurst, Wharton, and Phips may have shared in the work of persuasion.[29] Mather did meet, however, with several other leading men of affairs shortly before and after their appointment to the Privy Council in February 1689, and the circumstances suggest a connection with the progress of his petition. The council would have the final word on the report of its committee. Moreover, any interested councillor could and frequently did attend the committee's meetings.[30] Hence there was shrewd logic behind Mather's

---

[27] Order of the King of Council, Feb. 16, 1689, *N. Y. Col. Docs.*, III, 572. With the addition of Viscount Lumley later in the month, the thirteen-man committee contained six of "the immortal seven" who had invited William to England.

[28] Petition of Phips and Mather, [Feb. 18, 1689], C.O. 5/751, no. 2; also Increase Mather, *Autobiography*, 341.

[29] Increase Mather, Diary, Feb. 16, 1689. Mather may have met Powle the previous summer, and he certainly sought the help of Mordaunt and Devonshire at some time during this year: Murdock, *Increase Mather*, 198; Increase Mather, *Autobiography*, 341; *Andros Tracts*, II, 16. Mordaunt may have met Mather through Phips, a fellow Caribbean treasure-hunter.

[30] Bieber, *Lords of Trade*, 47–48; Edward R. Turner, *The Privy Council of England in the Seventeenth and Eighteenth Centuries, 1603-1784*, II, 330-331.

solicitation of Henry Sidney, Hugh Boscawen, and William, Earl of Bedford. In addition, Wharton was a council member, as was his son Thomas, recently installed as Comptroller of the Household. Another was Henry, Lord Delamere who later assisted Ashurst in his work for New England. All were ardent Whigs—Bedford, Edward Russell's uncle, and Sidney were father and brother to the martyrs of 1683. Boscawen, a West Country Presbyterian of Cromwellian vintage, proved an ally of particular value because of his frequent attendance at the committee of trade. Mather also discussed New England's plight with John Hampden, the radical and unstable son of yet another Whig privy councillor, Richard Hampden, one of the commissioners of the treasury. Mather, Ashurst, Boscawen, and Hampden conferred together in early February, and again, with the addition of Wharton, on the day before the petition was read to the committee. Presumably, they planned a common strategy. Mather consulted several eminent lawyers and hired three counsel at two guineas apiece.[31]

These preparations had their effect. At first glance it seems absurd to suppose that the matter of New England should in any way distract attention from the great events of the post-Revolutionary settlement. But the issue apparently became a symbolic test of political strength among the factions seeking office under the king they had created. On February 20, when the petition was read, Richard Hampden and Boscawen attended the committee. Two days later, when the Lords of Trade drew up their report, all the appointed members except Russell were present, together with Hampden, Boscawen, and two other councillors, Viscount Lumley and Sir John Lowther. Fifteen was a quite exceptional attendance for the commit-

---

[31] Narcissus Luttrell, *A Brief Historical Relation of State Affairs from September 1678 to April 1714*, I, 502–503; Mass. Hist. Soc., *Collections*, 6th ser., I (1886), 145n.; Increase Mather to Sir Henry Ashurst, Feb. 18, 1689, *ibid.*, 4th ser., VIII (1868), 117; Increase Mather, Diary, Jan. 9, Feb. 1, 3, 12, 19, 20, 25, 27, Mar. 4, and *sub* Mar., 1689. In February alone Mather met with Lord Wharton eight times, Ashurst seven, Boscawen and Hampden three, and Bedford twice. I have assumed that Mather's principal contact was with John rather than Richard Hampden since it was the former who later corresponded with Massachusetts and received the colony's official thanks.

tee—in 1689 and for three years after, the average was only five.[32]

But Mather may have stirred up too much attention, for he met with such limited success that, considering the king's expressed support for his petition, it amounted to a rebuff. The committee recommended that, pending a lasting settlement, Andros should be replaced by a provisional governor without authority to raise money by vote of governor and council alone. After a further flurry of lobbying at Whitehall, the King in Council accepted the report with the proviso that two commissioners, not a new governor, should be sent to administer New England. "Such merchants and planters as are at present in England"—in short, Mather and his friends—were to be allowed a voice in choosing one of the commissioners. In addition, the committee was instructed to prepare a draft of a new charter for New England.[33]

Mather had a promise of Andros's dismissal and the restoration of some form of representative government in New England. Yet he fell far short of his goal of reinstating the old Massachusetts charter and dismantling the Dominion into its component parts. Every line of the committee's report and the king's reply proclaimed an intention to preserve the Dominion as a coherent whole. A new charter would have to run the gauntlet of the tender mercies of the Plantation Office staff. The immediate cause of the debacle was Mather's failure to prove that the colonial charters had been illegally vacated. The testimony of clerks and attorneys involved in the suit revealed no flaw in the *scire facias* levied against Massachusetts. Indeed, former Attorney General Sir Robert Sawyer's rehearsal of the colony's illegalities probably backfired against Mather by reminding the committee that New England was not just another victim of Stuart tyranny. Whiggish re-

---

[32] Bieber, *Lords of Trade*, 47, 89; Journal of the Lords of Trade, Feb. 20, 22, 1689, *Randolph Letters*, II, 99n. Lumley was a moderate Whig, Lowther a Tory ally of Danby.

[33] Order of the King in Council, Feb. 26, 1689, *APC Col.*, II, no. 278; Mass. Hist. Soc., *Collections*, 4th ser., VIII (1868), 118.

spect for the sanctity of property (including offices and corporations) was matched by a concomitant reverence for the procedures of the common law.[34]

Yet the language of the committee's report, emphasizing that this was a matter deeply affecting the royal revenues and the security of the northern colonies, also suggests that Mather could hardly have succeeded even had he made a better case. To the committee, clearly, the status of the Massachusetts charter was subordinate to a much larger concern: how could New England and the rest of the American plantations best be administered at a time when England was preparing to engage all its resources in a European war? Since early manhood, William of Orange had fought to contain the expansion of Louis XIV's France. Having invaded England to force a reversal of the Stuarts' apathetic neutrality in foreign affairs, he now swiftly harnessed his new realm to the defense of Protestant Europe and the Dutch republic. "Hee hath such a mind to [attack] France," noted Halifax following one audience, "that it would incline one to think, hee took England onely in his way." William's legacy to his adopted country was an enduring involvement in the continental balance of power.[35]

The colonies, it was agreed, had a minor but significant part to play in this grand design. They furnished England with valuable raw materials and a growing market for its manufactures. A well-regulated transatlantic trade was the backbone of a self-sufficient merchant marine with reserves of trained seamen. Through the profits and taxes drawn from this trade, as merchants and colonial governors were at pains to point out, the colonies contributed substantially to the revenues of the crown. No less important, all this was wealth de-

---

[34] The official journal shows that Sawyer's testimony dominated the meetings of both February 20 and 22; see also the account of Morrice, "Entr'ing Book," II, 480–481. The materials in C.O. 5/855, foll. 14–15 (*CSP Col., 1689–1692*, no. 153) are probably those Sawyer submitted to the committee; they are not, as suggested in the calendar, abridged from a preceding letter by Randolph.

[35] Foxcroft, *Life and Letters of Halifax*, II, 219. For William and his ambitions, see Stephen B. Baxter, *William III and the Defense of European Liberty*, and G. C. Gibbs, "The Revolution in Foreign Policy," 59–79.

nied to the coffers of England's European rivals. In the days to come, and well into the following century, royal officials strove to conserve and consolidate these benefits while avoiding costly distractions from the European task in hand. Our interest, wrote Sir Robert Southwell to Secretary Nottingham in concluding a cogent summary of the need to preserve such a balance in colonial policy, "is for bare defence and the keeping of what already Wee have."[36]

Even to achieve this limited goal required a renewed commitment to the colonies' defense, and in a series of memoranda on the conditions of the American settlements, the committee of trade urged prompt action to meet the threat of French attack. In response, fleshing out a practice begun by the Stuarts, William and his ministers placed virtually every royal governorship in America, even the lucrative sinecures customarily bestowed on English courtiers, in the hands of experienced soldiers or prominent local residents. The king personally vetoed a number of civilian applicants. Plans were laid to send fresh supplies of military stores to America and the committee's staff spent long hours in the task of coordinating colonial defense and safeguarding the arteries of trade. As a veteran campaigner, William was provisioning his outlying dependencies for a long siege with little prospect of relief.[37]

No less than his predecessors, however, William recognized that some colonies were more valuable than others. England's own security was paramount, and the troubles in Ireland, coupled with the very real threat of a French invasion, required that all resources be husbanded for the protection of the mother country. Trade with the

---

[36] [Southwell?] to the Earl of Nottingham, Mar. 23, 1689, Blathwayt Papers, Hunt. Lib., printed in Michael G. Hall, Lawrence H. Leder, and Michael G. Kammen, eds., *The Glorious Revolution in America*, 69.

[37] Memoranda and reports of the Lords of Trade, Apr. 29–May 29, 1689, *CSP Col., 1689–1692*, nos. 94, 102, 113, 124, 145, 150; Orders of the King in Council, May 18, July 11, 22, Aug. 15, 29, 1689, *ibid.*, nos. 131, 132, 249, 279, 342–344, 384; Commissioners of Ordnance to Lords of Trade, July 20, Aug. 31, 1689, *ibid.*, nos. 278, 392; Foxcroft, *Life and Letters of Halifax*, II, 215, 216, 224. The names of those proposed and appointed to governorships in early 1689 can be found in C.O. 5/1, foll. 11, 12, 14, 18, 20, 21, 23–25; for biographical details of many of these men, see Webb, *The Governors-General*, Appendix.

colonies was restricted by frequent embargoes, to preserve merchant shipping from attack but principally to serve the navy's need for manpower.[38] Whatever could be spared, however, was assigned to the defense of the West Indies. William's first act of colonial business was to confirm a reorganization of the government of Jamaica, and letters sent to the colonial governors warning of imminent war with France also promised the dispatch of a naval squadron to the Caribbean.[39] Disorganization and penury at a Pepysless Admiralty delayed its departure for a year, but the protection of the sugar islands remained the fixed and guiding star of English strategy in America. No less than four expeditions were sent to their assistance during the 1690s. A full regiment of British regulars, followed in 1695 by a second, joined the independent companies stationed in Barbados and the Leeward Islands, all this despite the catastrophic ravages of disease which generally struck down half the crews and garrisons within a year of service. If Flanders was the cockpit of Europe, the Caribbean was the graveyard.[40]

In contrast with this prodigal expenditure of men and money, the mainland colonies were expected to provide for their own defence. Another island far to the north, Newfoundland, received substantial military aid because its fisheries and the English fleets that frequented them lay open to French raids from Acadia. But the Lords of Trade were never able to follow up their own recommendations for a general program of supervision and assistance. They clearly regarded the proprietary governments south of the Delaware as dangerously weak and incompetent—these colonies, they advised the king, should

---

[38] *APC Col.*, II, 117–122, 158–176, 219–235; more detailed lists can be found in C.O. 1/68, nos. 20, 31, 65.

[39] Prince of Orange to President of Jamaica, Jan. 11, Circular to colonial governors, Apr. 15, List of ships for the West Indies squadron, June 3, 1689, *CSP Col., 1689–1692,* nos. 6, 69, 169.

[40] William T. Morgan, "The British West Indies during King William's War (1689–97)," 378–409; a more detailed account is Josiah Burchett, *Memoirs of Transactions at Sea during the War with France.* For conditions of service in the West Indies see, for example, Memorials of Col. Henry Holt, June 14, [June], 1695, *CSP Col., 1693–1696,* nos. 1894, 1895, and R. E. Scouller, *The Armies of Queen Anne,* 244, 294n.

be sent "such directions as may better secure your Majesty's interests in those parts and put them in a condition of defence against the enimie."[41] Maryland could not be left under the control of its Catholic proprietor, Lord Baltimore. Yet all these issues were laid aside to await the resolution of more urgent problems.

As for the Dominion of New England, the Lords acknowledged its importance as the outlying bulwark of all English settlements in America, a bulwark, moreover, already under attack. But they were unwilling or unable to prescribe specific remedies to match their diagnosis. On the one hand they agreed that the Dominion, in its present form, infringed upon many of the English liberties vindicated by the Revolution. Nor was James's creation worth the risk of a rebellion by disgruntled colonists at such a critical time. On the other, royal authority had to be upheld to the extent that the colonies were adequately protected and trade kept within its proper channels. The dilemma—and the guidelines of future royal policy—were succinctly expressed in the conclusion of the committee's report on Mather's petition: the king should authorize "such a further Establishment, as may be lasting, and Preserve the Rights and Properties of the People of New England and yet Reserve such a Dependance on the Crowne of England, as shalbe thought requisite."[42] Yet this bland declaration of principle brought matters no closer to a practical solution. Three months after the report, the committee still sought refuge in a calculated ambiguity that mirrored its own disunity while reiterating the supreme necessity of a unified colonial defence. New England, New York, and the Jerseys, the committee suggested, should be granted a government that would enable their numerous inhabitants "not only to oppose by their united Forces, the French of Canada and Nova

---

[41] Report of the Lords of Trade, Apr. 26, 1689, *N. Y. Col. Docs.*, III, 574 (C.O. 5/1 foll. 4–5).

[42] Report of the Lords of Trade, Feb. 22, 1689, *APC Col.*, II, 125. This was the report as communicated to and endorsed by the Privy Council; in the transmission the word *Properties* was substituted for *Privileges*, a change to Mather's disadvantage, since the latter could be construed to promise a restoration of the charters. Cf. *Randolph Letters*, II, 99n. and Mass. Hist. Soc., *Collections*, 4th ser., VIII (1868), 118.

Scotia, but to carry on such further designs as your Majesty may find requisite for your Service without which union and Government the French may easily possess themselves of that Dominion and Trade of those parts, which are soe considerable to the Crowne."[43]

Mather recoiled from the implications of such a settlement. He continued to press his cause at court and, in a second audience with the king three weeks after the committee's report on his petition, he and Lord Wharton promised to stand guarantee for the correction of any irregularities committed by New England. William did not respond to Mather's argument that the prayers of the grateful colonists would benefit him more than an army of forty thousand men, but he agreed to recall Andros and bring him to account for his administration of the Dominion. Further, New England's former magistrates were to be empowered to proclaim the new reign.[44]

Phips sailed for Boston a few days later, and his account of the king's words upon his arrival late in May must have strengthened the hands of those in Massachusetts who pressed for the immediate resumption of charter rule.[45] Once again, however, Mather found that royal promises were more easily given than fulfilled. William's knowledge of New England was slight—it was the following year before Halifax "explained about New England to him which he did not before fully apprehend"—and he hesitated to recall a colonial governor before providing adequately for his successor. In mid-April, and in accordance with the council's decision two months before, he directed Secretary Shrewsbury to seek the advice of "those who have the most considerable interest in New England, New York and the Jerzeys" in

---

[43] Report of the Lords of Trade, Apr. 26, 1689, *N. Y. Col., Docs.,* III, 573. This report was drawn up at a meeting attended by Danby (now Carmarthen), Halifax, Capel, and the eccentric Whig, Charles Paulet, Duke of Bolton—an exceptionally discordant group.

[44] Increase Mather, *Autobiography,* 332; Morrice, "Entr'ing Book," II, 554.

[45] Sewall, *Diary,* I, 204; *N. Y. Col. Docs.,* III, 587–588; Andrews, *Narratives of the Insurrections,* 216.

preparing a settlement. But the order provided for the appointment of a single executive—not a pair of temporary commissioners—over the territories of the Dominion.[46] Mather would have gained only a Pyrrhic victory if Andros were merely superseded by another royal governor. For all his careful emphasis on the personal deficiencies of Andros, Mather was well aware that it was royal government in the shape of the Dominion rather than its representative that was intolerable to New England. Once William had in effect confirmed the Dominion by sending a new governor, Mather would have forfeited his opportunity to discredit it as an illegal and superfluous relic of Stuart tyranny.

Mather and his fellow colonists in London worked together to delay the appointment of a governor. There were visits to the office of Secretary Shrewsbury and expeditions to Hampton Court to attend meetings of the Privy Council. Mather had frequently discussed colonial affairs with Dr. Daniel Coxe, the influential proprietor of West New Jersey, and this energetic entrepreneur and land speculator now collaborated in a joint petition reminding the crown that the charters of the proprietary colonies—only one of which stood condemned—reserved the right of such appointments. The great majority of the colonists wished for charter rule, and a denial would so demoralize them as to hinder an effective defence of New England against the French. In response, Sir Robert Sawyer dug up the issue of the *quo warranto* issued against Massachusetts in 1635 and demanded to see a copy of the charter.[47] Sawyer, a well-connected High Church Tory,

---

[46] Foxcroft, *Life and Letters of Halifax*, II, 244; Order of the King in Council, Apr. 18, 1689, Mass. Hist. Soc., *Collections*, 4th ser., II (1854), 298.

[47] Sewall, *Diary*, I, 212, 215; "The humble petition of several persons having considerable interest in New England and the Jersies," [Apr.–May? 1689], Mass. Hist. Soc., *Collections*, 3rd ser., I (1825), 120–121. This document does not appear among the state papers relating to the colonies, but since the colonists' efforts were directed at the Privy Council rather than its committee of trade, this does not necessarily mean that the petition was not presented. Parts of the petition were incorporated in a later pamphlet: *Andros Tracts*, II, 226. For Coxe, his numerous ventures, and his earlier links with New England, see G. D. Scull, "Biographical Notice of Doctor Daniel Coxe of London," 317–337; Albright G. Zimmerman, "Daniel Coxe and the New Mediterranean Sea Company," 86–96; John E. Pomfret, *The Province of West New Jersey, 1609–1702*, 150–171; Viola Barnes,

seems to have been the stalking horse of diehard bureaucrats such as Blathwayt and Southwell who sought to sustain the Dominion. Both sides wanted delay, the New Englanders in order to prevent the dispatch of another governor, their opponents in the hope that Andros would be retained in office so as to teach that "factious and seditious place" a lesson.[48] The hearing before the council was twice postponed. Finally, on May 18, Mather, Sewall, Hutchinson, Appleton, and William Whiting took coach to Hampton Court with their two counsels and the son and nephew of Robert Thompson—"cost 21 shillings apiece, besides money to the Drivers," noted the thrifty Sewall. There the matter was indefinitely adjourned—*"sine Die."*[49]

The impasse was broken by news from New England. The first account of the Boston uprising reached London in the last week of June while Mather and Sewall were out of town, inspecting the petrified cheese of St. John's College and other curiosities of Cambridge University. "We were surpris'd with joy," wrote Sewall in his diary. Mather hastened to Hampton Court to urge the king to make known his approval of the colonists' action. William promised to give his secretary of state orders to this effect.[50] Mather's opponents, for their part, realized that there was no longer any advantage to be gained by delay. In mid-July, the Lords of Trade received a graphic account of the disintegration of the Dominion from Lieutenant Governor Nicholson in New York. They promptly added New York (but not New

---

"Richard Wharton," 248–249; Daniel Coxe to Governor Samuel Bradstreet, Oct. 10, 1684, Prince Papers.

[48] Morrice, "Entr'ing Book," II, 543, describes under date of Apr. 27, 1689, a clash at the committee of trade between the Earl of Nottingham "and all that party" who favored Andros's retention and the Duke of Bolton, who urged his removal: "thereupon the King said Andrews [Andros] should be removed." Nottingham, however, is not recorded as attending the meeting of Apr. 26 (note 43, preceding) and Morrice may be referring to a council meeting.

[49] Sewall, *Diary*, I, 216; Proceedings in Council, May 6, 9, 12, 1689, *APC Col.*, II, 130. Mather's counsel were "Mr. Ward and Hook," probably Edward Ward and John Hooke, the noted lawyers whose lives are given in Leslie Stephen and Sidney Lee, eds., *Dictionary of National Biography*.

[50] Sewall, *Diary*, I, 220, 222; Increase Mather, *Autobiography*, 332–333; Increase Mather to Thomas Hinckley, Sept. 12, 1689, Mass. Hist. Soc., *Collections*, 4th ser., V (1861), 209–210.

England) to the colonies for which lists of possible governors were being prepared for submission to the king. In a further meeting on July 29, they drew up a letter to New York ordering the proclamation of William and Mary and another to Boston requiring the return of Andros and his fellow prisoners to England.[51] Finally, after what was reported to be "hot discourse in Council last Sabbath-day [August 4], about sending a Governour to N[ew] E[ngland]," the committee on the following Saturday agreed upon a second letter to Massachusetts authorizing a continuation of the revolutionary government until a more orderly settlement could be reached.[52]

New York's difficulties doubtless accelerated this shift in policy. The security of Albany could not wait upon the reconstruction of the Dominion, and a governor was needed to bring order to the colony and take command of the two additional companies of British regulars ordered to New York.[53] Several influential politicians were already putting forward candidates for the post, and Carmarthen's choice, Col. Henry Sloughter, eventually won out over Nicholson, the Duke of Bolton's nominee.[54] But the root cause was the Boston revolt. Whatever its consequences for New England's peace and stability, it achieved what Mather in London had failed to accomplish in that it placed the burden of disturbing the status quo in New England back upon the shoulders of the crown and compelled English officials to negotiate with the colonies of the Dominion as individual units. They

---

[51] Lieutenant Governor Nicholson and others of New York to the Lords of Trade, May 15, 1689 (read in Council, July 16, 1689), *N. Y. Col. Docs.*, III, 574–576; List of Governors, July 19, 1689, C.O. 5/1, foll. 20, 24, 25; Order of the King in Council, July 25, Journal of the Lords of Trade, July 19, 29, Lords of the Privy Council to Nicholson, July 29, the king to Nicholson, July 30, to Massachusetts, July 30, 1689, *CSP Col., 1689–1692,* nos. 270, 291, 302, 304, 307, 309.

[52] Sewall, *Diary,* I, 233; Journal of the Lords of Trade, Aug. 10, 1689, C.O. 391/6, 247 (a meeting attended by Nottingham, Fauconberg, Mordaunt, and Speaker Henry Powle); the king to Massachusetts, Aug. 12, 1689, C.O. 5/751, no. 3 (Hutchinson, *History of Massachusetts-Bay,* I, 331n.).

[53] Order of the King in Council, Sept. 2, 1689, *APC Col.,* II, 141–142; Stanley Pargellis, "The Four Independent Companies of New York," 98–99.

[54] Sewall, *Diary,* I, 232; Carmarthen to Nottingham, Sept. 11, 1689, HMC, *Finch,* II, 245; Shrewsbury to Bolton, Sept. 10, 1689, *Calendar of State Papers, Domestic Series of the Reign of William and Mary, 1689–1690,* 248.

could no longer build a policy upon the assumption that the Dominion was a coherent and working whole. It was, in retrospect, a turning point in England's relations with the northern colonies. There were to be times when a loose confederation of colonies was placed under a single governor, but never again did Whitehall succeed in breaking down traditional boundaries to form a single consolidated northern province.

Meanwhile, the dispatch of the letter empowering the revolutionary government in Boston represented a considerable triumph for New England's cause. Ashurst, now designated by both Massachusetts and Plymouth as their representative at court, could justly boast to Governor Bradstreet how he and Mather had defeated "the malignant crew" who had tried to impose a governor upon New England.[55] Yet the letter afforded no more than a temporary respite. Even as Ashurst wrote, supplicants disappointed of office in the southern colonies were seeking the vacant governorship.[56] The fact of the matter was that Mather could not expect complete success while he remained entangled in Whitehall's administrative machinery. As his reluctant and ill-fated attempt to impugn the legality of the *scire facias* demonstrated, he could not outmaneuver the old guard of the Plantation Office on their own ground. Hence he had striven to confine the business of New England to those upper levels of government—the royal closet and council chamber—most susceptible to his special pleading. Yet even these channels were now constricting as the fluidity of a period of abrupt political change gave way to the resumption of bureaucratic routine. As the spring of 1689 blossomed into summer, therefore, the pace of Mather's lobbying at court slackened and he turned to pin his hopes upon a strategy that would place the matter of the New England charters beyond the grasp of Whitehall offi-

---

[55] Sir Henry Ashurst to Governor Bradstreet, Aug. 6, 1689, Prince Papers.

[56] Sewall, *Diary*, I, 233: "Sir William Waller, to prevent others as he says, has petition'd to be Governour." For Waller, a radical Whig and a distant relative of both Ashurst and Nottingham, see Foxcroft, *Life and Letters of Halifax*, II, 215, 224, and Stephen and Lee, *Dictionary of National Biography*. He was still interested in the governorship two years later: Increase Mather, Diary, May 6, 1691, Mass. Hist. Soc.

cialdom—the bill introduced into the House of Commons to restore all corporate charters, both municipal and colonial, forfeited since 1660.[57]

The seeds of this new strategy had been planted earlier in the year. The Convention Parliament met at Westminster on January 22. Within two weeks, a committee of the lower house had prepared a Declaration of Right which called for legislation to restore corporate charters, including those of the plantations, and protect them against writs of *quo warranto*. The clause was dropped in conference with the House of Lords only to be revived in a different form. On March 5, the Grand Committee for Grievances in the Commons unanimously resolved that "the late Prosecutions of *Quo Warranto's* against the . . . Cities, Two Universities, the Towns Corporate, Boroughs and Cinque Ports, and the Plantations; and the Judgments thereupon; and the Surrender of Charters to the Violation of their ancient Rights are illegal, and a Grievance."[58] The following week it proposed the introduction of a bill to restore these charters. The Commons accepted both reports. The Corporations Restoration Bill passed its first reading on April 30 and its second two days later.[59]

Closely though the bill corresponded with Mather's aims, its inclusion of the colonies and Mather's hand in securing this must be set in perspective. The Whigs, flushed with enthusiasm and self-confidence in the wake of having, as they conceived, "elected" William and Mary to the throne, were pressing for a broad range of restrictions upon the royal prerogative. Moreover, Parliament's right to intervene in colonial affairs traditionally within the preserve of the prerogative

---

[57] I have assumed Mather's waning interest in lobbying from his own silence and from Sewall's references to Mather's absences and excursions from London: Sewall, *Diary*, I, 215, 220–222, 233–237; *idem*, "The Diary of Samuel Sewall," 301–302.

[58] *Commons Journals*, X, 17, 23, 35, 41–42.

[59] *Ibid.*, 51, 105, 112, 119; Richard C. Simmons, "The Massachusetts Charter of 1691," 72.

was not yet the lively issue it was to become in later years. Like much else arising out of England's overseas expansion, it was undefined rather than openly contested: despite the bill's provision for the restoration of charters in all of England's dominions and territories, supporters of the colonial cause still felt it necessary to tack on an amendment—"and *New England,* and other Plantations"—to ensure the colonies' inclusion.[60] Neither was Mather alone in desiring such a clarification. Quite apart from the powerful corporations within England seeking to regain their ancient privileges, other colonies besides those of New England stood to benefit by a measure that, in its original form, established a precedent against any future confiscation of their charters. The evidence is lacking, yet it may be assumed that Daniel Coxe and the proprietors of the Carolinas, three of whom sat in the House of Lords, lent their support to the bill. Doubtless William Penn did likewise, although his friendship with James II now placed him out of favor and under suspicion of treasonable correspondence with the exiled king.[61] In sum, Mather's cause again profited by its harmony with the political currents of the moment.

Within this context, however, Mather himself clearly took the lead in shaping the Corporations Bill to serve colonial needs. His lobbying of the privy councillors now served a double purpose, since those such as Powle, Boscawen, Mordaunt, Delamere, and the Whartons were prominent parliamentarians. Simultaneously, he and Ashurst sought the help of other members less intimately connected to the court. In Mather's words, "I also became acquainted with the leading men in the convention parliament, particularly, Sr Edward Harley, Sr John Thomson, Mr Sacheveril, Alderman Love, Mr John Hampden, Sr John Somers, the three mr Foleyes, and others." In his diary, he wrote of meetings with several more—Sir William Ashurst, Sir John May-

---

[60] *Commons Journals,* X, 51; for the debate over Parliament's role, see Charles H. McIlwain, *The American Revolution;* Robert L. Schuyler, *Parliament and the British Empire;* and Harvey Wheeler, "Calvin's Case (1608) and the McIlwain-Schuyler Debate," 587–597.

[61] Joseph E. Illick, *William Penn the Politician,* 103–111.

nard, Sir Roland Gwynne, William Jephson, and Maj. John Wildman. Samuel Sewall solicited the help of an old business colleague, Thomas Papillon, now member of Parliament for Dover.[62] Even after William's accession, few of these men had sought or accepted office. Ardent believers in traditional English liberties, they ranged across the spectrum of late-seventeenth-century Whiggism, from the old-line country Puritanism of Harley and Paul Foley to the radical beliefs, shading into republicanism, of Hampden and Sacheverell. Most were Presbyterians, and in soliciting their aid Mather doubtless profited from his wide circle of acquaintances among London's dissenting clergy, particularly his friendship with the great Presbyterian divine Richard Baxter, a friendship cemented by Mather's support of proposals favored by Baxter for a union of Presbyterians and Congregationalists.[63] Many of these political figures were also associated by ties of blood and influence—Sir Henry Ashurst, for example, was related by marriage to the Thompsons, the Hampdens, and the Foleys, the latter being in turn kin to the Harleys. Ashurst, like Harley's precocious son Robert, sat in the Commons as member for one of Hugh Boscawen's pocket boroughs in Cornwall. Another Harley, Sir Edward's younger brother, was married to the sister of Mrs. Hercules Saltonstall Horsey of Newington Green.[64]

The political stature of these men and the ways in which they aided

---

[62] Increase Mather, *Autobiography*, 327; *idem, A Brief Account, Andros Tracts*, II, 275–276; *idem,* Diary, Dec. 1688–Mar. 1689; Sewall, *Diary*, I, 212–213, 218, 224. Papillon was the father-in-law of Mather's counsel, Edward Ward. Mather probably met John Wildman through acting as intermediary in the correspondence between regicide John Dixwell and his niece, the mother-in-law of Wildman's son: New Haven Historical Society, *Papers*, VI (1900), *passim;* Increase Mather, Diary, June 5, 1691, Mass. Hist. Soc.; Maurice Ashley, *John Wildman, Plotter and Postmaster*, 276.

[63] Baxter to Mather "at Major Thompsons house at Newington," n.d., R. Baxter Letters, I, 217–217v., Dr. Williams's Library; Murdock, *Increase Mather*, 266–267; Increase Mather, *Autobiography*, 338; Williston Walker, ed., *The Creeds and Platforms of Congregationalism*, 440–462; Bridenbaugh, *Mitre and Sceptre*, 32–34. For Baxter's friendship with many of those solicited by Mather, see the indexes in Frederick J. Powicke, *Baxter under the Cross;* William Orme, *The Life and Times of Richard Baxter;* and Geoffrey F. Nuttall, *Richard Baxter.*

[64] Sir Edward Harley to Sir Robert Harley, Mar. 30, [16]89, H. Fortescue to Robert Harley, Feb. 27, 1690, HMC, *Portland*, III, 435–436, 445.

Mather are evident in the course of the Corporations Bill through Parliament. Nine were members of the committee of thirty-nine which recommended legislation to restore the charters, and they and others formed a substantial proportion of subsequent committees appointed to consider the bill in its passage through the Commons.[65] Within such committees, leaders of the caliber of Paul Foley and Thomas Wharton customarily played a dominant role. Yet their influence alone might not be sufficient. Faced with the need to sway a wider audience than king and council, Mather also resorted to pen and printing press to publicize New England's cause.

Mather eventually published no less than five defenses of New England while in London, and these works stand alongside and yet in contrast to those being written by his son Cotton back in Boston. Cotton's interpretation of events in New England was designed to convince an aroused colonial populace of the need for moderation and patience; his father strove to portray these events in ways that would stir an English audience to sympathy and action.[66] The latter's piece, written during the last days of 1688, set the pattern of this approach. Entitled *A Narrative of the Miseries of New-England*, it described the threat to English interests posed by Andros's arbitrary rule over the Dominion. This *"French* Government"—he listed its abuses—was

---

[65] Sacheverell, Boscawen, Jephson, "Mr. Wildman," Thomas and Paul Foley, Richard and John Hampden, and Thomas Wharton: *Commons Journals*, X, 15. Sacheverell, Papillon, Thomas and Paul Foley, Wildman, Sr., Somers, Henry Ashurst, and "Mr. Hamden" sat on the crucial forty-seven-man committee appointed to consider the bill in May 1689; Sacheverell, both Wildmans, Somers, Paul Foley, and "Mr. Hamden" sat on the thirty-three-man committee created to revive the bill in October. Sacheverell, Edward and Robert Harley, Thomas Wharton, Thomas and Paul Foley, Boscawen, William and Henry Ashurst, Somers, and "Mr. Hamden" were members of a ninety-man committee which reported out the bill in January 1690. *Ibid.*, 119–120, 277, 312–313. On the role of these men in politics in 1689, see Douglas R. Lacey, *Dissent and Parliamentary Politics in England, 1661–1689*, chapter X.

[66] The reprinting of Increase Mather's London writings in the *Andros Tracts* alongside those published by Cotton and others in New England has led scholars to treat them as a single body of materials. Yet only one of Increase's defenses was reprinted in Boston at the time, and it is therefore hardly realistic to speak of their impact upon the collective New England "mind." Rather, his writings should be assessed in light of their purpose and the audience at whom they were aimed.

[*163*]

"a specimen of what was designed to be here in *England*." With the outbreak of an Indian war, speedy relief of the colonies was imperative, else they would fall into foreign hands. And "he that is sovereign of *New-England*," declared Mather in a phrase he later repeated in an audience with William, "may by means thereof (*when he pleaseth*) be Emperour of *America*."[67]

Mather distributed copies of the *Narrative* among members of the convention parliament, and with the introduction of the Corporations Bill his arguments touched off a brisk literary debate. In *Considerations Humbly Offered to the Parliament*, an anonymous writer recalled New England's past transgressions. The strategic importance of the northern colonies, he pointed out, was the very reason why it was essential to preserve the Dominion. To restore their charters would encourage an independence damaging to English trade. A second sheet listed the New England laws contrary to those of England which would be revived if the bill were passed. In reply, Mather denied that New England had disobeyed the Acts of Trade or resisted royal authority. A third anonymous tract repeated and amplified these charges, adding a caustic denunciation of the internal dissension which, before Andros's arrival, had exposed New England to French and Indian attack. Mather once more responded, first with a brief rebuttal and then in a longer pamphlet, *A Brief Relation of the State of New England*, both published in or around July 1689. In the light of news from Boston, he was now able to boast that the colonists had risen in support of William, "not knowing that He was then King." This was final proof, if any were needed, of their right "to partake in the common Deliverance" through the recovery of their ancient privileges.[68]

---

[67] [Increase Mather], *Miseries of New-England, Andros Tracts*, II, 5, 3; *The Present State of the New-English Affairs, ibid.*, 17; Increase Mather, *Autobiography*, 333; Murdock, *Increase Mather*, 212–213.

[68] Sewall, *Diary*, I, 217; *Considerations Humbly Offered to the Parliament* (London? May 1689), *An Abstract of Some of the Printed Laws of New England* (London? May 1689), *A Short Discourse Showing the Great Inconvenience of Joyning the Plantation Charters with Those of England* (London? 1689?), [Increase Mather], *New-England Vindicated* (London, 1689), and *A Brief Relation of the State of New England*, all reprinted in

Whether or not Blathwayt and Southwell actually wrote the anonymous tracts, they undoubtedly had a hand in this assault upon Mather's strategy. Chastened but not displaced by the revolution, they continued to advocate a greater royal supervision of the colonies. Indeed, the war with France, they maintained, made such a policy all the more essential. Their anxiety over the progress of the Corporations Bill was vividly expressed in a letter sent, probably by Southwell, to his kinsman, Secretary of State Nottingham, late in March 1689. The American plantations, he wrote, furnish a third of England's trade and much of its customs revenue.

> If New England be restored to the usurped Priviledges they had in 1660 and the old Proprietors of New Jersey, New York and other Islands and Places to what they pretend, It will so Confound the Present settlement in those Parts, and their Dependance on England, that 'tis hard to say where the Mischeif will stopp, or how farr the Act of Navigation will be over throwne thereby. Yett with such power and Ardour is this Designe carryed on and by those who perhapps suspect not the Intention of the Republicans who solicite them, that no Man dares open his Mouth to the Contrary for feare of being Crusht. Mr. Blathwayt, who best knows the truth and state of things dares not speake more than he has done, unless to his Majesty and my Lord Danby and to your Lordship alone. And 'tis of vast importance that an houre were sett apart to have this thing made plaine before it runns on in Parliament beyond Redresse.[69]

Fearful of reprisal, therefore, royal officials resorted to the anonymity of print. The three pamphlets addressed to Parliament all focused upon the specific issue of New England, and they bear unmistakable signs of having been prepared with materials drawn from the records of the Plantation Office—an early instance of the official "leak" de-

---

*Andros Tracts,* III, 3–9, 13–16, II, 137–147, 113–123, 149–170; and [Increase Mather], *A Further Vindication,* in Murdock, *Increase Mather,* facing 222 and 223. Murdock's pioneering analysis established this order; the pamphlets are also discussed in Thomas J. Holmes, *Increase Mather.* In *ibid.,* II, 637–641, Murdock analyzes yet another broadsheet contributed to this debate.

[69] [Southwell?] to Nottingham, Mar. 23, 1689, Hall, Leder, and Kammen, *Glorious Revolution in America,* 67.

signed to influence the formulation of policy.[70] They carefully skirted the treacherous quicksands of the prerogative. None questioned Parliament's authority to restore corporations or reorganize the colonies. Indeed, the final tract urged that the colonial charters be considered in a separate bill, a suggestion in harmony with the recommendation of the committee of trade in May 1689 that the condition of Maryland, Carolina, and Pennsylvania be referred to Parliament to secure their closer dependence on the crown.[71] Together, the pamphlets echoed the refrain made familiar by Randolph: with its charters restored, New England would once more be a nest of squabbling oligarchies, its "Abominable, Illegal way of Trade" a threat to English commercial supremacy and its aggressive insubordination a pernicious example to the other plantations. A minor but recurring theme was the damage which a return to charter rule would inflict on the scheme promoted by Wharton, Hutchinson, and several influential English backers for mining copper in New England. It exemplified the concern always uppermost in the minds of English policy makers—What circumstances would best encourage and protect English exploitation of the colonies?[72]

Mather agreed with his opponents about the critical importance of his country's trade and strategic position. New England, he declared, "is the Key of the *New World America*." But he sought to turn the issue to his advantage by arguing, in effect, that contented colonists gave better milk. Charter government had enabled the New Englanders to supply provisions to the West Indies and customs revenue to the royal treasury, all at no charge to the crown. Without the charters, they would be so discouraged that they would fall easy prey to foreign enemies. This still left him open to the rejoinder that "one entire Su-

---

[70] In addition, one of the pamphlets survives in draft in Attorney General Sir George Treby's handwriting: C.O. 5/856, no. 158xvii; *Andros Tracts*, III, 2.

[71] *A Short Discourse, Andros Tracts*, II, 146–147; Lords of Trade to the king, May 16, Minute of the Lords of Trade, May 25, 1689, William Hand Browne *et al.*, eds., *Archives of Maryland*, VIII, 100–101.

[72] *Considerations Humbly Offered, Andros Tracts*, III, 7–8; *A Short Discourse, ibid.*, II, 138, 144–145; [Mather], *New-England Vindicated, ibid.*, 120–121. See the following chapter for the subsequent fate of these schemes.

perintendancy" over the northern colonies would better secure their trade and defence, and in his final rebuttal Mather turned to the broader justification of New England's unique contribution to English overseas expansion, its religious origins, its schools and university, and its efforts to convert the Indians. He also sought to place the colonies in a constitutional context that would justify their inclusion in the bill. It was not true that their charters had been vacated "upon quite different reasons from those in England." On the contrary, "both the Charters in *England* and *New-England,* were taken away by the same sort of Men and on the same grounds, *viz.* in order to the Establishing of Arbitrary Government."[73]

Mather succeeded in diverting Parliament's attention from the sins of the colonies. Although Blathwayt plucked up courage and testified at Westminster against New England, the committee entrusted with the bill began an enquiry into Andros's government of the Dominion. Yet all this took time, and the bill's very breadth also worked to New England's disadvantage by compelling the committee to consider petitions from English municipal corporations affected by its passage.[74] The issue was still unresolved in August when Mather abruptly decided to accompany his fellow colonists back to Boston. It is difficult to accept his subsequent explanation that New England's affairs were so well advanced that nothing remained to be done. True, he had the letter authorizing a temporary continuation of the revolutionary government. But the bill, as Sewall observed at the end of July, was "despair'd of," bottled up by factional disputes over the conduct of the war. By the middle of August, it had no chance of passage before the conclusion of the session.[75] It is more likely that Mather realized that this might be his last chance to arrive back in Boston as his country's

---

[73] [Increase Mather], *A Brief Relation, Andros Tracts,* II, 160, 156–157, 162–170; *New-England Vindicated, ibid.,* 114, 119–120; *A Short Discourse, ibid.,* 145, 137; *Considerations Humbly Offered, ibid.,* III, 3; Murdock, *Increase Mather,* facing 223.

[74] Sewall, *Diary,* I, 216, 228–229; *Commons Journals,* X, 120, 233.

[75] *Commons Journals,* X, 271; Hall, ed., Increase Mather, *Autobiography,* 339; Sewall, *Diary,* I, 228, 232; Lacey, *Dissent and Parliamentary Politics,* 239–240; Horwitz, *Parliament, Policy and Politics,* 33–36.

savior. In his prayers, "the blessing which I especially begged for, was, That I might return to New England with good tidings." It was reported that Massachusetts was sending over "Envoys" to negotiate directly with the crown, and Mather had long feared that he might be superseded in his task or forced to share it with others distasteful to him. "Let none be joyned with me whom I cannot close with," he had admonished a political ally in Boston, ". . . an ox and an ass cannot plow together." Moreover, as Robert Harley's brother noted, "Toryism is now in the ascendant." New England might soon stand to lose more than it could gain from a negotiated settlement.[76]

But even as Mather's ship lay in the channel port of Deal, two days' sail out of London, his fifteen-year-old son Samuel contracted smallpox. The contrary wind shifted, and the Mathers were left behind as the vessel, carrying their fellow colonists Samuel Sewall and Thomas Brattle, departed for Boston.[77] In October, Increase and his convalescent son returned to London. Little is known about his activities during the winter of 1689, save for his redoubled dedication to parliamentary affairs. A second Corporations Bill was introduced into the new session, and although no record remains of its wording during its passage through the Commons, its form upon reaching the Lords suggests that Mather had again been both active and effective in promoting and countering opposition to his cause. As debated by the upper house, the bill carried amendments, evidently as a result of pressures from Whitehall, which ensured that none of its provisions would prejudice the crown's rights or alter the existing governments in New York, Pennsylvania, Maryland, Carolina, the Bermudas, or the West Indian colonies.[78] Yet no such exclusion was applied to the Jerseys or New England. Instead, the attack upon New England's

[76] Increase Mather, *Autobiography*, 342; Sewall, *Diary*, I, 232; Increase Mather to John Richards, Oct. 17, 1688, Winthrop Papers; Edward to Robert Harley, Mar. 26, 1689, HMC, *Portland*, III, 435.

[77] Increase Mather, *Autobiography*, 339–340; Increase Mather to [Lord Wharton], Sept. 11, 1689, Rawlinson Letters, 51, fol. 189, Bodleian Library.

[78] Increase Mather, *Autobiography*, 342; *Commons Journals*, X, 277, 284, 312–313; *House of Lords MSS.*, 1689–1690, 427, 423. What appears to be a draft of the bill without amendments, though dated Feb. 23, 1690/1, is in C.O. 1/67, no. 75.

charters was specifically condemned in the preamble to the bill prior to the clauses restoring all such confiscated charters. Writing to his father in Rhode Island some months later, Thomas Brinley reported that Mather had given twenty pounds (presumably to the clerk drafting the bill) to ensure this mention of New England.[79]

All these labors, however, were drowned beneath the rising tide of political factionalism. Even before the bill reached the Lords, it was encumbered with a penal amendment, the famous Sacheverell clause, which sought to disqualify from politics all those responsible for the confiscation of the charters. In a close vote on January 10, "the church party," principally composed of Tories, rallied and "routed Jack Presbyter."[80] The clause was expunged and the bill sent up to the Lords, but the contest strengthened William in his determination to put an end to parliamentary obstruction. He was now as disillusioned with the Whigs as they with him—John Hampden, he told Halifax, "was mad," Boscawen "a Blockhead." Although the bill reached a second reading in the Lords, it lapsed on January 27 when William first prorogued and then dissolved the convention parliament.[81]

Thus, wrote Mather with weary resignation, "a whole Year's *Sisyphean Labour* came to nothing." Even had the bill passed (and William

---

[79] Thomas Brinley to [Francis Brinley], May 28, 1690, Miscellaneous Manuscripts, R. I. Hist. Soc. The transcript of this letter published in Amer. Antiq. Soc., *Proceedings*, new ser., LXXXIII (1973), 245, misreads and omits this reference to Mather's payment.

[80] *Commons Journals*, X, 332–333; Anchitell Gray, *Debates in the House of Commons from the Year 1667 to the Year 1694*, IX, 510–520; Diary of Henry, Earl of Clarendon, Jan. 10, 1690, in Samuel W. Singer, ed., *The Correspondence of Henry Hyde, Earl of Clarendon, and of his brother, Lawrence Hyde, Earl of Rochester*, II, 301; Keith Feiling, *A History of the Tory Party, 1640–1714*, 270; Lacey, *Dissent and Parliamentary Politics*, 240–242. Of Mather's known friends in the Commons, eighteen of twenty voted for the Sacheverell clause, judging by the division list in John Oldmixon, *The History of England*, 36.

[81] *Commons Journals*, X, 329–330; Foxcroft, *Life and Letters of Halifax*, II, 224, 222; *Lords Journals*, XIV, 410, 419, 422, 429; Feiling, *Tory Party*, 266–267; Carswell, *Old Cause*, 78–79.

was determined that it should not), it would almost certainly have omitted the colonies from its provisions. Three days before the prorogation, the Lords agreed that the colonial charters should be considered separately, and one peer told Thomas Brinley that New England was excluded "as being in the forreigne Plantations and so belonging more Immediately to the king."[82] Discussion of the colonies' legal position, therefore, had served only to resurrect and strengthen the traditional view that they were among the king's personal possessions and hence under his direct control. Moreover, as Halifax's journals reveal, William himself now had a clearer perception of his rights and responsibilities in America. Although he continued to receive Mather's personal overtures with courtesy, he never again committed himself to restoring New England's ancient privileges.[83]

One misfortune now followed upon another. The new parliament which assembled in March 1690 was markedly more Tory and Anglican in its sentiments. John Hampden lost his seat in the Commons, and Henry Powle was not reelected Speaker. Mather spoke to several members about New England's needs at a time when it seemed that the Corporations Bill might be revived, but the project came to nothing and Parliament was soon adjourned until the fall of 1690. "There

---

[82] Increase Mather, *A Brief Account, Andros Tracts*, II, 276; Foxcroft, *Life and Letters of Halifax*, II, 243; *House of Lords MSS., 1689–1690*, 432; Thomas Brinley to [Francis Brinley], May 28, 1690, Miscellaneous MSS., R. I. Hist. Soc. From his Boston prison cell, John Palmer had expounded this viewpoint in detail, and it is possible that copies of his tract, in manuscript or as printed in Boston, had reached London by January 1690: Palmer, *An Impartial Account, Andros Tracts*, I, 35–40. Edward Arber, *The Term Catalogues, 1668–1709*, 321, shows that the London edition was not printed until June.

[83] Foxcroft, *Life and Letters of Halifax*, II, 244. I take Halifax's cryptic entry, *ibid.*, 246, that the king "said hee was glad to hear what Mr Hampbden said concerning Ld. Baltimore, and was resolved to put him in mind of his Agᵗ [Argument?] when New. England came into question" to refer to Hampden's inconsistency in demanding a change in the Catholic Baltimore's proprietorship of Maryland while supporting a restoration of the New England charters. Although there is little clear evidence of William's influence on colonial affairs, its importance can be inferred from the frequent delaying of decisions to await his return to London and his known domination of foreign policy in general. Thus Godfrey Davies, "The Control of British Foreign Policy by William III," in his *Essays on the Later Stuarts*, 91–95.

was an end of all endeavors to obtain releef by the Parliament," recorded Mather in his autobiographical journal. "No way was left but only to gett the best we could at the Court."[84] But at court, also, the political climate was changing for the worse. Halifax had resigned the Privy Seal; Mordaunt and Delamere were leaving the Treasury; and Shrewsbury, in poor health and eager to lay down his secretaryship, was soon to retire to the country accompanied by an indignant Thomas Wharton. The field was left clear for the ascendancy of Blathwayt's allies, Carmarthen and Nottingham, at the very moment when the matter of New England was again brought to the fore at Whitehall by the arrival in London of the new Massachusetts agents and the former rulers of the Dominion. Disheartened by his reverses and embittered by his country's ingratitude in sending new agents and failing to repay his expenses, Mather threatened to give up his mission and never return to New England.[85]

The most damaging setback, however, was yet to come. While the arrival of Andros and his subordinates confronted Mather with determined and well-informed opponents, it also offered a last chance of proving that the colonists had indeed risen in support of the cause of English liberty. After some delay, and by order of the committee of trade, the agents submitted a formal indictment. Andros and his accomplices had opposed the enterprise of the Prince of Orange; they had governed arbitrarily and without legal authority; and they had encouraged the Indians to attack New England. On April 17, 1690, the committee met to consider these charges. Once again, the colonists suddenly found themselves on the defensive. Speaking on behalf of Andros, Attorney General Sir George Treby dwelt on the harsh treatment of the prisoners during their long confinement, and

---

[84] Increase Mather to Thomas Hinckley, May 24, 1690, Mass. Hist. Soc., *Collections*, 4th ser., V (1861), 255; Increase Mather, *Autobiography*, 343; *Commons Journals*, X, 417.

[85] Luttrell, *Brief Historical Relation*, II, 38; Mather to Hinckley, May 24, 1690, Mass. Hist. Soc., *Collections*, 4th ser., V (1861), 255; Cotton to Increase Mather, May 17, 1690, in Cotton Mather, *Diary*, ed. Ford, I, 137–140.

in a "stormy Harangue," his fellow counsel and New England's inveterate opponent, Sir Robert Sawyer, recited the irrelevant and well-worn story of New England's offenses prior to the loss of the charter.[86]

In reply, after the charges had been read, the counsel for the agents, Edward Ward and Solicitor General Somers, began to discuss them point by point. At that moment, however, Joseph Dudley interposed a request that the agents would show their credentials and sign the charges so that the accused "might know who they had to answere, and to have satisfaction, if they clear'd themselves."[87] Dudley's intention was to intimidate the agents with the threat of a countersuit for damages. The stratagem succeeded. In discussion before the meeting, Cooke and Oakes had refused to sign the charges unless Mather and Ashurst would do likewise. They in turn had refused on the ground that they had not seen the evidence gathered in Boston. "Wee had bin children had wee done it upon their saying they could prove what was asserted," Mather later explained. One agent, probably Cooke or Oakes, now offered to sign the charges, but Somers and Ward held to their preconcerted strategy that the whole colony was presenting the case against Andros. The debate that followed quickly fastened upon the central issue of the nature of the revolution in New England. Who had imprisoned Sir Edmund Andros? Was it "the Country . . . the people of the place," as Somers asserted, who had risen "as we did here" to throw off the yoke of tyranny? Or was it, as Sawyer hotly retorted, merely "the Rabble spirited by the faction?" Several of the nine privy councillors attending the meeting—of Mather's known supporters, Powle, Boscawen, and Thomas Wharton were present—expressed their approval of the colonists' actions. One drew a barbed

---

[86] "Matters objected against Sir Edmund Andros . . . and others as occasions of the Imprisonment in New England." *Andros Tracts*, II, 176–177 (their answers to these charges, never read before the committee, are in *ibid.*, 178–188); Elisha Cooke to Simon Bradstreet, Oct. 16, 1690, Mass. Hist. Soc., *Proceedings*, XLV (1911–1912), 647. Sawyer, expelled from Parliament by the Whigs in December 1689, had just been triumphantly reelected.

[87] Thomas Brinley to [Francis Brinley], May 28, 1690, Miscellaneous MSS., R. I. Hist. Soc.

parallel between the seizure of Andros and the capture of the garrison at Hull during the Revolution in England. All knew that Carmarthen, now presiding over the hearing as Lord President of the Council, had been a leader in that enterprise.[88]

Finally, with the charges still unproved, Carmarthen brought the hearing to an end. By Cooke's account, it was no more than an adjournment; according to two other observers of the scene, Thomas Brinley and an anonymous friend of Sir Edmund Andros, the agents were forced to withdraw when they refused to show their credentials. Whatever the sequence of events, the result was the same. The committee agreed to report that since no one had come forward to accept responsibility for the charges, Andros and the others should be exonerated and set at liberty. A week later, the King in Council formally accepted the committee's recommendation.[89]

The agents had themselves left open this loophole by their failure to stand behind their complaints. Doubtless they remembered the crushing fines which Stuart courts had lately imposed upon those adjudged to have made malicious accusations. They were also the victims of unfavorable circumstances. As Governor Bradstreet admitted

---

[88] Elisha Cooke to Simon Bradstreet, Oct. 16, 1690, Mass. Hist. Soc., *Proceedings,* XLV (1911–1912), 648–649; Theodore B. Lewis, ed., "Sir Edmund Andros's Hearing before the Lords of Trade and Plantations, April 17, 1690," 244 (this account of the hearing, printed by Lewis from notes left by Increase Mather, seems contemporary, since it matches the language of Mather's letters at this time). The most detailed account of the hearing as it relates to Andros is given by Stephen Saunders Webb, "The Trials of Sir Edmund Andros," 45–53.

[89] Cooke to Bradstreet, Oct. 16, 1690, Mass. Hist. Soc., *Proceedings,* XLV (1911–1912), 649; Thomas Brinley to [Francis Brinley], May 28, 1690, Miscellaneous MSS., R. I. Hist. Soc.; "Memorandum of the Proceedings in the Council Chamber before the Committee of the Plantations, between Sir Edmund Andros, the other Gentlemen and the Agents for N. England," in Edith F. Carey, "Amias Andros and Sir Edmund, His Son," 59–60; Journal of the Lords of Trade, Apr. 17, 1690, *Randolph Letters,* II, 125n.; Order of the King in Council, Apr. 24, 1690, *Andros Tracts,* III, 41–43. All the contemporary accounts of the hearing differ in several important respects; Cooke's in particular, though the most detailed and most often cited, seems to evade or omit a number of important facts. Written six months after the hearing, it portrays a victory for backstairs official intrigue after Carmarthen abruptly terminated the proceedings. Yet other accounts, the business taken up by the committee after the withdrawal of the agents, and the official report prepared on the same day all suggest otherwise. Even the committee's journal is, no doubt deliberately, misleading in its brevity; and it is definitely inaccurate in stating that the charges against Andros were never read.

in a letter to Mather, the evidence sent over from Massachusetts to uphold the charges was thin. Legally, Andros could justify virtually all the acts which seemed so blatantly tyrannical to the colonists by reference to the letter and spirit of his instructions. To attack the governor's rule was to sail perilously close to questioning royal authority, and that in front of men who had for the most part cheerfully supported such policies almost until the end of James's reign. Had Andros been sent home earlier during the Whig ascendancy, the committee might have pressed an investigation. By the early months of 1690, however, attendance at its meetings had begun to reflect the turn in politics at large as Tories such as Carmarthen, Secretary Nottingham, the Earl of Pembroke (Sir Robert Sawyer's son-in-law), and Carmarthen's followers, Sir Henry Goodricke and Sir John Lowther, gained a slight but growing numerical advantage.[90] Simultaneously, the Whig campaign for vengeance was brought to an end by an Act of Grace which pardoned all save a few notorious offenders for past political actions. In these circumstances, the colonists' attempt to prosecute their former rulers was an embarrassing and impertinent reminder of the past. Small wonder that the committee accepted Carmarthen's decision to use the agents' refusal to sign the charges as an excuse to return this skeleton to the cupboard. As Sir John Somers cryptically remarked to Cooke, "if they will bring off thus, they may."[91]

A further ill consequence of the delay in returning Andros was the time it had allowed for the reports telling of New England's post-Revolutionary difficulties to reach alarming proportions. Initially, doubtless at the instance of Mather's friends at court, the Lords of Trade had ignored both the detailed accounts of the colonists' internal dissensions and military setbacks smuggled out by Edward Randolph from his prison cell in Boston and the grievances—"malicious informations" as Mather termed them—presented in person by two for-

---

[90] Bradstreet to Mather, Jan. 29, 1690, Hutchinson, *Papers*, II, 319; Journal of the Lords of Trade, Jan.–Apr., 1690, C.O. 391/6, 308–322.

[91] Cooke to Bradstreet, Oct. 16, 1690, Mass. Hist. Soc., *Proceedings*, XLV (1911–1912), 649.

mer Dominion officials, John Usher and Francis Nicholson.[92] Early in 1690, however, prodded by petitions and letters forwarded to them by the Privy Council and the Customs Commissioners, they at length commenced an investigation. At a meeting on February 25 attended by an array of leading Whigs and Tories, the reading of letters from Randolph and Governor Bradstreet together with the testimony of witnesses lately arrived from Boston and that of London merchants telling of the decay of New England's fisheries and timber trade combined to present a dismal picture of political turmoil, renewed evasion of the Acts of Trade, and frontier communities helpless in the face of Indian attack. Probably because Whigs and Tories were almost equally matched at the meeting, the committee's subsequent report merely described the situation without recommending a particular course of action.[93] Yet in echoing Randolph's exaggerated descriptions of events, it served to reemphasize that the committee was far more intent upon restoring strong and orderly government in the colonies than upon pursuing vague charges arising out of such government in the past. Nor did New England's evident difficulties substantiate the agents' contention that the Revolution there had been an all but unanimous popular uprising, a contention further cast into question when a group of some twenty "Gentlemen and merchants," including several New Englanders, assembled in support of Andros and his codefendants at the April hearing and when several petitions from New England appealing to the crown for aid and protection were produced and read at the Privy Council meeting which confirmed the committee's decision.[94]

---

[92] Increase Mather to [Lord Wharton], Sept. 11, 1689, Rawlinson Letters, 51, fol. 189, seeks the aid of Wharton, Monmouth, and Delamere in counteracting these accounts. Randolph's letters from Boston are in *Randolph Letters,* IV, 264–310, V, 20–31, VI, 287–332. For Usher's grievances and information, see *CSP Col., 1689–1692,* nos. 242, 337, 457; for his prolonged efforts to obtain repayment for his work as treasurer, see Jeffries Papers, II, 135–189, IV, 64–86, and *Mass. Acts and Resolves,* VII, 645–651, 719–720, VIII, 348–350, 419, 704–706.

[93] Journal of the Lords of Trade, Feb. 25, 1690, *Randolph Letters,* II, 121n. A copy of the merchants' petition is in C.O. 5/855, no. 65. Two reports by the committee are in *ibid.,* nos. 67, 69. No action was taken by the Privy Council.

[94] Thomas Brinley to [Francis Brinley], May 28, 1690, Miscellaneous MSS., R. I. Hist. Soc.; Petitions and Addresses from New England, [Jan. 1690], *CSP Col.,*

Mather, however, blamed only his fellow agents for the debacle. "Alas," he wrote to Richards in Boston, "the Agents lately come hither are become the Ridicule of the Town. . . . If they would have studyed to have gratified the enemies of N[ew] E[ngland] or to have exposed themselves or the Country they could not have done it more effectually." In his autobiographical memoir, Mather recalled how sympathizers such as Devonshire and John Hampden were "extremely Scandalized" by the news and how Lord Mordaunt had exclaimed that the agents had "cutt the throat of their Countrey" by failing to prove their charges against Andros.[95] Undeniably, Cooke and Oakes were, in the scornful phrase of one of Mather's allies, "two starched men," inflexible, fearful of exceeding their instructions, and convinced that every moment at the royal court held hidden perils for the unwary provincial.[96] Yet they were hardly more so than Mather himself had been six years before when he had incited the Boston freemen to resist all concessions to the crown. Moreover, they accurately embodied attitudes that lingered on in New England long after its leaders had recognized the need to come to terms with the crown and royal officials. In the short term, the conflict between the agents diverted their energies from their appointed task as each strove to justify his actions to those at home. From a longer perspective, it both mirrored the continuing debate among New Englanders over the nature of their relationship with London and marked the beginning of a personal rivalry between Mather, Cooke, and Oakes that was to reverberate through the next two decades of Massachusetts politics.

In the meantime, Mather reassessed his dwindling options and resources. His expenses had been heavy. "Whilst I attended at Whitehall," he wrote in 1689, "I was necessitated to give money to clerks,

---

*1689-1692,* nos. 740–743. See the following chapter for further analysis of these and similar petitions.

[95] Increase Mather to John Richards, May 1, 1690, Winthrop Papers; Increase Mather, *Autobiography,* 340–341.

[96] Increase Mather to John Richards, May 1, 1690, Winthrop Papers.

and to solicitors; sometimes 5 lb. [pounds]; sometimes 10 lb.; sometimes 30 lb.; sometimes 40 lb.; . . . I have borrowed 300 lb. and besides that, I have spent of my own money 150 lbs." Adding "dayly gratifications" bestowed on servants belonging to "persons of Quallitie" and "manie Visitts on Lawyers etc." he later estimated his official expenses at not less than £1,000. He borrowed £390 from a wealthy London merchant, Stephen Mason, £170 from Samuel Sewall, and £50 from Thomas Lake, the son of a former member of his congregation in Boston.[97] In December 1689, the Massachusetts General Court had voted a tax of one and a half rates, later translated into a credit of £2,000, to defray the agents' expenses. But when Cooke and Oakes arrived, they found difficulty in drawing upon their bills of exchange or the colony's letter of credit, and Randolph, with characteristic ingenuity, began proceedings to seize one of the cargoes of whale oil sent over to finance the agency. Letters back to Boston pleaded for further supplies of money. "Without it no g[ood] is to be done at Court," wrote Stephen Mason. "If money ca[nnot] be had in a public way, is there none among you that can le[nd] it? Where is the zeal of their fathers for God's glory?"[98]

These stringencies made the agents all the more anxious to avoid the costly labyrinth of Whitehall's bureaucracy. Mather briefly attempted to reverse the judgment against the Massachusetts charter by means of a writ of error transferring the case from the Court of Chancery to that of King's Bench, then presided over by a Whig Lord Chief Justice, Sir John Holt, but "an unexpected Providence" frustrated the attempt. Ultimately, therefore, he once more pinned his hopes upon a direct appeal to the crown. Again, his friends among

---

[97] Kenneth B. Murdock, "Increase Mather's Expenses as Colonial Agent," 200–204; Mason to Simon Bradstreet, May 26, 1690, Mass. Hist. Soc., *Collections,* 4th ser., V (1861), 256; Sewall, "Diary," 271, 284, 286, 288.

Mather's expenses were typical for the time: thus John C. Jeaffreson, *A Young Squire of the Seventeenth Century,* II, 29–30, and Higham, "Accounts of a Colonial Governor's Agent," 263–285.

[98] Orders of the General Court, Dec. 4, 1689, Nov. 7, 1690, *N. H. Laws,* I, 337, 450; *Andros Tracts,* III, 61–62; Randolph to the Lords of the Treasury, June 20, 1690, *Calendar of Treasury Books, 1689–1692,* 714; Stephen Mason to Simon Bradstreet, May 26, 1690, Mass. Hist. Soc., *Collections,* 4th ser., V (1861), 257.

the Dissenters furnished an introduction. William was on the point of leaving for a summer campaign in Ireland, but Mather gained the assistance of four ladies of Queen Mary's entourage—Lady Ann Clinton and Elizabeth, Countess of Anglesey, both members of dissenting congregations in London, and two Scottish Presbyterians, Jean, Countess of Sutherland and Madam Martha Lockhart.[99] The Countess of Sutherland, reported Mather in June 1690, "has 4 or 5 times sollicited the Queen to be kind to N.E." By October, Mary had promised that the colony's privileges would be restored.[100] There were other signs of official favor: in August, Mather obtained a legal opinion from Treby, Ward, and Somers that the Connecticut charter was still valid since it had not been vacated by the colony's submission in 1687.[101] Soon afterward came word of the success of New England's first counterattack since the overthrow of the Dominion, a naval expedition that had captured the French base at Port Royal in Acadia. The colonists, it seemed, were fulfilling Mather's pledge that the charter governments could adequately defend New England. All these favorable auspices encouraged the agents to take the decisive

---

[99] Increase Mather, *A Brief Account, Andros Tracts,* II, 276; *idem, Autobiography,* 328. Lady Anne Clinton was the wife of Boscawen's deceased wife's brother; the Countess of Anglesey was the mother-in-law of Sir John Thompson. Possibly Mather met the Countess of Sutherland and Madam Lockhart through William Carstares (note 20, preceding) and George Melville, Secretary of State for Scotland: Increase Mather to Thomas Hinckley, Sept. 12, 1689, Mass. Hist. Soc., *Collections,* 4th ser., V (1861), 211.

[100] Increase Mather to Richards, June 9, 1690, Winthrop Papers; *idem, Autobiography,* 328; James Porter to Robert Treat, Oct. 30, 1690, Conn. Hist. Soc., *Collections,* XXIV (1932), 40.

[101] Increase Mather to Robert Treat, Aug. 19, James Porter to Treat, Sept. 2, Oct. 30, William Whiting to Treat, Nov. 8, 1690, Conn. Hist. Soc., *Collections,* XXIV (1932), 37–41; *Conn. Records,* IV, 52, 54. Copies of the legal opinion, printed in Mass. Hist. Soc., *Collections,* 5th ser., IX (1885), 175–176, are preserved in Conn. Archives, Foreign Correspondence, II, 25d., and New England Colonial Records, State of Connecticut, 1664–1702, vol. 54, Connecticut State Library. Ward and Somers had appeared for the agents at the April hearing; and Treby, though then appearing for Andros, was remarkably sympathetic to the cause of proprietary charters, as shown by his reluctance to proceed against that of Maryland in 1690: Lois Green Carr and David William Jordan, *Maryland's Revolution of Government, 1689–1692,* 156.

step, early in November 1690, of petitioning the crown for a new charter for Massachusetts.[102]

This was not quite such a gamble as its ultimate consequences would suggest. Despite the risk that Whitehall would take the opportunity to resurrect the Dominion, Mather had reason to believe that he could obtain what farsighted colonists had always desired—a new charter embodying the powers of the old and adding those that Massachusetts had tacitly assumed in transforming itself from corporation to commonwealth. Until this was done, the colony would always remain vulnerable to charges such as those levelled by Randolph that it was exceeding its authority. Lawyers among Mather's Whig allies favored this course on the ground that the crown did not now have the power to reissue the old charter in its original form.[103] Lastly, the agents could not reasonably hope to stave off the mounting pressures within Whitehall for the appointment of a royal governor over New England without advancing proposals for an alternative settlement.[104] Even so, Cooke and Oakes still clung to the hope that the old charter could be restored and one of them, probably Cooke, refused to sign the petition to the crown.[105] Further disagreement ensued after William had referred the petition and the task of drafting a new

---

[102] Increase Mather, *A Brief Account, Andros Tracts,* II, 276–277. The petition does not survive in the official records, but it is presumably that described as presented on Nov. 6: Ichabod Wiswall to Thomas Hinckley, Nov. 10, 1690, Mass. Hist. Soc., *Collections,* 4th ser., V (1861), 278. Richard Simmons has plausibly suggested that it was similar to drafts surviving in Mass. Archives, XXXVII, 175 and 175a: Simmons, "Massachusetts Charter," 76.

[103] Charles Garth to Ringgold, Murdock, and Tilghman, Mar. 5, 1766, *Maryland Historical Magazine,* VI (1911), 295–296. While written long after the event Garth's account still seems plausible because it accords with the general trend of Whig thinking at the time.

[104] Thus Increase Mather, *Autobiography,* 340; *idem* to Richards, June 9, 1690, Winthrop Papers; James Porter to Robert Treat, Sept. 2, 1690, Conn. Hist. Soc., *Collections,* XXIV (1932), 39; Sewall, *Diary,* I, 268.

[105] Charles Lidgett to Francis Foxcroft, Nov. 5, 1690, *New England Historical and Genealogical Register,* XXXIII (1879), 407. Hutchinson, *History of Massachusetts-Bay,* I, 345n., states positively that Cooke refused to sign the petition, but other evidence suggests that Mather's principal disagreement was less with Cooke than with Oakes: Increase Mather to Richards, June 9, 1690, Winthrop Papers; Cooke to Simon Bradstreet, May 9, 1691, Prince Papers.

charter to a committee consisting of the crown's law officers, Treby and Somers, and Lords Chief Justice Holt and Pollexfen. Ichabod Wiswall, minister of Duxbury in Plymouth Colony and an ally of Elisha Cooke, had accompanied the agents to England at the request of the Boston government. He was infuriated to discover that Mather, invited to attend on the deliberations of this committee, had got Plymouth incorporated within the new grant. According to Mather, his surreptitious imperialism was in the colony's best interests. He claimed to have been instrumental in preventing Plymouth's inclusion in the commission of Governor Sloughter of New York; there was no chance that it could obtain a charter of its own, and it would certainly fall under New York's dominion were it not harnessed once and for all to the Bay mare. Wiswall protested, and Plymouth was struck out of the draft of the charter. "If you find yourselves thereby plunged into manifold miseries," wrote Cotton Mather to Hinckley from Boston, "you have none to thank for it but one of your own."[106]

Despite these differences, the proposals finally submitted to the king embodied almost everything that the agents could have desired. They had asked for the reestablishment of the Massachusetts Bay Company with all its lands and privileges, and with the additional right of government over Maine and New Hampshire. The deficiencies of the old patent were to be corrected by provisions empowering the officers and representative assembly elected by the freemen of the company (not the freeholders of the colony) to tax, legislate, and erect courts of judicature. Land titles were to be confirmed and the com-

---

[106] Increase Mather, *A Brief Account, Andros Tracts*, II, 277. This episode raises an interesting point of chronology. Cotton Mather's letter to Hinckley, describing Wiswall's intervention, has been dated as 26d. iim. 1690 (Apr. 26, 1690) in Mass. Hist. Soc., *Collections*, 4th ser., V (1861), 248, Murdock, *Increase Mather*, 403, and Kenneth Silverman, comp., *Selected Letters of Cotton Mather*, 24. This seems to be confirmed by its discussion in *Plymouth Records*, VI, 259, under a heading of June 1690. But both internal and circumstantial evidence shows that Mather's letter was commenting on events happening in England in the fall of 1690, and the ascribed dates of both the letter and the records are wrong. The events described in *Plymouth Records*, VI, 259, took place c. Feb. 1691 (Langdon, *Pilgrim Colony*, 238–239, perceives this misdating but not that of the letter). And Mather's letter was written not on 26d. iim. 1690 but on 26d. 11m. 1690—Feb. 26, 1691, the date also given in *The Prince Library, A Catalogue of the Collection of Books and Manuscripts which formerly belonged to the Reverend Thomas Prince*, 156.

pany invested with increased authority over the militia as in other matters of defence. By Cooke's account, which is corroborated by scattered documents in the English state papers, the committee of justices and law officers accepted this draft with three additions designed "to the end this colony be made more Imediately Dependent upon the crowne." All laws should be submitted to the king for his approval, civil suits involving more than a certain sum in debt or damages could be appealed to the King in Council, and all officials should take the oaths of allegiance prescribed by law. These were significant restrictions of the kind which the charter magistrates had stoutly resisted in earlier years. Yet they would not seriously impair the essential autonomy in the day-to-day exercise of godly rule which a restoration of the freemen's powers to choose the rulers of Massachusetts would permit. On January 1, 1691, by an order in council, William referred the various proposals with their supporting documents to the Lords of Trade for examination and report.[107]

Some thirty months after Mather had reached England, therefore, he was embarked upon what was to prove the final phase of his mission, the drafting of a new charter for Massachusetts. Within the closely knit world of royal government his diplomacy had come full

---

[107] Proposals of the agents, [Jan. 1, 1691], C.O. 5/855, no. 130; Proposals for making Massachusetts more dependent, [Dec. 1690?], C.O. 5/856, no. 158xxxiii (a version of this identified as proposals by the law officers and justices, and dated Dec. 24, 1690, is in Carte MSS., 81, fol. 754); Elisha Cooke to Simon Bradstreet, May 9, 1691, Prince Papers; Order of the King in Council, Jan. 1, 1691, Mass. Hist. Soc., *Collections*, 4th ser., II (1854), 301. This last order forwarded a collection of papers, not just the agents' proposals, and Cooke's invaluable letter shows that this collection consisted of a draft of a new charter with supporting documents. *CSP Col., 1689-1692*, no. 1443, provides a two-page calendar of over two hundred manuscript pages of documents bearing upon the preparation of the Massachusetts charter (C.O. 5/856, no. 158, foll. 418-523), and several of these clearly belong to the Dec. 1690 conferences of the agents and the legal committee. Among them are an abstract of Gorges's 1639 Maine charter (*ibid.*, no. 158xxii) endorsed, and mentioned by the agents in their proposals, as having accompanied the proposals and used as a model for broadening the powers of the old Massachusetts charter; a draft of the old charter modernized in this fashion with corrections and interlineations (*ibid.*, no. 158iii); and the agents' proposals set against the old charter with the legal committee's additions (*ibid.*, no. 158xxxiv).

circle, from Whitehall and St. James's Palace, to Westminster, and back to Whitehall again. Throughout, he had taken and held the initiative, playing upon James's political needs, enlisting new allies as they rose to power, and profiting from the currents of the post-Revolutionary settlement and the Whigs' innate sympathy for any measures likely to circumscribe the prerogative. Clearsighted and energetic in pursuit of his one supreme objective, he seemed once more upon the verge of success. Royal officials, by contrast, had still not settled upon a policy that would steer clear of the taint of James's discredited methods and yet avoid the opposite extreme of tamely permitting the colonists to reassert their old autonomy. Advocates of a stronger royal control such as Blathwayt and Southwell had been kept on the defensive by Mather's careful identification of his cause with that of the revolution in England—to oppose the one was made to seem disloyalty to the other. On the debit side, however, it was now more than two years since William's invasion, and this unity of theme and sentiment was dissolving into the more customary separation of colonial from English domestic affairs. Already the circumstances of Andros's acquittal gave warning of a more skeptical attitude toward New England's claims. Fresh accounts were filtering into Whitehall of the fortunes of the post-Revolutionary governments and the fate of their ambitious plans for a counterattack against the French. Even as the agents waited for the committee of trade to report on their proposals, therefore, circumstances on both sides of the Atlantic moved toward a new and more unfavorable conjunction, menacing all the advantages so laboriously won.

# IV

## "New England's Sad Condition": Transatlantic Interaction and the Fruits of Compromise

The negotiations that followed the referral of the agents' proposals to the committee of trade and concluded nine months later in October 1691 with the sealing of a new Massachusetts charter continued and built upon Mather's patient diplomacy in London. Yet a full explanation of their course and final outcome requires that they now be set in the larger context of the resumption of the transatlantic political ties interrupted by the Glorious Revolution. During the earlier years of his mission, Mather had been able to sway the course of royal policy through personal lobbying and backstairs politicking within the confines of Westminster and Whitehall; his reluctant acceptance by the end of 1691 of a settlement reimposing a royal governor upon Massachusetts was in large measure dictated by more impersonal and external circumstances—the course of events (and Whitehall's perception of those events) in New England, the changing climate of English politics, and the intervention of a group of colonists and former supporters of the Dominion who were opposed to Mather's stand. An understanding of these circumstances illuminates both the nature of the settlement and its acceptance in New England. From these and similar circumstances in later years, moreover, would come the enduring forces that governed New England's relations with London into the following century.

At the forefront of the mounting opposition to Mather and his fellow agents stood Andros, Randolph, and their colonial allies in London. Exhilarated by their acquittal and by a sympathetic reception from the king when Secretary Nottingham introduced them at an au-

dience at Kensington Palace a few days later, they had begun a vigorous campaign to discredit the post-Revolutionary governments in
New England. Andros prepared a lengthy vindication of his administration, and in May 1690 he submitted a detailed account of the dis-
astrous effects of its overthrow upon the colonists' security from
enemy attack. Randolph chimed in with a fervor heightened by his
unemployment—his post of collector of customs in New England had
already been assigned (as his sinecure of surveyor of the woods was
shortly to be) to a wealthy Rhode Islander, Jahleel Brenton. With the
aid of his friends among the customs commissioners, he launched an
investigation into the revival of illegal trade in New England, presenting a formidable list of shipowners who had violated the Navigation Acts during the period of his imprisonment. The true purpose of
the Boston revolutionaries, he charged, was "to Restore to themselves
a free Trade for their Vessells to all parts of Europe."[1] He and Dudley
may also have had a hand in the composition of two pamphlets published at this time which further embroidered upon the themes of
New England's trade and defense. A third, John Palmer's *An Impartial
Account*, was printed in London in June 1690.[2] All the while, Usher
and Brinley were forwarding to the Plantation Office a stream of
carefully chosen letters, from such towns as Newport, Salem, Marblehead, and Boston, telling of internal strife and military disaster. "Wee

---

[1] Thomas Brinley to [Francis Brinley], May 28, 1690, Miscellaneous MSS., R. I.
Hist. Soc.; Elisha Cooke to Simon Bradstreet, Oct. 16, 1690, Mass. Hist. Soc.,
*Proceedings*, XLV (1911-1912), 649-651; Answer of Andros to his instructions,
[Apr. 1690?], C.O. 5/855, no. 90; Andros's Account of the state of New England,
May 27, 1690, *N. Y. Col. Docs.*, III, 722-726; Randolph's account of irregular
trade in New England, 1690, *Randolph Letters*, V, 35-44; Michael G. Hall, *Edward
Randolph*, 133-134; Andrews, *Colonial Period*, IV, 150n. Brenton is known to have
met with Mather, and it is possible that the latter incited Brenton to supplant
Randolph: *Collections of the New-York Historical Society for the Year 1868* (New York,
1868), 298.

[2] C. D., *New-England's Faction Discovered, Andros Tracts*, II, 205-221 (see also An-
drews, *Narratives of the Insurrections*, 227-228); N. N., *A Short Account of the Present
State of New-England, Anno Domini 1690* (London, 1690) (a manuscript copy en-
dorsed "a malicious libel against New-England by a friend of Sir Edmund
Andros, Anno 1690" is in Miscellaneous Bound MSS., 1679-93, Mass. Hist.
Soc.); Palmer, *An Impartial Account, Andros Tracts*, I, 23-62. For other attacks on
Massachusetts, in print or manuscripts, see Perry, *Historical Collections*, III, 39-64,
and the materials forwarded by Randolph, *Randolph Letters*, VI, 312.

are heare in Great Confusion and without any Government. . . . Each Tub stands upon his owne bottome. . . . Wee are in a way of Utter Ruine unless God wonderfully prevents, we . . . have nothing but tumultuous Riotous actions and sore divisions among our Selves, Every man a Governor and I am afraid this people will growe soe unruly that Nothing butt an Imediate Governor from the King will or can rule them. . . . God grant the King may take our distressed State into consideration." One writer gleefully reported the cry of the soldiers in the streets of Boston after they had been fobbed off with paper debentures in lieu of pay for service in Maine: "God blesse King William, God blesse Sir Ed: Andros, and Damm all pumpkin states."[3]

Still more damaging, because they seemed to represent a genuine upsurge of popular feeling, were the petitions that began to arrive in London early in 1690. Sixteen settlers of Maine and fifty-eight inhabitants of Great Island in New Hampshire testified to the deplorable state of the frontier. Andros had cherished and protected them but the revolutionary government in Boston had abandoned all of eastern New England to the enemy. Three hundred lives had been lost, the fisheries and the trade in lumber and naval stores destroyed.[4] Two further petitions, from twelve citizens of Charlestown and forty-five men describing themselves as gentlemen and merchants of Boston, confirmed these reports, and another from the town's Anglican minister and churchwardens added details of the persecution of their

---

[3] Bullivant, "Journal," 106; Francis to Thomas Brinley, July 15, [James Lloyd?] to John Usher, July 10, Benjamin Davis to Edward Hull, July 31, 1689, Charles Redford to Sir Edmund Andros, Mar. 7, 1690, C.O. 5/855, nos. 29, 16, 68. See also *ibid.*, nos. 33, 40, 41, 62, 73–80. Many of these letters are endorsed as having been read to the committee at the meeting of May 29, 1690, attended by Carmarthen, Nottingham, Powle, Goodricke, and the Bishop of London: C.O. 391/6, 324–325.

[4] Petition and address of the inhabitants of Maine and the County of Cornwall, Jan. 25, 1690, C.O. 5/855, no. 55 (printed in *Andros Tracts*, I, 176–178); Petition of the inhabitants of Great Island and Narrative of the state of Great Island, May 15, 1690, C.O. 5/855, nos. 92, 93. The calendared version of the latter passes over an entire page (fol. 250) of forty-two signatures. Nathaniel Fryer, Sr., his son Nathaniel, and his two sons-in-law, John Hinckes and Robert Elliott, together with Shadrach Walton, seem to have led in drawing up the petition: Bullivant, "Journal," 107.

communicants.[5] A sixth petition circulated in Massachusetts later in the year depicted a divided and bankrupt country. It bore sixty-three signatures, twenty-six of which had appeared on earlier petitions.[6] All the petitions begged for royal assistance, the New Hampshire men seeking the return of a general governor and the Bostoners expressing their hope that royal commissioners would be dispatched or a governor and council appointed to rule the reunited colonies with the aid of an assembly elected by freeholders and inhabitants.

The agents strove to find an antidote for this "poyson" spread by those they denounced as "N[ew] E[ngland] toryes," and their alarm testified to its effect upon the negotiations for the charter. "The Toryes Labour to fill mens eares and hearts with horror on the account of the pretended desolation and confusion of New England and say the land will be ruined except a generall Governour be sent," wrote Wiswall back to Plymouth. "I believe some in NE will be ashamed when they heare the Extracts of their own writings."[7] Much of the discontent expressed in such writings clearly stemmed from immediate or parochial grievances—the resentment of settlers beyond the Merrimack over Boston's failure to defend them, the dislike of the Great Islanders for the domination of New Hampshire politics by the mainland towns, and the more general anxieties aroused as the heady rhetoric of revolution subsided into the grim realities of war and skyrocketing taxes. They were not the manifestoes of a new or coherent

---

[5] Address of sundry inhabitants of Charlestown, [Jan. 1690], C.O. 5/855, no. 59 (printed in Frothingham, *History of Charlestown*, 230–231); Address of divers gentlemen . . . of Boston, Jan. 25, 1690, of Samuel Myles, Francis Foxcroft, and Samuel Ravenscroft, Jan. 25, 1690, C.O. 5/855, nos. 56, 58 (the latter is printed in Mass. Hist. Soc., *Collections*, 3rd ser., VII [1838], 192–195).

[6] Address of divers inhabitants of Charlestown, Boston, and places adjacent, [presented in London, Apr. 9, 1691], C.O. 5/856, nos. 143–145. Again the printed calendar is a poor guide; it cites the address as it was printed in London with thirty-four signatures (also *Andros Tracts*, II, 236–239), but the manuscript petition (C.O. 5/856, fol. 392) had sixty-one signatures, including thirty-two of the thirty-four as printed, making sixty-three in all. Internal evidence indicates that this petition was circulated in New England in Nov. 1690.

[7] Cooke to Bradstreet, Oct. 16, 1690, Mass. Hist. Soc., *Proceedings*, XLV (1911–1912), 652; Wiswall to John Cotton, Oct. 17, 1690, Curwin Papers, III, 23, Amer. Antiq. Soc.

political movement. Yet the agents' alarm was understandable, for in the context of the traditional canons of New England political behavior these letters and petitions represented still another step in the colonists' gradual accommodation to the presence of royal authority. Their dispatch to London was in itself an open challenge to the competence and self-sufficiency of charter rule, a deliberate violation of the unwritten fundamental law barring appeals to an outside power which had governed the politics of colonies such as Massachusetts since the time in the 1640s when Robert Child had attempted to invoke the authority of the English parliament.

In composition also, as in tactics and intent, the petitioners of 1690 bore little resemblance to those moderates who had questioned the charter governments' intransigence a decade before. Almost without exception, the latter had been freemen and church members. Born into the colonial elite, many of them held high political office; they had worked for a compromise solution from within and through the structure of government. Indeed, of those who had accepted the necessity of an accommodation with the crown in the 1680s, Bradstreet, Stoughton, Saltonstall, Shrimpton, and Wait Winthrop were now leaders in the very Boston administration castigated in the petitions. Others, such as Bartholemew Gedney and a group of his political allies in Salem, though critical of their government's failure to obtain aid from England and reopen negotiations with the Iroquois, pointedly disclaimed any intention of bypassing its authority by appealing directly to the crown. Of the moderate faction, only Dudley and Usher remained irretrievably estranged from charter rule.[8]

In contrast, less than a tenth of the one hundred and sixty-three individuals who signed the six petitions can be identified as freemen even when the names of those then being nominated for freemanship are taken into account. In 1690, none sat in any of the General Courts

---

[8] Petition of Bartholemew Gedney and others, [c. Dec. 1690], *Doc. Hist. Maine,* V, 172-173. Only Nicholas Paige and John Pynchon, Jr. and Sr., can be identified as known former moderates among those signing the petitions. Dudley and Usher were already in London; two others who might have signed, Richard Wharton and Peter Bulkeley, were dead.

of New England. Only Nathaniel Fryer of Portsmouth held an official position of any importance. At least sixteen had served in government under Andros, however, and the brief taste of power had doubtless sharpened the edge of their discontent. Religious affiliations help to explain this pattern of exclusion from office under charter rule and service during the Dominion, for twenty-nine of the ninety-one subscribers to the three petitions circulated in Boston and Charlestown had contributed toward the construction of an Anglican church, and twelve were later churchwardens of the completed King's Chapel. Two more were reputed Quakers.[9]

The petitioners were heterodox in other respects. Those whose occupations are known were coastal merchants, frontier farmers, or seagoing captains and traders—additional evidence, perhaps, that they lacked the lineage and political influence which had endowed the moderates with landed estates through inheritance and opportunities for speculation. As the Massachusetts government hastened to inform London, some were "mear Strangers and transient Sojourners"—recent immigrants.[10] Others, however, were undeniably well established and prominent in the commercial life of the colony. John Nelson, Nicholas Paige, Nathaniel Byfield, and David Waterhouse of Boston and Laurence Hammond and Richard Sprague of Charlestown were all merchants who had been in the forefront of the revolution in April 1689 only to find themselves ousted as the Council of Safety succumbed to the popular pressure for a resumption of charter rule. Nelson had twice felt the sting of public disfavor. He had been relieved from command of the fort at Boston on suspicion of being too lax in his treatment of the imprisoned governor. Then, after he had

---

[9] Foote, *Annals of King's Chapel,* I, 89. This list undoubtedly includes some who were not Anglicans and who merely thought it politic to support what then, under Andros, seemed to be the coming religion. Most, however, were Anglicans. Three more petitioners not upon this list of subscribers later contributed to the furnishing of the church (*ibid.,* 117).

[10] Massachusetts to the agents, Oct. 14, 1691, Mass. Archives, XXXVII, 172; see also Simon Bradstreet to the Earl of Shrewsbury, Oct. 26, 1689, C.O. 5/855, no. 45 (this was not sent to the Lords of Trade, as stated in *CSP Col., 1689–1692,* no. 513), and the acute analysis in Thomas Danforth to Increase Mather, July 30, 1689, Hutchinson, *Papers,* II, 313.

helped to propose and organize the expedition against Port Royal, "the Country Deputies said he was a Merchant and not to be trusted," so the command was given to Sir William Phips.[11]

Nelson's experiences point to a further unifying theme in the petitions and ultimately to their larger significance. As the deputies knew and Phips took care to recall in his subsequent account of the Port Royal expedition, Nelson was intimately involved in trade with Acadia.[12] Some of the petitioners, such as those embattled on the frontier, would doubtless have sided with Phips in his belief that it was more patriotic to plunder the French than to do business with them. But the merchants of the Bay and the settlers beyond the Merrimack did agree about the urgent need for a stronger official commitment to defense and commercial expansion. Such a policy, they believed, could come only through renewed cooperation with England. Few wholeheartedly endorsed the autocratic ways of the Andros regime. Yet as Francis Brinley, another who signed the petitions, observed, "an oppressive government is to be preferred before an anarchy [though] a just and easy government, let the forme be how it will, is my wishes and desire."[13] Any government was better than none. Moreover,

---

[11] "A Particular Account," in Andrews, *Narratives of the Insurrections*, 202, 205–206; Bullivant, "Journal," 106. For Nelson's role in organizing the expedition, see the documents printed from Mass. Archives, XXXV, 160–162, 172–173, in *Doc. Hist. Maine*, V, 25–28, 30–31, and Sewall, *Diary*, I, 252, 255.

[12] *Journal of the Proceedings of the late Expedition to Port-Royal, on board their Majesties Ship, the Six-Friends, the Honourable Sr. William Phipps Knight, Commander in Chief*, 6–7 (also C.O. 5/855, no. 109). "Mr. Nelson's Warehouse" at Port Royal is mentioned three times. The enmity of Nelson and Phips was exacerbated by Nelson's attempt to protect the captured governor of Port Royal and the latter's property against Phips's breach of the terms of surrender; it culminated in Phips's refusal to help save Nelson from ten years of French imprisonment: Sewall, *Diary*, I, 271, 273; letter of Cotton Mather, Mar. 20, 1712, Mather Papers, Amer. Antiq. Soc.; petition of Nelson, Nov. 30, 1698, Mass. Archives, LXX, 389. Thus the rejection of Nelson as commander of the expedition is somewhat more than an example of antimerchant prejudice. Warden, *Boston*, 50, recasts the episode into an election for the General Court.

[13] Brinley to Wait Winthrop, May 6, 1689, Mass. Hist. Soc., *Collections*, 6th ser., V (1892), 21. Similarly, several of the Maine settlements placed security before ideological purity and petitioned that the brutal but evidently efficient English officers stationed with them by Andros be allowed to remain to organize their defense rather than being replaced or imprisoned: *Doc. Hist. Maine*, VI, 477–479. Fears of anarchy were a frequent theme of the letters to England.

whatever its faults, the Dominion had provided a glimpse of an alternative to the isolationism and constricting orthodoxy of charter rule. Prior to its coming, those such as the petitioners had cheerfully or at least silently acquiesced in their exclusion from the governing elite. Royal intervention had fomented disagreement among those already in office rather than between those in and out of power. Now, for the first time, emboldened by the Dominion and the misfortunes of its aftermath, a sizable and newly politicized faction within Massachusetts was appealing for action by the crown that would effectively put an end to charter rule. Very few members of this faction ever achieved high office, but this was relatively unimportant. The petitioners of 1690 had perceived that their influence did not necessarily depend upon their standing among their fellow colonists. Nor was the political horizon bounded by the shores of New England. The old world could be brought in to redress the balance of the new; influence and direction were to be found through an alliance with the royal government whose concern for colonial trade and security precisely matched their own. This implicit coalition of interest with Whitehall was to prove a lasting one throughout the American colonies: ninety years later, the loyalist cause found its most devoted adherents among the frontiersmen of the west and the traders of the Atlantic seaboard.

The agents struggled tenaciously to counter these assaults. They drew up answers to the charges filed by Andros and Randolph, and they submitted a memorial denigrating the subscribers of the petitions as opponents of the revolution and disappointed men of little estate.[14] But they found their way strewn with obstacles. Letters at-

---

[14] Answer to Randolph's Account, *Andros Tracts*, II, 127–134; Answer to Andros's Account, *ibid.*, III, 34–38; Ashurst, Cooke, Mather, and Oakes to the Lords of Trade, [Apr. 21, 1691], C.O. 5/856, no. 150. The memorial by the agents drew a prompt response listing the estimated wealth of sixty of the signers of the sixth petition (note 6, preceding). Forty-five were credited with estates ranging between one thousand and twelve thousand pounds each, and twenty-six were described as merchants: *ibid.*, no. 157.

tacking the New England governments were copied and read to the Privy Council and its committee of trade with suspicious alacrity while the agents waited in the antechambers of Whitehall for days on end to present their case. Meanwhile they were harassed by claims for damages and back pay brought by former officers of the Dominion. King William had once remarked of Blathwayt that, although dull, "hee had a good method." Clearly the secretary and his associates in the Plantation Office had already mastered the skills of shaping policy through procedural techniques and the manipulation of agenda.[15]

Moreover, the agents could not deny that, since the brief solace of Phips's capture of Port Royal, the news from New England had grown steadily worse. Even before the organization of this expedition, the New England governments had been considering more ambitious ways of taking the offensive by assaulting the main centers of French power in Quebec and Montreal. Plans for such a strategy were almost as old as royal interest in the northern colonies. In 1666 the crown had pressed Massachusetts and Connecticut to attack Canada, and Dongan had subsequently urged an overland assault up the Hudson valley, Randolph a thrust by sea down the St. Lawrence. The colonists themselves had been reluctant to disturb their peaceful coexistence with the French.[16] But these inhibitions melted as French designs became plain. By mid-1689, several perceptive leaders, among them Nicholas Bayard of New York, John Pynchon of Springfield on the Massachusetts frontier, and the commissioners of the New England Confederation meeting at Boston, were pressing for a revival of the scheme. The commissioners sent by Massachusetts to Albany in

---

[15] Cooke to Bradstreet, Oct. 16, 1690, Mass. Hist. Soc., *Proceedings*, XLV (1911–1912), 650–651; Petitions of John Riggs, [Apr. 25], of John Usher, Sept. 28, of Sir Edmund Andros, Sept. 28, 1691, *CSP Col., 1689–1692*, nos. 1429, 1791, 1792; Petition of Lt. James Weems, Feb. 26, 1691, *APC Col.*, II, no. 398; Cooke to Bradstreet, May 9, 1691, Prince Papers; Foxcroft, *Life and Letters of Halifax*, II, 226.

[16] Charles II to Massachusetts, Feb. 22, 1666, Mass. Hist. Soc., *Collections*, 2nd ser., VIII (1826), 101–102; Gov. John Winthrop, Jr., to Secretary of State Lord Arlington, Oct. 25, 1666, *ibid.*, 5th ser., VIII (1882), 101–103; *Mass. Records*, IV, pt. ii, 316, 328.

September were authorized to discuss such a project, and on his return Pynchon wrote to Bradstreet of his belief that "we shall never be quiet as long as we have those il Neighbors the French in Canida and at the eastward Girdling us about."[17]

The decisive impetus was given by the three-pronged French assault that fell upon the northern colonial frontier early the following year. In the snowy depths of winter, just before midnight on February 8, 1690, a party of Indians and Canadian *coureurs de bois* crept into Schenectady, twenty miles from Albany, and massacred the sleeping inhabitants. The news had scarcely reached New England when the two other war parties dispatched by Frontenac fell upon the eastern settlements beyond the Merrimack, beginning a series of raids which drove the line of English settlement back almost to the banks of the Piscataqua.[18]

The very scope of this assault, coupled with rumors of new French attempts to subvert the Iroquois from their alliance with the English, drew the colonial governments into prompt and unprecedented collaboration. Letters from Albany appealing for aid told of the Five Nations' request that New England prepare a naval expedition against Canada, and a delegation from the town, headed by Robert Livingston, followed in March to reemphasize the need for a concerted assault—"the only way is to strike at the head by taking Quebeck and then all the rest must follow." Albany's position was the more precarious because of its leaders' refusal to recognize the government of Jacob Leisler, New York's self-appointed ruler since the overthrow of the Dominion. Leisler was equally determined to display his

---

[17] Nicholas Bayard to Francis Nicholson, Aug. 5, 1689, *N. Y. Col. Docs.*, III, 611–612; Commissioners of the New England Confederation to Massachusetts, Oct. 25, Dec. 6, 1689, Mass. Archives, XXXV, 63, 106; Instructions to the commissioners sent to Albany, Aug. 1689, *ibid.*, CVII, 284; Pynchon to [Bradstreet], Dec. 5, 1689, *ibid.*, XXXV, 102–103; Arthur H. Buffinton, "The Isolationist Policy of Colonial Massachusetts," 175–177.

[18] Parkman, *Count Frontenac*, 208–234; Documents on the burning of Schenectady, *Doc. Hist. N. Y.*, I, 285–312; Charles Frost and Francis Hooke to Simon Bradstreet, Mar. 25, 1690, Moody, *Saltonstall Papers*, 195–196; John T. Hull, *The Siege and Capture of Fort Loyall, Destruction of Falmouth, May 20, 1690(O.S.), passim*.

authority, and he in turn sent out a call to neighboring colonies to assist in planning joint measures against the French.[19]

The New England governments needed little persuasion. Early in March, the Massachusetts General Court had decided that the emergency justified public sponsorship of the expedition in preparation against Port Royal, hitherto the private venture of a group of Bay merchants led by John Nelson. A week later, after both Livingston and an emissary from Leisler had arrived in Boston, the court ordered letters to be written to colonies as far south as Virginia and Maryland suggesting a meeting at New York "to Advise and Conclude on Sutable Methods in assisting each other for the Safety of the whole Land."[20] Probably because of the dispute between New York and Albany, Governor Bradstreet subsequently proposed that the meeting be held in Rhode Island—a location aptly symbolizing the way in which external threats were compelling New Englanders to sink old differences in a common cause. At length, however, after Albany had submitted to Leisler's authority, all fell in with the latter's proposal of an intercolonial conference at New York.[21] There, on May 1, 1690,

---

[19] The Convention of Albany to Massachusetts and Connecticut, Feb. 15, 1690, *Andros Tracts*, III, 114–115, Conn. Archives, War, II, 30; Jonathan Bull to Connecticut, Feb. 14, 1690, *ibid.*, 29; Colden, *History of the Five Nations*, 93–101; Albany Convention Records, Feb. 15, 27, 1690, Propositions of the Maquas and reply of the Albany officials, Feb. 25, 26, 1690, Leisler to the government of Maryland and to Governor Bradstreet, Mar. 4, 1690, *Doc. Hist. N. Y.*, II, 159, 171, 164–170, 181–185; Memorial of the Albany agents to Massachusetts, Mar. 20, 1690, *N. Y. Col. Docs.*, III, 697; Leder, *Robert Livingston*, 65–68. It has been suggested that the Iroquois were incapable of formulating the plans for a joint attack on Canada; W. D. Schuyler-Lightall, "The 'Glorious Enterprise,' " 1–37, assigns the plan to Pieter Schuyler and other Albany leaders who gave it weight by attributing it to the Iroquois. The evidence cited above, however, suggests that Parkman (*Count Frontenac*, 235) is correct in ascribing the plan to the Iroquois. Indeed, they clearly spoke of a combined attack by land and sea while the Albany magistrates, perhaps fearing an attack by Leisler, emphasized the need for a naval expedition.

[20] Orders of the General Court, Mar. 14, 19, 1690, *N. H. Laws*, I, 366, 370.

[21] Bradstreet to Connecticut, Mar. 24, to Leisler, Mar. 25, Gov. Henry Bull of Rhode Island to Bradstreet, Apr. 18, 1690, *Doc. Hist. Maine*, V, 63–67, 80; John Walley to Thomas Hinckley, Apr. 7, Governor and Council of Massachusetts to Hinckley, Apr. 11, Hinckley to Leisler, Apr. 17, 1690, Mass. Hist. Soc., *Collections*, 4th ser., V (1861), 233–234, 239, 242–244; Connecticut to Leisler, Apr. 11, Leisler to the governors of the neighboring provinces, Apr. 2, 1690, *Doc. Hist. N. Y.*, II, 232, 211.

commissioners from Connecticut, Plymouth, Massachusetts, and New York drew up plans for the dispatch of some eight hundred and fifty men to reinforce Albany with the expectation that they would launch an overland attack on Canada. The Iroquois undertook to provide twice as many warriors. Rhode Island promised (but never delivered) three hundred pounds. Massachusetts at first held back from any larger involvement. But in June, encouraged by the capture of Port Royal, the colony began preparations on a grand scale for a seaborne expedition aganst Quebec.[22]

Cotton Mather, ever concerned for his country's reputation abroad, held forth upon the service to England that a conquest of Canada would perform. Such an incentive had counted for little in the past, however, and at bottom the colonists were drawn to adopt an offensive strategy by motives of self-interest—a newly enlightened self-interest. Whatever the value of Frontenac's raids in rekindling Canadian morale, they had convinced New Englanders of the need to view their defense in continental terms. "By this action," wrote Bradstreet on hearing of the destruction of Schenectady, "the French have given us to understand what we may expect from them as to the frontier towns and seaports of New England." Reports from New York told of an impending attack upon Albany by twenty-five hundred of the enemy and the coming of a French fleet to Canada with two thousand more soldiers in the summer.[23] Should we not consider, wrote one pamphleteer, "whether we are now evidently reduced unto that extream Dilemma that either *New-England* or New-France must

---

[22] Agreement of the Commissioners, May 1, 1690, *Doc. Hist. N. Y.*, II, 239–240; Instructions to the Massachusetts Commissioners, Apr. 17, 1690, *Doc. Hist. Maine*, V, 76–78; William Stoughton and Samuel Sewall to John Pynchon, May 2, 1690, Mass. Hist. Soc., *Collections*, 2nd ser., VIII (1826), 238; Proposals of the Commissioners of Albany, May 3, 1690, *N. Y. Col. Docs.*, III, 712–714; Leisler to the Western Governments, May 13, to Governor Treat, May 29, 1690, *Doc. Hist. N. Y.*, II, 242, 254–256; *R. I. Records*, III, 273; Orders of the Massachusetts General Court, June 6, 7, 1690, *N. H. Laws*, I, 409, 411.

[23] Cotton Mather, *The Present State of New-England*, 33; Bradstreet to Hinckley, Mar. 11, Leisler to Hinckley, Apr. 3, 1690, Mass. Hist. Soc., *Collections*, 4th ser., V (1861), 230, 233; John Allyn to Fitz-John Winthrop, Mar. 3, 18, 1690, Winthrop Papers; *Propositions Made by the Sachems of the Three Maqua Castles;* Conn. Archives, War, II, 34–40.

unavoidably perish? Whether all our Encounters with several Bodies or Nations of *Indians* that may quarrel with us, be not meerly a lopping of Branches, whereas by an attack upon *Port Royal* and *Canada,* we fall upon the Root of all our Miseries?" As John Nelson tartly observed, "by a defensive warr nothing but bare defence cann be hoped for." A conquest of Canada would put an end to the French machinations held to be responsible for the hostility of the eastern Indians; and the mere attempt, Bradstreet believed, would "gain some reputation with the Five Nations," keeping alive the hope that some day the Iroquois would lend their aid to the struggle in Maine.[24]

By the beginning of August 1690, the forces of Connecticut and New York were encamped at Albany under the command of Fitz-John Winthrop. In Boston harbor, an armada of thirty-two vessels led by Phips awaited the embarkation of some two thousand men drawn from among the local friendly Indians and the militia regiments of Massachusetts and Plymouth. Leisler, desperate for the success that would sanctify his tottering regime in the eyes of officials in Whitehall, had solicited aid from as far afield as Barbados and Bermuda. But zeal and fair words could not make up for a fatal inexperience in the novel task of intercolonial collaboration. From the first the campaign was poorly planned and coordinated. Hartford could not decide whether the Albany venture was to be feint or full-scale attack. New York furnished less than half its quota of men and the Massachusetts contingent was diverted to the defense of the eastern frontier.[25] Under Winthrop's halfhearted leadership, the expedition marched a hundred miles to the shores of Lake Champlain only to find that there were not enough canoes for the final stage of the jour-

[24] *Further Quaeries, Andros Tracts,* I, 200; Proposals of John Nelson, Jan. 4, 1690, *Doc. Hist. Maine,* V, 26; Bradstreet to Hinckley, Mar. 11, 1690, Mass. Hist. Soc., *Collections,* 4th ser., V (1861), 230; (also Bradstreet to Governor Bull, Mar. 10, to Leisler, Mar. 25, 1690, Mass. Archives, XXXV, 284, 364).

[25] Governor and Council of Connecticut to Massachusetts, May 15, July 11, 1690, *Doc. Hist. Maine,* V, 96–98; Conn. Hist. Soc., *Collections,* XXI (1924), 323–324; Bradstreet to Leisler, May 30, 1690, *Doc. Hist. N. Y.,* II, 259.

ney to Montreal. The crowning blow was the failure of the Iroquois to provide more than a token contingent of warriors. As their sachems observed, smallpox was spreading among the tribes and within the English camp. But the explanation of one perceptive contemporary was no less convincing; the Indians were loath to assist in disturbing a balance of power that made their services so much in demand. On August 15, Winthrop and his officers bowed to the inevitable. Leaving behind a small raiding party to harass the settlements around Montreal, they began to retrace their steps to Albany.[26]

Meanwhile, the fleet at Boston waited in vain for a much needed cargo of ammunition requested from England.[27] The delay confounded the colonists' strategy of a simultaneous assault: the expedition set sail less than a week before Winthrop began his retreat, and contrary winds prevented its arrival until early October. Frontenac had just time enough to bring his forces back from Montreal where they had been guarding against the overland attack. Within a few days Quebec's garrison outnumbered its besiegers. Soon the river would be choked by ice. Phips, a resourceful sailor, proved an incompetent general. Thirteen hundred militia were landed, but before they could take up position, he squandered the fleet's supply of powder in a vain bombardment of the city's craggy walls. The troops ashore, under the uncertain—some said cowardly—leadership of Maj. John Walley of Plymouth, spent three days and nights, freezing and half-starved, in skirmishes with the enemy. Reembarkation became a rout, and five cannon were left behind. Nothing more could be done, and the fleet, buffeted by winter storms, straggled back to

---

[26] "Reflections upon the Affairs of New England," 334–336; Dunn, *Puritans and Yankees,* 290–294. Winthrop's letters and his journal of the expedition are in Mass. Hist. Soc., *Collections,* 5th ser., VIII (1882), 308–322, Conn. Archives, War, II, 102, 115, 117, 125.

[27] Green, "Two Narratives," 306; Danforth to Ashurst, Apr. 1, 1690, Hutchinson, *History of Massachusetts-Bay,* I, 337n.; Governor and Council of Massachusetts to the king, Mar. 29, 1690, C.O. 5/855, no. 71. These pleas were heard (*CSP Col., 1689–1692,* nos. 910, 911, 941), but the stores did not arrive until January 1691: Mass. Archives, Court Records, VI, Feb. 6, 1691, and John Cotton to Rowland Cotton, Jan. 31, 1691, Prince Papers.

Boston. Some ships were blown as far afield as the Caribbean, and several were wrecked or lost at sea.[28]

The failure of the "glorious enterprise" against Canada was a crippling blow. The casualties of battle were few, but disease and misadventure, the inevitable camp followers of any contemporary campaign, took a far higher toll. In all, some three or four hundred of Phips's men were lost—many of the Indians enlisted from Plymouth Colony were among those "thrown over" on the long voyage home.[29] The smallpox and dysentery which had reached Boston earlier in the year flared up within the crowded ships, and the soldiers scattered the infection on their return. More than half the men enlisted for Canada from Dorchester and Braintree, for example, died as a result of their service, and in Dorchester fifty-seven more inhabitants died in the epidemic that followed.[30]

The expeditions also bequeathed to the colonies a crushing burden of public debt. Connecticut ordered two fourpenny rates in 1690 and another of threepence in each of the next two years—"we had no 4 penny or 8 penny rates in Sir Edmund's time," remarked the embittered Gershom Bulkeley. The Plymouth General Court imposed two massive taxes, each of £1,350, in successive months, bringing the amount assessed in the twenty months since the revolution to nearly a tenth of the total rated property value of the colony.[31] Massachusetts

---

[28] Ernest Myrand, *Sir William Phips Devant Québec;* Walter K. Watkins, "The Expedition to Canada in 1690 under Sir William Phips," 111–232; *Report of the Public Archives of Canada for 1912,* 64–66; William J. Eccles, *Frontenac, the Courtier Governor,* 234–243; C. P. Stacey, *Introduction to the Study of Military History for Canadian Students,* 47–56.

[29] Sewall, *Diary,* I, 269, 279; *New England Historical and Genealogical Register,* XCIX (1945), 307–314. Some escaped shipwreck and passage to Barbados only to be impressed by the British navy: petition of Thomas Jackson, Mass. Archives, LXX, 507.

[30] John Duffy, *Epidemics in Colonial America,* 48; Sewall, *Diary,* I, 250, 259–262, 269–271; Winsor, *Memorial History of Boston,* II, 359–360 (of the 921 Dorchester inhabitants who died between 1657 and 1734, 103 died in the eighteen months after April 1691); Charles F. Adams, *Three Episodes of Massachusetts History,* 830. Disease also took a heavy toll in Rhode Island and Connecticut.

[31] *Conn. Records,* IV, 16, 37, 60, 84; Bulkeley, "Will and Doom," 193; *Plymouth*

had borrowed heavily from private citizens in expectation of a rich haul of furs and plunder from the French.[32] Having, as it were, doubled its stake, thrown, and lost, the Boston government found itself deeply in debt and still encumbered with the costly defense of the eastern frontier—four hundred men were kept in arms along and beyond the Merrimack during the summer, and noted Indian-fighter Benjamin Church led a raiding party to Casco Bay in September.[33] Despite the heavy taxes raised at the end of 1689, the General Court levied ten more rates in March, two and a half in July, and no less than twenty in November as the full extent of the government's obligations—estimated by some at over £40,000—became apparent.[34] Not even during King Philip's War had more than sixteen rates been levied in a single year.

Even had these taxes been promptly paid, they would not have been sufficient, and Massachusetts resorted to an expedient that was to characterize colonial finances for many years to come: the circulation of bills of credit as a paper currency. An issue of seven thousand pounds, then of forty, was authorized and the bills declared legal tender for all public payments. Essential though these bills were (and were to be for many years to come) for the financing of war and trade, their short-term effect was unsettling, for no provision was made for

---

*Records*, VI, 215, 220, 253, 255. Richard LeBaron Bowen, "The 1690 Tax Revolt of Plymouth Colony Towns," 4–14, gives a comprehensive account but overstates the tax burden through inadvertent duplication.

[32] Order of the General Court, June 6, 1690, *N. H. Laws*, I, 410–411; Sewall, *Diary*, I, 260; Fitz-John Winthrop to Robert Livingston, June 16, 1690, Mass. Hist. Soc., *Collections*, 5th ser., VIII (1882), 305; abstract of a letter from Boston, July 4, 1690, *Doc. Hist. Maine*, V, 132; petitions from John Richards, Timothy Thornton, *et al.*, [1691–1692], Mass. Archives, C, 416, 452.

[33] *N. H. Laws*, I, 409–410, 412–414, 433–434, 438, 441–444; Church, *History*, 177–196.

[34] *N. H. Laws*, I, 367, 425, 433, 450. The ten and twenty rates were in country pay (the latter with the poll tax lowered to twelvepence), the two and a half at the higher money rate. The comparative burden of the taxes can be seen in the Salem records, Essex Instit., *Historical Collections*, XLVIII (1932), 216–217, 312–314, 316–318, where the twenty rates amounted to nearly one thousand pounds of which a third came from poll money despite the lowering of the poll tax. For hostile but generally similar estimates of the colony's debt, see letter of Samuel Myles, Dec. 12, 1690, of James Lloyd, Jan. 8, 1691, extract from a letter of Dec. 8, 1690, C.O. 5/855, no. 127, 5/856, nos. 131, 138.

their redemption and they promptly depreciated from their face value by as much as one-third. A levy of eight thousand pounds annually for four years imposed early in 1691 was perhaps designed to serve as a sinking fund. Within a few months, the General Court twice moved to hasten its collection and then increased its yield by adjusting the rates by which provisions were accepted in lieu of money. The court also enacted customs duties on both imports and exports that were far broader in scope than those imposed by Andros. In a country where there was always a scarcity of liquid capital, the heavy expenditures of war led irresistibly to financial expedients that, as in England during these same years, were to have far-reaching repercussions on the structure of government.[35]

Considering the political difficulties that had followed the revolution in 1689, overt opposition to these harsh but necessary measures was remarkably infrequent. Several towns in Plymouth Colony continued to withhold payment of their taxes. In Rhode Island, the settlements on the mainland declined to contribute toward coastal defence despite Newport's success in repulsing a squadron of French privateers. Charlestown was still refractory, and Bulkeley and his Wethersfield friends held out against the Hartford government.[36] But this was the limit of popular discontent. Despite the grim tales of internal strife forwarded to London, the voters of Massachusetts continued to deliver resounding majorities to known supporters of the old charter. Compromisers such as Shrimpton, Stoughton, and Pynchon received among the lowest number of votes cast for those elected to

---

[35] *N. H. Laws*, I, 456, 457, 460, 463, 467, 474, 475, 477, 478, 490–492. In addition, the soldiers were paid with paper debentures, *ibid.*, 340, 347, 458. Ten thousand pounds of the paper money was retired late in 1691; Mass. Archives, Court Records, VI, Oct. 24, 1691. For its depreciation, see Francis Foxcroft to Charles Lidgett, Jan. 10, 1691, *New England Historical and Genealogical Register*, XXXIII (1879), 410; [Michael Perry?] to John Usher, [Jan. 1691], C.O. 5/856, no. 136; and [Cotton Mather and John Blackwell?], *Some Considerations on the Bills of Credit now passing in New-England*, in Andrew M. Davis, *Colonial Currency Reprints*, I, 204. On the effects of military expenditures, see P. M. G. Dickson and J. G. Sperling, "War Finance, 1689–1714," 284–315.

[36] Langdon, *Pilgrim Colony*, 233–234; *R. I. Records*, III, 275–276; Gov. John Easton of Rhode Island to Massachusetts, Nov. 17, 1691, Mass. Archives, XXXVII, 212; Order of the Massachusetts General Court, Dec. 11, 1691, *N. H. Laws*, I, 487; Bulkeley, "Will and Doom," 205; *Conn. Records*, IV, 34.

the council or failed of election altogether while their opponents, even when like Cooke, Oakes, and Phips they might be absent from the colony, moved ever higher in the electorate's esteem.[37] Nor were there significant changes in the composition of the General Courts elsewhere in New England.

What occurred was not a convulsion of the body politic, but its slow paralysis. Visitors and colonists alike remarked on New England's prostrate condition, the retrogression of its settlements, and the decay of its trade.[38] Such conditions pointed up the weakness that continued to lie at the heart of the colonists' difficulties—a widespread erosion of leadership and authority. Connecticut managed to regain its steady habits despite the bickering of the partisans of Fitch and Allyn. In Rhode Island, however, smallpox, factionalism, and a general distaste for public service threatened complete disruption. Not that there was much to save: in 1690, the colony treasury contained precisely £27/12/10d. and 269 pounds of wool.[39] And in Massachusetts, the tempo and business of government steadily diminished as an elderly board of magistrates, headed by the octogenarian and frequently bedridden Bradstreet, struggled with an unfamiliar world

---

[37] The names of those nominated and elected in Massachusetts as magistrates in May 1690 (with the votes cast) can be found in Mass. Archives, XXXVI, 54, and C.O. 5/855, no. 99; those elected in 1691 (with vote tallies) in *ibid.*, no. 146 (though the name of Samuel Appleton should replace that of Jeremiah Swaine); and those nominated and elected in 1692 (with vote tallies) in Mass. Hist. Soc., *Collections*, 3rd ser., X (1849), 120–121. Shrimpton and John Richards were replaced by Phips and Oakes in 1690; Pynchon and Stoughton failed of election, although the latter recovered his seat the following year.

[38] Thus Francis Foxcroft to Charles Lidgett, Jan. 10, Sept. 21, Oct. 8, 1691, *New England Historical and Genealogical Register*, XXXIII (1879), 408, and Jeffries Papers, VI, 53; Benjamin Davis to Francis Nicholson, Apr. 17, 1691, Blathwayt Papers, IV, Col. Wmsbg.; Notes taken by Samuel Sewall of Mr. Moody's sermon, Dec. 17, 1690, Commonplace Book of Samuel Sewall, Boston Public Library; Diary of Francis Borland for 1690, Edinburgh University Library (microfilm copy in Mass. Hist. Soc.); Bullivant, "Journal," 105; and, more rhetorically and apocalyptically, Randolph to Blathwayt, Mar. 14, 1693, *Randolph Letters*, VII, 433–434; "News From New England," *Doc. Hist. Maine*, V, 189–190; and the classic description in Hutchinson, *History of Massachusetts-Bay*, II, 9.

[39] General Treasurer's Accounts, 1672–1711, R. I. Archives, fol. 84; *R. I. Records*, III, 263, 273–274; Samuel G. Arnold, *History of the State of Rhode Island and Providence Plantations*, I, 523.

of debts, debentures, and incessant war.[40] The most dramatic break-down of central authority occurred in Plymouth Colony. On its western borders the withholding of taxes and numerous disputes over the election of militia officers swelled into a wholesale repudiation of government.[41] Here, the impact of the war exacerbated older divisions. Several of the western towns, including Bristol, Little Compton, and Freetown, had been settled late in the century, often from neighboring Rhode Island, by immigrants unfamiliar with the ideals and practices of the Pilgrim Fathers. Few had any regular Congregational ministry; Quakers and Baptists were numerous if not predominant in Swansea, Rehoboth, and Dartmouth.[42] Further, their insubordination was encouraged by the new royal government in New York in the hope that Plymouth might yet be incorporated into New York rather than Massachusetts. These problems were by no means insoluble, but the Plymouth leadership did nothing to rally it supporters. Gov. Thomas Hinckley was aged and indecisive, and his council gave him little assistance. By mid-1691, organized government had all but vanished from the colony.[43]

---

[40] I have drawn my conclusions about the winding down of the Massachusetts government from Mass. Archives, Court Records, VI, *passim;* for a particularly plaintive account of the colony's troubles and a plea for the "absolutely necessary" hastening of a royal settlement, see Bradstreet and the Massachusetts Council to the Agents, Nov. 29, 1690, *Andros Tracts,* III, 52–57. The average age of the Massachusetts magistrates present in New England in 1691 was sixty-two; Bradstreet was eighty-seven, and the governors of Plymouth, Connecticut, and Rhode Island were seventy-three, sixty-nine, and sixty-six respectively.

[41] Langdon, *Pilgrim Colony,* 228–229, 232–234, gives the best summary; Samuel H. Emery, *History of Taunton, Massachusetts,* 331–354, gives a more extended account of the difficulties in one town.

[42] Richard LeBaron Bowen, *Early Rehoboth,* I, 24–47, 69–88; *Our County and Its People,* 20–25, 32–33; William G. McLoughlin, *New England Dissent, 1630–1833,* I, 121–122. The close links of the county with the contagions of Rhode Island can be seen in the probate records printed in *New England Historical and Genealogical Register,* LXII (1908)–LXIV (1910).

[43] Hinckley to Governor Bradstreet of Massachusetts, Nov. 13, 1691, *Doc. Hist. Maine,* V, 307–308; *idem* to Increase Mather, Oct. 16, 1691, Mass. Hist. Soc., *Collections,* 4th ser., V (1861), 291; *idem* to Ichabod Wiswall, Oct. 17, 1691, *ibid.,* 296. Hinckley begs Wiswall to obtain "a few lines" from the crown to authorize a temporary government, the want of which has resulted in a widespread defiance of authority: *ibid.,* 295.

## Adjustment to Empire

Plymouth's collapse was unique, but everywhere the leaders of the administrations pieced together in 1689 bent beneath the weight of the burdens imposed by war and the fall of the Dominion. They were, of course, victims of circumstance. Yet their timidity at a time of little public opposition suggests that, as in the months immediately following Andros's overthrow, most still lacked confidence in their right and capacity to govern. The Dominion lay in ruins, but its very existence, as Randolph had prophesied, had unhinged the commonwealths of New England. A few colonists took matters into their own hands: besides those who appealed to London, the leaders of Salem banded together to organize their own defense, and two prominent landowners in the Narragansett country proposed an emergency meeting of all the settlers between Saybrook and Providence to make plans for the common safety.[44] Most, however, sank into a sullen and uncomprehending apathy that trembled on the verge of irrationalism and hysteria. Cotton Mather mirrored the public mood in his vacillation between benign prayers for tolerance and unity in one sermon and fulminations against Anglicans and malcontents in the next.[45] Only in the sudden epidemic of accusations of witchcraft centering upon the rural community of Salem Village in the early months of 1692, after word had come of the reimposition of royal government upon Massachusetts, did these violent undercurrents break out into the open. Hundreds were sent to prison and nineteen to the gallows. Students have long recognized that the Salem trials must be seen in the

---

[44] Petition of nineteen citizens of Salem, c. 1691, Mass. Archives, LXX, 194; Proposals of the Salem Committee of Militia, Oct. 31, 1691, *Doc. Hist. Maine,* V, 302–303; Richard Smith and John Fones to the men of Providence, Rochester [Kingstown], Apr. 1, 1690, R. I. Hist. Soc., *Collections,* III (1835), 222–223; John Greene to the freemen of Providence, Apr. 15, 1690, R. I. Hist. Soc. Manuscripts, V, no. 31. In Marblehead, Massachusetts, a crowd of sixty to seventy men stood to their own defense by forcibly preventing an emissary of the Boston government from removing cannon from the town's harbor fortifications for use in the Canada expedition: David Thomas Konig, *Law and Society in Puritan Massachusetts,* 166—a work which also contains an excellent account, in chapter VII, of the difficulties in Essex County during this period.

[45] Cotton Mather, *The Present State of New-England,* 21–22, 28, *Things to be Look'd For,* 55–57, 69, *Fair Weather, passim,* esp. 52; letters of Samuel Myles, Nov. 29, Dec. 12, 1690, C.O. 5/855, nos. 124,127.

context of a long and far-flung history of such episodes. Students of psychology and anthropology have furnished new and fruitful perspectives.[46] Yet such analyses, valuable as they are, should not obscure the no less essential issue of why the trials occurred at that particular time and place. Part of the answer lies in the peculiar circumstances of Salem Village. But other communities and colonies shared in the frenzy, and too little attention has been paid to the stifling, feverish atmosphere that pervaded all of Massachusetts, if not all New England, during these months.[47] It took much more than local mismanagement to inflate a parish scandal into a tragedy of historic proportions.

Indeed, to reverse the usual perspective, the mass of evidence pertaining to the trials sheds light upon the conditions that helped bring them forth. As "a PLOT of the Devil, against *New-England*," devoted to the "Hellish Design of *Bewitching* and *Ruining* our Land," witchcraft added a further horrid dimension to the French and Indian conspiracy of "Popery and Paganism" against the English colonies. Were not New Englanders "a People of God settled in those which were once the *Devil's* Territories?"[48] Some brought their anxieties into one symbolic focus: the invisible world manifested itself to the townsmen of Gloucester in the shape of a spectral army of French and Indians impervious to bullet and Bible. The testimony submitted at the Salem trials suggests the strength of other psychic preoccupations of the time—a hatred of Indians and those who associated with them, a fear

---

[46] As, most recently, John Demos, "Underlying Themes in the Witchcraft of Seventeenth-Century New England," 1311–1326; Frederick C. Drake, "Witchcraft in the American Colonies, 1647-62," 694–725; and Chadwick Hansen, *Witchcraft at Salem.* An excellent parallel study drawing upon the insights of anthropology is Alan Macfarlane, *Witchcraft in Tudor and Stuart England.* Paul Boyer and Stephen Nissenbaum, *Salem Possessed,* focuses upon local conflicts within Salem Village.

[47] Besides other towns in Essex County, Connecticut had its own witchcraft trials in the fall of 1692: *Conn. Records,* IV, 76n.; J. M. Taylor, *The Witchcraft Delusion in Colonial Connecticut,* 175–178; Wyllys Papers, 355–375, Annmary Brown Memorial Library, Providence, and Wyllys Papers, nos. 1–42, Connecticut State Library.

[48] Cotton Mather, *The Present State of New-England,* 38; idem, *The Wonders of the Invisible World* (London, 1693), reprinted in Drake, *The Witchcraft Delusion,* I, 3, 18, 15. *Ibid.,* 94–95, for Mather's account of the Devil versus New England which links Salem to the Andros Tyranny and the attacks of the "Tawnies" on the frontier.

of sexual license and its effect upon the sinews of society, and a suspicion of exotic outsiders and those who set themselves above their station.[49] And certainly the persecution of those whose deviant behavior seemed to reject, and thus to endanger, the well-being of society reveals the intensity of the colonists' anxieties as to their loss of purpose and community. In its own highly internalized way, perhaps, such a persecution was as much a rebuke to New England's leadership as the petitions to London—each sought their own remedies to a deteriorating situation as time-honored channels of recourse seemed to fail.

Back across the Atlantic, meanwhile, the atrophy of government in New England had important consequences for the charter negotiations in London. The embattled agents could neither rebut their opponents nor negotiate from a position of strength without information and support from those who had sent them. Nor could the committee of trade know more than it was told of conditions in the colonies. As in the other seaborne empires of the seventeenth century, the desire to organize and regulate the spread of colonization had outstripped the capacity to do so. Until such time as the systematic collection of information by a fair-minded bureaucracy replaced hearsay, lobbying, and propaganda, English policy making remained to a peculiar degree a product of perception rather than reality. Yet both Boston and Plymouth, the two governments most directly threatened by political change, took refuge in silence and allowed their cause to go by default. After the brief address forwarded in June 1689, Plymouth sent not a single letter to Whitehall. Massachusetts prepared several, but only one (which did not discuss the matter of the charter) reached Whitehall in the two years after March 1690. In

---

[49] Cotton Mather, *Decennium Luctuosum*, in Lincoln, *Narratives of the Indian Wars*, 243–246. These themes come out most particularly in the accusations levelled outside the normal bounds of village jealousies, as against Philip English, Hezekiah Usher, Nathaniel Saltonstall, and, especially, John Alden, accused by one of the afflicted girls of both commercial and sexual relations with the Indians: Calef, *More Wonders*, in Drake, *The Witchcraft Delusion*, III, 27. Alden was well known as an Indian trader.

October 1691 the General Court drew up a denunciation of those who had petitioned the crown; but by then it was too late.[50]

The two colonies were scarcely more communicative with their agents. Plymouth wished to obtain its own charter and, according to Governor Hinckley, was willing to pay for it, providing there were real prospects of success. Yet the Plymouth leadership was at a loss as to how to proceed: those with the necessary influence at Whitehall either had no interest in the colony or, like Mather, had other business in hand. Blathwayt had been Plymouth's previous contact at court, but he, as Mather told Hinckley, was now the chief among New England's enemies. The distracted governor was reduced to promising the colonists' prayers for the eternal reward of any who would serve them—hardly a marketable commodity at Whitehall— and to the equally unrealistic hope that a charter might be granted on credit or *sub forma pauperis.* Nearly two years passed. Finally, in response to Mather's warning that the colony would be joined to New York, the Plymouth General Court decided to appoint his friend, Sir Henry Ashurst, as its agent and raise two hundred pounds for his expenses. But the court also voted to refer a decision on the collection of the money to the towns. In consequence, while some contributed, others did not, and in October 1691 Hinckley informed Mather that the sum collected fell so far short that the court had ordered its return to the individual subscribers. Ichabod Wiswall, the one agent passionately concerned for Plymouth's autonomy, watched, embittered and unemployed, as Mather maneuvered to bring Plymouth within the Massachusetts orbit. "When I parted from your honor, Feb. the 5, *anno* '89 [i.e., 1690]," he wrote to Hinckley, "I little then imagined that it would have been August the 29, '91, before I should receive one line from you." But by this time, if not before, Hinckley and those

---

[50] Bradstreet to Secretary of State Nottingham, May 8, 1691, *N. Y. Col. Docs.,* III, 769; copy of Massachusetts petition to the king and letter to the agents, Oct. 14, 1691, Mass. Archives, XXXVII, 171, 172. A further petition from Massachusetts, of Dec. 16, 1690, was delivered directly to the king and does not appear in the official papers: *Andros Tracts,* II, 278; Elisha Cooke to Bradstreet, May 8, 1691, Prince Papers. Two other communications prepared in Massachusetts (printed in *Andros Tracts,* III, 43–45, 48–51 from copies in the Mass. Archives) never seem to have reached their destination.

he described as "sundry others of the most thinking men" were ready to accept incorporation into Massachusetts. With their authority in tatters, it must have seemed as if only the stronger government of the Bay could protect the remnants of a godly congregational commonwealth. The news of Plymouth's inclusion in the new charter found its leaders already resigned to their colony's demise.[51]

Massachusetts, by contrast, had a strong delegation of agents in England; where the colony failed was in the equally necessary task of guiding and assisting their work. Early letters had expressed Boston's hope that the charter and its ancient privileges would be restored; by 1691, Bradstreet and his council were pleading for an immediate settlement without mention of preconditions and terms. War and "the awfull Frowne of God in the disappointment of that chargable and hazardous Enterprize" against Quebec overwhelmed every other consideration—the more so since reliable reports from Canada told of Frontenac's resolve to treat all the English colonies as enemies of France without regard for their individual policies.[52] Samuel Sewall, for one, now saw the need for a union of the northern colonies and pressed home his point with two barrels of Indian scalps dispatched to Mather and another acquaintance in London. When Mather questioned the colony's request for military assistance, he was told that it took precedence over all other matters whatsoever, even (by implication) the winning of a charter. Nor did the Boston government send any further supplies of money—Mather had to borrow

---

[51] Increase Mather to Hinckley, Sept. 12, 1689, Hinckley to Ashurst, Feb. 4, 1690, to Mather, Feb. 4, 1690, John Cotton to Hinckley, Feb. 6, 1691, Hinckley to Mather, Oct. 16, 1691, to Wiswall, Oct. 17, 1691, Wiswall to Hinckley, Nov. 5, [1691], Mass. Hist. Soc., *Collections*, 4th ser., V (1861), 211, 225–229, 278–280, 287–297, 299; *Plymouth Records*, VI, 259–261; Langdon, *Pilgrim Colony*, 239, 242–244.

[52] Bradstreet to the agents, Nov. 29, 1690, *Andros Tracts*, III, 52–57; Bradstreet and the Massachusetts Council to the king, Mar. 29, 1690, C.O. 5/855, no. 71, to Secretary of State Nottingham, May 8, 1691, *N. Y. Col. Docs.*, III, 769–770; Declaration of Sylvanus Davis, [1690], *Doc. Hist. Maine*, V, 146–147. Davis's narrative (he was captured in Maine in May 1690 and exchanged by Phips at Quebec in October) evidently made a great impression on the Massachusetts leadership—thus the letter to the agents cited above (*Andros Tracts*, III, 54) and Samuel Sewall to Increase Mather, Dec. 29, 1690, Mass. Hist. Soc., *Collections*, 6th ser., I (1886), 114–115.

four hundred pounds from the New England Company and one hundred more from Stephen Mason. As he later observed, Massachusetts could not reasonably complain of the final settlement when it had abdicated its responsibilities.[53]

The critics of charter government lay under no such inhibitions. Phips's return from Quebec set off a fresh flurry of letters to the Plantation Office claiming that the venture—"a pumpkin ffleet . . . commanded by a man who never did Exploit above water" (a hit at Phips's treasure hunting)—had been doomed from the start.[54] Several of the letters and the petition from the men of Boston and Charlestown were rushed into print; Cooke ascribed the publication to "Mr Randolph and his associates." Blathwayt dispatched a blistering denunciation of Phips and New England to Secretary of State Nottingham. "The damage will not be theirs alone," he wrote, "the blow will reach all the other Plantations which are under his Majesty's Government and have an immediate effect upon the revenue of the customs and manufactures of England. This I foretold very early, as I foresee greater and irreparable mischief if not prevented by a higher hand, for how can it be otherwise while a mean and mechanical sort of people shall pretend to and abuse the highest acts of royal government under the color of an imaginary charter they have justly forfeited."[55] The former lieutenant governor of the Dominion, Francis Nicholson, now promoted to rule the lucrative province of Virginia,

---

[53] Sewall to Increase Mather, Dec. 29, 1690, "Memoranda," Dec. 2–5, 1690, Mass. Hist. Soc., *Collections,* 6th ser., I (1886), 115, 113–114; Increase Mather, *A Brief Account, Andros Tracts,* II, 292–293; Murdock, "Increase Mather's Expenses," 202–203; Letterbook, 1688–1761, of the Company for the Propagation of the Gospel in New England, 8, Alderman Library, University of Virginia, Charlottesville (microfilm copy in Massachusetts Historical Society).

[54] Letter of James Lloyd, Jan. 8, 1691, C.O. 5/856, no. 131. Other letters are C.O. 5/855, nos. 124, 127, 5/856, nos. 136–140. Their endorsements show that many were forwarded to Whitehall by Dudley, Usher, and Nicholson.

[55] *An Account of the late action of the New-Englanders under the command of Sir William Phips* (licensed for printing, Apr. 13, 1691); *The Humble Address of divers Gentry, Merchants, and others . . . Inhabiting in Boston, Charlestown, and places adjacent* (licensed for printing, Apr. 28, 1691; for the original version, see note 6, preceding); Cooke to Bradstreet, May 6, 1691, Prince Papers; Blathwayt to Nottingham, Mar. 6, 1691, *Calendar of State Papers, Domestic Series, of the Reign of William and Mary, 1690–1691,* 297–298.

echoed Blathwayt's concern. The war, he told Nottingham and the committee, would now spread to the frontiers of Maryland and Virginia. He enclosed the journal of Col. Cuthbert Potter, an emissary he had sent to New England with letters to acquaintances who also happened to be opponents of charter rule. Not surprisingly, Potter brought back tales of illegal trade and popular discontent.[56]

Mather could not deny the sorry state of New England: "No good tidings thence of a long time," he noted in his diary in January 1691. But he fought back as best he could. He renewed his solicitations at court and at Whitehall in alliance with Ashurst, Daniel Coxe, and Lord Wharton.[57] He drafted and later published a short pamphlet setting forth reasons why the New England charters should be confirmed, and he circulated copies among members of the Privy Council.[58] One of his friends—internal evidence and the sentiments typical of the "commonwealth" writers of the time suggests that Robert Thompson may have been responsible—wrote a virulent attack on the petitioners of Boston and Charlestown and their allies, chastising them as "the Publicans of New England," although the confused violence of his language probably did Mather's cause more harm than

---

[56] Lieutenant Governor Nicholson to the Lords of Trade, Nov. 4, to Nottingham, Nov. 4, 1690, to the Government of New England, n.d., Journal of Cuthbert Potter, July 6–Sept. 24, 1690, *CSP Col., 1689–1692*, nos. 1164, 1165, 1164iii, vii. For Potter's journal see also Newton D. Mereness, *Travels in the American Colonies, 1690–1783*, 3–11. Nicholson kept close watch on events in New England: thus Minutes of the Proceedings of the Virginia Council, June 5, 1690–Jan. 15, 1691, H. R. McIlwaine, ed., *Executive Journal of the Council of Colonial Virginia*, 118, 121, 130, 137–138, 140–141, and the depositions sent to England, *CSP Col., 1689–1692*, no. 1292.

[57] Increase Mather, Diary, Jan. 3, 1691, Mass. Hist. Soc. Mather consulted Coxe on Jan. 17, Feb. 5, and June 13, and he held numerous meetings with Ashurst and Lord Wharton through the rest of the year.

[58] Increase Mather, *A Brief Account, Andros Tracts*, II, 277. The pamphlet *Reasons for the Confirmation of the Charters belonging to the Several Corporations in New-England* is printed, together with variants from a second, almost identical version referring only to Massachusetts, in *Andros Tracts*, II, 225–229. A manuscript copy of the first version, endorsed "Published in Print July 1691," is in C.O. 5/856, no. 158xviii. A third version linked to the time when the judges and law officers were considering the agents' charter proposals is in Carte MSS. 81, foll. 758–759. A further attack upon Massachusetts, unusually well informed and criticizing the colonists' "antimonarchicall" principles, is in manuscript in C.O. 5/856, no. 158xix (foll. 473–483v.).

good.[59] On April 9, Madam Lockhart conducted him to a lengthy audience with the queen, who again promised her assistance. Mary professed her ignorance of the pamphlet attacks on New England, but she recollected its past religious disputes and its "bad condition" at the present time. Mather assured her that a just settlement would resolve all these problems and adroitly steered the conversation to the subject of toleration for Nonconformists, a topic close to Mary's heart.[60] A few hours later, however, John Nelson's uncle, Sir Purbeck Temple, placed the petition from Boston and Charlestown before the Privy Council. The council referred it to the committee of trade with instructions that the agents were to submit a written account of the condition of Massachusetts and the fate of the expedition against Canada. Phips, who had arrived from Boston five weeks previously, and all other interested parties were summoned to a full-scale hearing later in the month.[61]

The lines of battle were drawn, and the contest began in earnest upon the king's return from Holland. On April 18, five days after William's arrival in London, Mather presented the king with an address from Massachusetts and a petition signed by seventy-seven merchants "who have concerns in New England." Both asked for the restoration of charter privileges and the dispatch of frigates to Boston to aid in a second attempt upon Canada. Three days later, several of the merchants, headed by Ashurst's brother-in-law Alderman Sir Thomas Lane, accompanied the agents to the hearing before the committee of trade. Their appearance, according to Cooke, "did very much damp" a rival group of traders, led by Usher and Charles Lid-

---

[59] On this pamphlet, reprinted in *Andros Tracts*, II, 231–269, see Johnson, "The Humble Address," 241–249.

[60] Increase Mather, *Autobiography*, 333–335; this was presumably transcribed from the account in Mather's Diary, Apr. 9, 1691, Mass. Hist. Soc., although the queen's concluding words on religious toleration have been considerably expanded. Mather himself refrained from any commitment to such toleration.

[61] Order of the King in Council, Apr. 9, Minutes of the Lords of Trade, Apr. 17, 21, 1691, C.O. 5/856, nos. 143, 147, 149; Cooke to Bradstreet, May 9, 1691, Prince Papers.

gett, who had gathered to testify against the agents.[62] The Lords of
Trade listened to the agents' defence of the measure taken by the revolutionary governments of New England and then set a day for their
opponents to be heard. In the meantime, through William Blathwayt
and Secretary of State Sidney, they made a frank attempt to bargain.
Would the agents, they enquired, be willing to accept a new charter
"with as large priviledges and franchises as are enjoyed by any Corporation within their Majesties' dominions, leaving only to their
Majesties the power of commissionating a Governor and the Council
from time to time, The People being to meet once a year or oftner, as
the Governor shall think fit, by ther Representatives in an Assembly
(in the nature of a House of Commons) for the making of laws relating to property and the good government of the colony"?[63] In sum,
would they consent to a constitution which would make Massachusetts a royal colony similar to all others?

The agents' reply is unknown, but they evidently held back from
accepting a royal governor. This now became the central point at
issue. By Cooke's account, some of the Lords of Trade were not informed of the forthcoming meeting of the committee on April 27.
Alerted by the agents, however, they were on hand to question those
who proclaimed the necessity of royal government. To Carmarthen's
disgust, these witnesses made a poor showing. When Lidgett offered

---

[62] Luttrell, *Brief Historical Relation,* II, 208 (Nottingham had returned at the end of
March); Increase Mather, *A Brief Account, Andros Tracts,* II, 278; *idem,* Diary, Apr.
18, 1691, Mass. Hist. Soc.; Cooke to Bradstreet, May 9, 1691, Prince Papers. Neither the Massachusetts address nor the merchants' petition remains in the official
papers, but a copy of the latter is in Mass. Archives, XXXVII, 7. Mather helped
to draw it up: Diary, Apr. 13, 14, 16, 1691, Mass. Hist. Soc. Only four of the seventy-seven signers had signed the earlier petition, [Feb. 13, 1690], C.O. 5/855,
no. 65, hostile to the charter governments and sponsored by Thomas Brinley and
Jeremiah Johnson. The two groups could unite, however, on matters of common
concern: thus their May 14, 1690 petition against the Hudson Bay Company,
*House of Lords MSS., 1690–1691,* no. 271, and the 25 signatures on the Sept. 11,
1690 petition asking that ships be allowed to leave for New England, C.O. 1/68,
no. 7. The committee of trade obviously set great store by the merchants' opinions; unfortunately little as yet is known of their activities.

[63] The Massachusetts agents to the Lords of Trade, [read Apr. 21, 1691], Minute
of the Lords of Trade to Secretary Sidney [in Blathwayt's hand], Apr. 22, 1691,
C.O. 5/856, nos. 150, 151; Journal of the Lords of Trade, Apr. 21, 1691, C.O.
391/7, 7.

his own difficulties as an example of the severity of the Boston authorities in searching houses and preventing the dispatch of petitions, the
agents were able to reply that it was not the Bay government but
Lidgett's creditors, led by his own sister, who were besieging the
house. Unable to reach agreement on the form of the new charter, the
committee resolved to seek the king's opinion as to the appointment
of a royal governor.[64]

Mather wasted no time. On the very next day, by the intercession
of the Earl of Devonshire, he met with William in the royal bed-
chamber and besought him to approve the settlement drafted by the
committee of judges and law officers which allowed the governorship
to remain in the hands of the colonists. Because of religious differences, he added, "such a Governor will not suit with the people of
New England as may be very proper for the other England plantations."[65] William made no promises, and, at a council meeting on
April 30, he decided in favor of appointing a royal governor. Councillors in attendance reported to the agents that the king had justified
his decision by reference to the urgent need to provide for the defense
of the colonists of New England. In a time of war, "it was necessary
that a Military Man should be set over them," and William seems to
have envisioned the appointment of a kind of generalissimo—New
England's old bugbear of a "General Governor"—who would coordinate the forces of the several colonies. Nevertheless, Mather's plea
had not been in vain, for William also expressed his approval of the
settlement already drafted and declared that the colony should re-

---

[64] Cooke to Bradstreet, May 9, 1691, Prince Papers. Nottingham, Carmarthen,
Sidney, Powle, and the Bishop of London were at the meeting of April 21; they
were joined at that of April 27 by Pembroke, Goodricke, Lord Chief Justice Holt,
Capel, and Boscawen—no doubt it was these last three in particular that the
agents were glad to have in attendance.

The agents were correct in their attack upon Lidgett. Though the son and son-
in-law of wealthy men, he was in perpetual financial difficulties at this time; thus
the dramatic tale of his wild threats when cornered by his creditors in his study:
Thomas Newton to John Usher, Jan. 29, 1690, Jeffries Papers, III, 64. After leaving Boston a month later, he settled in London.

[65] Increase Mather, Diary, Apr. 28, 1691, Mass. Hist. Soc.; *idem, Autobiography,*
335–336.

ceive its former rights and privileges together with a governor suited to its idiosyncrasies and acceptable to its people.[66]

William returned to Holland two days later, and Mather quickly found that the royal guidelines left considerable room for interpretation and disagreement. The committee of trade had phrased its request for guidance in the form of two alternatives—did the king desire a royal governor who would "give His consent to all Laws and Acts of Government as in Barbados and the other Plantations, or [would he] leave the Power of making Laws to the People or officers appointed by them"? William had opted for a middle course between these two artificial extremes, but the resulting order in council repeated the phraseology of the committee's original minute so as to make it appear that the king favored the appointment of a colonial executive "as in Barbados," armed with veto powers over all acts of government. Mather detected the discrepancy, which he privately ascribed to the deliberate forgery of one of the clerks on the council. With testimony from several privy councillors that the king had not intended such a settlement, he sought in vain to have the order set aside.[67] For the moment, however, he was able to circumvent this piece of bureaucratic intrigue through his friendship with Treby and Somers—an alliance which Mather had cultivated by his liberal payments to the law officers and their clerks. When the draft of the Massachusetts charter was returned to Treby for revision, Mather per-

---

[66] Increase Mather, *A Brief Account, Andros Tracts,* II, 279-280; *idem, Autobiography,* 336; Cooke to Bradstreet, May 9, 1691, Prince Papers; Order in Council, Apr. 30, 1691, *APC Col.,* II, 125-126. For evidence as to William's intentions, see also the petition prepared for presentation to the queen, [late July 1691?], Mass. Hist. Soc., *Proceedings,* XII (1871-1873), 120-121, and Cotton Mather to John Cotton, Sept. 14, 1691, Cotton Mather, *Diary,* ed. Ford, I, 141—"a General, for all the united Colonies."

[67] Minutes of the Lords of Trade, Apr. 27, 1691, C.O. 5/905, 269; Order in Council, Apr. 30, 1692, *APC Col.,* II, 126; Cotton Mather to John Cotton, Sept. 14, 1691, Cotton Mather, *Diary,* ed. Ford, I, 140-141 (the editor's note here, and hence the comments of Jacobsen, *William Blathwayt,* 135, should be disregarded). As to the identity of the guilty clerk, the copy of the order in Addit. MSS., 34712, fol. 218, is signed by Richard Colinge, a veteran Whitehall bureaucrat and colleague of Blathwayt. Mather's efforts to discredit the order can be followed in his *A Brief Account, Andros Tracts,* II, 280, his Diary, May 7-9, 1691, Mass. Hist. Soc., and the petition to the queen cited in note 66, preceding.

suaded the attorney general to disregard the misleading order and work on the basis of the king's remarks in council. In consequence, the new draft which Treby presented to the committee on June 8 differed little from that drawn up six months before save for the addition of a royal governor without any power of veto and with carefully circumscribed powers of appointment.[68]

The king's preoccupation with his campaign in Flanders placed the responsibility for completing the details of the charter squarely upon the shoulders of the Lords of Trade. By an unhappy coincidence, the political situation in these critical months could scarcely have been more unfavorable to the pretensions of Massachusetts. Carmarthen's ascendancy was at its height. Monmouth, Wildman, and Sir Henry Ashurst were ousted from their official positions.[69] Shrewsbury had finally resigned in June 1690, and although the king's close friend, Henry Sidney, served with Nottingham as secretary of state from December of that year until March 1692, the latter retained sole charge of colonial affairs and most other business until his dismissal in November 1693. The duumvirate of Carmarthen and Nottingham, "Tom Tyrant," the prince of patronage, and "Dismal Daniel," the champion of the established church, was nowhere more evident than at meetings of the committee of trade. Between June and the end of September, when the Lords concluded their deliberations on the charter, they held fifteen meetings on the subject of New England. Carmarthen and his faithful henchman, Sir Henry Goodricke, lieu-

---

[68] Minute of the Lords of Trade, May 12, Order in Council, May 14, 1691, C.O. 5/905, 271–272; Draft of charter presented by the Attorney-General, June 8, 1691, C.O. 5/856, no. 166 (foll. 549–572). Mather met three times with Somers between March and June 1691, seven times with Treby, and on innumerable occasions, then and later, with Treby's clerk, S. Gwillym, spending many days at the Temple: Diary, *passim*, Mass. Hist. Soc. The diary also contains a list of Mather's expenses, Jan.–Dec. 1691; they record a total of 10 guineas paid to Somers, 15 shillings to his clerks, 10 guineas to Treby, 196 guineas to Gwillym, and 20 guineas to Mr. Harrington, who also seems to have held a clerical position. Undoubtedly, much of this money was in payment for the drafting and passage of the charter. Nevertheless, Mather must have reaped a harvest of influence.

[69] Andrew Browning, *Thomas Osborne, Earl of Danby and Duke of Leeds, 1632–1712*, I, 474–475, 486; Horwitz, *Revolution Politics*, 124–125; Luttrell, *Brief Historical Relation*, II, 204.

tenant general of the ordinance, attended every meeting, Nottingham eleven of fifteen, and Sir John Lowther, another of Carmarthen's associates, six. Henry Powle, now Master of the Rolls and Mather's frequent confidant, was present at four early meetings; Secretary Sidney and such Whig stalwarts (and appointed members of the committee) as Devonshire, Monmouth, Capel, and Richard Hampden attended none at all. Only Hugh Boscawen among Mather's supporters, secure in his kinship to the indispensable Sidney Godolphin at the Treasury, attended regularly during this period, ten times in all. The division within the committee noted by Elisha Cooke was, in effect, resolved by the withdrawal of one faction. Attendance dropped to between six and the bare quorum of three members. At most sessions, Carmarthen and the Tories were in a majority of three or four to one.[70]

With this orientation, the committee gave short shrift to Treby's proposals. "By such a charter as this," remarked one member, "the King's Governour would be made a *Governor of Clouts.*" Blathwayt was asked to prepare a comparison of the various documents and he responded, as expected, with a savage and well-informed attack on each and every concession offered to the agents. In his view, the entire history of Massachusetts—its illegal trade, its abuse of its former charter, and its "improper and irregular dispositions of land"—was one long argument against granting the colony greater powers than those allowed to Barbados and Virginia. He concluded on a more constructive note. Drawing an implicit distinction between the old proprietary grants and those incorporated since the Restoration, he pointed out that the council had already decided (in October 1690) to impose a royal governor on Maryland, the last colony retaining a charter of the first type. Hence it would be a retrograde and eccentric step not to do likewise in New England.[71]

---

[70] Journal of the Lords of Trade, June 8–Sept. 28, 1691, C.O. 391/7, 21–53. Others attending were Pembroke, four times, and John Egerton, Earl of Bridgewater, once.

[71] Increase Mather, *A Brief Account, Andros Tracts,* II, 281—in contemporary usage, "a king of clouts" signified a mere figurehead; Journal of the Lords of Trade, June 8, 1691, C.O. 391/7, 21; Commentary on the attorney general's draft, [June 25, 1691], C.O. 5/856, no. 170; Orders in Council, Aug. 21, Oct. 9, 1690, Browne

The Lords of Trade were receptive to schemes for a greater uniformity in colonial administration—a royal governor (Lionel Copley, one of Carmarthen's supporters) was duly dispatched to Maryland, and in the following year they attempted to remove both Pennsylvania and the Jerseys from their proprietors' control.[72] They were not distracted by a proposal from Sir William Phips that an expedition under his command would undertake to conquer Canada if only Massachusetts were restored to its former rights and privileges.[73] But in the knowledge of William's sympathy for New England they restricted their disagreement with Treby's draft to a lengthy list of amendments hammered out during a succession of meetings in early July. The agents advanced counterproposals of their own. Where the attorney general had suggested that the franchise remain in the hands of freemen chosen by the General Court, the committee insisted on a change to freeholder suffrage. The agents then proposed that freemen and freeholders together be permitted to elect both council and assembly; the committee compromised by proposing that the council be chosen by the assembly (rather than by the crown as in other royal colonies) and that the vote be restricted to freeholders and a token contingent of one hundred freemen to be named by the agents. Ultimately, all parties agreed upon a franchise limited to forty-shilling freeholders and inhabitants worth fifty pounds in money. Other questions were more easily decided. The General Court (here defined, apparently, as the assembly alone) was to choose the governor's council and all officials except for sheriffs, judges, and justices of the

---

*et al., Archives of Maryland,* VIII, 200, 207. For further analysis of Blathwayt's comments, see Simmons, "Massachusetts Charter," 77–78.

[72] Commission and Instructions to Lionel Copley, June 27, Aug. 26, 1691, Browne *et al., Archives of Maryland,* VIII, 263–280; Order of the Queen in Council, Mar. 10, Minute of the Lords of Trade, Apr. 18, Order of the Privy Council, May 12, Draft commission of Gov. Benjamin Fletcher, June 27, 1692, *CSP Col., 1689–1692,* nos. 2118, 2181, 2227, 2296.

[73] Proposal and petition of Sir William Phips, read in committee July 1, 1691, C.O. 5/856, nos. 171, 172. The scheme had been tentatively advanced earlier in the year (Agents to the Lords of Trade, read Apr. 21, 1691, C.O. 5/856, no. 150), and Luttrell (*Brief Historical Relation,* II, 237) had heard in May that New England had offered to conquer Canada and build ships for the navy in return for confirmation of the old charter.

peace. It was to meet at least once a year, in May. Its appointments, however, together with its legislation and all other acts of government, were to be subject to the veto of the governor, who could also decide on the time of its proroguing and dissolution. Finally, the committee instructed Treby to report the agents' objections.[74]

Mather was now placed in an agonizing position. Through the spring of 1691 he had continued to lobby at court among such intimates of the royal family as Henry Sidney and the queen's private secretary, Monsieur D'Alonne, and among members of the Privy Council—Devonshire; Charles Gerard, Earl of Macclesfield; Ralph, Earl Montagu; and the rising general, John Churchill, Earl of Marlborough.[75] He had prevailed upon two more friends of Richard Baxter, John Tillotson, the newly appointed Archbishop of Canterbury, and Francis Charlton, a former associate of Shaftesbury and a conspirator in the Rye House Plot of 1682, to speak with the king on New England's behalf.[76] Yet none of these men had any hand in the day-to-day administration of the colonies. The best that Mather could hope for was some further stroke of intervention by king or

---

[74] Journal of the Lords of Trade, July 2, 9, 17, 1691, C.O. 391/7, 30–36; Report of the attorney general on the minutes for the charter, [July 29, 1691], C.O. 5/856, no. 176 (*CSP Col., 1689–1692,* no. 1669 mistakenly gives forty pounds instead of 40s., and one hundred instead of fifty pounds—the latter figure is written in and is the one copied into the entry books); Proposals offered by the New England agents, [July? 1691], C.O. 5/856, no. 169. These undated proposals by the agents were evidently submitted after some of the amendments were made, since they ask for some of Treby's original draft to be restored. If they were submitted together and not piecemeal, the evidence would suggest that they were presented between the meetings of July 2 and July 9. Mather clearly tried to hold on to the freeman franchise, and Murdock's attempts to deny this (*Increase Mather,* 240–242) are not convincing, being grounded on incomplete and secondhand evidence.

[75] For Abel Tassin D'Alonne, see Mary F. Sandars, *Princess and Queen of England, Life of Mary II,* 137–138. For Mather's numerous meetings with D'Alonne and Sidney, see Diary, Mar. 6, 8, 24, 25, Apr. 16, 17, 22, 24, 25, May 19, June 6, 10, 1691, Mass. Hist. Soc., and *ibid.,* Apr. 16, 20, 21, May 7, 25, June 8, July 6, 1691 for his meetings with the privy councillors.

[76] Increase Mather, *Autobiography,* 336; *idem,* Diary, Jan.–Oct. 1691, Mass. Hist. Soc., records nine meetings with Charlton and five with Tillotson.

council, and William's absence and the hegemony of Nottingham and Carmarthen in council and committee as the queen's most trusted advisers made this possibility increasingly remote. Mather's predilection for associating with the high and the mighty—a strategy that had served him well in the past and from which he derived considerable personal pleasure—became a self-deluding diversion once the business of the charter had passed into the hands of the officials of the Plantation Office. Not until after the committee had agreed upon its amendments could Mather bring himself to negotiate with Blathwayt, and even then their meetings were conducted in an atmosphere of mutual mistrust.[77]

He also faced a challenge to one of the few legacies of the Dominion of which he could approve—the reunion with Massachusetts of the territories lying beyond the Merrimack. Earlier in the year, Samuel Allen, a merchant of London, had purchased Robert Mason's title to New Hampshire from Mason's two sons. Allen had also secured a contract from the navy commissioners to supply masts and spars to the annual value of twenty-two hundred pounds for seven years.[78] Citing these documents, he now petitioned to be sent out as governor of New Hampshire. Called upon to respond, the agents cast doubt upon the validity of Mason's title and pointed out that the province was so small and poor as to be quite unable to defend itself or support a separate government. Allen subsequently scaled down his proposals—he asked for a government "distinct from that of the Massachutes" to be subject to a general governor of New England on the pattern of the administration of the Leeward Islands, and he relinquished his claim to the southern half of Mason's grant, which on paper extended as far south into Massachusetts as Salem. His suit forestalled the inclusion of New Hampshire in the Massachusetts

---

[77] Mather met with Blathwayt and with William Bridgeman, the latter's colleague in the office of the secretary of state, on several occasions in the spring of 1691 but not with any regularity until the fall. Diary, *passim*, Mass. Hist. Soc. There is no record that Mather had any financial dealings with Blathwayt.

[78] *N. H. State Papers*, XXIX, 143–152; Allen's contract for ship timber, [Mar. 30, 1691], C.O. 5/924, foll. 5–6; William Henry Fry, *New Hampshire as a Royal Province*, 220.

charter and, since no general governor was appointed, Allen received an independent commission early in 1692.[79]

Allen had lent money to Robert Mason, and he may have conceived of the project as the only way to recover his investment. He had contacts with the mast traders of the Piscataqua through William Partridge, a Portsmouth shipwright, and he was undoubtedly encouraged in his application for political office by John Usher, who had territorial claims of his own in New Hampshire deriving from lands sold by Mason and the Million Purchase promoted by Richard Wharton. Allen appointed Usher his resident lieutenant governor—he himself did not visit New England until 1698—and Usher may have helped to finance the enterprise since, despite his subsequent marriage to Allen's daughter, he dunned his father-in-law for the repayment of debts that amounted to over four thousand pounds by 1713.[80]

It is less easy to explain why the committee of trade should have disregarded its own and the king's pronouncements on the need for a united New England to bestow the command of a frontier province on a city merchant without knowledge or experience of frontier conditions. The agents' account of the defenseless condition of New Hampshire was well-founded, as Usher promptly acknowledged upon his arrival there. Both Cooke and Mather agree that Allen gained the advantage because he was able to persuade the committee, perhaps

---

[79] Petitions of Samuel Allen, [Mar. 30], [July 29], [Sept. 2], Sept. 7, 11, 1691, [Jan. 11, 1692], the Massachusetts agents to the Lords of Trade, May 4, 1691, Order of the King in Council, Jan. 21, 1692, C.O. 5/924, nos. 1i, 4, 6, 7, 9, 11, 2, 12; Journal of the Lords of Trade, July 29, Sept. 3, 11, 1691, Jan. 11, 1692, C.O. 391/7, 33, 44, 47–49, 79; Cooke to Bradstreet, Sept. 11, 1691, Prince Papers; Commission and Instructions of Gov. Samuel Allen, Mar. 1, 3, 1692, *N. H. Laws*, I, 501–514. The committee, however, did reject an attempt by the Gorges family to reclaim its proprietary province of Maine.

[80] Randolph to Blathwayt, Apr. 2, 1688, *Randolph Letters*, VI, 252; Affidavit of Elisha Hutchinson, June 14, 1700, C.O. 5/931, no. 3xxiii; Sewall, *Diary*, I, 235; *N. H. State Papers*, XXIX, 138–141; Proprietors of the Million Purchase, [1685], Stephen Wesendunck to Usher, Oct. 27, 1695, Usher to Allen, July 7, 1703, Jan. 15, 1705, Jeffries Papers, IV, 111, III, 117, 131; Maine Hist. Soc., *Collections*, 2nd ser., VIII (1897), 191–192.

with the aid of the petition from Great Island sent over the previous year and the testimony of Thomas Graffort, a wealthy Anglican merchant of Portsmouth who had just arrived in London, that the people of New Hampshire wished for a separate government.[81] And as both Phips and Randolph reminded the committee, the forests of northern New England were a most valuable resource. No doubt its members came to believe that this timber could best be preserved from the sawmills of the Bay during a time of crisis in the struggle for naval supremacy if the soil and government of New Hampshire were administered by one committed to the mast trade with England.[82]

There is some evidence that the Lords of Trade acquiesced in Allen's ambitions for less creditable motives. A decade later, the Earl of Bellomont, then governor of Massachusetts, New Hampshire, and New York, charged that Allen had promised shares in his proprietary to an old associate, the Duke of Leeds, and to Lords Lonsdale and Leinster, presumably to ensure the success of his original application. Some time later, he had included Blathwayt in the deal after receiving from him a loan of three thousand pounds. Bellomont was a garrulous and partisan Whig with an obsessive dislike for Blathwayt, and he never substantiated his accusation. Nevertheless, it is at least superficially plausible. In 1691, Leeds and Lonsdale—Carmarthen and Sir John Lowther as they were then—dominated the committee; Leinster, the son of Marshal Schomberg, was high in the king's favor; and Blathwayt already had an interest in New Hampshire through his share in the Million Purchase and his friend Cranfield's promise to divide up the spoils of its government. Among Blathwayt's papers,

---

[81] John Usher to the Lords of Trade, Oct. 29, 1692, C.O. 5/924, no. 18; Cooke to Bradstreet, Sept. 10, Nov. 4, 1691, Prince Papers; Increase Mather to John Richards, Oct. 26, 1691, Winthrop Papers; *idem, A Brief Account, Andros Tracts,* II, 283.

[82] Randolph to the Lords of Trade, Oct. 13, 1691, *Randolph Letters,* V, 71–74; Phips to the Lords of Trade, [Sept. 2, 1691], C.O. 5/856, no. 184; see also the undated memorials submitted by Andros and Charles Lidgett on the same subject, *ibid.,* nos. 186, 187. Curiously, there is some evidence of an alliance between Allen and Phips: *Calendar of State Papers, Domestic Series, of the Reign of William and Mary, 1690–1691,* 485; *Calendar of Treasury Books, 1689–1692,* 1452, *1693–1696,* 359.

moreover, survives a written pledge by Allen to present him with a cargo of Spanish wine and fruit for every year Allen remained New Hampshire's governor.[83]

This was not the only subterranean current running beneath the placid surface of official business to complicate Mather's task. In April 1691, a new group of promoters revived the proposals advanced by Wharton and Hutchinson for the exploitation of minerals in New England and petitioned once more for a charter of incorporation. Led by Sir Matthew Dudley, the group was distinctly Whig and Nonconformist in character. It included two London aldermen, Sir Humphrey Edwin and Sir Thomas Lane, and several other merchants involved in the negotiations for the charter—Daniel Coxe, Robert Wolley, Jeremiah Johnson, Robert Hackshaw, Sir Samuel Thompson, and William, eldest son of Richard Wharton.[84] They were opposed before the Privy Council by the newly floated Company of Copper Miners in England and its governor, Sir Joseph Herne, a wealthy financier and Tory member of Parliament who traded to Newfoundland and the Indies in partnership with business interests in the West Country. Meanwhile, Sir William Phips, in alliance with an old associate of his treasure-hunting days and two New Englanders who had settled prosperously in London, Thomas Lake and Sir Stephen Evance, proposed yet a third company for the purpose of working copper mines in Acadia.[85] Mather had friends in at

---

[83] Bellomont to the Board of Trade, June 22, to Secretary Vernon, June 22, 1700, C.O. 5/861, nos. 45, 47; Jacobsen, *William Blathwayt*, 465–467; Samuel Allen to Edward Flower, n.d. (endorsed by Blathwayt), Blathwayt Papers, XII, Col. Wmsbg.

[84] Petition of Sir Matthew Dudley and others, Apr. 1691, C.O. 5/857, no. 6xii; Proceedings in Council, Sept. 17, 1691, *APC Col.,* II, 193. A relic of the group in the form of a circular, dated May 7, 1692, summoning its managers to a meeting "at Denings Coffee-House in Popeshead Alley" survives in Miscellaneous Bound MSS., 1679–93, Mass. Hist. Soc.

[85] Proceedings in Council, Apr. 28–July 7, 1692, *APC Col.,* II, 194–195; Proceedings in relation to the Company of Copper Miners, July 23, Aug. 13, 21, 1691, *Calendar of State Papers, Domestic Series, of the Reign of William and Mary, 1690–1691,* 459, 486, 498; Petition of Sir William Phips, Sir Steven Evans [Evance], Thomas Lake, John Smith, Thomas Porter, and Richard Frith, Jr., Aug. 3, 1691, *ibid.,* 485. For further analysis of these groups, see Johnson, "Adjustment to Empire," 636–637.

least two of the three groups, but he rightfully viewed their conflict with apprehension: it resurrected, at a most inconvenient moment, the old question of whether New England and its corporations should be governed directly from London. Thus his anonymous opponents during the debate over the corporations bill had charged the New England subscribers to the mining proposals with abandoning their solicitation for a patent on the grounds that the prospective restoration of charter rule would render unnecessary any reliance upon royal authority. At first, Dudley and his partners made rapid progress, assisted no doubt by their foresight in elevating Peregrine, Earl of Danby, Carmarthen's feckless and improvident son, to the governorship of their company. Ultimately, they were diverted to fruitless schemes for the production of naval stores. In the meantime, the various proposals were one more reason for the committee, and Carmarthen in particular, to keep a watchful eye upon the progress of the Massachusetts charter.[86]

These additional perplexities and the ordeal of attending upon the committee while it methodically reworked the draft which he and Treby had devised drove Mather to the point of collapse. At odds with his fellow agents and exhausted by his labors, he took to his bed in mid-July for five days with a fever.[87] His overwrought condition— he resorted to purging doses of Epsom waters, a renowned local cathartic—impelled him to an open display of his disappointment. He later recalled his anguished declaration to Treby and "some Ministers of State" that he would rather part with his life than accept amendments by the committee or any other restrictions that infringed upon the liberties and privileges of his country. The response was crushing: the ministers replied that the colonists' consent was "neither expected

---

[86] *Considerations Humbly Offered, Andros Tracts,* III, 7–8; [Increase Mather], *New-England Vindicated, ibid.,* II, 120–121; and *A Short Discourse, ibid.,* 144–145; Orders in Council, Oct. 9, 1691, Mar. 17, July 7, Sept. 12, 1692, C.O. 5/905, 411, C.O. 5/857, nos. 6, 6i, xiii, xiv; List of Governor and Assistants of the Company for working mines in New England, July 20, 1692, C.O. 5/857, no. 3. For the subsequent history of the project, see Eleanor Lord, *Industrial Experiments in the British Colonies of North America,* 6–7, 15–30.

[87] Increase Mather, Diary, July 1691, Mass. Hist. Soc.

nor desired." The agents were not plenipotentiaries from another sovereign state, and "if we declared we would not submit to the King's Pleasure, his Majesty was resolved to settle the Countrey and we must take what would follow."[88]

A more reasoned plea to the committee, drawn up with Ashurst's aid and citing the king's promises concerning New England, was no more effective. Cooke and Oakes, for their part, had held aloof from the negotiations—Cooke had refused to attend at Whitehall during Mather's illness—and they now urged delay until the king returned to England. Mather acquiesced, and together the agents petitioned the queen that either Treby's draft be accepted without alteration or the charter's completion be delayed until the king's return. At Mather's urging, Archbishop Tillotson persuaded Mary to write to her husband in support of this request. Mather also sent a copy of his objections to the committee's amendments to Secretary Sidney, who had accompanied William to Flanders.[89]

In the meantime, however, either because of some renewed disagreement with Cooke and Oakes or in order to preserve as many options as possible, Mather continued to negotiate with the committee. He was once more forced to give ground. In May, he had resigned himself to the appointment of a royal governor despite the forebodings of such friends as the Harleys that "this is parting with all." He had made further concessions, step by step, in July. By the end of the month, Treby was able to report to the committee that the agents— presumably Mather and Ashurst—accepted all save three of the amendments. They insisted only that there be a limit upon the time

[88] Increase Mather, *A Brief Account, Andros Tracts*, II, 281. His diary, July 24, 1691, Mass. Hist. Soc., records that he told Treby that "I would part with my life First than consent to Mr B[lathwayt?]'s Minutes which were fatal to the Life of N. E."

[89] Increase Mather, *A Brief Account, Andros Tracts*, II, 282 (together with the extracts from Calef's *More Wonders* and Mather's reply reprinted in *Andros Tracts*, II, 316, 319); Petition prepared for presentation to the queen, Mass. Hist. Soc., *Proceedings*, XII (1871–1873), 120–121; Increase Mather, Diary, July 17, 23–25, 1691, Mass. Hist. Soc. Cooke did take part in combating the claims of Samuel Allen and the Gorges family: thus his letters to Bradstreet, Sept. 10, Nov. 4, 1691, Prince Papers. Unhappily, only fragments of his correspondence with Isaac Addington, said by Ichabod Wiswall to give the inside story of the negotiations, have survived.

in which the king could disallow the colony's laws, that all officials, including judges, justices, and sheriffs, be chosen by the assembly, and that the governor should have no power of veto over appointments but only over legislation. The first issue was soon settled, but neither side was willing to give way on the others. The committee eventually agreed to ask for further guidance on the matter, a concession that can probably be attributed to the presence of Mather's friends, Powle and Boscawen, at the meeting since, for the first time in several months, Carmarthen and Goodricke were the only Tories in attendance. The Privy Council, in turn, with the queen presiding, instructed Secretary Nottingham to seek a decision from the king. Mather thereupon retired to the country for a month's convalescence at Francis Charlton's house in Totteridge, ten miles northwest of London and within walking distance of the healing waters of the medicinal well at Barnet.[90]

Nottingham duly forwarded the agents' objections to William in Flanders but in terms which demanded their rejection as a vote of confidence in the committee's work. His tone exemplified official attitudes toward the colonies as vividly as the snub administered to Mather the month before. "The Committee," he wrote to the king, "has made all the condescension to that people which could possibly consist with your sovereignty over them." To accept the colonists' demands "admitts them almost to a copartnership in government . . . since rewards and punishments will be put into their own hand." The committee has already offered Massachusetts "more than any of the plantations or of your kingdoms yet pretend to." Further concessions, Nottingham concluded, summoning up the venerable specter of the transatlantic conspiracy of dissent, will only encourage new demands by others in England.[91]

---

[90] Robert Harley to Sir Edward Harley, June 2, Edward Harley to Sir Edward Harley, June 13, 1691, HMC, *Portland,* III, 467, 468; Report of the Attorney-General, [July 29, 1691], C.O. 5/856, no. 176; Report of the Lords of Trade, July 29, 1691, *ibid.,* no. 177; Journal of the Lords of Trade, July 29, 1691, C.O. 391/7, 37–38; Order in Council, July 30, 1691, *APC Col.,* II, 126–127; Increase Mather, Diary, Aug. 8–Sept. 7, 1691, Mass. Hist. Soc.; William Page, ed., *The Victoria County History of Hertfordshire,* 329.

[91] Nottingham to the king, July 31, 1691, HMC, *Finch,* III, 187–188.

The letter produced its desired effect. On August 10, Sidney replied that the king had expressed his satisfaction with the committee's proceedings and his entire disapproval of the agents' objections. Mather was summoned back to London to find that nothing remained but acquiescence in the completion of the charter on the best remaining terms.[92]

This, at least, was the account that Mather later presented in justification of his actions. While essentially correct, it glosses over a more complex reality. In defending himself against Robert Calef's charge that he had made needless concessions to serve his own ends, Mather told of being called back to London "before I had been there [in the country] three weeks." He left the city on August 8, and he certainly returned on August 26 to meet with Blathwayt and Nottingham. He omitted to mention, however, a similar two-day visit to London earlier in the month, during which he met with Ashurst, Nottingham, and D'Alonne after Phips had travelled out to Totteridge to fetch him back. And at about this time, and before the arrival of Sidney's letter from Flanders, Nottingham wrote to his fellow secretary that the New England agents were now willing to accept the charter on the committee's terms and would not insist on their objections.[93] This can only refer to Mather and his friends. The simplest explanation is that Phips or the agents had already heard of William's decision, perhaps from the queen's secretary, D'Alonne, or from another of Mather's recent acquaintances with friends in high places, William

---

[92] Sidney to Nottingham, Aug. 10, 1691, *ibid.*, 199; also *Andros Tracts*, II, 320, 283.

[93] *Andros Tracts*, II, 283–284, 316–317, 319–321; Increase Mather, Diary, Aug. 8, 12–14, 26–28, 1691, Mass. Hist. Soc.; Nottingham to Sidney, Aug. 11 (?), Sidney to Nottingham, Aug. 20, 1691, HMC, *Finch*, III, 202, 220. All dates, even those of letters from Flanders, then using New Style dating, are uniformly in Old Style dating. A further chronological problem is that Nottingham's letter telling of the agents' submission is apparently dated August 11 but Mather did not return to London until August 12, consulting with Nottingham the following day (Mather's diary entries can be checked against others entered among his expenses). Perhaps Nottingham knew of the agents' submission before Mather's return, for it was Phips, as Nottingham informed the committee of trade on August 20, who told him of that submission (C.O. 391/7, 40); or perhaps Nottingham's letter, which contains a succession of news items, was not completed until August 13.

Paterson, the Scottish financier who was just beginning the meteoric career which encompassed the founding of the Bank of England and the promotion of the ill-fated Darien Company.[94] Or it may be that Mather repented of his support of Cooke and Oakes in their appeals for delay. The mutilation of Treby's draft had left him torn between conciliation and defiance; in seeking an end to this painful ambiguity he may have felt that even the chance of royal intervention would not prevent the eventual submission predicted by his opponents.

Whether or not Mather withdrew his objections before learning of William's response, the effect was the same. Despite the blasting of his hopes, he stood ready to proceed with the completion of the charter. His decision was the logical conclusion of three years of negotiation, and it can hardly be construed to his discredit. He recognized what others discounted or ignored, that Massachusetts could not depend upon the old charter. It was defective as an instrument of government and it could not withstand a second challenge from the crown.[95] Further, he knew of his country's need for a speedy settlement and that Whitehall would dispatch a governor with or without his consent. A gaggle of English soldiers—Nicholson, Sloughter, Copley—had already been appointed to rule the mainland colonies. Old enemies were returning to power, Randolph becoming surveyor general of the customs in America and Andros succeeding Nicholson in Virginia. Mather was well aware of these dangers. "If the new draft be not submitted to," he wrote in his diary, "that which is worse will be imposed—A strang[er] will be appoynted governor and Andros creatures will be of his council; there will be no Judges or Lawes but what they shall assent to and what a case is the Countrey in then?" As the

---

[94] W. A. S. Hewins in Stephen and Lee, *Dictionary of National Biography,* s.v. "William Paterson"; Paterson's identity is confirmed by his signature on a petition he presented with Mather, Aug. 27, 1691, C.O. 5/856, no. 183, the same as that reproduced in James S. Barbour, *A History of William Paterson and the Darien Company,* 154. Mather met with Phips and Paterson several times during these crucial weeks: Diary, July 31, Aug. 3, 7, 1691, Mass. Hist. Soc.

[95] Increase Mather, *A Brief Account, Andros Tracts,* II, 287, and the opinion on the old charter drawn up by John Hooke for John Hampden in Hutchinson, *History of Massachusetts-Bay,* I, 347n. A similar, briefer statement, also submitted as a report to "Mr. Hampden," is in C.O. 5/856, no. 158xxx.

first governor bent the twig, so would grow the tree. It was essential that "faithfull hands" should implement the new charter.[96]

Merely to acknowledge the sanity of Mather's pragmatism, however, is to neglect the extent to which his views had changed since the days when he had led the Boston freemen in opposition to any compromise with the crown's demands. Cooke and Oakes had learnt their lessons well, and it is scarcely surprising that they and other colonists believed that Mather had succumbed to the same corruptions he had detected in earlier agents and regarded him as a renegade from the cause he had helped to create. The entries confided to his diary during the summer of 1691 and the tortured repetitions in the *Brief Account* of his agency show that the choice was not an easy one to make. It was Mather's fate to prefigure rather than accompany New England's accommodation to empire, and he suffered accordingly. "Dulce est pro patria mori," he inscribed upon the flyleaf of his diary, but the tag rang hollow—a sacrifice for one's country was scarcely sweet if one returned to find it viewed as a betrayal.

William had authorized the immediate completion of the charter, and Mather returned to London late in August to find Blathwayt intent on rushing matters to a conclusion. By routing Attorney General Treby and his clerk from their refuge in the fashionable spa of Tunbridge Wells, the secretary managed to have a new draft of the charter ready for submission to the committee by the second week in September. Mather, though disconcerted by this haste, petitioned for several more amendments. Most were petty and procedural compared to what had gone before—the council's quorum and the times of its meetings, the forms of oath taking, and a request that the assembly be permitted to send its own agents to London in time of need, a remarkably farsighted prediction of the consequences of the imperial relationship and the expedient adopted by several colonial

---

[96] Increase Mather, Diary, fol. 1v., under date of Sept. 9, 1691, Mass. Hist. Soc. On the competition for the northern governorships, see Cooke to Bradstreet, Nov. 4, 1691, Prince Papers.

assemblies in the following century. The committee sanctioned these changes with the exception of the last. It also accepted a stipulation which went far toward ensuring the charter's acceptance in Massachusetts—the confirmation of all land grants previously made by the General Court and all property legally vested in the inhabitants.[97]

With the form of government decided, there remained the equally important issues of its boundaries and personnel. At Mather's request, Maine and Nova Scotia—Acadia as far as the St. Lawrence—were included in the new charter. His petition for New Hampshire was denied, but early in September, while he was once more at Totteridge, the committee agreed to incorporate Plymouth Colony into Massachusetts. Finally, the agents were invited to nominate the officers of the new government. Only in one respect did the colonists' solicitations redound to their disadvantage. As the future was to show, Phips nourished grandiose schemes for trading monopolies and landed proprietorships in northern New England which he endeavoured to advance by promoting the rich naval stores to be found in the region. The result was a provision in the charter reserving trees of a certain size for the king—a source of endless trouble in later years—and another forbidding the granting of land east of the Kennebec River without royal permission.[98]

Events now progressed with all the speed that Blathwayt could have desired. Mather scurried between the officials at Whitehall and

[97] Sidney to Nottingham, Aug. 20, 1691, HMC, *Finch*, III, 220. Blathwayt to Treby, Aug. 23, S. Gwillym to Blathwayt, Aug. 23, 1691, Draft charter for Massachusetts, [Sept. 6, 1691], Petition of I. Mather and William Paterson (on behalf of Ashurst), Aug. 27, 1691, Memorial of the Massachusetts agents, [Sept. 15, 1691], C.O. 5/856, nos. 181, 182, 189, 183, 192; Journal of the Lords of Trade, Aug. 20, Sept. 2, 3, 16, C.O. 391/7, 40–44, 50.

[98] Journal of the Lords of Trade, Sept. 3, 7, 9, 1691, C.O. 391/7, 44–49; Sir Henry Ashurst to Increase Mather, Sept. 3, 1691, in Hutchinson, *History of Massachusetts-Bay*, I, 349n. The draft charter drawn up in early September included Plymouth Colony (C.O. 5/856, fol. 635) but no other defined boundaries. It also set the line beyond which land grants were forbidden without royal permission at the Piscataqua (fol. 656); despite the committee's decision on Sept. 3 to move it east to Sagadahoc (the Kennebec), Mather had to protest to get this implemented. For Phips's plans, see his memorials, [Sept. 2, Nov. 10, 1691], C.O. 5/856, nos. 184, 203, and the following chapter.

his legal advisers at the Temple to make certain of the last details of the charter. Its final drafting entailed large expenditures—184 guineas alone for Treby's clerk Gwillym, and a further £65 in fees to secure its passage through the seals. Mather subsequently estimated the total cost at £270.[99] Cooke and Oakes refused to share in these expenses or to take part in the nomination of officers—from their point of view Massachusetts was being asked to purchase its own fetters and choose its own jailers. Cooke still professed to pin his hopes for a more favorable settlement on the intervention of the king, and he expressed his bitterness to Bradstreet that, "some being restless and impatient till that matter was irretrievable," the charter had passed the Great Seal three days before William's return on October 19. Whether or not Cooke seriously believed in the likelihood of a royal reprieve (since by Blathwayt's account William heartily approved of the settlement), Mather's alleged "rashness and imprudence" were a useful peg on which to hang a seemingly rational rejection of the charter.[100]

To Cooke's alarm, the charter was completed even before a governor and his deputy were selected. But, true to its agreement with the agents, the committee secured the appointment of all those whom Mather and Ashurst had nominated. Indeed, Nottingham twice escorted Mather to audiences with the king to forward the commissioning of Phips as the first governor of the province of the Massachusetts Bay.[101] To all appearances, it was a perfect choice. Phips had proved his loyalty and service to the crown by his conquest of Acadia and his recovery of the Caribbean treasure. With this bubble reputation he could pass as the "Military Man" the king desired for the government of New England. To the colonists, he was from among

---

[99] Increase Mather, Diary, Sept. 8–Oct. 9, 1691, and among his expenses under date Sept. 22, Nov. 12, 1691, Mass. Hist. Soc.; Murdock, "Increase Mather's Expenses," 203.

[100] Cooke to Bradstreet, Nov. 4, 1691, Prince Papers; Increase Mather to John Richards, Oct. 26, 1691, Winthrop Papers; *idem,* Diary, Sept. 17, Oct. 7, 13, 22, 1691, Mass. Hist. Soc.

[101] Increase Mather, *Autobiography,* 336–337; *idem,* Diary, Oct. 23, Nov. 4, 1691, Mass. Hist. Soc.

themselves, a local hero risen from rural obscurity and untainted with past political involvement or mercantile sophistication. And to the Mathers, he was peculiarly their own candidate. Cotton had baptized him into membership of their own Second Church and watched over his swift advancement to freemanship, military command, and the magistracy; Increase had tutored him in the ways of Whitehall.[102] This protean ability to appear attractive to both sides of the Atlantic became an essential qualification for executive power in Massachusetts; time was to reveal the temperamental deficiencies in Phips that lay behind the facade erected by his admirers.

With the rest of his nominations, Mather set the new government squarely in the center of Boston's political spectrum. The charter provided for the annual election by the General Court of twenty-eight assistants or councillors, of which at least eighteen were to be inhabitants or landowners in Massachusetts, four in Plymouth, three in Maine, and one in the country east of the Kennebec. Mather's nominees, who were to serve until May 1693, were listed in the charter. Three local leaders represented Maine. All four chosen from Plymouth were already serving as magistrates in the colony, as were eleven of the remaining twenty-one in Massachusetts. More significant in view of the tradition of political continuity in New England, however, was Mather's omission of six other Massachusetts assistants currently in office. All six—Cooke, Oakes, Thomas Danforth, and three more from rural communities—were diehard supporters of the old charter. Mather cut himself adrift from these traditional allies and followed his son's lead in extending an olive branch to the moderates and the merchants of the coastal towns. At Cotton's recommendation, Stoughton replaced Danforth as deputy governor. Bartholemew Gedney of Salem (who, like Stoughton, had served under both Andros and the old charter), John Richards, Adam Winthrop, John Joyliffe, Peter Sergeant, John Foster, and Richard Middlecott of Boston, and Joseph Lynd and Samuel Hayman of Charlestown, together

---

[102] Bullivant, "Journal," 105; Cotton Mather, *Life of Phips*, 54–62, and *idem, Diary*, ed. Ford, I, 148.

with Stephen Mason of London, were the ten new councillors from Massachusetts. Four were members of the Mathers' church. All save three had served on the Council of Safety, and only Mason (whose name Mather inserted in the charter in place of that of James Prentice, apparently in gratitude for his assistance) had not previously been elected by popular vote to some form of public office in Massachusetts. Isaac Addington, a friend and correspondent of Elisha Cooke, retained his place as secretary of the colony.[103]

These appointments completed a settlement that contained much of permanent value to Massachusetts, and indeed to all the New England colonies. With representative government formally reestablished, the Dominion became an unnatural hiatus rather than a precedent. In Mather's words, "the General Court ... hath, with the King's Approbation, as much power in *New-England* as the King and Parliament have in *England.*" It could tax, legislate, and erect courts capable of exercising full powers of judgment. Alone among colonial legislatures, the assembly was specifically empowered by charter to apportion representation within the province.[104] Equally unique was its right to elect the governor's council in conjunction with the outgoing members of that body—not even the House of Commons had any hand in selecting its upper house. Admittedly, the governor could now nominate and veto as never before. Yet as Mather pointed out, his appointments could only be made with the consent of the elected council, while the assembly controlled the purse strings of the province. And since there was no permanent appropriation for the governor's salary, in effect, "the People have a Negative on him." The colo-

---

[103] *Mass. Acts and Resolves,* I, 10–12; Nominations submitted by Mather and Ashurst, [Sept. 18, 1691], C.O. 5/856, nos. 193, 194. Mather seems to have made overtures to his more moderate opponents such as Charles Lidgett as early as 1690: thus Joshua Moody to Increase Mather, Jan. 28, 1691, J. Trumbull Collection, no. 16, Mass. Hist. Soc.

[104] Increase Mather, *A Brief Account, Andros Tracts,* II, 289. Other colonies had secured a de facto or, in the case of Virginia and Jamaica, a statutory right to control apportionment.

nists were also assured of all the liberties and immunities of native-born English subjects, and all Protestants were granted freedom of conscience in matters of religion. Where most of these privileges had been enjoyed only by prescriptive inflation of the patent of a trading company, they were now guaranteed by grant from the crown. "These things," concluded Mather from his vantage point in London, "are as a Wall of Defence about the Lord's Vineyard in that part of the World."[105]

In addition, the charter greatly expanded the vineyard's boundaries. It granted to the Boston government the dominion over the lands of northern New England that royal officials had sought to prevent since the Restoration. New Hampshire, Rhode Island and the Narragansett country, other neighbors who had felt the force of the Bay colony's expansion, retained a feeble independence. But Plymouth was annexed and the constriction which had threatened New England since the grant of Pemaquid to the Duke of York was forever removed. Well might Wiswall complain that "the whole of N[ew] E[ngland's] interests seem designed to be loaden on one bottom and her particular motions to be concentric to the Massachusetts tropic." And the charter added the authority to render this dominion effective. Besides confirming existing titles, whatever their "defect of Form," it permitted the General Court to grant new patents and establish townships. It contained no mention of quitrents. Nor could appeals in cases involving real property be carried to England. If nothing else, the new charter contained everything that a budding land speculator could desire.[106]

Thus in several respects, notably in the powers accorded to the provincial assembly at the expense of the autonomy of the upper house, Massachusetts received greater privileges from the crown than other colonies subject to direct royal control. By contrast, the govern-

---

[105] *Ibid.*, 290, 289; *Mass. Acts and Resolves*, I, 14.

[106] *Mass. Acts and Resolves*, I, 8–10, 15, 17; Wiswall to Thomas Hinckley, Nov. 5, 1691, Mass. Hist. Soc., *Collections*, 4th ser., V (1861), 301. This was Mather's interpretation of the provisions concerning appeals; it was later challenged by the crown.

ments simultaneously established in Maryland and New Hampshire were modelled according to the pattern of Virginia and the West Indian colonies where the crown appointed both the governor and his council. These privileges could not have been obtained without Mather's efforts; nor would the charter have been so complete and carefully detailed an instrument of government.

At the same time, there is no reason to credit Mather with averting a restoration of the Dominion in its old and restrictive form. Blathwayt and Southwell may have cherished some such intentions, but the committee held steadily to the purpose it had defined two years before—a settlement "as may be lasting, and Preserve the Rights and Properties of the People of New England and yet Reserve such a Dependance on the Crowne of England, as shalbe thought requisite." Uniformity in colonial administration, not the resuscitation of unwieldy and eccentric frontier provinces, was the goal; not a policy that might fritter away resources needed at home, but "bare defence and the keeping of what already Wee have."[107] In short, not nostrums but normalcy. Months before the committee took up the question of a new charter for Massachusetts, it had already recommended that a governor be sent to New York "with such a Commission and Instructions as are intended for the other Plantations." Hence Sloughter was instructed to summon an assembly of freeholders, a decisive and, as it proved, final, rejection of James Stuart's most radical departure from traditional policy. In similar fashion, the committee or its subordinates used a draft of the Virginia charter of 1676 in preparing the Massachusetts patent. For reasons both pragmatic and principled—ministers who had rallied to the banner of the Prince of Orange could scarcely deny representative government and security of property to other Englishmen, even though colonists—Whitehall had no intention of preserving a regime that had touched off armed rebellion in the plantations.[108]

---

[107] Report of the Lords of Trade, Feb. 22, 1689, *APC Col.*, II, 125; [Southwell?] to Nottingham, Mar. 23, 1689, in Hall, Leder, and Kammen, *Glorious Revolution in America*, 69.

[108] Memorandum of the Lords of Trade, Aug. 31, Commission of Colonel

## Transatlantic Interaction and Compromise

What endured was the insistence that Massachusetts recognize and submit to royal authority; on this point the crown and its servants achieved their object. In essence the final settlement had two interlocking parts: the committee enfolded the colony in a skeletal structure of royal government and permitted the agents to mask the structure's bones with the flesh of procedure and personnel. The king appointed the governor, his deputy, and the secretary of the colony. The governor in turn appointed judges, sheriffs, marshals, and justices of the peace with the advice and consent of his council. He held power to veto over laws and all other acts of government, including the election of councillors. Should legislation surmount this hurdle, it still ran the risk of falling before the more formidable barrier of disallowance by the King in Council. Massachusetts was brought to toe the common line in other respects. All public officers were required to take the prescribed oath of allegiance. Certain judicial causes could be appealed to the Privy Council, and admiralty jurisdiction was reserved to the crown. The declaration of liberty of conscience withdrew official sanction from the enforcement of Puritan orthodoxy, and the replacement of the primarily religious qualifications for colony-wide voting by a franchise open to the traditional forty-shilling freeholder and other inhabitants worth fifty (or, in the inaccurate copy of the charter sent to Boston, forty) pounds in estate destroyed the institutional underpinnings of sectarian politics in the colony.[109]

This framework, particularly the governor's veto and his control over the administration of justice, was well suited to the purpose of curbing that open defiance of the crown's commercial regulations and

Sloughter, Nov. 14, 1689, *N. Y. Col. Docs.,* III, 618, 624; Journal of the Lords of Trade, Oct. 28, 1689, C.O. 391/6, 284; Copy of preamble of Virginia charter adapted for Massachusetts, [June? 1691], C.O. 5/856, no. 167; David S. Lovejoy, "Virginia's Charter and Bacon's Rebellion, 1675-1676," 31-51.

[109] *Mass. Acts and Resolves,* I, 11-12, 363; for the consequences of the difference between the copies of the charter, see Ellis Ames in Mass. Hist. Soc., *Proceedings,* X (1867-1869), 370-375; and Robert E. Brown, *Middle-Class Democracy and the Revolution in Massachusetts, 1691-1780,* 21-24. Also note 74, preceding, for the evolution of this franchise; and Chapter 5, note 62, following, for its limited political consequences.

of Whitehall's efforts to provide redress to colonial petitioners that had done so much to precipitate royal intervention in the past. Whether the charter would also provide competent and responsible government was another matter, one which did not greatly trouble English officials. Their prime concern was a recognition of sovereignty, a reassertion of control.[110] Hence the concessions made to Mather may well have seemed a small price to pay for acceptance of the larger principle and the conclusion of so troublesome a matter. This would explain Nottingham's sudden cordiality toward Mather in the months following their agreement on the charter. The secretary introduced the agent a third time to the king at Whitehall and entertained him to dinner in company with Mather's friend and fellow minister, Dr. William Bates, and one of his own Anglican protégés, John Moore, Bishop of Norwich. Mather corresponded with Nottingham long after his return to New England, and their friendship was a measure of the committee's respect for Mather's achievement in cajoling and pressuring the English court into compromise with his proposals.[111] It was a measure also, perhaps, of official gratitude; the committee was well aware that Mather's decision to part company with his fellow agents and support the charter vastly improved its chances for acceptance by the unpredictable fanatics across the Atlantic.

On the pressing issue of defense, the charter said little save to cite this as the reason for annexing Plymouth to Massachusetts. The governor was given command of the militia, though in deference to the agents' request he was forbidden to declare martial law without the

---

[110] "I assure your Majesty," wrote Nottingham to the king in his letter of July 31, 1691, "here is no dispute in this matter between partys unless it be between them who would support your regal just authority and those who little by little would leave you none:" HMC, *Finch*, III, 188.

[111] Increase Mather, *Autobiography*, 337; *idem*, Diary, Nov. 6, 20, 1691, Mass. Hist. Soc.; Mather to Nottingham, June 23, 1692, Nov. 26, 1703, C.O. 5/751, no. 7, Addit. MSS., 29549, fol. 111. One remarkable tribute to Mather's reputation survives in Mass. Archives, XI, 59: a letter from one Jo. Combe to Mather, c. 1691, asking him to contact Lords Delamere or Monmouth through Ashurst to recommend Mr. Webb, the minister of Inniskilling, northern Ireland, for a bishopric.

council's agreement or to march troops out of the province without
the General Court's consent or that of the troops themselves. In
drafting Phips's commission, however, and in obedience to the king's
wishes, the committee tried once more to unite New England behind
a single military leader. In addition to the customary authority allowed to royal governors in naval affairs, which included the power to
erect vice-admiralty courts and to suspend captains of the Royal
Navy from their posts, Phips was appointed commander-in-chief of
the militias of all the New England colonies. A few months later,
Benjamin Fletcher, the newly chosen governor of New York, was similarly authorized to enlist men from the militia of the Jerseys.[112] It
was a device which aptly reflected the mixture of conservatism and
expediency that characterized the revolutionary settlement in
America. Except where they had no alternative but to take more decisive action, as in the case of the Massachusetts charter, the Lords of
Trade chose to settle for solutions to old problems that would leave
existing arrangements undisturbed. A vague expectation of intercolonial cooperation replaced the unsettling coercion of the Dominion.
Royal officials do not seem to have paused to consider whether semi-
autonomous colonies such as Rhode Island and Connecticut would
indeed surrender control of their armed forces to a neighboring royal
governor; the compromise between respect for New England's constitutional proprieties and the needs of its defense was too convenient
for its wisdom to be questioned.

To colonists in Massachusetts, however, Phips's military authority
opened a way to regain the assistance once provided by the now de-
funct New England Confederation, and royal officials did their best
to give substance to the plan by providing the sinews of war. They

---

[112] *Mass. Acts and Resolves,* I, 8, 18; Commission and Instructions to Sir William
Phips, Dec. 12, 31, 1691, Pubs. Col. Soc. Mass., *Collections,* II (1913), 69–75, C.O.
5/905, 265–394; Order of the Queen in Council, Mar. 10, 1692, C.O. 5/1037, no.
89; Commission for Benjamin Fletcher, governor of New York, as governor of
Pennsylvania, Oct. 21, 1693, *N. Y. Col. Docs.,* III, 859–860. Phips's instructions
omitted the usual phrases concerning the royal governor's duty to lead and encourage the Church of England. They did not, however, permit what Phips and
Mather had petitioned for, Nov. 9, 1691, C.O. 5/856, no. 202, that is, a liberty for
Massachusetts to coin its own money.

ordered the dispatch to Boston of over a thousand pounds worth of munitions, including two hundred barrels of powder.[113] Responding to the pleas of the merchants, they arranged for two frigates to be stationed off the New England coast. Plans were in preparation for a naval expedition that would sweep through the West Indies and then sail north to assist in a second assault upon Canada.[114]

Mather could cite these benefits as visible proof of the advantages of working in harmony with the crown. He well knew that the negotiation of a settlement in London did not ensure its acceptance in New England—indeed, past history indicated that the contrary was more often true—and he passed the months before he and Phips set sail for Boston in March 1692 in gathering support for the struggle that lay ahead. He wrote and published a *Brief Account* of his agency, justifying his actions, and appended to it an extract of a letter signed by thirteen eminent dissenting ministers, testifying to Mather's "inviolate Integrity, excellent Prudence and unfainting Diligence." Sir Henry Ashurst and Robert Thompson wrote in similar terms to the Massachusetts government, the latter adding a scathing criticism of those who had refused to help Mather "because their morose conceited Humours were not comply'd with." Thompson concluded by advising the colonists that "for the future if you shall have occasion to send Commissioners over you will send such as know how to distinguish between our Court and yours."[115] In one respect, Mather was

[113] Increase Mather to Richards, Oct. 26, 1691, Winthrop Papers; Sir Henry Ashurst to the Governor and Council of Massachusetts, Dec. 28, 1691, Curwin Papers, III, 41, Amer. Antiq. Soc.; Memorial of the agents, Oct. 1, 1691, C.O. 5/856, no. 200; Order of the Queen in Council, Oct. 8, 1691, C.O. 5/905, 397–398. Mather twice called at the Tower of London to secure ammunition for New England: Diary, Oct. 15, 17, 1691, Mass. Hist. Soc.

[114] Minutes of the Lords of Trade, Sept. 28, Oct. 6, 1691, Orders of the King in Council, Dec. 17, 1691, Jan. 14, 1692, Proposals for destroying the French Plantations in America, [June? 1691], *CSP Col., 1689–1692,* nos. 1788, 1805, 1956, 2008, 1560; Draft of instructions for Sir Francis Wheeler, [Oct. 21, 1691], *Calendar of State Papers, Domestic Series, of the Reign of William and Mary, 1690–1691,* 542–543; George H. Guttridge, *The Colonial Policy of William III in America and the West Indies,* 62–68, 74–75.

[115] Increase Mather, Diary, Oct. 5, 1691, Mass. Hist. Soc.—"Wrote Narrative of my Negotiations"; *idem, A Brief Account, Andros Tracts,* II, 273–298 (the text is dated Nov. 16, 1691); Ashurst to the Governor and Council of Massachusetts, Dec. 28,

fortunate. Wiswall had denounced Mather's role in the extinction of
Plymouth's independence and Cooke had gone so far as to suggest
that Massachusetts consider repudiating the entire settlement. But
whether morose or disconsolate, they made no attempt to carry their
protest to the people of the colony. Mather and Phips landed in Boston at dusk on May 14, a full six months before Cooke, Oakes, and
Wiswall slipped quietly back to their homes, "almost before any body
knew it."[116]

Even had the three agents reached Boston before Mather, it is unlikely that they could have excited Massachusetts into resistance. The
peace concluded with the Indians in November 1690 had broken
down the following spring, and throughout the remainder of the year,
the Abnaki ravaged the eastern frontier with a devastating war of at-
trition. Cattle were killed, settlers driven from their homes and crops.
An ill-equipped expedition under Captain John March was am-
bushed; it returned home "in a shattred Condition." And less than
four months before Mather's return, as if to remind the colonists of
the international context of the struggle, a force of French and Indians descended upon the town of York, killing and capturing over a
hundred of its inhabitants. Among the dead, shot down on his own
doorstep, was Shubael Dummer, the first minister (and second Harvard graduate) to perish in New England's wars.[117] Already the colony had lost the fruit of its only victory, the capture of Port Royal.
Unable to provide a garrison for the town—the Massachusetts militia
were of one mind in their distaste for such duties—the debt-ridden
Boston government had authorized a consortium of merchants led by

1691, letter of Robert Thompson, Jan. 1, 1692, Curwin Papers, III, 41, 33, Amer.
Antiq. Soc. (an extract from Thompson's letter addressed to William Stoughton
is in Mass. Archives CCXLII, 421). Also Joseph Thompson to Increase Mather,
Nov. 17, 1693, Mass. Archives, CVI, 380, and Ashurst to Cotton Mather, Dec. 28,
1691, Curwin Papers, III, 38, Amer. Antiq. Soc.

[116] Wiswall to Hinckley, Nov. 5, 1691, Mass. Hist. Soc., *Collections*, 4th ser., V
(1861), 299–301; Cooke to Bradstreet, Nov. 4, 1691, Prince Papers; Sewall, *Diary*,
I, 291, 299.

[117] Cotton Mather, *Decennium Luctuosum*, in Lincoln, *Narratives of the Indian Wars*,
228–232; *Doc. Hist. Maine*, V, 243–339.

John Nelson and Edward Tyng to use the town as a center for trade. No sooner had their caravan arrived in Acadia than it was snapped up, and Port Royal recaptured, by a cruising French frigate, at a loss to Boston commerce estimated by Sewall at eighteen thousand pounds.[118] Only an English naval patrol could curb this menace. Meanwhile, within the colony, the seeds of the witchcraft hysteria were taking root: as many as a hundred prisoners awaited the pleasure of the new governor. Clearly Massachusetts was in no condition to oppose any reasonable solution to its difficulties, especially one advocated by the most influential minister in the colony.

Thus, as in 1686, there was no resistance to the establishment of a royal government in Massachusetts. The predominant feeling was probably one of relief, for up until the end of 1691 persistent reports that Andros would return as governor had poised Cotton Mather and his friends "on the wing," ready to flee to his father in England.[119] No doubt some feared that Phips, like Joseph Dudley, would prove to be the opening wedge of some darker scheme. But the provisions of the charter, restoring a representative assembly and hedging the authority of the governor with safeguards, were quickly published for all to read, and London's prudence in allowing native New Englanders to man the new administration provided a somewhat spurious sense of continuity—fifteen of those named in the charter had been elected to the magistracy ten days before its arrival. Mather and Phips took care to observe the proper forms; the latter's installation was delayed a day to avoid profaning the Sabbath and the new governor gave broad assurances of his devotion to the principles and practices hallowed by tradition. The illusion was complete; a year later the congregation of the church at Plymouth counted among its blessings, be-

---

[118] Commission and instructions to Edward Tyng, July 20, 1691, Mass. Archives, XXXVII, 85, 86; Francis Foxcroft to Francis Nicholson, Oct. 26, to Jeremiah Johnson, Nov. 19, David Jeffries to John Usher, Nov. 19, 1691, *CSP Col., 1689–1692*, nos. 1857, 1910, 1911; Sewall, *Diary*, I, 282–283.

[119] Cotton Mather to [John Cotton], Dec. 8, 1691, Silverman, *Selected Letters of Cotton Mather*, 29; Samuel Ravenscroft to Francis Nicholson, Nov. 5, 1691, *CSP Col., 1689–1692*, no. 1875. Nicholson seems to have broadcast these rumors; ironically, it was he who was displaced by Andros when the latter was appointed governor of Virginia.

sides health, harvest, returning agents, repulsing the enemy at Wells, and "destroying caterpillars last summer," the fact that "the Government over us is yet in the hands of saints."[120]

Mather's return set an end to one phase of New England's adjustment to empire and inaugurated another. In retrospect, the Massachusetts charter of 1691 was remarkable less for its character than for the circumstances in which it emerged. Other colonies—Connecticut, Rhode Island, and Virginia—had solicited earlier in the century for such privileges with varying degrees of success. Massachusetts had gone its own way, self-contained and self-confident in its mission and ultimate strength. England's response was no less extreme—an alien regime imposed without care or consultation. A few saw the necessity (and personal advantage) of compromise, but they were a small minority distrusted by both sides. The Glorious Revolution came as a solvent to these congealed animosities. On the one hand, New England could feel that the mother country was once more worthy of allegiance; on the other, the crown abandoned its high-flying claims for the prerogative and its schemes for a wholesale reorganization of the American colonies. Above all, internal differences were submerged in opposition to a common enemy.

These circumstances were indispensable to the success of Mather's diplomacy. But they hardly detract from the achievements of a mission that, in terms of lasting results, must be judged the most notable of all the colonial agencies. The ministerial sneer that Mather was no plenipotentiary—a fact Wiswall and Cooke also emphasized in their letters home—concealed an uneasy consciousness that the contrary was closer to the truth. Mather had been, in effect, an independent mediator with talents and reputation enough on his own account to construct a new political equation out of the relationship between London and New England. Over the course of three years, he had put

---

[120] Joshua Broadbent to Francis Nicholson, June 21, 1692, *CSP Col., 1689–1692*, no. 2283; Sewall, *Diary*, I, 291; "Plymouth Church Records, 1620–1859," 172.

together a formidable coalition of allies ranging from Whig poten-
tates and Scottish ladies-in-waiting to London merchants and the
massed battalions of English Nonconformity. Some of these allies, no
doubt, were sincerely convinced by Mather's argument that colonists
and Englishmen had a common stake in the preservation of each
other's political freedoms; others he had brought to perceive the political capital to be gained at home by supporting dissenters abroad. To
royal officials, by bringing the weight of this coalition to bear, Mather
had shown that attempts to bring recalcitrant colonists to heel involved more than cranking up the inefficient machinery of English
government: they could also have unpleasant domestic consequences.
Mather had made the matter of Massachusetts a problem whose solution would pay political dividends at home, and in light of Whitehall's long-standing disdain for the colonists and their affairs this
strategy was undoubtedly a key to his success. To the colonists,
though few of them as yet perceived the lesson, Mather had demonstrated the advantages to be won by plying the corridors of Whitehall. In the past, the Massachusetts government had steered clear of
such entanglement; over the next decade it would come to accept the
necessity of maintaining a permanent, professional agency in London. If, in the end, the crown gained rather more than it conceded by
the settlement of 1691, this was not because of Mather's misjudgment
or his ambition to nominate the new government. Rather, both he
and royal officials in London became ever more aware of New England's weakness and the demoralization of its leadership. The
grounds for resistance were cut away from under Mather's feet. The
final settlement, a curious mixture of multiplicity in civil government
and unity in military command, mirrored the common determination of king and colonist to provide for a more effective defense of
New England without deranging its institutions.

The proof of this pudding lay in the eating of it. Massachusetts had
transformed one royal charter into the ark of its covenant; it remained to be seen what could be done with a second. But the times
were changed. America was caught up in the European struggle for
supremacy. The king's governor ruled in Massachusetts. In Boston,

Collector Jahleel Brenton was already battling traders in efforts to enforce the Acts of Trade. Elsewhere, the other New England colonies remained in suspense—New Hampshire watching for the arrival of Samuel Allen's lieutenant governor, John Usher, and Connecticut and Rhode Island waiting in apprehension to discover how Phips would execute his commission as generalissimo of their militia and whether his authority foreshadowed a new attempt at consolidation. In one way or another, royal government was now a permanent part of New England's political landscape.

# V

## Exploring a Settlement:
## Confusion and Conflict,
## 1692–1698

O n both sides of the Atlantic, the years following Mather's return
from London were a time of gradual adjustment to the new
order brought into being by the Glorious Revolution. In England, a
dozen years passed before the Act of Settlement in 1701 completed
the formal constitutional changes set in train by the overthrow of
James II. In New England, likewise, the imposition of royal government upon Massachusetts and New Hampshire was but the prelude
to its definition and explication in the arena of practical politics.
Even Rhode Island and Connecticut, for all their return to charter
rule, continued to feel and respond to the aftershocks of the political
disruption caused by the Dominion as well as the pressures exerted by
a London government still resolved to orchestrate colonial trade and
defense. By comparison with the previous decade's open confronta-
tions and sharp oscillations between defiance and authoritarianism,
the 1690s were a time of muted rivalries and grudging accommodation. A rough consensus as to the ways and forms of government
emerged; both colonists and royal officials moderated their expectations and demands. Yet serious political difficulties remained, rooted
in mutual uncertainties and exacerbated by the strains of war. Internal dissension followed external challenge. Only slowly did New
Englanders begin to perceive the opportunities as well as the tensions
and frustrations inherent in their closer relationship with the crown.

Overshadowing this relationship, and in large measure defining its
contours and development, lay the presence of incessant international
conflict. The War of the League of Augsburg—King William's

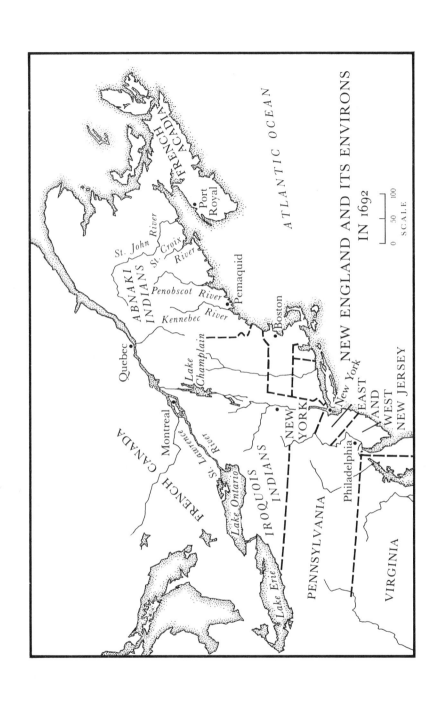

NEW ENGLAND AND ITS ENVIRONS
IN 1692

SCALE
0    50    100

ATLANTIC OCEAN

FRENCH ACADIA

Port Royal

St. John River

St. Croix River

ABNAKI INDIANS

Penobscot River

Kennebec River

Pemaquid

Boston

Quebec

Lake Champlain

New York

NEW YORK

Montreal

St. Lawrence River

FRENCH CANADA

IROQUOIS INDIANS

Lake Ontario

Lake Erie

EAST AND WEST NEW JERSEY

PENNSYLVANIA

Philadelphia

VIRGINIA

*Adjustment to Empire*

War—straggled to an indecisive close in 1697, but negotiations over colonial boundaries were still in progress when Louis XIV's acceptance of his grandson's inheritance of the Spanish empire in defiance of previous agreements with his European rivals precipitated a second and even more widespread conflict—the War of the Spanish Succession—which lasted until the Peace of Utrecht in 1713. Marlborough and Eugene battled the hitherto invincible armies of France on the fields of Flanders and Germany; rival fleets patrolled and skirmished in the strategic waters of the Mediterranean and Caribbean; and on the American mainland French and Spanish squadrons and raiding parties harassed the English settlements in South Carolina, Newfoundland, and Hudson's Bay. Nowhere in America was the struggle more bitter or prolonged than along the New England frontier. The massacre at York in 1692 was followed by further French and Indian attacks upon western Massachusetts and Maine, some penetrating as deeply as Lancaster, Groton, and Billerica, none more than thirty miles from Boston. To guard the frontier and overawe the Abnaki, the Massachusetts government built a strong fort at Pemaquid, Fort William Henry, near the mouth of the Kennebec. But in 1696 a French force captured both the fort and one of the English frigates patrolling the northern coasts. Laboriously assembled punitive expeditions counterattacked as far as French Acadia but accomplished little. Scarcely less demoralizing than these setbacks were the strains and costs of constantly garrisoning the frontiers against an enemy who might strike at any moment and vanish no less swiftly. The 1690s were indeed, as Cotton Mather declared, a *Decennium Luctuosum*, a sorrowful decade for the settlers of New England.[1]

Within the colonies, the war's consequences were capricious and often contradictory, opening the way for conquest yet inhibiting territorial expansion, crippling commerce and the northern fisheries, yet stimulating shipbuilding, the mast trade, and the expansion of the co-

---

[1] Cotton Mather, *Decennium Luctuosum*, in Lincoln, *Narratives of the Indian Wars*, 179–277. A useful narrative of events summarizing the main printed sources is given by Philip S. Haffenden, *New England in the English Nation, 1689–1713*, chapter III.

lonial merchant marine. In a number of towns, especially those best sheltered from attack, the population grew rapidly during the war years, seemingly as a result of internal migration from threatened areas of New England, the absence of any severe epidemics or crises of subsistence, and a sudden surge in the birth rate.[2] Migrants from surrounding communities moved to settle the relatively empty and secure lands between the Connecticut River and Narragansett Bay. In Massachusetts and New Hampshire as a whole, however, the rate of population growth appears to have been markedly less than in previous decades.[3] On the Massachusetts frontier, only two new towns were established, and an equal number were abandoned. Others were kept inhabited only by dint of laws confiscating the property of those who left their homes. All too many towns came to resemble the condition of Deerfield, whose inhabitants described themselves as "a Litle handful . . . in the Mouths of the Enemy," and Haverhill, where in 1694 all lived crammed "Top-full" in a few fortified garrison houses "much thronged with Children and Lice," not daring to venture out.[4]

At sea, even coastal trade had to sail in convoy for protection, and a visiting royal official later estimated that the war had cut Boston's

[2] Lockridge, "Population of Dedham," 321–322, 341; Philip J. Greven, Jr., *Four Generations*, 103, 180–185; Susan L. Norton, "Population Growth in Colonial America," 438. Hingham, by contrast, seems to have experienced a deceleration in population growth comparable to that of Massachusetts as a whole: Daniel Scott Smith, "The Demographic History of Colonial New England," 174–180.

[3] Mathews, *Expansion of New England,* 64–66; Richard L. Bushman, *From Puritan to Yankee,* 83 *et seq.;* Hutchinson, *History of Massachusetts-Bay,* II, 150. Massachusetts leaders frequently complained of the migration from the province into Rhode Island and Connecticut. For estimates of the population in the individual colonies, see U.S. Bureau of the Census, *Historical Statistics of the United States,* 756; these figures may be too high in absolute numbers but seem to be an accurate reflection of the pattern of population growth and internal migration suggested by the figures collected in Evarts B. Greene and Virginia D. Harrington, *American Population Before the Federal Census of 1790,* 8–73. Douglas R. McManus, *Colonial New England,* 68–69, provides some percentages of increase based on these figures.

[4] Petitions of the inhabitants of Deerfield, Feb. 18, Nov. 6, 1693, Feb. 22, 1694, Mass. Archives, CXII, 436, LXX, 199, CXIII, 57; Nathaniel Saltonstall to Rowland and Elizabeth Cotton, Aug. 23, 1694, Richard Saltonstall to Rowland Cotton, Aug. 16, 1695, Moody, *Saltonstall Papers,* 218, 242. The many town histories provide graphic details of frontier life at this time: see, for example, J. H. Temple, *History of North Brookfield.*

commerce by as much as two-thirds.[5] Yet even such hazards could open new paths to profit: privateering and its near (and often indistinguishable) relative, piracy, flourished as never before, bringing plunder and the unaccustomed jingle of hard currency to the ports of Rhode Island and the Bay.[6] The war sharpened both danger and opportunity, robbing John Higginson of Salem of the fishing ketches that were his livelihood, raising Andrew Belcher of Boston to a solid prosperity through the provisioning of colonial expeditions and visiting Royal Navy frigates, and propelling Samuel Lillie to dizzying heights of speculation in shipowning before consigning him to the ruin of a spectacular bankruptcy.[7]

In the realm of politics, too, the war's pressures quickened the pace of events. They hastened an unfolding of the constitutional legacies of the post-Revolutionary settlement, strengthening the claims of the representative assemblies to a voice in administrative matters and nourishing the growth of central government. As early as 1695, for example, the Boston government's annual expenditures had risen to over twenty-two thousand pounds, more than five times the amount of ten years before; nine-tenths were devoted to matters of defense.[8] The war perpetuated the colonists' dependence upon English military

---

[5] Gov. Fitz-John Winthrop to Gov. Joseph Dudley, Mar. 4, 1703, Mass. Hist. Soc., *Collections*, 6th ser., III (1889), 121–122; Robert Quarry to [the Commissioners of Customs?], Apr. 6, 1708, *ibid.*, 2nd ser., IV (1883), 153. Quarry's estimate seems high yet the toll taken by the French *guerre de course* was immense. The young Harvard graduate Henry Newman made three voyages to Spain during these years and his ship suffered French attack upon each occasion: Leonard W. Cowie, *Henry Newman*, 15.

[6] Curtis P. Nettels, *The Money Supply of the American Colonies before 1720*, 87–88; Craven, *Colonies in Transition*, 307–309. Piracy could bring strange fruits: in 1699 the Reverend Gurdon Saltonstall wrote of receiving 136 pounds of opium from a confiscated pirate cargo: Brock Collection, Box 256, Hunt. Lib.

[7] Rev. John Higginson to Nathaniel Higginson, Aug. 31, 1698 [1693], Essex Instit., *Historical Collections*, XLIII (1907), 183; John Higginson, Jr., to Nathaniel Higginson, Aug. 20, 1697, Mass. Hist. Soc., *Collections*, 3rd ser., VII (1838), 202; Bailyn, *New England Merchants*, 195; *Mass. Acts and Resolves*, VIII, 287–288, 384–385; Bernard Bailyn and Lotte Bailyn, *Massachusetts Shipping, 1697–1714*, 35, 68–70, 99.

[8] Accounts of Treasurer James Taylor of Massachusetts, June 29, 1694–May 29, 1695, Blathwayt Papers, BL 246, Hunt. Lib.

and naval resources, and the experience of battling in a common cause helped to reduce the suspicions and misunderstandings that had so long bedevilled relations between New England and Whitehall. Yet old antagonisms died hard, and only slowly through the 1690s did instability and experiment give way to a political culture built upon the heritage of the years of founding but oriented to accommodate the requirements of royal government.

The stage was set by events in London. Here, during the last years of the century, the bureaucratic mechanisms constructed by the Stuarts for the administration of the colonies were revised and strengthened. Widespread dissatisfaction with the depressed state of England's overseas trade and the losses incurred by French attacks upon ill-protected Atlantic convoys came to a head early in 1696, when a bill was introduced into the House of Commons for a council of trade to be appointed and controlled by Parliament. To forestall this intrusion upon the prerogative, King William and his ministers hastily pushed through plans already drafted for the replacement of the old committee of trade by a group of Lords Commissioners for Trade and Plantations, the body known to history as the Board of Trade. The board retained its predecessor's cumbersome dual function of supervising commercial as well as colonial affairs; the former was evidently intended to be its prime responsibility, since the majority of the eight men appointed commissioners were experts in the field of trade and only one, William Blathwayt, promoted from secretary of the old committee to full membership of the new board, was thoroughly conversant with conditions in the colonies.[9]

Parliament, meanwhile, turned to debate the one aspect of England's commerce that seemed only too fatally prosperous, the illegal trading charged against many colonists and, more recently, against Scottish merchants striving to break into the colonial trade. Edward

---

[9] Andrews, *Colonial Period*, IV, 280–293; Ian K. Steele, *Politics of Colonial Policy*, 10–18. After May 1696, therefore, the work of the body known as the Lords of Trade becomes that of the Board of Trade.

Randolph had just returned from a three-year tour of duty as surveyor general of the customs in America, bringing fresh facts and figures on such transgressions. He quickly persuaded his superiors at Whitehall to take advantage of the complaints aired in Parliament to propose new measures for the stronger enforcement of the Acts of Trade. In April 1696, a month prior to the commissioning of the Board of Trade, a new Navigation Act "for preventing Frauds and regulating Abuses in the Plantations" was passed. Drawn to Randolph's specifications, it effectively extended the English customs service to America, complete with all its powers and privileges. Governors, whether royal or proprietary, and other local officials were obliged to take oaths and give bond for their part in the enforcement of the acts; obstructive colonial laws were nullified; and, taking a logical though drastic step to circumvent the prejudices of local juries, the act permitted violations of the acts to be tried in vice-admiralty courts, instruments of the prerogative which operated without juries and under a judge directly appointed by the English admiralty. Such courts were duly established in the colonies the following year, their officers nominated by Randolph. Only the determined opposition of a coalition of proprietors and colonial agents thwarted his plans to complete the last link in the judicial chain thrown about colonial trade by the simultaneous appointment of royal attorneys general throughout the plantations.[10]

These reforms were an important step on the road toward a general administrative uniformity. Hitherto, the proprietary and chartered colonies had been linked to England by little more than their own spasmodic obedience to the laws of trade and their proprietors' allegiance to the crown. Among them, only Massachusetts had a royal governor. The act of 1696 and its aftermath implanted a microcosm of Whitehall within each colony, a group of permanent royal officials backed by their own special tribunal and responsible only to their su-

---

[10] Andrews, *Colonial Period*, IV, 156–174; Michael G. Hall, "The House of Lords, Edward Randolph, and the Navigation Act of 1696," 494–515; Nominations of Edward Randolph, July 31, 1696 [Feb. 1697], [Mar. 1697], *Randolph Letters*, V, 136–137, 162–163, VII, 500–501; Papers relating to the appointment of Law Officers, Aug. 25–Oct. 30, 1696, *ibid.*, V, 140–151.

periors in London. Other local courts could not assume jurisdiction, and cases could swiftly be transferred to England if the need arose. In matters of trade, at least, the new regulations subjected every colony to the direct supervision of the crown.

Further, as veteran administrators like Blathwayt and Randolph undoubtedly expected and desired, attempts to execute these reforms led swiftly toward a recognition of the need for even closer subjection. Experience demonstrated that the act of 1696 was carelessly drafted, allowing local officials to drag their feet and leaving loopholes through which the common law courts in the colonies could hamper or even prohibit the course of royal justice. Reports flooded in of the sanctuary afforded to pirates by colonial governments outside the crown's direct control. The new commissioners of the Board of Trade absorbed the lesson first learned by their predecessors twenty years before, that economic regulation, to be effective, must be supported on the spot by direct political authority. The answer, if *quo warranto*s were now out of style, lay in a further resort to the supreme legislative authority of Parliament. The act of 1696 had already reestablished Parliament's role in the regulation of trade and colonial affairs and it was soon followed by the Woollen Act of 1699, the first in a long line of measures designed to restrict the colonists in the manufacture of such items as iron and hats, prescribe the value of their coinage, and encourage their production of naval stores. An act for the suppression of piracy passed in 1700 set up courts in America armed with jurisdiction extending into the proprietary colonies, and a clause of the act made failure to obey the law grounds for the forfeiture of their charters.[11] From all sides—from Randolph, neighboring royal governors, and domestic opponents of the various proprietors—came complaints that the offending colonies harbored pirates and illegal traders, defied the new regulations, and refused to contribute to the common defense. Early in 1701, following a report from the Board of Trade sum-

---

[11] 10 William III, c. xvi, 11 William III, c. vii, 3 & 4 Anne, c. ix, 6 Anne, c. lvii, 5 George II, c. xxix, in *Statutes of the Realm.* One recommendation for the use of a *quo warranto* was made against Rhode Island, but it was never pursued: Board of Trade to the king, Dec. 21, 1697, *CSP Col., 1697–1698,* no. 1071.

marizing these charges, a bill for the "reunion" of the proprietary and chartered colonies with the crown was introduced into the House of Lords. Though it did not formally confiscate the colonies' charters, it voided all clauses in them that granted powers of government. All such powers would be "reunited, annexed, and vested" in the crown. Each of the New England colonies was specifically included in the bill.[12]

Despite the witnesses and evidence marshalled by Randolph, the bill failed to get beyond a second reading in the Lords before the session ended. A second attempt the following year was equally unsuccessful, as were subsequent bills brought forward in 1706 and 1715. The only fruit of the campaign was the New Jersey proprietors' voluntary surrender of their rights of government in 1702. It does not seem to have been a party issue. Whigs who might have supported the bill for its likely benefits for English merchants or its implicit recognition of Parliament's power over the colonies may have been alienated by so blatant a confiscation of the "property" represented by the proprietors' rights of government. Tories who could have been expected to favor an attack upon such strongholds of Nonconformity as New England and Pennsylvania probably felt little enthusiasm for a measure that added to the proliferation of government and the authority of an agency created by a Whig ministry. Blathwayt, writing to a colleague in the midst of the session, concluded that each party was striving to outdo the other in weakening the powers of the crown.[13] In retrospect, the Board of Trade tried to accomplish too much at a single stroke. Its frontal attack raised up a host of lobbyists, each demanding time to testify against the bill. Parliament was torn by factional rivalry and preoccupied with such matters as the Act of Settlement and the highly controversial treaties recently negotiated with

[12] Board of Trade to the king, May 26, 1701, in Louise P. Kellogg, "The American Colonial Charter," 286–287; Steele, *Politics of Colonial Policy*, 60–81; *House of Lords MSS., 1699–1702*, 314–315.

[13] William Blathwayt to George Stepney, Mar. 11, 1701, cited by Horwitz, *Parliament, Policy and Politics*, 283; Steele, *Politics of Colonial Policy*, 79–80. For a different view, that the bill was a party issue, see Olson, *Anglo-American Politics*, 100–105.

France. Colonial affairs were simply not important enough to merit precedence over other business. Once again, Englishmen shied away from establishing uniformity for its own sake and clung to the existing diversity.

The attempt to resume the government of the chartered and proprietary colonies marked the zenith of the Board of Trade's activity. At first it had struggled valiantly with the task of coordinating the numerous branches of royal government which now had dealings with America: after 1696, for example, even such a colony as Connecticut, outside the sphere of direct royal control, experienced a dramatic increase in the number of letters it received from Whitehall.[14] The board's thrice-weekly meetings, its hiring of additional clerks, and the diligent copying of correspondence into carefully cross-referenced entry books all evidenced its enthusiasm and its concern for system and detail. Yet the very volume of paper shuffling was a measure of its weakness as an instrument of government. Like the old committee, it possessed only advisory, not executive, functions. Those serving on the old committee, however, had also sat in the Privy Council where the final decisions were made. Blathwayt and his colleagues had no such access, and the principal ministers of state, though ex officio members of the board, seldom attended its meetings. There could be no more sessions like those witnessed by Increase Mather in 1691, during which politicians of the caliber of Nottingham and Carmarthen had debated and decided colonial affairs. Nor did the board possess powers of patronage or appointment save at the level of nominating members of the royal governors' councils. These weaknesses steadily reduced its role from one of formulating policy to that of collecting information and maintaining the status quo. By the early years of the new century, its freedom of action was

---

[14] Thus the letters copied in New England Records, State of Connecticut, 1664–1702, vol. 54, Conn. State Library. One, a good example of the care taken to regulate illegal trade, is printed in Conn. Hist. Soc., *Collections,* XXIV (1932), 137–147.

already being curtailed and its authority usurped by departments closer to the seats of power, particularly the Treasury and the office of the secretary of state. Three political purges in rapid succession, including the dismissal of Blathwayt in 1707, replaced its best administrators with inexperienced placemen. The board began a long decline into the politics of interest and apathy characteristic of its parent government during the years of Whig supremacy.[15]

Ultimately, therefore, even Whitehall's exceptional vigor following the reforms of the 1690s failed to produce the thorough changes in the structure of colonial government that might have sustained and institutionalized its efforts. In the immediate aftermath of the Glorious Revolution, Massachusetts, New Hampshire, Maryland, and Pennsylvania had all been brought into the fold of royal government. Thereafter, in terms of a further royalization, little was accomplished: indeed, the crown soon restored the administration of Pennsylvania and later, in 1715, that of Maryland to the hands of their proprietors. Even the extension of crown rule to New Jersey and, ultimately, to the Carolinas was more the consequence of the collapse of proprietary authority there than of royal pressure and the threat of legal or legislative action.

Other weaknesses besides those of the Board of Trade contributed to this outcome: the intensity of party rivalries during these years; the constant changes of personnel at the ministerial level; the waning of the monarchy's personal interest in matters relating to the colonies; and the uncertainties as to the wisdom and best means of involving Parliament in the work of colonial reorganization.[16] In the wake of James II's overthrow, moreover, the ideological purpose and readiness to cut procedural corners so evident in the 1680s had gone out of

---

[15] Steele, *Politics of Colonial Policy*, 27–30, 86–88, 92–100; Mark A. Thomson, *The Secretaries of State, 1681–1782*, 46–47; Dora M. Clark, *The Rise of the British Treasury*, 4–6; James A. Henretta, *"Salutary Neglect,"* 24–34. For the board's membership, see Addit. MSS., 30372, foll. 32v.–33; and *ibid.*, 15483, foll. 2–37 for its careful watch upon the membership of colonial councils, 1703–1711.

[16] For example, ten general elections in twenty years followed the Triennial Act of 1694, a record unequalled before or since in English politics. In addition, there were more than three times as many secretaries of state in the years 1689–1717 as in the equivalent period 1660–1688.

the conduct of colonial affairs. Officials such as the Whig philosopher John Locke, a member of the board from 1696 to 1700, placed a high value on due process and measured consultation—they were not prepared to press reform to the limits tested in the previous decade.[17] *Quo warrantos* were not employed, the colonists' right to representative government was never questioned, and even the attempts to remodel the charters were accompanied by careful assurances that existing laws would remain in force and all property rights would be protected and preserved. The legacy of James's reign lived on in the efforts of veteran administrators such as Blathwayt and Randolph to add a political uniformity to that imposed upon commerce by the Acts of Trade. Yet the truer continuity, as shown in both Whitehall's inability to impose such uniformity and its heightened respect for constitutional niceties, lay with the more moderate and pragmatic royalism of the decades preceding James's ascendancy. The character of the colonists' post-Revolutionary settlement reinforces the point: as in England itself, the improvised and, in part, wholly fortuitous arrangements patched together in the years immediately following William's succession ultimately attained authority and even sanctity less out of any widespread conviction that they deserved to be definitive than by virtue of their capacity to survive all attempts at alteration.

As for New England, it was no longer the peculiar target of Whitehall's displeasure. Traces of the old animosity remained, as in the contempt of royal officials for the ill-educated and disorganized settlers of Rhode Island, but memories of "the New England disease" were all but forgotten in the larger distinction between royal and proprietary governments. Indeed, during the attacks upon the latter, the Board of Trade concentrated its fire, and the majority of its charges, on William Penn.[18] Possibly, it viewed the great Quaker proprietor as still tainted by his association with James II and hence most vulner-

---

[17] Peter Laslett, "John Locke, the Great Recoinage, and the Origins of the Board of Trade, 1695–1698," 398–401.

[18] *House of Lords MSS., 1699–1702,* 318–355.

able to attack. More probably, their tactic reflected economic realities: Pennsylvania with its burgeoning port of Philadelphia was far more important than either Connecticut or Rhode Island to the integrity of the colonial system.

In consequence, New England attracted less attention. By and large, Whitehall intervened only when called upon to do so, as when complaints were brought against Gov. Sir William Phips of Massachusetts and when a case involving the disposition of an estate was appealed from the Connecticut courts to the Privy Council. In two important matters, however, it consciously took the initiative. The first concerned the further production of strategic commodities. While contemporaries were beginning to perceive that New England's principal value for England might lie in the markets it provided for English manufactures and the supplies it sent to the West Indies, royal officials still grasped eagerly at any scheme that would enable the northern colonies to contribute more directly to the mother country's resources. Hence they looked with favor on the export of such items as whale oil, furs, barrel staves, and the ships in which these goods travelled: by the 1690s, ships built in Massachusetts yards and sold in England were already a major source of the credits used to finance the importation of English goods.[19]

In particular, English administrators strove to encourage the production of the naval stores—timber, tar, pitch, turpentine, and resin—that would preserve maritime supremacy and reduce England's dependence on supplies from the Baltic. Such "returns," they perceived, would redress New England's chronic deficit in its balance of trade with England. Their character would encourage rather than infringe upon the market for English manufactures.[20] Sensing the fa-

---

[19] Nettels, *Money Supply*, 69, 73–76, 92–93; Bailyn and Bailyn, *Massachusetts Shipping*, 52–53; Joseph Goldenburg, *Shipbuilding in Colonial America*, 31–48. During the last years of the century, by official reckoning, New England imported goods from England valued at three times those it exported to England and such imports were about 30 percent of all English exports to the mainland colonies, about 15 percent of English exports to all the plantations: Emory R. Johnson *et al., History of Domestic and Foreign Commerce of the United States*, I, 120–121.

[20] Thus the remarks of Board of Trade member Abraham Hill, Jan. 14, 1698, in

vorable wind at Whitehall, the promoters of those projects for mining minerals in New England which had complicated Increase Mather's task back in 1691 trimmed their sails accordingly. Sir Matthew Dudley and his partners now petitioned for a charter of incorporation for the production of naval stores, and counterproposals came from Sir Henry Ashurst and Sir Stephen Evance, acting on behalf of Massachusetts, and from others including Customs Collector and Surveyor of the Woods Jahleel Brenton.[21] The crown, acting through the Lords and then the Board of Trade, proceeded with care. It was, in every sense, a knotty problem. Through Ashurst, the Massachusetts government provided a sample cargo of stores, but the commissioners of the Navy Board in London reported that the timber was unsound and the tar so corrosive as to burn up the very ropes it was supposed to protect. Even the great masts from the forests of New Hampshire, it was said, were "the most floaty," and weaker for their size than their Scandinavian counterparts. Labor and transport costs were greater. Mast merchant John Taylor concluded that "it rests with his Majestie to give life to such a Trade" by granting monopoly privileges and generous subsidies to its promoters.[22] At length, after receiving reports from special commissioners dispatched, at considerable expense, to survey conditions in New England, the Board of Trade recommended against giving any one group an exclusive grant and sought instead a policy more in tune with mercantilistic practices. It drafted a naval stores act, passed by Parliament in 1705, which paid bounties on such stores imported from the colonies in order to overcome their competitive disadvantage and thus stimulate production. In 1710,

---

Sloane Manuscripts, 2902, fol. 177v., British Library, and Edward Randolph to the Board of Trade, July 24, 1696, *Randolph Letters*, VII, 479–486.

[21] Nettels, *Money Supply*, 141–154; Lord, *Industrial Experiments*, 15–30; Joseph J. Malone, *Pine Trees and Politics*, 10–27; Proceedings in Council, 1694–1704, *APC Col.*, II, 193–198; HMC, *Portland*, VIII, 164; Papers relating to naval stores projects, Bernon Papers, R. I. Hist. Soc.

[22] Report of the surveyors of the stores sent from New England, [June 5, 1696], C.O. 5/859, no. 12iii; Sir Henry Ashurst to Massachusetts, Sept. 20, 1697, Mass. Archives, CVI, 410; J. R. Tanner, ed., *The Further Correspondence of Samuel Pepys, 1662–1679*, 18; John Taylor to Charles Montagu, July 2, 1695, Addit. MSS., 10120, fol. 77v.; Taylor to [John Povey], Mar. 20, 1694, C.O. 323/1, no. 80.

several thousand German refugees were sent into back-country New York in a vain attempt to establish a naval stores industry. All the while, London carefully provided for the naval protection of the fleet that returned each fall from the Piscataqua with its precious cargo of masts and spars.

Besides the matter of strategic commodities, the English government continued to seek more effective means of ensuring the security of the northern colonies. This became more than ever the central theme of royal policy toward New England. Its character and purpose, however, had altered. Backing away from the costly and authoritarian paternalism of the Dominion, royal officials worked to promote a greater local self-sufficiency in defense. Both the eastern frontier and Albany, "the only bulwark and safe guard of all Their Majestys plantacons on the main of America," lay open to attack. The vital friendship of the Iroquois was crumbling as the Indians perceived the divisions among the colonists. In response to repeated appeals from New York, the Lords of Trade procured the dispatch of royal letters commanding neighboring colonies to lend assistance and transferring command of the Connecticut militia from Phips to Governor Fletcher of New York. Later, they drew up a formal system of quotas—an idea that seems to have originated in New York—whereby each colony would furnish a specified number of men upon request. They also sent over two more companies of British regulars, together with a considerable quantity of munitions.[23]

In one way or another, all these plans proved ineffectual. Not even a personal visit to Hartford by Governor Fletcher could persuade the Connecticut government to offer more than token assistance, and the colonies to the south of New York were even less cooperative. As might have been expected, Rhode Island bluntly refused to concede

---

[23] Circular letter of Governor Sloughter to the northern colonial governments, July 11, 1691, *N. Y. Col. Docs.*, III, 785; the queen to the Governors of New England, Pennsylvania, Virginia, and Maryland, Oct. 11, 1692, Commission to Governor Fletcher, May 1, 1693, Memorandum of quotas, Aug. 21, 1694, *CSP Col., 1689-1692*, no. 2543, *1693-1696*, nos. 310, 1253; the king to the Colony of Connecticut, Mar. 3, 1693, Conn. Hist. Soc., *Collections*, XXIV (1932), 56–57; the queen to the governor of Rhode Island, Aug. 21, 1694, *R. I. Records*, III, 298–300; Pargellis, "The Four Independent Companies," 99.

to Phips the authority it had struggled so long to preserve from the demands of earlier Massachusetts leaders. Each colony, by a combination of excuses, protests to England, and outright defiance, effectively prevented the operation of the quota system.[24] The two companies of English regulars arrived in the spring of 1695. But, like the troops that preceded them, they were docked of thirty percent of their pay by the sublime bureaucratic logic that colonial money was worth that much less than sterling. Since the cost of living at Albany and New York was about double that in England and even the pitifully inadequate remainder of their pay was often months in arrears, these forces inevitably degenerated into a half-starved, ill-equipped, and, on one occasion, openly mutinous rabble whose numbers were decimated by desertion despite fresh drafts from England. So tattered were their uniforms, wrote the governor of New York to London in 1700 that "those parts of 'em which modesty forbids me to name, are expos'd to view; the women forced to lay their hands on their eyes as often as they pass by 'em."[25]

Thus, bureaucratic manipulation and colonial self-interest combined to leave the frontiers no better protected than before. It is not difficult to understand the recalcitrance of Connecticut and Rhode Island. They were snugly insulated from the main theaters of war, with only their coastlines open to attack. Both were convinced that a surrender of the power of the sword would fatally compromise their independence, a prospect rendered the more disagreeable by the venal and hectoring manner of the visiting representatives of royal

---

[24] *Conn. Records*, IV, 111–117; Fletcher to [Secretary Nottingham?], Oct. 28, 1693, C.O. 5/536, foll. 3–4; Phips to Nottingham, Feb. 20, 1693, C.O. 5/751, no. 23; Extract from a letter from Boston, [c. Mar. 1693], C.O. 5/857, no. 41; *R. I. Records*, III, 285–292.

[25] Governor Lord Bellomont to the Board of Trade, July 26, Oct. 28, Nov. 28, 1700, Robert Livingston to the Board of Trade, May 13, 1701, *N. Y. Col. Docs.*, IV, 687, 770, 781, 871–872; Duncan Campbell to Fitz-John Winthrop, Oct. 28, Nov. 8, 1700, Winthrop Papers; Report of William Blathwayt, Mar. 3, 1692, T. 64/88, 387; Report on the petition of the Four Companies of New York, Feb. 19, 1704, Addit. MSS., 10453, fol. 42.

authority.[26] Moreover, the nature of the war made such help as the two colonies could provide seem futile and unnecessary—false alarms were frequent, yet relief arrived too late in the event of a real attack. At the same time, Whitehall's dissatisfaction with this state of affairs is equally comprehensible. The northern colonies, reported the Board of Trade in 1696, are "so crumbled into little Governments" that they cannot present a united defense. "It is almost incredible that his Majestys Governor of New York in the middle of above forty thousand English that he has in his neighbourhood should say as he does, that he has but the four Companies his Majesty sent . . . to rely on for the defence of that frontier, in case of any attempt from the French."[27]

Confronted with a steady stream of letters from Boston and New York complaining of the inefficacy of the quota system, royal officials once more turned to consider some form of union of the northern colonies under the auspices of the crown. As usual, the ebb and flow of domestic politics played a part in shaping a solution. Following the dismissal from office of Nottingham in November 1693, the Whigs were again in the ascendant. Shrewsbury returned as principal secretary of state. Hence it was natural that, upon Phips's death in 1695, one of the secretary's followers, an ardent and impecunious Irish Whig, Richard Coote, Earl of Bellomont, should succeed to the vacant governorship of Massachusetts. It was well known, however, that the colony's assembly had refused to grant Phips a regular salary, a tactic that, it was believed in Whitehall, had driven the late governor to the questionable practices that had led to his recall. Upon Bellomont's representation, the Lords Justices administering England during the king's absence overseas recommended that the earl be made governor of both Massachusetts and New York, with his salary drawn in part from the royal revenues of the latter colony. Ostensibly, the

---

[26] William Pitkin to Fitz-John Winthrop, Oct. 27, 1693, Winthrop Papers; [Pitkin and John Allyn?], *Their Majesty's Colony of Connecticut Vindicated,* 41; Gershom Bulkeley, "Will and Doom," 242; The Case of Connecticut against Benjamin Fletcher, [Jan. 29, 1694], Conn. Hist. Soc., *Collections,* XXIV (1932), 84–85; Robert C. Winthrop Collection, II, 214a, Conn. State Library; Proceedings in Rhode Island, Sept. 4, 1702, *R. I. Records,* III, 461.

[27] Board of Trade to the Lords Justices, Sept. 30, 1696, *N. Y. Col. Docs.,* IV, 227.

appointment would provide for unity in defense while avoiding unnecessary subsidies from the English exchequer. In reality, the plan
had the added advantage of providing for the needy Bellomont at the
expense of Fletcher, a Tory appointee.[28] It was further cemented by a
complicated intrigue engineered by Robert Livingston (visiting London from New York and now Fletcher's opponent) by which Bellomont and four of the leading Whig ministers—Shrewsbury, Lord
Keeper Somers, Sidney, now Earl of Romney, and Sir Edward Russell—agreed to finance and profit from a privateering venture under
the command of Capt. William Kidd of New York. The scheme subsequently backfired in dramatic fashion when Kidd and his crew
strayed into piracy, precipitating a major political scandal. For the
moment, however, it gave influential backing to Bellomont's claim to
the two governments.[29]

A combination of circumstances—the powerful Blathwayt's opposition to Fletcher's recall, Bellomont's absence in Ireland, and the administrative reorganization of 1696—delayed this settlement for more
than a year. It was given new life by persistent reports of French plans
for a full-scale attack upon the northern colonies. In September, John
Nelson returned on parole from his French imprisonment to provide
additional details to the Board of Trade, as well as a memorial summarizing the dangers of colonial disunity. A week later, John Locke
drew up, and his fellow board members approved, a lengthy represen-

---

[28] Journal of the Lords of Trade, June 14, 27, July 4, 1695, C.O. 391/8, 51–59;
Memorial of the Lords Justices to the King, July 16, 1695, C.O. 5/859, no. 3;
Hutchinson, *History of Massachusetts-Bay*, II, 64n.; Secretary Shrewsbury to the
king, July 16, 1695, William Coxe, ed., *Private and Original Correspondence of Charles
Talbot, Duke of Shrewsbury, with King William, the Leaders of the Whig Party, and other
Distinguished Statesmen*, 94. For Fletcher's backers, Jacobsen, *William Blathwayt*,
142, 304, 310; for those of Bellomont, Stanley H. Friedelbaum, "Bellomont: Imperial Administrator," 22–40. Bellomont's appointment to both colonies had already been decided long before the committee of trade was informed: Sir Henry
Ashurst to Benjamin Jackson, May 6, 1695, Letterbook of Sir Henry Ashurst, fol.
116v.

[29] The most complete picture of the intrigues of 1695 which led to Fletcher's replacement by Bellomont is given by Leder, *Robert Livingston*, 101–116, and subsequent accounts have added little save for Jacob Judd, "Lord Bellomont and
Captain Kidd," 67–74. Somers and Shrewsbury were two of the seven Lords Justices.

tation recommending the appointment of a captain general to coordinate colonial defense.[30] The matter became the more urgent as word
came of a succession of military setbacks on the frontier. One expedition led by Frontenac in person had attacked and burnt the castles of
the Onondaga and Oneida Iroquois. Another, under Iberville, had
captured both the royal frigate *Newport* and the fort at Pemaquid, the
key to New England's eastern defenses. Urgent appeals for royal assistance soon arrived from Massachusetts.[31]

At this point, a group of merchants, colonists, and proprietors in
London took the lead in bringing both the union of the northern colonies and Bellomont's appointment to the point of decision. Seven
years of war had convinced them of the need to find a middle way
between the autocracy of the Dominion and the fragmentation of
charter rule. Across the Atlantic, others had already reached a similar
conclusion. The assembly of New Hampshire petitioned for annexation to Massachusetts; John Usher pressed for the appointment of a
general governor; and Samuel Sewall's brother Stephen, a Salem
merchant, wrote of his hope that England would send a "Viceroy . . .
a Great and Noble man that is a Soldier" to rule the squabbling colonists. As Sewall implied, Bellomont's social position and liberal political sympathies made him an ideal candidate in colonial eyes. Even
Fitz-John Winthrop, Connecticut's agent in London, who was on
guard against any policy that might infringe upon his colony's sov-

---

[30] Board of Trade to the Lords Justices, July 7, Memorial of Charles Pilsworth to
Blathwayt, May 9/19, 1696, Memorial of the New York agents, [1696], Board of
Trade to the Lords Justices, Sept. 30, 1696, *N. Y. Col. Docs.*, IV, 166–172,
227–230; Memorials of John Nelson, [Sept. 24, 1696], *ibid.*, 206–211, and C.O.
323/2, no. 12; Journal of the Board of Trade, Apr. 17, Sept. 16, 24, 1696, C.O.
391/8, 174, 391/9, 109–111, 139–140; William Popple to Lord Townshend, July
22, 1720, Historical Manuscripts Commission, *The Manuscripts of the Marquis
Townshend,* 296. Nelson had already presented two memorials to Shrewsbury similar to those he delivered to the Board of Trade: Historical Manuscripts Commission, *Report on the Manuscripts of the Duke of Buccleuch and Queensbury, K.G., K.T., Preserved at Montagu House, Whitehall,* II, pt. ii, 722–733.

[31] Eccles, *Canada under Louis XIV,* 194–195, 200–201. Details of the unprecedented
stream of letters appealing for help, from Massachusetts to the king, the Privy
Council, Somers, Blathwayt, Benjamin Jackson, Thomas Cooper, and agents
Constantine Phipps and Sir Henry Ashurst, Sept. 3–29, Dec. 5, 1696, can be
found in *Mass. Acts and Resolves,* VII, 122–123, 127–129, 513–516, 521 (and C.O.
5/859, no. 44i).

ereignty, admitted that the earl was "a very good man." The agent of
Massachusetts, Sir Henry Ashurst, warmly supported the appointment of his friend and fellow Whig, not least because Bellomont's success would frustrate the efforts of Joseph Dudley to secure the Massachusetts governorship. English and colonial merchants trading to
New England also endorsed a policy that seemed to promise a greater
security and uniformity of commercial life.[32]

These representatives of what contemporaries would have described as the New England "interest" were now willing to assist Livingston and his Whig friends in their well-orchestrated campaign for
the dismissal of Governor Fletcher. Early in 1697, just as testimony
attacking the latter's corrupt and autocratic rule began to flood into
Whitehall, several memorials were presented to the Board of Trade
declaring that only a union of the governments of the northern colonies could preserve them from utter destruction. Edmund Harrison
and Dr. Daniel Coxe, "as in the name of all," urged the appointment
of Bellomont. Both men, it should be noted, were involved in Livingston's dealings with Kidd—Harrison, a wealthy East India merchant
and a proprietor, with Coxe, of West Jersey, had provided much of
the capital for the venture.[33] Naturally, Fletcher's agents were op-

---

[32] Petition of New Hampshire assembly, petition of 232 inhabitants of New
Hampshire, [Apr. 6, 1693], C.O. 5/924, nos. 22i, ii (also *N. H. Provincial Papers*,
III, 36, 47, and *Randolph Letters*, VII, 414–415); Lt. Gov. John Usher to the Lords
of Trade, Jan. 31, July 14, 1693, Sept. 1694, Oct. 5, 1696, C.O. 5/924, nos. 19, 27,
40, C.O. 5/859, no. 35; Stephen Sewall to Edward Hull, Nov. 2, 1696, *ibid.*, no.
40; Fitz-John Winthrop to Wait Winthrop, July 13, 1695, Mass. Hist. Soc., *Collections*, 5th ser., VIII (1882), 324.

[33] Memorials of Edmund Harrison, of Henry Ashurst and Constantine Phipps, of
30 proprietors and inhabitants of the northern colonies, [Feb. 1, 1697], C.O.
5/859, nos. 60–62; Journal of the Board of Trade, Jan. 25, Feb. 1, 8, 11, 17, 22,
25, 1697, C.O. 391/9, 367–368, 383, 394–395, 398–399, 410–411, 391/10, 2–3, 8.
For Harrison, Coxe, and Kidd, see Bellomont to James Vernon, Mar. 7, 1700,
and Captain Kidd's Protest, HMC, *Portland*, VIII, 74–75, 79; and *Commons Journals*, XIII, 13–15, 444, 550. Ashurst and Harrison had added their names to the
petition of the proprietors and inhabitants (others signing included John Nelson,
David Waterhouse, Jeremiah Johnson, Samuel Penhallow, Henry Newman,
Thomas Newton, and Richard and Walter Mico) but later withdrew them on the
grounds that they—Ashurst and Harrison—favored only military and not civil
union: C.O. 391/9, 393.
The widespread support for Bellomont's appointment appears also to have
been part of an attempt by the representatives of the proprietary colonies to di-

posed to the plan, as were Winthrop, Jahleel Brenton of Rhode Island, and Samuel Allen, proprietor of New Hampshire. But public policy, private profit, and party spoilsmanship all pointed in the same direction. On February 25, after receiving belated assurances from Bellomont that he did indeed wish to be sent to what he somewhat casually referred to as "the West Indies," the Board recommended that a single governor be set over New York, Massachusetts, and New Hampshire with power as captain general to command the militias of Connecticut, Rhode Island, and the Jerseys. The king concurred and Bellomont was promptly appointed to the post.[34]

The episode revived memories of the Dominion and its structure: the Lords Justices had urged the king in 1695 that "the Government of New Yorke and New England may be united again, as not long since they were under Sir Edmund Andros," and after his appointment Bellomont asked for the same high salaries paid out of the royal revenues that Andros had enjoyed.[35] Like his predecessor, he was made commander-in-chief of all the northern colonies. But these parallels were deceptive. As finally constituted, Bellomont's government was not a consolidation but a confederation of three separate colonies, each with its own lieutenant governor, assembly, and civil administration. He was assigned only a small salary from the reve-

---

vert attention from Randolph's larger plans for vice-admiralty courts and royal attorneys general. Thus William Penn proposed his famous plan of union and joined in the attack upon Fletcher: "Mr. Penn's scheme," [Feb. 8, 1697], *N. Y. Col. Docs.,* IV, 296–297. For proprietorial collaboration at this time, see Jeremiah Basse to Fitz-John Winthrop, Nov. 14, 18, 1696, Mar. 13, 19, 1697, Winthrop Papers; Penn to Winthrop, Dec. 27, 1696, Winthrop to Penn, n.d., Mass. Hist. Soc., *Proceedings,* XII (1871–1873), 42.

[34] Memorials of Samuel Allen, Feb. 3, 1697, of Chidley Brooke and William Nicolls, [Feb. 8, 1697], of Ashurst and Harrison, [Feb. 11, 1697], C.O. 5/859, nos. 64, 68, 69; Memorial of Fitz-John Winthrop, Feb. 4, 1697, Mass. Hist. Soc., *Collections,* 5th ser., VIII (1882), 337; Bellomont to [the Earl of Bridgewater], Feb. 23, 1697, Ellesmere MSS., 9655, Hunt. Lib.; Board of Trade to the king, Feb. 25, 1697, Shrewsbury to the Board of Trade, Mar. 16, 1697, *N. Y. Col. Docs.,* IV, 259–261; Commissions of Bellomont as governor of New York, Massachusetts and New Hampshire, June 18, 1697, *CSP Col., 1696–1697,* nos. 1091–1093.

[35] Lords Justices to the king, July 16, 1695, Bellomont to William Popple, Apr. 9, 14, 1697, C.O. 5/859, nos. 3, 86, 89. Judging by Blathwayt's interpretation of what the Lords Justices meant, "New England" here had its common contemporary meaning of "Massachusetts": Jacobsen, *William Blathwayt,* 310.

nues of New York and none at all from Massachusetts or New Hampshire independent of the consent of their respective assemblies. He received no authority over Rhode Island and Connecticut save over their militia, and even this power was later abridged to apply only in time of war. As in 1691, Whitehall's solution to the problem of defense was cosmetic rather than realistic, the offspring of an alliance of colonial particularism and domestic political expediency.

In light of all the words expended in detailing the military advantages that would ensue from Bellomont's appointment, it was somewhat ironic that his governorship—he died in office at New York in March 1701, three years after his arrival—should have coincided with the one peaceful interval in a quarter-century of conflict. Nonetheless, his voluminous letters and the deepening disaffection of the Iroquois, which culminated in their treaty of neutrality with the French in 1701, kept the problem of the northern frontier in the forefront of Whitehall's deliberations.[36] Blathwayt had opposed a confederation of Massachusetts and New York from the beginning on the grounds that they were too different in government and too far apart geographically, especially while Rhode Island and Connecticut retained their charters.[37] Events vindicated his judgment. For all Bellomont's zeal, he was no more successful than Andros in superintending both an inaccessible frontier and twin provincial capitals over two hundred miles apart. Bellomont himself, afflicted by gout, went to Boston only once, travelling from New York to Newport by ship and then journeying overland in May 1699, returning fourteen months later. Even this brief absence brought protests, forwarded to the House of Commons in London, from New York merchants anxious to cut the tie with Massachusetts.[38] Moreover, by the time of Bellomont's death the Whigs were again in retreat at court and Blathwayt's influence

---

[36] Thus, for example, Board of Trade to the king, Apr. 24, Oct. 4, 1700, to Secretary of State Vernon, Oct. 1700, *N. Y. Col. Docs.,* IV, 639–641, 700–709.

[37] Jacobsen, *William Blathwayt,* 310–311; also Webb, "William Blathwayt, Imperial Fixer: Muddling Through," 395–396.

[38] Petition of merchants of New York, [Mar. 1700], Board of Trade to Bellomont, Apr. 29, 1701, *N. Y. Col. Docs.,* IV, 624, 854.

with his fellow members of the Board of Trade was at its height. There were rumors that Lord Cornbury, nephew of the Earl of Rochester, a Tory grandee recently appointed Lord Lieutenant of Ireland, would inherit Bellomont's province in its entirety. But Cornbury received only the government of New York. Massachusetts and New Hampshire were given to Blathwayt's longtime friend and client, Joseph Dudley.[39]

The exact circumstances of these appointments remain obscure. As in the case of Bellomont, they were presented to the Board of Trade as decisions already made. We cannot automatically assume that the right hand of Whitehall knew what the left intended. But in view of the fact that royal officials were then urging the passage of the bill against the chartered and proprietary governments, the decision to separate New York once more from New England would seem to be more a repudiation of the ungainly structure of Bellomont's province than of the concept of colonial confederation. Had the bill of 1701 become law, the board probably hoped to establish two northern governments, one grouped around the Hudson and including at least the western half of Connecticut, the other around the Massachusetts Bay, including Rhode Island, in the manner originally intended in 1685 and subsequently suggested by Randolph, John Usher, and Robert Livingston.[40] But it was not to be. The bills and its successors failed; Dudley clung to office in Massachusetts until 1715; and the arrangements made in 1701, save for the dissolution of the link between Massachusetts and New Hampshire in 1741 and a few minor boundary adjustments, endured for three-quarters of a century.

---

[39] Henry Newman to Fitz-John Winthrop, Aug. 5, 1701, Wait Winthrop to Fitz-John Winthrop, Dec. 23, 1701, Winthrop Papers; John Chamberlayne to Joseph Dudley, Sept. 22, 1702, Mass. Hist. Soc., *Collections,* 6th ser., III (1889), 530–531.

[40] Randolph to the Commissioners of Customs, Dec. 7, 1695, *Randolph Letters,* VII, 477; John Usher to William Blathwayt, Sept., 1698, *William and Mary Quarterly,* 3rd ser., VII (1950), 103–104; Livingston to the Board of Trade, May 13, 1701, *N. Y. Col. Docs.,* IV, 874; Livingston to [William Blathwayt], May 23, 1701, Blathwayt Papers, BL 149, Hunt. Lib.

In New England, therefore, as elsewhere, royal officials failed to effect the broad remodelling of colonial governments and boundaries that they had sought. The outlines established by the settlement of 1691 remained. In place of arbitrary subordination and consolidation, however, came influences of a subtler kind. The spirit and intent of Whitehall's reforming zeal left permanent marks upon New England's political development, and their impact was reinforced by the growing strength of economic and cultural ties. The result, when coupled with the absence of any major constitutional changes after 1691, was a significant change in the tone and style of New England's relations with the crown. In the years prior to the Glorious Revolution, these had resembled an open military engagement, a war of siege and skirmish, of scouts and informers, which culminated in a sudden coup, the establishment of the Dominion. After the Revolution, by contrast, the colonists offered no open resistance to the crown. Instead, by a process that may best be described as a political and cultural osmosis, a permeation through barriers rather than a demolition of them, the New England colonies slowly accommodated themselves to the ways and requirements of the mother country.

In part, these changes were simply the result of continued commercial expansion. By the last years of the century, New England's economic well-being, and that of Massachusetts in particular, depended more than ever upon the prosperity of their trade with England and other English colonies. Boston's immediate hinterland furnished little in the way of staple products or manufactured goods, and although New England as a whole was a net exporter of foodstuffs, Massachusetts remained dependent for its grain upon shipments from colonies as far south as Pennsylvania. Colony-wide shortages in the 1690s were eased only by emergency cargoes donated by charitable settlers in Connecticut.[41] In consequence, the merchants of the Bay necessarily

---

[41] Petition of Boston selectmen, June 1696, Mass. Archives, LIX, 219; Samuel Sewall, "Letter-Book of Samuel Sewall (1686–1729)," 5–8, 165, 181–186; Conn. Archives, War, III, 43b; Wyllys Papers, II, 39–41, Conn. Hist. Soc.; *Mass. Acts and Resolves*, I, 226, 249, 277; Cotton Mather, *Diary*, ed. Ford, I, 191, 196, 223; Benjamin Colman to Robert Wodrow, Jan. 23, 1719, Mass. Hist. Soc., *Proceedings*, LXXVII (1965), 113; "A Short Account of the Present State of N. E., A.D. 90," Miscellaneous Bound MSS., 1679–93, Mass. Hist. Soc. Even Connecticut several

continued to perfect their skills as middlemen and merchants in intercolonial and transatlantic trade. They still depended upon exports of the region's lumber and fish. Every one of the vessels recorded as leaving New Hampshire ports for destinations beyond New England in the twelve months after August 1, 1694, bore lumber and nearly two-thirds carried fish, while of those leaving Boston in the six months after March 25, 1688, at least sixty percent bore such cargoes, almost all bound for the Caribbean.[42] Well might the famous codfish subsequently hung in the Massachusetts Assembly facing the speaker's desk be a wooden replica, as a fitting tribute to the importance of New England's forests and fisheries to the province's economic health.

By the early years of the eighteenth century, however, this dependence was declining in conjunction with changes in the patterns of New England's trade. By the twelve months ending June 25, 1715, the next period for which adequate records survive, only forty percent of the vessels clearing from Boston carried lumber or fish. A greater proportion than before were sailing directly to England with naval stores and tropical commodities such as molasses and tobacco; still more, nearly one-sixth in 1714, were listed as carrying "European goods" to other colonies on the American mainland, principally New York, Virginia, and North Carolina. Not all these vessels were owned by New Englanders, but their numbers suggest the extent to which the Bay ports were becoming centers for the exchange and transhipment of goods in the Atlantic trading community. Further evidence comes from the figures kept in England as a record of the nation's balance of trade. Not only did the total value of New England's trade with England rise steadily between 1697 and 1714, despite the ravages of war, but its share of England's exports to the mainland American colonies increased considerably faster than its proportion-

---

times prohibited the export of grain and provisions during the 1690s: *Conn. Records*, IV, 16, 154, 157. For the importation of grain into Boston, Naval Office Lists, Mass. Entries, 1688, 1718, C.O. 5/848, 24–31, 103 *et seq.*

[42] Naval Office Lists, N. H., Clearings, C.O. 5/968, 1–6, Mass., Clearings, C.O. 5/848, 17–23. Van Deventer, *Emergence of Provincial New Hampshire*, 90, provides somewhat different figures for New Hampshire drawn from the same material.

ate population growth. More and more of these exports, it would seem, were being reexported from New England for sale elsewhere.[43]

The few surviving commercial letterbooks and ledgers kept by merchants during these years illustrate this growing interdependence and diversification. John Usher of Boston and New Hampshire, for example, imported a wide range of fabrics and manufactured goods from his many correspondents in London in return for his shipments of fish, naval stores, and tropical woods. His son-in-law, David Jeffries of Boston, established ties with traders in both London and England's West Country ports, purchasing cloths and linens with the bills of exchange obtained from the sale of fish in the markets of southern Europe. Cod and mackerel sent to Europe or the Caribbean were likewise the staple export of Salem merchants such as John Higginson and Philip English, who in return imported items such as Madeira wine, Spanish iron, and West Indian molasses—molasses which Philip English distilled into rum and traded to other colonies, notably Maryland and Newfoundland. Jonathan Corwin of Salem, Higginson's colleague upon the Massachusetts council for many years, sent lumber from his sawmill at Wells to the West Indies, importing cotton, sugar, and molasses; but the bulk of his trade was local, and he stocked his store with manufactured goods obtained from Boston, the prime port of call for vessels coming from England. In that city, merchants such as Thomas Fitch had steadily built up a trade in fabrics and hardware with almost every English colony in America, importing large supplies from William and John Crouch of London. Benjamin Davis specialized in the pharmaceutical trade, providing amateur physicians like the Reverend Gershom Bulkeley of Wethersfield with their medicines; Davis died in 1704 owing over £1,000 to English merchants, including £130 to the New England Company.[44]

---

[43] Naval Office Lists, Mass., Clearings, C.O. 5/848, 32–50; Emory Johnson *et al.*, *History of Domestic and Foreign Commerce*, I, 120–121; John J. McCusker, "The Current Value of English Exports, 1697 to 1800," 623.

[44] Jeffries Papers, II, III, VII, VIII, XVI–XVII, XIX–XXI (Usher and Jeffries); Account Book of John Higginson, 1646–1719, Higginson Family Papers, 1690–1760, Philip English Manuscripts, I, II, Ledger Books of Philip English, 1664–1718, Hathorne Papers, I, Curwen Papers, I, II, Ledger Book of Jonathan

A perennial problem all these traders faced was how to find suitable "returns" to pay for their English goods, especially in the face of dunning letters such as those received by David Jeffries, demanding specie and bills of exchange in payment rather than colonial commodities or shipping. A number, including Fitch and Davis, managed to obtain a share in the bills of exchange sent over by the New England Company, paying the company's representatives in Massachusetts and using the bills to finance their imports from London. A few fortunate colonists, like Samuel Sewall of Boston and Henry Wolcott of Windsor, Connecticut, still drew income from family estates in England with which they could purchase occasional cargoes. Wolcott also participated, through his brother in Salem, in the busy coastal trade between Connecticut and the Bay, buying such items as salt, nails, spices, rum, and dry goods, and sending back pork, peas, wheat—and his son, to Harvard College.[45]

Neither law nor geography aided the Bay ports in their quest for commercial prosperity. The Acts of Trade were designed to promote the direct rather than indirect exchange of colonial raw materials for English manufactured goods. Winds and currents favored the routes between Europe and the Caribbean, to the extent that passengers and

---

Corwin, 1658–1717, all in Essex Instit.; Letterbook of Thomas Fitch, 1702–1711, Amer. Antiq. Soc.; and, for the accounts and debts of Benjamin Davis, Jeffries Papers, V. These private papers also serve in some degree to confirm the accuracy of the official Naval Office Lists as a guide to the character of New England trade for they reveal very few voyages in which New Englanders invested that did not begin or end in New England ports. An excellent account of one family's fortunes is given by Byron Fairchild, *Messrs. William Pepperrell: Merchants at Piscataqua,* especially chapter IV. General contemporary descriptions of New England trade during the 1690s can be found in the letters of John to Nathaniel Higginson, Oct. 3, 1669 [1699], Aug. 29, 1700, Mass. Hist. Soc., *Collections,* 3rd ser., VII (1838), 208–210, 217–221; and Bellomont to the Board of Trade, Nov. 28, 1700, *N. Y. Col. Docs.,* IV, 789–797. Mass. Archives, LXI, 195–565, LXII, 1–327, CXIX, 69–168, contain a mass of material dealing with trade and maritime affairs during this decade but little that provides a coherent or systematic picture of either.

[45] Francis Clarke to David Jeffries, May 10, 1698, William and Sheldon Chambers to Jeffries and Charles Shipreeve, July 24, 1708, Jeffries Papers, VII, 66, VIII, 75; Kellaway, *New England Company,* 72–80, 181; Letterbook, 1688–1761, of the Company for the Propagation of the Gospel in New England, 1 *et seq.;* Sewall, "Letter-Book," 161, 207, 236–239; Allyn-Wolcott Family Papers, 1646–1797, Conn. State Library; Notebook of Henry Wolcott and Roger Wolcott Papers, I, Conn. Hist. Soc.

correspondence often travelled between England and the northern colonies by way of the West Indies, whether intentionally or no— Lord Bellomont, coming from England in 1698 and aiming for New York, was blown to Barbados. In winter, fogs and icebergs endangered the northern routes. In the face of all these impediments, the Bay merchants nonetheless achieved remarkable success. In 1700, Boston, with around six thousand inhabitants, was still the most populous town in English America, its fast-growing wharves and docks crowded with a merchant fleet built in local yards that probably placed Boston second only to London and Bristol among the empire's ports. As a commercial center it far surpassed its local rivals, paying almost a fifth of the province's taxes—the Reverend Benjamin Colman, with his customary sense of proportion, justly compared its metropolitan position to that of London. A second fifth was assessed from six other coastal towns, in ranking order Ipswich, Salem, Newbury, Watertown, Charlestown, and Dorchester.[46] Here, as in the flourishing settlements at New Castle and Portsmouth on the Piscataqua and at Newport in Rhode Island, mercantile oligarchies were beginning to set themselves apart from what was still a predominantly agrarian society. Drawn together by intermarriage and commercial correspondence, facing the sea and not the wilderness, they had more in common with each other and with their trading partners set around the rim of the Atlantic seaboard than with the rural communities of the interior of any individual colony.

Commerce brought other, more genteel influences in its wake. A number of colonists dispatched their sons to England in order that they might, in Fitz-John Winthrop's phrase, "enquire into the art and way of merchandizing" and benefit from what his nephew characterized as "the pollishing aires of Europe." Others studied law at London's Inns of Court.[47] The *Boston News-Letter*, from 1704 the first

---

[46] Bailyn and Bailyn, *Massachusetts Shipping*, 20, 24; *Mass. Acts and Resolves*, I, 439–441 (proportions which remain fairly constant, 1691–1713); Colman to Robert Wodrow, Jan. 23, 1719, Mass. Hist. Soc., *Proceedings*, LXXVII (1965), 109; Bridenbaugh, *Cities in the Wilderness*, chapters V–VI.

[47] Winthrop to Samuel Read, July 1699, Mass. Hist. Soc., *Collections*, 5th ser., VIII (1882), 364; John Winthrop to Fitz-John Winthrop, c. 1707, *ibid.*, 6th ser.,

newspaper regularly published in the colonies, filled its columns with
the fashions and scandals of London life and accounts of European
events to the virtual exclusion of colonial news. Private correspondence reveals the same curiosity about life beyond the boundaries of
New England. In 1706, Cotton Mather proudly listed in his diary the
names of some fifty correspondents scattered throughout Europe and
the American colonies. Benjamin Colman, minister of the Brattle
Street Church, was scarcely less diligent in cultivating the friends he
had made during a seven-year stay in England. The prospect of Protestant unity against the encroachments of Romish tyranny stirred up
an unprecedented collaboration among ministers of all denomina-
tions; both Mather and Colman, together with such prominent Boston laymen as Edward Bromfield and Samuel Sewall, were deeply interested in projects for religious union and universal moral
reformation. It was as if the temporary constriction of the frontier had
reoriented the minds of the colonists toward the common problems of
Anglo-American society.[48]

Other manifestations of this ecumenical spirit were less welcome to
orthodox New Englanders. The spread of religious toleration—only
slowly accepted and as grudgingly allowed despite its embodiment in
the charter—sowed tares among the seed of the choice grain scattered
in the wilderness. Quaker and Baptist ministers invaded New England in greater numbers than ever before, and their congregations established close ties with brethren in England attentive to any complaints of persecution.[49] Most alarming of all was the growth of

III (1889), 402; *Sibley's Harvard Graduates*, III, 356, 410, 413, IV, 43, 210, 383, V, 426; William Byrd to Benjamin Lynde, Feb. 20, 1736, *Virginia Magazine of History and Biography*, IX (1901-1902), 244; John M. Murrin, "The Legal Transforma-tion," 419-423.

[48] Cotton Mather, *Diary,* ed. Ford, I, 549-551; Cotton Mather, *The Diary of Cotton Mather, D.D., F.R.S., for the year 1712,* ed. William R. Manierre, 124; Joyce O. Ransome, "Cotton Mather and the Catholic Spirit," *passim;* Proposals for Corre-spondence among Protestant Dissenters, Colman Papers, I; Ebenezer Turell, *The Life and Character of the Reverend Benjamin Colman,* 47-49, 121-162, and Colman's letters in Mass. Hist. Soc., *Proceedings,* LIII (1919-1920), 67-84, LXXVII (1965), 105-142.

[49] "A Register of all the Publick Friends that Visited New England since the Year 1656," New England Yearly Meeting of Friends, Quaker Archives, R. I. Hist.

Confusion and Conflict

Anglicanism in New England, since the patronage of a royal governor might enable it to rival or even supplant the established Puritan church. After a decade of relatively peaceful coexistence, the truce was broken in 1702 by the arrival of missionaries from the Society for the Propagation of the Gospel in Foreign Parts. To the anger and dismay of Cotton Mather and his colleagues, this militant agency of "high-flying" Anglicanism proceeded to send funds and ministers to New England under the insulting pretext that the dissenting colonies were in need of further proselytization. King's Chapel in Boston once more became the fashionable place of worship for royal officials—and for merchants eager to show their accommodation to the changing order. Episcopal churches were established in several other coastal towns, particularly as minority factions within existing congregations realized that appeals to the society might secure official recognition for a separate church, together with subsidies and exemption from local taxes for ministerial maintenance. Resentful Puritans found that Governor Dudley, intent on currying favor with the society and its influential patrons, refused to check this heterodoxy.[50] Four Harvard graduates travelled to England to receive ordination as Anglican ministers, confirming colonial suspicions of the dangerous liberal tendencies loose at Cambridge under the presidency of Dudley's friend and ally, the urbane and cultivated John Leverett. The climax came in 1722 when at Yale, the college founded to reverse this tide, the

---

Soc., lists twenty-seven visitors, 1692–1700; twenty-four, 1701–1710; and thirty-one, 1711–1720. Much evidence of transatlantic Quaker communication can be found elsewhere in the records collected at Providence, as, for example, the Minutes of the Yearly Meeting of New England, 1683–1787, 3–81, and Earliest Discipline Manuscripts, 1672–1735, 43–65. Also Frederick B. Tolles, *Quakers and the Atlantic Culture*, 1–35; Edwin Bronner, "Intercolonial Relations among Quakers Before 1750,"3–17; and the excellent study by Susan B. Reed, *Church and State in Massachusetts, 1691–1740*, 86–147. There were some fourteen Baptist ministers in New England in 1700, mostly in Rhode Island; for their spread and struggles, see McLoughlin, *New England Dissent*, I, 113–162.

[50] E. L. Pennington, "The Reverend Samuel Myles and His Boston Ministry," 154–178; Ethyn Kirby, *George Keith (1638–1716)*, 125–137; Foote, *Annals of King's Chapel*, I, 117, 229–235; George C. Mason, *Annals of Trinity Church, Newport, Rhode Island*, I, 11, 25; R. I. Hist. Soc., *Collections*, IV (1838), 265–266; C. F. Pascoe, *Two Hundred Years of the S.P.G.*, II, 852–854; Reed, *Church and State in Massachusetts*, 148–189.

president and two of the tutors suddenly announced their conversion to the Church of England.[51]

There were signs, also, that the ways of English society were eroding the unique characteristics of New England life. Samuel Sewall, ever vigilant in such matters, mournfully recorded in his diary the increasing popularity of wigs, the fighting of duels, and his struggles to prevent the introduction of such English and, to his eyes, pagan practices as the naming of the days of the week and the observance of Christmas as a holiday. From Marblehead came a report of a "Bull baiting as they do in England."[52] Visitors remarked on the imported fashions and fabrics of Boston society: one writer, intending a compliment which Sewall, for one, must have wished undeserved, declared that here "a Gentleman from London might almost think himself at home." Wealthy citizens drove the streets in coaches attended by their servants and, in what was perhaps the most revealing instance of a turning to England as a reference point in determining social status and behavior, a number of colonists applied to London for coats of arms to sustain their claims to noble ancestry.[53] Breeding and connection, it appeared, were now hardly less important than sanctity as requisites for leadership. Few of these cosmopolitan habits had as yet taken root in rural areas where, as some later remembered with affectionate regret, a simpler and more modest way of life per-

---

[51] The graduates were Samuel Myles, William Vesey, Gershom Rawlins, and Dudley Bradstreet; another, Henry Newman, became secretary of the Anglican Society for Promoting Christian Knowledge. For Harvard in the 1690s, see Samuel Eliot Morison, *Three Centuries of Harvard*, 45–46, and Cowie, *Henry Newman*, 5–10. For the events at Yale, see Bridenbaugh, *Mitre and Sceptre*, 68–69.

[52] Sewall, *Diary*, I, 337, 351, 406, 475, 494, II, 678, 913, 1,000; Henry L. Seaver, "Hair and Holiness," 3–20; Josiah Cotton to Rowland Cotton, Oct. 17, 1702, Miscellaneous Bound MSS., 1701–1713, Mass. Hist. Soc.

[53] Bridenbaugh, *Cities in the Wilderness*, 253; New Haven Hist. Soc., *Papers*, VII (1908), 263–270; James Pierpont to Fitz-John Winthrop, Sept. 24, 1693, Mass. Hist. Soc., *Collections*, 6th ser., III (1889), 266–267; Winthrop to Pierpont, Feb. 15, 1698, Winthrop Papers; William Waldron to Richard Waldron, Apr. 15, 1723, Waldron Letters, Mass. Hist. Soc.; *New England Historical and Genealogical Register*, LXXX (1926), 371–376; *North American Review*, XCI (1860), 361; John M. Phillips, *American Silver*, 44–47.

sisted, ruled by the passage of the seasons and the demands of subsistence agriculture.[54] Less charitable contemporaries, such as the redoubtable Madam Sarah Knight of Boston, travelling overland to New York in 1704, wrote scathingly of rudimentary roads and even ruder society. In the meantime, the deepening cultural differences between coast and hinterland, expressed in popular tales about "a Hectoring Debauchee" from Boston and the children fathered by the Devil there, and in counterblasts against the "parcell of resolute rustics" in the provincial assembly, gave added weight to traditional political divisions between the port towns and the back country.[55]

A few colonists responded to these magnetic influences. Several of the brightest stars from Harvard's firmament chose to settle permanently in England. Its president, Increase Mather, hankered for the opportunity, such as would arise were he officially commissioned to obtain a royal charter for the college, that would permit him to mingle once more with England's leaders. His inability to secure the appointment—many remembered all too well what had happened last time Mather had gone to England on charter business—coupled with other frustrations, fostered his progressive alienation from Massachusetts life.[56] A number of New Englanders migrated to other colonies, and a steady stream of aspiring planters and merchants moved down the established lines of trade to try their fortune in the golden Caribbean. "I assure you," wrote Isaac Royall to John Usher from Antigua, "tis beyond thought I have Clerd above Six thousand

---

[54] Wolcott, "Memoir," 332: Thomas Prince, growing up in rural Massachusetts, recalled that until he came to Boston at the age of fifteen he had never heard a profane oath or curse: *The People of New-England Put in Mind of the Righteous Acts of the Lord,* 35.

[55] "The Journal of Madame Knight," in Perry Miller and Thomas H. Johnson, eds., *The Puritans,* II, 425–447; Hammond, "Diary," 147; John Winthrop to Fitz-John Winthrop, [June 1706], Mass. Hist. Soc., *Collections,* 6th ser., III (1889), 335.

[56] Josiah Quincy, *The History of Harvard University,* I, 467–477; Morison, *Harvard College,* II, 501–502; Increase Mather, *Autobiography,* 345–350; Middlekauff, *The Mathers,* 173–174.

pounds."[57] None left in the belief that godlier lives could be lived elsewhere, and most retained fond memories of their native land. But, like those who remained behind, they now knew themselves to be part of a larger transatlantic society, one perhaps more dangerous to body and soul, yet affording broad new vistas of opportunity beyond the moral and physical boundaries of New England.

Thus, in their several ways, economic and social contacts drew the colonists closer to the mother country. The most immediate and visible change, however, and one directly attributable to the settlement reached after the Glorious Revolution, was the marked and enduring extension of royal authority within New England. It was most evident, naturally, in Massachusetts and New Hampshire. Not all the Mathers' sermons extolling the virtues of the charter of 1691 as a stronger wall around the Lord's vineyard could erase the fact that the king's governor sat in Boston. His formal powers, if less than those given to Andros, were far greater than those held by his predecessors under the old charter. In appointing, with the advice and consent of the council, the sheriffs, justices of the peace, judges of probate, and all other officers pertaining to the administration of justice, the governor exercised a preponderant influence in the field of local administration, dominating the agencies that most directly touched the affairs of the average colonist. As captain general of the province, he had the exclusive power to bestow the coveted status of military rank: as Cotton Mather sourly noted in criticizing Gov. Joseph Dudley's adroit use of this authority, "the Influence which Preferments and Commissions have upon little Men, is inexpressible." Indeed, the executive power was at its height in time of war, extending to such delicate plums of patronage as the issuance of letters of marque to priva-

---

[57] *New England Historical and Genealogical Register*, XXX (1876), 64–67, XXXIV (1880), 408; Mathews, *Expansion of New England*, 66–69; *Sibley's Harvard Graduates*, III, 429, IV, 101–105, 297, 322–324; Cook, *John Wise*, 83–84; Royal to Usher, Apr. 18, 1706, Jeffries Papers, III, 132; Babette M. Levy, "Early Puritanism in the Southern and Island Colonies," 259–267.

teers and the appointment of commissioners to dispose of captured prizes.[58]

Further, the governor now held the initiative in political affairs. Providing that a General Court was held at least once a year in May, he could convene, adjourn, and dissolve its meetings at his convenience. It became customary for him to deliver an address at the beginning of each session, when he would comment upon the state of the province and suggest certain matters for the consideration of the General Court. He was the sole official channel for communication to or from the crown. Finally, although the governor's power of veto over appointments, legislation, and the appropriation of money was at best a blunt instrument for the shaping of policy, it did allow him to exert a decisive restraint upon any deviations from the established pattern of government.

In May 1692, however, as Governor Phips arrived in Boston, this pattern existed only on the parchment of the charter accompanying him and there seemed little likelihood that the executive's powers would be fully exercised. An exultant Cotton Mather gave thanks to the providence which, "instead of my being made a Sacrifice to wicked Rulers," had placed the government in the hands of men nominated by his father, many of them from Mather's own congregation, and whose leader was a man he had baptized and reckoned among his dearest friends. Publicly, he circulated a paper of advice in the form of political fables, in one of which the elephant—Phips—chided the assembled animals for fearing that he would serve as a "shoeing-horn" by which worse executives would later be imposed upon them. If he were such, the elephant continued, "yet I have at least obtained this for you, that you have time to shape your foot, so as, whatever shoe comes, it shall sit easy upon you."[59] The message

---

[58] [Cotton Mather?], *The Deplorable State of New-England*, 118*; Benjamin Marston to Joseph Dudley, Aug. 24, 1702, Chamberlain Collection, Ch.M.2.3.II, 219; Commission of Lieutenant Governor Stoughton to Stephen Sewall and John Higginson, Nov. 2, 1695, Saltonstall Papers, Folio XI, B, Mass. Hist. Soc.

[59] Cotton Mather, *Diary*, ed. Ford, I, 148; *Andros Tracts*, II, 328.

was clear: together, Phips and the General Court could mold the new government to such effect that even some future Andros would not be able to reverse its course.

This plan was promptly pursued. In a torrent of legislation—fifty-two laws were enacted by March of 1693, a record unequalled during the rest of the colonial period—Phips and his General Court went far toward reestablishing administrative institutions and procedures as they had existed prior to 1686. Once on the books, as Mather noted, this "Body of good Laws" could not be annulled without the court's consent.[60] Phips also set a precedent by allowing his council to choose the judges and other appointed officials instead of, as the charter provided, submitting his nominations for their advice and consent. Moreover the powers of these appointed officials were restricted in several important respects compared with those exercised by their English counterparts. The new laws, for example, provided for jurors to be chosen by the towns, not the sheriffs (a measure doubtless prompted by memories of the "Packt and pickt juries" of the Dominion) and for county treasurers to be elected to administer the taxes collected for county government.[61] And even where the charter's provisions could not be evaded, the old ways might silently survive: though the General Court dutifully enacted laws providing for the election of representatives by forty-shilling freeholders and those possessing an estate of forty pounds sterling, the one piece of evidence regarding its enforcement in the early 1690s suggests that the new requirements, if they permitted many non-church members to vote in provincial elections for the first time, were not interpreted to exclude those who had customarily voted. Nor, save for an initial flurry during Phips's administration, did the change in franchise result in the election of legislators significantly different in social standing or reli-

---

[60] *Mass. Acts and Resolves*, I, 27–109 (three acts are not printed here); Cotton Mather, *Life of Phips*, 123–124; Joseph Dudley to William Blathwayt, Feb. 25, 1693, Blathwayt Papers, IV, Col. Wmsbg. Judging by the language of the council records, the great bulk of this legislation originated in the lower house.

[61] Hutchinson, *History of Massachusetts-Bay*, II, 10; Lord Bellomont to the Board of Trade, Aug. 28, 1699, *CSP Col., 1699*, no. 746; Sewall, *Diary*, I, 301–302, 327; *Mass. Acts and Resolves*, I, 37, 63–64, 74–75.

gious and political beliefs from those chosen prior to 1692. To the contrary, as royalist John Usher complained to William Blathwayt of conditions under the new charter, "Att present itts Comon Wealth and nott Kingly Govermentt."[62]

Yet within a year of Phips's arrival the political consensus began to disintegrate. One reason was the antagonism ingrained within the format of the charter. Although relations between magistrates and deputies prior to 1686 had seldom been smooth, both groups had shared the same constituency and substantially the same ideals. Under the charter of 1691, not only were there two rival sources of political authority, the crown and the Massachusetts voters, but the structure of government, a replica of England's mixed and balanced constitution, was deliberately designed to accommodate and express the clash of conflicting interests.[63] As in other colonies coming under royal government, therefore, those taking office were all too often drawn into adopting the rhetoric, claims, and antagonisms attendant upon their position. Status shaped behavior; an adversary system created adversaries. Massachusetts leaders, with vivid memories of Andros, were especially sensitive to assertions of executive power: for example, agent Elisha Cooke, writing from London, had warned against allowing a royal governor any permanent revenues.[64] From the first, the new assembly jealously guarded its power of the purse, refusing to grant Phips or his appointed officials regular

---

[62] *Mass. Acts and Resolves,* I, 80 (a rare completed version of the precept printed here, from Dedham, Aug. 1693, is in Miscellaneous Manuscripts, HM 22304, Hunt. Lib.); Hammond, "Diary," 161–162; Usher to Blathwayt, Sept., 1698, *William and Mary Quarterly,* 3rd ser., VII (1950), 100. Although scholars have long taken the formal change from a franchise based on church membership to one based on property holding as a symbolic turning point, they have not shown that it had any significant political impact upon the character of those electing or elected to office. Nor did contemporaries speak of any such change. For a general account of the franchise after 1691, see Robert E. Brown, *Middle-Class Democracy,* chapters II and III.

[63] Corinne C. Weston, *English Constitutional Theory and the House of Lords, 1556–1832,* examines this theme; for its subsequent application to Massachusetts, see, for example, Breen, *Character of the Good Ruler,* 224.

[64] Cooke to Simon Bradstreet, Nov. 4, 1691, Prince Papers (Hutchinson, *History of Massachusetts-Bay,* I, 348n.). The colony had shown a similar caution before the Dominion: Viola Barnes, *Dominion of New England,* 58.

salaries and carefully defining the purpose and duration of revenue measures.

Phips was not the man to bear such suspicions patiently, and his personal ambitions soon swelled the rivalries latent in the charter into open dissension. Despite the cloak of sanctity thrown about him by the Mathers, Phips was at bottom a volatile blend of bluff sea dog and imaginative entrepreneur, a self-made man who had always pursued his own fame and fortune ahead of other, more patriotic loyalties. In 1683, he had quarrelled with the charter magistrates over what he deemed to be their failure to pay him due respect as commander of a king's ship, and his conquest of Port Royal in 1690 had been marred by his ruthless plundering of his captives.[65] As governor, he was soon appealing to London for authority to compel the assembly to pay him an annual salary and to replace Province Secretary Isaac Addington, Elisha Cooke's cousin and political ally, with a follower of his own. Later, he proposed to Blathwayt a scheme by which the two of them would divide the profits if Blathwayt would secure for him a monopoly of the colony's fur trade.[66]

In personality, as Cotton Mather delicately acknowledged, Phips "was of an Inclination cutting rather like a *Hatchet,* than like a *Razor,*" and his explosive temper led him, early in 1693, into successive hand-to-hand brawls on the Boston dockside with two royal officers, Captain Short of the frigate *Nonsuch* and Collector of Customs Jahleel Brenton. The fight with Short stemmed from their equal determination to profit from the sale of captured prize vessels and the hired-out labor of the frigate's crew. As for Brenton, two of the first acts passed under the new charter had effectively stripped the customs officers

---

[65] Journal of John Knepp, 1683–1684, Egerton MSS., 2526, foll. 8–13, 15; Viola Barnes, "The Rise of Sir William Phips," 277; Mass. Hist. Soc., *Collections,* 3rd ser., I (1825), 114–117; Mass. Archives, CCXLII, 403–404; Sewall, *Diary,* I, 271, 273.

[66] Phips to William Blathwayt, Oct. 12, 1692, Feb. 27 (twice), Sept. 11, 1693, Blathwayt Papers, V, Col. Wmsbg.; Petitions of Sir William Phips, [Apr. 3, 1693], [1693], C.O. 5/857, nos. 47, 95; letter of Elisha Hutchinson, Feb. 1, 1693 [1694], Mass. Hist. Soc., *Proceedings,* II (1844), 296. I have found no evidence that Phips offered the share in the fur monopoly in exchange for confirmation of the colony's laws, as stated by Lovejoy, *Glorious Revolution in America,* 373.

appointed by London of jurisdiction over the colony's trade and bestowed it upon others appointed by the governor. Brenton protested and tried to exercise his authority; Phips and a mob of supporters manhandled the collector and forced him to give up his seizures. Phips won both fights, but the spectacle was unsettling to those who remembered the dignity in office of a Leverett or a Bradstreet. Through both episodes, moreover, ran the thread of the governor's readiness to take the law into his own hands to protect his personal interests. Other evidence later gathered by his opponents suggests that he was also using his position to turn a quick profit in such ventures as privateering, the production of naval stores, trafficking with the Indians, and speculation in eastern lands.[67] All in all, he was behaving almost as badly as opponents of the new charter feared a royal governor might behave, and his plebeian manners—"the lowness of his Education and parts"—alienated even those few who had admired autocracy in the more dignified form of Andros.[68]

Matters came to a head with the election of 1693. Despite a blunt sermon from Increase Mather preached on the text of "I will Restore thy Counsellours as at the Beginning" and warning that the governor would veto any "Malecontents" put forward by the General Court, ten of the twenty-eight councillors named by Mather eighteen months before were left out and others, including Addington, Elisha Cooke, and former Deputy Governor Thomas Danforth, elected in

---

[67] Cotton Mather, *Life of Phips,* 19; for the charges against Phips, set out at much greater length than in the printed calendar, see C.O. 5/857, nos. 42, 44, 57, 87i, C.O. 5/751, nos. 19, 34, C.O. 5/924, no. 23, and, especially, C.O. 5/858, nos. 10i–xix, 42i–ii, 44 (*CSP Col., 1693–1696,* nos. 88, 224, 225, 247, 258, 293, 689i, 827i–xix, 1505i–ii, 1507). Duplicates of the evidence and much else relating to Phips's struggle with Short and Brenton are in Mass. Archives, LXI, 320–557. Viola Barnes, "Phippius Maximus," 532–553, provides a full account which, while accepting the accusations of the governor's opponents at face value and neglecting their share in the same abuses charged against Phips, provides a necessary corrective to those modern writers misled by Cotton Mather's hagiographic biography.

[68] Thus Testimony of Nathaniel Byfield, Francis Foxcroft, Giles Dyer, Daniel Allin, Thaddeus Mackarty, and David Waterhouse, Feb. 20, 1693, Blathwayt Papers, IV, Col. Wmsbg.; John Higginson to John How[e], Aug. 1, 1694, Moody, *Saltonstall Papers,* 214.

their place.[69] The numbers are slightly deceptive; at least two of the ten old councillors, Simon Bradstreet and John Joyliffe, were incapacitated, and another, the London merchant Stephen Mason, had remained in England. Two more, Addington and Lieutenant Governor Stoughton, had been named to office in the charter but were now formally elected to the council. Yet in view of the way in which magistrates were customarily reelected year after year in New England, the results were still a slap in the face to Mather and a demonstration of the colonists' preference for those who had served as old charter magistrates over those he had chosen in 1691. Phips, acting on what all believed to be Mather's advice, vetoed Cooke's election, raising a storm of protest from those who believed that the governor's veto was a dangerously arbitrary and divisive weapon which should have been left to wither from disuse. In the meantime, Phips had also aroused Stoughton's angry hostility by his necessary but high-handed intervention to stop the witchcraft proceedings pressed by the lieutenant governor and his fellow judges.[70]

A further challenge to the governor emerged out of the new House of Deputies elected in 1693. In what appears to have been a concerted bid to check Phips's headlong course, a number of the coastal merchants and gentry who had come to political prominence in the months after Andros's overthrow suddenly secured election as representatives, most of them sitting on behalf of country towns, a common practice under the old charter. They included several—Nathaniel Byfield, Francis Foxcroft, Benjamin Davis, Richard Sprague, and Dr. Daniel Allin—who had shown what opponents decried as their "tory" sympathies back in 1690 by signing the petitions sent to London appealing for royal intervention in New England. Also elected were the battered Jahleel Brenton and his brother Ebenezer, Byfield's brother-in-law. Only Sprague had previously served in the General

---

[69] Increase Mather, *The Great Blessing, of Primitive Counsellours,* 19; Sewall, *Diary,* I, 309.

[70] Sewall, *Diary,* I, 310; Samuel Stow to Wait Winthrop, Aug. 4, 1692, Mass. Hist. Soc., *Collections,* 6th ser., V (1892), 28; Phips to the Earl of Nottingham, Feb. 21, 1693, Mass. Hist. Soc., *Proceedings,* 2nd ser., I (1884–1885), 340–342; Stoughton to Blathwayt, Oct. 24, 1693, Blathwayt Papers, V, Col. Wmsbg.

Court. These men were doubtless inspired by the conviction that Phips was demeaning and distorting royal authority; a letter from Randolph, now briefly back in New England, also suggests that Byfield and Collector Brenton at least were seeking to curb the governor's usurpation of the hitherto handsome profits of Brenton's selective enforcement of the Acts of Trade.[71]

The new assembly promptly showed its mettle by dismissing John Phillips, the governor's "*Fidus Achates,* and very dear Friend" (and Cotton Mather's father-in-law), as province treasurer and then appointing a committee packed with opponents of the governor to investigate Phillips's accounts. Phips promptly dissolved the assembly and, after its successor failed to gather a quorum, summoned another in November. The new house, however, contained even more of his adversaries, including two additional "tories," John Cutler of Charlestown and Giles Dyer, the latter, like Francis Foxcroft, an Anglican who had held office during the Dominion.[72]

Phips was now in trouble in London as well as in Boston. Captain Short had finally escaped to England after several months of imprisonment; a pursuit by Phips had carried as far as New Hampshire, where the governor had boarded the ship carrying the captain back to London and seized his papers and personal belongings. Short complained at Whitehall of his mistreatment, and Jahleel Brenton sent over a list of charges accusing the governor of abusing his vice-admiralty powers and violating the Acts of Trade. From the governors of New York, New Hampshire, and even Rhode Island came further

---

[71] *Mass. Acts and Resolves,* VII, 20–21; Randolph to the Lords of Trade, Sept. 29, 1692, *Randolph Letters,* VII, 421–422; Barrow, *Trade and Empire,* 40–43. The traditional interpretation that sees a simple division between Phips and the Mathers on one hand and the old charter party on the other takes no account of the status and royalist sentiments of these opponents of Phips. This has led to such tortured explanations as that Mather meant Elisha Cooke and his allies when he spoke of "tories" in Boston (Thomas J. Holmes, *Cotton Mather,* II, 807; David Levin, *Cotton Mather,* 253) and to the wilder surmises, compounded by a confused chronology, of Warden, *Boston,* 45–47. Miller, *Colony to Province,* 175, perceives two parties— Phips and the eastern merchants contending against the assembly and the rural back country. The reverse—Phips allying himself with the rural house members against a group of merchants—is closer to the truth.

[72] *Mass. Acts and Resolves,* VII, 29–30, 376, 383; Cotton Mather, *Life of Phips,* 161; Sewall, *Diary,* I, 311.

reports of Phips's irascible behavior.[73] Spurred on by representations from the Commissioners of Customs, the Lords of Trade began an enquiry into Phips's conduct. A military success might have gilded over the governor's transgressions, and an opportunity seemed at hand when a force of English ships and soldiers sailed into Boston harbor in June 1693 to launch a new assault upon Canada. Unhappily, not only did the expedition arrive with its strength halved by diseases contracted during a stay in the Caribbean, but Phips, through a failure of communication, was given no time to make preparations to assist it, so that the scheme perished amid mutual recriminations and excuses.[74] Finally, by the fall of 1693, Joseph Dudley, the most formidable of the governor's opponents and the man widely regarded as his likely successor, had returned to England to lead the attack. Ignominiously shipped off to England in the wake of the Dominion's collapse, he had come back to America in 1691 as royal councillor and chief justice in New York. But, as one jealous New Yorker noted, Dudley "cannot forgett to be a N England man," and early in the following year he moved to Boston, still hoping for office in his native land.[75] There, in a further instance of the remarkable "tory" resurgence of 1693, he failed by only two votes to be elected to Phips's council in place of Elisha Cooke.[76] He soon perceived, however, that his chances of preferment were slight: "the present Masters of this Country," he told Blathwayt, "look upon Mee as a strange Creature

---

[73] Note 67, preceding, and Gov. Benjamin Fletcher to [William Blathwayt], Feb. 14, 1693, the Governor and Company of Rhode Island to the king and queen, Aug. 2, 1692, *CSP Col., 1693–1696*, nos. 84, 85, 524ii. Byfield, Foxcroft, Dyer, Allin, Thaddeus Mackarty, and David Waterhouse also sent a denunciation of Phips to Blathwayt, Feb. 20, 1693, with Dudley's assistance: Blathwayt Papers, IV, Col. Wmsbg.

[74] Guttridge, *Colonial Policy of William III*, 65–68, 74–75; Webb, "William Blathwayt, Imperial Fixer: Muddling Through," 381–393; *Mass. Acts and Resolves*, VII, 384–386.

[75] Kimball, *Public Life of Joseph Dudley*, 58–65; James Graham to Francis Nicholson, Apr. 6, 1691, Blathwayt Papers, X, Col. Wmsbg. Dudley also visited Boston in 1691: Dudley to [Governor Sloughter of New York?], July 23, 1691, Washburn Papers, VII, 18, Mass. Hist. Soc.

[76] Sewall, *Diary*, I, 309. The "Col. Dudley" spoken of by Sewall was the customary reference to Joseph Dudley at this time.

in their Forrest." Whitehall beckoned, and by mid-November Dudley was back at court, pressing for Phips's dismissal.[77]

In Massachusetts, the beleaguered governor strove to rally his supporters. After some consideration of sending Increase Mather back to defend him, Phips dispatched his secretary, Benjamin Jackson, to Whitehall to counter Dudley's attack.[78] Yet only a bare majority of the November assembly supported an address to the crown praising his record as governor. Hence Phips next sought to persuade the deputies to select a new speaker in place of Byfield, who was in correspondence with Dudley and had openly aided Captain Short in his efforts to escape to England.[79] Failing, he embarked upon a more sweeping purge of his opponents, including Byfield, by bringing forward a bill regulating the assembly with a clause banning the election of representatives who were not residents or freeholders of the towns for which they were chosen. The bill passed both houses by narrow margins after fierce debate. In consequence, few "tories" appeared in the assembly chosen the following May. Nonetheless, six

---

[77] Dudley to Blathwayt, Feb. 25, 1693, Blathwayt Papers, IV, Col. Wmsbg.; Sir Henry Ashurst to [William Stoughton], Nov. 14, 1693, Feb. 1, 1694, to Increase Mather, Nov. 14, 1693, Letterbook of Sir Henry Ashurst, foll. 91, 93, 92v.

[78] Increase Mather, *Autobiography*, 345; Sir Henry Ashurst to [Stoughton], Feb. 1, 1694, to [Sir William Phips], [Mar. 1694], to Increase Mather, June 11, 1694, Letterbook of Sir Henry Ashurst, foll. 93, 94v., 103v.; Petition of Benjamin Jackson, Jan. 5, 1694, C.O. 5/858, no. 2.

[79] *Mass. Acts and Resolves*, VII, 32, 388, 391; Sewall, *Diary*, I, 314; Extracts of the minutes of the House of Representatives, Nov. 21, 1693, C.O. 5/857, no. 86; Phips to the Earl of Nottingham, Apr. 6, to the Lords of the Admiralty, Apr. 6, 1693, C.O. 5/751, no. 34, C.O. 5/857, no. 50 ("Bye" in the printed calendar should read "Byfield"); Affidavit of Nathaniel Byfield, [Aug. 1694], Mass. Archives, LXI, 474–475; Francis Foxcroft and Giles Dyer also aided Short (*ibid.*, 466), and some months earlier Byfield had aided another shipmaster persecuted by Phips to escape: Byfield to John Usher, Mar. 13, 14, 1693, Jeffries Papers, III, 81, 82.

The account of the vote in Hutchinson, *History of Massachusetts-Bay*, II, 59, is based on the eight-page printed "Letter from New England" dated Nov. 1, 1694, a copy of which is in C.O. 5/858, no. 41A. Hutchinson, however, mistranscribes it: twenty-three (not twenty-four) of fifty representatives, including Byfield, voted against the address. The council minutes, Mass. Archives, Court Records, VI, for Nov. 16, 1693, show that five councillors (Stoughton, Addington, Peter Sergeant, Wait Winthrop, and William Bradford) did not sign the address although they were present when this was done. This address should not be confused with the second, similar address sent a year later, as cited in note 82, following.

towns elected nonresidents, whereupon Phips, in a scene painfully reminiscent of King Charles I's pursuit of the Five Members in 1642, personally invaded the lower house to drive out the offending delegates, including Byfield, Foxcroft, Davis, and Thomas Dudley, Joseph Dudley's nephew.[80] Not even a blistering election sermon preached the same day by yet another Dudley associate, his brother-in-law the Reverend Samuel Willard, pointedly denouncing unjust rulers and laws made to strengthen particular interests, could deter Phips from banishing his opponents.[81]

Phips's purge broke the back of open opposition to his administration within the General Court. It also, whether by reason of his own changing convictions or the pledges he may have needed to carry through the purge, drew him closer to those still hankering for the old charter and away from the Mathers' tutelage. In the election of 1694 he withheld his veto when Elisha Cooke was chosen to the council, and by September he was promising to procure from England a restoration of the old charter and all its privileges, a suggestion which, though welcomed by the representatives, can hardly have endeared him to the Mathers.[82] Yet Byfield and his friends laughed last, for by the fall of 1694 Phips was on the verge of leaving Massachusetts for England, recalled from office to answer the charges levelled against him. With him, by royal command, went a mass of evidence, most of it unfavorable, gathered with remarkable alacrity by Secretary Addington and Lieutenant Governor Stoughton, who now assumed the

---

[80] *Mass. Acts and Resolves*, I, 147; Nathaniel Byfield to Joseph Dudley, June 12, to John Usher, July 12, 1694, C.O. 5/858, nos. 31, 35. The bill was carried with twenty-four or twenty-five dissenting votes in the house and by nine to eight in the council, with Phips not voting: "Letter from New England," [Nov. 1, 1694], C.O. 5/858, no. 41A; Sewall, *Diary*, I, 315; [Thomas Dudley] to William Blathwayt, Dec. 3, 1693, Blathwayt Papers, IV, Col. Wmsbg.; Extract from the minutes of the House of Representatives, Nov. 22, 1693, C.O. 5/857, no. 86 (which adds the name of Benjamin Browne of Salem to Sewall's list of those opposing the bill). Six out of seven representatives sitting for Bristol County opposed the bill.

[81] Willard, *The Character of a Good Ruler*, 27.

[82] Sir William Phips's Remarks to the Massachusetts Assembly, Sept. 14, 1695 [1694], Blathwayt Papers, BL 245, Hunt. Lib.; Vote of the Representatives, Sept. 20, 1694, *Mass. Acts and Resolves*, VII, 451; Address of the Council and Assembly of Massachusetts to the king and queen, Oct. 31, 1694, C.O. 5/858, no. 41.

administration of the province. His case was never decided; arriving in London in January 1695, he died the following month of a sudden illness.[83]

Phips's departure eased the political tensions within Massachusetts. His successor, William Stoughton, had worked with Joseph Dudley to introduce royal government to New England ten years before. Yet he had disengaged himself from the worst excesses of the Andros regime and quickly returned to public esteem. In sharp contrast to Phips, he exuded a reassuring continuity with patterns of past leadership. Reserved and austere, scrupulous in his attention to what he saw as his duty and the letter of the law, he displayed neither his predecessor's self-seeking ambitions nor his boisterous temperament. He had not sought his post: one cause of his breach with Phips was his conviction, expressed in letters to England, that his old friend Dudley was still best fitted to be governor. In the meantime, believing, as he wrote to Blathwayt, that it had been Phips's "misfortune to doe too many things upon his own opinion," he instinctively turned back to the time-honored practice of governing in harmony with a consensus of the council.[84] Elisha Cooke remained a councillor and was chosen by his colleagues to the added dignity of Judge of the Superior Court. Byfield returned to the assembly as representative for Boston, resumed the speakership, and in 1699 moved to the council, having married his daughter to Stoughton's heir. Without the constant provocation of a governor such as Phips, and hampered by the nonresidency law, most of the other purged "tories" stayed out of province politics. Stoughton himself cemented this stability and displayed his firm loyalty to the new charter and its ties to England by blocking all

---

[83] The king to Sir William Phips, Feb. 15, 1694, Pubs. Col. Soc. Mass., *Transactions*, XI (1906–1907), 342–343; Fitz-John Winthrop to Wait Winthrop, Mar. 6, 1695, Mass. Hist. Soc., *Collections*, 5th ser., VIII (1882), 326; Cotton Mather, *Life of Phips*, 187–192.

[84] Stoughton to Blathwayt, Oct. 23, 1693, Nov. 14, 1694, Blathwayt Papers, IV, Col. Wmsbg. For Stoughton's legalistic scruples, see Sewall, *Diary*, I, 278–279, 348.

attempts by nostalgic assemblymen to petition the crown for a restoration of the colony's "ancient privileges."[85] The great bulk of his lengthy stewardship—Bellomont did not arrive in Boston until May 1699, four and a half years after Phips had left—was taken up with matters of defense as the frontiers remained under siege from French and Indian attack.

Nonetheless, even Stoughton's conciliatory rule could not extinguish the constitutional rivalries ignited during Phips's brief tenure of office. Like other aspects of New England life, these too were showing the effects of a closer relationship with England. Under the old charter, when deputies and magistrates had clashed over such issues as the latter's claims to discretionary and veto powers, both sides had appealed to Biblical authority and the letter of the charter. By 1694, the Massachusetts representatives had turned to take their stand upon their right to "use and exersize such Powers & Privileges here as the house of comons in England may & have usually done there." Following in the Commons's footsteps, the representatives fastened upon the crucial issue of financial control. In a lengthy controversy extending over several sessions, they protested against the payment of salaries by authority of governor and council alone and strove to intrude upon the realm of executive policy by requiring that their appropriations be expended only in predesignated ways. An act passed in 1694 ratified these claims. Though later disallowed by the crown, it effectively established guidelines for the future which assumed all powers not expressly reserved by charter to the executive to be subject to the supervision of the legislature. Other laws consolidated this control in providing for the lower house's right to audit government accounts and (here going beyond the powers claimed by the Commons in England) to appoint those charged with collecting provincial revenues.[86]

---

[85] *Mass. Acts and Resolves*, VII, 450–451 and n., 518; Sewall, *Diary*, I, 322; Mass. Archives, Court Records, VI, Dec. 1, 3, 1696.

[86] Breen, *Character of the Good Ruler*, 58–86, 123–133, *Mass. Acts and Resolves*, VII, 33–34, 392–394, 409–412, I, 163, 170, 230. For subsequent disputes in the 1690s over these issues, *ibid.*, VII, 534–537, 540–542. For contemporary English parliamentary practice, see Dennis Rubini, *Court and Country, 1688–1702*, 68–92, and J. A. Downie, "The Commission of Public Accounts and the Formation of the Country Party," 33–51.

More generally, the representatives steadily refined their conduct of affairs over the course of the decade, establishing their right to "the accustomed priviledges of an English assembly" in such matters as freedom of speech, freedom from arrest while in session, and control over their own procedures, and carrying their bills through the customary three readings, committee study, and engrossment as practiced in the House of Commons.[87] Like their English counterparts, they kept "a Booke," a formal journal of their proceedings.

The loss of this journal makes it difficult to determine whether any particular group or individuals led this surge of self-assertion. Some of the procedures adopted in the 1690s, such as the assembly's hand in the auditing of accounts and the choosing of the colony treasurer, had existed prior to 1686, although then exercised by both houses of the General Court. There was a blending of old practices and new claims within the framework of the constitutional scenario imposed by the charter of 1691. Yet it is significant that these procedures were most firmly pressed and most vociferously identified with English precedent during the months when Byfield and his fellow "tories" sat in the assembly, prior to Phips's purge. These "tory" members formed an effective alliance, which fragmentary evidence suggests endured throughout the decade, with the towns of the former Plymouth Colony, particularly those in Bristol County where Byfield and the Brentons were landowners and where many of the inhabitants were resisting incorporation into Massachusetts in the hope of joining with

---

[87] *Mass. Acts and Resolves,* VII, 390–393, 533–534, I, 88–90. For pre- and post-1692 procedure on a bill, compare, for example, Mass. Archives, LXI, 269 with *ibid.,* 314, 318, 344, LXII, 256, and CXIX, 26, 62, with *ibid.,* 74–79, 94, 107. The record of the passage of a typical money bill reads: "In the House of Representatives June 21:99 Read a first time Read 21 June 99 a Second Tyme Read a 3d tyme 22 June 1699 Voted to be Engrossed Ordered to be sent up to his Excellency and Council for Concurrence. In Council June 22 1699. Read a first time and ordered to be read a second time to morrow morning. 23rd Read a Second time and committed to a Committee of the whole board. 26.4.99 Agreed to—Read in Council July 11, 99 and past to be Engrossed": Mass. Archives, CXIX, 162. Other bills were often drafted and debated by joint committees appointed by both houses. For a brief description of the meeting of such committees, and their intercommuning "in the green chamber over the secretary's office," see William Bassett to Roland Cotton, June 23, 1699, Miscellaneous Bound MSS., 1694–1700, Mass. Hist. Soc.

neighboring Rhode Island.[88] The "tories" themselves lived in or close to Boston and so were able to give their full attention to assembly business, no small advantage when most of the representatives were busy farmers. As a group, they also possessed markedly greater wealth and social status than the great majority of their colleagues. With these advantages they emerged as the natural leaders of the house, dominating the committees formed to draft reports and legislation.[89] All had close ties with England: some, such as Francis Foxcroft, Giles Dyer, and Byfield himself, had been born and raised there. Though strong supporters of the establishment of royal government in Massachusetts, they feared that in Phips's hands it was being perverted into a means for resuscitating the broad discretionary powers formerly wielded by the old charter magistrates. Hence they naturally turned to the time-honored procedures used in England to curb an overbear-

---

[88] For the struggle in Bristol County and between Massachusetts and Rhode Island, which produced some of the liveliest official language of the period, see *Mass. Acts and Resolves*, VII, 492–494, 544, 658–668, 700–701, and, generally, the correspondence in Mass. Archives, II, 59–75. Its religious overtones—towns such as Swansea and Rehoboth had strong Baptist and Quaker congregations—are described by McLoughlin, *New England Dissent*, I, 121 *et seq.*

The political ties between the "tories" and Bristol County are evident in the election returns: Jahleel and Ebenezer Brenton, Byfield, and Giles Dyer all sat for Bristol County towns. They are also apparent in the only two "division lists" of the period, that giving the twenty-one names of those opposed to the act banning nonresident representatives in 1693 and a dissent to the appointment of Wait Winthrop as agent in 1701 signed by fifteen representatives: Sewall, *Diary*, I, 315; Blathwayt Papers, BL 255, Hunt. Lib. In the first, of the twenty-two names (in a house of seventy-five), twelve were either representatives of Boston or of Bristol County towns or were Bostoners sitting for other towns. In the second, the fifteen names included two of the four Boston representatives and ten of the thirteen Plymouth representatives (five of six from Bristol County). A further indication of the strength of the Bristol group is the fact that four of the eleven private acts passed 1693–1700 gave particular benefit to those in the county: *Mass. Acts and Resolves*, VI, 3–33. Also "Gleanings from the Ancient Records of Bristol, R. I.," 162–163. For the town of Bristol and those associated with its founding, see Richard LeBaron Bowen, *Early Rehoboth*, I, chapter IV, and Munro, *History of Bristol, passim*. The lingering resentment of the Plymouth towns over their incorporation by Massachusetts is apparent in Nathaniel Byfield to John Usher, July 12, 1694, C.O. 5/858, no. 35, and, particularly as it related to a fervent dislike of the Mathers, John Cotton to Joanne Cotton, July 6, 1698, Miscellaneous Bound MSS., 1694–1700, Mass. Hist. Soc.

[89] Thus *Mass. Acts and Resolves*, VII, 383, 392, 410, 411. Probably, also, this group benefited from the high turnover in the numbers of representatives during the 1690s: see Chapter 7, following.

ing executive. Ironically, it was those most loyal to the crown who most effectively began the work of limiting the powers of the crown's representative.

To the north, in New Hampshire, the return of royal government likewise heightened political tensions, but for reasons which produced a somewhat different pattern of response. Here, in contrast to the situation in other New England colonies, independence from external authority was not a major issue, except for the form such authority should take. Accustomed to government from Boston and convinced that the province could not defend its borders out of its own scanty human and financial resources, most New Hampshire settlers continued to hope, as in 1690, for union with Massachusetts. Even the royal lieutenant governor, John Usher, arriving in August 1692 to rule on behalf of the absentee governor, Samuel Allen, soon urged Whitehall to place the province under a general governor of New England.[90] Rather than a desire for independence, therefore, New Hampshire's political alignments reflected the old anxieties that royal intervention had aroused long before the coming of the Dominion—the fear that outside claimants backed by the crown would dispossess the settlers of their lands. In Massachusetts, this issue, so central to the overthrow of Andros's regime, had been defused by Mather's careful drafting of the charter and by the subsequent passage of acts for "the quieting of possessions and the setling of titles."[91] In New Hampshire, the issue was perpetuated by the crown's ill-conceived decision to entrust the province's government to those who had purchased Robert Mason's claims to its lands. Nothing could have been more damaging to Whitehall's hopes for a strong and unified royal government there, for as long as this intermingling of private and public interests con-

---

[90] Petition of New Hampshire assembly, petition of 232 inhabitants of New Hampshire, [Apr. 6, 1693], C.O. 5/924, nos. 22i, ii; Usher to the Lords of Trade, Jan. 31, July 14, 1693, Sept. 1694, *ibid.,* nos. 19, 27, 40; *N. H. Provincial Papers,* III, 36, 47.

[91] *Mass. Acts and Resolves,* I, 10, 41, 299.

tinued, it ensured that the great majority of the settlers would regard the crown's representatives with suspicion and mistrust.

Usher at first attempted to conciliate his subjects by accepting long-established local leaders such as Richard Waldron and William Vaughan into his council and by agreeing to postpone any major challenge to existing land titles for as long as the province remained at war. By early 1693, however, he was already disillusioned with his post, complaining, like Cranfield before him, of its poverty and the opposition of "an ungrateful people." The province's assembly, with the backing of Waldron and Vaughan, worked to frustrate his administration, refusing him any form of salary, withholding province records, and in 1695 refusing to vote appropriations for government and defense unless Usher would join in a petition to the crown seeking annexation to Massachusetts.[92]

In New Hampshire, moreover, as in neighboring Massachusetts, personal foibles exacerbated political divisions. A prosperous Boston bookdealer and stationer by profession, timorous and high-strung to the point of incoherency in speech and writing, Usher was ill equipped to rule a rough and vigorous frontier province; physically, at least, Phips would have cut a far better figure in the job. Seldom has a royal executive inspired so little respect—on one occasion a local constable deliberately confiscated Usher's saddle, on another a militia officer "turned his britch upon the Lt. Governor" and contemptuously relieved himself in the latter's presence.[93] Usher soon chose to spend most of his time back within the genteel security of Boston society, far from the marauding Indians and the formidable marcher barons of his council. From there he quarrelled with Phips

---

[92] Usher to the Lords of Trade, Jan. 31, 1693, C.O. 5/751, no. 18; *idem* to the Earl of Nottingham, Jan. 31, 1693, C.O. 5/751, no. 18; *N. H. Provincial Papers*, II, 73, 87, III, 36, 47, 176, XVII, 636–637; William Redford to Usher, Mar. 12, Nov. 19, 1694, Jeffries Papers, III, 95, 98. Like other royal governors except those of Massachusetts, Usher could nominate and suspend members of his council.

[93] *N. H. Provincial Papers*, II, 134, 199–201. Usher's personality comes through most clearly in his many letters in C.O. 5/924, Blathwayt Papers, VI, Col. Wmsbg., and Jeffries Papers, III, IV. Usher's brother, Hezekiah, was hardly less idiosyncratic, as his appearances in Sewall's diary and his will (*Historical Magazine,* 2nd ser., IV [1868], 120–126) reveal.

over the aid he demanded for his province's defense, badgered his dwindling band of supporters with incomprehensible instructions, and bombarded Whitehall with querulous letters complaining of his mistreatment and the machinations of a "commonwealth" faction working to subvert "Kingly Government" in both Massachusetts and New Hampshire.[94] The existence of such an intercolonial coalition cannot be traced beyond Usher's feverish meanderings. Yet the ties of sympathy and sentiment between the two provinces were clearly strong enough to invite such an interpretation: during the 1690s New Hampshire legislators copied many of their laws verbatim from those then being enacted in Massachusetts.[95]

Ultimately, in 1696, Usher's opponents tired of trying to frustrate him into quitting, and they persuaded the London government to appoint a local shipbuilder and timber merchant, William Partridge, in his place. Usher discovered a sudden fondness for the post he had so long disparaged, and a comic opera succession struggle ensued, with Partridge's supporters taking over the government and Usher declaring his province in rebellion. There was much mustering of militia and reading of proclamations. Governor Samuel Allen suddenly appeared from London, reviving Usher's hopes, only for Allen's authority to be superseded in turn by the arrival of the Earl of Bellomont in New England. Bellomont reestablished Partridge as lieutenant governor but then decided that the wealthy merchant's profiting from the timber trade to continental Europe made him unfit to hold

---

[94] Usher believed that Elisha Cooke and Elisha Hutchinson in Boston were in league with Vaughan, Waldron, and the Reverend Joshua Moodey of Portsmouth; in another letter he cited Cooke, Hutchinson, Danforth, Wait Winthrop, Eliakim Hutchinson, John Foster, Jonathan Corwin, and Samuel Shrimpton as "persons against Kingly Government": Usher to Blathwayt, Dec. 20, 1695, and undated note, Blathwayt Papers, VI, Col. Wmsbg. A very similar alignment was given by Sir Henry Ashurst in recommending these and others to Bellomont, c. Aug., 1697: Letterbook of Sir Henry Ashurst, fol. 144. By the mid-1690s, Robert Elliott and his father-in-law, Nathaniel Fryer, were Usher's only remaining allies on the New Hampshire council and these turned to oppose him by 1698: Jeffries Papers, III, 87, 90, 108.

[95] Compare, for example, *Mass. Acts and Resolves*, I, 30–34, 48–49, 84–88, 142–143, 225–226, 298–299, 312–314, with *N. H. Laws*, I, 527–531, 683–684, 595–600, 691–692, 680–683, 687–689. See also note 10, Chapter 7, following.

the office. Usher, in consequence, was eventually reappointed lieutenant governor, and he and Allen, their alliance reforged by Usher's marriage to Allen's daughter, began court proceedings to establish their territorial claims. The only real sufferers by these scenes were those compelled to be the audience, the settlers exposed to physical and legal threats to the security of their homesteads because of the disordered state of government.[96]

Within each of the two New England colonies now directly ruled by London, the return of royal government touched off flurries of political conflict and jockeyings for power. In character, these rivalries displayed little of the kind of deep-seated uncertainty regarding the legitimacy of government evident during the months following Andros's overthrow and preceding Mather's return with the charter—that period melodramatically remembered by Samuel Willard in his election sermon of 1694 as "the short *Anarchy* accompanying our late *Revolution.*" Rather, they represented the colonists' response to the new legitimacy received from England, a testing of that settlement's powers and procedures and of the boundaries between its component parts. And as in England during these same years, the evident importance of shaping the direction and contours of government while they still remained malleable intensified and embittered factional disputes. In Boston, Wait Winthrop cried out against "the ruine of the antient liberty of this country" by "the pride, ambition, avarice" of those who had once served Andros but were now deluding "our honest country representatives" with "studied fair speaches and pretentions." His opponents replied in kind, denouncing measures like Phips's nonresidency law as deliberate proscriptions of the governor's political opponents. "I doe not know that ever I saw the Council run upon with such a height of Rage before," lamented Sewall after a heated clash between the two houses in 1696. "Never," wrote William Redford to his patron, Lieutenant Governor Usher, from New Hamp-

[96] *N. H. Provincial Papers,* II, 209–226, 259, 268, 276–282, 293, 313–316, 357, 406; Van Deventer, *Emergence of Provincial New Hampshire,* 53.

shire, "was there so crooked a generation as this since the Deluge."[97]

Whitehall took little immediate part in these disputes, and its attempts to pursue the remodelling of New England in the 1690s were, as we have seen, almost wholly ineffective. Yet a closer examination reveals that its influence could work in less direct and deliberate ways. Just as the basic structure of royal government in Massachusetts and New Hampshire had channelled politics into English patterns, so the institutions with which the colonists fleshed out this structure were slowly molded into closer conformity with the crown's desires by the persistence and continuity of London's administrative procedures. Every royal governor, for example, was required by his instructions to send back copies of all laws and of all journals of his council and assembly, as well as detailed reports describing the nature and legality of his colony's trade, the conditions of its finances and defenses, and the structure of its government.[98] Not all these tasks were adequately performed—the copies of New Hampshire's laws and journals forwarded by Usher provoked the Board of Trade to describe them as "so ill-written and ill-digested that they are neither legible or intelligible."[99] Their mere existence, however, coupled with the board's initial diligence in demanding satisfactory responses, stimulated both the greater definition of colonial government and its gradual, if at times somewhat cosmetic, accommodation to London's ways.

The crown's most effective and pointed weapon in this process was its right to disallow colonial laws. Approximately one-sixth of the laws passed in Massachusetts during the 1690s, including fifteen of the fifty-two enacted at the first General Court meeting under the

---

[97] Willard, *Character of a Good Ruler*, 3; Wait Winthrop to Sir Henry Ashurst, [1699], Mass. Hist. Soc., *Collections*, 6th ser., V (1892), 49–50 (both Stoughton and Byfield had held office under Andros); Nathaniel Byfield to Joseph Dudley, June 12, 1694, C.O. 5/858, no. 31; Sewall, *Diary*, I, 363; Redford to Usher, Oct. 8, 1694, Jeffries Papers, III, 97.

[98] Thus, for example, Instructions for the Earl of Bellomont, Aug. 31, 1697, *N. Y. Col. Docs.*, IV, 284–292, and to Gov. Joseph Dudley, Apr. 6, 1702, *N. H. Laws*, II, 13–29.

[99] Board of Trade to Usher, Aug. 3, 1697, *CSP Col., 1696–1697*, no. 1222. Secretary Isaac Addington of Massachusetts, by contrast, took considerable care: thus his letters to Blathwayt, July 16, 1692–Jan. 25, 1698, Blathwayt Papers, II, Col. Wmsbg.

new charter, were subsequently nullified by the Privy Council, as were over half of those enacted during the same decade and forwarded to London from New Hampshire. They included many of the laws reestablishing old charter ways, now struck down for being contrary to English law or infringing upon the royal prerogative.[100] It was an irksome and wholly negative tactic: in 1699 the news of the disallowance of an act establishing courts passed four years before caused the sudden dissolution of the Massachusetts Superior Court in the midst of its proceedings. "A grate disappointment to many people, there being neer forty actions depending and hardly five or six issued," noted Judge Wait Winthrop. Sections of this particular act were passed four times before the assembly finally submitted to language agreeable to the lawyers at Whitehall. In one instance the cup was too bitter to be swallowed; despite the remonstrances of the Mathers and their allies, the General Court refused to pass any bill incorporating Harvard that reserved to the crown the right to appoint an official Visitor to supervise the college. As a result, Harvard never obtained the royal charter that Increase Mather, its president, so much desired.[101] In general, however, colonial legislators gradually learned by trial and error which provisions were likely to incur the confusion and inconvenience of disallowance. Hence colonial codes were shaped, willingly or no, into conformity with Whitehall's wishes. The proportion of laws disallowed steadily decreased, and, save for a single private act, none from Massachusetts were struck down during Dudley's administration, though this was doubtless due in part to the growing laxity of officials in London. The effect was akin to that of an inattentive rider curbing an unruly mount; frequent excursions from

---

[100] *Mass. Acts and Resolves,* I, 109, 767–787; *N. H. Laws,* I, 709–711, 644–652, 859–863 (though news of some of these disallowances seems never to have reached New Hampshire); *APC Col.,* II, 840–845; and, generally, Joseph H. Smith, "Administrative Control of the Courts of the American Plantations," 1210–1263.

[101] Wait Winthrop to Fitz-John Winthrop, May 1, 1699, Mass. Hist. Soc., *Collections,* 5th ser., VIII (1882), 551; Sewall, *Diary,* I, 408–409; Morison, *Harvard College,* II, 509–518, 523–530.

the straight and narrow did not prevent spasmodic progress toward a common destination.

Such discipline, in milder form, was also brought to bear upon the two colonies in New England that had quietly resumed their old charter governments. Neither Connecticut nor Rhode Island was obliged to submit legislation for the crown's approval. Nonetheless, the Board of Trade demanded and received copies of the two colonies' laws, and in 1704 complaints presented in London prompted the Privy Council to disallow a law regulating admiralty jurisdiction in Rhode Island and a second, the following year, penalizing Quakers and other "Hereticks" in Connecticut.[102] A further and keener weapon for regulating the two colonies' affairs was the crown's insistence on "the inherent right" of appeal from courts in the American plantations irrespective of their form of government. Indeed, since such appeals to the King in Council were virtually the only procedural chink in the armor of the autonomy of the corporate colonies, they became the principal means by which the larger question of those colonies' position within the imperial system was decided. For Rhode Island, this did not prove to be a major issue during the 1690s, for appeals from its courts were few and the colony raised no formal objection to the principle. Only in later years did the notorious chaos of its legal system produce a large number of appeals.[103]

The Connecticut government, on the other hand, insisted that its charter reserved final jurisdiction to the colony's own courts, and it stood by this argument in two famous cases brought before the Privy Council in 1699 and 1706: these were the disposition of the estate of a

---

[102] *APC Col.,* II, 457, 832, 852; Dunn, *Puritans and Yankees,* 349; Reed, *Church and State in Massachusetts,* 98–101.

[103] Order of the King in Council, Mar. 9, 1699, C.O. 5/1258, no. 8, and Conn. Archives, Foreign Correspondence, I, 78; Petition of Francis Brinley, [Feb. 23, 1699], C.O. 5/1258, no. 9i; Gov. Samuel Cranston to the Board of Trade, July 21, 1699, C.O. 5/1259, no. 9; *R. I. Records,* III, 562, IV, 49; Joseph H. Smith, *Appeals to the Privy Council,* 141–142, 246, 641–642; Harold D. Hazeltine, "Appeals from Colonial Courts to the King in Council, with Special Reference to Rhode Island," 299–350.

New London merchant, John Liveen, and the protest of the Mohegan Indians against the colony's appropriation of their lands. As Gov. Fitz-John Winthrop pointed out, both cases were politically inspired. His own brother-in-law, Edward Palmes, in league with Liveen's stepsons, John and Nicholas Hallam, had a guiding hand in pressing the cases to the point of appeal, and they were abetted by speculators eager to shake the Connecticut government's hold upon vast areas of unsettled land upon its eastern border and by neighboring royal governors, Cornbury of New York and Dudley of Massachusetts, who hoped to weaken and even dismember the colony. Connecticut survived the attack and won its two legal battles (the Privy Council upheld the judgments of the Connecticut courts even though, incredibly, the Mohegans' charges were not finally dismissed until 1773), but it lost the war. The door of appeals to London remained open, although rusty with disuse.[104] At the time, moreover, the two cases endangered the very survival of charter rule, for they drew the colony into the spotlight of Whitehall's attention at a moment when royal officials were looking for excuses to remodel the chartered governments or at least subject them to crown-appointed executives. In 1701 and again in 1705, the refusal to allow appeals was one of the principal charges pressed against Connecticut and (unjustifiably) Rhode Island as a prelude to the parliamentary bills designed to curb their autonomy.[105]

Yet at no time during these years did Whitehall succeed in obtaining the formal structural changes it desired, and by comparison with

[104] Winthrop to Sir Henry Ashurst, June 2, Nov. 25, 1700, Winthrop Papers; Dunn, *Puritans and Yankees*, 295–296, 331–343; Joseph H. Smith, *Appeals to the Privy Council*, 138–151, 422–442. Strictly speaking, the Mohegan case began as a complaint made in London by Nicholas Hallam on behalf of the Indians, not as an appeal from a colonial court. Ironically, it was Connecticut that appealed to the Privy Council against the findings of a commission led by Dudley and Palmes which had been set up to investigate the matter.

[105] Report of the Board of Trade, Apr. 23, 1701, C.O. 324/7, 446; Charges against Connecticut, [Mar. 26, 1705], C.O. 5/1292, 142; *R. I. Records*, IV, 12, 15; R. R. Hinman, ed., *Letters from the English Kings and Queens . . . to the Governors of the Colony of Connecticut together with the answers thereto from 1635 to 1749*, 328.

their royally governed neighbors, Connecticut and Rhode Island had little regular contact with the crown, less indeed than any other American colony. They continued to elect their own rulers each spring; they remained overwhelmingly rural and agricultural in their way of life; and they were shielded by geography from direct involvement in the war. In these circumstances, it might have been expected that both colonies would have swiftly resumed the tranquil political courses they had followed prior to their incorporation in the Dominion. The fact that they did not, coupled with the character of their difficulties, reemphasizes how marked was the watershed in New England's political development created by the Dominion and the Revolution.

The clearest evidence of each colony's problems during the 1690s was its open political factionalism. Connecticut's leaders, like Phips and Mather in Massachusetts, faced opposition on both flanks. A "tory" remnant loyal to Andros, led by Edward Palmes and Gershom Bulkeley and centered upon Bulkeley's parish of Wethersfield, appealed to neighboring New York for assistance against those they viewed as rebels and usurpers at Hartford, lending color to the New Yorkers' arguments that Connecticut should be reduced to greater dependence upon the crown.[106] A more immediate threat within the colony came from the followers of the bellicose Capt. James Fitch who had forced a swift resumption of the charter in 1689. As one opponent bitterly remarked, Fitch was "soe expert in the act of flatery that he makes many of the people beleive that he is the cheife patron of theire charter privelages." Bulkeley accused the old guard leaders of feathering their own nests during their government of the colony;

---

[106] Conn. Hist. Soc., *Collections,* III (1895), 73, 242; Address of Palmes, Bulkeley, and William Rosewell, Sept. 16, 1692, *ibid.,* XXIV (1932), 49–52; Objections against the Government of Connecticut, *N. Y. Col. Docs.,* III, 849–854; Governor Fletcher to the Lords of Trade, Nov. 10, 1693, *ibid.,* IV, 72; Bulkeley to Fletcher, Apr. 5, Sept. 15, Oct. 30, 1693, *CSP Col., 1693–1696,* nos. 245, 611v, 650xviii; Bulkeley and thirty-four others to Fletcher, [Jan. 1694?], Robert C. Winthrop Collection, II, 212a–c. Palmes, a New London merchant, had tried and failed to be elected a Connecticut magistrate in the 1670s. Like Bulkeley, he had served as a justice of the peace during the Dominion. He also signed one of the petitions to London circulated in 1690: *Conn. Records,* III, 388; C.O. 5/856, fol. 392.

Fitch added charges of mismanagement and favoritism in the distribution of land.[107] The even flow of Connecticut politics, barely resumed since the disruptions of the Dominion period, dissolved into a flurry of debate. Moderates like Samuel Willis, William Pitkin, and Secretary John Allyn retained their seats as magistrates for a time with the aid of a change in election procedures which made it more difficult for malcontents to veto the reelection of incumbents.[108] But death, and disgust at the trend of events, thinned their ranks as Fitch and his cohorts steadily gained the advantage. In 1696 Fitch captured control of a committee set up to revise the colony's laws. The exasperated Willis protested that while Fitch remained "the principle Minister of State," it was impossible for "gentlemen"—an exclusive club in which Willis clearly saw himself as possessing hereditary membership—to receive or administer justice. "This Languishinge Colony," he told Fitz-John Winthrop, "is now declyned to almost the Lowest Ebb of Democracy if it does not border upon Anarki," and he asked his friend to seek direction from England to ensure "that persons of such low extract and Education may be improved in such usefull matters as they are fitt for and not to governe theire betters."[109]

Willis needed to look no further than Rhode Island to perceive what the consequences of such "Anarki" might be. That colony's co-

---

[107] Samuel Willis to Wait Winthrop, Apr. 22, 1702, Mass. Hist. Soc., *Collections,* 6th ser., V (1892), 112; Bulkeley, "Will and Doom," 110, 196, 214–216, 237–238, 257–258; Ellen D. Larned, *History of Windham County, Connecticut,* I, 128, 145, 151; Conn. Archives, Civil Officers, 1st ser., I, 75.

[108] *Conn. Records,* IV, 12, 81, 223. The interpretation of these procedures provided by Bushman, *From Puritan to Yankee,* 90, is more convincing than that of Dunn, *Puritans and Yankees,* 294–295; see also Bulkeley, "Will and Doom," 160, 251. Nonetheless, Dunn's account of Fitz-John Winthrop's career still provides the best analysis of Connecticut in these years: *Puritans and Yankees,* 294–319. Somewhat narrower in scope and less reliable in detail is Robert M. Bliss, "A Secular Revival," 139–146.

[109] *Conn. Records,* IV, 161, 182, 191; Willis to Fitz-John Winthrop, Dec. 25, 1697, Sept., 1693, James Pierpont to Winthrop, Jan. 17, 1698, Mass. Hist. Soc., *Collections,* 6th ser., III (1889), 31, 16–17, 267; Willis to Winthrop, Oct. 8, 1693, Winthrop Papers. Pitkin died in 1694, Allyn in 1696; Willis lost his seat as assistant in 1693.

hesion had long depended upon the negative force of its neighbors' hostility; if its settlers did not hang together in mutual toleration, they were sure to be persecuted separately. In this respect, at least, little had changed. Land speculators, headed by the heirs of the Atherton partners, continued to dabble in the troubled Narragansett country with tacit assistance from the Hartford and Boston governments; by the last years of the century conflict between the tenants of the various claimants had risen to the level of open border warfare. On the other side of the colony, the secessionist feelings among the towns of southwestern Massachusetts, particularly in Bristol County, provoked several near riots and a heated exchange of insults between Boston and Newport.[110] Such difficulties were familiar; far more deadly was the abrupt erosion of traditional loyalties within the colony itself that followed upon the resumption of charter rule. For several years after 1692, organized central government appears to have all but vanished from Rhode Island.[111] Official positions lay vacant; taxes went unpaid; disputes between the towns over lands and boundaries proliferated, unchecked by any superior authority; and, as in the other New England colonies, a group of "tories" appeared, prominent merchants and landowners such as Francis Brinley, Samuel Gorton, Peleg Sanford, and Nathaniel Coddington, who intrigued to bring the colony under closer royal control. Even the agent commissioned to present Rhode Island's defense in London, the ubiquitous Jahleel Brenton, influential here as in Massachusetts through his family's

---

[110] Thus, for example, Memorials of the Connecticut and Rhode Island Commissioners, June 29, 30, Dec. 8, 1698, Conn. Hist. Soc., *Collections,* XXIV (1932), 150–154; Mass. Hist. Soc., *Collections,* 5th ser., IX (1885), 196–205; Robert C. Winthrop Collection, I, 46–48; and note 36, Chapter 1, preceding. For the Rhode Island–Massachusetts boundary, note 88, preceding, and Boundary Documents, Rhode Island and Massachusetts, I, *passim,* R. I. Archives.

[111] *R. I. Records,* III, 288. The gap in the records of the Rhode Island General Court is apparently more than a documentary loss; it is paralleled by a similar gap in the continuously paged General Treasurer's Accounts, 1672–1711, foll. 84–86. James, *Colonial Rhode Island,* 113, observes a similar break, 1687–1693, in the records of the colony's General Court of Trials. A few town records do show the occasional election of deputies, and Brinley in 1693 writes of a "so-called assembly" as sitting. Thus there may have been a form of government without its substance.

far-flung landholdings, promptly sought upon his arrival in England to undermine the colony's independence.[112]

The political leaders who remained in office within Rhode Island, most of them Quakers, hardly measured up to Willis's aristocratic standards. Following complaints to London from within and without the colony, the Board of Trade sent Bellomont to Newport in 1699 to investigate reports of illicit trade and to adjudicate the border with Connecticut. He reported back in vigorous terms. The colony's attorney general, he noted, was "a poor illiterate Mechanick," its deputy governor "a brutish man of very corrupt or no principle in Religion." Indeed, the latter, John Green of Warwick, was said to be a Familist (a follower of Samuel Gorton, one of Rhode Island's most notorious early settlers) who openly asserted that "it was no more sin in the Light of God for one man to lye with another mans wife than for a Bull to leap a Cow upon the Common." As for the colony's administration, Bellomont judged it to be "the most Irregular and Illegal that ever any English Government was." Its most striking characteristic, according to the testimony forwarded with his report, was the lack of statutory law and judicial procedure. "Their law," declared one witness, "is what the Clerke pleases who carries the same in his pockett it

---

[112] *Early Records of the Town of Providence*, XI, 5–6; *R. I. Records*, III, 307, 323–325, 331, 347–348, 353, 372, 380–382, 413, 574–576; Francis Brinley to Samuel Gorton, Nov. 21, 1693, R. I. Hist. Soc., Manuscripts, X, 147; Brinley to Blathwayt, Dec. 29, 1692, Blathwayt Papers, XI, Col. Wmsbg.; Edward Randolph to the Board of Trade, May 30, 1698, *Randolph Letters*, V, 185–188; Samuel G. Arnold, *History of Rhode Island*, I, 552, 554; Jahleel Brenton to the Board of Trade, [Feb. 14, 1699], C.O. 5/1257, no. 48. Brinley was the uncle of Coddington and of Sanford's wife. Others who seem to have favored royal control or at least opposed the existing government to the point of cooperating with its external enemies were Caleb and Josiah Arnold, Ludovic Updike, Nathaniel Waterman, and John Fones. Most of these men had also signed the 1686 address of Rhode Islanders willing to submit immediately to the crown: *R. I. Records*, III, 195. Brinley, Fones, Coddington, and Updike were linked to the Atherton partners. Brenton seems to have played a lone hand, playing off one side against the other: thus Samuel Willis to Fitz-John Winthrop, Aug. 13, 1698, Mass. Hist. Soc., *Collections*, 6th ser., III (1889), 36; Elisha Hutchinson to Fitz-John Winthrop, Feb. 22, 1698, Winthrop Papers; and Josiah Wolcott to Henry Wolcott, Feb. 15, 1698, Roger Wolcott Papers, I, 30a. For Brenton's wealth and family background, see John O. Austin, *The Genealogical Dictionary of Rhode Island*, 254. Among his land interests in Rhode Island was a share, with Samuel Sewall and Caleb and Josiah Arnold, of the great Pettaquamscut Purchase in the southeast Narragansett country: R. I. Hist. Soc., *Collections*, III (1835), 279–281.

seldome or ever lying anywhere for Publick view but should it, it would avail but little the same being so torne and wrote in such an unintelligible hand that in many places it cannot be read; so that what the Clerk saith is alwaies taken for Law although directly contradictory to an act of their own Assembly." In Francis Brinley's judgment, "will and Multitude" and not "reason and law . . . sway the Scepter in this Government."[113] Incoherent in structure and beset from all sides, Rhode Island seemed about to go the way of New Haven and Plymouth colonies. "Att Rhode Island they are all in a staunce and cannot agree upon anything so that now may be the best time to settle the Narragansetts," wrote one of the Atherton proprietors in 1698; another expressed his hope that the colony could soon be entirely dismembered.[114]

Willis's lamentations to the contrary, Connecticut never fell so low: it had fewer enemies, greater internal cohesion, and a stronger heritage of centralized rule. Yet by comparison with their past accomplishments both governments were clearly in dire straits during the 1690s, and it was a measure of their common plight that sober observers such as Josiah Wolcott of Salem should by 1698 perceive Connecticut as scarcely better able to manage its affairs than "that contemptible Government" of Rhode Island.[115] Both colonies' politics, moreover, were marked by an alarming readiness to question the sanctity of government and the extent of its powers, a skepticism far more fundamentally subversive of authority than the predominantly procedural and tactical issues then being debated within New England's two royal colonies.

The contrast points up the way in which the Dominion and its af-

---

[113] Bellomont to the Board of Trade, Nov. 27, 1699, *R. I. Records*, III, 387 (inaccurately transcribed), C.O. 5/1259, fol. 144; Testimony of Francis Brinley and Ludovic Updike, Sept. 29, 1699, *ibid.*, fol. 171 (also the similar testimony of John Easton, *ibid.*); Testimony of Jo. Hearne, *ibid.*, fol. 196; Brinley to Thomas Newton, Aug. 20, 1699, *ibid.*, fol. 203; Bellomont to William Popple, Nov. 6, 1699, C.O. 5/861, no. 3.

[114] Elisha Hutchinson to Fitz-John Winthrop, Feb. 22, 1698, Winthrop Papers; Wait Winthrop to Fitz-John Winthrop, Sept. 28, 1696, Mass. Hist. Soc., *Collections*, 5th ser., VIII (1882), 524.

[115] Josiah Wolcott to Henry Wolcott, Feb. 15, 1698, Roger Wolcott Papers, I, 30a.

termath left different legacies in different places. In Massachusetts and New Hampshire, as we have seen, political differences were fought out within the structures of government newly imposed by the crown, structures which at least bound up, if they did not entirely heal, the wounds inflicted by the Dominion. Within Rhode Island and Connecticut such wounds at first seemed slight, for London had never pressed proceedings against their charters to the point of confiscation, and only a few ardent royalists such as Brinley and Bulkeley persisted in treating charter rule as null and void. Yet some wounds did fester, for neither did London bestow any new or more comprehensive powers to strengthen the hand of governments now weakened by the debates and dissensions stirred up during the process of resuming charter rule. Squeezed between the conflicting and encroaching demands of crown and "Multitude," the two colonies' traditional leaders maintained their places only to suffer, if in milder form, the same erosion of their capacity to govern which had reduced their counterparts in Massachusetts to desperation prior to the coming of the charter of 1691.

In both colonies, moreover, as in New Hampshire, one issue in particular expressed and exacerbated the leadership's plight; this was the granting of titles to land. Such grants could spark intercolonial conflict, and by the end of the century Connecticut was enmeshed in boundary disputes with all three of its neighbors; these disputes on occasion flared into miniature border wars.[116] More often, and with more damaging consequences for the authority of government, strife erupted within the colonies themselves. Here again the Dominion left its mark for, as Richard Bushman has shown, the threat of its coming had greatly accelerated the process whereby common and hitherto unassigned lands were divided among individual owners.[117] Terri-

---

[116] The materials on such disputes are voluminous. See, for example, on Connecticut, the three volumes in Conn. Archives, Colonial Boundaries, I (Rhode Island), II (New York), III (Massachusetts), and Clarence W. Bowen, *Boundary Disputes of Connecticut, passim.*

[117] Bushman, *From Puritan to Yankee,* 44–47; *ibid.,* 83–103, provides an excellent and more detailed account of "the politics of land." Bushman somewhat overstates the threat of royal government as the cause of this change; as other studies

tories relinquished by the Indians were a further source of contention: James Fitch's power, for example, rested upon the vast acreage in eastern Connecticut which he claimed by virtue of a deed of gift from Chief Oweneco of the Mohegans, and in Rhode Island towns such as Providence and Warwick fought bitterly over territory ceded by the tribes.

The result, by the 1690s, was a tangle of conflicting claims that closely matched, and did much to perpetuate, the principal political divisions within each colony. Could title be obtained directly from the crown, as New England's royalists believed? Could it be secured by gift or purchase from the Indians, "native right," as Fitch and his followers maintained? Or was it based upon the authority of charter government, as interpreted by the ruling group of magistrates? In practice, the matter was even more complex than these divisions suggest, for the more resourceful claimants (like the Atherton proprietors) were skilled in blending together various kinds of title to bolster their cases.[118] In the process, one government's internal opponents often became another's allies: Fitch and Palmes enlisted the patronage of Governor Cranston of Rhode Island while from within that colony dissidents such as Brinley and Coddington looked to Massachusetts and Connecticut for aid.[119] As in the years before the coming of the Dominion, territorial disputes between and within the New

---

show, it was also part of a larger struggle throughout New England whereby established settlers sought to exclude newcomers from sharing in the common lands: Mead, *Connecticut as a Corporate Colony*, 65–70; Akagi, *Town Proprietors of New England*, 50–60, 124–138. Nonetheless, the challenge of the Dominion undoubtedly hastened and further institutionalized this process.

[118] Thus, for example, the account by Francis Brinley in R. I. Hist. Soc., *Publications*, new ser., VII (1900), 69–94. Nathaniel Coddington to Fitz-John Winthrop, Nov. 8, 1706, Winthrop Papers, provides three similar divisions—"Mortgage men" (claimants through the Atherton proprietors and backed by Connecticut), "Nenegrates agents" (native right purchasers and trustees backed by Rhode Island), and squatters claiming title from England.

[119] Thus Gov. Fitz-John Winthrop to Sir Henry Ashurst, July 15, 1703, Mass. Hist. Soc., *Collections*, 6th ser., III (1889), 134; Deposition of James Fitch and Samuel Mason, July 10, 1703, Nathaniel Coddington to Gov. Joseph Dudley, Nov. 9, 1705, *CSP Col., 1704–1705*, nos. 1424xlviii, lv; and *R. I. Records*, III, 396–399.

England colonies continued to undermine their governments' authority and encourage a resort to the authority of the crown.


To most New Englanders, therefore, and especially to their leaders, the decade following the Glorious Revolution remained a confused and confusing time, a period of transition and reassessment. Few coherent themes emerged save those of friction and diversity, in part because of the pressures of war and the haphazard character of the post-Revolutionary settlement imposed by England, in part because the colonists themselves remained wary and uncertain about their present status and future course. The old alignment of like-minded and like-modelled Puritan commonwealths embodied in the New England Confederation had given way to a bewildering variety of forms—royal government, royal government under a new charter, and restored though enfeebled charter rule. Moreover, the region's traditional moral and political leader, Massachusetts, had changed the most: toleration was now the former Bible Commonwealth's official creed, and visible affluence, not visible sanctity, its formal criterion of citizenship. Its executive had passed into alien, if sympathetic, hands: Rome's procurator ruled in Israel. No clear pattern of how these new forms would unfold and coexist had yet emerged. The political momentum still rested with the crown, but Whitehall's direction of affairs—vigorous in intention, ineffective in execution, and verging upon incompetence in appointment—had served to disrupt rather than stabilize the political scene. Even where the New England governments had tempered their ways to conform to royal supervision, they had responded more to structural pressures than to any coherent imperial policy.

The colonists themselves were still feeling their way in this new universe. Save for such outbursts as Willard's attack upon Phips in 1694 and the Mathers' monotonous and, to judge by the Massachusetts assembly's response, notably unpersuasive reiteration of the new charter's blessings, there had been a striking absence of the kind of wide-ranging political debate which had flourished during the years prior

[*304*]

to Increase Mather's return from London. Royal authority was nowhere openly denied. Yet in political practice if not in theory a significant domestic response to Whitehall's pressures and the colonists' own internal difficulties was beginning to emerge. It was fostered in Massachusetts and New Hampshire, as we have seen, by the need to flesh out and interpret the structures of royal government. Lacking such a stimulus, it was as yet barely apparent amid the disorders afflicting Rhode Island and Connecticut. Its character can best be traced by turning back to the theme that was so important in the first months after the Dominion's overthrow and now leads forward into the new century, the colonists' conduct of their ties with the English crown.

# VI

## Agents and Office Seekers: The Evolution of Transatlantic Politics, 1692–1715

Late in December 1691, as Increase Mather carried the new charter back to Boston, Sir Henry Ashurst wrote from London to extol the blessings which their joint endeavors had conferred upon Massachusetts and to offer his services "in the Quality of an Agent." A decade later, he urged these services as indispensable: "I can't imagine," he wrote to Governor Lord Bellomont and the General Court, "that you Ever needed an Agent more than now for . . . in So uncertain a time when interests are often pushing att one another there may happen thinges to be offer'd which att so great a distance you can't avoid being ignorant of and without an agent to watch Every turn it may be impossible for you to prevent."[1]

Sir Henry's concern was far from disinterested; he was keenly aware of the profit and prestige that could accrue from an agent's post. Yet, as New England's leaders came to appreciate, he expressed an important truth. Confronted by such vigorous bodies as the Board of Trade and by bills threatening further regulation of the charters, no colony, not even Rhode Island and Connecticut, could afford to isolate itself from the process of decision making in London. Moreover, the character of that process—complex, deliberate, and highly susceptible to the interplay of political factions and special interests—afforded abundant opportunity for the colonists themselves to influence Whitehall's measures and appointments. Such involvement could also furnish them with potent weapons of office and influence

---

[1] Ashurst to Massachusetts, Dec. 28, 1691, Apr. 30, 1700, Curwin Papers, II, 41, Amer. Antiq. Soc., *Mass. Acts and Resolves*, VII, 685. Also Ashurst to William Stoughton, Oct. 22, 1692, to Increase Mather, Oct. 18, 1692, Letterbook of Sir Henry Ashurst, foll. 84–84v.

in fighting their own domestic battles. A quarter of a century earlier, royal administrators had been the first to recognize the political handicaps imposed by ignorance of transatlantic conditions: "Things," noted the Committee of Trade in 1675, "at this distance and where no person appeares on the other side seeme very dark."[2] Randolph and his successors had bridged that void. Now, with the crown having secured its information and a new authority, New Englanders in their turn were drawn to reach back across the seas, seeking a voice in what had become their government. The ties they established shaped both London's conduct of colonial affairs and the colonists' own perception, and hence their utilization, of their relationship with England. These ties thereby became the key element of the new political systems which crowned the post-Revolutionary settlement in New England.

The most conspicuous change in the character of New England's ties with the London government in the years after the Glorious Revolution was their steady regularization. Between the restoration of Charles II and the coming of the Dominion, such contact had been sought only upon demand—the carefully circumscribed "messengers" grudgingly dispatched by Massachusetts—or in times of special need, as when Connecticut and Rhode Island sent agents to negotiate for their charters in the 1660s. Most colonial leaders, particularly those in Massachusetts, had held to the belief that collaboration with the crown was likely to be useless if not positively dangerous—he who is silent, they seemed to have held, does not consent. Familiarity bred corruption. These suspicions were never wholly dispelled. In the last years of the century, however, each colony moved closer toward establishing a permanent agency to represent its interests in London, a purpose fully accomplished by the early decades of the next.

As usual, and despite its mistrust of the English court, Massachusetts led the way. Its dispatch of Cooke and Oakes in 1690, carrying

---

[2] Committee of Trade to the Lord Treasurer, May 1, 1675, C.O. 5/903, 23.

the commission which empowered them to work with Mather and Ashurst in seeking a restoration of the old charter, marked a turning point in the colony's dealings with the London government. Henceforth, while its leaders showed no great willingness to obey the crown's instructions in such matters as the governor's salary or the rebuilding of the fort at Pemaquid, they took care that their responses were presented and recorded at Whitehall. Ashurst performed this task through the 1690s, together with such routine work as ensuring that copies of the province's laws were presented for the crown's approval. Massachusetts also employed Constantine Phipps, an English relative of Governor Phips and an accomplished London lawyer, to act with Ashurst as agent.[3]

Neighboring colonies ultimately followed this lead. Connecticut came face to face with the problem of regular contact with England in 1692 when it wished to send an address to the crown protesting the grant to Phips of authority over the colony's militia. Rebuffed by those they asked for assistance—"through your owne fault there was not a man to be found in England that could and would serve you," wrote Increase Mather to Governor Treat—and fearful lest their correspondence should fall into Phips's hands, the Connecticut magistrates turned to the unlikely medium of the Royal Navy for help. A messenger was dispatched to Boston with instructions to approach Capt. Robert Fairfax of the frigate then in harbor, present the address, and, "if he give no repulss to it that is vehement" (for even landlocked Hartford knew of the uncertain temper of frigate captains), offer him five pounds to take the address, unopened, to Whitehall.[4] Fairfax's response is not recorded, but the address never

---

[3] The correspondence of Phipps and Ashurst with Massachusetts can be found scattered through Mass. Archives, III, XX, CVI. Phipps was appointed by means of Governor Phips (*Mass. Acts and Resolves*, VII, 685) and Ashurst described him as Phips's "Coszen": Ashurst to [Lieutenant Governor Stoughton], Nov. 14, 1693, Letterbook of Sir Henry Ashurst, fol. 90v.

[4] Increase Mather to Robert Treat, Aug. 19, 1690, drafts of letters from the Connecticut Council to Captain Fairfax and William Whiting, Nov. 25, 1692, Conn. Hist. Soc., *Collections*, XXIV (1932), 38, 55–56.

reached its destination, and the incident doubtless helped convince the magistrates of the wisdom of sending an agent from among themselves to London. The result, spurred on by the news that command of the colony's militia had been transferred to the even more distasteful hands of Governor Fletcher of New York, was Fitz-John Winthrop's mission to London in 1693. Winthrop could not revoke Fletcher's power or prevent the appointment of Bellomont as captain general of all New England. But, during a four-year stay in London, he preserved Connecticut's charter and won procedural concessions from the crown which effectively prevented external interference, a success plainly revealing the advantages of direct negotiation.[5] Prior to Winthrop's return, Secretary John Allyn informed him of the magistrates' desire that he should "engage som honest freind at Court" on Connecticut's behalf "so that we have wherewith all to Answer for ourselves," and Winthrop may have reached an understanding with Sir Henry Ashurst before his departure from London.[6] In any event, Winthrop's return and election to the governorship of Connecticut was speedily followed by Ashurst's commissioning as the colony's official agent in the dispute over the Narragansett lands.[7] Subsequently, Ashurst defended the colony in the struggle over the charters and the cases appealed to the Privy Council. His decade of service to the colony came to an end shortly before his death in 1711 when Gov. Gurdon Saltonstall dropped him in favor of younger and more influential counsel.[8]

---

[5] Dunn, *Puritans and Yankees*, 298–314.

[6] Allyn to Winthrop, Oct. 19, 1696, Winthrop Papers; also Governor Treat and the Connecticut Council to Winthrop, Oct. 28, 1695, Conn. Hist. Soc., *Collections*, XXIV (1932), 116.

[7] Ashurst's commission, dated Oct. 15, 1699, is printed from Conn. Archives, For. Corr., II, 65, in Hinman, *Letters*, 279–280; a manuscript copy with an unsigned copy of Ashurst's instructions, June 2, 1700, is in Miscellaneous Bound MSS., 1694–1700, Mass. Hist. Soc. Also Connecticut to the Board of Trade, Oct. 15, 1699, Conn. Hist. Soc., *Collections*, XXIV (1932), 163, and Ashurst to Wait Winthrop, Feb. 5, 1701, Mass. Hist. Soc., *Collections*, 6th ser., V (1892), 80.

[8] Ashurst's breach with Saltonstall can be followed in the letters in Mass. Hist. Soc., *Collections*, 6th ser., V (1892), 191–199, 204–214, 222–223.

The two smaller colonies were slower to appreciate the advantages of a permanent agency. The ubiquitous Ashurst rendered occasional services to New Hampshire during these years, as when he swung his influence behind the appointment of William Partridge in place of John Usher as lieutenant governor.[9] But factional disputes within the colony limited its formal representation in London to a series of visits by special envoys, Partridge's son Richard and another father and son, William and George Vaughan.[10] The increasing frequency of these missions, coupled with the hope of protecting the province's landowners from the claims of proprietor Samuel Allen and his heirs, led in 1709 to the employment of Henry Newman, a New Englander living in London, as agent.[11] Newman became New Hampshire's permanent representative eleven years later and retained the post until 1737. In similar fashion, a succession of colonists, Christopher Almy, Jahleel Brenton, and William Wharton, son of land speculator Richard Wharton, represented Rhode Island's interests at court with varying degrees of loyalty and success until Richard Partridge was appointed agent with a salary of forty pounds a year. Partridge, who had stayed on in London following his service to New Hampshire,

---

[9] *N. H. Laws*, I, 694; Ashurst to New Hampshire, Apr. 24, 1700, *N. H. Provincial Papers*, III, 125; *ibid.*, 126, 139, XIX, 730; Ashurst to William Popple, Jr., Aug. 1, 1702, C.O. 5/862, no. 123. Ashurst claimed credit for Partridge's appointment (and reported receiving one hundred pounds for it) in a letter to William Vaughan and Richard Waldron, July 6, 1696 (Letterbook of Sir Henry Ashurst, fol. 120v.), a claim substantiated by other evidence: thus Bellomont to the Board of Trade, Nov. 28, 1700, *N. Y. Col. Docs.*, IV, 795; Samuel Allen to Blathwayt, Nov. 28, 1698, Blathwayt Papers, XII, Col. Wmsbg. Allen, however, though fiercely opposed to Partridge by 1698, is recorded two years earlier as the petitioner seeking Usher's replacement by Partridge: *APC Col.*, II, no. 630.

[10] *N. H. Laws*, I, 706–708, II, 90; *N. H. Provincial Papers*, III, 157–158, 353–355, 371, 375, 382, 469, XIX, 730, 734, 738–739. Lieutenant Governor Usher later claimed that much larger sums amounting to several thousands of pounds had been paid to the agents for presents and other expenses without a full accounting but there is no way to ascertain the truth of these charges, a task rendered the more impossible by the dense fog of Usher's prose: Jeffries Papers, IV, 59, 70; *CSP Col., 1710–1711*, nos. 335, 508iv, 510ii.

[11] *N. H. Provincial Papers*, III, 412, 417–418, 508–510, 779–780; Samuel Penhallow to Henry Newman, Nov. 25, 1710, Nov. 14, 1711, Belknap Papers, 1664–1744, Mass. Hist. Soc.; Cowie, *Henry Newman*, 202–222.

represented Rhode Island and no less than five other colonies at one time or another for more than forty years.[12]

Gradually, therefore, as individual missions became more frequent, the New England governments came to recognize the advantages of uninterrupted representation at Whitehall. One such advantage was financial for, as small governments such as Rhode Island and New Hampshire found to their cost, the travel and living expenses of a colonist sent upon a special mission could amount to a substantial portion of a colony's total budget, far more than the salary paid to a resident agent. More generally, as the Rhode Island assembly noted in appointing Partridge in 1715, not only did a colony have routine business to transact in England, but its interests could be seriously damaged for want of an agent in place at the crucial moment. An anonymous observer in Massachusetts some years earlier was still more explicit. Unless the province dispatched an agent prepared to give full attention to its affairs, he declared, it would not obtain the supplies necessary for its defense; it would be in danger of being "new modelled" in Parliament's forthcoming investigation of the plantations; laws would go unconfirmed; and only an agent on the spot could ensure the appointment of "such a Governor as may be Agreeable to N-England in our perswasion About matters of religion."[13]

[12] *R. I. Records*, III, 292, 295, 297, 331, 368, 372, 380–382, 403–405, 409–412, 464, 560, IV, 63–64, 125, 187–188; Marguerite Appleton, "Richard Partridge," 293–309. Details of Almy's and Brenton's expenses are in Boundary Documents, Rhode Island and Massachusetts, I, R. I. Archives. Wharton, acting for Rhode Island from 1703, was apparently first introduced as agent by William Penn, whom the colony had at some point commissioned to look after its interests in London. Wharton had assisted Penn in the past and was referred to in the colony as "Agent" and as "solicitor to Sir William Penn, our agent": *R. I. Records*, IV, 64, 125; R. I. Hist. Soc., Manuscripts, I, 99; Mass. Hist. Soc., *Collections*, 6th ser., III (1889), 103, 289.

[13] *R. I. Records*, IV, 187; Memorial in Miscellaneous Bound MSS., 1694–1700, Mass. Hist. Soc., probably written in 1698 or early 1699 by a colonist opposed to Ashurst and sympathetic to closer ties with England. See also the reasons cited by the House of Representatives, Sept. 1694, *Mass. Acts and Resolves*, VII, 450–451. For examples of the large sums spent in funding those sent on missions to England, amounting to as much as half the revenue raised by general taxation in some years, see *R. I. Records*, III, 418, 465, 541; *N. H. Provincial Papers*, III, 160, 375.

## Adjustment to Empire

A competent agent, in sum, could both help his colony and hinder its opponents. In the course of 1697, for example, acting on behalf of Massachusetts, Ashurst worked to ensure Bellomont's commissioning as governor and Joseph Dudley's continued exclusion from office; advanced the cause of his own joint venture with the Boston government for the production of naval stores while combatting the schemes of a rival group; arranged for the dispatch of arms and ammunition to the province and protested against proposals that disbanded soldiers and women convicts should also be exported to New England; collected money for Harvard College in the midst of defending the province's boundaries against the ancient and now revived claims of the Duchess of Hamilton; and, all the while, shepherded the laws passed in Massachusetts through the various agencies necessary to secure their confirmation by the crown.[14]

How was all this accomplished? Ashurst's letters to New England reveal how a knowledgeable representative could link and lubricate the mechanisms of imperial administration. "I am here looked upon as your Agent," he wrote in 1700, "and am Sent for often to all the Offices, of the Councill, Committee of Trade, Treasury and admiralty etc., to answer to questions and Solicite . . . relating to your Affaires, and tis from me that the Officers Expect all fees and gratifications for doing your Buisness which are not inconsiderable for a common reference is 52 shillings, the Sollicitour [-General] has had fourteen pounds att a time and the attorney [-General] Severall fees in passing your laws."[15] Small wonder that Whitehall officials en-

---

[14] *CSP Col., 1696–1697,* nos. 603, 652, 688, 695, 704, 751, 800, 827, 1005, 1023, 1152, 1189, 1195, 1202, 1328, 1361, *1697–1698,* no. 7; Ashurst to Massachusetts, June 28, Aug. 25, 20, Sept. 20, 1697, Jan. 25, 1698, Mass. Archives, CVI, 406–415; Letterbook of Sir Henry Ashurst, foll. 129–157 (numerous letters to correspondents in Massachusetts).

[15] Ashurst to Massachusetts, Apr. 30, 1700, *Mass. Acts and Resolves,* VII, 684. Four years later the price of a "reference" had risen to £3/2/6d. (Ashurst to Gov. Fitz-John Winthrop, Sept. 9, 1704, Hinman, *Letters*), although an official list of the same year cites the sum of £2/6/8d.—3½ medieval marks (Blathwayt Papers, BL 300, Hunt. Lib.). Whitehall veteran John Povey, writing Oct. 12, 1698, to Rhode Island, cited a list of charges for issuing a letter confirming a judgment of 1684, including £7/12/- for himself and the other clerks of the Privy Council, £15 for the Secretary's office (of the Board of Trade), £6 to the Attorney General, and

couraged the growth of the agency system, not only because of the steady stream of fees and gratuities they could expect to receive but for its contribution to administrative efficiency. It was Ashurst whom Secretary William Popple of the Board of Trade called upon in 1698 to persuade the crown's law officers to give their opinion on some laws of Massachusetts that had been gathering dust in their files for nearly two years.[16] Often, only an agent could effectively coordinate the work of the various departments required to carry through a complex operation such as the dispatch of troops and supplies to America. The fact that an agent was specifically empowered to represent a colony eased London's perennial problem of negotiating with governments three thousand miles away. For all these reasons, the Board of Trade encouraged the stationing of permanent agents in London; others chosen by such colonies as Virginia, Barbados, and the Leeward Islands joined those appointed by New England.[17] In 1705, the Board ordered all agents to follow Ashurst's example and register their credentials at the Plantation Office.[18]

An agent such as Ashurst moved freely in Westminster as well as in Whitehall. Sir Henry sat in four of the six parliaments of William's reign, and his connections to such potent political families as the Foleys, Boscawens, and Harleys enabled him, or so he boasted, to influence any bill affecting the colonies. His acquaintance with "great people," as during the days in the summer of 1697 when he was a house guest at the country estate of the Earl of Orford, a Whig gran-

---

£30–35 to the Clerk of the Hanaper and Great Seal: Boundary Documents, R. I. and Mass., I, no. 7, R. I. Archives.

[16] Popple to Ashurst, May 3, 1698, *CSP Col., 1697–1698*, no. 420.

[17] Thus, for example, Journal of the Board of Trade, Oct. 15, 1697, and the Board's subsequent letters to various colonial governors on the value of appointing an agent: *CSP Col., 1696–1697*, no. 1373, *1697–1698*, nos. 252, 259, *1701*, no. 823, *1712–1714*, no. 324, *1719–1720*, nos. 217, 217i. Also Lillian M. Penson, *The Colonial Agents of the British West Indies*, 250–254, and Ella Lonn, *The Colonial Agents of the Southern Colonies*, 57–60. Michael Kammen, *A Rope of Sand*, chapter I, provides a brief overview.

[18] *Journal of the Commissioners for Trade and Plantations*, I, 225. Earlier, Ashurst had been requested by the Board to present his commission as Connecticut's agent in writing: Journal of the Board of Trade, Dec. 5, 1700, C.O. 391/13, 265.

dee, paid political dividends. Thus when Connecticut's appeal against a judgment favoring the colony's Mohegan Indians came to a hearing before the Privy Council, Ashurst persuaded the Dukes of Devonshire and Somerset to put in a special appearance. This tactic, coupled with his employment of eminent and expensive counsel on behalf of the colony, won a partial reversal of the judgment.[19]

But if the need for agents was generally admitted, a colony such as Massachusetts was still reluctant to commit itself to the expense and responsibility of a formal appointment. Throughout the 1690s, Ashurst labored long and hard on Boston's behalf. "I have been 8 years your public servant," he wrote in 1697, "and two thirds of that tyme I have spent in your actuall Service and about £1200 of my owne Money." Year after year, he pressed for reimbursement and the settlement of a regular salary—the little Caribbean island of Nevis, he reported, paid its agent £300 a year and £100 for expenses. "Nothing is to be done here without money.... Had we money to greaze the Wheels, your laws would all pass but you would have us worke without straw."[20] The Massachusetts government, however, only intermittently remitted money for his expenses and never granted any regular income. Nor, despite his repeated pleas for greater recognition, did it ever entrust him with more than a general authority to act, in effect, as the colony's answering service in Whitehall.[21]

---

[19] Ashurst to William Partridge, Aug. 25, 1697, Letterbook of Sir Henry Ashurst, fol. 154; Ashurst to Governor and Council of Connecticut, May 21, 1706, Mass. Hist. Soc., *Collections*, 6th ser., III (1889), 324–326; Joseph H. Smith, *Appeals to the Privy Council*, 427n. Ashurst frequently lauded the strength of his political connections; to judge by this rather unreliable evidence, his most consistent patrons were Lord Somers, Hugh Boscawen, Edward Harley, the Earls of Bridgewater and Pembroke (the latter his political patron for his seat of Wilton), and the Dukes of Devonshire and Somerset.

[20] Ashurst to [the Massachusetts council?], Sept. 20, 1697, Mass. Archives, CVI, 411; similarly, Ashurst to Penn Townsend, Nehemiah Jewett, and James Converse, Aug. 30, 1697, to Cotton Mather, Aug. 30, 1697, Letterbook of Sir Henry Ashurst, foll. 151, 152. Ashurst was perhaps referring to the group of agents then representing the Leeward Islands: Penson, *Colonial Agents*, 70. He was simultaneously seeking a salary of one hundred pounds from New Hampshire.

[21] For grants to Ashurst, of money and of 1,000 acres of land, see Mass. Archives, CVI, 381, 382, 387, 454a, LXI, 531, CXIII, 194. Much of this money passed by

Ashurst's frustrations symbolized the difficulties of representing a New England colony, particularly one in the throes of adjusting to the reimposition of royal government. Ever mindful of the sinister changes that had overtaken a Dudley and a Mather in London, the colonists hesitated to grant any agent there, especially an Englishman, more than minimal powers. Nor, in this context, was Ashurst's inability to obtain a salary a personal failure: the Massachusetts assembly of the 1690s allowed no one such a privilege, not even its own doorkeeper and clerk. Compounding this parsimony was the colonists' innate conviction, long evident in their dealings with their "messengers" abroad, that to serve so godly a commonwealth was in itself sufficient reward. Full reimbursement would come hereafter, from a higher power.

Sir Henry genuinely believed in New England's transcendent mission, and in his plaintive letters complaining of his mistreatment he always stopped just short of resigning his position. Yet exploitation could run both ways, and in time the colonists came to perceive the disadvantages of having the kind of agent who would serve them for little official reward. In close harness with Ashurst's ideological loyalties, for example, as his private correspondence reveals, ran a keen desire to profit by his connection with New England. One early scheme he proposed to his old trading partner William Stoughton, nipped in the bud by the now lieutenant governor's reluctance to take advantage of his official position, envisaged a jointly sponsored privateering venture, similar to the one launched by Sir William Phips and to that which later entangled Bellomont and his English backers in the piracies of Captain Kidd.[22] Notably more successful was

---

way of the New England Company. A. C. Goodell, the careful editor of the *Mass. Acts and Resolves,* suggests (VII, 436) that neither Phipps nor Ashurst was regularly commissioned as agent during this period, but in fact both were duly commissioned and instructed: Ashurst to Increase Mather, Nov. 14, 1693, Letterbook of Sir Henry Ashurst, fol. 92v.; letter of Elisha Hutchinson, Feb. 1, 1693 [1694], Mass. Hist. Soc., *Proceedings,* II (1835–1865), 297; Mass. Archives, Court Records, VI, Oct. 30, 31, Nov. 2, 1694.

[22] Ashurst to [Stoughton], Nov. 14, 1693, Letterbook of Sir Henry Ashurst, fol. 90v. The two had traded with each other, Ashurst dispatching such goods as "Coarse clothes of sad mixtures for the winter ware," since 1684.

Ashurst's strategy for benefiting from London's interest in encouraging the production of colonial naval stores, as when he persuaded Massachusetts to finance a trial shipment of stores which he then sold to the crown for the inflated price of more than £3,000.[23] Later, given the opportunity through his influence with Lord Chancellor Somers to nominate the highly paid commissioners sent to New England to investigate its potential for further production, he demanded an appropriate reward for his favor—"You may place £100 to my Account presently for that service," he wrote to commissioner William Partridge. Indeed Partridge's nomination and his earlier promotion to lieutenant governor of New Hampshire (a success which put another £100 in Ashurst's pocket) were steps in a larger plan by which he and Ashurst were to split all subsequent profits and share in contracts negotiated with the Navy Board, with Ashurst supplying the necessary political muscle in London.[24] Another enterprise began when Ashurst and his business partner, the New England-born London banker Sir Stephen Evance, provided credit for the mounting of an English expedition to recapture settlements in Newfoundland conquered by the French and secured an official pledge of repayment for up to £4,000 worth of provisions to be furnished from Massachusetts. Ashurst then sent over his own merchandise to pay the debt and claimed the money from the crown.[25] When in 1700 he piously informed the General Court that he had "always sett my private concerns and yours

[23] Malone, *Pine Trees and Politics*, 12, 24, 161 n. 21; Commissioners of the Navy to the Lords of the Treasury, June 10, 1696, Invoice presented by Sir Henry Ashurst, [Aug. 17, 1696], C.O. 5/859, nos. 13, 20.

[24] Ashurst to Partridge, June 10, Aug. 4, 25, Oct. 2, 1697, Jan. 25, 1698, to Cotton Mather, Oct. 20, 1697, to William Vaughan and Richard Waldron, July 6, 1696, Letterbook of Sir Henry Ashurst, foll. 134, 136v., 153, 156, 158, 156v., 120v. Bellomont's opposition seems to have wrecked this scheme; Partridge later offered Ashurst a thousand pounds for the governorship of Massachusetts: Ashurst to Increase Mather, May 10, 1710, Mass. Hist. Soc., *Collections*, 6th ser., V (1892), 218.

[25] Ellesmere MSS., 9682, Hunt. Lib.; Ashurst to Massachusetts, June 28, 1697, to Treasurer James Taylor, June 28, July 29, 1697, to Stoughton, July 22, 1697, Letterbook of Sir Henry Ashurst, foll. 133v., 134, 135v., 136; the king to Lieutenant Governor Stoughton, Mar. 18, 1697, *CSP Col., 1696–1697*, no. 823. For a comparable profiting from war contracts half a century later, see Robert Zemsky, *Merchants, Farmers, and River Gods*, 191–209.

upon the Same foot," some must have cynically reflected that this indeed was the problem.[26]

In addition, the very fervor of Ashurst's commitment to New England and its purposes soon made him a partisan figure in the colony he served, an embroilment that was to blight the career of many another agent. As a known ally of the Mathers, Ashurst had supporters among members of the council, notably his nephew Peter Sergeant, but few in the lower house where, like the Mathers, he drew opposition from both sides of the political spectrum. Nor were his relations with successive chief executives close: Phips he regarded as monstrously ungrateful ("he had been noe more governour than Lord Lieutenant of Ireland if itt had not been for me"); Stoughton remained cool to the repeated overtures of the man who persisted in obstructing Joseph Dudley's return to power; and Bellomont, as Ashurst mournfully informed Cotton Mather, preferred his own ties to London and "thinks it his interest I should not be Agent."[27] As the Mathers' political influence weakened during the 1690s, so also did Ashurst's position. He was alive to the danger, especially after Nathaniel Byfield proposed his replacement as agent by Blathwayt, and he strove hard to broaden his political base by opening a correspondence with almost every notable political leader in Massachusetts, even his old opponent, Elisha Cooke.[28] He also managed to oust Byfield as vice-admiralty judge in favor of councillor Wait Winthrop.[29] But Winthrop had little political influence beyond his family name,

---

[26] Ashurst to Massachusetts, Apr. 30, 1700, *Mass. Acts and Resolves,* VII, 684.

[27] Ashurst to Stoughton, Oct. 22, 1692, to Peter Sergeant, Dec. 13, 1699, to [Cotton Mather], Feb. 1, 1701, Letterbook of Sir Henry Ashurst, foll. 84, 175v., 189.

[28] Ashurst to Wait Winthrop, Aug. 25, 1697, Mass. Hist. Soc., *Collections,* 6th ser., V (1892), 39-40. Letterbook of Sir Henry Ashurst, foll. 130-154 (Jan.-Aug., 1697), has copies of letters written to John Phillips, John Saffin, Eliakim Hutchinson, John Foster, Stoughton, Sergeant, Cooke, James Taylor, William Browne, Cotton and Increase Mather, Wait Winthrop, Penn Townsend, Nehemiah Jewett, James Converse, and Isaac Addington.

[29] Ashurst to Winthrop, May 5, June 6, 1699, Mass. Hist. Soc., *Collections,* 6th ser., V (1892), 43-44. He had earlier tried to secure the place for Peter Sergeant and Elisha Cooke.

and by the last years of the century Ashurst had effectively lost his post. When, in 1701, the council proposed that he be requested to present an address and solicit on its behalf at court, the assembly insisted that his fellow agent Constantine Phipps should be employed instead.[30] Phipps continued to serve as agent for the colony until as late as 1707, although with decreasing frequency.[31]

From Ashurst's perspective, the fact that Phipps was employed at all added ideological insult to financial injury, for Phipps was widely known for extreme Tory sympathies and as a man who had risen through marriage into the family of the very Sir Robert Sawyer whose denunciations of the Boston uprising had imperilled Mather's agency in 1690.[32] Ashurst's sneer, that Phipps was "only a councill to plead which anyone could do for money" was accurate: he failed to perceive, however, that this mechanical talent was precisely the quality the leaders of the Bay required. Phipps was an honest, competent, and persuasive lawyer prepared to follow instructions, just as he had done in both defending and prosecuting dissenting ministers in the courts of Charles II. He had no factional or commercial ties to the colony. Such a man was well suited to the agent's task of bureaucratic drudgery and constant vigilance—Ashurst himself, who sometimes retired from London to his country home in Oxfordshire or to take the waters at Tunbridge Wells, admitted as much in declaring that he would hire a clerk to assist him if the colony would only remit a regular salary. But the General Court remained deaf to his appeals, and

---

[30] *Mass. Acts and Resolves*, VII, 695. By this time, Ashurst was already refusing to act for the colony: Board of Trade to Massachusetts, May 20, 1701, Mass. Archives, LI, 122, and C.O. 5/909, 417. Nathaniel Byfield reported to Joseph Dudley, Aug. 7, 1701, that a vote of the assembly had just declared that Ashurst had been dismissed as agent two years before: Blathwayt Papers, BL 256, Hunt. Lib.

[31] Phipps to Massachusetts, May 16, 1700, Dec. 11, 1701, Apr. 17, Aug. 1, 1702, Mass. Archives, III, 73–74a, LI, 137–143, *Mass. Acts and Resolves*, VIII, 37, 316, 108; Attorney General Northey to the Board of Trade, Mar. 28, 1707, C.O. 5/864, no. 177; Gov. Joseph Dudley to Samuel Penhallow, Jan. 22, 1707, Belknap Papers, 1664–1744, no. 29.

[32] Robert Dunlop in Stephen and Lee, *Dictionary of National Biography*, s.v. "Phipps, Sir Constantine," and Jeaffreson, *Young Squire*, II, *passim*.

Dudley's triumphal return as governor in 1702 effectively barred the door against Sir Henry's further employment by Massachusetts.[33]

Ashurst's talents and loyalties were better suited to the more dramatic role of defending a colony's virtue against the Whitehall dragon than to the mundane hack work of representing a royal government. It was fitting, therefore, that he should have fought his last battles as agent in the service of Connecticut, the colony that many (including the founders of Yale) believed was assuming the mantle of godly leadership relinquished by Massachusetts. With the backing of Gov. Fitz-John Winthrop, he even secured the promise of a regular salary of one hundred pounds a year. Thus fortified, he plunged with reawakened zest into combat with the colony's internal and external foes: "I serve a good God in a glorious cause, and so I go on chearfully."[34] During these years, as Richard Dunn has shown, he rendered his adopted colony real service.[35] Yet once again his agency ended in disillusionment and in ways that revealed his inherent limitations as an agent. His hatred of Dudley, "that wicked Hamon," whom he viewed as the serpent of his imagined paradise, swelled into an obsession that absorbed his energies and Connecticut's resources. His alliance with Wait and Fitz-John Winthrop again exposed him to charges of serving particular interests, for some viewed his labors in such matters as defending land titles and rebutting the claims of Edward Palmes and the Hallams as catering more to the Winthrops' personal concerns than to the business of the colony.[36] In addition, his expertise in fending off Whitehall's interventions seemed less necessary and even overzealous as royal officials turned to take up plans for

---

[33] Letter of Elisha Hutchinson, Feb. 1, 1693 [1694], Mass. Hist. Soc., *Proceedings*, II (1835–1865), 297; Ashurst to [the Council of Massachusetts], Sept. 20, 1697, Mass. Archives, CVI, 412.

[34] *Conn. Records*, IV, 469; Ashurst to Gov. Gurdon Saltonstall, Aug. 25, 1708, Hinman, *Letters*, 336.

[35] Dunn, *Puritans and Yankees*, 332–352.

[36] *Ibid.*, 333, 341; and see, for Ashurst's pursuit of Dudley, his correspondence with Wait Winthrop, 1707–1710, Mass. Hist. Soc., *Collections*, 6th ser., V (1892), 140 *et seq.*, and Ashurst to [Robert Harley], c. 1708, HMC, *Portland*, X, 62.

a joint Anglo-colonial offensive against the French. The break came after Fitz-John Winthrop's death; his successor in the governorship, Gurdon Saltonstall, evaded further requests for payment and finally turned to, of all people, Col. Francis Nicholson, ardent Anglican and one-time lieutenant governor of the Dominion, to deliver the colony's addresses. "Is thy servant a dog that he should doe so?" cried an embittered Ashurst. "I reade in my Bible that it had like to have cost Jehosaphat his life for joyning with Ahab." Even Connecticut, it seemed, had come to need a workaday agent at Whitehall more than an aging paladin.[37]

Who could be such an agent? Among the candidates who felt themselves called, but were never chosen, were several who acted as personal representatives of the royal governor in Boston. As newly arrived colonial executives soon discovered to their cost, the English Treasury held fast to the ancient principle that a silent wheel was in no need of grease. Perpetual solicitation at Whitehall was required to extract even the payments officially scheduled for salaries and the upkeep of troops stationed in the colonies. Moreover, the complicated system of monetary exchange and the chronic shortage of coin and reliable bills of exchange made these items a lucrative official perquisite. Hence Bellomont engaged Sir William Ashurst, Sir Henry's brother, and John Champante, a London merchant, to act on his behalf, while Dudley established a correspondence with John Chamberlayne, a noted political journalist and man about court.[38] Cham-

---

[37] Ashurst to Wait Winthrop, May 10, 1710, to Saltonstall, May 16, 1710, Mass. Hist. Soc., *Collections,* 6th ser., V (1892), 221, 222. The bulk of Ashurst's correspondence with Connecticut can be found in Conn. Archives, Foreign Correspondence, II, 65–107c, and in the Winthrop Papers, portions of each being printed in Hinman, *Letters,* and Mass. Hist. Soc., *Collections,* 6th ser., V (1892). Scattered letters survive elsewhere, as in the Talcott and Saltonstall Papers, Conn. Hist. Soc.

[38] Leder, *Robert Livingston,* 135, 137–138, 149; Edward P. Lilly, *The Colonial Agents of New York and New Jersey,* 47–56; Bellomont to Champante, Sept. 6, 1699, Rawlinson Manuscripts, A 272, fol. 60, Bodleian Library; Francis Wyatt in Stephen and Lee, *Dictionary of National Biography,* s.v. "Chamberlayne, John"; and Chamberlayne's correspondence with Dudley in Mass. Hist. Soc., *Collections,* 6th ser., III (1889), 526–547. Chamberlayne later acted, through Dudley's management, as agent for the Pawtuxet proprietors: *Rhode Island Historical Tracts,* 2nd ser., IV (1896), 109–111; R. I. Hist. Soc., *Collections,* X (1902), 370.

pante's name was put forward for the Massachusetts agency and Chamberlayne evidently had a promise of the office from Dudley, but their close ties to the executive weighed against their employment by the General Court. Sir William, indeed, was asked to serve as agent in 1709 (he refused). But this was long after Bellomont's death, and the lower house pressed for the appointment principally because of Dudley's known dislike of the Ashurst family.[39]

Rather than employ such men, the colonists reasserted their old preference for agents who were of native birth and breeding. "Agents who are strangers to the particular circumstances of the Country cannot possibly do what is needfull to be done for us," warned one writer, and the Massachusetts assembly echoed his sentiment in requesting the commissioning of "one from amongst our selves to Joyne with those in England."[40] This was more easily said than done, and in Massachusetts during the 1690s such an appointment was repeatedly frustrated by the factional crosscurrents the matter stirred up within the General Court. Increase Mather longed to return as agent, if only on behalf of Harvard, but found his way barred by his old opponents Cooke and Danforth, backed by the lower house. This alliance in turn pressed for the dispatch of an emissary to seek "the restoration of as many of our Ancient Priviledges as may be obtained," but failed to circumvent the veto imposed by Stoughton and a majority of the council.[41] A last attempt, promoted by Cooke and Wait Winthrop

---

[39] Champante to Bellomont, Aug. 20, Sept. 20, Nov. 2, 1700, to Thomas Weaver, Feb. 27, 1701, Board of Trade to Massachusetts, May 20, 1701, Mass. Archives, III, 78–79, LI, 122; Sewall, *Diary,* II, 627–628, 632–633, 640; Votes of the General Court, Aug. 26–Nov. 11, 1709, Feb. 6–11, 1710, Mass. Archives, XX, 117–123, 127–132, 143; *Mass. Acts and Resolves,* IX, 106–108; Increase Mather to Sir William Ashurst, Dec. 5, 1709, [Jan. 19, Feb. 13, 1710], Pubs. Col. Soc. Mass., *Collections,* XLIX (1975), 228–231; John Leverett to Timothy Woodbridge, Feb. 1709 [1710], Conn. Hist. Soc., *Collections,* XXI (1924), 359.

[40] Memorial in Miscellaneous Bound MSS., 1694–1700, Mass. Hist. Soc.; *Mass. Acts and Resolves,* VII, 451.

[41] See the references in note 85, Chapter 5, preceding; and John Cotton to Rowland Cotton, [Dec. 10, 1696?], Miscellaneous Bound MSS., 1694–1700, Mass. Hist. Soc. Ashurst refused to deliver an address sent to London by the assembly alone, seeking the old Massachusetts charter with some additions: Ashurst to [Speaker] Penn Townsend and [Representatives] Nehemiah Jewett and James Converse, Aug. 30, 1697, Letterbook of Sir Henry Ashurst, fol. 151.

after the deaths of Bellomont and Stoughton in the spring of 1701 had left the council in control, put forward Winthrop's name as agent. Both houses initially concurred. But when Winthrop demanded a wide-ranging authority to negotiate a settlement returning Massachusetts to what he vaguely termed "the pure order of the Gospell" as established by the colony's founders and then sought a fund of two thousand pounds to be disbursed in England at his discretion, the lower house rebelled. One group of representatives, mostly from former Plymouth Colony towns, charged him with aiming at "an illimited and unreasonable power which may be of fatal consequences to this province." Subsequently, seven councillors, also principally those representing the old Plymouth territories and headed by Nathaniel Byfield, refused to sign his commission as agent.[42] In consequence, debate dragged out until September, at which point the news of Dudley's appointment as governor cut the ground from under Winthrop's feet and ended all further plans for his agency.[43] Not until a decade later, in 1710, after Sir William Ashurst had refused the post, did Massachusetts politicians finally agree on the appointment of a native-born agent, Jeremiah Dummer, then already resident in London.[44]

---

[42] Wait Winthrop to the General Court, Aug. 6, 1701, Mass. Hist. Soc., *Collections*, 6th ser., V (1892), 94; Dissent of fifteen representatives, [Aug. 1701], Blathwayt Papers, BL 255, Hunt. Lib.; Mass. Archives, Court Records, VII, Aug. 9, 1701; Dunn, *Puritans and Yankees*, 275–279. Many of the relevant documents are printed, from Mass. Archives, XX, 41–72, in *Mass. Acts and Resolves*, VII, 293, 300, 301, 306–307, 676, 682, 694–695; much additional information on the struggles inside the council and the roles of Cooke and Winthrop is given in Nathaniel Byfield to Joseph Dudley, Aug. 7, 1701, Blathwayt Papers, BL 258, Hunt. Lib. Of the twenty-two councillors attending the August 9 meeting, Byfield, Barnabas Lothrop, John Thacher, William Browne, John Phillips, Samuel Partridge, and Isaac Addington did not sign Winthrop's commission; the first three were among the four councillors representing the Plymouth territories; the fourth was not present.

[43] Hutchinson, *History of Massachusetts-Bay*, II, 97, plausibly suggests (though no contemporary evidence survives to this effect) that the real reason for Winthrop's mission was to secure his appointment as governor; hence its hasty abandonment after news of Dudley's success.

[44] For Dummer's career, see *Sibley's Harvard Graduates*, IV, 454–468. Despite the Reverend John Barnard's belief that he had been instrumental in securing Dummer's appointment in 1709, it was more probably due to Sir William Ashurst's recommendation backed by a letter from twenty-eight London merchants, May

Elsewhere in New England, however, the preference for such agents was given full rein. Save for Sir Henry Ashurst, in fact, every one of those empowered to represent Connecticut, Rhode Island, and New Hampshire in London in the 1690s was a New Englander. And when, as was increasingly the case, the colonists looked for more permanent representation in England, they turned to those who had migrated from their midst. William Wharton, for example, continued his father's maverick role by acting for a variety of "anti-establishment" New England causes—Rhode Island, Connecticut's internal opponents, Sir Matthew Dudley's scheme for naval stores, and John Usher's claim against Massachusetts for money expended while treasurer of the Dominion.[45] All three of those who might be termed the first generation of regularly commissioned and paid permanent agents—Richard Partridge, Henry Newman, and, on behalf of Massachusetts after 1710 and Connecticut after 1712, the great Jeremiah Dummer—were likewise New England born and bred, Newman and Dummer having graduated from Harvard.[46] Only much later, whether in the belief that there were now some Englishmen who could be trusted to understand New England or because fewer Harvard men were migrating to London, did the colonial governments employ such notable English-born agents as Jasper Mauduit, Richard Jackson, John Thomlinson, and Dennys De Berdt.[47]

---

5, 1710, just prior to Dummer's actual appointment: John Barnard, "Autobiography of the Rev. John Barnard," 208; Samuel Sewall to Sir William Ashurst, Nov. 21, 1710, Mass. Hist. Soc., *Collections*, 6th ser., I (1886), 404; Sewall, *Diary*, II, 640, 643–644; Increase Mather to Sir William Ashurst, Dec. 5, 1709–Nov. 8, 1710. Pubs. Col. Soc. Mass., *Collections*, XLIX (1975), 228–231, 236–237; Mass. Archives, XX, 144, 158–163.

[45] Note 12, preceding; Mass. Hist. Soc., *Collections*, 6th ser., III (1889), 254, 377, 380; *CSP Col., 1702–1703, 1704–1705*, indexes, *sub* "Wharton, William"; John Ive to John Usher, July 24, Nov. 11, 1703, June 24, 1704, Jeffries Papers, II, 135, 137, 139.

[46] *Conn. Records*, V, 360–362. Not all these men were salaried, but they were paid with a regularity that was the nearest that some colonies could bring themselves to bestowing a salary.

[47] Kammen, *Rope of Sand*, 323–326. Long residence in England could render even a native-born agent suspect: in the 1720s, for example, sentiment reappeared for sending "Persons born amongst us" as agents: *New-England Courant*, Jan. 14, 1723.

The years immediately following the Glorious Revolution, therefore, marked a significant turn toward a regularization and ultimately an institutionalization of New England's relations with England. Sir Henry Ashurst set the stage for this transition, and, having
proven the utility of a permanent agency, he was also the first to suffer from the parochialism that characterized its early development. In
a sense this was fitting, for by the first years of the new century
Ashurst had become a relic of a bygone era, the last of a generation of
influential Englishmen who served the Puritan colonies in the belief
and hope that they were the undefiled remnant of the reformed religion and its "good old cause." For all his schemes for personal profit,
he treasured most the meaning and status of his position. His expectations of New England were necessarily extravagant, and their progressive disappointment mirrored the extent to which the colonists'
ways and needs were changing. "I perceive," he wrote dolefully to his
faithful correspondent, Wait Winthrop, "that your young men have
little regard to the old cause that brought them thar, but ar for high
church and arbitrary. *O tempera, O mores.* I shall be able to stop the
tide but a litle while." And indeed he had no comparable successors;
no colony ever again boasted a baronet as its agent.[48] The New England Company, which he had used as the financial arm of his agencies, returned to its charitable work of funding Boston merchants and
Indian education—roughly in that order.[49] The spirit of the dissenting connection lived on in the work of such notables as Thomas
Hollis, Isaac Watts, and Daniel Neal. But it was many years before it
reasserted its true strength in transatlantic politics. The transition to

---

[48] Ashurst to Winthrop, May 8, 1698, Mass. Hist. Soc., *Collections*, 6th ser., V
(1892), 41. Ashurst himself was keenly aware that "none of the plantations have
an agent of my figure": to Fitz-John Winthrop, Mar. 25, 1702, Conn. Archives,
Foreign Correspondence, II, 70b–c. For a curious account of Sir Henry's last
hours, William Stratford to Edward Harley, Apr. 16, 1711, HMC, *Portland*, VII,
30.

[49] Ashurst drew at least fourteen hundred pounds sterling from New England
sources, 1694–1711, through the New England Company (of which his brother
was governor, 1696–1719): Letterbook, 1688–1761, of the Company for the Propagation of the Gospel in New England, 14, 54, 59, 72–74, 82, 93, 102.

a permanent agency replaced the freewheeling personal diplomacy of Mather and Ashurst with administrative procedures contained within the governmental framework, together with the type of agent best suited to exploit them.

Clearly, developments in Whitehall paved the way for this transition. Once the Board of Trade's attacks upon the charters eased, agents could settle into the routine business of judicial appeals, the review of legislation, and the representation of their colonies' needs. Such needs were particularly pressing in time of war, and it is significant that the New England governments turned to skilled lobbyists such as Jeremiah Dummer during the years when schemes for Anglo-colonial military cooperation finally blossomed into elaborate expeditions against Canada and Port Royal. Yet such influences should not obscure the magnitude of the adjustment that had taken place inside Massachusetts and, to a lesser degree, in the other New England colonies. In the 1680s the deputies of the Bay had held out to the last against compromise with the crown; a decade later their successors were pressing for the dispatch of agents to England. This is not to suggest that the colonists now sought permanent refuge in the mother country's comforting embrace. They were hardly less suspicious of Whitehall's intentions than before. Instead, just as the leaders of Massachusetts had learned how to "improve" their new charter, so experience had brought knowledge of how best to live within the constraints of the imperial system. The best defense against royal policy, for example, might be to participate in its formulation. The road back to New England's "ancient Priviledges" could lead by way of Whitehall. As in the subtler arts of self-defense, the colonists were coming to appreciate how to roll with their opponent's blow and turn its force to their own advantage.

The character of this adjustment can best be seen in what might be termed the voluntary aspects of colonial cooperation. Such issues as appeals and the attack upon the charters virtually required a response if a colony's case were not to go by default. But there were other matters where the colonists ventured uninvited. Ranging in substance and importance from personal grievances and solicitations to the crucial question of whom the crown should appoint as governor, they reveal the ways in which New Englanders were mastering the skills needed to profit from their transatlantic relationship.

Some of these solicitations proceeded through official intergovernmental channels, a prime example being the colonists' requests for military assistance and supplies. On several occasions, Massachusetts appealed for a stronger English naval presence on the New England coast to guard its fishing fleets and convoys against pirates and the French privateers swarming out of Port Royal. In response, additional frigates were sent. Often requested, also, were arms and ammunition, which remained in critically short supply, so much so that in 1696 the Boston government ordered a fast packet boat to London for the express purpose of collecting a cargo of gunpowder and other military stores. Well aware of how decisions were made in Whitehall, the colony strove to win a hearing for its needs beyond the confines of the Board of Trade: in 1696 and again in 1700 it reinforced its addresses to the crown by seeking aid with a scattering of letters to prominent English politicians soliciting their personal support.[50] Later, perceiving that even decisions meant little unless translated into action, Massachusetts dispatched a special emissary, Capt. Nathaniel Cary, to London to secure a shipment of twenty cannons promised for the colony's coastal defenses. After twelve months of navigating between government offices and much "treating" of their various functionaries, Cary escorted his precious cargo back to Boston late in 1705.[51]

---

[50] *CSP Col., 1696–1697*, nos. 483, 498, 1023ii, 1024, *1704–1705*, nos. 451, 452; *Mass. Acts and Resolves*, VII, 126, 127–129, 518; George Vaughan to the Earl of Sunderland, HM 22280, Hunt. Lib.; and note 31, Chapter 5, preceding. Among the politicians solicited in 1700 were Attorney General Trevor, Somers, Charles Montague, Secretary of State James Vernon, James [Hugh?] Boscawen, John Smith, and the Dukes of Shrewsbury and Bedford: Mass. Archives, CVI, 475–478a, XX, 32.

[51] List of ordnance requested by Massachusetts, May 22, 1703, English Manuscripts, 187, Boston Public Library; Board of Trade to the Queen, Nov. 7, 1704, C.O. 5/751, no. 58; *Mass. Acts and Resolves*, VIII, 78, 382–384, 548–552. The quest proved expensive: the ship commissioned to carry Cary to London was captured by the French at a cost to the province, with its cargo, of nearly £1,000, and Cary was later paid some £325 (including £5 as his ransom from a French prison) for his services.

## The Evolution of Transatlantic Politics

Outside official channels, the most revealing measure of the colonists' readiness to take advantage of their ties to England was the proliferation of interest groups seeking protection and favors from the crown. Emboldened by the vistas opened up by the Dominion, religious minorities protested against the reestablishment of Puritan orthodoxy. Local Quakers petitioned against "Priest rates," taxation for the support of a Congregational ministry, and forwarded accounts of their "sufferings" to Whitehall by way of the powerful Quaker communities in England. London Friends, in turn, led by William Crouch, a prominent trader to New England, repeatedly solicited the Board of Trade and Privy Council to repeal obnoxious laws and protect their fellow sectaries. Anglicans complained in similar fashion, employing the good offices of the Bishop of London and their church's Society for the Propagation of the Gospel in Foreign Parts. New England's Baptists likewise turned to present their case in England. By the 1720s these pressures, relayed back across the Atlantic by official letters of enquiry and news of the disallowance of a number of the offending laws, had significantly eased the disabilities imposed upon dissenters from the New England way.[52]

Other groups pursued more material goals. New England merchants trading to and visiting London had long gathered with their English colleagues upon "the New England Walk" within the city's Royal Exchange and in surrounding taverns and coffeehouses: in 1706, visiting colonist Nathaniel Saltonstall asked for letters to be sent to him at "the Sun or N. England Coffee house behind the Royal Exchange."[53] These traders now regularly petitioned the crown in support of particular commercial or political measures and for protection for their shipping. In turn, they were often called in for consultation by the Board of Trade. Though most were Englishmen, a

---

[52] Reed, *Church and State in Massachusetts,* 22–23, 88 *et seq.;* McLoughlin, *New England Dissent,* 144, 158-159, 182-224. Crouch traded with John Usher among others and was the principal supplier of Thomas Fitch: Jeffries Papers, III, 121-122; Letterbook of Thomas Fitch, 1702-11.

[53] *CSP Col., 1675-1676,* no. 889; Saltonstall to Roland Cotton, Jan. 14, 1706, Miscellaneous Bound MSS., 1701-13, Mass. Hist. Soc.; Penson, *Colonial Agents,* 180-182; Bryant Lillywhite, *London Coffee Houses,* 387-390, 557-558, plate 4.

number were New England born, others had relatives there, and all were in close touch with colonial opinion.[54] In 1696, Massachusetts appealed to this lobby, "our Countrymen in London with such Gentlemen as are concerned in Trade hither," to aid its agents in presenting its request for aid.[55]

In some instances, these interest groups extended and refined strategies formulated in earlier years. The Atherton proprietors continued to petition in London in support of their claims to land in the Narragansett country, though more, it would seem, as a means of pressuring Connecticut and Rhode Island to give way than in hope of obtaining a favorable royal settlement.[56] These two governments, in their turn, were forced to account for their own fierce contest over the disputed territories. One tactic profitably employed in a facet of this prolonged dispute was a repetition of that practiced by the Atherton proprietors and Lord Culpeper back in 1681, the obtaining from the crown of an "impartial" commission of enquiry stacked with commissioners known to be committed to one's own side. Such a commission was established to resolve the Mohegan Indians' complaints presented at court by Nicholas Hallam as part of his campaign against the Connecticut government. Its members, evidently nominated by Hallam, were either known sympathizers of the Indians within the colony or "tories" from Rhode Island and Massachusetts led by Gov. Joseph Dudley. This panel met in August 1705 and in a few hours

---

[54] Thus, for example, Mass. Archives, XXXVII, 7 (1691), XX, 144 (1710), C.O. 5/859, no. 81 (1697), C.O. 5/863, no. 63 (1703), C.O. 5/752, no. 6 (1713?), C.O. 5/866, nos. 44i, ii, 47, 48v (1715), Miscellaneous Manuscripts, HM 8258, Hunt. Lib. (c. 1711).

[55] Lieutenant Governor Stoughton to Thomas Cooper and Benjamin Jackson, Dec. 5, 1696, *Mass. Acts and Resolves,* VII, 521. The consequence was the petition of 1697 (C.O. 5/859, no. 81) with fifty-nine signatures, including such New Englanders in London as Cooper and Jackson, John Nelson, Benjamin Gillam, Gilbert Bant, Shadrach Walton, and John Colman.

[56] Petitions of Wait Winthrop and others, May 22, 1695, of Samuel Sewall and others, Jan. 27, 1697, of the Proprietors of the Mortgaged Lands of the Narragansett Countrey, [Nov. 13, 1705], of Wait Winthrop and others, [May 11, 1710], *CSP Col., 1693–1696,* no. 1844i, *1696–1697,* no. 636, *1704–1705,* no. 1451i, *1710–1711,* no. 231i; Mass. Hist. Soc., *Collections,* 6th ser., V (1892), 104, 150.

rendered judgment in favor of the Indians on all points.[57] Jahleel Brenton, one of the Massachusetts members, must have particularly relished Hallam's ploy, for a decade earlier, during his contest with Sir William Phips, he had persuaded the Commissioners of Customs to recommend the appointment of a no less partisan panel composed of all the leading members of the Byfield faction to investigate his charges against the governor.[58] Similar scenarios were played out with different casts in other American colonies during these years. They revealed that royal government, for all its administrative reforms, was still highly susceptible to manipulation by particular interests. Equally, they demonstrated that the crown was in no way prejudiced as to whom it surrendered its impartiality—it did not discriminate in its discrimination. Colonists too could secure royal backing, particularly if they presented themselves in person at Whitehall, emphasized the value of their cause in strengthening royal government, and greased the appropriate wheels.

The lesson sank home, particularly among those already looking to the crown for advancement or redress, and the years after the Glorious Revolution witnessed a steady rise in the numbers of office and favor seekers making their way to the fount of patronage in London. Following in the footsteps of William Dyre, the first New Englander to parlay a visit to Whitehall into a post in the colonial customs service, his fellow Rhode Islander Jahleel Brenton returned in 1691 with the twin positions of collector of customs and surveyor of the woods in New England. Harvard graduate Benjamin Lynde studied law in London and came back, through Randolph's favor, as attorney general and advocate of Massachusetts's new vice-admiralty court.

---

[57] Case of the Mohegan Indians, [Feb. 1, 1704], Board of Trade to the queen, Mar. 9, 1704, Proceedings of the Commissioners sent to the Board of Trade, Aug. 23, 1705, *CSP Col., 1704–1705,* nos. 56, 171, 1312.

[58] Commissioners of Customs to the Lords of Trade, Jan. 4, 1694, C.O. 5/858, no. 1.

Another Massachusetts lawyer originally nominated for the post, Thomas Newton, made several voyages to England before his solicitations established him as customs comptroller in Boston. William Tailer sought payment in London for his military services to the province and returned as its lieutenant governor. Such appointments could sometimes be won by proxy, as when Sir Henry Ashurst obtained for Wait Winthrop a vice-admiralty judgeship and for William Partridge the posts of lieutenant governor of New Hampshire and commissioner to investigate the production of naval stores. Randolph's nomination for the personnel of New England's vice-admiralty courts brought office to several prominent "tories," including Byfield, Lawrence Hammond, Peleg Sanford, and Nathaniel Coddington.[59]

Solicitation in person or by proxy was clearly prudent, for Englishmen too were hungry for the growing number of offices at the crown's disposal. New Englanders saw again the phenomenon first evident during the Dominion and already grimly familiar to colonists elsewhere, the arrival of migrants more concerned with farming the populace than the land. Sworn in with Thomas Newton before Governor Dudley in 1707, for example, was John Jeckyll, an Englishman whose powerful connections at court had won him Brenton's position as collector. Captain John Shackmaple took up residence in New London as collector of Connecticut, and Charles Story arrived in 1697 to begin a lengthy administrative career in New Hampshire with a commission as vice-admiralty judge. Thomas Povey, a needy cousin of William Blathwayt, served for some years as lieutenant gov-

---

[59] John Cotton to Rowland Cotton, Jan. 30, 1691, Prince Papers; Edward Randolph to William Popple, Mar. 17, 1697, Randolph's nominations, July 31, 1696, Mar. 1697, [1696], *Randolph Letters*, V, 165, 137, 163, VII, 501; Jeremiah Dummer to [Governor Dudley], June 5, 1711, Miscellaneous Bound MSS., 1701–13, Mass. Hist. Soc.; Petition of Thomas Newton, [July 6, 1706], *Calendar of Treasury Books, 1705–1706,* 698; Barrow, *Trade and Empire,* 81 (though Newton's previous official service had been with the vice-admiralty courts, and he was not yet, as here described, a former attorney general of Massachusetts). Another New Englander (later Newton's predecessor as province attorney general) who benefited by Ashurst's patronage was John Valentine, who came back from London as clerk of the naval stores commission: Ashurst to [Massachusetts], Aug. 14, 1699, Letterbook of Sir Henry Ashurst, foll. 146v.–147; also Mass. Archives, CVI, 410.

ernor of Massachusetts. Others, such as Nathaniel Kay and Charles Blechyden, the collectors at Rhode Island and Salem, were transferred to New England after many years' service in the British customs system, the first of a long line of such appointments that prompted one English observer in mid-century to remark that America had become "the hospital of Great Britain for her decayed courtiers and abandoned worn-out dependants."[60]

Simultaneously, a more vigorous group of newcomers rose to office attached to the coattails of the various royal governors. Benjamin Jackson, from Cheshire in England, came over as Phips's secretary and worked on his patron's behalf in Boston and then in London. In 1698 he returned to New England as one of the naval stores commissioners nominated by Ashurst. This seems to have ended his official career.[61] Bellomont's secretary, Robert Armstrong, showed greater staying power. Naval officer in New Hampshire until Bellomont's death in 1701, he went back to London, acted on behalf of the claims of Usher and Samuel Allen and returned in 1710 as the province's collector, a post to which he later added that of deputy surveyor of the woods. He thereby assumed the duties of John Bridger, another Englishman who had first visited New England as another of the naval stores commissioners and come back in 1706 to begin an eventful term of office as surveyor general of the woods, charged with the thankless task of protecting the timber reserved to the crown in the

---

[60] Sewall, *Diary*, I, 574; Barrow, *Trade and Empire*, 78–80; Gov. Joseph Dudley to [William Blathwayt], Feb. 1, 1706, Blathwayt Papers, BL 265, Hunt. Lib.; *N. H. Provincial Papers*, II, 206, 670; Letter of Gen. John Huske, May 5, 1758, in Robert Phillimore, comp., *Memoirs and Correspondence of George, Lord Lyttelton, 1734–1773*, II, 604. Barrow's contention (*Trade and Empire*, 81) that "Stackmaple" was a native of New London is contradicted by Connecticut historians: Conn. Hist. Soc., *Collections*, IV (1892), 235n.; Frances Manwaring Caulkins, *History of New London, Connecticut, From the First Survey of the Coast in 1612, to 1852*, 239; also Conn. Archives, Trade and Maritime Affairs, I, 53, and Robert Quary to the Commissioners of Customs, Apr. 6, 1708, Mass. Hist. Soc., *Collections*, 2nd ser., IV (1888), 151.

[61] Sir William Phips to William Blathwayt, Feb. 27, 1693, Blathwayt Papers, V, Col. Wmsbg.; Mass. Archives, LXI, 539, CVI, 403; Ashurst to Jackson, May 6, 1695, Jan. 25, 1698, to [Massachusetts], Aug. 14, 1697, Letterbook of Sir Henry Ashurst, foll. 116v., 158v., 146v.–147.

forests of New Hampshire and Maine.[62] New Hampshire, indeed, partly because governors like Usher had few friends within the province and partly because of the scarcity of those willing and able to serve in administrative positions, proved to be particularly hospitable to aspiring placemen as a succession of newcomers, most of them Englishmen—Story, William Redford, Thomas Newton, Henry Penny, and Samuel Penhallow—held the principal bureaucratic offices.

These appointments drew New England within the network of American patronage commanded by the crown, a network that reached extensive proportions by the latter half of the eighteenth century. More significant in the short term, however, was their effect in propelling colonists who had hitherto held back from involvement with Whitehall into taking a hand in transatlantic politics. The arrival of such English interlopers was not merely a check to the ambitions of the Byfields and Brentons ready to serve the crown and eager to monopolize the available places; it also alarmed those who abhorred such a quest for office yet recognized the dangers of allowing its rewards to fall into the hands of outsiders. To traditionalists such as Samuel Sewall, every such appointment was a further nail in the coffin of New England's political and spiritual health. After witnessing a London lawyer, William Atwood, sworn in as vice-admiralty judge in 1701, Sewall mournfully recorded in his diary that "thus a considerable part of Executive Authority is now gon out of the hands of New England men." All too often, moreover, as he noted with equal sorrow, it was passing into the hands of enthusiastic Anglicans: John Bridger, for example, strove hard to gather Episcopalian congregations in Newbury and Portsmouth.[63] The ways of Andros and

---

[62] Malone, *Pine Trees and Politics*, 57–87 (as "Thomas" Armstrong and "Jonathan" Bridger); Barrow, *Trade and Empire*, 81–82. Another who came over in hopes of preferment from a new governor (although the governor never came) was the noted physician and author, Dr. William Douglass: Douglass to Cadwallader Colden, Feb. 20, 1721, *Collections of the New-York Historical Society for 1917* (New York, 1918), 114.

[63] Sewall, *Diary*, I, 456. Sewall's watch upon whether the new arrivals chose the Anglican method of oathtaking can be followed in *ibid.*, 470, 493, 574, II, 834. For Bridger's religious activities, and Sewall's anxieties, Perry, *Historical Collections*, III,

his "crew of Abject persons," still vividly remembered, seemed to be flooding back. Was it not incumbent upon New Englanders themselves to play a part in stemming the tide? The delicate blend of personal and public interest that could inspire such a resolve is evident in the sentiments of Wait Winthrop, about to embark upon the abortive plan to serve as agent: loud in his denunciation of those "factors and strangers" who sought office for their own advantage, he was yet willing, as he told Sir Henry Ashurst, to accept a suitably remunerative post "to save the best interest here and keep this people from that slavery which they were growing under and have almost forgot alredy."[64]

Varied as these motives were, they forged an effective coalition of common interests that in time was able to exert, though in no very organized or consistent fashion, considerable influence at Whitehall. This coalition was seldom apparent in such minor matters as the appointment of customs officers and vice-admiralty judges, functionaries whose powers to annoy could, it was learned, be effectively disarmed by local courts or by quiet "arrangements" with those whose activities they were supposed to supervise. Rather, it focused upon the selection of the royal governor, the one official whose authority reached into every corner of colonial life and whose appointment determined the disposition of a host of lesser posts in government. Nowhere, indeed, is the increasing sophistication of the colonists' participation in transatlantic politics during the 1690s more apparent than in the train of events that led to Joseph Dudley's succession to the governorship of Massachusetts in 1701.

Dudley himself, of course, cannot fairly be regarded as representative of his fellow countrymen's changing ways. As patriotic contemporaries hastened to point out, he was living proof that not all the advantages of blood and breeding could save a man from the innate

99–106; Fulham Palace Manuscripts, IV, 44–45, 94, Archives of the Bishop of London, Lambeth Palace Library (microfilm in Library of Univ. of California, Berkeley); Sewall, "Letter-Book," 416–421; Reed, *Church and State in Massachusetts,* 161–162. Jeckyll, Povey, Kay, and Newton were also active Anglicans.

[64] Ashurst to Winthrop, May 8, 1698, Winthrop to Ashurst, July 25, 1698, Mass. Hist. Soc., *Collections,* 6th ser., V (1892), 41, 5th ser., VIII (1882), 535.

depravities of his nature. Having sold his birthright for the presidency of the Dominion, he had stayed loyal to Andros and suffered accordingly. Returning to New York as the colony's chief justice in 1691, he had further tarnished his reputation by presiding at the trial and execution of Jacob Leisler, the rebel leader soon celebrated as a martyr in the Protestant cause.[65] But Dudley, as even his most bitter opponents admitted, was a man of beguiling charm and enormous political dexterity; he was, as one obituary later noted, "visibly form'd for Government." Back in England to press the charges against Sir William Phips, he gained the patronage of Lord John Cutts, a renowned soldier recently appointed governor of the Isle of Wight. Cutts made Dudley his lieutenant governor and arranged his election as deputy mayor and in 1701 member of Parliament for Newton, one of the island's rotten boroughs.[66]

Dudley, however, regarded his new offices as but the means to his ultimate goal of returning to Massachusetts as governor, and his prolonged maneuverings during these years prefigure the "succession politics" that were to be so marked a feature of Anglo-colonial relations in the following century.[67] He seized every opportunity to harass the existing occupant of the governor's chair, pressing the charges against Phips and contriving his arrest for debt upon the governor's arrival in London in 1695. Later, or so Sir Henry Ashurst believed, he aided those attacking Bellomont over the Kidd affair.[68] He served as

---

[65] Kimball, *Joseph Dudley*, 58–64; also, Chapter V, preceding. Dudley did try to delay Leisler's execution (Leder, *Robert Livingston*, 75–76; Lovejoy, *Glorious Revolution in America*, 356–357), but the lasting hatred he aroused in Leisler's admirers, and their continued efforts to discredit him, can be seen in Jacob Melyen to Jacob Schellinger, July 30, 1691, to Abraham Gouverneur, June 25, 1692, Letterbook of Jacob Melyen, Amer. Antiq. Soc.

[66] *Boston News-Letter*, Apr. 4–11, 1720; Appointment of Joseph Dudley as lieutenant governor of the Isle of Wight, Apr. 12, 1694, *Calendar of State Papers, Domestic Series, of the Reign of William and Mary, 1694–1695*, 96; Kimball, *Joseph Dudley*, 65–71; William Page, ed., *The Victoria History of Hampshire and the Isle of Wight*, 266; Sir Robert Worsley to Dudley, Nov. 19, 1701, Nov. 21 [1701], C. E. French and F. L. Gay Papers, Mass. Hist. Soc.

[67] Thus John A. Schutz, "Succession Politics in Massachusetts, 1730–1741," 508–520; and Leonard Woods Labaree, *Royal Government in America*, 44–49.

[68] Sir Henry Ashurst to Benjamin Jackson, May 6, 1695, to Increase Mather, Apr. 23, 1700, Letterbook of Sir Henry Ashurst, foll. 116v., 177v.; Joseph Dudley to

Cutts's local political agent in order to enlist that nobleman's influence at court on his behalf.[69] And he was prepared to be all things to all men. While assuring his correspondents at home of his devotion to New England, he was also writing to William Blathwayt of his "Long declared Resolution to keep that Goverment in a Strict dependance upon the Crown and Goverment of England and that they be made usefull and serviceable and that the Church of England there may be easy and upon an Equall foot with others and that the Acts of Trade may be carefully observed."[70] He "insinuated" himself, as Ashurst put it, with the veteran Presbyterian statesman (and Ashurst's brother-in-law) Richard Hampden and boasted to Blathwayt of the English dissenting ministers he had brought to support his candidacy. Simultaneously, he was ingratiating himself with prominent Anglicans such as the Archbishop of Canterbury, the Bishops of London and St. Asaph, and the Tory Earls of Rochester and Jersey, and promising to put his membership in the Anglican Society for the Propagation of the Gospel in Foreign Parts to good use once he was back in Boston as governor. "I do not fayle every day to Make My Attendance somewhere," he wrote in the last months before his appointment was completed.[71]

---

William Blathwayt, Feb. 25, 1693, Nov. 23, 1695, Feb. 9, 1697, Blathwayt Papers, IV, Col. Wmsbg.

[69] For part of Cutts's correspondence with Dudley, 1695–1700, see Mass. Hist. Soc., *Proceedings,* 2nd ser., II (1885–1886), 173–192, and Chamberlain Collection, G.4. 36., Boston Public Library; also Historical Manuscripts Commission, *Report on the Manuscripts of Mrs. Frankland-Russell-Astley of Chequers Court, Bucks.,* 81, 83, 94. For Cutts's lobbying for Dudley, Sir William Trumbull to William Blathwayt, July 7, 1696, Historical Manuscripts Commission, *Report on the Manuscripts of the Marquess of Downshire,* I, pt. ii, 677, and James Vernon to the Duke of Shrewsbury, June 2, 7, 1698, in James Vernon, *Letters Illustrative of the Reign of William III from 1696 to 1708,* II, 93, 98.

[70] Dudley to [Blathwayt], July 29, 1701, Dudley Papers, Mass. Hist. Soc.

[71] Ashurst to Increase Mather, June 11, 1694, Letterbook of Sir Henry Ashurst, fol. 104; Dudley to [Blathwayt], July 22, 26, 29, Aug. 5, 12, 1701, Dudley Papers; Godfrey Dellius to Paul Dudley, Sept. 16, 1701, Mass. Hist. Soc., *Collections,* 6th ser., III (1889), 523; Ernest Hawkins, *Historical Notices of the Missions of the Church of England in the Northern American Colonies,* 23–25. Evidence of the support given Dudley by the English dissenting ministers can be seen in the letter of John Quick and eight others, Aug. 13, 1701, Hutchinson, *History of Massachusetts-Bay,* II, 91n. (a copy in Cotton Mather's hand dated Aug. 19 is in Curwin Papers, II, 40,

His efforts did not go unchallenged. "An honest New Englishman," wrote Sir Henry Ashurst to Cotton Mather, "is one who neither loves nor cares for D[udley] whose soule is as black as his hatt and would ruin both you and I if in his power." When Sir William Phips died in London and Dudley seemed likely to succeed him as governor, Ashurst used his position as a member of Parliament to promote a bill drawn up by Constantine Phipps reversing the attainder of Jacob Leisler. This tactic sparked a parliamentary investigation of the New York trial and the exposure of Dudley's part in it. The unfavorable publicity forced Dudley to withdraw his candidacy, clearing the way for the appointment of Bellomont.[72] Six years later, after Bellomont's death, Ashurst was once more in the forefront of the opposition: "I have harrased my body day and night," he told Wait Winthrop. With the help of his old ally, Stephen Mason, and by resurrecting the ghost of Leisler once more, he succeeded in delaying the passage of Dudley's commission for six long months, driving the unfortunate candidate to frenzies of anxiety. I pray, Dudley besought Blathwayt in July 1701, "that I may see my family and Country again, my Lord Cornbury seems to hasten and Mr. Selwyn [the newly appointed governors of New York and Jamaica] and if I have not the Kings favor soon I shall be left behind and truly Sir that would be the Greatest Misfortune of My whole life to lose so many years Service and Just Expectation from so Just and Good a Master for a business of ten years distance [the Leisler trial]."[73]

---

Amer. Antiq. Soc., and two further copies, one in Dudley's hand and adding mention of a further letter of endorsement from the Reverend John Howe, are in Blathwayt Papers, BL 259, Hunt. Lib.). Dudley also cited the help of Mr. [John?] Shower in writing to Lord Portland in his favor: Dudley to [Blathwayt], Aug. 12, 1701, Dudley Papers.

[72] Ashurst to Mather, Aug. 30, 1697, Letterbook of Sir Henry Ashurst, fol. 152; Hutchinson, *History of Massachusetts-Bay*, II, 64n.; Leo F. Stock, *Proceedings and Debates of the British Parliaments Respecting North America*, 113–117; *Collections of the New-York Historical Society for the Year 1868* (New York, 1868), 348–357; Documents relating to the Act reversing Leisler's attainder, [May 3, 1695], *CSP Col., 1693–1696*, no. 1803.

[73] Ashurst to Winthrop, July 10, 1701, Memorial of Ashurst to the Lords Justices, [Nov.? 1701], Mass. Hist. Soc., *Collections*, 6th ser., V (1892), 89–92; Sir William Ashurst to Thomas Hopkins, Nov. 13, 1701, *Calendar of State Papers, Domestic Series, of the Reign of William and Mary, 1700–1702*, 445; Stephen Mason to Elisha Cooke,

But at length his years of lobbying paid off. The political atmosphere was favorable, with the tide of Whitehall opinion against the chartered governments at its height and royal officials receptive to Dudley's promises to strengthen Massachusetts's dependence upon the crown. Besides the backing of the bishops and Tories he had solicited, Dudley secured at least the acquiescence if not the active support of such moderates in the government as Lord Treasurer Godolphin, Secretary of State James Vernon, Lord Keeper Sir Nathan Wright, Speaker Robert Harley (an important channel to the dissenting community), and William's new army commander, the Earl of Marlborough, the latter swayed in Dudley's favor by his old comrade in arms, Lord Cutts. At the king's side in Holland, Blathwayt worked on his client's behalf.[74] Back in Whitehall, agent Constantine Phipps discreetly recognized that Dudley "hath deservedly a great interest at Court" and also lent his aid. Ashurst's principal patron, Lord Somers, meanwhile, was fully occupied fighting for his political life against charges of impeachment. Sir Henry found himself, as he expressed it, "standing at the stake alone."[75] A last hurdle suddenly arose when King William died in March 1702, but Dudley managed

---

July 7, 1701, Moody, *Saltonstall Papers*, 267–268, and Sept. 23, 1701, Winthrop Papers; Secretary Vernon to the Board of Trade, June 18, 1701, Journal of the Board of Trade, Nov. 13, 1701, Commission and Instructions of Dudley as governor of New Hampshire and Massachusetts, Dec. 11, 1701, *CSP Col., 1701*, nos. 553, 1001, 1066–1069; Dudley to [Blathwayt], July 22, 1701, Dudley Papers. Dudley's anxieties were doubtless heightened by the weakening of the Tories' influence at court: Horwitz, *Parliament, Policy and Politics*, 299. As late as December, 1701, it was rumored in New England that Cornbury would receive Massachusetts as well as New York.

[74] Dudley to [Blathwayt], July 22–Aug. 22, 1701, Dudley Papers; Dudley to Robert Harley, Nov. 1, 1701, Portland Manuscripts, B.M. Loan, 29/134, British Library; Godfrey Dellius to Paul Dudley, Sept. 16, 1701, Mass. Hist. Soc., *Collections*, 6th ser., III (1889), 523. Godolphin, Wright, Jersey, and the Archbishop of Canterbury were all among the Lords Justices at this time, the body before which Ashurst and Dudley clashed in July: Ashurst to Wait Winthrop, July 10, 1701, *ibid.*, 6th ser., V (1892), 89. Ashurst ascribed Dudley's success to the influence of Rochester, Godolphin, the Bishop of London, and Blathwayt in particular: to Cotton Mather, July 17, to [Massachusetts], July 18, 1701, Letterbook of Sir Henry Ashurst, foll. 198v., 196v.

[75] Phipps to Lieutenant Governor Stoughton, Dec. 11, 1701, Mass. Archives, LI, 137; Ashurst to [Massachusetts], July 10, 1701, Letterbook of Sir Henry Ashurst, fol. 192v.

to get his commission renewed and sailed for Boston the following month.

Dudley's return to Massachusetts as governor was the personal triumph of one who had perceived far earlier than most of his fellow New Englanders the implications of the growth of royal authority in America and the ways by which such authority could be enlisted to advance his own ambitions. Equally notable, however, and unduly neglected, is the extent to which the colonists themselves participated in his odyssey. As early as 1693, Dudley had regained enough of his old prestige within Massachusetts to come within two votes of election to the council by the Tory-infiltrated General Court. Though back in England the following year, he remained in close contact with his friends at home, and Phips's antics soon led a number of influential colonists, among them Lieutenant Governor Stoughton, Secretary Addington, Speakers Nathaniel Byfield and John Leverett, and the Reverend John Higginson of Salem, to look to Dudley as his successor. Higginson's letter to a Presbyterian colleague in London, John Howe, criticizing Phips and recommending Dudley, reveals the mixture of patriotic sentiment and hardheaded calculation that inspired their choice. In contrast to Phips's uncouth ways—"the lowness of his Education and parts, his Natural passionateness, his unacquaintedness with the Affairs of Government"—Dudley was "of an Honorable family, Educated at our Colledge, a learned pious man, a member of the Church at Roxbury, of accomplished abilitys every way, one that is known amongst us and thoroughly knows the affairs of N[ew] E[ngland]." Moreover, added Higginson:

> If we should have a high Church of England-man or some Huffing Hectoring Blade (who it may be having don Service in the Warre is to be rewarded with Some government abroad, as at Barbadoes N. York Ec.) or if any hungry courtier or any Stranger that knows not N. E. (as Exodus 1.8) and will not reguard the Interest of these Churches, But the contrary, it may be a great affliction to us, if Strangers and those that hate us should [rule] over us. Therefore I do humbly and earnestly recommend to yourself, and Such as you know to be cordiall friends to N. E., to consider for us, whither

there can be anyone found fitter for us in this present State of things, then this Honoured Gentleman Mr. D.[76]

Joseph Dudley, in sum, was the man most nearly cast in New England's traditional mold of godly, genteel leadership who yet also seemed acceptable to Whitehall.

Ashurst thwarted these plans in 1695, but upon Bellomont's death, this Dudleian "party," as Wait Winthrop christened it, moved smoothly into action. Acting Governor Stoughton and Byfield on the council obstructed attempts to send Winthrop over as agent and possible rival candidate. Speaker Leverett wrote to deny Ashurst's claim to speak for Massachusetts. Addington and Byfield were put forward for the lieutenant governorship to complete the Dudley ticket. Moreover, Dudley was able to produce the names of other colonists, among them William and Richard Partridge (who had now deserted their alliance with Ashurst), William Vaughan, Richard Waldron, David Waterhouse, "Mr. Richards," Jeremiah Dummer, Benjamin Gillam, the Reverend John Danforth, and "young Woodbridge," who either by letter or in person supported his appointment.[77]

---

[76] Chapter 5, note 76, preceding; Higginson to How[e], Aug. 1, 1694, Moody, *Saltonstall Papers,* 214–215. Those whom contemporaries referred to as the "party" backing Dudley for governor can be identified from such evidence as Sir Henry Ashurst to [Increase?] Mather, May 5, 1695, Hutchinson, *History of Massachusetts-Bay,* II, 64n.; Wait Winthrop to Ashurst, [Aug.–Sept., 1699], Mass. Hist. Soc., *Collections,* 6th ser., V (1892), 47; John Leverett to John Cotton, Oct. 9, 1695, Saltonstall Papers, Fol. XI, C; and the events of Phips's administration. Both Leverett and his former pupil, Henry Newman, visited Dudley in England: thus Godard Oakes's letter of attorney to Leverett, *ibid.,* Fol. XI, D, and Newman to Fitz-John Winthrop, Feb. 27, 1697, Winthrop Papers. Reports reaching New England of Dudley's progress during these years can also be found in James Noyes to Samuel Sewall, Mar. 12, 1694, *New England Historical and Genealogical Register,* XLIX (1895), 286; Stephen Wesendunck to John Usher, Mar. 15, 1695, Jeffries Papers, III, 16; John Cotton to Rowland Cotton, May 18, 1694, Miscellaneous Bound MSS., 1694–1700, Mass. Hist. Soc.

[77] Wait Winthrop to Sir Henry Ashurst, [Aug.–Sept., 1699], Ashurst to Winthrop and others, July 10, 1701, to Winthrop, Mar. 25, 1701, Mass. Hist. Soc., *Collections,* 6th ser., V (1892), 47, 89–91, 109 (a more legible version of the July 10 letter is in Letterbook of Sir Henry Ashurst, foll. 192v.–193); Dudley to [Blathwayt], Aug. 22, 1701, Dudley Papers; Stephen Mason to Elisha Cooke, Sept. 23, 1701, Winthrop Papers; Byfield to Dudley, Aug. 7, 1701, "Extracts from Severall Letters from New England," [Apr. 3–Oct. 28, 1701], Blathwayt Papers, BL 258, 256, Hunt. Lib.

Finally, Dudley crowned his triumph by winning over the Mathers, those ministers, he told Speaker Robert Harley, "whom Sir H. Ashurst has call'd his pole starrs." A honeyed letter to Cotton pointed out the dangerous consequences of the appointment of an alien governor and of the continued federation of Massachusetts with New York, especially at a time when the crown was pressing changes upon the colonies: "Interest and management will be very different from what sometimes they have been." He would value the Mathers' guidance in correcting his past mistakes. "Absence," he concluded, "has given Mee a true Vallue of My Country and the Religion and Virtue that dwells in it to a show of which I have a right by my birth and Education and if I may obtain a short enjoyment of it in My age which is Now come upon mee I shall gladly tell my tale and hope to dye in peace."[78] This elegant plea arrived just as the Mathers, at odds with Bellomont over the government of Harvard and his favoring of the Cooke faction, and furious at the latter's attempts to recover the old charter, were seeking new channels of political influence. Clasping this seemingly humbled sheep to their bosoms, they responded with florid letters of support. The outgunned Ashurst could muster letters only from four of his Massachusetts correspondents, Cooke, Wait Winthrop, Elisha Hutchinson, and Peter Sergeant; and, to his stupefaction, he found Dudley hailed as both the prerogative and the popular choice.[79]

Judging by the talk of violent resistance and even assassination which greeted Dudley in Boston, Ashurst's indignation was well

---

[78] Dudley to Harley, Nov. 1, 1701, Portland MSS., B.M. Loan, 29/134; Dudley to [Cotton Mather], May 10, 1701, Curwin Papers, II, 41, Amer. Antiq. Soc.

[79] Cotton Mather to Dudley, Aug. 25, 1701, Silverman, *Selected Letters of Cotton Mather*, 64–66; letter of Increase Mather, Aug. 7, 1701 in "Extracts from Severall Letters," Blathwayt Papers, BL 256 Hunt. Lib.; Sewall, *Diary*, I, 452; Sir Henry Ashurst to Wait Winthrop, July 10, 1701, to [Increase Mather], May 5, 1701, to Cotton Mather, July 17, 1701, Letterbook of Sir Henry Ashurst, foll. 192v., 191v., 198v.; Ashurst to Increase Mather, Mar. 25, 1702, Hutchinson, *History of Massachusetts-Bay*, II, 92n. The Mathers' emotions during these months are evident in Cotton's hysterical outburst against the startled and unoffending Sewall: Sewall, *Diary*, I, 454–456. For Bellomont's opinion of "Mr. Mather's selfishnesse and pedantick pride," see his letter to Sewall, Aug. 14, 1700, *New England Historical and Genealogical Register*, XIX (1865), 236.

founded.[80] Dudley had won the battle by concentrating his slim but mobile forces precisely when and where they were needed. As significant as this "popular" participation in Dudley's appointment, moreover, are the signs that it was the key to his ultimate confirmation. Despite the array of court influence that had secured him nomination to the post, Ashurst had been able to block the passage of his commission by claiming that Dudley's past record made him unacceptable to the people of Massachusetts. Dudley, in turn, had beaten Ashurst at his own game by showing that, so far as the evidence available in London could show, it was Ashurst who lacked popular backing. "If either your Counsel or Representatives had addressed against him and sent itt to mee," Ashurst complained to Wait Winthrop, "hee could not have gone."[81] This is not to imply that Whitehall officials stood ready to appoint the colonists' choice; they looked, above all, for a governor who would preserve "a due dependence" upon the crown. Yet, as in earlier days when appointing Phips or seeking a compromise short of confiscating the Massachusetts charter, they were alive to the troubles abroad and pressures at home likely to follow upon ignoring colonial sentiment in either appointing or maintaining a governor. This sensitivity, and the colonists' perception of its existence and the ways by which it could be engaged, functioned as a safety valve for the imperial system, ensuring a certain measure of instability and insecurity among officeholders but forestalling the explosion of insurrection. It was in large measure the utilization of these channels of communication and intrigue across the Atlantic that ensured for three-quarters of a century that the events of 1689 were indeed a revolution that made other revolutions unnecessary.

---

[80] George Larkin to the Board of Trade, Oct. 14, 1701, C.O. 5/862, no. 79; Deposition of Joshua Gee, Sept. 21, 1702, Chamberlain Collection, F.1.5.

[81] Ashurst to Winthrop, Mar. 25, 1702, Mass. Hist. Soc., *Collections*, 6th ser., V (1892), 109.

Long the besieger, Dudley was soon himself besieged by those who had profited by observing his tactics. Intrinsic to any prolonged episode of "succession politics" was the period of reckoning when the new governor's campaign promises came home to roost, and Dudley had scattered his with desperate abandon. Anglicans who had expected, as one wrote back to London, that the governor would "give all possible encouragement to the congregation of the Church of England in this place" found Dudley's subsequent response lukewarm and their share in the fruits of office disappointing. An internal split within their Boston congregation intensified the complaints sent back to England. In consequence, when the Boston Anglican merchant Charles Hobby visited London in 1704 and sought to displace Dudley from the governorship, he received the favor of the Bishop of London, an ardent advocate of the spread of the Church of England in America.[82] Ironically, he also bore the good wishes of the Mathers, whose alliance with Dudley had lasted for less than a week after the latter's arrival in Boston. Cotton recorded in his diary how he had urged the new governor not to be unduly influenced by either him and his father or Byfield and Leverett; "the Wretch went unto these Men and told them, that I had advised him, to be no ways advised by them: and inflamed them into an implacable Rage against me." In the following year, the Mathers wrote to Increase's old acquaintance

---

[82] George Keith to John Chamberlayne, June 11, 1702, Hawkins, *Historical Notices,* 30; Joseph Dudley and others to the Archbishop of Canterbury, Dec. 23, 1703, Rev. Samuel Myles to Archdeacon Beveridge, Jan. 4, 1704, Perry, *Historical Collections,* III, 74–76; John Chamberlayne to Dudley, Aug. 16, 1704, Mass. Hist. Soc., *Collections,* 6th ser., III (1889), 545; Dudley to [William Blathwayt], July 30, 1705, Blathwayt Papers, BL 262, Hunt. Lib.; Dudley to the Bishop of London, Aug. 1, 1705, Fulham Papers, IV, 11; Increase Mather to [Samuel Penhallow?], Dec. 4, 1704, Belknap Papers, 1664–1744, no. 16; Members of the Church of England in Boston to the Board of Trade, Feb. 4, 1706, C.O. 5/864, no. 63. Hobby had returned to Massachusetts from Jamaica shortly before Dudley's arrival. Promoted by the governor to colonel of the Boston regiment, he fell out with the governor over privateering ventures he mounted with his brother-in-law, John Colman. He may also have travelled to London to help in pressing the Mason-Allen claims to New Hampshire since he appears to have been financially involved with these claims even before he bought a share in them in 1706: *N. H. Provincial Papers,* XXIX, 167–172; Jeffries Papers, XV, 114. For Hobby's career, see Alison Olson in George W. Brown *et al., Dictionary of Canadian Biography,* II, 288–290.

and adversary the Earl of Nottingham, now again secretary of state, to urge Dudley's replacement by Hobby.[83]

To judge by the reports flowing back to Boston, Hobby came close to success. News arrived in quick succession that he had received a knighthood and the backing of several powerful ministers and would soon be governor. "A fine *hobby*," punned a Connecticut minister with earthy humor, "will mount our *bay* jade." Dudley, preoccupied by the war and by his quarrels with Rhode Island and Connecticut, was slow to shore up his defenses in London, and not until early 1706, judging by letters to Blathwayt, did he perceive the seriousness of the threat to his position.[84] His problems deepened as he came under suspicion within Massachusetts of complicity in the activities of several merchants caught trading with the French under the pretext of exchanging prisoners.[85] In mid-1707, a petition was presented to the queen calling for his removal. The majority of its twenty signers were merchants and others in London concerned with New England, the most prominent being Ashurst's and Mather's old ally, Stephen Mason, and Nathaniel Higginson, a son of the Reverend John, who had prospered in the service of the East India Company. New Englanders signing included William Partridge (turncoat yet again), Thomas Newton, William Wharton, John Hinckes of New Hampshire, and John Calley, a lawyer and former representative of Marblehead.[86]

---

[83] Cotton Mather, *Diary*, ed. Ford, I, 465; Cotton Mather to Lord Nottingham, Nov. 26, 1703, Increase Mather to [Lord Nottingham], Dec. 8, 1703, Pubs. Col. Soc. Mass., *Transactions*, XIX (1916–1917), 153–156 (the recipient of these letters is sometimes identified as Lord Hatton, but this transcription, from Addit. MSS., 29549, foll. 109–111, correctly gives Nottingham as the recipient).

[84] Sewall, *Diary*, I, 531, 537; Cotton Mather to Samuel Penhallow, Dec. 4, 1704, Silverman, *Selected Letters of Cotton Mather*, 70; Increase Mather to [Penhallow?], Dec. 4, 1704, Belknap Papers, 1664–1744, no. 16; Rev. James Noyes to Fitz-John Winthrop, Aug. 29, 1706, Mass. Hist. Soc., *Collections*, 6th ser., III (1889), 346; Dudley to [Blathwayt], Feb. 1, Apr. 13, 1706, Blathwayt Papers, BL 265, 264, Hunt. Lib.; Luttrell, *Brief Historical Relation*, VI, 152.

[85] George M. Waller, *Samuel Vetch, Colonial Enterpriser*, 82–99, is the best treatment of this complex episode.

[86] Hutchinson, *History of Massachusetts-Bay*, II, 118n. Partridge's defection may have surprised Dudley as much as it had done Ashurst eight years before: recommending him for a customs post in 1706, the governor had characterized him as "truly the best man in New Hampshire notwithstanding all his faults": Dudley to [Blathwayt], Feb. 1, 1706, Blathwayt Papers, BL 265, Hunt. Lib.

The petition was backed by two pamphlets printed in London with Ashurst's assistance and containing material supplied at least in part by the Mathers, accusing the governor of crimes ranging from condoning illegal trade to accepting bribes.[87] Dudley's position was further eroded by the ignominious failure of an attempt to capture the French base at Port Royal and, in London, by the appointment of the Earl of Sunderland, a Whig sympathetic to Ashurst's suit, as secretary of state, and by a subsequent purge of Tories, including William Blathwayt, from the Board of Trade. In September 1707, Ashurst jubilantly informed Wait Winthrop "that I have, after all my paines, expence, and labor for so many yeares removed for-ever from being your oppresive Governer Mr. D."[88]

Yet the reports of Dudley's political demise once more proved premature. Again, he managed to mobilize his supporters at the crucial moment. Exerting all his political influence, he secured votes from both houses of the Massachusetts General Court condemning the Mason-Higginson petition, and his rebuttal of its charges, likewise printed as a pamphlet in London, was backed by a spate of counter-petitions praising his administration from the General Courts, minis-

---

[87]Philopolites [Cotton Mather?], *A Memorial of the Present Deplorable State of New-England*, [Cotton Mather?], *The Deplorable State of New-England*, both reprinted in Mass. Hist. Soc., *Collections*, 5th ser., VI (1879), 33*–64*, 97*–131*; Thomas J. Holmes, *Cotton Mather*, II, 664–671, I, 240–263. Evidence of Ashurst's hand in the printing of the second work beyond that cited by Holmes can be found in Ashurst to the Earl of Sunderland, Nov. 17, [1708], Miscellaneous MSS., HM 22272, Hunt. Lib., but Ashurst disclaims authorship ("the booke is just as it came over from New England") and there is too much evidence to the contrary to credit the suggestion of Richard Bushman that Ashurst authored *The Deplorable State:* Bushman, "Corruption and Power in Provincial America," 86 n. 15. Thus, in particular, the close parallels between passages in the work and Cotton Mather's letter in Silverman, *Selected Letters of Cotton Mather*, 74–76. Two of the letters printed in *A Memorial* (Mass. Hist. Soc., *Collections*, 5th ser., VI [1879], 40*–43*) were also printed in a London journal, *The Observator* (vol. VI, 35, June 28–July 2, 1707), signed J. M. and Robert Armstrong, a copy of which, brought into New Hampshire, was ordered to be burned by the public hangman: *N. H. Provincial Papers*, II, 567, XVII, 704; Sewall, *Diary*, I, 577.

[88]Ashurst to Winthrop, Sept. 29, 1707, Mass. Hist. Soc., *Collections*, 6th ser., V (1892), 152; Lord Treasurer Godolphin to the Duke of Marlborough, June 17, 1707, Henry L. Snyder, ed., *The Marlborough-Godolphin Correspondence*, II, 823. In his letter of Nov. 17, [1708], Ashurst claimed to have Sunderland's promise of Dudley's dismissal: Miscellaneous MSS., HM 22272, Hunt. Lib.

ters, merchants, and militia officers of both Massachusetts and New Hampshire. Early in 1708, the Privy Council dismissed the charges as "frivolous," and the Board of Trade later assured him of its support. "There is not one stone he hath left unturn'd to keepe him in," reported a chastened Ashurst. "He is a person of such insinuation, such parts, that only Satan himself hath greater."[89]

Within Massachusetts, the storm clouds lingered. The Mathers reached new heights of fury as Dudley took his revenge by persuading the General Court to approve the election of his ally John Leverett as president of Harvard, thwarting their hopes of regaining their influence over the college. Cotton and Increase responded with vituperative public letters denouncing the governor's "reign of bribery."[90] The much respected Samuel Sewall rebelled against Dudley's hard-driving management of the Council, withdrew his vote exonerating the governor from the charges of complicity in illegal trade, and placed the reasons for his dissent in print. Subsequently, he wrote to England to express his support for the appointment of Nathaniel Higginson as governor.[91] In the wake of these public criticisms, the elections of 1708 strengthened the forces opposed to Dudley in the

---

[89] Sewall, *Diary*, I, 574–578; Mass. Archives, XX, 109, 111, Court Records, VIII, Nov. 1, 4, 7, 20, 21, 28, 1707; *Boston News-Letter*, Nov. 24–Dec. 1, 1707; *A Modest Enquiry into the Grounds and Occasions of a Late Pamphlet*, 65\*–95\*, especially 84\*–94\*; John Nelson to William Popple, Feb. 11, 1706, Joseph Dudley to the queen, Nov. 10, 1707, Addresses of the Council and Assembly, Officers, and Ministers of New Hampshire, Oct. 22, 1707, C.O. 5/864, nos. 72, 73, 231ii, 235iv–vi; Dudley to Lord Treasurer Godolphin, Nov. 10, 1707, Address of 40 ministers, Feb. 13, 1708, *Calendar of Treasury Papers, 1702–1707*, 547–549, *1708–1714*, 10; Henry Newman to Benjamin Colman, June 7, 1707, *New England Historical and Genealogical Register*, V (1851), 59; *N. H. Provincial Papers*, III, 350–352; Proceedings in Council, June 12, 1707–Jan. 22, 1708, *APC Col.*, II, no. 1029; Luttrell, *Brief Historical Relation*, VI, 185, 193, 260; Kimball, *Joseph Dudley*, 188 (although the endorsed copy of the pamphlet cited in *ibid.*, 188n. cannot now be found in the official papers); Board of Trade to Dudley, July 23, 1708, C.O. 5/912, 481; Ashurst to Wait Winthrop, Aug. 24, 1708, Mass. Hist. Soc., *Collections*, 6th ser., V (1892), 173.

[90] Morison, *Harvard College*, II, 548–556; Increase Mather to Joseph Dudley, Jan. 20, 1708, Cotton Mather to Dudley, Jan. 20, 1708, Mass. Hist. Soc., *Collections*, III (1810), 126–134.

[91] Sewall, *Diary*, II, 578–580 (a copy in Sewall's hand is in Curwin Papers, III, 87, Amer. Antiq. Soc.); Sewall to Sir Henry Ashurst, Feb. 25, 1708, to Higginson, Mar. 10, 1708, Mass. Hist. Soc., *Collections*, 6th ser., I (1886), 359–363.

General Court, encouraging the representatives to address Whitehall in protest against his political tactics.[92] But Dudley, now securely anchored to his political base in London, rode out these local squalls. Nathaniel Higginson died, removing one rival, and Dudley managed to win back Hobby's allegiance, probably by agreeing to further the errant colonel's military ambitions—Hobby led a Massachusetts regiment to the capture of Port Royal in 1710 and became lieutenant governor of the new crown colony of Nova Scotia.[93]

A last internal challenge to Dudley's rule arose in 1714 when he was menaced simultaneously by the ambitions of a group of merchants seeking to promote a private bank, by the resurgent discontent of a faction of Boston's Anglicans, and by the formidable figure (weighing in, on his own pair of scales, at over two hundred and fifty pounds) of Nathaniel Byfield, once Dudley's close ally but now his embittered opponent. Linking and, it would seem, directing these forces, was Byfield's former son-in-law William Tailer, an Anglican who was a leading supporter of the bank and at odds with Dudley since his unexpected return from England with a commission as the province's lieutenant governor.[94] Late in the year, Byfield went to London to seek a charter for the bank and to solicit for the governorship. He failed in both aims. Yet his presence there helped to ensure

---

[92] Joseph Dudley to the Board of Trade, July 10, 1708, C.O. 5/865, no. 6; Philopolites, *The Deplorable State,* 101*; and, for the election of 1708, Chapter 7, note 83 following.

[93] Sir Henry Ashurst to Increase Mather, Oct. 10, 1709, Mass. Hist. Soc., *Collections,* 6th ser., V (1892), 199.

[94] Kimball, *Joseph Dudley,* 167–174; Andrew M. Davis, *Currency and Banking in the Province of Massachusetts-Bay,* II, 82–87; Hutchinson, *History of Massachusetts-Bay,* II, 154–159; Attestation of Samuel Myles, Feb. 17, 1714, Mass. Hist. Soc., *Collections,* VII (1801), 216–217; Gov. Jonathan Belcher to Lt. Gov. David Dunbar, July 23, 1733, *ibid.,* 6th ser., VI (1893), 336; Byfield to John Leverett, June 19, July 21, 1714, Moody, *Saltonstall Papers,* 314–316; Sewall, *Diary,* I, 479. The combination of "out-groups" such as the disgruntled Anglicans and the heirs of the old-charter faction behind the bank scheme is evident in the 240 signatures on the two petitions presented in London in 1715, C.O. 5/866, nos. 44i, ii. Launched by a group headed by Elisha Cooke, Jr., William Payne, Oliver Noyes, and John Colman, men generally suspicious of royal authority, the private bank project seems to have passed increasingly into the hands of those willing to take its case to England.

that Dudley's term of office, begun at Queen Anne's accession, would not long survive her death. Early in 1715, as part of the political spoils seized by the triumphant Whigs, the governorship of Massachusetts was given to an English army officer, Colonel Elizeus Burges.[95]

A glance back at the successive candidacies of Hobby, Higginson, and Byfield reveals the extent to which the colonists were now prepared to trim their hopes to the realities of imperial politics. No longer did they put forward those such as Wait Winthrop whose visions of a restoration of Massachusetts's ancient privileges ensured his instant rejection at Whitehall. Instead, they effectually acknowledged Dudley's own fitness for his office by endeavoring to supplant him with men who shared many of his outward characteristics, if rarely his political skills. Cotton Mather laid out the necessary qualifications in his effusive (and doubtless bitterly regretted) description of Dudley in 1701 as "a gentleman that is our own countryman, and perfectly understands how to serve the King, as well as how to ease the people."[96] Hobby, Higginson, and Byfield were all native New Englanders. Like agents Dummer and Newman, they were men "from amongst our selves." Yet each was able or willing to present himself in person at Whitehall, and each had won sufficient renown beyond the borders of New England to make plausible the belief that they would be acceptable in London—Hobby through his commercial contacts and service in Jamaica, Higginson through his prominence as governor of Madras in India, and Byfield by reason of his office as vice-admiralty judge and his family connections in England. True, Hobby was an Anglican and a man of notoriously supple morals. To the Mathers, however, the first characteristic offered but one more opportunity to recommend him to such as Nottingham and the Bishop of

---

[95] Petition of Nathaniel Byfield to be governor of Massachusetts and New Hampshire, [1715], Egerton MSS., 929, fol. 146; Jeremiah Dummer to Benjamin Colman, Jan. 15, 1714 [1715], Mass. Hist. Soc., *Collections*, V (1798), 197–198.

[96] Mather to Dudley, Aug. 25, 1701, Silverman, *Selected Letters of Cotton Mather*, 66.

London. As for the second, desperate diseases—the reign of the "Wretch" and "Apostate" Dudley and the exclusion of the Mathers from their proper role as "faithful monitors" of the government—demanded desperate remedies.

The failure of these candidacies, moreover, points to the tactics and qualifications that could maintain a governor in office. Perpetually exposed to complaints by reason of his position, a royal governor could not afford to take refuge in dignified silence, and Dudley took every opportunity to extol his administration's achievements both in London and at home. He kept the Board of Trade constantly informed of events. He showered flattering and solicitous letters upon such powers at Whitehall as Marlborough, Godolphin, and Godolphin's successor as Lord Treasurer, Robert Harley, as well as Lord Weymouth and William Blathwayt.[97] He strove to allay the suspicions of the Bishop of London, explaining how his powers to help local Anglicans were circumscribed by a legislature "amongst whom is not one of the Church of England, not so much as a favourer as I know of." He worked to disarm the London Quakers' suspicions of his administration's attitude toward their sect. He also kept alive his ties to English Congregationalist and Presbyterian communities by cultivating the friendship of Sir William Ashurst, Sir Henry's more moderate brother and governor of the New England Company.[98] Within Massachusetts and New Hampshire, meanwhile, Dudley regularly

---

[97] Dudley to the Duke of Marlborough, 1708, 1709, Historical Manuscripts Commission, *The Manuscripts of the Duke of Marlborough,* 35, 37; Dudley to Harley, July 7, 1712, Portland MSS., B.M. Loan, 29/134; Dudley to Blathwayt, May 9, 1705–Apr. 13, 1706, Blathwayt Papers, BL 269, 260–265, Hunt. Lib.; Viscount Weymouth to John Chamberlayne, July 9, 1703, Mass. Hist. Soc., *Collections,* 6th ser., III (1889), 541; Sir Henry Ashurst to Wait Winthrop, Aug. 24, 1708, *ibid.,* 6th ser., V (1892), 173–174.

[98] Dudley to Bishop Henry Compton, Aug. 1, 1705, Fulham Palace MSS., IV, 11; Dudley to Sir William Ashurst, Nov. 15, 1710, John W. Ford, ed., *Some Correspondence between the Governors and Treasurers of the New England Company in London and the Commissioners of the United Colonies in America, the Missionaries of the Company, and Others,* 92; Jeremiah Dummer to [Joseph Dudley], Feb. 19, 1711, Miscellaneous Bound MSS., 1701–13, Mass. Hist. Soc.; Hutchinson, *History of Massachusetts-Bay,* II, 140.

addressed the assembled General Courts on the state of each province and outlined his future policies.[99]

To both sides of the Atlantic, the governor could boast of some telling successes. At a time when the Board of Trade despaired of achieving any intercolonial cooperation in defense, he dispatched two companies of volunteers, the first ever to leave New England in royal service, for the protection of Jamaica.[100] He secured the persons and plunder of a group of privateers turned pirates and, following their trial and public execution, forwarded nearly eight hundred ounces of gold worth over four thousand pounds to a grateful English treasury.[101] Most important of all, despite the ill-success of his expeditions into Maine and against Port Royal, his defense of the frontiers was so energetic and tenacious that only two major settlements, Deerfield and Haverhill, were seriously damaged during the thirteen years of his governorship. To judge by the language of the colonists' petitions on his behalf in 1707 and by the praise extended by officials in Whitehall, it was this capacity to protect his subjects through policies that even the suspicious Sewall acknowledged as "truly Excellent" that was Dudley's strongest card in his fight to stay in office, and the one that none of his domestic rivals could match.

Dudley also benefitted from the lingering distaste still felt by many colonists for their ties to the London government. Traditionalists such as Elisha Cooke deplored what they saw as the governor's corrupt and autocratic rule, yet hesitated to acknowledge London's right to intervene by appealing to the crown for redress. Their opposition, therefore, rarely extended beyond domestic politics and so posed no direct threat to Dudley's tenure of office. Conversely, those who did appeal could seldom muster much popular backing. The Nathaniel Higgin-

---

[99] Dudley's speeches can be found in *N. H. Provincial Papers,* III, 271 *et seq.,* and, in his own hand, in Mass. Archives, CVIII, 1–106 (1702–1712).

[100] Herbert L. Osgood, *The American Colonies in the Eighteenth Century,* I, 401–402; Pubs. Col. Soc. Mass., *Transactions,* XVIII (1915–1916), 84–93.

[101] *Mass. Acts and Resolves,* VIII, 386–398; Dow and Edmonds, *Pirates,* 99–115. For the political effects of the gold's arrival, Cotton Mather to Stephen Sewall, May 2, 1706, Silverman, *Selected Letters of Cotton Mather,* 71.

son petition of 1707 is a case in point. Apparently assembled by Ashurst and his old ally Stephen Mason after Hobby had declined to bell the cat by pressing charges of his own, it drew neither the signatures of the leading London merchants trading to New England nor any widespread backing from the colonists themselves, save for those such as Thomas Newton and William Partridge who were themselves ambitious for royal office.[102] As a matter of strategy, therefore, a governor in Dudley's position was well advised to incur a measure of domestic opposition by his royalist stance if he could thereby guard against those who might unseat him by presenting themselves to London as more committed to preserving a due dependence upon the crown.

Domestic opposition, moreover, could be disarmed by the realization that a governor's removal was likely to bring down a remedy worse than the disease. Such was the case during Dudley's last years in office. By 1711, with the Tories firmly in power in England and dissenting meetinghouses under siege by the London mob, it had become clear that in regard to the governorship, as Sir William Ashurst informed Increase Mather in a letter widely circulated within Massachusetts, "you are much better as you are at present. For as Things are here now, we cannot expect any Change for the better."[103] Three years later, when Queen Anne's death threatened Dudley's continuation in office, the Mathers wrote to Ashurst to urge him, albeit with restrained enthusiasm, to use his influence to secure Dudley's retention. "I believe," wrote Increase, "the generality of the people had rather have him continued than to have one sent from England especially one whose sentiments in Religion shall differ from what is the general profession of this Country." Rebutting, in effect, his own attack upon Dudley six years before, he added: "Whether he has bin guilty of such Notorious Bribery as some say is none of my business to

---

[102] Hutchinson, *History of Massachusetts-Bay,* II, 118n.; Joseph Dudley to the queen, Nov. 10, 1707, C.O. 5/864, no. 231ii (foll. 455v.–456). Of the twenty signers of the Higginson petition, only Mason's name appears on other contemporary petitions of those trading to New England, such as those cited in note 54, preceding.

[103] Sewall's memorandum of Ashurst's letter to Mather, Jan. 31, 1711, Mass. Hist. Soc., *Collections,* 6th ser., I (1886), 411; also *ibid.,* 6th ser., V (1892), 231.

enquire. Since his estate is here, it is in his Interest to Seeke the well-fare of the Country." Bribes paid to Dudley, in other words, at least did not swell the deficit in the province's balance of payments. Cotton, unlike his father, still cherished hopes for the success of Hobby, then in London, especially now that King George's accession had returned the Whigs to power. But, he wrote to Ashurst, "I perceive that some are even still of the opinion that we had better still have [Dudley] for our Governor than some that may be *strangers* to us, or *not of our nation.*"[104] Not all could swallow this bitter cup; led by Oliver Noyes of Boston, a close ally of Elisha Cooke and a leader of the group promoting the private bank, the representatives declined to join in an address to the crown seeking Dudley's retention. Later, when the usual letters authorizing governors to remain in office following the sovereign's death did not arrive, the council in a curious fit of legalism spurred on by long-suppressed resentment briefly superseded Dudley from his post.[105] Yet they made no attempt to precipitate his removal. Clearly, even the governor's most bitter enemies had learned to calculate the risks of seeking his replacement.

Indeed, as essential as the task of advancing candidates for the governorship had become that of dissuading others from accepting the post; the events that followed Dudley's fall from office in 1715 demonstrated that here too the colonists were now taking the initiative. At the root of the Mathers' endorsement of Dudley lay their fear that, given the crown's concern for colonial defense and its preference for military men as governors, some army veteran—"a disbanded, boisterous, terrible *Flanderkin*"—would be imposed upon Massachusetts. Save that Colonel Burges, the new governor named in January 1715,

---

[104] Increase Mather to Ashurst, Nov. 22, 1714, Miscellaneous MSS., HM 22310, Hunt. Lib.; Cotton Mather to Ashurst, Oct. 12, 1714, Silverman, *Selected Letters of Cotton Mather*, 153–154. Increase also spoke in similar terms even prior to news of the queen's death: Letter of June, 1714, Increase Mather Letters, typescript, Mass. Hist. Soc. Dudley had mellowed also: indeed his funeral sermon hints at the onset of senility: Benjamin Colman, *Ossa Josephi*, 41.

[105] Sewall, *Diary*, II, 771; Jeremiah Dummer to Benjamin Colman, Jan. 15, 1714 [1715], Mass. Hist. Soc., *Collections*, V (1798), 198; Worthington C. Ford, "The Governor and Council of the Province of the Massachusetts Bay, August 1714–March 1715," 327–361. Dudley's declining health may also have prompted the council to take action.

had served in Spain rather than Flanders, he was otherwise the embodiment of such fears, hard-bitten, profane, a known rake and duellist, John Higginson's "Huffing Hectoring Blade . . . that knows not N. E. . . . and will not Reguard the Interest of these Churches."[106] Yet Burges was no Andros. While still in London, his favors were openly for sale and they found a ready market amid the colonists' domestic factionalism. The wealthy Byfield, thwarted in his own candidacy, purchased William Tailer's continuance as lieutenant governor. Through Burges and Tailer, it was hoped, the private bank group would achieve its goals. In similar fashion, George Vaughan of New Hampshire secured that province's lieutenant governorship over strenuous objections from the Board of Trade.[107] Agent Jeremiah Dummer, by contrast, had incurred the new governor's enmity (forcibly expressed in Burges's threats to slit Dummer's throat) for his attempts to retain Dudley in office. Back in Boston, therefore, Tailer and his allies worked to discredit Dummer by spreading stories of his Tory associates and rakish behavior. To friends in London, Tailer wrote of the steady weakening of "Governor Dudley's interest" and of his plans to assign the agency to Londoner Thomas Sandford, an old friend of his ally in the assembly, Oliver Noyes.[108]

The Dudleians' cause seemed lost. But Byfield made the fatal error of returning to Massachusetts in the fall of 1715 with copies of the new administration's commissions in order to establish Tailer as act-

---

[106] Cotton Mather to Sir William Ashurst, Oct. 12, 1714, to Wait-Still Winthrop, Oct. 6, 1712, Silverman, *Selected Letters of Cotton Mather*, 153, 107; John Higginson to John How[e], Aug. 1, 1694, Moody, *Saltonstall Papers*, 215; Albert Matthews, "Colonel Elizeus Burges," 360–372. On the appointment of army officers, Webb, *The Governors-General*, 463–464 and Appendix; William Byrd, *The Secret Diary of William Byrd of Westover, 1709–1712*, 159.

[107] Dexter, *Extracts from the Itineraries*, 202; William Tailer to Captain Mathews, June 28, 1715, to Francis Nicholson, June 30, 1715, William Tailer Letterbook, Belknap Papers, 1664–1744, no. 70, Mass. Hist. Soc.; *N. H. Provincial Papers*, II, 677; Governor Burges to the Board of Trade, [June 17, 1715], Board of Trade to Secretary Stanhope, Aug. 3, 1715, *CSP Col., 1714–1715*, nos. 470, 547. Burges himself showed little enthusiasm for the private bank: Burges to the Board of Trade, [Aug. 4, 1715], *ibid.*, no. 550i.

[108] Matthews, "Colonel Elizeus Burges," 363–365; Sewall, *Diary*, II, 804, 808, 815, 834; William Tailer to Jeremiah Dummer, July 1, Sept. 3, 1715, to Thomas Sandford, June 3, Sept. 3, 1715, William Tailer Letterbook.

ing governor. Perhaps Burges never intended to follow. In any event, left unchaperoned, he harkened to Dummer's arguments that a royal governor could expect only meager rewards in Massachusetts; for a thousand pounds sterling advanced by Dummer and another New Englander then in London, Jonathan Belcher, he was induced to resign his governorship. In April 1716, the post fell to Samuel Shute, another army colonel but of very different reputation, descended from a renowned dissenting family and a graduate of Charles Morton's Newington Green Academy.[109]

The news of Burges's defection abruptly turned the tables on the Byfield-Tailer faction. Tailer worked frantically to stay in office under Shute. "Now is the time to know if I have any friends left." But to no avail. "Those two Villains Belcher and Dummer," aided by Sir William Ashurst, secured his replacement as lieutenant governor by Dummer's brother William, who was Joseph Dudley's son-in-law. Another Dudley relative, Josiah Willard, purchased the post of province secretary from the English army officer appointed by Burges. Jeremiah Dummer was reappointed agent and continued in his handsome allowance of three hundred pounds sterling a year. George Vaughan lost his lieutenant governorship of New Hampshire. Governor Shute, though courted by all factions upon his arrival in Boston late in 1716, moved in to lodge with Attorney General Paul Dudley, the old governor's son, a decision widely taken to mean, as Sewall mournfully noted, "that he is deliver'd up to a Party." Tailer, humiliated, went off to London to solicit an army pension.[110]

---

[109] Jonathan Belcher to Benjamin Colman, May 31, 1716, Colman Papers, I, Mass. Hist. Soc.; Belcher to the Massachusetts General Court, read Nov. 27, 1718, Mass. Archives, XX, 182–184. Possibly not all the money went to Burges, who assured Tailer "on his honour" he had none of it. Further, there is a hint that some of the initiative (and perhaps some of the money for the plan) came from Dudleians in Massachusetts: Tailer to Oliver Noyes, Feb. 9, 1717, to Thomas Sandford, Oct. 20, 1715, William Tailer Letterbook.

[110] Tailer to Paul Mascarene, July 7, 1716, to [Samuel] Woodward, Sept. 1716, to Oliver Noyes, Feb. 9, 1717, William Tailer Letterbook; Sir William Ashurst to Increase Mather, Mar. 10, 1718, Belknap, *History of New Hampshire*, III, 257–259; Hutchinson, *History of Massachusetts-Bay*, II, 161n.; Sewall, *Diary*, II, 821, 833–834; John Nelson to Henry Lloyd, May 24, Oct. 14, 1717, *Collections of the New-York Historical Society for the Year 1926* (New York, 1927), 218, 224.

Born out of such domestic intrigues, Shute's administration proved troubled and divisive. Six years after his arrival, the disheartened governor simply abandoned the province and returned to England. Yet for aspiring politicians such as Jonathan Belcher, the lesson was plain. Colonists prepared to dabble in the murky and expensive waters of English politics could secure not only lesser prizes but the disposition and perhaps even the possession of the governorship itself. Moreover, the waning influence of the Board of Trade and the departure from its ranks of members who, like Blathwayt, had enjoyed close ties with those in real power made such backstairs fixing easier to arrange. Those who now dominated colonial appointments, Stanhope (Burges's patron) and, after him, Townshend and Newcastle, were party politicians with little interest in or knowledge of the colonies. The Burges episode demonstrated how easily personal obligations and party spoilsmanship could override larger considerations of policy. Fifteen years later, Belcher turned this knowledge to good account in obtaining the governorship of Massachusetts for himself.[111]

The colonists' perceptions of the complex strategies required to secure and hold public office in governments bound into closer dependence upon the crown had a significant effect upon the character of New England's political life in the years following the Glorious Revolution. Naturally, this influence was greatest in those colonies where the crown and its representatives had the most offices to bestow. In Rhode Island and Connecticut, "succession politics" remained almost entirely a domestic matter since their colonists retained the right to choose their own governors and local officials—"an inestimable priviledge," as a weary Jeremiah Dummer informed a friend in Connecticut after a year's hard labor in promoting the succession of Governor Shute.[112] The few dissidents such as Peleg Sanford and

---

[111] Steele, *Politics of Colonial Policy*, 149–150; Henretta, *"Salutary Neglect,"* 23–34, 82–93.

[112] Dummer to Timothy Woodbridge, July 6, 1716, Pubs. Col. Soc. Mass., *Transactions*, VI (1899–1900), 179.

Nathaniel Coddington who accepted royal appointments soon found that such a tactic eroded rather than strengthened their domestic political influence as resentful colonists united against those inviting external intervention. Powerfully as London's supervision affected the two colonies' political development in other ways, their charters effectively screened out the temptations proffered by the crown's array of patronage.

In Massachusetts and New Hampshire, however, the twin sources of political authority embodied in the structure of royal government gave politics a Janus face, turned both to England and to the electorate at home. In each colony, a strong and numerous group remained, centered in the assembly but also represented on the council, which distrusted all collaboration with the crown. The adherents of this group strove to preserve their influence in local affairs and to balance and confine executive power. Set apart from this "country" faction were those who stood ready to participate in the work of royal government. "Courtiers" by reason of duty, inclination, or ambition, less fearful than their fellows of England's corrupting influences, they looked to the crown and its representatives for office and advancement.

During the early years of the eighteenth century, as Timothy Breen has shown, these divisions took on increasing clarity and ideological substance from sermons and pamphlets upholding one persuasion or the other.[113] Court advocates preached the virtues of order and paternal leadership, country writers the necessity of popular vigilance to avert the stifling of liberty by an overmighty government. Court charges that their opponents were little better than "republicans"

---

[113] Breen, *Character of the Good Ruler,* 203–269. Carefully as Breen qualifies his conclusions, I question the picture he presents in three respects: his treating of New England as a single unit during these years; his assumption that the themes of the debates that emerged after 1715 are also those of the two decades prior to 1715; and his tacit equation of ideological and political divisions. In the course of writing this present study I have, by contrast, been more impressed by the differing pace of political development in the various colonies, by the slowness with which coherent ideological divisions appeared after 1689, and by the way in which politicans varied their rhetoric to match their political needs. Nonetheless, Breen's study remains an excellent guide to the development of Puritan political ideas.

[355]

and "commonwealthmen" provoked counterepithets of "Jacobite" and "tory." Party lines began to emerge. Yet the precision and significance of these divisions should not be exaggerated. They were slow to develop: by comparison with the circumstances that were fostering strong party rivalries in England, truly divisive ideological issues were fewer, reverence for authority greater, and the press, the indispensable vehicle for spreading party fervor in England, remained more closely controlled, less highly developed, and essentially apolitical.[114] Not until Governor Shute's administration, and then only in Massachusetts, did a substantial literature of political opposition bloom, drawing upon the writings of English critics of court rule and expressed in such irreverent journals as the Franklins' *New-England Courant*.

Moreover, to accept these divisions as a sufficient explanation of the actual workings of politics is to neglect the composite loyalties and shifting factionalism that pervaded the two colonies' political life in the years following the return of royal government, a complexity arising out of the interweaving of traditional New England attitudes and beliefs with the obligations and opportunities of the connection with the crown. Samuel Sewall, for example, a charter magistrate become royal councillor, never abated his suspicions of Dudley's autocratic ways and vigorous employment of his powers of patronage. Yet

---

[114] For a different picture, suggesting that in Massachusetts and New Hampshire, as in most other American colonies during these years, coherent parties had emerged, paralleling and to a large degree corresponding to those which had emerged in England, see Olson, *Anglo-American Politics,* especially 75–118. Olson's analysis furnishes a highly stimulating overview, but I believe she exaggerates both the coherency and bipolarity of party groupings in New England and the degree of ideological and practical correspondence between these groupings and Whig-Tory divisions in England. Consistent political connections did exist, as between Dudley and the Tories and Bellomont and the Whigs, but all too many others straddled ideological boundaries or shifted according to need and circumstance. From the colonial perspective one reason for this was that differences between Whigs and Tories on colonial policy were slight, certainly slighter than those separating colonists and Englishmen. Also, the issues shaping politics in New England were on the whole quite different from those fueling "the rage of party" in England; only occasionally were the colonists willing or able to take advantage of English party rivalries by portraying their concerns in terms of English issues. For these reasons, and because of the interpretative framework advanced in the text, I have not found Dr. Olson's argument convincing for explaining New England politics of this period.

Sewall also remained deeply committed to the maintenance of executive authority and himself solicited for offices of profit upon occasion. Even Elisha Cooke and his son Elisha, Jr., long among the most prominent critics of royal authority, were not so completely "country" in their attitudes as to refuse office when it was offered.[115] Thrust into a new political context, members of the old ruling group responded in different ways. The majority, like Sewall, clung to their status and sense of duty in striving to infuse the new order with some remnants of the old tradition of godly magistracy. Others, with the Cookes, perceived greater virtue (and greater opportunity to cultivate their own local political interests) in yearnings for the old charter and opposition to Dudley and his successors. A few followed Dudley and Usher in wholeheartedly embracing the aims and perquisites of royal government. Throughout, attitudes and actions mirrored the changing realities of power and position. Samuel Willard, for example, whose blast against Governor Phips in 1694 is often cited as a classic early exposition of a ruler's responsibilities to his people, came to have a new appreciation of a people's obligations to their rulers once his brother-in-law Joseph Dudley had returned to power.[116] Conversely, the Mathers, gallant apologists for Phips's deeds, denounced the self-same practices when they were pursued in rather more modest fashion by Governor Dudley. Their philippics were not empty rhetoric, for they helped to legitimize criticism of authority and thereby sowed the seeds of subsequent country assaults. Yet they must also be perceived as they were by contemporaries, within the context of the province's shifting factionalism.

A prime example of the sinuous course a contemporary might follow in pursuit of influence and office was the career of Nathaniel Byfield. Son of a prominent English dissenting minister, Byfield early

---

[115] Sewall, *Diary*, II, 856, 808, I, 327, 473. Elisha Cooke, Sr., was a justice of the Superior Court and briefly a judge of probate in Suffolk County; Elisha, Jr., was clerk to the Superior Court. For the latter's political career, see *Sibley's Harvard Graduates*, IV, 349–356.

[116] Compare Willard, *Character of a Good Ruler, passim,* with his *A Compleat Body of Divinity*, 620, 631–636, 655 (sermons preached 1703–1704).

displayed the makings of a politician when, soon after his arrival in New England in 1674 at the age of twenty-one, he pleaded Biblical chapter and verse (Deut. 24:5) in claiming that his recent marriage exempted him from being drafted to fight the Indians. His scruples did not deter him from settling on land taken from the defeated tribes at Mount Hope, later Bristol, Plymouth Colony, where he lived in considerable state—a census of 1688 credits him with two children and the exceptional number, for New England, of eleven servants.[117] A minor officeholder in the Dominion, he moved to Boston early in 1692 and into a profitable partnership with Jahleel Brenton, the newly appointed collector of customs who was his relative by marriage.[118] There, as we have seen, he led the Tory opposition to Phips within the house of representatives. Excluded by the residency act, he returned as representative for Boston and was later chosen to the council. He vigorously championed Dudley's candidacy for the governorship and the latter in turn unsuccessfully proposed Byfield as his lieutenant governor.[119] For several years after Dudley's return, the two worked harmoniously together, with Byfield serving on committees and diplomatic missions and the governor establishing him in undisputed leadership of Bristol County as judge of its courts of common pleas and probate and colonel of its militia. Later Dudley obtained from Whitehall his ally's reappointment as vice-admiralty judge. But in June 1710 came a parting of the ways when, following Byfield's "unmannerly and rude behaviour" to the governor and council and "his peremptory refusal to obey their order directed to

---

[117]Amer. Antiq. Soc., *Proceedings*, new ser., XXXI (1921), 46; *New England Historical and Genealogical Register*, XXXIX (1885), 173-175, LII (1898), 135-141; *Heraldic Journal*, II (1886), 126-127; Richard LeBaron Bowen, *Early Rehoboth*, I, 75-76; Munro, *History of Bristol, passim*.

[118] *Early Records of the Town of Providence*, XVII, 90; Samuel Sewall to John Cotton, Feb. 22, 1692, Curwin Papers, III, 20, Amer. Antiq. Soc.; and Chapter 5, preceding. Although Byfield wrote a detailed description of the overthrow of Andros, he was still in Bristol at the time: *Andros Tracts*, I, 1-10; John Walley and Nathaniel Byfield to Wait Winthrop, Apr. 22, 1689, Winthrop Papers.

[119] Byfield to Dudley, Aug. 7, Sept. 22, Oct. 18, 1701, Blathwayt Papers, BL 258, 257, Hunt. Lib.; Sir Henry Ashurst to Wait Winthrop, Mar. 25, 1702, Mass. Hist. Soc., *Collections*, 6th ser., V (1892), 109.

him as Judge of Probate," he was suspended from all his civil offices.[120] Thrust into the political wilderness, he embarked upon his vain mission to London for the governorship and the private bankers, a defiance that cost him his vice-admiralty position as well. For a few years after Dudley's fall he recovered his seat on the council but his new political alliance with Elisha Cooke, Jr., sealed by his marriage to the latter's sister-in-law, resulted in his being negatived by Shute in 1720 and for several years thereafter. Not until the last years of his long life did he win back a governor's favor, ironically that of Jonathan Belcher, who had helped frustrate his and William Tailer's ambitions fifteen years before.[121]

Byfield also typified the breed of vigorous and acquisitive politicians who were coming to the fore in New England's royal governments. Placing spoilsmanship above the old traditions of consensus, he urged Dudley to purge from the council those who had opposed his appointment as governor. He had many brushes with Sewall, who recorded how Byfield had "swell'd grievously" and insulted his fellow judges when denied a favorable verdict. Years after Byfield's death, an old opponent remembered how "that Proud base Monster. . . . a Snorting vile Fellow" had stacked the courts of Bristol County against him.[122] Byfield's career, indeed, provides a rare insight into the way in which local and personal rivalries could fuel provincial politics, a link doubtless underlying many of the factional divisions of

---

[120] Minutes of the Massachusetts Council, June 30, Oct. 23, 1702, *CSP Col., 1702,* nos. 679, 1091; List of civil and military officers, Dec. 1702, *ibid., 1702-1703,* no. 30v; William H. Whitmore, *The Massachusetts Civil List for the Colonial and Provincial Periods, 1630-1774,* 68, 99, 102. Byfield's appointment to the Superior Court, however, was blocked by the council, and in 1703 he failed to be reelected councillor. Whitmore, *ibid.,* 48, errs in stating that Byfield was again on the council in 1704, a year, in fact, in which he returned to live in Bristol. His dominance of Bristol County can be followed in *Mass. Acts and Resolves,* VII, VIII, *passim.*

[121] Jeremiah Dummer to John White, June 25, 1715, Pubs. Col. Soc. Mass., *Transactions,* XIV (1911-1913), 366. For a contemporary assessment of Byfield and "his flaming Zeal for his honour," see Charles Chauncy, *Nathanael's Character Display'd.* He was probably the author of a short "country" pamphlet, *A Letter from a Gentleman in Mount Hope to His Friend in Treamount.*

[122] Byfield to Dudley, Aug. 7, 1701, Blathwayt Papers, BL 256, Hunt. Lib.; Sewall, *Diary,* I, 398; Thomas Coram to Benjamin Colman, Sept. 21, 1738, Sept. 23, 1735, Mass. Hist. Soc., *Proceedings,* LVI (1922-1923), 46-47, 31.

the time but all too often imperceptible for want of fuller evidence. One source of Byfield's Toryism, it would seem, was his feud with John Saffin, another settler in Bristol whose senior status and defense of the old charter won him the county leadership and a seat in the Massachusetts council during the 1690s.[123] Dudley gave Byfield victory by purging Saffin from office. In the meantime, however, Byfield had become involved in a second bitter dispute with another Bristol inhabitant, Nathaniel Blagrove, over the administration of a will. The case dragged on for a decade, driving the choleric Byfield to new heights of outrage, and appears to have been the immediate cause of his confrontation with the council and dismissal from office in 1710.[124]

Such divisions and their interweaving at the various levels of government, long a feature of English political life, had begun to emerge prior to the loss of the Massachusetts charter.[125] But they grew in both importance and intensity with the coming of royal government and its concentration of patronage in the hands of a single executive. Not only were the fruits of office and influence more alluring than ever before, but they were also far more likely to be abruptly snatched away by a change of administration. Dudley's arrival, for example, and the swift transition of power during 1715 and 1716 from Dudley to Tailer and then to Shute saw a heavy turnover in such lucrative offices as sheriff and judge of probate. Even legal proceedings could be affected: thus the fortunes of Elisha Cooke's seventeen-year lawsuit against Col. Nicholas Paige, Dudley's longtime ally and relative by marriage, rose and fell in precise accordance with whether the Dud-

---

[123] For Saffin, slave trader and poet, see Harold S. Jantz, "The First Century of New England Verse," 273–279; Pubs. Col. Soc. Mass., *Transactions*, I (1893), 85–113; and John Saffin, *John Saffin: His Book*.

[124] *Mass. Acts and Resolves*, VIII, 650–657.

[125] Thus, for example, in seventeenth-century Essex County, Robert Wall, *Massachusetts Bay*, 35–39, 69–78; Richard P. Gildrie, *Salem, Massachusetts, 1626–1683*, 88–104, 123–139; and Jonathan M. Chu, "Madmen and Friends," 58–66, 88–90, 101–110, 145–151. Much more work needs to be devoted to tracing such connections; excellent examples of what has been accomplished in English history are A. Hassell Smith, *County and Court Government and Politics in Norfolk, 1558–1603*, and Thomas Garden Barnes, *Somerset, 1625–1640*.

leians or Cooke and his allies held the upper hand.[126] The stakes of
power were rising, and the fickleness of London's favor, the tactics
and alliances necessary to secure it, and the rewards and retribution
which followed success or failure all fostered the growing politiciza-
tion of New England life.

Politics within early eighteenth-century Massachusetts and New
Hampshire, therefore, though superficially divided between court
and country, can more usefully be described as factional within a
fundamentally tripartite form—a country persuasion suspicious of
the ways of royal government and two fluid groups of office seekers
distinguished from each other more by the fact of their success or failure than by their attachment to ideological issues. First apparent in
the 1690s, with the rivalries of the Phips, Byfield, and old charter factions within Massachusetts and those of Usher, Partridge, and settlers
nostalgic for Boston's old authority within New Hampshire, this tri-
plicity became strongly marked by the last years of Dudley's administration. The appearance of a simple polarity persisted for, like Byfield after 1715, those who failed to secure office or fell from power
slipped smoothly into verbal alliance with their erstwhile opponents
of the country persuasion. Paul Dudley, for example, the governor's
son and an expert spoilsman, though perennially at odds with the
younger Cooke, did not hesitate to make common cause with him, to
the wonder of contemporaries, when he himself was out of favor with
subsequent administrations. Jonathan Belcher, at first a loyal supporter of Governors Dudley and Shute, joined forces with Cooke and
his friends in the late 1720s and, upon winning the governorship, replaced his longtime ally William Dummer (whom Belcher had first
lifted to office) with his former opponent William Tailer as lieutenant
governor. Once in office, of course, he and Cooke soon parted com-

[126] *Mass. Acts and Resolves,* VII, 507–511; Sewall, *Diary,* I, 119, 128, 339, 457, 463;
Joshua Moodey to Increase Mather, July 10, 1688, Mass. Hist. Soc., *Collections,*
4th ser., VIII (1868), 365; Mellen Chamberlain, *A Documentary History of Chelsea,* I,
635–650, II, 1–43. The antecedents of the case can be found in Edmund S. Morgan's classic "A Boston Heiress and Her Husbands," 499–513. Cooke's attempt to
get relief through a private bill got as far as a second reading, June 10, 1702, and
then no further. Dudley arrived as governor the following day.

pany.[127] In New Hampshire, leaders such as William Partridge and George Vaughan displayed a similar talent for trimming their sails to the prevailing political winds across the Atlantic. The crown's patronage, and the factionalism it engendered, had become an integral and determinative part of the two colonies' politics.

Looking back upon New England's relations with England in the quarter-century since the Glorious Revolution, a pattern of change stands out—from charter to royal government, from "messengers" to permanent agents, from isolation from Whitehall to the intricacies of succession politics. The prime impetus for this change had come from the crown, as its imposition of royal government and the consolidation of its systematic regulation of colonial trade and politics drew New Englanders closer within the imperial orbit. The pressures of war deepened this dependence. Yet dependence did not mean subjection, and by the early years of the eighteenth century, much of the initiative had passed to the colonists themselves. Reaching back along the lines of authority, exploring the corridors of Whitehall's labyrinth, they had learned the value of participating in the London government's deliberations and how best to turn its procedures to their own account. Such participation, they found, could check threatening measures at their source, win military assistance, and give them an informal but significant voice in the making of decisions and appointments. And as the vigor and coherence of English colonial policies withered in the heat of domestic party rivalries, the colonists reached out to take advantage of—and thereby helped to quicken—this decay. In vain did the Board of Trade protest Secretary Stan-

---

[127] For the careers of Dudley, Cooke, Belcher, and Vaughan, see *Sibley's Harvard Graduates*, IV, 42–54, 349–356, 434–449, 308–314; and Zemsky, *Merchants, Farmers, and River Gods*, 99–129. Some particular comments upon their changing rivalries and alliances can be found in William Waldron to Richard Waldron, Nov. 11, 1723, Waldron Letters, Mass. Hist. Soc.; William Douglass to Cadwallader Colden, Nov. 20, 1729, *Collections of the New-York Historical Society for the Year 1917*, 238; Jonathan Belcher to Horace Walpole, Jan. 21, 1740, Mass. Hist. Soc., *Collections*, 6th ser., VII (1894), 264–268.

hope's appointment of George Vaughan as lieutenant governor of New Hampshire and reach back into its files to repeat Bellomont's strictures against appointing colonists, especially those engaged in the timber trade, to such a position.[128] Even more clearly than their English counterparts, colonial office seekers profited by the increasing subordination of public policy to private interest.

Finally, too, these changes lead us back to take up the story of New England's internal political development, for they reveal a sophistication and sense of direction that had been sorely lacking amid the confusions of the 1690s. Some elements of a stronger synthesis had begun to appear as the colonists strove to infuse their new forms of government with the spirit and practice of the old. It remains to be seen to what extent these were brought to fruition.

---

[128] Board of Trade to Stanhope, Aug. 3, 1715, *CSP Col., 1714–1715,* no. 547; Bellomont to the Board of Trade, Apr. 23, 1700, *ibid., 1700,* no. 354 (p. 192).

# VII

## Conclusion: Resurgence and Synthesis, 1698–1715

"**D**eservedly is it called *New England*," Cotton Mather told Governor Bellomont and the assembled Massachusetts General Court in 1700: "for *England,* that bravest Lady of *Europe,* has nowhere in *America,* a Daughter that so much Resembles her. . . . It is no Little Blessing of God that we are a part of the *English Nation.*"[1] Through the last years of the seventeenth century, New Englanders had come to accept, and in some cases even to embrace, a closer link to the crown. Yet such a course had visibly failed to bring domestic tranquility in its wake. On the contrary, Whitehall's reshuffling of its schemes for colonial defense, its attentive ear to wealthy malcontents, and its constant sniping at charter governments, together with the unsettling consequences of the colonists' own first dabblings in transatlantic politics, had all tended to inhibit the growth of a stable political order. The wounds inflicted upon the colonists' self-confidence and sense of purpose by the Dominion and its aftermath remained unhealed. The troubled administrations of Phips and Usher, Connecticut's factionalism, and the virtual dissolution of central government within Rhode Island all marked the 1690s as a period of political crisis within New England.

Ultimately, the waning of Whitehall's pressures and the colonists' growing ability to counter royal authority or even turn it to their own account helped ease these strains. More important in the short term, however, and plainly visible by the turn of the century, was a resurgence of political confidence and consensus among the colonies themselves. Shaped by the character of the crown's constraints and making

---

[1] Cotton Mather, *A Pillar of Gratitude,* 10, 32–33.

skilful use of the weapons forged in adjusting to these ties, it drew strength and assurance from New England's cherished heritage of godly aristocratic rule. A sense of renewed continuity eased the pangs of change. This resurgence, moreover, was embodied and perpetuated by reforms in government that likewise blended old traditions with new and, for the most part, more specifically English procedures. Other aspects of New England society followed a similar path. The result was diversity rather than uniformity as each colony's particular circumstances fostered different solutions. Seen in concert, however, these solutions exemplify the theme which more than any other summarizes the Glorious Revolution's legacy to New England, the simultaneous growth and more careful definition of government and its functions.

The cutting edge of this resurgence was the reappearance of strong, sustained leadership within the New England colonies. In 1698, the year of Bellomont's arrival in New York, Samuel Cranston and Fitz-John Winthrop were elected governors of Rhode Island and Connecticut respectively. Repeated expressions of popular support extended their service to a lifetime tenure. Cranston held office until his death in 1727, longer than any other governor who served in the American colonies; when Winthrop died in 1707, the Connecticut General Court, in an unprecedented gesture of respect, chose his close friend and confidant, Gurdon Saltonstall, to replace him. Saltonstall, the only ordained minister ever to govern an American colony, filled the post with distinction until his death in 1724. Bellomont's period of office was brief, but his successor, Joseph Dudley, remained in office for thirteen years, until 1715.

Cranston, Winthrop, Saltonstall, and Dudley—a comparison suggests that circumstances now favored a specific combination of qualities for leadership. All four were native-born New Englanders of distinguished social pedigree; all save Saltonstall, the descendant of three generations of Massachusetts magistrates, were the sons of former governors. Hence, they could draw upon traditional loyalties within New England, as well as the deference still accorded to the prerogatives of birth and breeding. Cranston and Winthrop, for example, presented a reassuring image of gentility to those alarmed by the pretensions of the "Multitude," or the crudity of such as James Fitch. Yet both could rally their governments around the banner of charter privileges with stirring denunciations of those internal critics, "snakes in the grass and vipers that gnaw out the bowells of their mother," who "hath been and daily are plotting and conniving . . . who strain things to the greatest hight Imaginable makeing Mountains out of Mole Hills." "I am of that opinion," concluded Cranston in a speech to the Rhode Island Assembly prior to Bellomont's visit in 1699, "we had better like men spend the one halfe of our Estates to Maintain Our priviledges than that we with Our children should be brought under bondage and Slavery."[2] Dudley, as the crown's representative and because of his collaboration in the Dominion, was less trusted. Yet as we have seen, there were many in Massachusetts who worked for and welcomed his appointment. However blackened, Dudley was at least a native sheep.

In their origin and upbringing, therefore, and in their conviction that such things mattered, these leaders had much in common. Indeed, they often conducted intercolonial relations by means of personal letters among themselves, as befitted one gentleman and head of state to another. "It is our dutys," wrote Cranston to Winthrop in an effort to heal a boundary dispute, "we being the chieff or head pilots, to make knowne the dainger to the people and exhort them to labour for their owne preservation and safety." Dudley's appeal to Saltonstall for help in expediting a court decision in Connecticut "because I know this matter must needs be under your influence" struck this chord of common social sympathies directly. "We are some

---

[2] Samuel Willis to Fitz-John Winthrop, Dec. 25, 1697, Fitz-John Winthrop to the General Assembly of Connecticut, [Oct. 1701], [Oct. 1705], Mass. Hist. Soc., *Collections,* 6th ser., III (1889), 31, 524–525, 290; Speech of Samuel Cranston, Aug. 21, 1699, C.O. 5/1259, no. 34 (foll. 119–119v.).

of us English gentlemen, and such is your owne family," he told Saltonstall, "and we should labor to support such famalyes because truly we want them."[3] New England's tradition of genteel rule, sorely weakened by the events of the preceding decade, revived in more secular form with the reassertion of the English model from which it had originally sprung.

At the same time, these men moved with confidence in the world of Anglo-American interest and connection. Dudley and Winthrop, of course, had become familiar with Whitehall's ways during their years in London. Once in office, all four were assiduous in cultivating their English contacts by means ranging from gifts of furs and walnut wood to letters professing friendship and respect for such bureaucrats as Blathwayt and William Popple, permanent secretary to the Board of Trade. Ceremonial occasions and the board's requests for information brought prompt response.[4] These precautions undoubtedly helped to allay Whitehall's suspicions of the nature of government in New England. Indeed, it would seem that Winthrop and Cranston were kept in office precisely because they could offer this kind of reassurance, evidence of a growing sophistication among the colonial electorate. Cranston's career is especially revealing. Rhode Island's relations with the crown had long been clouded by the reluctance of its Quaker governors, on grounds of conscience, to take the oaths of office required by English law. Quaker scruples had also impeded participation in New England's defense. Cranston, a "Demy-Quaker . . . only put in to serve the Quakers turn" in the opinion of one opponent, willingly subscribed to the oaths, eliminating a constant source

[3] Cranston to Winthrop, May 28, 1701, Mass. Hist. Soc., *Collections*, 6th ser., III (1889), 70; Dudley to Saltonstall, [May 1708], *ibid.*, 6th ser., V (1892), 170.

[4] Thus, besides the official correspondence summarized in *CSP Col.*, see, for example, Fitz-John Winthrop to Blathwayt, July 1, 1698, to Popple, July 1, Oct. 27, 1698, to the Board of Trade, July 1, Oct. 27, 1698, to William Cowper, Nov. 12, 1698, Mass. Hist. Soc., *Collections*, 5th ser., VIII (1882), 344–347, 352–356; Winthrop to the Earl of Manchester, July 29, 1702, to the Earl of Nottingham, July 29, 1702, *ibid.*, 6th ser., III (1889), 109–111; Saltonstall to [the Earl of Oxford], Sept. 10, 1711, HMC, *Portland*, V, 89; and Chapter 6, note 97, preceding. Examples of Cranston's careful prose can be seen in *R. I. Records*, IV, 54–60, 73, 108.

of friction and complaint.[5] Nor did he shrink from organizing the colony's defense and even sending contingents to help neighboring colonies against the French. With such associates as John and William Wanton of Newport, brothers of Quaker upbringing who led the colony's military and naval forces during these years and later in turn succeeded to the governorship, Cranston represented a new breed of colonial leader who accurately perceived that the best hope of preserving local autonomy lay in a measure of pragmatic conformity to Whitehall's demands. The Dominion had shown the consequences of refusing to bend. Only by setting their own houses in order could the colonists ward off further visitations by royal officials or the ultimate calamity of a remodelling of their governments.[6]

Under this guidance, the New England colonies embarked upon a remarkably widespread movement for the reform and institutionalization of government, one in no way orchestrated by its participants but coherent in retrospect because of the extent to which common problems prompted a resort to similar solutions. In part, it was a natural response to the deepening complexity of colonial life as such matters as defense, paper money, land distribution, compliance with imperial regulations, and correspondence with Whitehall came to require a greater attention to administrative routine and a more professional and centralized government. More immediately, however, this movement reemphasized the disruption wrought by the Dominion and its aftermath in that the colonists were clearly striving to reconstruct the tattered fabric of political legitimacy in New England. For the central theme of these reforms was one of definition—of laws and courts and offices and procedures. Massachusetts had led the way, even before 1698, when it had fleshed out the new charter's skeleton with a variety of such measures, many of which, particularly those concerning taxation, courts, and fees, were adopted verbatim by

---

[5] Journal of the Board of Trade, Aug. 8, 1699 (testimony of Jahleel Brenton), C.O. 391/12, 140. An excellent, though undocumented, account of Cranston's administration is given in James, *Colonial Rhode Island,* 119–155, an expansion of his briefer, documented "Colonial Rhode Island and the Liberal Rationalized State," 178–182.

[6] James, *Colonial Rhode Island,* 123–124.

New Hampshire: other colonies still followed the Bay horse even with a royal governor in the saddle.[7] Pressure of a more imperative kind came from Whitehall's request in 1698 for copies of all colonial legislation. Connecticut forwarded a bundle of printed and manuscript statutes, New Hampshire printed its laws for the first time, and Rhode Island scraped together two blotched and disordered abstracts which drew the contemptuous scorn of Bellomont and officials at Whitehall. The effect was salutary, and each colony set to work to draft a more uniform and presentable legislative code.[8]

The character of these reforms was as significant as their extent. As with earlier aspects of the post-Revolutionary settlement, the reforms blended ancient practice with a novel acceptance of English forms and procedures. The Massachusetts assembly's claim to "the accustomed priviledges of an English assembly" was followed by Rhode Island's and Connecticut's adoption, in 1696 and 1698, of a bicameral form of legislative organization complete with speakers and such procedural devices as committees of the whole house. Both colonies reorganized local administration along English lines by strengthening (or, in the case of Rhode Island, creating) county government and by subordinating the towns more firmly to the central authorities.[9] Massachusetts and New Hampshire restructured their judicial systems in similar fashion, transferring the jurisdiction of the old court of assis-

---

[7] *Mass. Acts and Resolves,* I, esp. 27–103; and compare *ibid.,* 3–34, 48–49, 84–88, 142–143, 225–226, 289–299, 312–314, with *N. H. Laws,* I, 527–531, 683–684, 595–600, 689–690, 687–689. Connecticut also copied a number of the new laws passed in the Bay in the 1690s: compare *Acts and Laws of His Majesties Colony of Connecticut in New-England,* 13–14, 40–44, 72–74, 103–105, 107–108, with *Mass. Acts and Resolves,* I, 255, 316–321, 208–210, 58–59, 114.

[8] *Conn. Records,* IV, 332, 343, 362; Fitz-John Winthrop to the Board of Trade, Oct. 27, 1698, Mass. Hist. Soc., *Collections,* 5th ser., VIII (1882), 352; Francis Fane, *Reports on the Laws of Connecticut,* 11–16; *N. H. Laws,* I, 638–642; *R. I. Records,* III, 330, 346, 376, 378, 388, 398, 493, 534, 558; James, "Rhode Island," 179.

[9] Chapter 5, note 87, preceding; *R. I. Records,* III, 313, 477–479; Message of Rhode Island Council to Assembly, Mar. 23, 1697, R. I. Hist. Soc. Manuscripts, I, 75; *Conn. Records,* IV, 235, 260, 266–268, 282, 376; Samuel Willis to Fitz-John Winthrop, Dec. 5, 1699, Mass. Hist. Soc., *Collections,* 6th ser., III (1889), 44; Bruce C. Daniels, "The Political Structure of Local Government in Colonial Connecticut," 46–51 (although this useful study does not, in my opinion, take sufficient account of the strengthening of the central government's authority accomplished by these reforms).

tants and county quarter courts to a superior court, an inferior court
of common pleas, and a general sessions of the peace, the latter two
dealing with civil and criminal matters as in England. Every colony
made greater use of that archetypal English official, the justice of the
peace, a title first introduced into Massachusetts and Connecticut
during the Dominion. Indeed, the basic form of the new judicial system was almost identical to that created by Andros, and in some instances, as John Murrin has noted, the colonists copied the language
of the acts passed at that time.[10] The creation in the two royal colonies of a separate judiciary (although many of its members also sat in
the council or assembly) was an important step toward the English
separation of law making from law administering and away from the
traditional concentration of all branches of government in the General Court. The process was more gradual in Rhode Island and Connecticut, where the General Courts retained their powers of appointment and only gradually relinquished those of original and appellate
jurisdiction. But it was during these years that English precedent and
the requirements of royal government initiated in New England the
separation of governmental functions later enshrined as constitutional principle.

These institutional reforms leave unresolved the vexed question of
whether there was a concomitant "reception" of English law.[11] Con-

---

[10] *Mass. Acts and Resolves,* I, 72–76, 283–287, 367–375; *N. H. Laws,* I, 541–544,
662–666; John M. Murrin, "Review Essay," 260, and, more generally, "Anglicizing an American Colony: The Transformation of Provincial Massachusetts,"
164–173. The parallels cited by Murrin are not always exact, and a number of
the laws he lists have clear roots in the old charter legislation passed prior to the
Dominion. But there are no New England precedents for *N. H. Laws,* I, 190–194,
197–200, 202–204, and they are plainly followed in Massachusetts in *Mass. Acts
and Resolves,* I, 72–76, 70–71, 49–51, 69–71. The ancestry of the Dominion legislation is as yet unclear, but *N. H. Laws,* I, 190–194, the legislation establishing
courts in the Dominion, has been compared to a Jamaica act of 1681: Hamlin
and Baker, *Supreme Court,* I, 57, n. 46. The title "justice of the peace" was used in
Maine after 1665: Robert E. Moody, ed., *Province and Court Records of Maine,*
xvi–xx.

[11] Thus Julius Goebel, Jr., "Kings Law and Local Custom in Seventeenth-Century New England," 416–448; Zechariah Chafee, Jr., "Records of the Suffolk
County Court, 1671–1680," xxviii–xxxv; *idem,* "Colonial Courts and the Common Law," 132–159; and Anton-Herman Chroust, *The Rise of the Legal Profession
in America,* I, 4–17, for debate and further references. See also, for contemporary

temporaries disagreed as to its necessity. Francis Brinley in Rhode Island and Samuel Willis in Connecticut urged that their governments accept all the laws of England as valid. But these were men who feared that New England was falling into "the dreges of a democraticall anarkie" and believed that English common law procedures would have spared them personal legal misfortunes.[12] Others were equally convinced that "a naked Administration of the English Lawes here" would be ruinous; Connecticut, claimed William Pitkin, was entitled, because of its particular local circumstances, to enact "municipal Lawes" even though they might conflict with English "Regal" law.[13] Bellomont reported in 1699 that the Massachusetts council was divided on the issue, "the sour part" asking "with some warmth" what the laws of England had to do with them and "the most understanding gentlemen" being zealous for their adoption. A year later, Rhode Island declared its acceptance of English law in cases not covered by the colony's own statutes. Yet this placed no restriction upon any laws that the colony might choose to pass, and the whole exercise was probably designed more for show than effect, as another instance of Cranston's ability to mask his government's self-sufficiency with a facade of dependence designed to impress officials at Whitehall.[14]

---

discussion of the issue, Michael Kammen, *People of Paradox*, 40–42; Joseph H. Smith, *Appeals to the Privy Council*, 464–522; and *idem*, "The English Criminal Law in Early America," 3–60.

[12] Brinley to William Blathwayt, Dec. 29, 1692, Blathwayt Papers, XI, Col. Wmbg.; Willis to Fitz-John Winthrop, Oct. 8, 1693, Sept. 1693, Aug. 13, 1698, Oct. 6, 1701, Apr. 21, 1697, Winthrop Papers and Mass. Hist. Soc., *Collections*, 6th ser., III (1889), 16, 37, 80, V (1892), 38. For Willis's legal misfortunes, see Conn. Hist. Soc., *Collections*, XXI (1924), 281 *et seq.*, esp. 296–297; Wyllys Papers, II, *passim*, Conn. Hist. Soc.; and Conn. Archives, Private Controversies, III, 213–259.

[13] William Pitkin to Fitz-John Winthrop, Oct. 27, 1693, Winthrop Papers. Also Eleazer Kimberley to Abraham Pierson, Oct. 1, 1701, John Elliott to Pierson, [Oct. 1701], Franklin B. Dexter, ed., *Documentary History of Yale University, 1701–1745*, 11–14; Gov. Jonathan Law to Francis Wilks, Mar. 24, 1742, Conn. Hist. Soc., *Collections*, XI (1907), 27–30; and *The Case of Massachusetts Colony Considered* in Simmons, "The Massachusetts Revolution of 1689," 8.

[14] Bellomont to the Board of Trade, Aug. 28, 1699, *CSP Col., 1699*, no. 746; *R. I. Records*, III, 425, 374 (cf. *ibid.*, I, 157). The argument persisted that English law was not binding because the colonists were not represented in Parliament: *Mass.*

Clearly, some who might have favored a more explicit reception of English law held back for fear it would serve as an opening wedge for the further intrusion of English authority. How to secure the blessings of the one without incurring the burdens of the other could hardly be answered short of eventual independence from England and the transmutation of the rights of Englishmen into the rights of man. Most New Englanders, in the meantime, held to the fine line trodden by their forebears, proclaiming on the one hand that they followed the "fundamental" laws of England and denying on the other that they were subject to English legislation, save perhaps that specifically aimed at the colonies. Or, as the Board of Trade sourly charged in 1705, "they do not allow of the Laws of England . . . otherwise than as it may serve a turn for themselves."[15] These were ambiguities better left unresolved.

Meanwhile, however, the colonists were finding that the ways if not the substance of English law could indeed "serve their turn" and for reasons as compelling as the pressures exerted by Whitehall. There was truth in Gershom Bulkeley's criticism of New England's laws as confusing and inconsistent, "neither flesh nor good fish." Merchants trading to and between the colonies and landowners anxious to protect their titles were no longer willing to accept a situation where individual courts and assemblies (or in Rhode Island, as Bellomont was told, the assembly's clerk) "declared" the law as the spirit moved them, as if in some medieval moot.[16] Such uncertainties served only to benefit the growing number of English-trained lawyers now practising in colonial courts. Connecticut's law concerning intestate estates, for example, "a mixture," in Bulkeley's opinion, "of the Judi-

---

*Records*, V, 200; William Atwood to the Board of Trade, Dec. 29, 1701, *CSP Col., 1701*, no. 1122.

[15] Hutchinson, *Papers*, I, 226–227; *Mass. Records*, V, 200; George Larkin to the Board of Trade, Oct. 14, 1701, *CSP Col., 1701*, no. 945; Charges exhibited against Rhode Island and Connecticut, [Mar. 26, 1705], *ibid., 1704–1705*, nos. 975i, 976i.

[16] Conn. Hist. Soc., *Collections*, XXI (1924), 347; Testimony of Jo. Hearne, [Sept. 1699], C.O. 5/1259, fol. 196. One response to the difficulties faced by merchants was a compilation designed to help them, *An Abridgment of the Laws in Force and Use in Her Majesty's Plantations*.

ciall Law of Moses, and of the Common Law of England, with a smacke of the Custome of Gavelkind," spawned a weary round of appeals within the colony and to the Privy Council.[17] Such litigation could be as costly for its participants as it was damaging to colonial autonomy: Sir Henry Ashurst submitted a bill of £270 for his aid in the Mohegan case, and the Reverend James Noyes of Stonington complained of spending £204 in fees defending a farm worth £1,000 against a Rhode Islander who had hired a New York lawyer to fight the case in England.[18] Colonists no less than royal officials came to perceive the need to clarify and codify legal forms and procedures.

These themes of strong leadership and institutional reforms came together in a general strengthening of the prestige and authority of central government. A powerful impetus came from the many settlers exhausted by the endless bickering over questions of boundary and title, for it was plain that peace was impossible until every government was strong enough to enforce its decisions. External pressures— the war and London's threats to intervene—combined with internal reforms to foster the settlement of old disputes. Cranston, for example, took the lead in mediating the forty-year conflict over the Narragansett country. "Our contending," he pointed out to Winthrop in 1701, "doth lay us both open for others to take the greater advantage against us. . . . Perhaps you think there is noe dainger of yours, soe you will doe your indevors to overthrow us and thereby strengthen yourselves; but I would pray you not to flatter

---

[17] Conn. Hist. Soc., *Collections,* XXI (1924), 347; Joseph H. Smith, *Appeals to the Privy Council,* 537–584; George L. Haskins, "The Beginning of Partible Inheritance in the American Colonies," 1280–1315. For the influx of lawyers, Murrin, "Legal Transformation," 419–423, and, for the accompanying importation of law books, Worthington C. Ford, *The Boston Book Market, 1679–1700,* Appendices. An example of the heightened complexity and sophistication which resulted is the trial of Capt. John Quelch for piracy: *Mass. Acts and Resolves,* VIII, 392–393.

[18] Ashurst to Connecticut, May 21, 1706, Nathaniel Coddington to Fitz-John Winthrop, Oct. 10, 1706, Mass. Hist. Soc., *Collections,* 6th ser., III (1889), 326, 356; Samuel Sewall to Ashurst, Oct. 16, 1706, *ibid.,* 6th ser., I (1886), 337; Noyes to Wait Winthrop, Oct. 8, 1706, to Samuel Sewall, Dec. 2, 1707, Winthrop Papers.

yourselves with such expectations, for you may assure yourselves that if wee splitt you will sinke; for wee are both upon one bottom and I am apte to conclude as many rents and leaks on your part as on ours, if not some trunnell holes open." Rebuffed by Winthrop, Cranston appealed to Deputy Governor Robert Treat as one not personally involved in the contest. "I am Shure it is Intrest that hath obstructed hetherto and not so much the Government," he told Treat, "For my part I am sicke and weary in Liveing thus in Contention."[19] This flanking movement, it appears, brought results. Perhaps Cranston was able to exert further leverage through his ties with James Fitch who, after a two-year exclusion from power, had returned to the Connecticut council in 1700. Whatever the reasons, in May 1703 a Connecticut boundary commission dominated by legislators from the western corner of the colony, the old New Haven government which was also Treat's political base, agreed with Cranston's commissioners upon an eastern boundary line which gave Rhode Island most of the disputed territory, including the Narragansett country. During these years, also, Connecticut reached agreements in its boundary disputes with Massachusetts and New York, while Rhode Island laid out its northern and eastern borders.[20]

These settlements were not finally ratified until years (in one instance over a century) later, and while they quieted they did not still the domestic wrangling over land titles within each colony. In Connecticut, in particular, Fitch and his "native right" claimants re-

[19] Cranston to Winthrop, May 28, 1701, Winthrop to Cranston, June 20, 1701, Mass. Hist. Soc., *Collections,* 6th ser., III (1889), 70, 73-75; Cranston to Treat, July 17, 1701, Winthrop Papers. Cranston also suggested to Treat that the two colonies should maintain a single agent at joint expense in London.

[20] *Conn. Records,* IV, 399; *R. I. Records,* III, 474-475, IV, 4, 30, 63, 83, 86, 218, 235; Wait Winthrop to Fitz-John Winthrop, Dec. 9, 1701, Mass. Hist. Soc., *Collections,* 6th ser., V (1892), 105; Deposition of James Fitch and Samuel Mason, July 10, 1703, *CSP Col., 1704-1705,* no. 1424xlviii. Winthrop's correspondence suggests that the old New Haven Colony long remained an essentially separate political unit within Connecticut, as did Plymouth within Massachusetts after 1692, and it may be that the New Haveners were prepared to concede Connecticut's eastern claims because of the western territory—the towns of Bedford and Rye—which Winthrop had just surrendered to New York. On these and Connecticut's other boundary conflicts, Clarence W. Bowen, *Boundary Disputes of Connecticut,* and Roland M. Hooker, *Boundaries of Connecticut.*

mained a disruptive force for several decades to come.[21] Judged in comparison to the confusions of the 1690s, however, each colony had made substantial progress toward possessing, for the first time, well-defined territorial boundaries. New England was at least freeing itself from the baleful influence of the Stuart monarchy's overlapping grants and charters. Such progress, in turn, was both a measure and a reinforcement of the heightened status of the central governments. It could also provide them with resources above and beyond (and free of the constraints accompanying) those furnished by taxation. Rhode Island, for example, anticipating the federal government's practice in the nineteenth century, derived several thousand pounds from selling off its "public lands" in the Narragansett country.[22]

No less effective than the task of defining colonial boundaries in strengthening the hand of government was that of defending them from enemy attack. At first, as in the months following Andros's overthrow, the war had exposed the weaknesses of those in power. Not until the five years of peace that followed the Treaty of Ryswick in 1697 did the colonists' domestic resurgence take hold. This breathing space, however, was turned to good effect, for by the time that war returned to New England in the summer of 1703, the colonial governments showed themselves both better prepared to meet the shock and ready as they had not been since the expeditions of 1690 to work together in New England's defense. Massachusetts and New Hampshire forces, together with a force of Indians from Connecticut, strove to protect the settlements in Maine; Connecticut sent several hundred militia to garrison the towns of western Massachusetts; and even Rhode Island, hitherto totally unresponsive to its neighbors' appeals for aid, voted men and money for the common defense and then in 1707 sent an armed sloop and a force of soldiers to join those from Massachusetts and New Hampshire in the unsuccessful assault upon Port Royal. Later, every New England colony contributed to the ex-

---

[21] Bushman, *Puritan to Yankee,* 93–103.

[22] MS. Act of 1708, R. I. Archives; *R. I. Records,* IV, 51, 62, 149–150; Arnold, *History of Rhode Island,* II, 37; General Treasurer's Accounts, 1672–1711, fol. 157, R. I. Archives.

peditions which finally captured Port Royal in 1710 but failed to conquer Canada the following year.[23] Each government continued to complain in anguished tones of its unique burdens and its neighbors' importunities; in fact, however, they displayed a new capacity for co-operation, even to the point of regaining the military initiative by carrying the war into enemy territory.

Within the individual colonies, the war accentuated the dependence of the towns upon the central governments. The work of the standing councils empowered to act in the intervals between the legislative sessions swelled under the pressure of day-to-day emergencies and the need to sustain outlying communities constantly threatened with attack. In such vulnerable forward areas as Hartford County in Connecticut, York County in Maine, and along the seacoast, defensive arrangements were coordinated by special councils of war or committees of safety made up of magistrates and veteran local commanders.[24] Permanent garrisons were stationed in a chain of specially designated frontier towns whose inhabitants were forbidden to desert their homes (and whose spiritual security was maintained by subsidies paid to their ministers).[25] Flying columns and marching parties, often using the Indians' own device of snowshoes to travel in dead of winter, were sent out to keep the enemy at a distance. Smaller groups

---

[23] Osgood, *American Colonies in the Eighteenth Century,* I, chapter XIII; Haffenden, *New England in the English Nation,* chapters VI–VII; Gerald S. Graham, ed., *The Walker Expedition to Quebec;* [Walter K. Watkins], "The Expeditions against Port Royal in 1710 and Quebec in 1711," 81–143. The volume of business imposed by the war is evident in all the administrative records of the period: see, for example, Mass. Archives, Executive Records of the Council, III–VI (transcripts of the material calendared in *CSP Col.* up until the end of 1703, such material then being omitted from the calendar).

[24] *Conn. Records,* IV, 14, 27, 442–443, 458, 462, 535, V, 32; Petition of Waterbury to the Hartford Council of War, Jan. 20, 1707, Robert C. Winthrop Collection, II, 180; *Mass. Acts and Resolves,* VII, 185; Minutes of the Council of War at Kingstown, Mar. 15, 1704, Governor and Council, Miscellaneous Papers, 1652–1704, R. I. Archives. A large number of letters from leaders of the Hartford Council are in the Winthrop Papers.

[25] *Mass. Acts and Resolves,* I, 194, 293, 402, 547, VII, 34, 88, 113, 126, 173, VIII, 36, 42, 84, 101, XXI, 833; *Conn. Records,* IV, 463, V, 86; Mass. Archives, LXX, 380, LXXI, 871–876; *New England Historical and Genealogical Register,* L (1896), 339–345; Dudley to the Board of Trade, Feb. 1, 1706, *CSP Col., 1706–1708,* no. 69 (p. 31).

were directed "to lye out by Night and Scout in the Day" around the towns.[26] Experience proved the militia to be a ponderous and un-wieldy weapon for such tasks. Hence the central governments took the lead in sponsoring its supplementation and gradual replacement as an active fighting force by the volunteer regiments (often including companies of friendly Indians) raised by such *condottieri* as Benjamin Church, and by the packs of bounty hunters that formed in response to the rewards, raised as high as one hundred pounds in 1704, paid for enemy Indian scalps. War as well as government was becoming pro-fessionalized.[27]

Defensively, these measures proved remarkably effective. Offen-sively, though the colonists now showed the will to strike back, they still lacked the necessary equipment and leadership: the expedition against Port Royal in 1707, for example, was a dismal failure even though the attackers outnumbered the town's French defenders by more than three to one. Within the borders of New England, how-ever, despite incessant enemy attacks, casualties and material damage were less than those suffered during King Philip's War over a much briefer span of time. Histories of the conflict, both then and later, have focused upon its dramatic incidents and setbacks, such as the fa-mous midnight sacking of Deerfield early in 1704. More typical, how-ever, was the reception given a second and stronger French and In-dian force later that same year. Repulsed from the town of Lancaster, it was driven back by a rapid concentration of the Connecticut troops stationed in western Massachusetts and detachments of militia mobi-lized from the counties surrounding Boston.[28] Such was the pattern of the frontier war, with the enemy battering, and occasionally break-

---

[26] Printed circular directed to Capt. Henry True, Aug. 14, 1706, Miscellaneous MSS., HM 688, Hunt. Lib. A graphic picture of the strategy of frontier defense can be drawn from the letters of Col. William Whiting and Col. Samuel Par-tridge in Mass. Hist. Soc., *Collections,* 6th ser., III (1889), 168 *et seq.,* and from the more varied documents in Mass. Archives, LXXI. "Flyeing armies," "moveing bodies," and "marching partys" had first been extensively used in the 1690s.

[27] Richard Johnson, "Search for a Usable Indian," *passim,* esp. 639–641; *Mass. Acts and Resolves,* I, 558–559.

[28] *Mass. Acts and Resolves,* VIII, 420–427. Dudley reported that the French were repelled, "with the Triumph only of three children carried away": to the Board of Trade, Oct. 10, 1704, C.O. 5/863B, no. 118.

ing, the links of the chain of frontier towns but with reinforcements always close at hand and backed by the central governments' determination never to abandon a threatened town. Well might Dudley boast to Whitehall of his success in maintaining the borders he had inherited. More significantly for the prestige of government, contemporaries recognized his achievement. "By the good Providence of Almighty God [and] the Courage, Care and Prudence of Colonel Dudley," testified the New Hampshire General Court, "we have been exceedingly preserved, beyond what has been in former Wars." New England had at last found a frontier strategy.[29]

But this protection was purchased at a high and politically momentous price. During the summer of 1704, for example, the period of the French attack upon Lancaster, Dudley had as many as nineteen hundred men under arms, perhaps one-sixth of the province's able-bodied men. In consequence, and following the trend established in the 1690s, the Boston government's expenditures mounted to nearly forty thousand pounds in the year ending May 1705, more than four-fifths of which were spent on defense.[30] Large sums were devoted to strengthening coastal fortifications, over six thousand pounds alone in three years for the rebuilding of Castle Island in Boston harbor under the abrasive direction of Col. Wolfgang Romer, a German engineer sent out from England.[31] Except for New Hampshire, other colonies escaped more lightly in proportional terms, but an examination of their financial records reveals a similar massive increase in their an-

---

[29] Dudley to the Board of Trade, Mar. 1, 1709, *Doc. Hist. Maine*, IX, 252; Address of the Council and Representatives of New Hampshire, July 25, 1706, *A Modest Inquiry*, 94*; see also *ibid.*, 89*-90*. For a similar tribute, George Vaughan to Constantine Phipps, Nov. 15, 1706, Rawlinson MSS., C 379.

[30] Dudley to the Board of Trade, July 13, 1704, *Doc. Hist. Maine*, IX, 190; Accounts of Treasurer James Taylor, May 31, 1704–May 31, 1705, *Calendar of Treasury Books, 1706–1707*, 204–205; Mass. Archives, CXXII, 209–236. With moneys outstanding, the accounts totalled over fifty thousand pounds, a sum which rose to over ninety thousand pounds, by 1711: *Mass. Acts and Resolves*, VIII, 122, IX, 179.

[31] The rebuilding of the castle and the province's clashes with Romer can be followed in *Mass. Acts and Resolves*, VII–IX. Other coastal fortifications were built or renovated during these years at Saco, Casco, Winter Harbor (Maine), Great Island (New Hampshire), Boston Neck, Newport, New London, and Saybrook. Much of this work was begun in the five-year interval of peace ending in 1703.

nual charges. Connecticut, for example, which claimed contributions of some five thousand pounds to the defense of Albany during the 1690s, spent double that sum in the three years after 1702 in aid to western Massachusetts alone.[32] The expeditions of 1709-11 left every colony deep in debt: Rhode Island's accounts, hitherto rarely amounting to more than a few hundred pounds a year, suddenly rose to an average annual total of over sixty-three hundred pounds during these three years, less than half of that total funded by current taxation. Connecticut's accounts averaged twice this sum during the same period. By 1711, the Massachusetts treasury was estimated to be one hundred and twenty thousand pounds in arrears.[33]

Inevitably, these expenditures brought new and heavier taxation. In Massachusetts, in the decade after July 1703, the taxes levied upon polls and estates by the General Court totalled approximately a quarter of a million pounds, more than the total it had levied for the previous eighty years of the colony's history. A tenth more, at least, came from excise and import duties. One effect was to accentuate the trend, apparent ever since King Philip's War, whereby a colonist paid a greater share of his taxes to the central government than to his local community, heightening the former's prestige and importance as it became the principal collector (and dispenser) of public moneys.[34] In addition, the prolonged burden of these taxes, extending over a quar-

---

[32] Gov. Robert Treat and the Connecticut Council to Fitz-John Winthrop, Nov. 12, 1696, Conn. Hist. Soc., *Collections*, XXIV (1932), 127; Conn. Archives, War, III, 61, 67a-c; Account of Peter Burr and John Winston, Oct. 18, 1705, Wyllys Papers, Annmary Brown Memorial Library. For the war's burden upon New Hampshire, Van Deventer, *Emergence of Provincial New Hampshire*, 69-70.

[33] General Treasurer's Accounts, 1672-1711, foll. 145-157, R. I. Archives; Conn. Archives, Finances, I, 1-38; Mass. Archives, III, 124.

[34] Breen, "War, Taxes, and Changing Political Brokers," 10. For the comparative burden of town and province taxes, 1689-1715, see for example: figures in *Boston Records*, VII, 226, 241, VIII, 35, 72; Francis Jackson, *History of the Early Settlement of Newton*, 220; *Milton Town Records, 1662-1729*, 190-198, 245-250; *Watertown Records*, II, 133, 177, 199; and Deloraine Pendre Corey, *The History of Malden, Massachusetts, 1633-1785*, 362-363, with the figures for the province taxes for these towns in *Mass. Acts and Resolves*, I, *passim*. Depending on the sums levied for ministerial salaries, the largest local expense, province levies were often double and sometimes even, for the larger and wealthier communities, quadruple local taxes during the war years, falling back to rough parity in times of peace. Small additional sums were assessed for the expenses of county government.

[379]

ter of a century, impelled further administrative reforms. Each colony endeavored to improve the efficacy of its revenue-gathering machinery. Massachusetts abandoned the old system of country rates and, after a period of experimentation in the 1690s, opted for the more certainly productive method of assessing each town for a specified portion of the tax.[35] New Hampshire followed suit. Rhode Island, finding "that the manner of rating towns by guess is no suitable or certain rule," experimented briefly with taxing according to the appraised value of estates before returning to its former practice of assessing each town for an allotted amount and bolstering it with better methods of collection. Only Connecticut retained the traditional system of country rates.[36]

A further incentive for such reform in Massachusetts was the need for taxes in specified amounts to provide a sinking fund for the retirement of the province's paper currency. The scarcity of liquid capital in New England and the absence of banks and corporations with funds of credit prevented the colonies from adopting the English government's solution of financing the war through loans raised from private citizens upon the open market. Hence Massachusetts covered its deficits by printing increasing quantities of the paper bills of credit first issued in 1690. The cost of the expeditions of 1709-11 compelled each of the other New England colonies to follow suit. This currency served an essential function in colonies chronically short of hard currency and, at first, after an initial confusion and depreciation in Mas-

---

[35] Charles H. J. Douglas, *The Financial History of Massachusetts from the Organization of the Massachusetts Bay Company to the American Revolution*, 60–72; H. H. Burbank, "The History of Polls and Property in Massachusetts, 1630–1775," Burbank Papers, Baker Library, Harvard Business School, confirms the importance of these reforms (which also considerably reduced the disproportionate burden of the poll tax) and suggests, on page 21a, that, during the 1690s in particular, Massachusetts was trying to bring its taxation into line with methods used in England. English direct taxation and the debate over the merits of subsidies (i.e., rates) and assessments are examined by Chandaman, *English Public Revenue*, chapter V.

[36] Maurice H. Robinson, *A History of Taxation in New Hampshire*, 28–32; *N. H. Laws*, I, 524–526, 554, 563, II, 68 (a law which transferred to the governor's justices of the peace the power to appoint tax assessors); Jeffries Papers, IV, 52; *R. I. Records*, III, 277, 301–303, 343, 484–486; *Conn. Records*, IV, 262, 439–440, V, 127–128, 334.

sachusetts in the early 1690s, sound management preserved the paper's nominal value. Without it, Governor Dudley told the Board of Trade, Massachusetts could not have fought the war. But as its volume grew, and provision for its redemption was extended further and further into the future in the years after the expeditions against Canada, New England was drawn into a spiral of monetary depreciation and economic inflation that was to be a potent issue in colonial politics for many years to come. More internally divisive in its effects than the war, it displayed no less clearly the growing importance and complexity of the business now handled by the central governments.[37]

Interwoven with this consolidation and definition of government was a burgeoning of executive power. In Rhode Island and Connecticut, Cranston and Winthrop received new authority to appoint local officials; their salaries were doubled; and, with their councils, they played a more active and decisive role during the times when their legislatures were not in session. In Connecticut, Winthrop and his council were commissioned to draft a wide range of bills to reform and "methodize" the judicial and financial structure.[38] For the first time, the colony's governor exercised formal powers of patronage as Winthrop carefully sifted the names of those who solicited office (or were nominated by his political allies) before appointing the naval of-

[37] Nettels, *Money Supply,* 253–277, 199–200; Dudley to the Board of Trade, Dec. 1, 1713, *CSP Col., 1712–1714,* no. 509. For depreciation of New England currency after 1711, Felt, *Historical Account of Massachusetts Currency,* 83, 135; Henry Bronson, "A Historical Account of Connecticut Currency," 52 (separately paginated); N. H. Hist. Soc., *Collections,* V (1837), 258; John J. McCusker, *Money and Exchange in Europe and America, 1600–1775,* 131–155; and, generally, William De Witt Metz, "Politics and Finance in Massachusetts." For parallel problems and their solution in Europe, see Dickson and Sperling, "War Finance, 1689–1714," 284–315.

[38] *R. I. Records,* III, 309, 345–346, 351, 417–418, 430, 432, 439, 445, 451, 489, 566, IV, 5; General Treasurer's Accounts, 1672–1711, fol. 86, 1711–1727, fol. 7, R. I. Archives; *Conn. Records,* IV, 179, 225, 261–262, 268, 279, 302, 329–330, 348–349; Conn. Archives, Finances, I, 1; Dunn, *Puritans and Yankees,* 321–322; Bliss, "Secular Revival," 147. The Rhode Island governor's salary, first paid in 1695 (ten pounds) had risen to thirty pounds by 1698 and one hundred pounds by 1712; over the same period that of the governor of Connecticut rose from eighty to two hundred pounds.

ficers who kept watch upon the colony's trade. He even received a polite enquiry from an English Winthrop who, having lost his government job in Ireland, sought employment in New England.[39]

The two governors served their own interests with these reforms. Cranston used his authority to good effect and personal profit in forwarding a variety of schemes for the parcelling out of western Rhode Island; several of the measures passed in Connecticut had the happy and deliberate effect of clipping the wings of Captain Fitch, Winthrop's deadly rival in the sale and settlement of the lands stretching north from New London to the Massachusetts border.[40] The scanty surviving evidence tells us little of Cranston's conception of his role beyond the striking fact of his willingness and capacity to hold the governorship longer than his eight predecessors in office put together. Winthrop's correspondence, however, documents the ideological purpose underlying legislative action in showing that he returned from his London agency determined to invest colonial government with more of the dignity and authority of its English counterpart. "There seems a slowness to Exert all the authority which the King's Gracious Charter does allow," he told the Reverend James Pierpont soon after his return from London and three months before his election to the governorship. "A Government Easy and indulgent beyond what is fitting brings a Contempt upon it and makes rude and angoular persons bold and unsafe to the Government." Winthrop commented with approval on the reverence shown to judges and justices in England. "But in this wilderness (eyther from principles of too fond familiarity or not remembring the rules abroad) they are wanting to introduce such fitting formes and customes as should support the honor of the Courts and give them a reputation and character abroad in other parts of the world. I hope the Contin-

---

[39] Robert Treat to Winthrop, Aug. 1, 13, Sept. 8, 1698, Winthrop to Treat, Aug. 10, 24, 1698, Winthrop Papers, and Mass. Hist. Soc., *Collections,* 5th ser., VIII (1882), 350–351; James Pierpont to Winthrop, Sept. 12, 1704, John Hodson to Winthrop, Sept. 11, 1702, Jonathan Winthrop to Fitz-John Winthrop, London, Oct. 10, 1699, Winthrop Papers.

[40] James, *Colonial Rhode Island,* 138–145; Dunn, *Puritans and Yankees,* 317, 323, 328–330.

ued instance of the King's grace that has given new life to the Government will encourage every one in his station to proceed vigourously in such steps as may strengthen their hands to Governe." Cranston probably held similar if less openly elitist and Anglocentric opinions.[41]

The character of the "fitting formes and customes" subsequently adopted in Connecticut plainly reflected its governor's new-found appreciation of "the rules abroad." Within the colony, moreover, Winthrop's propositions were eagerly embraced by local gentry like Samuel Willis and by an influential group of ministers headed by Saltonstall, Pierpont, and Timothy Woodbridge of Hartford. These men feared a breakdown of order and established religion in the colony, a threat exemplified by Fitch's activities and, in particular, by the passage shortly before Winthrop's return from London of a law which sharply reduced the ministers' security in their posts and, ultimately, their salaries.[42] Indeed, a number of the themes of Winthrop's platform were first expressed by his close friend Saltonstall who on the day of the law's passage had preached a blistering election sermon attacking those who were weakening or perverting authority, emphasizing the colony's ties to "the English Israel" ("We are a little branch of that Vine; our Civil Life and Liberty is bound up in theirs") and calling for "a man of Courage," some Connecticut counterpart to King William, who would restore "the two great things, that are the grand Interests of a People; *Religion* and *Property*."[43] But neither Saltonstall nor Winthrop managed to practice all the powers for which

[41] Winthrop to [Pierpont], Feb. 15, 1698, Winthrop Papers (internal evidence shows that this letter was not to Abraham Pierson, as usually cited). Cranston's admiration for the image of genteel leadership is evident in his subsequent attempts to reestablish ties with his aristocratic Scottish relatives: *New England Historical and Genealogical Register*, LXXIX (1925), 58, LXXX (1926), 370–378.

[42] *Conn. Records*, IV, 198–201, 225, 259, 267; Ministers of Fairfield County to the General Court, Oct. 13, 1698, Conn. Hist. Soc., *Collections*, XXIV (1932), 155–159; the ministers' answer to objections and resentments, Oct. 13, 1695, Robert C. Winthrop Collection, II, 267a–c.

[43] Gurdon Saltonstall, *A Sermon Preached before the General Assembly of the Colony of Connecticut*, 23, 57, 31; also Samuel Willis to Fitz-John Winthrop, Sept. 1693, Mass. Hist. Soc., *Collections*, 6th ser., III (1889), 16–17. For the relief afforded the clergy under Winthrop's administration, *Conn. Records*, IV, 267, 287, 316.

they preached. Working within a constitutional framework that granted the colony's executives none of the independent authority exercised by a royal governor in neighboring Massachusetts or New York, they remained, as did Cranston in Rhode Island, essentially first among equals in their governments, with their power to act and appoint still closely circumscribed. By comparison to their immediate predecessors, however, the three governors' success was striking. Their personal predominance was marked, and they had moved far toward achieving a settlement that hewed closer to English forms while preserving their colonies' unique heritage and freedom from external control.

In Massachusetts and New Hampshire, meanwhile, Bellomont and Dudley proved adept in enlarging the role assigned to them by charter. Where Phips and Stoughton had allowed their councils to assume the task of nominating judges and other royal officials, Bellomont insisted upon the governor's right to nominate, with the council's role restricted to signifying approval or dissent.[44] Dudley preserved this power and added to it by his vigorous use of the governor's authority to veto councillors, a power not exercised since Phips's negative of Cooke in 1693. In 1703 Dudley settled old scores by vetoing five councillors, including Cooke, Cooke's fellow agent in 1690, Thomas Oakes, and Sir Henry Ashurst's cousin, Peter Sergeant. In all, he used his veto thirteen times, four times on Cooke. Within council meetings, he refused to allow decisions to be made by secret ballot.[45]

Bellomont and Dudley also displayed considerable skill in wooing their constituents, albeit in very different ways. Bellomont drew upon the deference accorded to a real live earl, the first ever to rule in the mainland colonies: his entry into Boston in May 1699 escorted by twenty companies of soldiers and watched, as one witness recorded, by "such a vast concourse of people as my poor eys never saw the like

---

[44] Chapter 5, note 61, preceding; Bellomont to the Board of Trade, Aug. 28, 1699, Minutes of the Massachusetts Council, July 14–17, Sept. 7, 1699, *CSP Col., 1699*, nos. 746, 633, 768. Bellomont also seems to have been the first governor to impose his personal veto upon a bill: Mass. Archives, Court Records, VII, July 18, 1699.

[45] Mass. Archives, Court Records, VII–IX, *passim;* Sewall, *Diary*, I, 470.

before" was the grandest ceremonial occasion yet staged in New England.[46] He was also an ardent and forthright Whig who gladdened the hearts of his Puritan audience with high-flown speeches extolling the General Court's parliamentary status and denouncing the sins of Stuart autocracy, heresies that drew from the Board of Trade a caution lest, in reflecting upon "his Majesty's Royal Progenitors," he "alienate the minds of that people from monarchy itself."[47] In time, perhaps, his determination to assert his own constitutional powers and enforce the Acts of Trade—no less a part of Whiggism—would have prompted disillusion and conflict. While it lasted, however, his brief tenure of office was long remembered as a time of exceptional cooperation in government, and Bellomont reaped a golden reward in the form of the largest "presents" (two thousand pounds in two years) ever given to a Massachusetts governor.[48]

Dudley's contemporaries knew his past transgressions far too well for any such rhetorical strokings to have carried conviction. Nor did he make the attempt: his speeches as governor were the blunt injunctions of an intensely practical man of affairs, devoid even of the appeals for sympathy as a native-born New Englander with which he had bolstered his climb back into office. Taking a different tack, he speedily passed on the lessons he had learned as Lord Cutts's political manager in England: his arrival in 1702 was followed by a shake-up of his government's civil and military list unprecedented since the convulsions of the 1680s. Indeed, a number of those now appointed to high office, such as Francis Foxcroft, Nicholas Paige, John Nelson,

---

[46] John Marshall, "John Marshall's Diary," 153. A poem written for the occasion by Benjamin Tompson is in Jantz, "First Century of New England Verse," 381–383.

[47] Board of Trade to Bellomont, Apr. 11, 1700, *CSP Col., 1700*, no. 312; Bellomont's speeches are in C.O. 5/860, no. 65ii, 66ii; C.O. 5/861, no. 31ii; and Mass. Archives, Court Records, VII, June 2, 1699, May 30, 1700, and *N. H. Provincial Papers*, III, 66.

[48] Hutchinson, *History of Massachusetts-Bay*, II, 84–87; *Mass. Acts and Resolves*, I, 394–395, 437. Bellomont's knowledge and use of parliamentary procedure are abundantly evident in Mass. Archives, Court Records, VI, with the Earl turning his council into a committee of the whole and moving in and out of the chair to offer amendments to bills.

Benjamin Davis, Giles Dyer, John and Samuel Legg, Nathaniel Byfield, and the Brentons, had first entered government during the time
of the Dominion or had stood out as "tories" after its fall.[49] Several
were Anglicans. Dudley also installed his two sons in office, the eldest,
Paul, becoming attorney general, advocate of the admiralty court, a
justice of the peace, and a register of probate. His two elder daughters
he married to the sons of Wait Winthrop and Samuel Sewall.[50]

Dudley's highly personal style of government was equally evident
in his day-to-day conduct of affairs. Where previous administrations
had delegated the defense of the frontiers to a ponderous body of
commissioners, he himself directed operations by means of terse notes
dispatched to his commanders in the field dealing with matters as
small as the type of headgear to be worn by frontier scouts.[51] Local
concerns such as bridge building and militia appointments received
the same minute attention. "I pray you not to Disturb yourselfs," he
wrote to the New Hampshire council, "but to Lett me know what you

---

[49] Mass. Archives, Executive Records of the Council, III, June 29, 30, July 2, 6, 8,
Oct. 23, 1702 (*CSP Col., 1702*, nos. 679, 696, 704, 728, 1091); List of civil and military officers, Dec. 1702, C.O. 5/863A, no. 4v. Among the appointments to which
the council did not consent were those of Byfield and Nathaniel Thomas, Dudley's Plymouth allies, to the province Superior Court, Jahleel Brenton to be a
justice of the peace, and Samuel Legg to be an Inferior Court judge. The ripest
plums of patronage, the judgeships of probate, fell to Dudley's allies, among
them Isaac Addington, John Appleton, John Leverett, Thomas, and Byfield.

[50] Whitmore, *Civil List*, 80, 126. William Dudley also served as his father's representative in the missions to Canada and the 1707 expedition to Port Royal. For
Dudley's attempt to prefer Paul to such offices as province secretary, advocate
general of the admiralty court, and probate judge, see Dudley to [Blathwayt],
Feb. 15, 1706, Blathwayt Papers, BL 260, Hunt. Lib.; *CSP Col., 1704-1705*, no.
422; and Sewall, *Diary*, II, 790. Dudley also tried to impose William on Harvard
as its treasurer in 1713, precipitating a breach with his old ally, John Leverett.

[51] Thus, for example: Mass. Archives, LXXI, 308, 335, 370, 389, 713, 727; Dudley
to Maj. William Vaughan, Dec. 19, 1706, to Capt. Jas. Davis, Oct. 22, 1706,
Chamberlain Collection; to Capt. Stephen Sewall, Sept. 24, Nov. 27, 1706, Cur-
win Papers, I, 65, III, 43, Amer. Antiq. Soc.; to Col. Thomas Noyes, Mar. 3, 1709,
Jan. 27, 1710, Appleton Papers, Washburn Papers, VII, both Mass. Hist. Soc.; to
Samuel Penhallow, July 30, 1710-Mar. 17, 1712, Belknap Papers, 1664-1744; to
Capt. John Lane, Nov. 5, 1702, *New England Historical and Genealogical Register*,
XVII (1863), 331-332. Many others are to be found in such collections as the
Winthrop Papers or, printed, in *N. H. Provincial Papers*, II, and *Doc. Hist. Maine*,
IX.

want and I shall give orders for it."[52] In addition, Dudley conducted what was in effect his own foreign policy. Proposals to the French in Canada for an exchange of prisoners led to a succession of visits to Boston and Quebec by each side's emissaries and developed, in 1705, into negotiations for a treaty of neutrality to bring a local truce to the northern colonies.[53] The treaty was never concluded and Dudley's intentions in the matter remain obscure. Keen to obtain both military intelligence and the return of English captives from Canada, he also seems to have spun out negotiations to delay a resumption of French border raids for as long as possible. A side benefit was the opportunity to gratify some of his mercantile allies with a profitable trade to Quebec and Acadia under the guise of exchanging prisoners.

Dudley's penchant for playing a lone hand rebounded upon him in 1706 when several of the merchants he had sent to Canada were accused of selling supplies to enemy Indians, precipitating an angry scandal and uniting the governor's enemies in the hope that he could be forced from office. The result was the Mason-Higginson petition presented to the queen.[54] Yet Dudley's handling of this crisis only served to show that he was as skilled at guiding the political currents within his government as he was in defending his political base at Whitehall. He encouraged the angry representatives to try the offending merchants for treason, knowing that their assumption of such jurisdiction would eventually ensure Whitehall's overturning of the

---

[52] Dudley to [New Hampshire Council], Aug. 16, 1708, C. E. French Papers, 1701-1740.

[53] Arthur H. Buffinton, "Governor Dudley and the Proposed Treaty of Neutrality, 1705," 211-229; *Mass. Acts and Resolves*, VIII, 497-503, 510-514, 538, 541-545; a further and shorter draft of a treaty of neutrality is in Parkman Papers, XXX, 439-442, Mass. Hist. Soc. For later contacts between Quebec and Boston during these years, *Mass. Acts and Resolves*, VIII, 186-189, 618, 641-642; John Stoddard, "Stoddard's Journal," 21-42; and *Collections de manuscrits contenant lettres, mémoires, et autres documents historiques relatifs à la Nouvelle France*, II, 520-522, 537-539—the latter concerning a French emissary sent to persuade "les Bostonnais" who live in "une espèce de République" that the British forces coming to help in the expedition against Canada were really designed to crush New England's independence.

[54] Chapter 6, preceding; Waller, *Samuel Vetch*, 83-93.

merchants' convictions upon appeal. He kept a tight hand upon Boston's newly established journal, the *News-Letter*. And just when Cotton Mather and his allies felt confident of blocking a vote absolving Dudley of complicity with the illegal trading, they found to their disgust and fury that the governor had won the backing of Nathaniel Jewett of Ipswich, an influential leader of the old charter group in the lower house, through whose influence the house at length passed a motion condemning the charges brought against the governor.[55] Jewett's reward was an appointment as justice of the peace, and the whole episode, in Cotton Mather's eyes, demonstrated all too plainly Dudley's diabolical skill in winning over opponents by his generous hospitality, glib tongue, and command of patronage—"the Caresses of the *Table,* which are enough to Dazzle an Honest Countryman," the governor's "Mixture of *Coaksing* and *Bouncing,* and Confident Assertions of Things," and the allurement of the titles he could bestow.[56]

Dudley's tenure of office abounds with similar examples of his political dexterity—his close attendance upon the day-to-day workings of the Massachusetts assembly, his trading of the old Harvard College charter for the appointment of his ally Leverett as president, and his balancing of the Puritan and Anglican claims upon his favor. In New Hampshire, he won popular support (together with the first regular salary, one hundred and fifty pounds a year, ever granted to a royal governor in New England) by his efforts to defend the province and

---

[55] The identity of Jewett, whom Mather calls only a "sowgelder" and representative of Ipswich, is established by his appointment as justice, Dec. 4, 1707, and by the pamphlet of 1694 which identifies the then Speaker of the assembly (Jewett) as "a practising Sow-gelder"; [Cotton Mather?], *Deplorable State of New-England,* 118*; Cotton Mather to Stephen Sewall, Dec. 13, 1707, Silverman, *Selected Letters of Cotton Mather;* 75; C.O. 5/858, fol. 126. Jewett, characterized by Samuel Sewall as one of the "Old-Charter Men" and by Increase Mather in 1702 as one "soundly for the true interest of the Churches and country," was one of the very few representatives who had served almost uninterruptedly since 1692; hence his appointment as chairman of the committee assigned to draw up charges against the merchants: Sewall to Timothy Woodbridge, Feb. 1, 1720, Conn. Hist. Soc., *Collections,* XXI (1924), 393; Mather to Mr. Speaker [James Converse], [Oct. 1702], Pubs. Col. Soc. Mass., *Collections,* XLIX (1975), 196; *Mass. Acts and Resolves,* VIII, 183.

[56] [Cotton Mather?], *Deplorable State of New-England,* 118*, 114*. These pages in the tract bear abundant signs of Mather's authorship.

to arrange a settlement in the battle over the Mason-Allen claims.[57] A compromise he negotiated in 1705 whereby the province would purchase part of Samuel Allen's title and recognize the remainder collapsed when Allen suddenly died and his heir was persuaded by John Usher to appeal his cause to London. But Dudley's steady pressure for a decision and his refusal to commit himself to backing Allen paid off when the Privy Council dismissed Allen's appeal and effectively confirmed existing titles.[58] The governor's popularity in New Hampshire undoubtedly owed much to his good fortune in having Usher as his deputy, for the latter only had to make one of his infrequent visits to the province to arouse feelings that made any other ruler seem a blessing: "If he be a weeke in Hampshire," Dudley told Blathwayt, "he puts all there into a flame." Usher's increasing withdrawal from his post—he made only four short visits to the province while the assembly was in session in the nine years after 1706—did much to restore political harmony.[59] Dudley usually attended assembly sessions, and when in Boston he supervised province affairs through frequent correspondence with New Hampshire councillor and treasurer Samuel Penhallow.[60]

---

[57] *N. H. Laws*, II, 57, 64; Fry, *New Hampshire as a Royal Province*, 101–102, 221–239; Paul Dudley to William Blathwayt, Mar. 20, 1705, Joseph Dudley to [Blathwayt], May 9, 1705, Blathwayt Papers, BL 267, 269, Hunt. Lib. Also George Vaughan to Constantine Phipps, Nov. 15, 1706, Rawlinson MSS., C 379.

[58] Joseph H. Smith, *Appeals to the Privy Council*, 157.

[59] Dudley to Blathwayt, July 30, 1705, Blathwayt Papers, BL 262, Hunt. Lib.; Usher's concerns are displayed in his letter to the Board of Trade, [July, 1709], *CSP Col., 1708–1709*, no. 663. Van Deventer, *Emergence of Provincial New Hampshire*, 138, 264–265, suggests that after 1705 Usher created a faction in New Hampshire politics by means of political and economic favors. Usher praised some New Hampshire councillors and attacked others in his rambling correspondence with Whitehall, but I have found no evidence, either in the official papers or in his private correspondence in the Jeffries Papers, of such influence building. Although Usher was appointed the resident executive of the province, he attended only a quarter of the council meetings, 1703–1715; Dudley attended more council sessions than he during these years and twice as many when the assembly was in session.

[60] Dudley's extensive correspondence with Penhallow, 1703–1712, is in Belknap Papers, 1664–1744. He was also in frequent communication with the leader of the province's defense forces, his half-brother's grandson, Colonel Winthrop Hilton.

Within each colony, therefore, executive authority grew stronger during the first years of the new century. Yet this conclusion needs careful qualification to reveal its ultimate significance. Only in Rhode Island and Connecticut was this strengthening formally embodied in legislative acts and resolves; in the royal colonies the assemblies carefully refrained from any similar expression of support. Nor were the consequences of such strengthening uniform across New England: from the first, Bellomont and Dudley exercised far greater powers than did their counterparts in Connecticut and Rhode Island. Such differences reflected the diversity of political structures now established in New England; in particular, they point to the ways in which this diversity, in conjunction with the pressures exerted by internal dissensions, Whitehall, and the war, was fostering two quite different patterns of political thought and behavior. In Rhode Island and Connecticut, stronger leadership won broad support because it served to combat both domestic division and external challenge. In the royal colonies, by contrast, with the crown's representative already inside the gates and occupying the governor's chair, to bolster the executive was to augment rather than diminish external control. Consequently, a more complex pattern emerged in these latter colonies. The colonists conceded to a Dudley or a Bellomont the power to rule—and even the necessity of such power in such a time of crisis. But, especially in Massachusetts, they also strove to hedge in their governor with a vigilant watch upon his pretensions and a countervailing insistence upon their own rights as subjects. Such a response, in turn, reveals a further dimension of our larger theme of the growth of government: paradoxically (and as modern Americans have discovered to their cost), to circumscribe government was also to stimulate its institutional growth through codification and definition. Limiting the business of government became a part of the business of government.

Clearly, the traumatic experience of the Dominion and its aftermath prepared the ground for this response. Andros's summary demolition of the very cornerstones of the New England way left an indelible memory of the dangers of government unrestrained by any ties of law or precedent. In effect the colonists had found themselves hoist on the very petard they had so often exploded against dissidents and royal officials. Spurning the pleas of those who claimed the rights of "Free-born English-men," the Massachusetts magistrates had consistently denied the validity of English law in New England.[61] It was precisely this argument that a Dominion official used to counter John Wise's appeal to Magna Carta and his English rights in 1687. The colonists, he warned, should not think that the laws of England followed them to the ends of the earth, adding that Wise and his fellows had "no more previledges . . . than not to be Sould for Slaves."[62] A second official, Judge John Palmer, rammed home the point with his pamphlet demonstrating the legality of Andros's rule and expounding the duty of nonresistance to duly constituted rulers.[63] Only too plainly, the sword of unlimited authority could cut both ways.

The fears of arbitrary power heightened by the Dominion were freely aired in the debates that followed its overthrow. Andros had invaded the property and English liberties of his subjects.[64] In themselves, however, these arguments are no certain evidence of a sudden transformation of New England's political thinking. Most were specifically written to convince English readers that the Boston uprising was not a revolution of the saints but a microcosm of their own against James II, and those addressed directly to the colonists, such as the broadsheets circulated in May 1689, were far more concerned with securing a resumption of charter rule, to "set up our *Hedge of Government* about us, that we may *sit under our Vines and Fig-trees,* and there

[61] Bishop, *New England Judged,* 189; Remonstrance and Petition of Robert Child and others, [1646], Hutchinson, *Papers,* I, 216; Winthrop, *Journal,* II, 297.

[62] Mass. Archives, XXXV, 138–139; Thomas F. Waters, *Ipswich in the Massachusetts Bay Colony, 1633–1700,* 246–247, 260, 262, and George A. Cook, *John Wise,* 50–52, show that John West (or possibly West and Robert Mason) made these remarks. As early as 1707, however, the still prevalent legend was taking hold that they were uttered by Dudley: Mass. Hist. Soc., *Collections,* 5th ser., VI (1879), 36* (corrected, 105*).

[63] [John Palmer], *The Present State of New-England;* also Palmer, *An Impartial Account, Andros Tracts,* I, 21–62.

[64] In particular, *The Revolution in New England Justified, Andros Tracts,* I, 65–131, and A. B., *An Account of the Revolution, ibid.,* II, 191–201.

may be *none to make us afraid,*" than with considering whether such government would involve any further Andros-style excesses of authority.[65] Had Massachusetts managed to retain its old charter, the great bulk of the rhetoric of opposition to authority would most likely have faded away as quickly as it had arisen. In "rehedged" Connecticut and Rhode Island, for example, there was no attempt to shackle executive power.

In Massachusetts, however, the new charter and the return of a royal governor revived the danger of alien and overbearing leadership. The political divisions that followed reinvigorated libertarian strains in colonial thought that had long been repressed by the need for unity in the face of threatened external encroachment. Increasingly, moreover, colonial writers responded to English authority by clothing their discussions of government in the language of the Whig beliefs that had triumphed in the Glorious Revolution in England. It is not easy to trace the transmission of these ideas, and they assume no clear pattern in New England until the early decades of the eighteenth century. Some were inherent in the philosophical heritage of "the good old cause" preserved on both sides of the Atlantic. They were made the more palatable to colonial tastes by the strong contractual element in Puritan theology. Judging by the output of New England's printing presses, a sampling admittedly skewed by the Mathers' intimidating dominance of the period's sermon literature, it was they who first made this Whig terminology the common coin of political debate.[66] Increase's ardent defense of his agency—or, more accurately, his interpretation of what it had achieved—helped recast the vocabulary of Massachusetts politics even as his charter transformed the structure of its government. Seeking the return of the colony's "auncient priviledges," he had ended up thanking William for the "English liberties" of the new patent. The one formula over-

---

[65] Simmons, "The Massachusetts Revolution of 1689," 12. Also Chapter 2, note 147, preceding. For interpretations stressing a more abrupt shift in colonial beliefs, see Miller, *Colony to Province,* 157–160, and Breen, *Character of the Good Ruler,* 150–167.

[66] Miller, *Colony to Province,* 157–163; Breen, *Character of the Good Ruler,* 182–183; and, set in a different context, Middlekauff, *The Mathers,* 214.

lapped the other; but it left Mather with no choice but to convince his countrymen of the validity of the argument he had composed to soothe an English audience, that the revolution in New England had been fought to defend the rights of Englishmen. The charter, in encapsulating these rights, had preserved the fundamentals of the New England way: it was "a MAGNA CHARTA, whereby Religion and English Liberties, with some peculiar Priviledges, Liberties, and all Mens Properties, are Confirmed and Secured . . . to Them and their Posterity for evermore."[67] Back in Boston, and through the 1690s, father and son played endless variations upon this single theme, the blessing—"all *Christian Liberties* and all *English Liberties*"—which the charter had bestowed.[68]

Simultaneously, the Mathers and their allies sought to define more explicitly the "Libertyes and Immunities" guaranteed in the charter. At their urging, and as part of the body of legislation fleshing out the structure of the new government, the Massachusetts assembly passed an act "setting forth general priviledges" which rehearsed the principles of England's Magna Carta and added further guarantees concerning the security of land titles, the right to bail, and the illegality of taxation without representative consent. Similar laws were passed or proposed in other royal colonies, notably New York, during these years.[69] The clear intent was to establish a body of fundamental law in the manner of the famous English declarations of 1215 and 1689 which would forever prevent a repetition of the Dominion's tyranny.[70]

---

[67] Increase Mather, *A Brief Account, Andros Tracts*, II, 296.

[68] Cotton Mather, *Optanda*, 89–90; *idem, Winter-Meditations*, 49–50; *idem, Life of Phips*, 53, 117; Increase Mather, *Great Blessing*, 21–22.

[69] Increase Mather, *A Brief Account, Andros Tracts*, II, 295; *Mass. Acts and Resolves*, I, 14, 40–41.

[70] Evarts B. Greene, *Provincial America, 1690–1740*, 70–72, and, excluding the Massachusetts law, Lovejoy, *Glorious Revolution in America*, 358–363, 369–370, note these parallels. The New York law, passed in May 1691, seventeen months before that of Massachusetts, is printed in Hall, Leder, and Kammen, *Glorious Revolution*, 121–123. As Lovejoy (*Glorious Revolution in America*, 116, 358) observes, this New York law was in turn modelled upon the 1683 New York Charter of Libertyes which itself drew for its language upon such English documents as Magna Carta and the Petition of Right. The language and organization of the Massachusetts

It was a further step beyond advancing these claims to deploy them as a weapon against the executive, and one which the Mathers themselves did not take. Their background, their commitment to the structure of the new order, and their passionate desire to preserve within it the true faith and church of the old disposed them to work with and not against authority—they sought to be the powers behind, not the dissidents confronting, the governor's chair; even when, at a later date, they turned on Dudley, they denounced his abuse of his office, not its powers. Instead, as we have seen, it was Byfield and the Tories who took the lead in countering executive pretensions through the medium of the house of representatives and its assertions of "the accustomed priviledges of an English Assembly."[71] As in England, the struggle to define the rights of the subject became intertwined with the conflicts between the various branches of government. During the 1690s, these Tory tactics, in conjunction with the character of the governors appointed to Massachusetts, delayed what seems in retrospect to have been an inevitable confrontation between a royal executive and those still deeply suspicious of any form of external authority. With the return of Dudley and his ally Byfield to power in 1702, however, the divisions that were to dominate provincial politics for the next three-quarters of a century quickly reemerged.

Dudley himself undoubtedly sharpened and accelerated these divisions. His purge of officeholders and promotion of Anglicans, his bullying of subordinates and disregard for protocol, and his evident ambition to expand his powers aroused immediate anxiety and resentment. Samuel Sewall feared that the governor's repeated vetoes of councillors were disturbing the balance of the "three Members"— the constituent elements—of government.[72] John Saffin, one of those

---

act strongly suggest that it was inspired by the 1691 New York act. Perhaps, although the New York act was passed by an assembly dominated by opponents of Leisler, its text was taken to Boston by a Leislerian refugee such as Abraham Gouverneur.

[71] *Mass. Acts and Resolves*, VII, 390; also *ibid.*, 34, 393, I, 170.

[72] Samuel Sewall to Stephen Sewall, June 3, 1704, Curwin Papers, I, 3, Amer. Antiq. Soc.; Sewall, *Diary*, I, 470, 472, 547, 578. An indication, perhaps, of the popular concern was the record number of voters at the Boston elections of 1703: *ibid.*, 482.

excluded, urged every man "true to the Interest of his Countrey . . . to obstruct the Streame of Innovation of the State of things respecting our Libertys both civill and Sacred; the omission of which where of may tend to the Detriment, if not the ruine of the Publicke weale." Later, after Dudley and his family had narrowly escaped drowning when the ice on the Charles River broke beneath their sled, Saffin pointed the moral of this sign of divine displeasure, and drew the parallel with the time of the Dominion, in verse. "Your Excellency knowes," he wrote,

> That you Designe (your actions don't conceale)
> a Totall Change in Church, and commonweale
> is the Opinion of most Thinking men
> We must return to Egypt once agen
> ah! Let it not be said that you now dare
> to pull down that your Father helped to Reare.[73]

Other critics pointed to Dudley's nepotism and to his son Paul's indiscreet remark that Massachusetts would never be worth living in "for Lawyers and Gentlemen" until the charter was taken away. An incident in 1705 epitomized the family's peremptoriness and hauteur: denied passage for their coach by some local farmers, the governor and his younger son drew their swords, attacked the men, and finally had them clapped into prison.[74]


Understandably, therefore, even while the Massachusetts legislators acknowledged the value of Dudley's vigorous leadership, they never let his "*Coaksing* and *Bouncing*" seduce them into any formal strengthening of his powers. On the basis of its past record and present membership, the council might have been expected to take the lead in circumscribing the governor. It was elected and not ap-

---

[73] Saffin, *His Book,* 75, 81.

[74] [Cotton Mather?], *Deplorable State of New-England,* 109*; Sewall, *Diary,* I, 532–536. One of the governor's opponents in this fracas, John Winchester, promptly secured election to the assembly as Brookline's first representative, where he doubtless did his best to obstruct Dudley's policies.

pointed; as late as the time of Dudley's arrival, over half its members had served as magistrates prior to 1692; and it enjoyed a remarkable continuity of membership, averaging less than three changes a year in its twenty-eight-man composition between 1692 and 1715. During the 1690s, moreover, except when the assembly had taken the initiative during the first years of Phips's administration, it had assumed a dominant role in government, drafting the bulk of the legislation passed by the General Court and directing affairs through its powerful standing committees.[75] Events proved, however, that under a governor of Dudley's caliber the council had little opportunity in practice to check the chief executive's power or indeed to exercise any significant independent role. Overawed by Dudley's vetoes and deprived of its initiative in making appointments, it all too often found itself trapped in the middle or even drawn in on the governor's side in Dudley's clashes with the lower house. Furthermore, as Dudley frequently pointed out to Whitehall, because of the lower house's preponderant role in its selection, it was not a completely reliable instrument of executive power. At bottom, its weaknesses were constitutional rather than personal. Placed, in effect, between king and Commons, between prerogative and popular authority, the council could not even claim to be a House of Lords, for it possessed no independent power base or constituency of its own. Its members, men generally of conscience and integrity, hardly merited the violent abuse—"Pusillanimous . . . Obsequious . . . the Tools of their Governour's particular Designs"—poured upon them by Dudley's opponents; rather, they were prisoners of their station, condemned to serve more as buffer than as balance in the province's mechanism of government.[76]

---

[75] Thus, for example, Mass. Archives, Court Records, VI, July 7, Nov. 17, 1693, May 31, Nov. 28, 1695, May 27, 28, June 8, 1697, VII, June 22, 1700, Feb. 24, 1701. From July 1701 to June 1702, after the deaths of Bellomont and Stoughton, the Massachusetts council ruled the province.

[76] [Cotton Mather?], *Deplorable State of New-England*, 97*, 114*, 113*; Leonard Woods Labaree, *Royal Government in America*, 167–168; Hutchinson, *History of Massachusetts-Bay*, II, 7; William Douglass, *A Summary, Historical and Political, of the First Planting, Progressive Improvements, and Present State of the British Settlements in North-America*, I, 486. I have also drawn these conclusions from a general reading of the

## Resurgence and Synthesis

In consequence, the representatives reassumed and held the initiative. Like the Commons in England, they were always careful to make themselves indispensable to the continuance of government (and thereby circumscribed the executive) by limiting the term of legislation authorizing taxation and the governor's powers in military affairs to a single year or some similar brief period, renewing such authority as the need arose.[77] Defying the crown's explicit instructions, they refused Dudley a regular salary, holding him instead on a short financial leash by doling out, in biennial instalments, an allowance of five hundred pounds a year, not even enough to meet the governor's incidental expenses according to one of his supporters.[78] The length to which they were prepared to carry such stringency was demonstrated by the sad case of Thomas Povey. A needy English relative of William Blathwayt, Povey accompanied Dudley to Massachusetts as his lieutenant governor only to find that the General Court refused to allow him any money save as captain of isolated Castle William in Boston harbor, and then only if he spent three days a week there—a rather more subtle method of quarantining an unwelcome English official than that employed when Andros had been imprisoned in the island castle back in 1689. Povey, understandably discouraged, sailed for England in 1706, never to return.[79] In like fashion, New Hampshire legislators strove to starve the inimitable John Usher from his post but discovered that in this case the lieutenant governor's great wealth and even greater vanity made him impervious to all their insults.

council's records for the period, Mass. Archives, Court Records, VI–IX, and Executive Records of the Council, II–VI.

[77] Thus, for example, *Mass. Acts and Resolves,* I, 491, 519, 552, 566. The London government was well aware of the effect of these and other short-term acts in limiting executive authority and forestalling royal disallowance: Board of Trade to Bellomont, Feb. 3, 1699, *CSP Col., 1699,* no. 73; Leonard Woods Labaree, *Royal Government in America,* 247 *et seq.*

[78] Henry R. Spencer, *Constitutional Conflict in Provincial Massachusetts,* 70–72; Kimball, *Joseph Dudley,* 95–97; *Mass. Acts and Resolves,* VIII, 293–294, 339–341; John Nelson to Mr. Popple, Feb. 11, 1706, C.O. 5/864, nos. 72, 73.

[79] *Mass. Acts and Resolves,* VIII, 75, 378–380; Members of the Church of England to the Board of Trade, Feb. 4, 1706, C.O. 5/864, no. 63.

Simultaneously, the Massachusetts lower house maintained and consolidated the powers it had asserted in the 1690s. Once again, the war and its voracious appetite for men and money accelerated constitutional development. For even as military necessity enhanced the day-to-day authority of the executive, it also compelled a governor to work closely with his legislature and thereby established precedents and practices that gave the latter a larger voice in administrative affairs. The representatives' prime weapon, as before, was their expansion of their right to participate in the levying of taxation into a comprehensive system of detailed appropriation and audit. Despite Dudley's protests, they prescribed salaries, gratuities, and rates of pay, laid down the duties of officials, and effectively dictated policy by refusing to supply funds for some purposes (notably the rebuilding of Fort William Henry at Pemaquid) and earmarking grants for others with such precision as to prevent their being used in any other fashion. Like the English House of Commons, they insisted upon the redress of grievances before they would proceed to the granting of revenue. All the while, they kept a tight watch upon expenditures, down to such items as the excessive cost of the candles burned at Castle William and the quantity of ingredients for wine-punch allowed to those careening the province galley. They showed an increasing reluctance even to confer with the council in the framing of money bills. Actions they perceived as a challenge to their powers they heatedly protested: the council's vote of fifty pounds to Lieutenant Governor Povey was "arbitrary, and Illegall, a violation of our English, and Charter Priviledges, and Rights and if Precedentiall, of pernicious and fatell Consequence, to all her majesties subjects within this Province." And in the manner of English representative bodies everywhere, they justified such fiery rhetoric by reference to a mythic past which traced Parliament's right to control expenditures as far back as the thirteenth century, to the reign of Henry III.[80]

---

[80] Henry R. Spencer, *Constitutional Conflict*, 95–105, 115–121; *Mass. Acts and Resolves*, VIII, 649, 379, 341. For an example of this supervision, exerted over the governor's freedom to run up expenses during his travels about the province, Mass. Archives, Court Records, VIII, July 2, Oct. 26, Nov. 3, 1708.

The house was equally sensitive to any apparent threat to its independence or that of the General Court as a whole. In 1705, with the council's support, it forced Dudley to back down from his attempt to veto its choice of Thomas Oakes as speaker, the former agent whom Dudley regarded as "a known Comon-Wealth's man."[81] Together, the two houses were quick to counter the governor's attempts to engineer a more submissive council by means of his patronage: in 1703, for example, to Dudley's fury, the two houses refused to reelect to the council Nathaniel Byfield, John Appleton, Nathaniel Thomas, and Barnabas Lothrop, all men upon whom Dudley had bestowed the lucrative office of judge of probate the previous year.[82] Five years later, in the wake of the illegal trading scandal, three of Dudley's supporters were purged and several others only narrowly reelected.[83] These actions, it would seem, were more the consequence of partisan political feeling than of any principled objection to members of the General Court accepting administrative office. The old-charter practice whereby leaders were at once executives, legislators, and judges lived on—almost all the justices of the Massachusetts Superior Court during these years, for example, simultaneously sat as councillors—and there was no attempt to enact "place" bills of the kind regularly introduced into the English Parliament to bar those holding offices of profit from the crown from sitting in the legislature. Clearly, however, to accept office or to side too ardently with the executive was to invite suspicion and even retribution from one's constituents no less than

---

[81] Sewall, *Diary*, I, 523–524; Dudley to the Board of Trade, July 25, 1705, *CSP Col., 1704–1705*, no. 1274, (p. 588).

[82] Sewall, *Diary*, I, 486; Lyman H. Weeks and Edwin M. Bacon, *A Historical Digest of the Provincial Press*, 44; Thomas Cushing to John Cushing, June 4, 1703, Cushing Papers, 1644–1780, Mass. Hist. Soc. Dudley then vetoed five councillors, including four of the five chosen in the place of those excluded.

[83] Sewall, *Diary*, I, 594–595; [Cotton Mather?], *Deplorable State of New-England*, 101*; Dudley to the Board of Trade, July 10, 1708, *CSP Col., 1708–1709*, no. 33. The three were Penn Townsend, John Thacher, and Simon Stoddard (the other voted off, Benjamin Browne, soon died); Andrew Belcher and Samuel Appleton were only narrowly reelected. The contemporary evidence does not support the belief of Hutchinson, *History of Massachusetts-Bay*, II, 130–131, that the men left off were opponents of Dudley. In the previous year, the governor's ally John Leverett had been dropped from the council.

from one's colleagues in the General Court: Nathaniel Jewett lost his seat for selling out to Dudley in 1707, and only a small proportion of his fellow justices of the peace, despite their prominence in local affairs, ever sat in the lower house in any one session.[84]

The consistency of purpose underlying the house's actions seems the more remarkable in light of what we know of the fluidity of its membership. Each time the members assembled between 1692 and 1715 (and, with few exceptions, well into the eighteenth century), more than half of them had not served in the preceding house. The average length of service of each representative during the twenty-six assemblies of this period was less than two and two-thirds terms, a third less than the average term served during an equal period of time in Massachusetts prior to 1686. Many towns regularly represented year after year, notably Medfield, Marblehead, Salisbury, Hadley, and Plymouth, rarely elected the same representative from one assembly to another. Over forty percent of all the representatives served only a single term.[85] Though some elections were contested, as in Boston, the bulk of the evidence during this period points to a seat in the house being regarded more as a burden than a privilege: especially in the 1690s, some chosen refused to serve, and Josiah Wolcott's lament—"I am foarst to serve in the Assembly"—contains no hint of mock humility.[86] Involuntary absence from home in an agricultural

---

[84] Bushman, "Corruption and Power," 72; Gerald E. Aylmer, "Place Bills and the Separation of Powers," 45–69; Geoffrey Holmes, *British Politics in the Age of Anne,* 130–136; Murrin, "Review Essay," 260–261. The absence of J.P.s from the assembly must be seen in the context of the very high turnover in the membership of the lower house. Nonetheless, the contrast with English practice is marked. Suspicion of the office continued to run high: the office of a justice of the peace, declared John Adams years later, "is enough to purchase and corrupt allmost any Man." Lyman H. Butterfield, ed., *Adams Family Correspondence,* 116.

[85] Michael Zuckerman, *Peaceable Kingdoms,* 209–211, 178, and Murrin, "Review Essay," 259, provide some data for these years, to which I have added tables of each town's representatives constructed from the lists in *Mass. Acts and Resolves,* VII–IX. For the twenty-three years before 1686, I have used the lists in Robert E. Wall, Jr., "The Membership of the Massachusetts General Court, 1634–1686." The figures for average length of service given here do not take account of service outside the bounds of each of the two periods selected, 1663–1686 and 1692–1715.

[86] Josiah Wolcott to Henry Wolcott, May 31, 1699, Roger Wolcott Papers, I, 32; and, for refusals to serve, *Mass. Acts and Resolves,* VII, 104n., 105n., 239n., 333n.,

economy was always onerous, but the greater incidence of such reluctance to serve under the new charter than the old suggests other reasons as well: a distaste for complicity in the work of royal government, the burden of longer sessions, and the added anxiety of leaving one's home and family in a time of war and frequent border raids.

A similar fluidity of membership did not inhibit the pretensions of other eighteenth-century colonial assemblies, and a closer look at the composition of the Massachusetts house points to the source of its strength by revealing an inner core of long-serving members. Sixty-one of the 725 representatives who sat in the house between 1692 and 1715 served nearly a third of the total number of terms, averaging nearly ten terms apiece. Ten sat in thirteen or more of the twenty-six assemblies. Long service was no certain guide to political prominence, and some of these men stood out only by their continued presence year after year. Others, such as Penn Townsend, John Clark, and Thomas Hutchinson, all of Boston, had promising careers cut short when they were promoted (or, in some cases, it would seem, pushed upstairs) to the council. Overall, however, to judge by those who held the speakership and sat on the most important committees, this core group dominated the assembly's proceedings.[87] Particularly prominent were such veterans as James Converse of Woburn, John Burrill of Lynn, Nehemiah Jewett of Ipswich, Thomas Oliver of Cambridge,

---

VIII, 162n., IX, 5n. Other examples can be found in many of the surviving records of the towns. This reluctance, rather than any agreement to rotate the holding of a much sought-after office, would seem to be the reason why in some towns a remarkably high proportion of the population served as representative— in Braintree, Wrentham, Medfield, Sherburne, Duxbury, and Yarmouth, for example, the number of individuals serving as representatives, 1692–1715, exceeded 10 percent of the number in their militia in 1690. For a somewhat different analysis, but one based upon a much more extensive and sophisticated examination of political leadership at the town level, see Edward M. Cook, Jr., *The Fathers of the Towns*, esp. chapter II.

[87] Although no single source for committee membership exists prior to 1715, due to the loss of the house journals, many committee assignments are recorded in *Mass. Acts and Resolves*, VII–IX, to which I have added additional data gathered from Mass. Archives, XX, XXX, XXXI, LXI, LXII, LXX, LXXI, C, CI, CXIX, and, especially, Court Records, VI–IX, in a desire to emulate the method pursued by Jack P. Greene, *The Quest for Power*, 463–495. For high turnover in other eighteenth-century assemblies, see Robert J. Dinkin, *Voting in Provincial America*, 68.

all speakers of the house, and William Dennison of Roxbury and Samuel Phipps of Charlestown. Boston's four representatives, double the number allowed to any other town, were always a powerful force, especially when, as in the first years of Dudley's administration, the town returned the same quartet—Ephraim Savage, Samuel Checkley, Elizur Holyoke, and Dudley's bugbear, two-time speaker Thomas Oakes—for six years in a row. Bostonians, indeed, held the speakership during nine of the twenty-six assemblies.[88]

Lacking the house journals, we cannot be entirely certain of the part played by this core of leaders. Very few—only three of our sixty-one—had sat as deputies prior to 1686. Yet it seems logical to assume that it was these leaders—men "soundly for the true interest of the Churches and country" as Increase Mather characterized them in 1702—who formulated and preserved the house's "undoubted privileges" and inspired the tenacious spirit so apparent in its often turbulent relations with Dudley.[89] Their influence must have been all the greater amid the inexperience of most of their colleagues. In their conservative cast of mind and their distaste for court attitudes and connections, they resembled the country members of Queen Anne's

---

[88] A similar dominance continued in the five years after 1715 under the long speakership of John Burrill of Lynn, when such long-serving Boston-area legislators as Oliver Noyes and Elisha Cooke, Jr., of Boston, Jonathan Remington of Cambridge, Charles Chambers of Charlestown, Samuel Thaxter of Hingham, William Dudley of Roxbury, Francis Fulham of Weston, with John Stoddard of Northampton, effectively monopolized the most important committees (I am indebted for this information to the researches of Mr. Bill Yedor). Absent from the names cited here and above, it may be noted, is that of Elisha Cooke, Sr., long lauded as the leader of the "patriot" party in Massachusetts. Cooke, Sr., who died in 1715, was certainly a prominent opponent of Dudley and the new charter, but the contemporary evidence that he dominated or formally organized such opposition is even slimmer than the number of offices he held—hence the ingenious but not necessarily convincing argument that he was always "working behind the scenes." In fact, he seems to owe most of his posthumous fame to his foresight in giving his son, undoubtedly a leading critic of royal government in the 1720s and 1730s, the same name as himself, thus making the name of Elisha Cooke a synonym for political leadership.

[89] Increase Mather to Mr. Speaker [James Converse], [Oct. 1702], Pubs. Col. Soc. Mass., *Collections*, XLIX (1975), 196, speaking of Samuel Phipps, Oliver, Jewett, and Dennison. For the value of having the aid of a leader like Converse, and a testimony to his influence, see the petition of John Wilson, Oct. 15, 1701, Mass. Archives, LXX, 543.

House of Commons. Unlike those English squires, however, they were not inveterate backbenchers: they ran their house. Nor were they backwoodsmen: after the mid-1690s, following Phips's nonresidency law and the ebbing of the brief Tory tide within the house, almost all these leaders came from the towns bordering on or within a few miles of Massachusetts Bay. Such proximity to the seat of government in Boston helps to explain their predominance in assembly affairs. Significantly, also, these towns lay within the province's cradle and heartland, the area least dependent upon executive authority for protection and where old charter traditions were most deeply rooted.

Plainly, therefore, to employ the terms *court* and *country* to describe the ideological differences at the center of Massachusetts politics during these years should not be taken to imply a struggle between coastal town and rural back country. Rather, the dimensions of the contest were historical and constitutional, between those representing (or competing for) the crown's authority and those who, hankering after the old ways, were yet being drawn to express their opposition within the structure of the new. This division, moreover, was becoming as much one between the levels of government as between its branches as the political attitudes and practices now established at the center of affairs diverged from those sustained and cherished in the localities. A similar contrast, less sharply etched, can be glimpsed elsewhere in New England. The outcome, Edward Cook has plausibly suggested, was two political cultures, one local and the other provincial, one predominantly egalitarian and consensual in its social and political beliefs and the other placing a greater emphasis upon the need for hierarchy and deference to one's superiors.[90] The division

---

[90] Edward M. Cook, *Fathers of the Towns*, 117–118. Cook's suggestion, as he perceives, helps to explain why scholars, approaching the question of the nature of Massachusetts politics from different directions, from the center of government and from the towns, have arrived at such different conclusions. Still unclear, for example, is whether local power was increasing or decreasing in relation to that of the central government during the course of the late seventeenth and early eighteenth centuries; thus compare Zuckerman, *Peaceable Kingdoms*, esp. 16–45, with Murrin, "Review Article," 257–270; David Grayson Allen, "The Zuckerman Thesis and the Process of Legal Rationalization in Provincial Massachusetts," 443–460; John W. Putre, "Town and Province in Early Eighteenth-Century Massachusetts," *passim*, and Lockridge, *New England Town*, 135–138. My own

# Adjustment to Empire

between the two was never absolute and its roots can be traced back into seventeenth-century New England and in turn to English society, but it was sharpened and given much clearer institutional form by the coming of royal government. Much of the colonial assemblies' strength and importance in the eighteenth century derived from their capacity to link these cultures and to express the needs of local particularism at the center.

Constitutional conflict bred skepticism and dissent, and a final instance of the way in which old ideals and new circumstances came together to form a weapon against executive power was the gradual transformation of contemporary conceptions of the nature of government and political authority. Even before the attack upon the charters, some had questioned the magistrates' discretionary powers. Save for a militant few, however, New Englanders did not doubt the need for a certain measure of discretion. Rulers were chosen for their obedience to God, not man, and there was no place for tenderness when a holy commonwealth's survival lay at risk. Preachers depicted rulers as nursing fathers, steersmen, pilots, shepherds, keepers—benevolent experts who could and should be trusted to care for those under their command. "Leave the guidance of the ship to those that are at the helm," urged Jonathan Mitchell, "jostle not into their Places nor refuse to acquiesce in their Conclusions." It was "commonly they that raise the loudest Out-cry against *Governors* for Robbing the people of their Liberties," declared Urian Oakes in 1673, who "either design or *eventually* prove to be the greatest Oppressors of them. . . . Nothing makes way more for Tyranny and Oppression, then an undue Affectation of Liberty."[91] Twenty years later, Samuel Willard expressed

analysis, doubtless shaped by approaching the matter from a study of the central governments, leads me to the conclusion stated earlier in Chapter 7, that the power, prestige, and regulatory authority of these central governments increased significantly during the first years of the eighteenth century, due in large part, however, to circumstances—war and the crisis of the 1690s—which were not as pressing later in the century.

[91] Jonathan Mitchell, *Nehemiah on the Wall in Troublesome Times*, 7, 25; Urian Oakes, *New-England Pleaded With*, 51, 52; also William Stoughton, *New-England's True Interest*, 34; Thomas Shepard, *Eye Salve*, 51.

the very different perspective inspired by memories of the Dominion and the presence of a royal governor: "A People are not made for Rulers," he told Phips, "But Rulers for a People."[92]

The transition was not as swift and decisive as this contrast would suggest. Ministers continued to preach the duty of obedience to rulers who would uphold a godly order in church and state. A heightened loyalty to the English crown helped ease suspicions of its representatives, and fear of tyranny was matched by an equal apprehension of the dangers of mobbish anarchy. Even a Dudley could win the restrained endorsement of a Willard or Solomon Stoddard, and in 1704 the Reverend Ebenezer Pemberton of Boston's South Church plainly sided with the governor in his conflict with the legislature.[93] Further, attitudes toward authority continued to fluctuate according to the realities of power and position: one's ally could be trusted, one's enemy could not. Overall, however, the broad stream of political thought within which these different currents ran was increasingly colored by a more skeptical and less reverent attitude toward those in power. The vocabulary of patriarchal authority gave way to that of obligation and contract, and talk of a ruler's duties replaced the reiteration of his God-given privileges. "The management of Civil Government is not left to the Arbitrary will and pleasure of men," declared Joseph Sewall, "No! Rulers must walk by Rule in their Administrations, taking care that the Ruled enjoy their Rights and Properties." Other writers, especially those who took part in the warm political debates of the 1720s, stressed the necessity of a continual watch upon those in power to preserve the people's liberties. Opposition to authority became acceptable, even respectable. The way was prepared for those who, in the course of the century, would draw a net of theory around executive authority, even to the point of urging the overthrow of rulers who abused their office. Leaders who had

---

[92] Willard, *Character of a Good Ruler*, 15.

[93] Ebenezer Pemberton, *A Christian Fixed in His Post, passim;* also *idem, The Divine Original and Dignity of Government Asserted,* 80–81, 93–96. For Pemberton's loyalties, see Sewall, *Diary,* II, 637–638, 646–647.

been "as Gods" became as suspect as Puritan sinners before their maker.[94]

By the end of Dudley's administration, therefore, both political theory and practice were setting firmer bounds upon executive power. Well might Governor Shute complain eight years later, following his ignominious retreat to London, that the Massachusetts representatives "are in a manner the whole Legislative and in a Good measure the Executive Power of the Province."[95] Yet Shute's bitter comment misleads if it is taken to mean that the lower house was now running the government. The governor might find his prerogatives eroded and his powers circumscribed. He might lack the prestige and patronage by which the crown and its ministers in England were able to guide proceedings and build a majority in Parliament.[96] But he retained extensive powers to appoint officials and administer the day-to-day affairs of government, as well as a fundamental independence by virtue of drawing his authority from across the Atlantic, beyond his subjects' immediate control. In consequence, royal government in the colonies preserved and accentuated a division of function of a kind that was fast disappearing in England where the crown, dabbling in parliamentary waters, was caught and drawn into complete subordination to the legislature. In America, by contrast, despite a period during the Revolution when the legislatures in effect overthrew and captured the executive, a formal separation of powers survived to become an essential component of American conceptions of constitutional government. Such a development, of course, was not unique to New England. Yet it was there that its evolution was most clearly marked because of the unique degree to which all governmental

---

[94] Joseph Sewall, *Rulers must be Just, Ruling in the Fear of God,* 31; also, generally, Breen, *Character of the Good Ruler,* chapter VII; Clinton Rossiter, *Six Characters in Search of a Republic,* chapter IV; Richard D. Brown, *Revolutionary Politics in Massachusetts,* 8–14; Alice M. Baldwin, *The New England Clergy and the American Revolution,* 25–27, 39–40.

[95] Memorial of Samuel Shute to the King, [1723], Perry, *Historical Collections,* III, 121.

[96] Bernard Bailyn, *The Origins of American Politics,* 72–80.

functions had once been concentrated in the hands of its General Courts. Far from developing along parallel lines, old and New England were in practice set upon intersecting and then diverging constitutional courses.

Two questions remain. What forces and motives shaped this pattern of political development? What was its significance in the larger context of New England's "adjustment to empire" in the years following 1689? Plainly, the colonists' political institutions and practices were brought into closer conformity with English ways, whether by an adoption of Dominion precedents and parliamentary procedure, a submission to Whitehall's discipline of disallowance and appeal, or a desire to invest government with a dignity and order culled from "the rules abroad." The prime cause of this greater conformity was the extension of royal government within and around New England, in part because of the combination of example and supervision which such government provided, but also because the institutional framework it imposed upon Massachusetts and New Hampshire transformed the character of political life in the two provinces, reorienting the attitudes and actions of those who remained hostile to royal authority hardly less than of those who strove to turn it to their advantage. Succession politics, the quest for royal and gubernatorial favor, and the increasing depth and complexity of the rivalry between executive and legislature all evidenced the effect of the colonists' more formal ties to the crown. Ideologically, government so blatantly sprung not from God but from Caesar lost much of its aura of religious purpose: the Puritan concept of a Bible Commonwealth, in Perry Miller's phrase, evolved into the philosophy of a government limited by the law of the land; Christian liberty was translated into those liberties guaranteed by statute.[97] The role of direct royal government in spurring these changes stands out by a comparison with affairs in Connecticut, for

---

[97] Miller, *Colony to Province*, 297, 171.

there, under restored charter rule, the traditional language and practice of politics persisted much longer and with less overt challenge than in Massachusetts.

Yet it is equally apparent that after the initial changes stemming from the reimposition of royal government, Whitehall's policies were neither as coherent nor as vigorously pursued as the flow of correspondence across the Atlantic would suggest. Closer examination reveals the familiar debris of Stuart bureaucracy, of overlapping and often contradictory instructions, of projects floated but never fulfilled, and orders given but never carried out—the knots in a string of endless expedients. The same cautious pragmatism that had tempered the crown's involvement in New England affairs before the 1680s reemerged, heightened by the turmoil of English domestic politics and the country's entanglement in a European war. Military assistance was forthcoming, but it was not accompanied by any further schemes for a political reorganization. Whitehall's legacy lay in the structures of government imposed in the 1690s rather than in any subsequent reforms or disciplined supervision.

Within these structures, moreover, even in the two royally governed provinces of Massachusetts and New Hampshire, much of the spirit and many of the forms of the old order plainly continued to infuse and impart a distinctive cast to the workings of the new. The colonists' opposition to executive power may have employed the terminology of English Whiggism, but it was inspired by the same profound belief in the necessity of godly rule that had shaped the New England magistracy prior to 1686. Similarly, just as the Massachusetts representatives fleshed out the new charter by reenacting many of their old laws, so they drew upon such traditional procedures as their participation in the auditing of accounts and the appointment of the colony treasurer in establishing what they now defined as "the accustomed priviledges of an English assembly." The relative weakness of this heritage in New Hampshire, coupled with that province's more exposed and dependent position, suggests why the New Hampshire assembly was always more submissive to royal authority. Its strength and significance in Massachusetts, by contrast, stands out from a further comparison, with New York; in that colony, where a representative assembly had existed only briefly prior to 1691, it was many years before the lower house was able to gain a comparable control over financial affairs.[98] In sum, ideals and procedures that had been an integral part of government under the old charter became weapons in the hands of those who now sought to limit discretionary power. Confronted by the king's governor in Boston, Puritanism in Massachusetts reassumed some part of what it had always retained in England, its vigor as an ideology of political opposition.

New England's accommodation to royal authority, therefore, was clearly far more complex than a simple submission to the crown. Not deference or coercion, but the pressures of war, the ties of trade, a desire to escape further royal intervention, and a need for alternative sources of political legitimacy were its underlying motives. The colonists did not surrender their unique heritage, and they retained a lively suspicion of Whitehall's intentions in this marriage of convenience. It was these mixed motives and emotions that gave the post-Revolutionary settlement its hybrid character. For even as New Englanders accepted the crown's solution, they adapted it in such a way as to retain much of their old independence. Royal authority was more widely recognized than ever before. It had become an integral part of what the colonists recognized as duly constituted government. Yet it was everywhere circumscribed by institutional checks and by the careful definition of roles and responsibilities. The shaping of government to English forms and procedures likewise cut both ways, for if it matched New England more closely to the pattern of empire it also ensured that the crown would not again be able, as in the 1680s, to erect an arbitrary regime in a legal vacuum.

Other aspects of the post-Revolutionary political settlement show this same spirit of pragmatic adaptation. In time, as we have seen, the colonists learned how to turn even their closer ties to England to advantage. A show of cooperation with Whitehall gave no excuse for the stern measures that open defiance might have prompted, and New

---

[98] Charles W. Spencer, *Colonial Wars and Constitutional Development in New York, passim*.

England leaders soon realized that their own representations or those of their agents could give them significant influence in shaping policy and appointing governors and other officials. A few, notably Joseph Dudley and, later, Jonathan Belcher, built careers at the point where imperial policy and colonial nativism met, balancing the desires of the one for a peaceable dependence upon the crown against the other's longings for rulers who would be "from amongst our selves" and of native "Family and Interest."[99] At worst, participation in the formulation of policy could offer abundant opportunities for its frustration. Bureaucracy could be impeded with its own procedures and choked with its own red tape.

Further, even what had once appeared to be the crown's fetters could be beaten into armor. Just as the Massachusetts colonists had turned the royal grant of 1629 into the ark of their covenant, "a free donation of absolute government" and *"an Original Contract,"* so their descendants came in time to view the charter of 1691 as an extension of the old which shielded them no less completely from further royal and parliamentary intervention. Cautiously advanced by agent Jeremiah Dummer in his famous *Defence of the New-England Charters* of 1721, this reinterpretation soon took firm hold back in Boston. "Our charter privileges," wrote the Reverend William Waldron to his brother in 1723, "are founded upon a Differing Bottom from what others are. Our Charter is an Act of Justice to us. Our Forefathers had these and Those Immunities and freedoms granted to them as a Condition of their Settlement and Enlargement of the Kings Dominions, now we having complyed with our Conditions cant in Justice be dispossesed of our Charter privileges, they belong to us unalienably whereas the Generality of other charters are Acts of Grace and Mercy which are theirs only during pleasure." Acts of Parliament have no force with us, royal official John Bridger was told, for we have a char-

---

[99] *Mass. Acts and Resolves,* VII, 451; [Cotton Mather?], *Deplorable State of New-England,* 104*; and, among many other expressions of such sentiment, Wise, *Churches Quarrel Espoused,* 33, and Ebenezer Gay, *The Duty of People to Pray for and Praise their Rulers,* 32.

ter.[100] So accustomed were the colonists to employing such a weapon and so easily did its character suit it for such a purpose that the new charter became encapsulated within the mythology of the old. True, the charter and the royal government it brought had helped to ensure that the vision to be protected was now more secular and more English in form than the Bible Commonwealth of yesteryear. Yet the transformation was striking: by the struggles of the 1760s and 1770s, most colonists, belatedly vindicating Cotton Mather's defense of his father's work, had come to regard the settlement of 1691, once distrusted as an alien imposition, as the keystone of their liberties.[101]

Nor was this theme of adaptation, of old wine placed in new bottles, confined to the political arena. The story of New England's religious development during these years has been well and often told, though not always with a full appreciation of its larger context. Confronted by royal government and by the threat of unrestrained (and now, it appeared, perhaps unrestrainable) sectarian incursions, clergy and colonists struggled long and hard to preserve the essentials of Puritan orthodoxy. Some, with the Mathers, strove to renew as far as possible the old alliance between church and state and work within it. Others responded by opening up church membership to all of godly and sober life and by espousing a less Calvinistic creed.[102] Many of these changes were rooted in tendencies long implicit within Puritan doctrine. Yet they were perceptibly shaped by New Eng-

---

[100] Winthrop, *Journal*, II, 315; *The Revolution in New England Justified, Andros Tracts,* I, 126; Dummer, *A Defense of the New-England Charters,* 5; William Waldron to Richard Waldron, Nov. 25, 1723, Waldron Letters; John Bridger to the Board of Trade, July 14, 1718, *CSP Col., 1717–1718,* no. 616; and, generally, Theodore B. Lewis, "A Revolutionary Tradition, 1689–1774," 424–433, and Murrin, "Review Essay," 258–259 (although Murrin is mistaken in his assertion here that the Massachusetts Superior Court once declared the charter to be "no law").

[101] See, for example, John Adams, *The Works of John Adams,* II, 171, IV, 114, 128; Joseph Warren, *An Oration, Delivered 5 March, 1772,* 8; Richard D. Brown, *Revolutionary Politics in Massachusetts,* 109; and Bernard Bailyn, *The Ideological Origins of the American Revolution,* 190–193.

[102] See, most recently, the studies of Robert G. Pope, *The Half-Way Covenant;* James P. Walsh, "Solomon Stoddard's Open Communion," 97–114; E. Brooks Hollifield, *The Covenant Sealed;* David D. Hall, *The Faithful Shepherd;* and Lucas, *Valley of Discord.*

land's closer contact with the outside world and by the circumstances of the post-Revolutionary settlement. In particular, many ministers supported efforts to combat heterodoxy by a more tightly centralized and in form distinctly Presbyterian discipline over congregational autonomy. "It is high time for us to leave our Independency," wrote Gershom Bulkeley, "if we do not meane that the Gospell shall take its leave of us."[103] The outcome testified to the impact of New England's political fragmentation. In Connecticut, where church and state still stood in close alliance, the new college of Yale was founded to train clergy free from the taint of Harvard's liberalism, and in 1708 ministers and magistrates combined under the leadership of Governor the Reverend Gurdon Saltonstall to enact the Saybrook Platform, which authorized clerical consociations within each county to oversee local congregations and preserve religious uniformity. With the Platform were enacted the *Heads of Agreements,* the terms for a union of English Congregationalists and Presbyterians which Increase Mather had helped to draft in 1691 during his stay in London. In royally governed Massachusetts, however, similar proposals foundered in the face of a lack of official support and a fear, most cogently expressed in the famous counterblasts of Andros's old opponent, John Wise, of the larger implications of such a centralization of authority.[104]

The contrast and its causes were plain, and they impelled Massachusetts ministers toward new ways of revitalizing religion. They made increasing use of informal ministerial associations to uphold clerical authority; again led by Cotton Mather, many veered away from their traditional reliance upon an alliance of church and state to embrace a new and more ecumenical basis for a united Christian order in the preaching of the programs of moral reform and evangelical piety already widely advocated by English and continental Protestant clergy. For Mather, such an emphasis upon "Christian Union" served to strengthen his cherished ties to overseas churches and to

---

[103] Bulkeley to Benjamin Davis, June 24, 1700, Jeffries Papers, V, 19.

[104] J. William T. Youngs, Jr., *God's Messengers,* 69–78; Williston Walker, *Creeds and Platforms,* 440–523; Wise, *Churches Quarrel Espoused,* and *idem, A Vindication of the Government of the New-England Churches.*

furnish new weapons with which to counter the insulting pretensions of the Anglican missionaries invading New England, those "Tools of Contention" who "deparave and molest Religion under the pretense of propagating it." Above all, however, his course and the courses of his colleagues were determined by a clear-sighted recognition that the state neither could nor would enforce the old orthodoxy as it had existed prior to 1686. From these new tactics would ultimately blossom an American pietism which led toward the evangelistic revivals of mid-century.[105] In a number of ways, therefore, the pattern of the colonists' religious development during these years mirrored that of their politics—responding to external pressures and controls, drawing upon new forms and ideas (often from the very forces that pressed in upon them), and grafting these fresh shoots upon their deeply rooted devotion to their seventeenth-century heritage to produce a reinvigorated, if now quite differently structured and defined, New England way.

Over the forty years since 1675, the New England colonists had passed through greater and more far-reaching changes than in any previous period of their short history. For more than half these years, they had suffered under wars of unprecedented scale and severity; royal government had come and gone and come again, and John Winthrop's city upon a hill had descended into a hubbub of internal strife and division. The region's rapid geographical expansion had come to a halt: in 1715, New England's boundaries stood no further advanced and in areas such as Maine well behind those of 1675. Worcester, for example, first settled in 1674, was abandoned during King Philip's war, resettled in 1684 only to be again abandoned, and not finally reestablished until the coming peace in 1713.

Within these boundaries, society and politics had altered in style as

---

[105] Cotton Mather to Robert Wodrow, Sept. 17, 1715, *Diary*, ed. Ford, II, 327; Cotton Mather, *Diary*, ed. Manierre, 45; Middlekauff, *The Mathers*, 220–230, 305–319; and Chapter 5, note 48, preceding. For the moral reform movement in England, see Dudley Bahlman, *The Moral Revolution of 1688.*

well as substance. Ministers and magistrates had bewailed the rise of worldliness almost from the first day of settlement, but by 1715, as warring factions exchanged volleys of pamphlets over matters of currency and banking, as the governorship of Massachusetts went on sale to the highest bidder, and as ministers punctuated their sermons with public complaints of the inadequacy of their salaries, it was plain that the pursuit of wealth and power—what Wait Winthrop denounced as the prevalence of "private interest"—was now, at the least, much more openly admitted and accepted than ever before.[106] Nowhere was this more apparent than in the upper reaches of politics, as the work of government, swollen in scope and complexity and responding to London's demands, became more formal in character and, in every sense, more businesslike. The task of ruling, once the ill-requited responsibility of those called to office by God and His elect, was fast developing into a full-time, well-rewarded, and highly competitive profession.[107] Socially, also, these leaders were increasingly set apart by their full-bottomed wigs and fine wardrobes, their carriages and coats of arms, all visible (and very English) trappings of gentility and authority. No longer, after Joseph Dudley's return, could one expect to meet the chief executive of Massachusetts as Samuel Sewall met William Stoughton late in 1697, carting ears of corn from his barn. Only in a nightmare would the dignified Samuel Cranston have imagined himself greeting a visitor with the artless informality of one of his im-

---

[106] Wait Winthrop to Fitz-John Winthrop, Oct. 27, 1701, Winthrop Papers.

[107] Between 1675 and 1715, for example, the annual sums paid to the governors of the various colonies rose from one hundred to five hundred pounds in Massachusetts (Shute was soon to be paid twelve hundred pounds a year during most of his term of office), from eighty to two hundred in Connecticut, and from no regular salary to one hundred pounds in Rhode Island. Allowances paid to other officials rose much more slowly but there was a considerable expansion of the civil list, especially because of the expansion of the judiciary. Similarly, although the sums allowed as fees (the other principal, and, in some cases, sole, income from official service) did not rise much above the levels prescribed back in the old charter period, they proliferated markedly in number, as administrative procedures became more complex, especially in the royal governments. Indeed, a comparison shows that colonial lawmakers in the 1690s followed the forms established during the period of the Dominion, although reducing the scale of the fees then permitted: compare *N. H. Laws*, I, 107, 250, 546–553 (a "copy of all the fees as they were settled in the time of Sir Edmund Andrews": *N. H. Provincial Papers*, III, 5), with *Mass. Acts and Resolves*, I, 84–88, 145, and *N. H. Laws*, I, 596–600, II, 146–150.

mediate predecessors as governor of Rhode Island who, as Ezra Stiles later told the tale, emerged from his hayfield stripped to the waist and strode back to his house with his shirt hanging off the end of his rake handle.[108] By 1715, those in authority maintained and indeed demanded the deference and ceremony they deemed proper to their station.

These changes, in turn, point to the growing social and political predominance of the group to which such leaders almost invariably belonged, the merchants and gentry of the coastal towns. Drawn together by ties of common interest and intermarriage, keenly attuned to England's ways and demands, and well circumstanced by location, wealth, and leisure to participate in the work of an ever busier government, these men now filled a much larger proportion of the administrative and executive posts, especially in the two royal colonies. By 1715, thirteen of the eighteen councillors chosen to represent the territory of Massachusetts (as distinct from that of Plymouth or Maine) lived in Boston; all the rest save one, frontier lord John Pynchon, came from the commercial seaports of Salem, Ipswich, and Marblehead.[109] In New Hampshire, the merchants of Portsmouth

---

[108] Sewall, *Diary*, I, 380; Dexter, *Extracts from the Itineraries*, 134.

[109] The proportion of Bostonians and other coastal residents in the council rose steadily under the new charter. By the mid-1690s, for example, three-quarters of those elected for the Massachusetts territory came from the three towns of Boston, Charlestown, and Salem, more than twice the proportion of twenty years before. The great majority of them were connected by ties of blood or marriage, creating an extended political family, a "cousinage," at the head of affairs. In addition, they were more regular in their attendance upon council meetings and other governmental business than were their colleagues coming from communities more distant from Boston. It was during these years, I believe, rather than prior to 1689 as stated by Bailyn (*New England Merchants*, 143, 169), that men who can properly be described as merchants first came to assume a significant and enduring role in province government, most notably through their membership of the council. Yet even then their rise cannot accurately be described as that of a coherent economic class or group; nor can its significance be understood by means of simply dividing the community into "merchants" and "non-merchants." The more accurate division during this period, I would suggest, is one which takes as much account of geographical location and social standing as of occupational specialization, one closer though not wholly corresponding to that found by Jackson Turner Main to have existed three-quarters of a century later, between "Cosmopolitans" living in urban and commercially oriented regions and "Localists" remote or alienated from such interests: Main, *Political Parties Before the Constitution*, chapter 13; and,

and New Castle attained a similar dominance.[110] One consequence
was to give an economic dimension to the constitutional rivalry between executive and legislature as the governor and his council confronted a still overwhelmingly rural lower house. More broadly, the
transition further illuminates the changing character of New England's politics. On the one hand, even those whose birth and family
name all but guaranteed them political office now saw no stigma attached to a career in "trade"—"A Winthrop A Signor of bills," mar-
velled Samuel Sewall in 1716 on finding that Adam, great-grandson
of the noble Governor John, was helping to issue bills of credit for the
province.[111] On the other, the entry into politics of many who had
hitherto held aloof plainly reflected their belief that the rewards of
office had come to outweigh its burdens, a proposition some then attempted to prove true once set in place.[112] If rising men like Jonathan
Belcher drew any moral from the complexities of the new order, it
was von Clausewitz's dictum given a Yankee twist—politics could be
the continuation of business by other means. The way stood prepared
for the vigorous promotion of private interest through public office, as
in the fever of land speculation that followed peace on the frontier,
that was to become common in New England by mid-century.[113]

---

for an analysis specifically concerned with Massachusetts and employing similar
categories, Van Beck Hall, *Politics Without Parties: Massachusetts, 1780–1791*. For
the rise of similar elites within the councils of other mainland American colonies
in the early eighteenth century, see Leonard Woods Labaree, *Conservatism in Early
American History*, chapter I.

[110] Van Deventer, *Emergence of Provincial New Hampshire*, 135–138, 212–221, provides an excellent analysis; a second study, Ralph Peter Barry, "The New Hampshire Merchant Interest, 1609–1725," likewise sees the merchants as dominant by
1720. Barry seeks to trace the emergence of a "merchant interest"—and its rivalry
with a "lumber interest" within the province—back into the first years of founding, but he does so with uneven success and at a cost, I believe, of exaggerating
the significance and coherence of such a division and the province's preoccupation with internal affairs.

[111] Sewall, *Diary*, II, 823. Adam's mercantile career proved less than successful:
Kellaway, *New England Company*, 214–215.

[112] Thus Wait Winthrop to Sir Henry Ashurst, July 25, 1698, Mass. Hist. Soc.,
*Collections*, 5th ser., VIII (1882), 534.

[113] Akagi, *Town Proprietors of the New England Colonies*, 175–287; Douglas E. Leach,
*The Northern Colonial Frontier, 1607–1763*, 171–176; and Moody, "The Maine
Frontier," 357–448.

## Resurgence and Synthesis

Overall, therefore, New England's course during these years lay toward a more pluralistic and openly acquisitive society which more closely resembled that of the mother country. This was not so much a secularization or declension of society as a whole as it was a steady loosening of the intimate political and ideological ties between church and state, spiritualizing the one and secularizing the other. No less reverence was rendered to God in New England's meetinghouses; but the things rendered to Caesar were now shaped more by the needs of everyday life and the influence of royal government than by the transcendent goal of a Bible Commonwealth. In society as in politics, and in large part, I have suggested, because of the external forces pressing in upon New England, what had once been unified, discretionary, and interdependent was being separated, defined, and stratified.

Yet change may preserve or reestablish as well as erode, and a glance back from 1715 must end by emphasizing how much of the New England of forty years before remained, if often in quite different guise. New settlement had never entirely ceased during the war years, though it was largely confined to eastern Connecticut and western Rhode Island; with the coming of peace in 1713 fresh migrants were soon moving north and west to burst beyond New England's old borders.[114] They carried with them what successive generations had carefully cherished, a heritage of local life and autonomy, of closely knit communities and town meetings, which had changed little over half a century and which continued to stand in sturdy (and, ultimately, violent) contrast to the ways of royal government for many years to come.[115] Much more had altered at the level of central government, of course, especially in Massachusetts and New Hampshire,

---

[114] Mathews, *Expansion of New England*, 64–66; Bushman, *Puritan to Yankee*, 83, 291–292. A good example of this internal migration can be seen in the movement of Benjamin Sabin and his family who spread from Rehoboth, Plymouth Colony, north and west into Massachusetts and Connecticut: *New England Historical and Genealogical Register*, XXVI (1882), 52–58, 324–325; Clarence W. Bowen, *The History of Woodstock, Connecticut*, I, 20–64.

[115] This local life is best, if somewhat idealistically, depicted by Zuckerman, *Peaceable Kingdoms*.

but even here the colonists retained a much greater measure of control over their own affairs than had seemed likely twenty years before during the internal confusions and external threats of the 1690s. And as long as magistrates of the caliber of Samuel Sewall stood near the head of affairs, public life in New England, despite its more visible pursuit of private advantage, maintained standards of frugality and disinterested service very different from the ardent spoilsmanship of officeholders in England and such colonies as Virginia.[116]

Change, too, could reveal new ways of defending traditional positions or help repair old weaknesses. As we have seen, many of the alterations in the forms and practice of politics during these years significantly strengthened the colonists' ability to preserve much of their old autonomy. Within New England as a whole by 1715, moreover, renewed military cooperation, the settlement of boundary disputes, and the progressive regularization of political and economic relations had noticeably eased the intercolonial rivalries that had so often prompted royal intervention in earlier years. Old animosities died hard, and as late as 1710, troops from Massachusetts and Rhode Island gathering for the expedition against Port Royal refused to join together for prayers. Yet at least the two colonies' forces now took the field side by side, not face to face; and this greater harmony was confirmed by the subsequent collaboration of the two colonies' governments in constructing a bridge over the Pawtucket River, the road laid out between Providence and eastern Connecticut in 1714, and the Rhode Island assembly's voting of twenty shillings a year to provide Governor Cranston with a weekly copy of the *Boston News-Letter*.[117] Such a lifting of the virtual state of quarantine long imposed upon "Rogue Island," indeed, points to a still broader trend: the New

---

[116] Edmund S. Morgan, *American Slavery, American Freedom*, 208. Thus, for example, Andrew Belcher, long Massachusetts commissary general, never made even a fraction of the huge fortunes amassed in England by John Churchill and James Brydges, respectively captain general and paymaster general of the army: see Belcher's petition, *Mass. Acts and Resolves*, VIII, 627.

[117] Bostonian Society, *Publications*, III (1906), 28; *R. I. Records*, III, 542, IV, 119, 135–136; *Mass. Acts and Resolves*, IX, 285, 313, 452; Isabel S. Mitchell, *Roads and Road-Making in Colonial Connecticut*, 21.

## Resurgence and Synthesis

England colonies, compelled to stand together as a strategic unit, drawn into greater economic interdependence and physical proximity by the expansion of settlement, and with their political and institutional development set upon converging paths, were now moving rapidly—perhaps more rapidly than at any time before or after—toward the self-conscious regional identity so renowned and cherished by the late eighteenth and early nineteenth centuries. A new dominion of New England, its bonds now cerebral and social rather than political, was taking shape. It would prove both more enduring than its predecessor and considerably less pliant to the will of its nominal overlords in London.

In sum, what has been justly termed an anglicization of government and society was only in small part a royalization, a stricter subordination to Whitehall.[118] The colonists' allegiance was given to English constitutionalism rather than to the crown. Hence, to look ahead, we can more easily understand why they asserted the one to the eventual denial of the authority of the second as the crown appeared to abandon constitutional procedures in its attempts to restructure imperial administration in the 1760s. New England's loyalty was never absolute or unthinking: its dependence was conditional, the outcome of a careful accommodation to particular circumstances. A similar if less striking pattern appears in other colonies as New York, Maryland, and, later, New Jersey and the Carolinas passed under royal government, and Pennsylvanians struggled to define the terms of their own holy commonwealth. They too sought to shape their political development around the rights and status of Englishmen, a strategy that both acknowledged and yet defended against imperial power.[119] In some respects, it would seem, they followed in New Eng-

---

[118] Murrin, "Anglicizing an American Colony," a provocative and original study of the evolution of Massachusetts's military and legal institutions in the eighteenth century.

[119] Thus Julius Goebel, Jr., "The Courts and the Law in Colonial New York," 21–27; Michael Kammen, *Colonial New York,* 128–140; Newton D. Mereness, *Maryland as a Proprietary Province,* 207, 257–277; M. Eugene Sirmans, *Colonial South Carolina,* 62–63, 68–69, 96; Gary B. Nash, *Quakers and Politics,* 134, 266–267; and, more generally, Evarts B. Greene, *Provincial America,* 70–71, and Lovejoy, *Glorious Revolution in America,* index, *sub* "Rights of Englishmen."

[*419*]

land's footsteps. Virginia had the greatest experience in reconciling autonomy with royal government, but contemporaries agreed that, so far as resistance to royal authority was concerned, New England's example— "the New England disease"—was the more infectious.[120] In this light, the years immediately after the Glorious Revolution, when New Englanders first learned how to live with but not necessarily under royal government, can be seen as more broadly formative for the subsequent course of events in English America than we have hitherto realized.

More importantly, however, New England's experience reminds us that this pattern of colonial political development was not merely one doomed to eventual disruption. If we can turn away our eyes from the blinding light of 1776, we can perceive that the settlement which followed the Glorious Revolution was much more than an uneasy juxtaposition of disparate and ultimately irreconcilable elements. It was a creative synthesis which initiated a period of political stability lasting for three-quarters of a century, a substantial proportion of the period of European settlement in America. We have grown accustomed to contrasting England's Augustan calm with the turmoil of colonial factionalism. America's political system, it is said, was "anomalous in its essence, lacking in what any objective observer would consider a minimal degree of functional integration."[121] The contrast, though pertinent, is overdrawn. After passing through violent political tempests in the late seventeenth and early eighteenth centuries, both England and its American colonies emerged into calmer seas ruffled by the clash of interest groups but essentially devoid of major political crises, in large part, indeed, because their systems' toleration and even encouragement of such clashes relieved the pressures that might otherwise have ended in explosion. For many years, especially while common dangers and opportunities drew colonies and mother country together, political practice overrode or circumvented constitutional anomalies in England and America alike. The ambivalent

---

[120] Evarts B. Greene, *Provincial America*, 198; Observations upon the proposals of Thomas Ludwell of Virginia, [1674?], *CSP Col., 1675–1676*, no. 403.

[121] Bailyn, *Origins of American Politics*, 63–64, 124.

character of New England's adjustment to empire helps to explain the circumstances and rhetoric of the final rupture. But the extent to which this adjustment satisfied a wide variety of needs on both sides of the Atlantic also explains why this rupture did not occur until 1776, three generations after crown and colonist had wrought a settlement out of the Glorious Revolution.

# Bibliography

PRIMARY SOURCES

Manuscripts

Alderman Library, University of Virginia, Charlottesville
 Letterbook, 1688–1761, of the Company for the Propagation of the
  Gospel in New England, microfilm copy in the Massachusetts
  Historical Society
American Antiquarian Society, Worcester, Massachusetts
 Curwin Papers
 Letterbook of Thomas Fitch
 Letterbook of John Hull, 1670–1685
 Massachusetts Manuscripts, Colonial, 1659–1787
 Diaries of Increase Mather
 Mather Papers
 Letterbook of Jacob Melyen
Baker Library, Harvard Business School, Cambridge, Massachusetts
 Burbank Papers
Bodleian Library, Oxford University, Oxford
 Letterbook of Sir Henry Ashurst, Ashurst Manuscripts
 Carte Manuscripts
 Rawlinson Letters
 Rawlinson Manuscripts
Boston Public Library, Boston, Massachusetts
 Chamberlain Collection
 Cotton and Prince Papers
 Commonplace Book of Samuel Sewall
 English Manuscripts
British Library, London
 Additional Manuscripts
 Egerton Manuscripts
 Portland Manuscripts
 Sloane Manuscripts
Annmary Brown Memorial Library, Providence, Rhode Island
 Wyllys Papers
Colonial Williamsburg, Williamsburg, Virginia
 Blathwayt Papers

Connecticut Historical Society, Hartford
  Miscellaneous Letters
  Saltonstall Papers
  Talcott Papers
  Notebook of Henry Wolcott
  Roger Wolcott Papers
  Wyllys Papers
Connecticut State Library, Hartford
  Allyn-Wolcott Family Papers
  Connecticut Archives: Civil Officers, Colonial Boundaries, Ecclesiastical
    Affairs, Finance, Foreign Correspondence, Indians, Miscellaneous,
    Private Controversies, Trade and Maritime Affairs, War
  New England Colonial Records
  Robert C. Winthrop Collection
  Wyllys Papers
Edinburgh University Library, Edinburgh
  Diary of Francis Borland, microfilm copy in the Massachusetts
    Historical Society
Essex Institute, Salem, Massachusetts
  Ledger Book of Jonathan Corwin
  Curwen Papers
  Philip English Papers and Ledger Books
  Hathorne Papers
  Account Book of John Higginson, Jr.
  Higginson Family Papers
Harvard University, Cambridge, Massachusetts
  College Papers
Henry E. Huntington Library, San Marino, California
  Blathwayt Papers
  Brock Collection
  Ellesmere Manuscripts
  Miscellaneous Manuscripts
Lambeth Palace Library, London
  Fulham Palace Manuscripts, microfilm copy in the library of the
    University of California at Berkeley
Massachusetts Historical Society, Boston
  Appleton Papers
  Belknap Papers
  Colman Papers
  Cushing Papers
  Dudley Papers
  C. E. French Papers
  F. L. Gay Papers

# Bibliography

Jeffries Papers
Diary of Increase Mather for 1691
Increase Mather Letters, typescript
Miscellaneous Bound Manuscripts
Parkman Papers
Prince Papers
Saltonstall Papers
William Tailer Letterbook, Belknap Papers
J. Trumbull Collection
Waldron Letters
Washburn Papers
Winthrop Papers
Massachusetts State House, Boston
  Massachusetts Archives, volumes II, III, XX, XXX, XXXI, XXXV–XXXVII, LI–LIX, LXI, LXII, LXX, LXXI, C, CI, CVI–CVIII, CXIX, CXXVI–CXXIX, CCXL–CCXLII; Court Records, volumes VI–IX; Executive Records of Council, volumes II, III
Public Record Office, London
  Admiralty Papers, 51
  Colonial Office Papers, 1, 5, 324, 388, 389, 391
  Treasury Papers, 64
Rhode Island Historical Society, Providence
  Bernon Papers
  Manuscripts
  Miscellaneous Manuscripts
  Quaker Archives: Earliest Discipline Manuscripts; Minutes of the Yearly Meeting of New England
Rhode Island State House, Providence
  Rhode Island Archives: Boundary Documents; Miscellaneous Papers; General Treasurer's Accounts
Society for the Propagation of the Gospel in Foreign Parts, London
  Correspondence Received, Series A and B, microfilm copy in the library of the University of Washington, Seattle
Dr. Williams's Library, London
  Richard Baxter's Letters
  Roger Morrice, "Entr'ing Book"

Published

*Abridgment of the Laws in Force and Use in Her Majesty's Plantations, An.* London, 1704.
*Account of the late action of the New-Englanders under the command of Sir William Phips, An.* London, 1691.

Adams, John. *The Works of John Adams.* Edited by Charles Francis Adams. 10 vols. Boston, 1850–1866.

Andrews, Charles M., ed., *Narratives of the Insurrections, 1675–1690.* New York, 1915.

"Andros Records." American Antiquarian Society, *Proceedings,* new ser., XIII (1899–1900): 237–268, 463–499.

Arnold, James N., ed. *Records of the Proprietors of the Narragansett, otherwise called the Fones Record.* Providence, R.I., 1894.

B., A. *Seasonable Motives to Our Duty and Allegiance.* Philadelphia, 1689.

Barnard, John. "Autobiography of the Rev. John Barnard." Massachusetts Historical Society, *Collections,* 3rd ser., V (1836): 177–243.

Bates, Samuel A., ed. *Records of the Town of Braintree, 1640 to 1793.* Randolph, Mass., 1886.

Bishop, George. *New England Judged not by Man's But by the Spirit of the Lord.* London, 1661.

Boston. *New-England Courant.*

———. *Reports of the Records Commissioners of the City of Boston.* 39 vols. Boston, 1876–1909.

———. *Boston News-Letter.*

"Boxford Town Records, 1685–1706." Essex Institute, *Historical Collections,* XXXVI (1900): 41–103.

Browne, William Hand, *et al.,* eds. *Archives of Maryland.* 72 vols. Baltimore, 1883–.

Bulkeley, Gershom. "Will and Doom, or the Miseries of Connecticut by and under an Usurped and Arbitrary Power, 1692." Connecticut Historical Society, *Collections,* III (1895): 62–269.

Bullivant, Benjamin. "Journal of Dr. Benjamin Bullivant." Massachusetts Historical Society, *Proceedings,* XVI (1878): 101–108.

Burchett, Josiah. *Memoirs of Transactions at Sea during the War with France.* London. 1703.

Butterfield, Lyman H., ed. *Adams Family Correspondence.* Vol I. Cambridge, Mass., 1963.

[Byfield, Nathaniel?] *A Letter from a Gentleman in Mount Hope to His Friend in Treamount.* Boston, 1721.

Byrd, William. *The Secret Diary of William Byrd of Westover, 1709–1712.* Edited by Louis B. Wright and Marion Tinling. Richmond, Va., 1941.

Canada. *Report of the Public Archives of Canada for 1912.* Ottawa, 1912.

Chauncy, Charles. *Nathanael's Character Display'd.* Boston, 1733.

Church, Thomas. *The History of Philip's War . . . also, of the French and Indian Wars at the Eastward, in 1689, 1690, 1692, 1696, and 1704.* Edited by Samuel E. Drake. 2nd ed. Boston, 1928.

Colden, Cadwallader. *The History of the Five Indian Nations Depending on the Province of New-York in America.* Ithaca, N. Y., 1964.

# Bibliography

*Collections de manuscrits contenant lettres, mémoires, et autres documents historiques relatifs à la Nouvelle France.* 4 vols. Quebec, 1883.

Colman, Benjamin. *Ossa Josephi, or the Bones of Joseph, Consider'd.* Boston, 1720.

Connecticut. *Acts and Laws of His Majesties Colony of Connecticut in New-England.* Boston, 1702.

——. *The Public Records of the Colony of Connecticut.* Edited by J. Hammond Trumbull and C. J. Hoadly, 15 vols. Hartford, 1850–1890.

Coxe, William, ed. *Private and Original Correspondence of Charles Talbot, Duke of Shrewsbury, with King William, the Leaders of the Whig Party, and other Distinguished Statesmen.* London, 1821.

Davenport, John. *The Letters of John Davenport, Puritan Divine.* Edited by Isabel M. Calder. New Haven, 1937.

Davis, Andrew M., ed. *Colonial Currency Reprints, 1682–1751.* Prince Society Publications, vols. XXXII–XXXV. Boston, 1910–1911.

Dexter, Franklin B., ed. *Documentary History of Yale University, 1701–1745.* New Haven, 1916.

——. *Extracts from the Itineraries and Other Miscellanies of Ezra Stiles.* New Haven, 1916.

Douglass, William. *A Summary, Historical and Political, of the First Planting, Progressive Improvements, and Present State of the British Settlements in North-America.* London, 1760.

Drake, Samuel E., ed. *The Witchcraft Delusion in New England.* 3 vols. Roxbury, Mass., 1866.

"Dudley Records." Massachusetts Historical Society, *Proceedings,* 2nd ser., XIII (1899–1900): 226–286.

Dummer, Jeremiah. *A Defense of the New-England Charters.* Boston, 1721.

Emmison, Frederick G., ed. *Early Essex Town Meetings: Braintree, 1619–1634; Finchingfield, 1626–1634.* Chichester, England, 1970.

Evelyn, John. *The Diary of John Evelyn.* Edited by Esmond S. De Beer. Vol. III. Cambridge, 1955.

Fane, Francis. *Reports on the Laws of Connecticut.* Edited by Charles M. Andrews. Publications of the Acorn Club, vol. XII. New Haven, 1915.

Field, Edward, comp. *Tax Lists of the Town of Providence during the Administration of Sir Edmund Andros.* Providence, R. I., 1895.

Forbes, Allyn B., ed. *Winthrop Papers, 1498–1649.* 5 vols. Boston, 1929–1947.

Ford, John W., ed. *Some Correspondence between the Governors and Treasurers of the New England Company in London and the Commissioners of the United Colonies in America, the Missionaries of the Company, and Others.* London, 1897.

Gay, Ebenezer. *The Duty of a People to Pray for and Praise their Rulers.* Boston, 1730.

Gill, Obadiah, *et al. Some Few Remarks upon a Scandalous Book.* Boston, 1701.

"Gleanings from the Ancient Records of Bristol, R. I." *Narragansett Historical Register,* III (1884–1885): 59–66, 157–163, 205–215, 276–281.

Graham, Gerald S., ed. *The Walker Expedition to Quebec.* Naval Records Society, vol. XCIV. London, 1953.

Great Britain. *Acts of the Privy Council in England, Colonial Series.* Edited by W. L. Grant and James Munro. 6 vols. London, 1908–1912.

———. *Calendar of State Papers, Colonial Series, America and West Indies.* Edited by W. Noel Sainsbury *et al.* 44 vols. London, 1860–1969.

———. *Calendar of State Papers, Domestic Series, of the Reign of Charles II.* Edited by Mary A. E. Green *et al.* 28 vols. London, 1860–1939.

———. *Calendar of State Papers, Domestic Series, of the Reign of Anne.* Edited by Robert Pentland Mahaffy. 2 vols. London, 1916–1924.

———. *Calendar of State Papers, Domestic Series, of the Reign of William and Mary.* Edited by William J. Hardy. 11 vols. London, 1895–1937.

———. *Calendar of Treasury Books.* Edited by William A. Shaw. 32 vols. London, 1904–1969.

———. *Calendar of Treasury Papers.* Edited by Joseph Redington. 6 vols. London, 1868–1889.

———. Historical Manuscripts Commission. *Report on the Manuscripts of the Duke of Buccleuch and Queensbury Preserved at Montagu House, Whitehall.* 3 vols. London, 1899–1926.

———. Historical Manuscripts Commission. *Report on the Manuscripts of the Marquess of Downshire.* 4 vols. London, 1924–1940.

———. Historical Manuscripts Commission. *The Manuscripts of Lord Kenyon. Fourteenth Report,* Appendix. London, 1894.

———. Historical Manuscripts Commission. *Report on the Manuscripts of the Late Allen George Finch Esq. of Burley-on-the-Hill, Rutland.* 4 vols. London, 1913–1965.

———. Historical Manuscripts Commission. *Report on the Manuscripts of Mrs. Frankland-Russell-Astley of Chequers Court, Bucks.* London, 1900.

———. Historical Manuscripts Commission. *The Manuscripts of the House of Lords.* 3 vols. London, 1889–1895. New ser. 11 vols. London, 1906–1962.

———. Historical Manuscripts Commission. *The Manuscripts of His Grace the Duke of Marlborough. Eighth Report,* Appendix I. London, 1881.

———. Historical Manuscripts Commission. *Calendar of the Manuscripts of the Marquess of Ormonde Preserved at Kilkenny Castle.* New ser. 8 vols. London, 1902–1920.

———. Historical Manuscripts Commission. *The Manuscripts of His Grace the Duke of Portland Preserved at Welbeck Abbey.* 10 vols. London, 1891–1931.

———. Historical Manuscripts Commission. *The Manuscripts of the Marquis Townshend. Eleventh Report,* Appendix, Part IV. London, 1887.

———. House of Commons. *Journals.* London, 1742–.

# Bibliography

————. House of Lords. *Journals.* London, 1767–.

————. *Journal of the Commissioners for Trade and Plantations.* 14 vols. London, 1920–1938.

————. *Statutes of the Realm.* 11 vols. London, 1810–1828.

Green, Samuel A., ed. "Two Narratives of Sir William Phips's Expedition to Quebec." Massachusetts Historical Society, *Proceedings,* 2nd ser., XV (1901–1902): 283–320.

Grey, Anchitell. *Debates in the House of Commons from the Year 1667 to the Year 1694.* 10 vols. London, 1769.

Hammond, Lawrence. "The Diary of Lawrence Hammond." Massachusetts Historical Society, *Proceedings,* 2nd ser., VII (1891–1892): 144–172.

Higginson, John. *The Cause of God and His People in New-England.* Cambridge, Mass., 1663.

Hill, Don C., ed. *Early Records of the Town of Dedham.* 6 vols. Dedham, Mass., 1886–1936.

Hinman, R. R., ed. *Letters from the English Kings and Queens . . . to the Governors of the Colony of Connecticut together with the answers thereto from 1635 to 1749.* Hartford, 1836.

Hubbard, William. *The Happiness of a People.* Boston, 1676.

Hull, John. "Diaries of John Hull." American Antiquarian Society, *Transactions and Proceedings,* III (1857): 109–316.

*Humble Address of divers Gentry, Merchants, and others . . . Inhabiting in Boston, Charlestown, and places adjacent, The.* London, 1691.

Hutchinson, Thomas. *Hutchinson Papers.* Prince Society Publications, vols. II–III. Albany, 1865. A reprint of Thomas Hutchinson, *A Collection of Original Papers Relative to the History of the Colony of Massachusetts-Bay.* Boston, 1769.

Johnson, Edward. *Johnson's Wonder-working Providence, 1628–1651.* Edited by J. Franklin Jameson. New York, 1910.

*Journal of the Proceedings in the Late Expedition to Port-Royal, on board their Majesties Ship, the Six-Friends, the Honourable Sr. William Phipps Knight, Commander in Chief.* Boston, 1690.

Lewis, Theodore B., ed. "Sir Edmund Andros's Hearing before the Lords of Trade and Plantations, Apr. 17, 1690: Two Unpublished Accounts." American Antiquarian Society, *Proceedings,* new ser., LXXXIII (1973): 241–250.

Lincoln, Charles H., ed. *Narratives of the Indian Wars, 1675–1699.* New York, 1913.

Luttrell, Narcissus. *A Brief Historical Relation of State Affairs from September 1678 to April 1714.* 6 vols. Oxford, 1857.

McIlwaine, H. R., ed. *Executive Journal of the Council of Colonial Virginia.* Vol. I. Richmond, Va., 1925.

Maine. *Documentary History of Maine.* Maine Historical Society, *Collections,* 2nd ser., I–XXIV. Portland, 1869–1916.

Manchester, Mass. *Town Records of Manchester.* Salem, 1889.

Manross, William W., comp. *The Fulham Papers in the Lambeth Palace Library.* Oxford, 1965.

Marshall, John. "John Marshall's Diary." Massachusetts Historical Society, *Proceedings,* 2nd ser., I (1884): 148–164.

Massachusetts. *Acts and Laws, of Her Majesties Province of the Massachusetts-Bay in New England.* Boston, 1714.

———. *Acts and Resolves, Public and Private, of the Province of the Massachusetts Bay.* Edited by Abner C. Goodell and Melville M. Bigelow. 21 vols. Boston, 1869–1922.

———. *The Colonial Laws of Massachusetts. Reprinted from the Edition of 1672 with the Supplements through 1686.* Edited by William H. Whitmore. Boston, 1890.

———. *Records of the Governor and Company of the Massachusetts Bay in New England.* Edited by Nathaniel B. Shurtleff. 5 vols. Boston, 1853–1854.

Mather, Cotton. *The Diary of Cotton Mather.* Edited by Worthington C. Ford. 2 vols. New York, 1957.

———. *The Diary of Cotton Mather, D.D., F.R.S., for the Year 1712.* Edited by William R. Manierre II. Charlottesville, Va., 1964.

———. *Fair Weather.* Boston, 1692.

———. *The Life of Sir William Phips.* Edited by Mark Van Doren. New York, 1929.

———. *Magnalia Christi Americana.* London, 1702.

———. *Optanda. Good Men Described, and Good Things Propounded.* Boston, 1692.

———. *A Pillar of Gratitude.* Boston, 1700.

———. *The Present State of New-England.* Boston, 1690.

———. *The Serviceable Man.* Boston, 1690.

———. *Souldiers Counselled and Comforted.* Boston, 1689.

———. *Things to be Look'd For.* Boston, 1691.

———. *Winter-Meditations.* Boston, 1693.

———. *The Wonderful Works of God.* Boston, 1690.

[Mather, Cotton?] *The Deplorable State of New-England.* London, 1708. Reprinted in Massachusetts Historical Society, *Collections,* 5th ser., VI (1879): 97*–131* (separate pagination).

Mather, Increase. *The Autobiography of Increase Mather.* Edited by Michael G. Hall. Worcester, Mass., 1962. Reprinted from American Antiquarian Society, *Proceedings,* new ser., LXXI (1961): 271–360.

———. *An Earnest Exhortation to the Inhabitants of New-England.* Boston, 1676.

———. *The Great Blessing, of Primitive Counsellours.* Boston, 1693.

[Mather, Increase.] *The Necessity of Reformation.* Boston, 1679.

# Bibliography

Mather, Samuel. *The Life of the Very Reverend and Learned Cotton Mather.* Boston, 1729.

Mereness, Newton D., ed. *Travels in the American Colonies, 1690–1783.* New York, 1916.

Miller, Perry, and Johnson, Thomas H., eds. *The Puritans.* Rev. ed. 2 vols. New York, 1963.

Milton, Mass. *Milton Town Records, 1662–1729.* Milton, 1930.

Mitchell, Jonathan. *Nehemiah on the Wall in Troublesome Times.* Cambridge, Mass., 1671.

*Modest Enquiry into the Grounds and Occasion of a Late Pamphlet, A.* London, 1707. Reprinted in Massachusetts Historical Society, *Collections,* 5th ser., VI (1879): 65*–95* (separate pagination).

Moody, Robert E., ed. *Province and Court Records of Maine.* Vol. III. Portland, Me., 1947.

———. *The Saltonstall Papers, 1607–1815. Vol. I: 1607–1789.* Massachusetts Historical Society, *Collections,* LXXX (1972).

Morison, Samuel E., ed. "Charles Morton's *Compendium Physicae.*" Publications of the Colonial Society of Massachusetts, *Collections,* XXXIII (1940).

New Hampshire. *Laws of New Hampshire.* Edited by Albert S. Batchellor. 10 vols. Manchester, 1904–1922.

———. *Provincial, State and Town Papers of New Hampshire.* Edited by Nathaniel Bouton *et al.* 40 vols. Concord, 1867–1943.

New York. *The Documentary History of the State of New York.* Edited by Edmund B. O'Callaghan. 4 vols. Albany, 1887.

———. *Documents Relative to the Colonial History of the State of New York.* Edited by Edmund B. O'Callaghan and Berthold Fernow. 15 vols. Albany, 1853–1887.

Oakes, Urian. *New-England Pleaded With.* Cambridge, Mass., 1673.

[Palmer, John.] *The Present State of New-England impartially considered in a Letter to the Clergy.* Boston, 1689.

Pemberton, Ebenezer. *A Christian Fixed in His Post.* Boston, 1704.

———. *The Divine Original and Dignity of Government Asserted.* Boston, 1710.

Perry, William S. *Historical Collections Relating to the American Colonial Church.* Vol. III. Hartford, 1873.

Phillimore, Robert, comp. *Memoirs and Correspondence of George, Lord Lyttelton, 1734–1773.* 2 vols. London, 1845.

Philopolites [Cotton Mather?] *A Memorial of the Present Deplorable State of New-England.* London, 1707. Reprinted in Massachusetts Historical Society, *Collections,* 5th ser., VI (1879): 33*–54* (separate pagination).

[Pitkin, William, and Allyn, John?] *Their Majesty's Colony of Connecticut Vindicated.* Boston, 1694.

"Plymouth Church Records, 1620–1859: Part I." Publications of the Colonial Society of Massachusetts, *Collections,* XXII (1920).

Plymouth Colony. *Records of the Colony of New Plymouth in New England.* Edited by Nathaniel B. Shurtleff and David Pulsifer. 12 vols. Boston, 1855–1861.

Powers, Zara Jones, ed. *New Haven Town Records. Vol. III: 1684–1769.* New Haven, 1962.

Preston, Howard W., ed. *The Letter Book of Peleg Sanford of Newport.* Providence, R. I., 1928.

*The Prince Library. A Catalogue of the Collection of Books and Manuscripts which formerly belonged to the Reverend Thomas Prince.* Boston, 1870.

Prince, Thomas. *The People of New-England Put in Mind of the Righteous Acts of the Lord.* Boston, 1730.

*Propositions Made by the Sachems of the Three Maqua Castles.* Boston, 1690.

Providence, R. I. *Early Records of the Town of Providence.* 21 vols. Providence, 1892–1915.

Randolph, Edward. *Edward Randolph: Including his Letters and Official Papers from the New England, Middle, and Southern Colonies in America, with Other Documents Relating Chiefly to the Vacating of the Royal Charter of the Colony of Massachusetts, 1676–1703.* Edited by Robert N. Toppan and Alfred T. S. Goodrick. Prince Society Publications, vols. XXIV–XXVIII, XXX–XXXI. Boston, 1898–1909.

"Reflections upon the Affairs of New England." Connecticut Historical Society, *Collections,* XXI (1924): 324–339.

Rhode Island. *Acts and Laws, of His Majesties Colony of Rhode-Island, and Providence-Plantations, in America.* Boston, 1719.

———. *Records of the Colony of Rhode Island and Providence Plantations in New England.* Edited by John R. Bartlett. 10 vols. Providence, 1856–1865.

Saffin, John. *John Saffin: His Book (1665–1708).* Edited by Caroline Hazard. New York, 1928.

Salem, Mass. "Salem Town Records." Essex Institute, *Historical Collections,* vols. XL–XLIX (1904–1913), LXII–LXIX (1926–1933).

Saltonstall, Gurdon. *A Sermon Preached before the General Assembly of the Colony of Connecticut.* Boston, 1697.

Sewall, Joseph. *Rulers must be Just, Ruling in the Fear of God.* Boston, 1724.

Sewall, Samuel. "The Diary of Samuel Sewall." Massachusetts Historical Society, *Collections,* 5th ser., V (1878).

———. *The Diary of Samuel Sewall, 1674–1729.* Edited by M. Halsey Thomas. 2 vols. New York, 1973.

———. "Letter-Book of Samuel Sewall (1686–1729)." Massachusetts Historical Society, *Collections,* 6th ser., I (1886).

Shepard, Thomas. *Eye-Salve.* Cambridge, Mass., 1673.

Silverman, Kenneth, comp. *Selected Letters of Cotton Mather.* Baton Rouge, La., 1971.

Singer, Samuel W., ed. *The Correspondence of Henry Hyde, Earl of Clarendon, and of his brother, Lawrence Hyde, Earl of Rochester.* London, 1828.

# Bibliography

Smith, Joseph H., ed. *Colonial Justice in Western Massachusetts (1639–1702): The Pynchon Court Record*. Cambridge, Mass., 1961.

Snyder, Henry L. ed. *The Marlborough-Godolphin Correspondence*. 3 vols. Oxford, 1975.

Stock, Leo F. *Proceedings and Debates of the British Parliaments Respecting North America*. Vol. II. Washington, D.C., 1927.

Stoddard, John. "Stoddard's Journal." Edited by Sylvester Judd. *New England Historical and Genealogical Register*, V (1851): 21–42.

Stoughton, William. *New-England's True Interest*. Cambridge, Mass., 1670.

Tanner, Joseph R., ed. *The Further Correspondence of Samuel Pepys, 1662–1679*. London, 1929.

———. *Pepys' Memoires of the Royal Navy, 1679–1688*. Oxford, 1906.

Turell, Ebenezer. *The Life and Character of the Reverend Benjamin Colman*. Boston, 1749.

Vernon, James. *Letters Illustrative of the Reign of William III from 1696 to 1708*. Edited by G. P. R. James. 3 vols. London, 1841.

Warren, Joseph. *An Oration, Delivered 5 March, 1772*. Boston, 1772.

Watertown, Mass. *Watertown Records*. Vol. II. Watertown, 1900.

Whitmore, William H., ed. *The Andros Tracts. Being a Collection of Pamphlets and Official Papers issued during the Period between the Overthrow of the Andros Government and the Establishment of the Second Charter of Massachusetts*. Prince Society Publications, vols. V–VII. Boston, 1868–1874.

Willard, Samuel. *The Character of a Good Ruler*. Boston, 1694.

———. *A Compleat Body of Divinity*. Boston, 1726.

———. *The Sinfulness of Worshipping God with Men's Institutions*. Boston, 1691.

Winthrop, John. *Winthrop's Journal "History of New England," 1630–1649*. Edited by James K. Hosmer. 2 vols. New York, 1908.

Wise, John. *The Churches Quarrel Espoused*. New York, 1713.

———. *A Vindication of the Government of the New-England Churches*. Boston, 1717.

Wolcott, Roger. "A Memoir for the History of Connecticut, 1759." Connecticut Historical Society, *Collections*, III (1895): 321–336.


SECONDARY WORKS

Adams, Charles F. *Three Episodes of Massachusetts History*. Vol. II. Boston, 1903.

Adams, James Truslow. *The Founding of New England*. Boston, 1921.

———. *Revolutionary New England, 1691–1776*. Boston, 1923.

Akagi, Roy H. *The Town Proprietors of the New England Colonies: A Study of Their Development, Organization, Activities, and Controversies, 1620–1770*. Philadelphia, 1924.

Allen, David Grayson. "The Zuckerman Thesis and the Process of Legal

Rationalization in Provincial Massachusetts." *William and Mary Quarterly*, 3rd ser., XXIX (1972): 443–460.

Allen, Myron O. *The History of Wenham.* Boston, 1860.

Anderson, Terry Lee. *The Economic Growth of Seventeenth-Century New England: A Measurement of Regional Income.* New York, 1975.

Andrews, Charles M. *British Committees, Commissions, and Councils of Trade and Plantations, 1622–1675.* Baltimore, 1908.

———. *The Colonial Period of American History.* 4 vols. New Haven, 1934–1938.

———. *Guide to the Materials for American History, to 1783, in the Public Record Office of Great Britain.* 2 vols. Washington, D.C., 1912–1914.

Andrews, Charles M., and Davenport, Frances G. *Guide to the Manuscript Materials for the History of the United States to 1783 in the British Museum, in Minor London Archives, and in the Libraries of Oxford and Cambridge.* Washington, D.C., 1908.

Appleton, Marguerite. "Richard Partridge, Colonial Agent." *New England Quarterly*, V (1932): 293–309.

Arber, Edward. *The Term Catalogues, 1668–1709.* Vol. II. London, 1905.

Archdeacon, Thomas J. *New York City, 1664–1710: Conquest and Change.* Ithaca, N.Y., 1976.

Arnold, Samuel G. *History of the State of Rhode Island and Providence Plantations.* 2 vols. New York, 1859–1860.

Ashley, Maurice. *John Wildman, Plotter and Postmaster.* London, 1947.

Austin, John O. *The Genealogical Dictionary of Rhode Island.* Albany, N. Y., 1887.

Aylmer, Gerald E. "Place Bills and the Separation of Powers: Some Seventeenth-Century Origins of the 'Non-Political' Civil Service." Royal Historical Society, *Transactions*, 5th ser., XV (1965), 45–69.

Bahlman, Dudley. *The Moral Revolution of 1688.* New Haven, 1957.

Bailyn, Bernard. *The Ideological Origins of the American Revolution.* Cambridge, Mass., 1967.

———. *The New England Merchants in the Seventeenth Century.* Cambridge, Mass., 1955.

———. "The New England Merchants in the Seventeenth Century: A Study in the History of American Society." Ph.D. dissertation, Harvard University, 1953.

———. *The Origins of American Politics.* New York, 1968.

Bailyn, Bernard, and Bailyn, Lotte. *Massachusetts Shipping, 1697–1714: A Statistical Study.* Cambridge, Mass., 1959.

Baldwin, Alice M. *The New England Clergy and the American Revolution.* Durham, N.C., 1928.

Bancroft, George. *History of the United States of America from the Discovery of the Continent.* 23rd ed. Vol. II. Boston, 1870.

# Bibliography

Banks, Charles E. *Topographical Dictionary of 2,885 English Emigrants to New England, 1620-1650.* Edited by Elijah E. Brownell. Philadelphia, 1937.

Barbour, James S. *A History of William Paterson and the Darien Company.* Edinburgh, 1907.

Barnes, Thomas Garden. *Somerset, 1625-1640: A County's Government during the "Personal Rule."* Cambridge, Mass., 1961.

Barnes, Viola. *The Dominion of New England: A Study of British Colonial Policy.* New Haven, 1923.

———. "Phippius Maximus." *New England Quarterly,* I (1928): 532-553.

———. "Richard Wharton, a Seventeenth Century New England Colonial." Publications of the Colonial Society of Massachusetts, *Transactions,* XXVI (1924-1926): 238-270.

———. "The Rise of Sir William Phips." *New England Quarterly,* I (1928): 271-294.

Barrow, Thomas C. *Trade and Empire: The British Customs Service in Colonial America, 1660-1775.* Cambridge, Mass., 1976.

Barry, Peter Ralph. "The New Hampshire Merchant Interest, 1609-1725." Ph.D. dissertation, University of Wisconsin, 1971.

Baxter, Stephen B. *William III and the Defense of European Liberty.* New York, 1966.

Beer, George L. *The Old Colonial System, 1660-1754.* 2 vols. New York, 1913.

———. *The Origins of the British Colonial System, 1578-1660.* New York, 1908.

Belknap, Jeremy. *The History of New Hampshire.* 3 vols. 2nd ed. Dover, N. H., 1812.

Bieber, Ralph Paul. *The Lords of Trade and Plantations, 1675-1696.* Allentown, Pa., 1919.

Bjork, Gordon C. "The Weaning of the American Economy: Independence, Market Changes, and Economic Development." *Journal of Economic History,* XXIV (1964): 541-560.

Bliss, Robert M. "A Secular Revival: Puritanism in Connecticut, 1675-1708." *Journal of American Studies,* VI (1972): 129-152.

Bloom, Jeanne Gould. "Sir Edmund Andros: A Study in Seventeenth Century Colonial Administration." Ph.D. dissertation, Yale University, 1962.

Bowen, Clarence W. *The Boundary Disputes of Connecticut.* Boston, 1882.

———. *The History of Woodstock, Connecticut.* 8 vols. Norwood, Mass., 1923-1935.

Bowen, Richard LeBaron. *Early Rehoboth.* 4 vols. Rehoboth, Mass., 1945-1950.

———. "The 1690 Tax Revolt of Plymouth Colony Towns." *New England Historical and Genealogical Register,* CXII (1958): 4-14.

Boyer, Paul, and Nissenbaum, Stephen. *Salem Possessed: The Social Origins of Witchcraft.* Cambridge, Mass., 1974.

[*435*]

Brebner, John B. *New England's Outpost: Acadia Before the Conquest of Canada.* New York, 1927.

Breen, Timothy H. *The Character of the Good Ruler: A Study of Puritan Political Ideas in New England, 1630–1730.* New Haven, 1970.

———. "War, Taxes, and Changing Political Brokers: The Ordeal of Massachusetts Bay, 1675–1692." Unpublished paper.

Breen, Timothy H., and Foster, Stephen. "The Puritans' Greatest Achievement: A Study of Social Cohesion in Seventeenth-Century Massachusetts." *Journal of American History,* LX (1973): 5–22.

Bridenbaugh, Carl. *Cities in the Wilderness: The First Century of Urban Life in America, 1625–1742.* 2nd ed. New York, 1955.

———. *Fat Mutton and Liberty of Conscience: Society in Rhode Island, 1636–1690.* Providence, 1974.

———. *Mitre and Sceptre: Transatlantic Faiths, Ideas, Personalities, and Politics, 1689–1775.* New York, 1962.

———. *Vexed and Troubled Englishmen, 1590–1642.* New York, 1968.

Bronner, Edwin. "Intercolonial Relations among Quakers Before 1750." *Quaker History,* LVI (1967): 3–17.

Bronson, Henry. "A Historical Account of Connecticut Currency, Continental Money, and the Finances of the Revolution." New Haven Historical Society, *Papers,* I (1865): 1–192 (separately paginated).

Brown, B. Katherine. "The Controversy over the Franchise in Puritan Massachusetts, 1954 to 1974." *William and Mary Quarterly,* 3rd ser., XXXIII (1976): 212–241.

Brown, George W., *et al.,* eds. *Dictionary of Canadian Biography.* 6 vols. Toronto, 1966–1979.

Brown, Richard D. *Revolutionary Politics in Massachusetts: The Boston Committee of Correspondence and the Towns, 1772–1774.* Cambridge, Mass., 1970.

Brown, Robert E. *Middle-Class Democracy and the Revolution in Massachusetts, 1691–1780.* Ithaca, N. Y., 1955.

Browning, Andrew. *Thomas Osborne, Earl of Danby and Duke of Leeds, 1632–1712.* 3 vols. Glasgow, 1944–1951.

Buffinton, Arthur H. "Governor Dudley and the Proposed Treaty of Neutrality, 1705." Publications of the Colonial Society of Massachusetts, *Transactions,* XXVI (1924–1926): 211–229.

———. "The Isolationist Policy of Colonial Massachusetts." *New England Quarterly,* I (1928): 158–179.

———. "New England and the Western Fur Trade, 1629–1675." Publications of the Colonial Society of Massachusetts, *Transactions,* XVIII (1915–1916): 160–192.

———. "The Policy of Albany and English Westward Expansion." *Mississippi Valley Historical Review,* VIII (1922): 327–366.

———. "The Policy of the Northern English Colonies towards the French to the Treaty of Utrecht." Ph.D. dissertation, Harvard University, 1925.

Bushman, Richard L. "Corruption and Power in Provincial America." In *The Development of a Revolutionary Mentality*, 63–91. Library of Congress Symposia on the American Revolution. Washington, D.C., 1972.

————. *From Puritan to Yankee: Character and the Social Order in Connecticut, 1690–1765*. Cambridge, Mass., 1967.

Caplan, Niel, ed. "Some Unpublished Letters of Benjamin Colman." Massachusetts Historical Society, *Proceedings*, LXXVII (1965): 101–142.

Carey, Edith F. "Amias Andros and Sir Edmund, His Son." Guernsey Society of Natural Science and Local Research, *Transactions*, VII (1913–1916): 36–66.

Carr, Lois Green, and Jordan, David William. *Maryland's Revolution of Government, 1689–1692*. Ithaca, N. Y., 1974.

Carswell, John. *The Old Cause: Three Biographical Studies in Whiggism*. London, 1954.

Cass, F. C. *History of East Barnet*. London, 1885–1892.

Caulkins, Frances Manwaring. *History of New London, Connecticut. From the First Survey of the Coast in 1612, to 1852*. New London, 1852.

Cederberg, Herbert R., Jr. "Wages and Prices in Eighteenth-Century England and the Thirteen Colonies." M.A. thesis, University of California, Berkeley, 1962.

Chafee, Zechariah, Jr. "Colonial Courts and the Common Law." Massachusetts Historical Society, *Proceedings*, LXVIII (1944–1947): 132–159.

————. "Introduction" to "Records of the Suffolk County Court, 1671–1680." Publications of the Colonial Society of Massachusetts, *Collections*, XXIX–XXX (1933): xvii–xciv.

Chalmers, George. *Political Annals of the Present United Colonies from the Settlement to the Peace of 1763*. Part I: London, 1780. Part II: New York, 1868. Reprinted, New York, 1968.

Chamberlain, Mellen. *A Documentary History of Chelsea*. 2 vols. Boston, 1908.

Chandaman, C. Douglas. *The English Public Revenue, 1660–1688*. Oxford, 1975.

Channing, Edward. *A History of the United States*. Vol. II. New York, 1908.

Chroust, Anton-Herman. *The Rise of the Legal Profession in America*. 2 vols. Norman, Okla., 1965.

Chu, Jonathan M. "Madmen and Friends: Quakers and the Puritan Adjustment to Religious Heterodoxy during the Seventeenth Century." Ph.D. dissertation, University of Washington, 1978.

Clark, Charles E. *The Eastern Frontier: The Settlement of Northern New England, 1610–1763*. New York, 1970.

Clark, Dora M. *The Rise of the British Treasury*. New Haven, 1960.

Conley, Patrick T. "Rhode Island Constitutional Development, 1636–1775." *Rhode Island History*, XXVII (1968): 55–63, 74–94.

[*437*]

Cook, Edward M., Jr. *The Fathers of the Towns: Leadership and Community Structure in Eighteenth-Century New England.* Baltimore, 1976.

Cook, George A. *John Wise, Early American Democrat.* New York, 1952.

Cooperman, Roslyn R. "The Free Worker in Colonial Massachusetts." M.A. thesis, University of California, Berkeley, 1945.

Corey, Deloraine Pendre. *The History of Malden, Massachusetts, 1633–1785.* Malden, 1899.

Cowie, Leonard W. *Henry Newman: An American in London, 1708–43.* London, 1956.

Craven, Wesley Frank. *The Colonies in Transition, 1660–1713.* New York, 1968.

———. *The Southern Colonies in the Seventeenth Century.* Baton Rouge, La., 1949.

Currier, John J. *History of Newbury, Massachusetts, 1635–1902.* Boston, 1902.

Daniels, Bruce C. "The Political Structure of Local Government in Colonial Connecticut." In *Town and County: Essays on the Structure of Local government in the American Colonies,* edited by Bruce C. Daniels, 44–71. Middletown, Conn., 1978.

Daviault, Pierre. *Le Baron de St. Castin, Chef Abenaquis.* Montreal, 1946.

Davies, Godfrey. *Essays on the Later Stuarts.* San Marino, Calif., 1958.

Davis, Andrew M. *Currency and Banking in the Province of Massachusetts-Bay.* 2 vols. New York, 1901.

Davis, Ralph. "English Foreign Trade, 1660–1700." *Economic History Review,* 2nd ser., VII (1954–1955): 150–166.

Davisson, William I. "Essex County Price Trends: Money and Markets in Seventeenth-Century Massachusetts." Essex Institute, *Historical Collections,* CIII (1967): 144–185.

Demos, John. *A Little Commonwealth: Family Life in Plymouth Colony.* New York, 1970.

———. "Underlying Themes in the Witchcraft of Seventeenth-Century New England." *American Historical Review,* LXXV (1969–1970): 1311–1326.

Dickson, P. M. G. *The Financial Revolution in England, 1688–1756.* London, 1967.

Dickson, P. M. G., and Sperling, John G. "War Finance, 1689–1714." In *The New Cambridge Modern History.* Vol. VI, edited by J. S. Bromley, 284–315. Cambridge, 1970.

Dinkin, Robert J. *Voting in Provincial America.* Westport, Conn., 1977.

Douglas, Charles H. J. *The Financial History of Massachusetts from the Organization of the Massachusetts Bay Company to the American Revolution.* New York, 1892.

Dow, George F., and Edmonds, John H. *Pirates of the New England Coast, 1630–1730.* Salem, Mass., 1923.

# Bibliography

Downie, J. A. "The Commission of Public Accounts and the Formation of the Country Party." *English Historical Review*, XCI (1976): 33–51.

Drake, Frederick C. "Witchcraft in the American Colonies, 1647–62." *American Quarterly*, XX (1968): 694–725.

Duffy, John. *Epidemics in Colonial America.* Baton Rouge, La., 1953.

Dunn, Richard S. "The Downfall of the Bermuda Company: A Restoration Farce." *William and Mary Quarterly*, 3rd ser., XX (1963): 487–512.

———. "Imperial Pressures on Massachusetts and Jamaica, 1675–1700." In *Anglo-American Political Relations, 1675–1775*, edited by Alison Gilbert Olson and Richard Maxwell Brown, 52–75. New Brunswick, N. J., 1970.

———. *Puritans and Yankees: The Winthrop Dynasty of New England, 1630–1717.* Princeton, 1962.

———. *Sugar and Slaves: The Rise of the Planter Class in the English West Indies, 1624–1713.* Chapel Hill, N. C., 1972.

Eccles, William J. *Canada under Louis XIV, 1663–1701.* Toronto, 1964.

———. *Frontenac, the Courtier Governor.* Toronto, 1959.

Edmonds, John H. "Captain Thomas Pounds, Pilot, Pirate, Cartographer, and Captain in the Royal Navy." Publications of the Colonial Society of Massachusetts, *Transactions*, XX (1917–1919): 29–84.

Emery, Samuel H. *History of Taunton, Massachusetts.* Syracuse, N. Y., 1893.

Fairchild, Byron. *Messrs. William Pepperrell: Merchants at Piscataqua.* Ithaca, N. Y., 1954.

Feiling, Keith. *A History of the Tory Party, 1640–1714.* Oxford, 1924.

Felt, Joseph B. *An Historical Account of Massachusetts Currency.* Boston, 1839.

Foote, Henry W. *Annals of King's Chapel.* 2 vols. Boston, 1882–1896.

Ford, Worthington C. *The Boston Book Market, 1679–1700.* Boston, 1917.

———. "The Governor and Council of the Province of the Massachusetts Bay, August 1714–March 1715." Massachusetts Historical Society, *Proceedings*, 2nd ser., XV (1901): 327–361.

Foster, Stephen. *Their Solitary Way: The Puritan Social Ethic in the First Century of Settlement in New England.* New Haven, 1971.

———. "The Massachusetts Franchise in the Seventeenth Century." *William and Mary Quarterly*, 3rd ser., XXIV (1967): 613–623.

Foxcroft, Helen C. *Life and Letters of Sir George Savile, Bart., First Marquis of Halifax.* 2 vols. London, 1898.

Friedelbaum, Stanley. "Bellomont: Imperial Administrator. Studies in Colonial Administration During the Seventeenth Century." Ph.D. dissertation, Columbia University, 1955.

Frothingham, Richard. *History of Charlestown, Massachusetts.* Charlestown, Mass., 1845–1849.

Fry, William Henry. *New Hampshire as a Royal Province.* New York, 1908.

Gibbs, G. C. "The Revolution in Foreign Policy." In *Britain after the Glorious*

*Revolution, 1689–1714,* edited by Geoffrey Holmes, 59–79. London, 1969.

Gildrie, Richard P. *Salem, Massachusetts, 1626–1683: A Covenant Community.* Charlottesville, Va., 1975.

Goebel, Julius, Jr. "The Courts and the Law in Colonial New York." In *History of the State of New York,* edited by Alexander C. Flick, III, 3–43. New York, 1933.

————. "King's Law and Local Custom in Seventeenth-Century New England." *Columbia Law Review,* XXXI (1931): 416–448.

Goldenburg, Joseph. *Shipbuilding in Colonial America.* Charlottesville, Va., 1976.

Gookin, F. W. *Daniel Gookin, 1612–1687.* Chicago, 1912.

Gottfried, Marion. "The First Depression in Massachusetts." *New England Quarterly,* IX (1936): 655–678.

Greene, Evarts B. *The Foundations of American Nationality.* Rev. ed. New York, 1935.

————. *Provincial America, 1690–1740.* New York, 1905.

Greene, Evarts B., and Harrington, Virginia D. *American Population Before the Federal Census of 1790.* New York, 1932.

Greene, Jack P. *The Quest for Power: The Lower Houses of Assembly in the Southern Royal Colonies, 1689–1776.* Chapel Hill, N. C., 1963.

Greven, Philip J., Jr. *Four Generations: Population, Land, and Family in Colonial Andover, Massachusetts.* Ithaca, N. Y., 1970.

Guttridge, George H. *The Colonial Policy of William III in America and the West Indies.* Cambridge, 1922.

Haffenden, Philip S. "The Crown and the Colonial Charters, 1675–1688." *William and Mary Quarterly,* 3rd ser., XV (1958): 297–311, 452–466.

————. *New England in the English Nation, 1689–1713.* Oxford, 1974.

Haley, Kenneth H. D. *The First Earl of Shaftesbury.* Oxford, 1968.

Hall, David D. *The Faithful Shepherd: A History of the New England Ministry in the Seventeenth Century.* Chapel Hill, N. C., 1972.

Hall, Michael G. *Edward Randolph and the American Colonies, 1676–1703.* Chapel Hill. N. C., 1960.

————. "The House of Lords, Edward Randolph, and the Navigation Act of 1696." *William and Mary Quarterly,* 3rd ser., XIV (1957): 494–515.

————. "Randolph, Dudley, and the Massachusetts Moderates, in 1683." *New England Quarterly,* XXIX (1956): 513–516.

Hall, Michael G.; Leder, Lawrence H.; and Kammen, Michael G., eds. *The Glorious Revolution in America: Documents on the Colonial Crisis of 1689.* Chapel Hill, N. C., 1964.

Hall, Van Beck. *Politics Without Parties: Massachusetts, 1780–1791.* Pittsburgh, 1972.

Hamlin, Paul M., and Baker, Charles E. *Supreme Court of Judicature of the Province of New York, 1691–1704.* 3 vols. New York, 1959.

# Bibliography

Hansen, Chadwick. *Witchcraft at Salem.* New York, 1969.

Harlow, Vincent. *A History of Barbados, 1625–1685.* Oxford, 1926.

Harris, F. R. *The Life of Edward Mountagu, K.G., First Earl of Sandwich (1625–1672).* 2 vols. London, 1912.

Haskins, George Lee. "The Beginnings of Partible Inheritance in the American Colonies." *Yale Law Review,* LI (1942): 1280–1315.

———. *Law and Authority in Early Massachusetts: A Study in Tradition.* New York, 1960.

Haskins, George Lee, and Ewing, Samuel E. "The Spread of Massachusetts Law in the Seventeenth Century." *University of Pennsylvania Law Review,* CVI (1958): 413–418.

Haswell, Jock. *James II, Soldier and Sailor.* London, 1972.

Hawkins, Ernest. *Historical Notices of the Missions of the Church of England in the Northern American Colonies.* London, 1845.

Hazeltine, Harold D. "Appeals from Colonial Courts to the King in Council, with Special Reference to Rhode Island." American Historical Association. *Annual Report for the Year 1894.* Washington, D.C., 1895.

Heimert, Alan. *Religion and the American Mind: From the Great Awakening to the Revolution.* Cambridge, Mass., 1966.

Henretta, James A. *"Salutary Neglect": Colonial Administration under the Duke of Newcastle.* Princeton, N. J., 1972.

Henripin, Jacques. *La Population Canadienne au Début de XVIIIe Siècle.* Travaux et Documents de l'Institut Nationale d'Études Demographiques, no. 22. Paris, 1954.

Higham, C. S. S. "The Accounts of a Colonial Governor's Agent in the Seventeenth Century." *American Historical Review,* XXVIII (1922–1923): 263–285.

Hill, Christopher. *The Century of Revolution, 1603–1714.* Edinburgh, 1961.

Hollifield, E. Brooks. *The Covenant Sealed: The Development of Puritan Sacramental Theology in Old and New England, 1570–1720.* New Haven, 1974.

Holmes, Geoffrey. *British Politics in the Age of Anne.* London, 1967.

———, ed. *Britain after the Glorious Revolution, 1689–1714.* London, 1969.

Holmes, Thomas J. *Cotton Mather: A Bibliography of His Works.* 3 vols. Cambridge, Mass., 1940.

———. *Increase Mather: A Bibliography of His Works.* 2 vols. Cleveland, 1931.

Hooker, Roland Mather. *Boundaries of Connecticut.* New Haven, 1933.

Horwitz, Henry. *Parliament, Policy and Politics in the Reign of William III.* Manchester, England, 1977.

———. *Revolution Politics: The Career of Daniel Finch, Second Earl of Nottingham, 1647–1730.* Cambridge, 1968.

Hull, John T. *The Siege and Capture of Fort Loyall, Destruction of Falmouth, May 20, 1690 (O.S.).* Portland, Me., 1885.

Hutchinson, Thomas. *The History of the Colony and Province of Massachusetts-Bay.* Edited by Lawrence S. Mayo. 3 vols. Cambridge, Mass., 1936.

Illick, Joseph E. *William Penn the Politician: His Relations with the English Government.* Ithaca, N.Y., 1965.

Jackson, Francis. *History of the Early Settlement of Newton.* Boston, 1854.

Jacobsen, Gertrude. *William Blathwayt: A Late Seventeenth Century English Administrator.* New Haven, 1932.

James, Sydney V. *Colonial Rhode Island: A History.* New York, 1975.

———. "Colonial Rhode Island and the Beginnings of the Liberal Rationalized State." In *Essays in Theory and History: An Approach to the Social Sciences,* edited by Melvin Richter, 165–185. Cambridge, Mass., 1970.

Jantz, Harold S. "The First Century of New England Verse." American Antiquarian Society, *Proceedings,* new ser., LIII (1943): 219–508.

Jeaffreson, John C. *A Young Squire of the Seventeenth Century.* 2 vols. London, 1888.

Jenkins, William Sumner. *A Guide to the Microfilm Collection of Early State Records.* Washington, D.C., 1950.

Johnson, Allen, and Malone, Dumas, eds. *Dictionary of American Biography.* 22 vols. New York, 1928–1944.

Johnson, Emory, *et al. History of Domestic and Foreign Commerce of the United States.* 2 vols. Washington, D.C., 1915.

Johnson, Richard R. "Adjustment to Empire: War, New England, and British Colonial Policy in the Late Seventeenth Century." Ph.D. dissertation, University of California, Berkeley, 1972.

———. "The Humble Address of the Publicans of New-England: A Reassessment." *New England Quarterly,* LI (1978): 241–249.

———. "Politics Redefined: An Assessment of Recent Writings on the Late Stuart Period of English History, 1660–1714." *William and Mary Quarterly,* 3rd ser., XXXV (1978): 691–732.

———. "The Search for a Usable Indian: An Aspect of the Defense of Colonial New England." *Journal of American History,* LXIV (1977): 623–651.

Jones, Frederick R. *History of Taxation in Connecticut.* Baltimore, 1896.

Jones, G. F. Trevallyn. *Saw-Pit Wharton: The Political Career from 1640 to 1691 of Philip, Fourth Lord Wharton.* Sydney, Australia, 1967.

Judd, Jacob. "Lord Bellomont and Captain Kidd: A Footnote to an Entangled Alliance." New-York Historical Society, *Quarterly,* XLVII (1963): 67–74.

Judd, Sylvester. *History of Hadley.* Rev. ed. Springfield, Mass., 1905.

Judson, Margaret A. *The Political Thought of Sir Henry Vane the Younger.* Philadelphia, 1969.

Kammen, Michael G. *Colonial New York: A History.* New York, 1975.

# Bibliography

————. *People of Paradox: An Enquiry into the Origins of American Civilization.* New York, 1972.

————. *A Rope of Sand: The Colonial Agents, British Politics, and the American Revolution.* Ithaca, N. Y., 1968.

Kaye, Percy L. *English Colonial Administration under Lord Clarendon, 1660–1667.* Baltimore, 1905.

Kellaway, William. *The New England Company, 1649–1776: Missionary Society to the American Indians.* London, 1961.

Kellogg, Louise P. "The American Colonial Charter." American Historical Association. *Annual Report for the Year 1903.* Part I. Washington, D.C., 1904.

Kenyon, John P. *Revolution Principles: The Politics of Party, 1689–1720.* Cambridge, 1977.

————. *Robert Spencer, Earl of Sunderland, 1641–1702.* London, 1958.

Kimball, Everett. *The Public Life of Joseph Dudley: A Study of the Colonial Policy of the Stuarts in New England, 1660–1715.* New York, 1911.

Kirby, Ethyn. *George Keith (1638–1716).* New York, 1942.

Konig, David Thomas. *Law and Society in Puritan Massachusetts: Essex County, 1629–1692.* Chapel Hill, N. C., 1979.

Labaree, Benjamin. *Colonial Massachusetts: A History.* Millwood, N. Y., 1979.

Labaree, Leonard Woods. *Conservatism in Early American History.* Ithaca, N. Y., 1948.

————. *Royal Government in America: A Study of the British Colonial System Before 1783.* New Haven, 1930.

Lacey, Douglas R. *Dissent and Parliamentary Politics in England, 1661–1689: A Study in the Perpetuation and Tempering of Parliamentarianism.* New Brunswick, N. J., 1969.

Langdon, George D., Jr. *Pilgrim Colony: A History of New Plymouth, 1620–1691.* New Haven, 1966.

Larned, Ellen D. *History of Windham County, Connecticut.* Worcester, Mass. 1894.

Laslett, Peter. "John Locke, the Great Recoinage, and the Origins of the Board of Trade, 1695–1698." *William and Mary Quarterly,* 3rd ser., XIV (1957): 370–402.

Leach, Douglas E. *Flintlock and Tomahawk: New England in King Philip's War.* New York, 1958.

————. *The Northern Colonial Frontier, 1607–1763.* New York, 1966.

Leder, Lawrence H. "The Politics of Upheaval in New York, 1689–1709." New-York Historical Society, *Quarterly,* XLIV (1960): 203–212.

————. *Robert Livingston, 1654–1728, and the Politics of Colonial New York.* Chapel Hill, N. C., 1961.

Levin, David. *Cotton Mather: The Young Life of the Lord's Remembrancer, 1663–1703.* Cambridge, Mass., 1978.

Levy, Babette M. "Early Puritanism in the Southern and Island Colonies." American Antiquarian Society, *Proceedings,* new ser., LXX (1960): 69–348.

Lewis, Theodore B. "Land Speculation and the Dudley Council of 1686." *William and Mary Quarterly,* 3rd ser., XXI (1974): 255–272.

———. "Massachusetts and the Glorious Revolution, 1660–1692." Ph.D. dissertation, University of Wisconsin, 1967.

———. "A Revolutionary Tradition, 1689–1714: 'There was a Revolution here as well as in England.'" *New England Quarterly,* XLVI (1973): 424–438.

———. "Royal Government in New Hampshire and the Revocation of the Charter of Massachusetts, 1679–1683." *Historical New Hampshire,* XXV, no. 4 (1970): 3–38.

Lewis, Theodore B., and Webb, Linda M. "Voting for the Massachusetts Council of Assistants, 1674–1686: A Statistical Note." *William and Mary Quarterly,* 3rd ser., XXX (1973): 625–634.

Lilly, Edward P. *The Colonial Agents of New York and New Jersey.* Washington, D.C., 1936.

Lillywhite, Bryant. *London Coffee Houses: A Reference Book of Coffee Houses of the Seventeenth, Eighteenth, and Nineteenth Centuries.* London, 1963.

Lockridge, Kenneth A. *A New England Town: The First Hundred Years.* New York, 1970.

———. "The Population of Dedham, Massachusetts, 1636–1736." *Economic History Review,* 2nd ser., XIX (1966): 318–346.

Lonn, Ella. *The Colonial Agents of the Southern Colonies.* Chapel Hill, N. C., 1945.

Lord, Eleanor L. *Industrial Experiments in the British Colonies of North America.* Baltimore, 1898.

Lovejoy, David S. "Equality and Empire: The New York Charter of Libertyes, 1683." *William and Mary Quarterly,* 3rd ser., XXI (1964): 493–515.

———. *The Glorious Revolution in America.* New York, 1972.

———. "Virginia's Charter and Bacon's Rebellion, 1675–1676." In *Anglo-American Political Relations, 1675–1775,* edited by Alison Gilbert Olson and Richard Maxwell Brown, 31–51. New Brunswick, N. J., 1970.

Lucas, Paul R. "Colony or Commonwealth: Massachusetts Bay, 1661–1666." *William and Mary Quarterly,* 3rd ser., XXIV (1967): 88–107.

———. *Valley of Discord: Church and Society along the Connecticut River, 1636–1755.* Hanover, N. H., 1976.

McCully, Bruce T. "The New England-Acadia Fishery Dispute and the Nicholson Mission of August 1687." Essex Institute, *Historical Collections,* XCVI (1960): 277–290.

# Bibliography

McCusker, John J. "The Current Value of English Exports, 1697 to 1800." *William and Mary Quarterly*, 3rd ser., XXVIII (1971): 607–628.

———. *Money and Exchange in Europe and America, 1600–1775: A Handbook.* Chapel Hill, N. C., 1978.

Macfarlane, Alan. *Witchcraft in Tudor and Stuart England: A Regional and Comparative Study.* London, 1970.

McIlwain, Charles H. *The American Revolution: A Constitutional Interpretation.* New York, 1923.

McLachlan, Herbert. *English Education under the Test Acts: Being the History of the Nonconformist Academies, 1662–1820.* Manchester, England, 1931.

McLoughlin, William G. *New England Dissent, 1630–1833: The Baptists and the Separation of Church and State.* 2 vols. Cambridge, Mass., 1971.

McManus, Douglas R. *Colonial New England: An Historical Geography.* New York, 1975.

Malone, Joseph J. *Pine Trees and Politics: The Naval Stores and Forest Policy in Colonial New England, 1691–1775.* London, 1964.

Main, Jackson Turner. *Political Parties Before the Constitution.* Chapel Hill, N. C., 1973.

Mason, Bernard. "Aspects of the New York Revolt of 1689." *New York History*, XXX (1949): 165–180.

Mason, George C. *Annals of Trinity Church, Newport, Rhode Island.* 2 vols. Newport, 1890–1894.

Mathews, Lois K. *The Expansion of New England: The Spread of New England Settlement and Institutions to the Mississippi River, 1620–1865.* Boston, 1909.

Matthews, Albert. "Colonel Elizeus Burges." Publications of the Colonial Society of Massachusetts, *Transactions*, XIV (1911–1913): 360–372.

Mead, Nelson P. *Connecticut as a Corporate Colony.* Lancaster, Pa., 1906.

Menard, Russell R. "Immigrants and Their Increase: The Process of Population Growth in Early Colonial Maryland." In *Law, Society, and Politics in Early Maryland,* edited by Aubrey C. Land, Lois Green Carr, and Edward C. Papenfuse, 88–110. Baltimore, 1977.

Mereness, Newton D. *Maryland as a Proprietary Province.* New York, 1901.

Metcalfe, John G., comp. *Annals of Mendon.* Providence, R. I., 1880.

Metz, William De Witt. "Politics and Finance in Massachusetts." Ph.D. dissertation, University of Wisconsin, 1945.

Middlekauff, Robert. *The Mathers: Three Generations of Puritan Intellectuals, 1596–1728.* New York, 1971.

Miller, Perry. *Errand into the Wilderness.* Cambridge, Mass., 1956.

———. *The New England Mind: From Colony to Province.* Beacon paperback ed. Boston, 1961.

Mitchell, Brian R., and Deane, Phyllis, eds. *Abstract of British Historical Statistics.* Cambridge, 1962.

Mitchell, Isabel S. *Roads and Road-Making in Colonial Connecticut.* New Haven, 1933.

Moody, Robert E. "The Maine Frontier, 1607 to 1763." Ph.D. dissertation, Yale University, 1933. Published Xerographically, Ann Arbor, Mich., 1968.

Morgan, Edmund S. *American Slavery, American Freedom: The Ordeal of Colonial Virginia.* New York, 1975.

———. "A Boston Heiress and Her Husbands: A True Story." Publications of the Colonial Society of Massachusetts, *Transactions,* XXXIV (1942): 499–513.

———. *Visible Saints: The History of a Puritan Idea.* New York, 1963.

Morgan, William T. "The British West Indies during King William's War (1689–97)." *Journal of Modern History,* II (1930): 378–409.

Moriarty, G. Andrews. "Barbadian Notes." *New England Historical and Genealogical Register,* LXVII (1913): 360–371, LXVIII (1914): 177–181.

———. "New England and Barbadian Notes." *Journal of the Barbados Museum and Historical Society,* XIV (1947): 164–167, XV (1948): 132–136.

Morison, Samuel Eliot. *Harvard College in the Seventeenth Century.* 2 vols. Cambridge, Mass., 1936.

———. *Three Centuries of Harvard.* Cambridge, Mass., 1936.

Munro, Wilfred H. *The History of Bristol, R. I., The Story of the Mount Hope Lands.* Providence, R. I., 1880.

Murdock, Kenneth B. "Increase Mather's Expenses as Colonial Agent." Publications of the Colonial Society of Massachusetts, *Transactions,* XXVII (1927–1930): 200–204.

———. *Increase Mather: The Foremost American Puritan.* Cambridge, Mass., 1925.

Murrin, John M. "Anglicizing an American Colony: The Transformation of Provincial Massachusetts." Ph.D. dissertation, Yale University, 1966.

———. "The Legal Transformation: The Bench and Bar of Eighteenth-Century Massachusetts." In *Colonial America: Essays in Politics and Social Development,* edited by Stanley N. Katz, 415–449. Boston, 1971.

———. "Review Essay." *History and Theory,* XI (1972): 226–275.

Muth, Philip A. "The Ashursts, Friends of New England." Ph.D. dissertation, Boston University, 1967.

Myrand, Ernest. *Sir William Phips Devant Québec: Histoire d'un Siège.* Quebec, 1893.

Nash, Gary B. *Quakers and Politics: Pennsylvania, 1681–1726.* Princeton, N. J., 1968.

Nenner, Howard. *By Colour of Law: Legal Culture and Constitutional Politics in England, 1660–1689.* Chicago, 1977.

Nettels, Curtis P. *The Money Supply of the American Colonies Before 1720.* Madison, Wis., 1934.

# Bibliography

Norton, Susan L. "Population Growth in Colonial America: A Study of Ipswich, Massachusetts." *Population Studies*, XXV (1971): 433-452.

Noyes, Sybil; Libby, Charles T.; and Davis, Walter. *Genealogical Dictionary of Maine and New Hampshire*. Portland, Me., 1928-1939.

Nuttall, Geoffrey F. *Richard Baxter*. London, 1965.

Ogg, David. *England in the Reign of Charles II*. 2 vols. Oxford, 1934.

————. *England in the Reigns of James II and William III*. Oxford, 1955.

Oldmixon, John. *The History of England during the Reigns of King William and Queen Mary, Queen Anne, King George I*. London, 1735.

Ollard, Richard L. *Pepys: A Biography*. New York, 1975.

Olson, Alison Gilbert. *Anglo-American Politics, 1660-1775: The Relationship between Parties in England and Colonial America*. New York, 1973.

Orme, William. *The Life and Times of Richard Baxter*. London, 1830.

Osgood, Herbert L. *The American Colonies in the Eighteenth Century*. 4 vols. New York, 1924-1925.

————. *The American Colonies in the Seventeenth Century*. 3 vols. New York, 1904-1907.

*Our County and Its People: A Descriptive and Biographical Record of Bristol County, Massachusetts*. Boston, 1899.

Page, William, ed. *The Victoria County History of Hampshire and the Isle of Wight*. Vol. V. London, 1912.

————. *The Victoria County History of Hertfordshire*. Vol. II. London, 1908.

Palfrey, John Gorham. *History of New England*. 5 vols. Boston, 1858-1890.

Pargellis, Stanley. "The Four Independent Companies of New York." In *Essays in Colonial History Presented to Charles McLean Andrews by his Students*, 98-123. New Haven, 1931.

Parkman, Francis. *Count Frontenac and New France under Louis XIV*. Boston, 1880.

————. *A Half-Century of Conflict*. Boston, 1892.

Pascoe, C. F. *Two Hundred Years of the S. P. G.* 2 vols. London, 1901.

Payne, James Bertrand. *An Armorial of Jersey*. N.p., 1859.

Pennington, E. L. "The Reverend Samuel Myles and His Boston Ministry." *Historical Magazine of the Protestant Episcopal Church*, XI (1942): 154-178.

Penson, Lillian M. *The Colonial Agents of the British West Indies: A Study in Colonial Administration, Mainly in the Eighteenth Century*. London, 1924.

Phillips, James D. *Salem in the Seventeenth Century*. Boston, 1933.

Phillips, John M. *American Silver*. New York, 1949.

Plumb, John H. *The Growth of Political Stability in England, 1675-1725*. London, 1967.

Polf, William Andrew. "Puritan Gentlemen: The Dudleys of Massachusetts, 1576-1686." Ph.D. dissertation, Syracuse University, 1973.

Pomfret, John E. *The Province of West New Jersey, 1609-1702: A History of the Origins of an American Colony*. Princeton, N. J., 1956.

Pope, Robert G. *The Half-Way Covenant: Church Membership in Puritan New England.* Princeton, N. J., 1969.

Potter, Elisha. "The Early History of Narragansett: With an Appendix of Original Documents." Rhode Island Historical Society, *Collections*, III (1835): 1–315.

Powicke, Frederick J. "The Reverend Richard Baxter and his Lancashire Friend, Mr. Henry Ashurst." *Bulletin of the John Rylands Library*, XIII (1929): 309–325.

———. *The Reverend Richard Baxter under the Cross (1662–1691).* London, 1927.

Powicke, Sir F. Maurice, *et al. Handbook of British Chronology.* 2nd ed. London, 1961.

Putre, John W. "Town and Province in Early Eighteenth-Century Massachusetts: A Study in Institutional Interaction." Ph.D. dissertation, State University of New York at Stony Brook, 1973.

Quincy, Josiah. *The History of Harvard University.* 2 vols. Boston, 1840.

Ransome, Joyce O. "Cotton Mather and the Catholic Spirit." Ph.D. dissertation, University of California, Berkeley, 1966.

Records, Ralph H. "Land as a Basis for Social and Economic Discontent in Maine and Massachusetts to 1776." Ph.D. dissertation, University of Chicago, 1936.

Reed, Susan B. *Church and State in Massachusetts, 1691–1740.* Urbana, Ill., 1914.

Reich, Jerome R. *Leisler's Rebellion: A Study of Democracy in New York, 1664–1720.* Chicago, 1953.

Reid, John G. *Maine, Charles II and Massachusetts: Governmental Relationships in Early Northern New England.* Portland, Me., 1977.

Ritchie, Robert C. *The Duke's Province: A Study of New York Politics and Society, 1664–1691.* Chapel Hill, N. C., 1977.

Robinson, Maurice H. *A History of Taxation in New Hampshire.* New York, 1903.

Rossiter, Clinton. *Six Characters in Search of a Republic.* New York, 1964.

Rubini, Dennis. *Court and Country, 1688–1702.* London, 1967.

Sachse, William L. *The Colonial American in Britain.* Madison, Wis., 1956.

Sandars, Mary F. *Princess and Queen of England, Life of Mary II.* London, 1913.

Savage, James. *A Genealogical Dictionary of the First Settlers of New England.* 4 vols. Boston, 1860–1862.

Schutz, John A. "Succession Politics in Massachusetts, 1730–1741." *William and Mary Quarterly*, 3rd ser., XV (1958): 508–520.

Schuyler, Robert L. *Parliament and the British Empire: Some Constitutional Controversies Concerning Imperial Legislative Jurisdiction.* New York, 1929.

Schuyler-Lightall, W. D. "The 'Glorious Enterprise': The Plan of Campaign for the Conquest of New France, Its Origin, History, and Connection with the Invasion of Canada." *Canadian Antiquarian and Numismatic Journal,* 3rd ser., III (1920): 1–37.

Scouller, R. E. *The Armies of Queen Anne.* Oxford, 1966.

Scull, G. D. "Biographical Notice of Doctor Daniel Coxe of London." *Pennsylvania Magazine of History and Biography,* VII (1883): 317–337.

Seaver, Henry L. "Hair and Holiness." Massachusetts Historical Society, *Proceedings,* LXVII (1944–1947): 3–20.

Shipton, Clifford K. "Immigration to New England, 1680–1740." *Journal of Political Economy,* XLIV (1936): 225–239.

———. "The Shaping of Revolutionary New England, 1680–1740." *Political Science Quarterly,* L (1935): 584–597.

Sibley, John L., and Shipton, Clifford K. *Biographical Sketches of Those Who Attended Harvard College.* 17 vols. Cambridge, Mass., 1873–1975.

Simmons, Richard C. "The Massachusetts Charter of 1691." In *Contrast and Connection: Bicentennial Essays in Anglo-American History,* edited by H. C. Allen and Roger Thompson, 66–87. Athens, Ohio, 1976.

———. "The Massachusetts Revolution of 1689: Three Early American Political Broadsides." *Journal of American Studies,* II (1968): 1–12.

———. "Studies in the Massachusetts Franchise, 1631–1691." Ph.D. dissertation, University of California, Berkeley, 1965.

Sirmans, M. Eugene. *Colonial South Carolina: A Political History.* Chapel Hill, N. C., 1966.

Smith, A. Hassell. *County and Court Government and Politics in Norfolk, 1558–1603.* Oxford, 1974.

Smith, Daniel Scott. "The Demographic History of Colonial New England." *Journal of Economic History,* XXXII (1972): 165–183.

Smith, Joseph H. "Administrative Control of the Courts of the American Plantations." *Columbia Law Review,* LXI (1961): 1210–1263.

———. *Appeals to the Privy Council from the American Plantations.* New York, 1950.

———. "The English Criminal Law in Early America." In *The English Legal System: Carryover to the Colonies: Papers Read at a Clark Library Seminar, November 3, 1975,* 1–60. Los Angeles, 1975.

Snow, Vernon F. "The Concept of Revolution in Seventeenth-Century England." *Historical Journal,* V (1962): 167–174.

Spencer, Charles W. *Colonial Wars and Constitutional Development in New York.* New York, 1915.

Spencer, Henry R. *Constitutional Conflict in Provincial Massachusetts.* Columbus, Ohio, 1905.

Stacey, C. P. *Introduction to the Study of Military History for Canadian Students.* 5th ed. Ottawa, 1960.

Steele, Ian K. *Politics of Colonial Policy: The Board of Trade in Colonial Administration, 1696–1702.* Oxford, 1968.

Stephen, Leslie, and Lee, Sidney, eds. *Dictionary of National Biography.* 63 vols. London, 1885–1903.

Sutherland, James. *Defoe.* London, 1937.

Taylor, J. M. *The Witchcraft Delusion in Colonial Connecticut.* New York, 1958.

Temple, J. H. *History of North Brookfield.* North Brookfield, Mass., 1887.

Thomson, Mark A. *The Secretaries of State, 1681–1782.* Oxford, 1932.

Thornton, Archibald P. *West-India Policy under the Restoration.* Oxford, 1956.

Tolles, Frederick B. *Quakers and the Atlantic Culture.* New York, 1960.

Trelease, Allen W. *Indian Affairs in Colonial New York: The Seventeenth Century.* Ithaca, N. Y., 1960.

Turner, Edward R. *The Privy Council of England in the Seventeenth and Eighteenth Centuries, 1603–1784.* 2 vols. Baltimore, 1927–1928.

Tuttle, Charles W. "New Hampshire in 1689–1690." Massachusetts Historical Society, *Proceedings,* XVII (1879–1880): 218–228.

U.S. Bureau of the Census. *Historical Statistics of the United States, Colonial Times to 1957.* Washington, D.C., 1960.

U.S. Department of Labor. Bureau of Labor Statistics. *History of Wages in the United States from Colonial Times to 1928.* Bulletin no. 499. Washington, D.C., 1929.

Van Deventer, David E. *The Emergence of Provincial New Hampshire, 1623–1741.* Baltimore, 1976.

Walker, Williston. *The Creeds and Platforms of Congregationalism.* New York, 1893.

Wall, Robert E., Jr. *Massachusetts Bay: The Crucial Decade, 1640–1650.* New Haven, 1972.

———. "The Membership of the Massachusetts General Court, 1634–1686." Ph.D. dissertation, Yale University, 1965.

Waller, George M. *Samuel Vetch, Colonial Enterpriser.* Chapel Hill, N. C., 1960.

Walsh, James P. "Solomon Stoddard's Open Communion: A Reexamination." *New England Quarterly,* XLIII (1970): 97–114.

Ward, Harry M. *The United Colonies of New England, 1643–90.* New York, 1961.

———. "Unite or Die": Intercolony Relations, 1690–1763.* Port Washington, N. Y., 1971.

Warden, Gerald B. *Boston, 1689–1776.* Boston, 1970.

———. "Boston Politics, 1692–1765." Ph.D. dissertation, Yale University, 1966.

Washburn, Wilcomb E. *The Governor and the Rebel: A History of Bacon's Rebellion in Virginia.* Chapel Hill, N. C., 1957.

Waters, Thomas F. *Ipswich in the Massachusetts Bay Colony, 1633–1700.* Ipswich, Mass., 1905.

Watkins, Walter K. "The Expedition to Canada in 1690 under Sir William

# Bibliography

Phips." In *Year-Book of the Society of Colonial Wars in the Commonwealth of Massachusetts,* no. 4. Boston, 1898.

[Watkins, Walter K.] "The Expeditions against Port Royal in 1710 and Quebec in 1711." In *Year-Book of the Society of Colonial Wars in the Commonwealth of Massachusetts,* no. 3. Boston, 1897.

Webb, Stephen Saunders. " 'Brave Men and Servants to His Royal Highness': The Household of James Stuart in the Evolution of English Imperialism." *Perspectives in American History,* VIII (1974): 55–80.

———. *The Governors-General: The English Army and the Definition of Empire, 1569–1681.* Chapel Hill, N. C., 1979.

———. "Officers and Governors: The Role of the British Army in Imperial Politics and the Administration of the American Colonies, 1689–1722." Ph.D. dissertation, University of Wisconsin, 1965.

———. "The Trials of Sir Edmund Andros." In *The Human Dimensions of Nation Making: Essays on Colonial and Revolutionary America,* edited by James Kirby Martin, 23–53. Madison, Wis., 1976.

———. "William Blathwayt, Imperial Fixer: From Popish Plot to Glorious Revolution." *William and Mary Quarterly,* 3rd ser., XXV (1968): 3–21.

———. "William Blathwayt, Imperial Fixer: Muddling Through to Empire, 1689–1717." *William and Mary Quarterly,* 3rd ser., XXVI (1969): 373–415.

Weeden, William B. *Economic and Social History of New England, 1620–1789.* 2 vols. Boston, 1890.

Weeks, Lyman, and Bacon, Edwin M. *A Historical Digest of the Provincial Press.* Boston, 1911.

Western, John R. *Monarchy and Revolution: The English State in the 1680s.* London, 1972.

Weston, Corinne C. *English Constitutional Theory and the House of Lords, 1556–1832.* New York, 1965.

Wheeler, Harvey. "Calvin's Case (1608) and the McIlwain-Schuyler Debate." *American Historical Review,* LX (1955–1956): 587–597.

Whitmore, William H. *The Massachusetts Civil List for the Colonial and Provincial Periods, 1630–1774.* Albany, N. Y., 1870.

Williamson, William D. *History of the State of Maine.* 2 vols. Hallowell, Me., 1839.

Willis, William. *History of Portland from 1632 to 1864.* Rev. ed. Portland, Me., 1865.

Winship, George P. *The New England Company of 1649 and John Eliot.* Prince Society Publications, vol. XXXVI. Boston, 1920.

Winsor, Justin. *The Memorial History of Boston.* 4 vols. Boston, 1880–1883.

Youngs, J. William T., Jr. *God's Messengers: Religious Leadership in Colonial New England, 1700–1750.* Baltimore, 1976.

Zemsky, Robert. *Merchants, Farmers, and River Gods: An Essay on Eighteenth-Century American Politics.* Boston, 1971.

Zimmerman, Albright G. "Daniel Coxe and the New Mediterranean Sea Company." *Pennsylvania Magazine of History and Biography,* LXVI (1952): 86–96.

Zuckerman, Michael. *Peaceable Kingdoms: New England Towns in the Eighteenth Century.* New York, 1970.

# Index

A

Abnaki Indians, 125; wars with, 85–86, 122, 237

Acadia, 227; French settlement in, 85; New England's relations with, 85–86, 178, 189, 387. *See also* Nova Scotia; Port Royal

Acts of Trade. *See* Navigation Acts

Addington, Isaac, 94, 95, 279, 280, 339; as secretary of Massachusetts, 230, 278, 284, 338

Agents, colonial: advantages of using, 306–307, 311–312, 320; and Board of Trade, 313; colonists' increasing acceptance of, 240; of Connecticut, 61, 308–309, 319–320, 323; desire for native-born, 321–323; financing and payment of, 176–177, 311, 314, 319; of Massachusetts, 37, 38, 49, 117, 130, 307–308, 312–319, 321–323; as "messengers," 38, 42, 307; of New Hampshire, 310, 311, 323; requested for Massachusetts assembly, 226; of Rhode Island, 21, 61, 310–311, 323; of royal governors, 320–321; and significance of their dispatch, 130, 305–307. *See also names of individual agents*

Agencies: establishing of permanent, 307–323

Albany, 58, 129, 192; aid to, 127, 194; strategic importance of, 126, 127, 256

Allen, Samuel: claims of, 310, 331, 389; as proprietor and governor of New Hampshire, 217–218, 241, 262, 289, 291–292

Allin, Daniel, 280

Allyn, John, 111–113, 200, 298, 309

Almy, Christopher, 310

Andros, Sir Edmund, 59, 139, 150, 155, 158, 238, 391; as governor of the Dominion of New England, 51, 62, 73–88, 90–91; as governor of Virginia, 225; imprisoned, 91, 99; trial of, 171–176; vindicates his administration, 183–184, 190

Anglesey, Countess of. *See* Annesley, Elizabeth

Anglesey, Earl of. *See* Annesley, Arthur

Anglicanism: and Boston uprising, 91, 99–100, 105; during the Dominion of New England, 77–78; as factor in royal policy, 74, 335, 342; growth of, in New England, 271, 332, 413; hostility to, 132, 271, 413

Anglicans: opposition to charter rule, 188; seek aid from London, 185, 327, 342

Annesley, Arthur, Earl of Anglesey, 34, 143

Annesley, Elizabeth, Countess of Anglesey, 178

Appeals to England, 21, 40, 83, 181, 295–296, 373; in Massachusetts charter of 1691, 231, 233

Appleton, John, 157, 399

Armstrong, Robert, 331

Army, English, in America, 25, 60, 74, 153, 256, 282; condition of, 257

Ashurst, Henry (c. 1614–1680), 39

Ashurst, Sir Henry (1645–1711): as

Connecticut agent, 309, 314, 319–320, 373; English political ties of, 162, 213, 313–314; and Increase Mather, 144, 148, 161, 208, 222, 224, 228, 236, 317; as Massachusetts agent, 117, 159, 261, 306, 308, 312–319; and Massachusetts politics, 317–318, 341; and naval stores, 255, 313, 316; as New Hampshire agent, 310; opposes Joseph Dudley, 312, 317, 319, 334–337, 339–341, 344–345, 350; as Plymouth Colony agent, 108, 159, 205; profits as agent, 315–317; views of New England's role, 315, 324; and Wait Winthrop, 330, 333, 340–341

Ashurst, Sir William, 321, 322, 353; as Bellomont's agent, 320; and Increase Mather, 161, 350; and Joseph Dudley, 348

Assemblies, colonial: crown's attitude towards, 35n.65. *See also* Representative government; *and names of individual colonies' assemblies*

Atherton proprietors, 20, 68, 72, 299, 301, 303; appeal to London, 21, 44, 47–48, 328; political influence of, 20n.36, 49. *See also* Narragansett country.

Atwood, William, 332

Authority: criticism of, 357, 404–406; views as to sources of, 101,104, 115. *See also* Executive; Leadership in New England.

*B*

Baltimore, Lord. *See* Calvert, Charles

Banks: proposals for, 72, 346, 346n. 94, 351, 352

Baptists, 201, 270, 327

Barbados, 15, 24, 195, 212

Bates, William, 234

Baxter, Richard, 162, 216

Bayard, Nicholas, 191

Bedford, Earl of. *See* Russell, William

Belasyse, John, Lord, 140

Belasyse, Thomas, Viscount Fauconberg, 147

Belcher, Andrew, 126, 246

Belcher, Jonathan, 353, 354, 359, 361, 410, 416

Bellomont, Earl of. *See* Coote, Richard

Bentinck, Hans Willem, 145

Bermuda, 32, 195

Blagrove, Nathaniel, 360

Blathwayt, William, 51, 73, 76, 82, 165, 167, 277, 282, 317, 330, 367, 397; attempts to win support of, 46–47, 219–220, 278; and Board of Trade, 247, 292; on colonial union, 263; and English colonial policy, 52, 53, 207; and Increase Mather, 141, 217; and Joseph Dudley, 335, 337, 343, 348, 389; and Massachusetts charter of 1691, 210, 214, 226; on New England's role, 35–36; and New Hampshire, 219; on Parliament and the colonies, 250; and Plymouth Colony, 205; political skills of, 191

Blechyden, Charles, 331

Board of Trade: creation of, 247; and colonial agents, 312–313; on colonial disunity, 258; and colonial regulation, 249–252, 264–265; on colonists and English law, 372; declining influence of, 251–252, 362–363; and New England, 253–265. *See also* England, colonial policy of; Lords of Trade and Plantations

Bolton, Duke of. *See* Paulet, Charles

Booth, Henry, Lord Delamere, 149, 161, 171

Boscawen, Hugh, 149, 161, 162, 169, 172, 214, 223, 313

Boston, 185; as commercial center,

359, 414, 418; on changing New
England ways, 78, 272, 332; income
from England, 268; and Joseph
Dudley, 345, 349, 386; in London,
84, 157, 162, 167; on loss of char-
ter, 70, 71; on Massachusetts poli-
tics, 292, 353, 394, 416; political
loyalties of, 67, 356–357; religious
views of, 270; strategic perceptions
of, 206
Sewall, Stephen, 260
Seymour, Charles, Duke of Somerset,
314
Shackmaple, John, 330
Shaftesbury, Earl of. *See* Cooper,
Anthony Ashley
Shipbuilding in New England, 254
Short, Captain Richard, 278, 281,
283
Shrewsbury, Earl of. *See* Talbot,
Charles
Shrimpton, Samuel, 82, 94, 100, 120,
187, 199
Shute, Samuel, 353–354, 356, 359; on
Massachusetts politics, 406
Sidney, Henry, Earl of Romney, 149,
210, 213, 214, 216, 222, 224, 259
Sloughter, Henry: governor of New
York, 158, 180, 225, 232
Small, Robert, 90
Society for the Propagation of the
Gospel in Foreign Parts, 271, 327,
335
Society for the Propagation of the
Gospel in New England. *See* Com-
pany for the Propagation of the
Gospel in New England
Somers, Sir John, 161, 178, 180, 212,
259, 316, 337; at trial of Andros,
172–174
Somerset, Duke of. *See* Seymour,
Charles
Southwell, Sir Robert, 152, 165

Spencer, Charles, third Earl of Sunderland, 344
Spencer, Robert, second Earl of Sunderland, 140
Sprague, Richard, 120–121, 280; petitions England, 120, 188
Stanhope, James, 354, 362–363
Stanley, Nathaniel, 110, 112
Steele, James, 110
Stiles, Ezra, 415
Stoddard, Solomon, 405
Story, Charles, 330, 332
Stoughton, William, 9, 68, 72, 187,
199, 414; acting governor of Massachusetts, 284–285, 321, 384; lieutenant governor of Massachusetts,
229, 280; Massachusetts agent, 37,
42, 49; role in Boston uprising, 94,
98, 100; and Sir Henry Ashurst,
315, 317; supports Joseph Dudley,
285, 338, 339; and witchcraft trials,
280
"Succession politics": in Massachusetts and New Hampshire, 333–354,
407
Sunderland, Earl of. *See* Spencer,
Charles; Spencer, Robert
Sutherland, Countess of. *See* Gordon,
Lady Jean

*T*

Tailer, William, 359; lieutenant governor of Massachusetts, 330,
352–353, 361; opposes Joseph Dudley, 346
Talbot, Charles, Earl of Shrewsbury,
147, 148, 155, 171, 213, 258, 259
Taxation: during the Dominion of
New England, 73, 74–75; political
effects of, 379; rising, 129, 197–198,
379–380. *See also* Money, paper; *and
names of individual colonies,* taxation
in
Taylor, John, 255

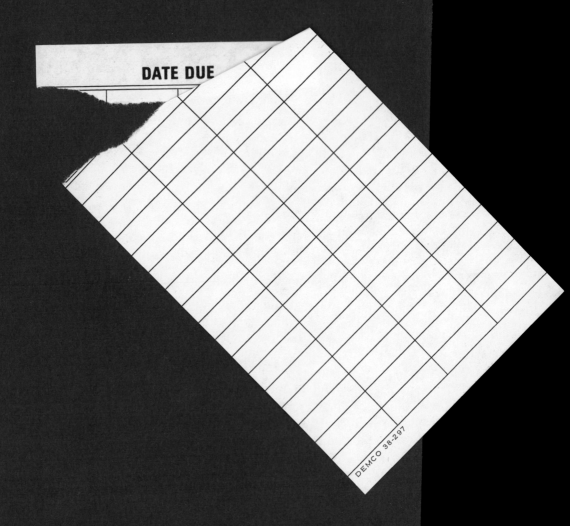

**DATE DUE**

DEMCO 38-297